CENTURY 21®
ACCOUNTING

CENTURY 21® ACCOUNTING

FOURTH EDITION   ADVANCED COURSE

ROBERT M. SWANSON
Professor Emeritus of Business Education
and Office Administration
Ball State University
Muncie, Indiana

KENTON E. ROSS, CPA
Professor of Accounting
East Texas State University
Commerce, Texas

ROBERT D. HANSON
Associate Dean
School of Business Administration
Central Michigan University
Mount Pleasant, Michigan

Published by

B47 **SOUTH-WESTERN PUBLISHING CO.**

CINCINNATI   WEST CHICAGO, IL   CARROLLTON, TX   LIVERMORE, CA

ISBN: 0-538-02470-4

Library of Congress Catalog Card Number: 87-60958

2 3 4 5 6 7 8 9 10 11 12 13 14 15 16 17 18 19 20 D 6 5 4 3 2 1 0 9 8

Printed in the United States of America

Preface

This fourth edition of CENTURY 21 ACCOUNTING, Advanced Course, is the second in a two-volume series available for use in a two-year accounting program. The chapter narrative and end-of-chapter learning activities are directed toward the knowledge and skills needed by students preparing for an accounting position following high school graduation. These learning activities also serve students who desire advanced preparation for the study of accounting in college.

The revisions made for this edition are based on suggestions received from classroom teachers, accounting students, and on changes occurring in the accounting profession. Accounting concepts and practices described in this textbook are in agreement with the *Statements of Financial Accounting Standards* issued by the Financial Accounting Standards Board.

TEXT ORGANIZATION

This edition retains the spiral approach to learning. Accounting procedures are described, applied and practiced, then reinforced. In each part new topics are presented that build on previous learnings. Learning progresses from the simple to the complex. End-of-chapter activities provide application and practice. The reinforcement activities in the textbook and the three business simulations provide realistic practice and strengthen the learnings.

Part 1 describes the accounting profession, its framework, and eleven commonly-accepted accounting concepts. Notations are made throughout the text to highlight applications of these accounting concepts.

Part 2 describes an accounting cycle for a departmentalized merchandising business organized as a corporation. This part provides a review of general accounting procedures for a merchandising business. The material also provides a foundation of knowledge and procedures for corporate accounting that will be used in Parts 3–7.

Part 3 describes automated accounting for a departmentalized merchandising business organized as a corporation. Topics presented include performing file maintenance, recording daily transactions, and completing end-of-fiscal-period work. Each chapter is followed by a computer application that can be completed using a micro-computer. These computer applications provide students with hands-on experience using microcomputers to complete an automated accounting cycle.

Part 4 describes accounting for uncollectible accounts, plant assets, prepaid expenses, accrued expenses, unearned revenue, accrued revenue, and promissory notes. This part builds on what students learned in their first year of accounting study. Computer Application 4 provides for the use of a microcomputer to input plant asset data, figure depreciation, and print depreciation schedules.

Part 5 describes the organizational structure, acquisition of additional capital, and financial analysis and financial statement preparation for a corporation. This material expands student learning from first-year accounting and from Parts 2–4 of this text. Computer Application 5 provides for the use of a microcomputer to complete end-of-fiscal-period work for a corporation.

Part 6 describes management accounting. Topics presented include inventory planning and valuation, budgetary planning and control, use of accounting information for making management decisions, and financial statement analysis. Computer Application 6 provides for the use of a microcomputer to complete financial statement analysis.

Part 7 describes cost accounting for a merchandising business and for a manufacturing business. Emphasis is placed on accounting procedures for preparing departmental responsibility statements for a merchandising business and for determining product cost information for a manufacturing business.

Part 8 describes accounting for two noncorporate organizations: (1) partnerships and (2) not-for-profit organizations. Accounting procedures are described for forming a partnership, dividing partnership earnings, and liquidating a partnership. Accounting for and reporting financial information for not-for-profit organizations are described with special emphasis on governmental organizations.

The Appendix describes the capabilities and basic parts of an electronic spreadsheet and the general application of spreadsheets to accounting activities. The Appendix introduces students to an additional use of computers in accounting. This material is provided as a supplementary topic for the advanced accounting course.

FEATURES

Important features of this fourth edition of CENTURY 21 ACCOUNTING, Advanced Course, include the following.

* *Competency-based program.* The text is organized as a complete, competency-based instructional program. General behavioral goals are listed on each part opener of the text. Enabling performance tasks are listed at the beginning of each chapter. Terminal performance objectives are provided in the Teacher's Reference Guide. The end-of-chapter practice material and the testing program that accompanies the textbook are an integral part of the competency-based program.

- *Professional accounting fields and concepts.* A new Chapter 1 introduces students to professional accounting fields through a description of the accounting framework and the accounting concepts which guide accounting practice.

- *Inventory planning and valuation.* A new chapter in Part 6 describes planning for and valuing of merchandise on hand. This material builds on and expands what students learned in their first year of accounting study.

- *Accounting for not-for-profit organizations.* Two new chapters in Part 8 describe not-for-profit accounting with special emphasis on accounting for governmental organizations.

- *Financial statement analysis.* Emphasis is placed on financial statement analysis which is now introduced in Part 2 and integrated throughout the remainder of the text.

- *Automated accounting.* Three completely revised chapters in Part 3 describe automated accounting and emphasize the use of microcomputers. Automated accounting is integrated throughout the remainder of the text through the use of computer applications. These computer applications provide for the use of microcomputers to automate problems from the textbook.

- *Microcomputer software.* Software is available to automate the computer application problems. The software that accompanies *Advanced Automated Accounting for the Microcomputer* and the template diskette are needed to complete these problems. The template diskette contains opening data for computer application problems. The time-consuming activity of key-entering account titles, account numbers, and beginning balances is eliminated.

- *Charts of accounts.* Complete charts of accounts are given at the beginning of each part. These charts provide students with easy reference to account titles and general ledger organization as they study the chapters and complete the practice work.

- *Color-coded accounting forms.* Distinctive background tints are used for journals, ledgers, and financial statements. The same colors are used throughout the text to help students identify the accounting forms.

- *Reinforcement activities.* Three reinforcement activities are provided in the text to strengthen learnings.

- *Business simulations.* Three business simulations are available to further strengthen learnings and add realism.

- *Working papers and study guides.* Accounting forms needed to complete end-of-chapter application and enrichment problems are provided in the working papers that accompany this text. A study guide is provided for each chapter.

- *Testing program.* An extensive testing program is available. One problem test is provided for each chapter except Chapter 1. Seven objective tests are provided with each test covering several chapters. A bank of test questions is provided on microcomputer diskette.

ACKNOWLEDGMENTS

The authors express their sincere appreciation to all persons who have contributed to this edition of CENTURY 21 ACCOUNTING, Advanced Course. The people who contributed to this fourth edition include the following. (a) High school teachers who shared their classroom experience and suggested ways to make the material more learnable. (b) Professional accountants who advised about accounting procedures and trends. (c) Students who suggested changes based on their learning experiences. (d) The authors of *Advanced Automated Accounting for the Microcomputer* who coordinated their software with the content of this textbook.

Robert M. Swanson
Kenton E. Ross
Robert D. Hanson

Contents

PART 4
GENERAL ACCOUNTING ADJUSTMENTS

PART 5
CORPORATION ACCOUNTING

PART 6
MANAGEMENT ACCOUNTING

PART 7
COST ACCOUNTING

PART 8
OTHER ACCOUNTING SYSTEMS

1
Professional Accounting

GENERAL BEHAVIORAL GOALS

1. Know terminology related to the framework of accounting and the forms of business organization.
2. Understand the framework of accounting, the forms of business organization, and how accounting standards are developed.
3. Understand applications of accounting concepts.

1 Accounting Framework and Concepts

ENABLING PERFORMANCE TASKS

After studying Chapter 1, you will be able to:
a. Define accounting terms related to the framework of accounting and the forms of business organization.
b. Identify the framework of accounting, the forms of business organization, and how accounting standards are developed.
c. Identify applications of accounting concepts.

Reliable financial information is needed to successfully operate a profit-making business. Business owners and managers use financial information to evaluate current operations and plan future operations. For example, are profits adequate? Should prices be increased or decreased? Should new or different products be sold? Should new equipment be bought? Should the business be expanded? Should additional employees be hired? Planning, keeping, analyzing, and interpreting financial records is called accounting. Orderly records of a business' financial activities are called accounting records.

Governmental and other not-for-profit organizations, such as churches, schools, and social clubs, also need good financial information for successful operation. For example, is the money available through taxes, dues, or donations adequate to operate the organization? Should nonprofit services be increased or decreased? Should new equipment be bought? Should additional employees be hired?

ACCOUNTING PROFESSION

Accounting is a growing profession. This growth is primarily due to the increase in number, size, and complexity of businesses, governmental

3

units, and other not-for-profit organizations. This growth is also due to continual changes in federal tax reporting requirements. Accounting employment is usually in private accounting, public accounting, or governmental/not-for-profit accounting.

Private accounting

Persons employed in private accounting work for only one business. These persons may perform a variety of duties. In small organizations they may do all of the summarizing, analyzing, and interpreting of financial information for management. In larger organizations they may share accounting responsibilities with other accounting employees.

Many private accountants are referred to as management accountants. A private accountant who has the required education and experience and passes a required examination may be granted a Certificate in Management Accounting (CMA). The CMA certificate is granted by the National Association of Accountants (NAA). The CMA certificate signifies professional status in private accounting.

Public accounting

Persons employed in public accounting may work independently or as a member of a public accounting firm. Public accountants sell services to individuals, businesses, governmental units, or other not-for-profit organizations. A public accountant who has the required education and experience and passes a required examination is designated as a Certified Public Accountant (CPA). The CPA designation is granted by the American Institute of Certified Public Accountants (AICPA). The CPA certificate signifies professional status in public accounting.

Governmental/not-for-profit accounting

Some persons employed in governmental/not-for-profit accounting work for a governmental agency (federal, state, county, or city). The Internal Revenue Service is an example of a governmental agency that employs large numbers of accountants. These persons may also work for other not-for-profit organizations such as hospitals, churches, schools, or foundations.

ACCOUNTING FIELDS

Prominent accounting fields are financial accounting, managerial accounting, cost accounting, tax accounting, accounting systems, and auditing.

Financial accounting

The recording of a business' financial activities and the periodic preparation of financial reports is called financial accounting. Financial accounting provides financial reports primarily for use by persons *external* to the organization. External users of financial accounting information include creditors, investors, bankers, and governmental units. Chapters 2 through 15 and Chapters 23 through 26 of this textbook describe the framework of financial accounting.

Managerial accounting

The analysis, measurement, and interpretation of financial accounting information is called managerial accounting. Managerial accounting provides information for *internal* decision making concerning daily operations as well as planning and control of future operations. Chapters 16 through 19 of this textbook describe the framework of managerial accounting.

Cost accounting

The determination and control of costs of a business enterprise is called cost accounting. Cost accounting provides information for *internal* decision making concerning the costs of operating merchandising and manufacturing businesses. Owners and managers use cost information for controlling current operations and planning for the future. Chapters 20 through 22 of this textbook describe the framework of cost accounting.

Tax accounting

The preparation of tax returns as well as tax planning is called tax accounting. Tax accountants prepare tax returns for their employer or client. Tax accountants must keep up to date on changes in tax regulations as well as court decisions on tax cases.

Accounting systems

Procedures which provide for financial information which will be helpful to management are called accounting systems. The systems accountant works in the design and implementation of accounting systems. Therefore, a systems accountant must be familiar with the uses and various types of electronic equipment which might make the accounting system more efficient. Chapters 6 through 8 and Computer Applications 1 through 6 of this textbook describe the framework of accounting systems utilizing electronic equipment.

Auditing

The independent reviewing and issuing of an opinion on the reliability of accounting records is called auditing. An auditor examines the records which support the financial records of a business to assure that generally accepted accounting principles (GAAP) are being followed. Also, an auditor is responsible for determining whether policies and procedures prescribed by management are being followed.

FORMS OF BUSINESS ORGANIZATION

The accounting information recorded, reported, analyzed, and interpreted may vary according to the type and form of business organization. A business is organized as either a (1) proprietorship, (2) partnership, or (3) corporation.

Proprietorship

A business owned by one person is called a proprietorship. A proprietorship is also known as a sole proprietorship. A proprietorship has a number of advantages and disadvantages.

Advantages of a proprietorship

1. A proprietorship is easy to establish.
2. The money needed to start a proprietorship need not be large.
3. A proprietorship provides complete independence for the owner. The owner has the satisfaction of making all decisions and assumes all profits or losses.

Disadvantages of a proprietorship

1. A proprietorship has limited potential for growth. Proprietorships are limited to the investment of the owner. Frequently, this investment is too small for future growth.
2. A proprietorship depends on the managerial skills of only one person. If the owner has limited managerial skills, the business may fail.
3. A proprietorship has unlimited liability. The owner is personally liable for all business debts.

Partnership

A business in which two or more persons combine their assets and skills is called a partnership. A partnership has a number of advantages and disadvantages.

Advantages of a partnership

1. A partnership is easy to establish.
2. The number of partners is unlimited. A partnership agreement is generally established which specifies each partner's investment, duties, and share of the business' profit or loss.
3. A partnership has good growth potential. Combining the assets and skills of more than one person increases investment and adds to the business' growth potential.

Disadvantages of a partnership

1. Partners have unlimited liability. As with a proprietorship, each of the owners (partners) is liable for all business debts.
2. Conflicts may develop among partners in managing a partnership. The partners may not agree on the solution to partnership problems. This potential for conflict often makes partnership management decisions difficult and ineffective.

Corporation

An organization with the legal rights of a person and which may be owned by many persons is called a corporation. The ownership of a profit-making corporation is divided into units. Each unit of ownership in a corporation is called a share of stock. Total shares of ownership in a corporation are called capital stock. An owner of one or more shares of a corporation is called a stockholder. A corporation has a number of advantages and disadvantages.

Advantages of a corporation

1. A corporation, with the legal right to act as a person, may buy, own, and sell property in its corporate name.
2. A corporation's life is independent of its owners. A corporation's life may be for a specified time, which is renewable, or it may be unlimited.
3. Unlike a proprietorship or partnership, a stockholder is not liable for a corporation's debts. Thus, a stockholder can never lose more than the amount paid for stock.
4. A corporation has good growth potential. Additional stock may be issued to provide funds for future growth.

Disadvantages of a corporation

1. The net income of a corporation is subject to double taxation — first as corporate income and later as stockholders' personal income. A corporation's net income, after payment of income tax, may be distributed to stockholders. This net income distribution is considered personal income to the stockholders and thus is subject to personal income tax.

2. A corporation has greater government regulation than either proprietorships or partnerships. Corporations come into existence under state and federal laws. Corporations are generally required to prepare more reports for both federal and state governments.

ACCOUNTING STANDARDS

The accounting profession is guided by principles and concepts to provide standardization and consistency in the work performed. A number of organizations provide assistance and influence in the development of these principles and concepts.

The Financial Accounting Standards Board (FASB) is responsible for the development of standards for financial accounting and reporting. When problems occur, the FASB studies the issues and develops recommended solutions which are distributed for review by the various accounting organizations and individual accountants. Once accepted by the accounting profession, the FASB publishes statements of financial accounting standards and financial accounting concepts. These statements are recognized by the professional accountant as generally accepted accounting principles (GAAP) which must be followed.

The American Institute of Certified Public Accountants (AICPA) is an organization of practicing certified public accountants (CPA's). The AICPA is the oldest and most influential of all organizations which guide the development of accounting principles and concepts. Administering and grading the uniform CPA examination is one of the primary roles of the AICPA.

The National Association of Accountants (NAA) is an organization of accountants concerned with how accounting information is used within an enterprise to direct business operations. Of all accounting organizations, the NAA has one of the largest memberships.

The Securities and Exchange Commission (SEC) is a governmental agency established by an act of Congress. This agency issues regulations that must be followed in the preparation of financial statements and other reports filed with the Commission. The primary role of the SEC is to regulate the issuance of stock by corporations and the trading of stock by the general public.

The Internal Revenue Service (IRS) is a governmental agency which issues regulations defining income for federal income taxation. Accounting for income tax has an influence on the development of accounting practices and concepts.

ACCOUNTING CONCEPTS

Accounting employees follow concepts commonly accepted by the profession as guides for reporting and interpreting accounting information.

The accounting procedures described in this textbook are based on the application of accepted concepts. Eleven commonly accepted concepts are described in this chapter.

CONCEPT: Going Concern

Financial statements are prepared with the expectation that a business will remain in operation indefinitely.

New businesses are started with the expectation that they will be successful. Accounting records and financial statements are designed as though businesses will continue indefinitely.

A business bought store equipment for $20,000.00. The store equipment is expected to last 10 years. Yearly depreciation therefore is recorded and reported based on the expected life of the equipment. After four years of the expected 10 year life of the equipment, the book value (cost less accumulated depreciation) of the equipment is $12,800.00. If the business ended operations and the equipment had to be sold, the amount received may be less than $12,800.00. However, accounting records are maintained with the expectation that the business will remain in operation indefinitely, and the cost will be allocated over the usable life of the equipment. The equipment value therefore remains $12,800.00 on the records regardless of what the equipment may be worth when sold.

A business is expected to continue successfully even if the owner retires or sells the business. If a business is sold, the new owner is expected to continue the business' operations.

CONCEPT: Business Entity

A business' financial information is recorded and reported separately from the owner's personal financial information.

A business owner usually owns personal items as well as business items. A business' financial records and reports must not be mixed with an owner's personal records and reports. For example, a business owner may buy insurance to protect the business and insurance to protect the owner's home. Only the insurance obtained for the business is recorded in the business' financial records. The insurance purchased for the owner's personal home is recorded in the owner's personal financial records. One bank account is used for the business and another for the owner. A business exists separately from its owner.

CONCEPT: Accounting Period Cycle

Changes in financial information are reported for a specific period of time in the form of financial statements.

Periodically, accounting records are summarized and reported to business owners and managers. The time period for which financial statements are prepared depends on the needs of the business. An accounting period may be one month, three months, six months, or one year. For tax purposes every business prepares financial statements at the end of each year.

CONCEPT: Historical Cost

The actual amount paid or received is the amount recorded in accounting records.

The actual amount paid for an item in a business transaction may be different from the value. Also, the value of an item sold may be different from the actual amount received.

Office equipment is valued at $15,000.00 and advertised at a sale price of $12,000.00. A business arranges to buy the equipment for $10,000.00. The amount recorded in the accounting records for the office equipment is the historical cost, $10,000.00 — the actual amount paid.

Business A bought a computer for $10,000.00. The historical cost of the computer according to the accounting records of Business A is $10,000.00. Business A decides two months later to sell the computer. Business A sells the computer to Business B for $8,000.00. For Business B, the historical cost of the computer is $8,000.00.

CONCEPT: Adequate Disclosure

Financial statements should contain all information necessary for a reader to understand a business' financial condition.

Accurate and up-to-date financial information about a business is needed by many persons. These persons include owners, managers, lenders, and investors. All important financial information must be adequately and completely disclosed on financial statements.

A business reports only the total liabilities of $125,000.00 on its balance sheet. However, the total liabilities include $25,000.00 in current liabilities and $100,000.00 in long-term liabilities. Therefore, the balance sheet does not adequately disclose the nature of the liabilities. The critical information not disclosed is that $25,000.00 is current and due within a few months.

CONCEPT: Consistent Reporting

In the preparation of financial statements, the same accounting concepts are applied in the same way in each accounting period.

Business decisions are based on the financial information reported on financial statements. Business decisions are often made by comparing current financial statements with previous financial statements. Accounting information recorded and reported differently each accounting period makes comparisons from one accounting period to another impossible. Unless a change is necessary to make information more easily understood, accounting information is reported in a consistent way for each accounting period.

A business reported the following on its income statement for August:

Sales...	$125,000.00
Operating Expenses.................................	100,000.00
Net Income from Operations.......................	$ 25,000.00

The same business reported the following on its income statement for September:

Sales...	$125,000.00
Cost of Merchandise Sold...........................	60,000.00
Gross Profit on Sales	$ 65,000.00
Operating Expenses.................................	40,000.00
Net Income from Operations.......................	$ 25,000.00

The two income statements are reported differently. Thus, the reader cannot compare all items on the two reports.

CONCEPT: Matching Expenses with Revenue

Revenue from business activities and expenses associated with earning that revenue are recorded in the same accounting period.

Business activities for an accounting period are summarized in financial statements. To adequately report how a business performed during an accounting period, all revenue earned as a result of business operations must be reported. Likewise, all expenses incurred during the same accounting period in producing the revenue must be reported. Matching expenses with revenue gives a true picture of business operations for an accounting period.

A business had sales of $150,000.00 in December. Expenses recorded for December were $100,000.00. Depreciation of $10,000.00 for December was not recorded with the expenses. To report accurate financial information, all expenses associated with earning revenue must be recorded in the same accounting period. Therefore, $110,000.00 should have been reported as expenses associated with earning the revenue of $150,000.00. The matching of expenses with revenue results in an accurate report of net income, $40,000.00, for December ($150,000.00 sales *minus* total expenses of $110,000.00 *equals* $40,000.00 net income).

CONCEPT: Materiality

Business activities creating dollar amounts large enough to affect business decisions should be recorded and reported as separate items in accounting records and financial statements.

Business transactions are recorded in accounting records and reported in financial statements in dollar amounts. How the amounts are recorded and reported depends on the amount involved and the relative importance of the time needed to make business decisions. Dollar amounts which are large generally will be considered in making decisions about future operations. A separate accounting record therefore is kept for these items. Dollar amounts which are small and not considered important in decision making may be combined with other amounts in the accounting records and financial statements.

Buying an office desk lamp for $15.95 represents an amount small enough to have little importance in decision making. Therefore, this amount may be combined with other unimportant amounts in one accounting record. The total amount of these unimportant items is reported as a separate item on financial statements.

Buying a computer for $16,000.00 represents an amount large enough to be considered important for future decision making. Therefore, a separate accounting record will be kept for the computer. The historical cost, $16,000.00, will also be reported separately on a balance sheet.

CONCEPT: Objective Evidence

Each transaction is described by a business document that proves the transaction did occur.

Only business transactions that actually did occur should be recorded in accounting records. The amounts recorded in accounting records must be accurate and true. One way to check the accuracy of accounting records is to check the original business papers containing details of transactions. For example, a check stub is the original business paper for cash payments. A sales invoice is the original business paper for goods sold. A receipt is the original business paper for cash received. Every entry in accounting records is supported by a business paper. When accounting information reported on financial statements needs to be checked or verified, an accountant can first check the accounting record. If the details of an entry need further checking, an accountant may then check the business papers as the objective evidence that the transaction did occur.

CONCEPT: Realization of Revenue

Revenue from business transactions is recorded at the time goods or services are sold.

A business may sell either goods or services. Cash may be received at the time of sale or an agreement may be made to receive payment at a later date. Regardless of when cash is actually received, the sale amount is recorded in the accounting records at the time of sale.

A business sells office furniture for $1,000.00. The business agrees to an initial payment of $200.00 with the remaining balance to be divided into four monthly payments of $200.00 each. The full $1,000.00 of revenue is recorded at the time of sale even though $800.00 will be paid later.

CONCEPT: Unit of Measurement

All business transactions are recorded in a common unit of measurement—the dollar.

All transactions are recorded in accounting records in terms of money. Useful nonfinancial information may also be recorded to describe the nature of a business transaction.

If part of the accounting information is financial and part is nonfinancial, financial statements will not be clear. A shoe store owner reporting only the number of shoes sold (nonfinancial) and the dollar amounts (financial) paid for expenses cannot determine net income. If the number of shoes sold and the expenses are both reported in dollar amounts (financial), the profit can be figured. Total expenses (financial) subtracted from money taken in from shoe sales (financial) equals profit. All values recorded in accounting records and reported on financial statements are reported in a common unit of measurement—the dollar.

Throughout this textbook, materials and procedures are described which apply to one or more of the concepts. In the chapters that follow, each time a concept application occurs, a concept reference is given.

ACCOUNTING TERMS

What is the meaning of each of the following?

1. accounting
2. accounting records
3. financial accounting
4. managerial accounting
5. cost accounting
6. tax accounting
7. accounting systems
8. auditing
9. proprietorship
10. partnership
11. corporation
12. share of stock
13. capital stock
14. stockholder

QUESTIONS FOR INDIVIDUAL STUDY

1. How do business owners and managers use financial information?
2. For whom does a person in private accounting work?
3. What signifies professional status in private accounting?
4. Who grants the Certificate in Management Accounting (CMA)?
5. For whom does a person in public accounting work?
6. What signifies professional status in public accounting?
7. Who grants the Certified Public Accountant (CPA) certificate?
8. For whom does a person in governmental or not-for-profit accounting work?
9. What are the prominent accounting fields?
10. What external units use a business' accounting information?
11. How is managerial accounting information used?
12. How is cost accounting information used?

13. What are three advantages of the proprietorship form of business organization?
14. What are two disadvantages of a partnership form of business organization?
15. What are four advantages of a corporate form of business organization?
16. What accounting organization is responsible for the development of standards for financial accounting and reporting?
17. What accounting organization is responsible for the administering and grading of the CPA examination?
18. What accounting organization is primarily concerned with how accounting information is used within an enterprise for directing business operations?
19. What is the primary role of the Securities and Exchange Commission (SEC)?
20. What governmental agency issues regulations for determining income for federal income taxation?
21. The expectation that a business will remain in operation indefinitely is an application of which accounting concept?
22. Recording and reporting a business' financial information separately from the owner's financial information is an application of which accounting concept?
23. Reporting changes in financial information for a specific period of time in the form of financial statements is an application of which accounting concept?
24. Recording the actual amount paid or received is an application of which accounting concept?
25. Reporting all accounting information necessary for a reader to understand a business' financial condition is an application of which accounting concept?
26. Reporting accounting information in the same way each year is an application of which accounting concept?
27. Recording in the same accounting period the revenue from business activities and expenses associated with earning that revenue is an application of which accounting concept?
28. Recording and reporting separately those business activities that create dollar amounts large enough to affect business decisions is an application of which accounting concept?
29. Recording in accounting records the information from details on a business paper is an application of which accounting concept?
30. Recording revenue from business transactions at the time goods or services are sold is an application of which accounting concept?
31. Recording in a common unit of measurement information about all business transactions is an application of which accounting concept?

CASES FOR MANAGEMENT DECISION

CASE 1 Mary Jason operates a video tape rental service. She records and reports accounting information on the basis of one-month accounting periods. The money earned from rentals is recorded in the accounting records at the time the tapes are rented to customers. Expenses for operating the business are recorded in the accounting records when actually paid. Is Ms. Jason following accepted accounting concepts? Explain.

CASE 2 Mark Mason does the accounting for Superior Office Supply. After transactions are recorded, Mr. Mason destroys the business papers containing the information for the entries. Richard Trent, a CPA, suggests that the business papers be kept for future reference. Mr. Mason argues that once a transaction has been recorded, the business paper is of no value. With whom do you agree? Explain.

CASE 3 Will Taft decides to buy a new truck for his business. Truck dealer A has a new truck listed at a price of $15,000.00. Truck dealer B has the identical truck on sale at a price of $13,500.00. Mr. Taft buys the truck from dealer B for $13,500.00. Because Mr. Taft feels the value of the new truck is really $15,000.00, he records the price of the new truck in his accounting records at $15,000.00. Do Mr. Taft's procedures follow accepted accounting concepts? Explain.

CASE 4 Susan Peitz operates a service business. She allows payment for services to be made at a later date. Mrs. Peitz records the sale of services in her accounting records at the time of sale even though she may not have received payment. Is Mrs. Peitz following accepted accounting concepts? Explain.

2
Departmentalized Accounting

GENERAL BEHAVIORAL GOALS

1. Know accounting terminology related to a departmentalized merchandising business organized as a corporation.
2. Understand accounting concepts and practices related to a departmentalized merchandising business organized as a corporation.
3. Demonstrate accounting procedures for a departmentalized merchandising business organized as a corporation.

SUPERGOLF
Chart of Accounts

Balance Sheet Accounts

(1000) ASSETS

1100   Current Assets

1105   Cash
1110   Petty Cash
1115   Accounts Receivable
1120   Allowance for Uncollectible Accounts
1125-1   Merchandise Inventory—Clothing
1125-2   Merchandise Inventory—Equipment
1130   Supplies—Office
1135   Supplies—Store
1140   Prepaid Insurance

1200   Plant Assets

1205   Office Equipment
1210   Accumulated Depreciation—Office
          Equipment
1215   Store Equipment
1220   Accumulated Depreciation—Store
          Equipment

(2000) LIABILITIES

2105   Accounts Payable
2110   Employees Income Tax
          Payable—Federal
2115   Employees Income Tax
          Payable—State
2120   Federal Income Tax Payable
2125   FICA Tax Payable
2130   Sales Tax Payable
2135   Unemployment Tax
          Payable—Federal
2140   Unemployment Tax
          Payable—State
2145   Hospital Insurance Premiums Payable
2150   Life Insurance Premiums Payable

(3000) STOCKHOLDERS' EQUITY

3105   Capital Stock
3110   Retained Earnings
3115-1   Income Summary—Clothing
3115-2   Income Summary—Equipment
3120   Income Summary—General

Income Statement Accounts

(4000) OPERATING REVENUE

4105-1   Sales—Clothing
4105-2   Sales—Equipment
4110-1   Sales Returns and
          Allowances—Clothing
4110-2   Sales Returns and
          Allowances—Equipment
4115-1   Sales Discount—Clothing
4115-2   Sales Discount—Equipment

(5000) COST OF MERCHANDISE

5105-1   Purchases—Clothing
5105-2   Purchases—Equipment
5110-1   Purchases Returns and
          Allowances—Clothing
5110-2   Purchases Returns and
          Allowances—Equipment
5115-1   Purchases Discount—Clothing
5115-2   Purchases Discount—Equipment

(6000) OPERATING EXPENSES

6100   Selling Expenses

6105   Advertising Expense
6110   Credit Card Fee Expense
6115   Depreciation Expense—Store
          Equipment
6120-1   Salary Expense—Clothing
6120-2   Salary Expense—Equipment
6125   Supplies Expense—Store

6200   Administrative Expenses

6205   Bad Debts Expense
6210   Depreciation Expense—Office
          Equipment
6215   Insurance Expense
6220   Miscellaneous Expense
6225   Payroll Taxes Expense
6230   Rent Expense
6235   Salary Expense—Administrative
6240   Supplies Expense—Office

(7000) INCOME TAX

7105   Federal Income Tax

The chart of accounts for Supergolf is illustrated above for
ready reference as you study Part 2 of this textbook.

2 Recording Purchases and Cash Payments

ENABLING PERFORMANCE TASKS

After studying Chapter 2, you will be able to:
a. Define accounting terms related to departmental purchases and cash payments.
b. Identify accounting concepts and practices related to departmental purchases and cash payments.
c. Record departmental purchases, purchases returns and allowances, and cash payments.
d. Identify banking practices.
e. Reconcile a bank statement.

Accurate and up-to-date financial information is needed to make decisions about a business' operations. Financial information is needed to prepare financial statements and various tax reports. The recording, summarizing, and reporting of financial information may be done by hand or by machine. Business size, type, and complexity determine how financial information and records are kept and reported. Accounting concepts and practices however are the same regardless of procedures and equipment used.

ACCOUNTING PRINCIPLES

Anything of value that is owned is called an asset. An amount owed by a business is called a liability. Financial rights to the assets of a business are called equities. The value of the owner's equity is called capital. In a corporation the value of the owner's equity is referred to as stockholder's equity.

An equation showing the relationship among assets, liabilities, and capital is called an accounting equation. The accounting equation may be stated as assets = equities. More commonly the equation is stated as assets = liabilities + capital. The accounting equation is shown in the following T account.

Accounting Equation	
(LEFT side) Assets	(RIGHT side) Liabilities + Capital

The equation is often viewed as forming a "T." Assets are listed on the left side of the T and equities (liabilities and capital) on the right side of the T. Total assets must always equal total liabilities plus capital.

ACCOUNTING RECORDS

Accounting records show changes and the current value of each asset, liability, and capital (or stockholders' equity) account. In the United States, the values are stated in dollars and cents. *(CONCEPT: Unit of Measurement)*

> The concept reference above indicates the application of a specific accounting concept. For a complete statement and explanation of the concepts, refer to Chapter 1.

Information about business transactions is first obtained from original business papers. A business paper from which information is obtained for a journal entry is called a source document. Each journal entry must be supported by a source document proving that a transaction did occur. *(CONCEPT: Objective Evidence)* Common source documents include receipts, check stubs, cash register tapes, invoices, and memorandums. A source document describes in detail the information about a transaction.

Journals

A form for recording accounting information in chronological order is called a journal. A journal used to record only one kind of transaction is called a special journal. Businesses with many transactions of the same kind commonly use four special journals.

1. Purchases journal — for all purchases on account
2. Cash payments journal — for all cash payments
3. Sales journal — for all sales on account
4. Cash receipts journal — for all cash receipts

When a business uses special journals, another journal is also used for entries that cannot be recorded in special journals. A journal with two amount columns used to record transactions that cannot be recorded in a special journal is called a general journal.

All journals include amount columns for recording the dollars and cents of a transaction. *(CONCEPT: Unit of Measurement)* The general journal, for example, has two amount columns. The *left* amount column is headed Debit. The *right* amount column is headed Credit. An entry recorded in a debit column is called a debit. An entry recorded in a credit column is called a credit. The "T" described previously in the accounting equation is also present in a general journal's debit and credit amount columns as shown in Illustration 2-1.

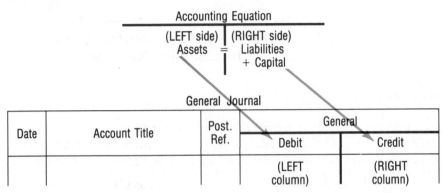

Illustration 2-1
Relationship of "T" in the accounting equation and general journal

Recording both debit and credit parts of a transaction is called double-entry accounting. The accounting equation is the basis for all double-entry accounting. Two accounting principles are common to double-entry accounting. (1) The total value of things owned by a business (assets) *equals* the total value of claims of outsiders (liabilities) and claims of owners (capital). (2) Debits equal credits for each business transaction recorded.

Accounts

Journal entries are recorded in chronological order by transaction date. Periodically, information is sorted to summarize like kinds of information. An accounting form used to sort and summarize changes in a specific item is called an account. The basic elements of an account form are the two amount columns used to record debit and credit amounts from a journal. The two amount columns form a "T" as shown in Illustration 2-2.

Debit	Credit
(LEFT column)	(RIGHT column)

Illustration 2-2
Two amount columns
of an account

The difference between the totals of amounts in an account's Debit and Credit columns is called an account balance. Each business transaction causes a change in two or more account balances. Increases in an account's balance are recorded in the same column as its normal balance. Decreases in an account's balance are recorded in the column opposite its normal balance. The normal balances of different classifications of accounts are shown in Illustration 2-3.

Assets		=	Liabilities		+	Capital	

Any Asset Account			**Any Liability Account**			**Any Capital Account**	
DEBIT column Normal balance Increase +	CREDIT column Decrease −		DEBIT column Decrease −	CREDIT column Normal balance Increase +		DEBIT column Decrease −	CREDIT column Normal balance Increase +

						Any Revenue Account	
						DEBIT column Decrease −	CREDIT column Normal balance Increase +

						Any Cost Account	
						DEBIT column Normal balance Increase +	CREDIT column Decrease −

						Any Expense Account	
						DEBIT column Normal balance Increase +	CREDIT column Decrease −

Illustration 2-3
Normal balances
of accounts

Asset account balances are increased by debits and decreased by credits. Liability, capital, and revenue account balances are increased by credits and decreased by debits. Cost and expense account balances are increased by debits and decreased by credits.

Ledgers

A group of accounts is called a ledger. A ledger that contains all accounts needed to prepare financial statements is called a general ledger. A ledger that is summarized in a single general ledger account is called a subsidiary ledger. An account in a general ledger that summarizes all accounts in a subsidiary ledger is called a controlling account. Two subsidiary ledgers and two general ledger controlling accounts are commonly used.

Subsidiary Ledgers	**Controlling Accounts**
Accounts Receivable Ledger	Accounts Receivable
Accounts Payable Ledger	Accounts Payable

Accounts for customers buying merchandise on account are kept in an accounts receivable ledger. Separate accounts are kept in an accounts payable ledger for vendors to whom money is owed.

DEPARTMENTALIZED ACCOUNTING

Management decisions depend on accounting information about each phase of a business. Accounting information about the kinds of merchandise that produce the greatest or the least profit is needed. When a business has two or more departments, accounting information is needed about how well each department is doing.

An accounting system showing accounting information for two or more departments is called a departmental accounting system. In a departmental accounting system, gross profit is figured for each department. The general ledger therefore must include a number of separate departmental accounts. Shoe stores, furniture stores, computer stores, department stores, and sporting goods stores are examples of firms that commonly organize on a departmental basis.

A business that purchases and sells goods is called a merchandising business. Supergolf, the merchandising business described in Part 2, is a corporation organized on a departmental basis. The business sells golf clothing and golf equipment, such as clubs, balls, and golf carts.

> A business may have two types of equipment: (1) equipment purchased for sale to customers and (2) equipment used in the operation of the business. Supergolf purchases and sells golf equipment. Supergolf also has office equipment and store equipment that is used in the operation of the business.

Supergolf uses a departmental accounting system. Accounting information is recorded and reported for two departments: (1) Clothing, and (2) Equipment. Sales are made to individuals as well as to golf clubs and school systems. Supergolf expects to make money and to continue in business indefinitely. *(CONCEPT: Going Concern)* The separate departmental accounts for Supergolf are in the chart of accounts, page 18. The accounts for the clothing department are indicated by a *-1* after the account number. Accounts for the equipment department are indicated by a *-2* after the account number.

DEPARTMENTAL PURCHASES ON ACCOUNT

A departmentalized business records a purchase on account in the same way as a business with a single department except for two differences. (1) Each purchase invoice has a notation placed on it showing to which department the purchase applies. (2) Each department has a separate purchases debit column in the purchases journal.

Journalizing purchases on account

All departmental purchases on account are recorded in a purchases journal. Supergolf's purchases journal has special Purchases Debit columns for each department—Clothing and Equipment. Supergolf's purchases journal for June, 1988, is shown in Illustration 2-4.

	DATE	ACCOUNT CREDITED	PURCH. NO.	POST. REF.	ACCOUNTS PAYABLE CREDIT	PURCHASES DEBIT CLOTHING	PURCHASES DEBIT EQUIPMENT	
1	1988 June 1	Turfco, Inc.	336		945 00		945 00	1
2								2

PURCHASES JOURNAL   PAGE 11
1   2   3

Illustration 2-4
Departmental purchases
journal

The purchase invoice is the source document for each entry in the purchases journal. (CONCEPT: *Objective Evidence*)

GENERAL LEDGER

Purchases — Equipment

945.00 |

Accounts Payable

| 945.00

ACCOUNTS PAYABLE LEDGER

Turfco, Inc.

| 945.00

June 1, 1988.
Purchased golf equipment on account from Turfco, Inc., $945.00. Purchase Invoice No. 336.

The analysis of this transaction is shown in the T accounts.

In the general ledger, Purchases — Equipment is increased by a $945.00 debit. Accounts Payable is increased by a $945.00 credit. In the accounts payable ledger, Turfco, Inc., is increased by a $945.00 credit.

The details of Purchase Invoice No. 336 are recorded on line 1 of the purchases journal, Illustration 2-4. The date, *1988, June 1*, is written in the Date column. The vendor name, *Turfco, Inc.*, is recorded in the Account Credited column. The purchase invoice number, *336*, is entered in the Purch. No. column. Since only purchase invoice numbers are written in the column, no identifying letter is necessary. The credit amount, *$945.00*, is written in the Accounts Payable Credit column. The debit amount, *$945.00*, is recorded in the Purchases — Equipment Debit column.

Posting from a purchases journal

Transferring information from journal entries to ledger accounts is called posting. Supergolf keeps vendor accounts in an accounts payable ledger. Individual amounts in the purchases journal's Accounts Payable Credit column are posted daily to the appropriate vendor accounts. Posting line 1 from the purchases journal to an accounts payable ledger account is shown in Illustration 2-5.

The date, *1988, June 1*, is written in the account's Date column. The journal page number, *P11*, is placed in the Post. Ref. column. The amount, *$945.00*, is recorded in the Credit column. Since there is no previous balance in this account, the amount in the Credit column is also the balance of the account. Therefore, this amount, *$945.00*, is also written in the Credit Balance column. The vendor number, *270*, is placed in the purchases journal's Post. Ref. column to show that posting is complete.

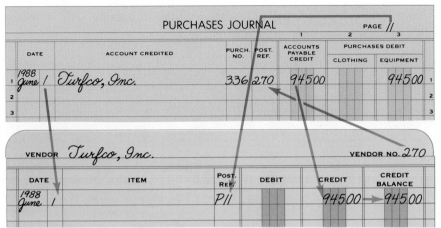

Illustration 2-5
Posting from a purchases journal to an accounts payable ledger account

The purchases journal is proved and ruled at the end of each month. A journal is proved by adding each column and then proving that the sum of the debit column totals equals the sum of the credit column totals. Double lines are then ruled across the amount columns. Each amount column total is posted to the general ledger account named in the column heading. Posting an amount column total from the purchases journal to a general ledger account is shown in Illustration 2-6.

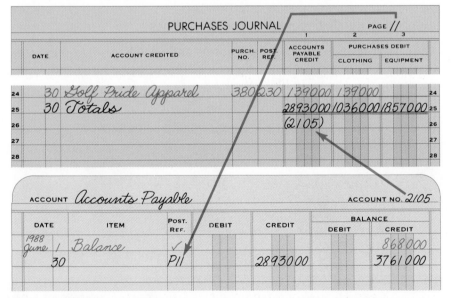

Illustration 2-6
Posting a total from a purchases journal to a general ledger account

To indicate that the posting came from the purchases journal, page 11, *P11* is written in the ledger account's Post. Ref. column. The account number, *2105*, is written in parentheses immediately below the purchases journal's column total to show that the amount has been posted.

Supergolf's departmental purchases journal, Illustration 2-7, is shown after all posting has been completed.

	DATE	ACCOUNT CREDITED	PURCH. NO.	POST. REF.	ACCOUNTS PAYABLE CREDIT	PURCHASES DEBIT		
						CLOTHING	EQUIPMENT	
1	1988 June 1	Turfco, Inc.	336	270	94500		94500	1
11	30	Ecolo-Golf Co.	358	220	392000	392000		11
12	30	Golf Pride Apparel	359	230	139000	139000		12
13	30	Totals			2893000	1036000	1857000	13
14					(2105)	(5105-1)	(5105-2)	14
15								15

PURCHASES JOURNAL   PAGE 11

Illustration 2-7
Departmental purchases journal after posting has been completed

DEPARTMENTAL PURCHASES RETURNS AND ALLOWANCES

Merchandise may be returned to a vendor for several reasons. The merchandise may be unsatisfactory. The merchandise may not be what was ordered. Also, merchandise may be received in damaged condition. When merchandise is returned, the vendor usually gives the buyer credit.

Journalizing purchases returns and allowances

Supergolf records all purchases returns and allowances in a purchases returns and allowances journal. Supergolf's purchases returns and allowances journal is shown in Illustration 2-8.

PURCHASES RETURNS AND ALLOWANCES JOURNAL   PAGE 6

	DATE	ACCOUNT DEBITED	DEBIT MEMO. NO.	POST. REF.	ACCOUNTS PAYABLE DEBIT	PURCHASES RETURNS AND ALLOWANCES CREDIT		
						CLOTHING	EQUIPMENT	
1	1988 June 3	Keno Golf Products	22	240	6450		6450	1
2	4	Ecolo-Golf Co.	23	220	12630	12630		2
3	7	Classic Golf Supply	24	210	9600		9600	3
4	8	Turfco, Inc.	25	270	4950		4950	4
5	13	Golf Pride Apparel	26	230	18600	18600		5
6	20	Nova Golf Carts	27	250	6500		6500	6
7	23	Universal Golf Supply	28	280	56000		56000	7
8	27	Softouch Golf Equip.	29	260	34000		34000	8
9	30	Totals			148730	31230	117500	9
10					(2105)	(5110-1)	(5110-2)	10
11								11

Illustration 2-8
Departmental purchases returns and allowances journal

Details of a purchases return or allowance may be stated in a letter, or the buyer may issue a debit memorandum. When returning merchandise or requesting an adjustment, Supergolf uses a debit memorandum. A debit memorandum is the source document for a purchases returns and allowances transaction. *(CONCEPT: Objective Evidence)*

> Before journalizing a purchases return or allowance, some buyers wait for written notice from the seller. This written notice is usually in the form of a credit memorandum received from a seller. When this procedure is followed, a buyer uses the credit memorandum from the seller as the transaction's source document. *(CONCEPT: Objective Evidence)*

An account that reduces a related account on financial statements is called a contra account. Purchases—Equipment is a cost account. Therefore, an account showing deductions from a purchases account is a contra cost account. Purchases Returns and Allowances—Equipment is one of Supergolf's contra cost accounts. Purchases returns and allowances are kept in a separate account and not deducted directly from the purchases account. This procedure helps the business see what proportion of the merchandise was returned to vendors.

June 3, 1988.
Returned damaged golf equipment to Keno Golf Products, $64.50, from Purchase Invoice No. 333. Debit Memorandum No. 22.

The analysis of this transaction is shown in the T accounts. In the general ledger, Accounts Payable is decreased by a $64.50 debit. Purchases Returns and Allowances—Equipment is increased by a $64.50 credit. In the accounts payable ledger, the vendor account, Keno Golf Products, is decreased by a $64.50 debit.

The details of Debit Memorandum No. 22 are recorded on line 1 of the purchases returns and allowances journal, Illustration 2-8. The date, *1988, June 3,* is written in the Date column. The vendor name, *Keno Golf Products,* is recorded in the Account Debited column. The debit memorandum number, *22,* is entered in the Debit Memo. No. column. The debit memorandum amount, *$64.50,* is written in the Accounts Payable Debit column. The credit amount, *$64.50,* is written in the Purchases Returns and Allowances—Equipment Credit column.

GENERAL LEDGER	
Accounts Payable	
64.50	
Purchases Returns and	
Allowances—Equipment	
	64.50
ACCOUNTS PAYABLE LEDGER	
Keno Golf Products	
64.50	

Posting from a purchases returns and allowances journal

Purchases returns and allowances are posted in the same manner as purchases on account. Each amount written in the Accounts Payable Debit column is posted daily to the vendor account written in the Account Debited column. To indicate that posting came from the purchases returns and allowances journal, page 6, *PR6* is recorded in the Post. Ref. column of the account. The vendor number for Keno Golf Products, *240*, is placed in the Post. Ref. column on line 1 of the journal to indicate completion of posting.

Sometimes a purchases return or allowance is made after a vendor has been paid in full. This situation might happen if an invoice is paid very soon after it is received. When this happens, the vendor account after posting has a debit balance instead of a normal credit balance. This debit balance reduces the amount to be paid for future purchases. An account balance that is opposite the normal balance is called a contra balance. A contra balance is shown by enclosing the amount in parentheses in the account's Balance column.

A purchases returns and allowances journal is proved, ruled, and posted at the end of each month. Each amount column total is posted to the general ledger account named in the column heading. The account number is written below the journal's column total to show that the amount has been posted. Supergolf's departmental purchases returns and allowances journal, Illustration 2-8, is shown after all posting has been completed.

DEPARTMENTAL CASH PAYMENTS

Most of Supergolf's cash payments are made by check. Therefore, check stubs are the source documents for most cash payments. *(CONCEPT: Objective Evidence)*

Journalizing cash payments

All cash payments are recorded in a cash payments journal. Supergolf's cash payments journal, shown in Illustration 2-9, has two debit columns—General Debit and Accounts Payable Debit. The journal also has four credit columns—General Credit, a Purchases Discount Credit column for each of the two departments, and Cash Credit.

Cash payment on account

Purchases on account are expected to be paid within the credit period agreed upon. A seller may encourage early payment by allowing a deduction from the invoice amount. A deduction that a seller allows on an invoice amount to encourage prompt payment is called a cash discount. A cash discount on purchases taken by a buyer is called a purchases discount.

A purchases discount is usually stated as a percentage that can be deducted from the invoice amount. For example, the terms of an invoice may be written as *2/10, n/30*. The expression 2/10 means that a 2% discount may be deducted if payment is made within 10 days of the invoice date. The expression n/30 means that payment of the invoice amount must be made within 30 days of the invoice date. No discount can be deducted however if payment is made after 10 days from the invoice date. Supergolf takes advantage of all discounts allowed by vendors.

DATE	ACCOUNT TITLE	CK. NO.	POST. REF.	GENERAL DEBIT	GENERAL CREDIT	ACCOUNTS PAYABLE DEBIT	PURCH. DISCOUNT CR. CLOTHING	PURCH. DISCOUNT CR. EQUIPMENT	CASH CREDIT	
1988 June 1	Classic Golf Supply	315	210			62500		1250	61250	1
1	Supplies – Office	316	1135	13600					13600	2
1	Rent Expense	317	6230	150000					150000	3
3	Ecolo-Golf Co.	318	220			45000	900		44100	4
4	Supplies – Store	319	1135	8950					8950	5
4	Miscellaneous Expense	320	6220	3900					3900	6
4	Universal Golf Supply	321	280			86000		1720	84280	7
30	Supplies – Office	330	1130	16400					40200	16
	Supplies – Store		1135	13600						17
	Advertising Expense		6105	5600						18
	Miscellaneous Expense		6220	4600						19
30	Miscellaneous Expense	331	6220	7300					7300	20
30	Miscellaneous Expense	M18	6220	1280					1280	21
30	Credit Card Fee Expense	M19	6110	44000					44000	22
30	Totals			1962000	183000	4394000	14530	33350	6125120	23
				(✓)	(✓)	(2105)	(5115-1)	(5115-2)	(1105)	24

CASH PAYMENTS JOURNAL — PAGE 13

A purchases discount reduces the amount previously recorded in the purchases account. The account Purchases Discount—Equipment is in the cost of merchandise division of Supergolf's general ledger. Purchases discounts are kept in separate accounts and not deducted directly from the purchases accounts. This procedure helps the business see what proportion of purchases on account were allowed purchases discounts. An account that reduces a related account on financial statements is known as a contra account. The purchases discount accounts are contra cost accounts.

June 1, 1988.
Paid on account to Classic Golf Supply, $612.50, covering Purchase Invoice No. 331 for equipment, $625.00, less 2% discount, $12.50. Check No. 315.

The analysis of this transaction is shown in the T accounts. In the general ledger, Accounts Payable is decreased by a $625.00 debit. Cash is decreased by a $612.50 credit. Purchases Discount—Equipment is increased by a $12.50 credit. In the accounts payable ledger, Classic Golf Supply is decreased by a $625.00 debit.

The entry on line 1, Illustration 2-9, shows the cash payment to Classic Golf Supply in which there is a purchases discount. The date, *1988, June 1,* is written in the Date column. The vendor name, *Classic Golf Supply,* is recorded in the Account Title column. The check number, *315,* is entered in the Ck. No. column. The debit amount, *$625.00,* is written in the Accounts Payable Debit column. The credit

Illustration 2-9
Departmental cash payments journal

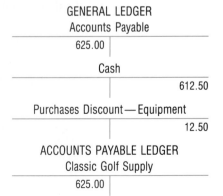

GENERAL LEDGER
Accounts Payable

| 625.00 | |

Cash

| | 612.50 |

Purchases Discount—Equipment

| | 12.50 |

ACCOUNTS PAYABLE LEDGER
Classic Golf Supply

| 625.00 | |

amount, *$12.50,* is recorded in the Purchases Discount — Equipment Credit column. The credit amount, *$612.50,* is entered in the Cash Credit column.

Cash payment for supplies

June 1, 1988.
Bought office supplies for cash, $136.00. Check No. 316.

Supplies — Office

| 136.00 |

Cash

| | 136.00 |

The analysis for this transaction is shown in the T accounts. Supplies — Office is increased by a $136.00 debit. Cash is decreased by a $136.00 credit.

The entry on line 2 of the cash payments journal, Illustration 2-9, shows the cash payment for supplies. The date, *1,* is written in the Date column. The account title, *Supplies — Office,* is recorded in the Account Title column. The check number, *316,* is entered in the Ck. No. column. The debit amount, *$136.00,* is written in the General Debit column. The credit amount, *$136.00,* is written in the Cash Credit column.

Cash payment for an expense

June 1, 1988.
Paid rent expense, $1,500.00. Check No. 317.

Rent Expense

| 1,500.00 |

Cash

| | 1,500.00 |

The analysis of this transaction is shown in the T accounts. Rent Expense is increased by a $1,500.00 debit. Cash is decreased by a $1,500.00 credit.

The entry on line 3 of the cash payments journal, Illustration 2-9, shows the cash payment for an expense. The date, *1,* is written in the Date column. The account title, *Rent Expense,* is recorded in the Account Title column. The check number, *317,* is entered in the Ck. No. column. The debit amount, *$1,500.00,* is written in the General Debit column. The credit amount, *$1,500.00,* is written in the Cash Credit column.

Cash payment to replenish petty cash

Supergolf deposits all cash receipts in a bank. Some money however is kept on hand for making small cash payments and for making change at the cash register.

An amount of cash kept on hand and used for making small payments is called petty cash. Supergolf has a petty cash fund of $500.00. A petty cash fund is replenished whenever the amount on hand becomes low. Supergolf replenishes petty cash whenever the fund drops below $100.00.

To replenish petty cash, a check is written for the amount spent from the fund. The check is cashed and the money placed back in the petty cash fund. Regardless of the amount remaining, the petty cash fund is always replenished on the last business day of each fiscal period. This procedure assures that all expenditures are recorded during the fiscal period in which actually made. *(CONCEPT: Matching Expenses with Revenue)*

June 30, 1988.
Replenished petty cash. Charge the following accounts: Supplies — Office, $164.00; Supplies — Store, $136.00; Advertising Expense, $56.00; Miscellaneous Expense, $46.00; total, $402.00. Check No. 330.

The analysis of this transaction is shown in the T accounts. The accounts increased by debits are: Supplies — Office, $164.00; Supplies — Store, $136.00; Advertising Expense, $56.00; and Miscellaneous Expense, $46.00. Cash is decreased by a $402.00 credit, the total amount needed to replenish petty cash. When Check No. 330 is cashed and the $402.00 is placed back in the petty cash fund, the fund again totals $500.00.

Supplies — Office	
164.00	

Supplies — Store	
136.00	

Advertising Expense	
56.00	

Miscellaneous Expense	
46.00	

Cash	
	402.00

The entry on lines 16 through 19 of the cash payments journal, Illustration 2-9, shows the cash payment to replenish petty cash. The date, *30*, is entered once in the Date column, line 16. The account titles are written in the Account Title column. The check number, *330*, is entered once in the Ck. No. column, line 16. The debit amounts are recorded in the General Debit column. The credit amount is written in the Cash Credit column.

Posting from a cash payments journal

Cash payments are posted in a similar manner as purchases on account and purchases returns and allowances. Supergolf posts daily to the general ledger each amount written in the cash payments journal's General Debit and General Credit columns. Also, each amount written in the Accounts Payable Debit column is posted daily to the accounts payable ledger. The cash payments journal is abbreviated as *CP* in the Post. Ref. column of the ledger accounts.

At the end of each month, the cash payments journal is proved and ruled. Totals of the special amount columns are then posted to their respective accounts in the general ledger. The general ledger account number for each respective account is written in parentheses immediately below the total. A check mark is written in parentheses below the totals of the General Debit and General Credit columns to show that these totals are not posted. Supergolf's departmental cash payments journal, Illustration 2-9, is shown after all posting has been completed.

BANKING PRACTICES

Banks keep detailed records of their depositors' checking accounts. Records are kept of all deposits, all checks paid, and miscellaneous charges.

Miscellaneous charges include checking account and credit card service charges.

A report of deposits, withdrawals, and bank balance sent to a depositor by a bank is called a bank statement. Bank statements are commonly sent to depositors monthly. A bank usually includes all canceled checks listed on the statement.

Reconciling a bank statement

A depositor should check the bank statement for accuracy as soon as it is received. Any errors found should be reported immediately to the bank. The bank balance is compared with the checkbook balance. Bringing information on a bank statement and a checkbook into agreement is called reconciling a bank statement.

Supergolf uses the steps and the form shown in Illustration 2-10 when reconciling the bank statement each month.

RECONCILIATION OF BANK STATEMENT   Date *June 30, 1988*

1. Enter CHECKBOOK BALANCE as shown on check stub.
2. Enter and add bank charges to obtain TOTAL BANK CHARGES.
3. Deduct TOTAL BANK CHARGES from CHECKBOOK BALANCE to obtain ADJUSTED CHECKBOOK BALANCE.
4. Enter BANK BALANCE as shown on bank statement.
5. Enter and add the amounts of any outstanding deposits recorded on the check stubs but not listed on the bank statement to obtain TOTAL OUTSTANDING DEPOSITS.
6. Add TOTAL OUTSTANDING DEPOSITS to BANK BALANCE to obtain TOTAL.
7. Sort all checks included in the statement numerically or by date issued.
    a. Check off on the check stubs of the checkbook each of the checks paid by the bank.
    b. Enter the check numbers and amounts of checks still outstanding.
    c. Add the outstanding checks to obtain TOTAL OUTSTANDING CHECKS.
8. Deduct TOTAL OUTSTANDING CHECKS from TOTAL to obtain ADJUSTED BANK BALANCE.
9. The ADJUSTED CHECKBOOK BALANCE and the ADJUSTED BANK BALANCE should agree, proving that both the checkbook balance and the bank balance are correct.

(1) CHECKBOOK BALANCE .... $ 33,231.55   (4) BANK BALANCE .... $ 20,525.23

BANK CHARGES

Description	Amount	
Service Charge	12	80
Credit Card Charge	440	00

OUTSTANDING DEPOSITS

Date	Amount	
6-30	12,728	52

(5) ADD TOTAL OUTSTANDING DEPOSITS .... $ 12,728.52

(6) TOTAL .... $ 33,253.75

(2) DEDUCT TOTAL BANK CHARGES ... $ 452.80

OUTSTANDING CHECKS

CK. NO.	Amount	
330	402	00
331	73	00

(7) DEDUCT TOTAL OUTSTANDING CHECKS .... $ 475.00

(3) ADJUSTED CHECKBOOK BALANCE . $ 32,778.75   (8) ADJUSTED BANK BALANCE .... $ 32,778.75

Illustration 2-10
Printed form for
reconciling a bank
statement

An adjusted checkbook balance and an adjusted bank balance must be the same. The reconciliation, Illustration 2-10, shows that both balances are the same, $32,778.75.

Journalizing bank charges

All bank charges listed on a bank statement are considered cash payments. Even though no checks are issued, each bank charge is recorded in a cash payments journal.

Supergolf has two bank charges. One charge is for bank service in maintaining the checking account. The other charge is a fee based on a percentage of the total of credit card sales deposited with the bank. No check stubs are available to serve as source documents for recording these two bank charges. Therefore, memorandums are prepared showing the details of each service charge. *(CONCEPT: Objective Evidence)*

June 30, 1988.
Recorded bank service charge, $12.80. Memorandum No. 18.

The analysis of this bank service charge transaction is shown in the T accounts. Miscellaneous Expense is increased by a $12.80 debit. Cash is decreased by a $12.80 credit.

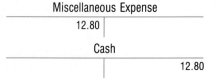

June 30, 1988.
Recorded bank credit card charge, $440.00. Memorandum No. 19.

The analysis of this bank credit card charge transaction is shown in the T accounts. Credit Card Fee Expense is increased by a $440.00 debit. Cash is decreased by a $440.00 credit.

The bank service charge and credit card charge are recorded on lines 21 and 22 of the cash payments journal, Illustration 2-9. The date is written in the Date column. The account titles are recorded in the Account Title column. The memorandum numbers are entered in the Ck. No. column and identified by the letter *M*. The debit amounts are written in the General Debit column. The credit amounts are written in the Cash Credit column.

ACCOUNTING TERMS

What is the meaning of each of the following?

1. asset
2. liability
3. equities
4. capital
5. accounting equation
6. source document
7. journal
8. special journal
9. general journal
10. debit
11. credit
12. double-entry accounting
13. account
14. account balance
15. ledger
16. general ledger
17. subsidiary ledger
18. controlling account
19. departmental accounting system
20. merchandising business
21. posting
22. contra account
23. contra balance
24. cash discount
25. purchases discount
26. petty cash
27. bank statement
28. reconciling a bank statement

QUESTIONS FOR INDIVIDUAL STUDY

1. What determines how financial information and records are kept and reported?
2. Supporting each journal entry with a source document to prove that a transaction did occur is an application of which accounting concept?
3. What five source documents are mentioned in this chapter?
4. What four special journals are commonly used by businesses with many transactions of the same kind?
5. What two accounting principles are common to double-entry accounting?
6. What is the normal balance side of asset accounts? of liability accounts? of capital accounts? of revenue accounts? of cost accounts? of expense accounts?
7. What is the name of the general ledger controlling account that summarizes all accounts in an accounts receivable subsidiary ledger?
8. What is the name of the general ledger controlling account that summarizes all accounts in an accounts payable subsidiary ledger?
9. What types of businesses commonly organize their accounting records on a departmental basis?
10. What two types of equipment might a business have?
11. Which accounting concept applies to Supergolf's expectation to make money and continue in business indefinitely?
12. What accounts are affected, and how, by a purchase on account by Supergolf's equipment department?
13. For what reasons might merchandise be returned to a vendor?
14. What source document does Supergolf use for a purchases returns and allowances transaction?
15. Why does Supergolf record purchases returns and allowances amounts in a separate account?
16. What accounts are affected, and how, by a purchases return of equipment transaction?
17. What is the source document for most entries in a cash payments journal?
18. Why would a seller allow a deduction from an invoice amount?
19. When the terms of a purchase invoice are 2/10, n/30, what payment options are available?
20. What accounts are affected, and how, by a cash payment on account transaction for equipment which includes a purchases discount?
21. How often does Supergolf replenish its petty cash fund?
22. Why is a petty cash fund always replenished on the last day of each fiscal period regardless of the amount remaining in the fund?
23. How often does Supergolf post individual amounts in a cash payments journal's Accounts Payable Debit column?
24. What three items do banks keep records of for their depositors' checking accounts?
25. What two bank charges are paid by Supergolf?

CASES FOR MANAGEMENT DECISION

CASE 1 Alice Walters manages a shoe store. The store's general ledger includes a single sales account and a single purchases account. Periodically, Miss Walters has an accountant review her accounting records and procedures. The accountant recommends that Miss Walters change to a departmentalized accounting system. The accountant recommends that separate revenue and cost accounts be kept for the two types of merchandise sold — men's shoes and women's shoes. Miss Walters objects to the accountant's recommendation. She sees no advantage to complicating the accounting system by having separate departmental revenue and cost accounts. With whom do you agree? Why?

CASE 2 Juan Reyes manages a furniture and appliance store. He has found that his bank statement and checkbook reconcile without error month after month. In order to save the time spent reconciling his bank statement each month, Mr. Reyes decides to make the reconciliation once every six months. His daughter, who helps with the business' accounting, disagrees with this practice. With whom do you agree? Why?

APPLICATION PROBLEMS

PROBLEM 2-1 Journalizing and posting departmental purchases on account and purchases returns and allowances

Adolfo Footwear, Inc., has two departments: Men's Shoes and Women's Shoes. The ledgers are given in the working papers accompanying this textbook. The balances are recorded as of August 1 of the current year.

Instructions: 1. Record the following selected transactions on page 16 of a purchases journal and on page 7 of a purchases returns and allowances journal. Source documents are abbreviated as follows: debit memorandum, DM; purchase invoice, P.

Aug. 1. Purchased women's shoes on account from Bond Shoes, $1,250.00. P283.
    2. Purchased women's shoes on account from Catalina Shoes, Inc., $2,130.00. P284.
    4. Purchased men's shoes on account from Artex Footwear, $965.00. P285.
    6. Returned defective men's shoes to Dade-Shoes, Inc., $165.00, from P280. DM36.
    9. Purchased men's shoes on account from Delta Distributors, $845.00. P286.
    13. Purchased men's shoes on account from Gamex Shoes Unlimited, $1,135.00. P287.
    15. Returned defective women's shoes to Bond Shoes, $75.00, from P283. DM37.
    18. Purchased women's shoes on account from Sanz Shoes, $268.00. P288.
    20. Returned defective men's shoes to Artex Footwear, $120.00, from P285. DM38.
    23. Returned defective women's shoes to Perstel Shoes, $55.00, from P281. DM39.
    24. Purchased women's shoes on account from Catalina Shoes, Inc., $893.00. P289.
    27. Purchased men's shoes on account from Dade-Shoes, Inc., $1,045.00. P290.
    30. Purchased women's shoes on account from Bond Shoes, $1,360.00. P291.
    31. Returned defective women's shoes to Catalina Shoes, Inc., $140.00, from P289. DM40.

2. Post individual items from the purchases and purchases returns and allowances journals.
3. Prove and rule the purchases journal. Post the totals.
4. Prove and rule the purchases returns and allowances journal. Post the totals.

PROBLEM 2-2 Figuring purchases discounts and amounts due

Vista Color, Inc., a departmentalized merchandising business, takes advantage of all purchase discounts allowed by vendors. The selected purchases on account given below are to be paid within the discount period.

Purch. No.	Purchase Amount	Discount Percentage
26	$1,340.00	2%
27	845.00	1%
28	1,560.00	2%
29	936.00	2%
30	1,475.00	1%
31	780.00	1%
32	295.00	2%
33	650.00	2%

Instructions: Use a form similar to the one below. Figure and enter the discount amount in Column 4 and the amount due in Column 5 for each purchase number. The amounts figured for Purch. No. 26 are given as an example.

1	2	3	4	5
Purch. No.	Purchase Amount	Discount Percent	Discount Amount	Amount Due
26	$1,340.00	2%	$26.80	$1,313.20

PROBLEM 2-3   Journalizing and posting departmental cash payments

Velez Sporting Goods has two departments: Ski Clothing and Ski Equipment. The ledgers are given in the working papers accompanying this textbook. The balances are recorded as of November 1 of the current year.

Instructions: 1. Record the following selected transactions on page 15 of a cash payments journal. Source documents are abbreviated as follows: check, C; memorandum, M.

Nov.   1.   Paid November rent, $1,500.00. C303.
     2.   Paid telephone bill, $110.00. C304. (Miscellaneous Expense)
     4.   Paid on account to Webster Ski Apparel, $867.30, covering P287 for ski clothing, $885.00, less 2% discount, $17.70. C305.
     5.   Paid for advertising, $83.50. C306.
     8.   Paid on account to Sportstown, Inc., $1,237.50, covering P288 for ski equipment, $1,250.00, less 1% discount, $12.50. C307.
    10.   Bought supplies for cash, $83.75. C308.
    13.   Paid on account to Century Sportswear, $943.74, covering P289 for ski clothing, $963.00, less 2% discount, $19.26. C309.
    15.   Paid miscellaneous expense, $33.50. C310.
    17.   Bought supplies for cash, $52.00. C311.
    21.   Replenished petty cash. Charge the following accounts: Supplies, $79.00; Advertising Expense, $83.40; Miscellaneous Expense, $39.60. C312.
    23.   Paid on account to United Skis, $1,803.20, covering P290 for ski equipment, $1,840.00, less 2% discount, $36.80. C313.
    27.   Paid on account to United Skis, $1,430.80, covering P292 for ski equipment, $1,460.00, less 2% discount, $29.20. C314.
    30.   Recorded bank service charge, $14.30. M26.
    30.   Recorded bank credit card charge, $388.20. M27.

  2. Post individual items from the cash payments journal.
  3. Prove and rule the cash payments journal. Post the totals.

PROBLEM 2-4   Reconciling a bank statement

On October 28 of the current year Delta, Inc., received its bank statement from First National Bank.

Instructions: Prepare a bank statement reconciliation on a form similar to the one in this chapter. The bank statement is dated October 27. The following additional information is needed.

Bank statement balance, October 27	$32,820.00
Bank service charge for October	11.80
Bank credit card charge for October	425.20
Balance on Check Stub No. 363	38,860.00
Outstanding deposit, October 27	6,152.75
Outstanding checks:	
No. 361	89.50
No. 362	460.25

ENRICHMENT PROBLEMS

MASTERY PROBLEM 2-M   Journalizing departmental purchases and cash payments

Creative Decorating, Inc., has two departments: Paint and Wallpaper. All purchases on account are subject to a 2% discount if payment is made within the discount period.

Instructions: 1. Record the following selected transactions for November of the current year. Use page 18 of a purchases journal, page 6 of a purchases returns and allowances journal, and page 16 of a cash payments journal. Source documents are abbreviated as follows: check, C; debit memorandum, DM; purchase invoice, P.

Nov. 1. Paid November rent, $1,350.00. C273.
  1. Paid for advertising, $82.50. C274.
  2. Purchased wallpaper on account from Julian Wallcovering, $750.00. P262.
  3. Paid on account to Astro Paint, covering P259 for paint, $460.00, less 2% discount. C275.
  3. Purchased paint on account from Trail-Color, Inc., $840.00. P263.
  5. Paid on account to Julian Wallcovering, covering P261 for wallpaper, $745.00, less 2% discount. C276.
  7. Returned defective paint to Trail-Color, Inc., $88.00, from P263. DM28.
  8. Purchased paint on account from Zep Paint Co., $388.00. P264.
  11. Bought supplies for cash, $82.50. C277.
  14. Purchased wallpaper on account from Famis, Inc., $550.00. P265.
  14. Paid on account to Julian Wallcovering, $750.00, covering P262 for wallpaper. No discount. C278.
  16. Returned defective wallpaper to Collazo Wallpaper, $122.50, from P260. DM29.
  17. Paid on account to Trail-Color, Inc., $752.00, covering P263 for paint, $840.00, less DM28 for $88.00. No discount. C279.
  18. Paid on account to Zep Paint Co., covering P264 for paint, $388.00, less 2% discount. C280.
  18. Purchased paint on account from Trail-Color, Inc., $1,120.00. P266.
  18. Returned defective wallpaper to Famis, Inc., $75.00, from P265. DM30.
  21. Bought supplies for cash, $62.30. C281.
  23. Purchased wallpaper on account from Collazo Wallpaper, $336.00. P267.
  24. Paid on account to Famis, Inc., covering P265 for wallpaper, $550.00, less DM30 for $75.00 and less 2% discount. C282.
  24. Purchased paint on account from Astro Paint, $726.40. P268.
  26. Bought supplies for cash, $43.00. C283.
  28. Paid on account to Trail-Color, Inc., covering P266 for paint, $1,120.00, less 2% discount. C284.
  29. Replenished petty cash. Charge the following accounts: Supplies, $47.10; Advertising Expense, $62.50; Miscellaneous Expense, $91.40. C285.

2. Prepare a bank statement reconciliation for November 30 of the current year. The bank statement is dated November 29. A comparison of the bank statement and Creative Decorating's check stubs shows the information below.

Bank statement balance, November 29...............................	$16,378.00
Bank service charge for November...................................	10.20
Bank credit card charge for November	392.80
Balance on Check Stub No. 286....................................	18,480.00
Outstanding deposit, November 29..................................	3,040.60
Outstanding checks: Nos. 283, 284, 285	

3. Record the following transactions.

Nov. 30.   Recorded bank service charge, $10.20. M31.
     30.   Recorded bank credit card charge, $392.80. M32.

4. Prove and rule the journals.

CHALLENGE PROBLEM 2-C   Recording purchases at net amount and using the account Discounts Lost

Introductory remarks: Some businesses record purchases at the net amount to be paid when the cash discount is taken. For example, merchandise is purchased for $500.00 with a 2% discount allowed if the account is paid within 10 days. The discount will reduce the price from $500.00 to $490.00. To record this purchase on account transaction, Purchases is debited for $490.00 and Accounts Payable is credited for $490.00. When the account is paid, Accounts Payable is debited for $490.00 and Cash is credited for $490.00. Purchases returns and allowances are also recorded at the discounted amount.

If the discount period expires before payment is made, then the entry in the cash payments journal for the example above would be as follows: Accounts Payable is debited for $490.00, Discounts Lost is debited for $10.00, and Cash is credited for $500.00. Because almost all cash discounts are taken, there are few entries involving the discounts lost account. For this reason, no special amount column is provided for the account in the cash payments journal. Instead, the amounts debited to this account are recorded in the General Debit column.

Instructions: 1. Record the transactions for Mastery Problem 2-M following the method described above. Use page 14 of a purchases journal, page 7 of a purchases returns and allowances journal, and page 15 of a cash payments journal.
    2. Prove and rule the journals.

3 Recording Sales and Cash Receipts

ENABLING PERFORMANCE TASKS

After studying Chapter 3, you will be able to:
a. Define accounting terms related to departmental sales and cash receipts.
b. Identify accounting concepts and practices related to departmental sales and cash receipts.
c. Record departmental sales, sales returns and allowances, and cash receipts.
d. Prove cash.

A departmental accounting system provides valuable decision-making information about the results of business operations. Gross profit from operations for each department is one type of information available through a departmental accounting system. Determining gross profit from operations helps a business manager answer at least two major questions. (1) Is each department earning an appropriate gross profit on operations? (2) If not, which items might be causing the problem? Records of departmental sales and cost of merchandise sold are necessary to determine departmental gross profit from operations.

DEPARTMENTAL SALES ON ACCOUNT

Supergolf makes sales on account to individuals, golf clubs, golf leagues, and schools. Supergolf sells golf clothing such as shirts, jackets, and hats with team or club emblems imprinted on each item. Likewise, Supergolf sells both standard and specialized golf equipment including clubs, bags, balls, and golf carts.

Journalizing sales on account

Supergolf records all departmental sales on account in a sales journal. The journal has one debit column — Accounts Receivable Debit. The journal also has three credit columns—Sales Tax Payable Credit and special Sales Credit columns for Clothing and Equipment. Supergolf's departmental sales journal is shown in Illustration 3-1.

		SALES JOURNAL				PAGE 13		
					1	2	3	4
DATE	ACCOUNT DEBITED	SALE NO.	POST. REF.	ACCOUNTS RECEIVABLE DEBIT	SALES TAX PAYABLE CREDIT	SALES CREDIT		
						CLOTHING	EQUIPMENT	
1988 June 1	Greenview Golf League	101		504 00	24 00	480 00		1
30	Stuart Schools	126		180 00		180 00		26
								27
								28

A sales invoice is prepared in duplicate for each sale on account. *(CONCEPT: Objective Evidence)* Each sales invoice shows the amount of merchandise sold by department.

The customer is given the original copy of the sales invoice. The duplicate copy is kept by Supergolf for journalizing the transaction. Supergolf records all departmental sales at the time of sale, regardless of when payment is made. *(CONCEPT: Realization of Revenue)*

June 1, 1988.
Sold clothing on account to Greenview Golf League, $480.00, plus sales tax, $24.00; total, $504.00. Sales Invoice No. 101.

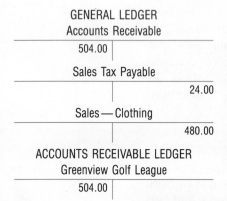

GENERAL LEDGER
Accounts Receivable

| 504.00 | |

Sales Tax Payable

| | 24.00 |

Sales — Clothing

| | 480.00 |

ACCOUNTS RECEIVABLE LEDGER
Greenview Golf League

| 504.00 | |

The analysis of this transaction is shown in the T accounts. In the general ledger, Accounts Receivable is increased by a $504.00 debit. Sales Tax Payable is increased by a $24.00 credit. Sales—Clothing is increased by a $480.00 credit. In the accounts receivable ledger, Greenview Golf League is increased by a $504.00 debit.

The details of Sales Invoice No. 101 are recorded on line 1 of the sales journal, Illustration 3-1. The date, *1988, June 1*, is written in the Date column. The customer name, *Greenview Golf League*, is recorded in the Account Debited column. The sales invoice number, *101*, is entered in the Sale No. column. Since only sales invoice numbers are written in this column, no identifying letter is necessary. The debit amount, *$504.00*, is recorded in the Accounts Receivable Debit column. The credit amount, *$24.00*, is entered in the Sales Tax Payable Credit column. The credit amount, *$480.00*, is written in the Sales—Clothing Credit column.

Not all customers are required to pay a sales tax. Many state agencies supported by local and state government and nonprofit educational institutions are exempted from paying a sales tax. These exemptions vary from state to state. Line 26 of the sales journal, Illustration 3-1, shows a sale on account to a school which is not required to pay sales tax.

Posting from a sales journal

Supergolf keeps customer accounts in an accounts receivable ledger. Individual amounts in the sales journal's Accounts Receivable Debit column are posted daily to the appropriate customer accounts. Posting line 1 from the sales journal to an accounts receivable ledger account is shown in Illustration 3-2.

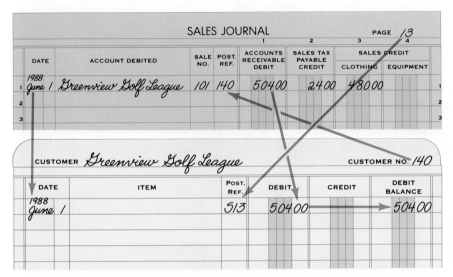

Illustration 3-2
Posting from a sales
journal to an accounts
receivable ledger account

The date, *1988, June 1*, is written in the account's Date column. The journal page number, *S13*, is placed in the Post. Ref. column. The amount, *$504.00*, is recorded in the Debit column. The account balance, *$504.00*, is entered in the Debit Balance column. The customer number, *140*, is recorded in the sales journal's Post. Ref. column indicating completion of posting.

The sales journal is proved and ruled at the end of each month. Each amount column total is posted to the general ledger account named in the column heading. Posting a column total from the sales journal to a general ledger account is shown in Illustration 3-3, page 42.

To indicate that the posting came from the sales journal, page 13, *S13* is written in the ledger account's Post. Ref. column. The general ledger account number, *1115*, is entered in parentheses immediately below the sales journal's column total to show that the amount has been posted. All amount column totals are posted in the same way.

Supergolf's sales journal, Illustration 3-4, is shown after all posting has been completed.

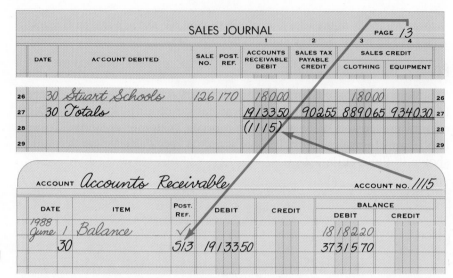

Illustration 3-3
Posting a total from a
sales journal to a general
ledger account

Illustration 3-4
Departmental sales
journal after posting has
been completed

DEPARTMENTAL SALES RETURNS AND ALLOWANCES

Merchandising businesses normally have some merchandise returned because a customer may have received the wrong size, the wrong style, damaged, or unsatisfactory goods. Merchandise may be returned by a customer for a credit on account or a cash refund. Credit may also be granted without having the damaged or unsatisfactory merchandise returned.

Journalizing sales returns and allowances

Supergolf records all sales returns and allowances in a sales returns and allowances journal. Supergolf's departmental sales returns and allowances journal for June, 1988, is shown in Illustration 3-5.

					SALES RETURNS AND ALLOWANCES JOURNAL			PAGE 5	
					1	2	3	4	
DATE	ACCOUNT CREDITED	CREDIT MEMO. NO.	POST. REF.	ACCOUNTS RECEIVABLE CREDIT	SALES TAX PAYABLE DEBIT	SALES RETURNS AND ALLOWANCES DEBIT			
						CLOTHING	EQUIPMENT		
1988 June 2	Alex Grant	43	130	131 25	6 25		125 00		1
7	Stuart Schools	44	170	88 00		88 00			2
15	Greenview Golf League	45	140	34 13	1 63		32 50		3
21	Larry Bissell	46	110	89 25	4 25		85 00		4
22	Easy-Golf	47	120	71 40	3 40	68 00			5
24	Parkside Golf Club	48	160	136 50	6 50	130 00			6
30	Helene Vega	54	180	42 00	2 00		40 00		12
30	Totals			956 35	41 35	380 00	535 00		13
				(1115)	(2130)	(4110-1)	(4110-2)		14

Illustration 3-5
Departmental sales returns and allowances journal

Details of a sales return or allowance may be stated in a letter, or a seller may issue a credit memorandum. When a customer returns merchandise or requests an adjustment, Supergolf issues a credit memorandum. A credit memorandum is the source document for a sales returns and allowances transaction. (*CONCEPT: Objective Evidence*)

An account that reduces a related account on financial statements is known as a contra account. Sales—Equipment is a revenue account. Therefore, an account showing deductions from a sales account is a contra revenue account. Sales Returns and Allowances—Equipment is one of Supergolf's contra revenue accounts. Sales returns and allowances are kept in a separate account and not deducted directly from the sales account. This procedure helps the business see what proportion of the merchandise sold was returned by customers.

June 2, 1988.
Granted credit to Alex Grant for equipment returned, $125.00, plus sales tax, $6.25, from Sales Invoice No. 100; total, $131.25. Credit Memorandum No. 43.

The analysis of this transaction is shown in the T accounts. In the general ledger, Sales Tax Payable is decreased by a $6.25 debit. The contra revenue account, Sales Returns and Allowances—Equipment, is increased by a $125.00 debit. Accounts Receivable is decreased by a $131.25 credit. In the accounts receivable ledger, Alex Grant is decreased by a $131.25 credit.

Details of Credit Memorandum No. 43 are recorded on line 1 of the sales returns and allowances journal, Illustration 3-5. The date, *1988, June 2*, is written in the Date column. The customer name, *Alex Grant*, is recorded in the Account Credited column. The credit memorandum number, *43*, is entered in the Credit Memo. No. column. The credit amount, *$131.25*, is written in the Accounts Receivable

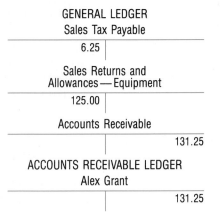

GENERAL LEDGER
Sales Tax Payable

6.25	

Sales Returns and Allowances—Equipment

125.00	

Accounts Receivable

	131.25

ACCOUNTS RECEIVABLE LEDGER
Alex Grant

	131.25

Credit column. The debit amount, *$6.25,* is recorded in the Sales Tax Payable Debit column. The debit amount, *$125.00,* is entered in the Sales Returns and Allowances — Equipment Debit column.

Posting from a sales returns and allowances journal

Individual postings are made daily from the sales returns and allowances journal. Each amount written in the Accounts Receivable Credit column is posted daily to the customer account named in the Account Credited column. The amount in the Accounts Receivable Credit column, line 1, is posted as a credit to Alex Grant's account in the accounts receivable ledger. To indicate that posting came from page 5 of the sales returns and allowances journal, *SR5* is recorded in the Post. Ref. column of the subsidiary ledger account. The customer number, *130,* is placed in the Post. Ref. column of the journal to indicate completion of posting.

> Sometimes a sales return or allowance is granted after a sale on account has been paid in full by a customer. This situation might happen if a sales invoice is paid very soon after the sale is made. When this happens, the customer account after posting has a credit balance instead of a normal debit balance. The credit balance, a contra balance, reduces the amount to be received from a customer for future sales on account. When a three-column account form is used, a contra balance in a customer account is shown by enclosing the amount in parentheses.

A sales returns and allowances journal is proved and ruled at the end of each month in the same manner as a sales journal. Each amount column total is posted to the general ledger account named in the column heading. The account number is written below the journal's column total to show that the amount has been posted. Supergolf's departmental sales returns and allowances journal, Illustration 3-5, is shown after all posting has been completed.

DEPARTMENTAL CASH RECEIPTS

Supergolf keeps a record of all cash receipts. The sources of most cash receipts are (1) cash received on account from customers, and (2) cash and credit card sales.

Journalizing cash receipts

Supergolf records all cash receipts in a cash receipts journal. The journal has five credit columns — General Credit, Accounts Receivable Credit, Sales Tax Payable Credit, and a Sales Credit column for each of the two departments. The journal also has five debit columns — General Debit, Sales Tax Payable Debit, a Sales Discount Debit column for each of the two departments, and Cash Debit. Supergolf's departmental cash receipts journal for June, 1988, is shown in Illustration 3–6.

DATE	ACCOUNT TITLE	DOC. NO.	POST. REF.	GENERAL DEBIT	GENERAL CREDIT	ACCOUNTS RECEIVABLE CREDIT	SALES TAX PAYABLE DEBIT	SALES TAX PAYABLE CREDIT	SALES CREDIT CLOTHING	SALES CREDIT EQUIPMENT	SALES DISCOUNT DEBIT CLOTHING	SALES DISCOUNT DEBIT EQUIPMENT	CASH DEBIT	
1988 June 1	Parkside Golf Club	R89	160			1701 00	1 62				32 40		1666 98	1
4	✓	T4	✓					590 00	4860 00	6940 00			12390 00	2
6	Greenview Golf League	R90	140			504 00	48				9 60		493 92	3
7	Larry Bissell	R91	110			2352 00	2 24					44 80	2304 96	4
7	Easy-Golf	R92	120			903 00	86					17 20	884 94	5
11	✓	T11	✓					532 50	4370 00	6280 00			11182 50	6
30	Stuart Schools	R108	170			399 00					7 98		391 02	17
30	✓	T30	✓					587 50	5620 00	6130 00			12337 50	18
30	Totals					16830 25	15 80	2521 50	23520 00	26910 00	127 00	189 00	69449 95	19
						(1115)	(2130)	(2130)	(4105-1)	(4105-2)	(4115-1)	(4115-2)	(1105)	20

Illustration 3-6
Departmental cash receipts journal

Cash received on account

Each customer is expected to pay the amount due within the credit terms agreed upon. To encourage early payment, a deduction on the invoice amount may be granted. A deduction that the seller allows on the invoice amount to encourage prompt payment is known as a cash discount. A cash discount on sales is called a sales discount. Supergolf sells on account using terms 2/10, n/30. These terms mean that a 2% sales discount may be deducted if sales on account are paid within 10 days of the invoice date. All sales on account must be paid within 30 days of the invoice date.

At the time a sale is made, Sales Tax Payable is credited for the sales tax liability on the total sales invoice amount. When payment is received within a discount period, the sales tax liability is reduced by the amount of sales tax on the sales discount. Two amounts must be figured when cash is received on account within a discount period: (1) sales discount, and (2) sales tax on sales discount. When Supergolf receives cash on account, a receipt is prepared as the source document. (*CONCEPT: Objective Evidence*)

June 1, 1988.
Received on account from Parkside Golf Club, $1,666.98, covering Sales Invoice No. 96 for clothing, $1,701.00 ($1,620.00 plus sales tax, $81.00) less 2% discount, $32.40, and less sales tax, $1.62. Receipt No. 89.

Sales discount and sales tax on sales discount for Parkside Golf Club are figured as follows.

Sales discount:

Sales Invoice Amount × Sales Discount Rate = Sales Discount
$1,620.00   ×   2%   = $32.40

Sales tax reduction:

Sales Discount × Sales Tax Rate = Sales Tax Reduction
$32.40   ×   5%   = $1.62

GENERAL LEDGER

Cash

| 1,666.98 | |

Sales Tax Payable

| 1.62 | |

Sales Discount — Clothing

| 32.40 | |

Accounts Receivable

| | 1,701.00 |

ACCOUNTS RECEIVABLE LEDGER

Parkside Golf Club

| | 1,701.00 |

The analysis of this transaction is shown in the T accounts. In the general ledger, Cash is increased by a $1,666.98 debit. Sales Tax Payable is decreased by a $1.62 debit, the sales tax amount on the sales discount amount. Sales Discount—Clothing is increased by a $32.40 debit. Accounts Receivable is decreased by a $1,701.00 credit. In the accounts receivable ledger, Parkside Golf Club is decreased by a $1,701.00 credit.

The details of Receipt No. 89 are recorded on line 1 of the cash receipts journal, Illustration 3-6. The date, *1988, June 1,* is written in the Date column. The customer name, *Parkside Golf Club,* is recorded in the Account Title column. The document number, *R89,* is entered in the Doc. No. column. The credit amount, *$1,701.00,* is written in the Accounts Receivable Credit column. The debit amount, *$1.62,* is recorded in the Sales Tax Payable Debit column. The debit amount, *$32.40,* is entered in the Sales Discount—Clothing Debit column. The debit amount, *$1,666.98,* is written in the Cash Debit column.

Cash and credit card sales

Supergolf sells merchandise to customers for cash. Also, merchandise is sold to customers who have a credit card that shows they have an account with a bank credit card system. Supergolf's bank accepts credit card slips in much the same way it accepts checks for deposit. The bank increases Supergolf's bank account balance for the total amount of the credit card sales slips deposited. Because the bank account balance is increased at the time of deposit, Supergolf records credit card sales and cash sales as one transaction. Sales transactions involving cash and credit cards therefore are all recorded as cash sales.

Supergolf uses a cash register to record all cash and credit card sales. Each transaction is printed on a paper tape that is given to a customer as a receipt. The cash register also internally accumulates data about total sales.

A credit card slip is prepared for credit card sales. However, the sale is still recorded on the cash register.

At the end of each week, the cash register prints a total of all cash and credit card sales for the week. The tape is removed from the cash register and identified with a *T* and the date. Supergolf uses a cash register tape as the source document for cash and credit card sales. *(CONCEPT: Objective Evidence)*

> *June 4, 1988.*
> *Recorded cash and credit card sales for June 1-4: clothing, $4,860.00; equipment, $6,940.00; plus sales tax, $590.00; total, $12,390.00. Cash Register Tape No. 4.*

The analysis of this transaction is shown in the T accounts. In the general ledger, Cash is increased by a $12,390.00 debit. Sales Tax Payable is increased by a $590.00 credit. Sales — Clothing is increased by a $4,860.00 credit. Sales — Equipment is increased by a $6,940.00 credit.

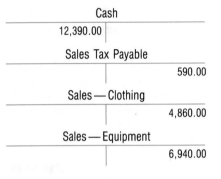

The details of Cash Register Tape No. 4 are recorded on line 2 of the cash receipts journal, Illustration 3-6. The date, 4, is written in the Date column. A check mark is placed in the Account Title column to show that no account title needs to be written for this transaction. The cash register tape number, T4, is recorded in the Doc. No. column. A check mark is also placed in the Post. Ref. column to show that amounts on this line do not need to be posted individually. The amount credited to Sales Tax Payable, *$590.00*, is entered in the Sales Tax Payable Credit column. The amount credited to Sales — Clothing, *$4,860.00*, is written in the Sales — Clothing Credit column. The amount credited to Sales — Equipment, *$6,940.00*, is recorded in the Sales — Equipment Credit column. The amount debited to Cash, *$12,390.00*, is entered in the Cash Debit column.

Posting from a cash receipts journal

Individual postings are made daily from the cash receipts journal. Supergolf posts daily to the general ledger each amount written in the cash receipts journal's General Debit and Credit columns. Also, each amount written in the Accounts Receivable Credit column is posted daily to the accounts receivable ledger. To indicate that the posting came from page 11 of the cash receipts journal, *CR11* is recorded in the ledger account's Post. Ref. column. The respective ledger account number is written in the Post. Ref. column of the journal to indicate completion of posting.

> Transactions involving entries in the General Debit and Credit columns of a cash receipts journal are described in Chapter 10.

At the end of the month, the cash receipts journal is proved and ruled. Totals of the special amount columns are then posted to their respective accounts in the general ledger. The general ledger account number is written in parentheses immediately below the total. A check mark is written in parentheses below the totals of the General Debit and Credit columns to show that the totals are not posted. Supergolf's departmental cash receipts journal, Illustration 3-6, is shown after all posting has been completed.

PROVING CASH

Determining that the amount of cash on hand agrees with the accounting records is called proving cash. Supergolf figures the cash proof at the end of June as shown below.

Cash on hand at the beginning of the month................ (June 1, 1988, balance of cash account in general ledger)	$24,580.00
Plus total cash received during the month .... (Cash Debit column total, cash receipts journal, Illustration 3-6)	69,449.95
Total	$94,029.95
Less total cash paid during the month .... (Cash Credit column total, cash payments journal, Illustration 2-9, Chapter 2)	61,251.20
Equals cash on hand at the end of the month...............	$32,778.75

The last check written in June, 1988, was Check No. 412. The checkbook balance after the last check had been written and after the last deposit was made is $32,778.75. Since the checkbook balance is the same as the cash balance on hand, cash is proved.

ORDER OF POSTING FROM JOURNALS

Businesses post transactions affecting vendor and customer accounts frequently during the month so that balances of subsidiary ledger accounts are kept up to date. Supergolf posts to subsidiary ledger accounts daily. General ledger account balances are needed only when financial statements are prepared. Therefore, posting to general ledger accounts may be done less frequently than posting to subsidiary ledgers. However, all transactions, including special amount column totals, must be posted at the end of a fiscal period. The recommended order in which to post journals is listed below.

1. Sales journal.
2. Sales returns and allowances journal.
3. Purchases journal.
4. Purchases returns and allowances journal.
5. General journal.
6. Cash receipts journal.
7. Cash payments journal.

This posting order generally places the debits and credits in the accounts in the order the transactions occurred.

ACCOUNTING TERMS

What is the meaning of each of the following?

1. sales discount

2. proving cash

QUESTIONS FOR INDIVIDUAL STUDY

1. What is one type of management information available through a departmental accounting system?
2. What two questions will departmental gross profit from operations help a manager answer?
3. What two types of information are needed to determine departmental gross profit from operations?
4. Why does Supergolf prepare a sales invoice in duplicate?
5. Recording all departmental sales at the time of sale is an application of which accounting concept?
6. What accounts are affected, and how, when merchandise for a department is sold on account?
7. How often does Supergolf post the individual amounts in the Accounts Receivable Debit column of the sales journal?
8. Why might a customer return merchandise?
9. How does Supergolf confirm sales returns and allowances?
10. Why are sales returns and allowances kept in a separate account and not deducted directly from the sales account?
11. What accounts are affected, and how, when departmental merchandise sold on account is returned?
12. How often does Supergolf post from a sales returns and allowances journal?
13. When might a customer account in the subsidiary ledger have a credit balance

14. instead of its normal debit balance? When a three-column subsidiary account form is used, how is a contra balance indicated in a customer account?
15. What are two types of cash receipts recorded by Supergolf?
16. Why does Supergolf offer a sales discount on sales on account?
17. What two amounts must be figured when cash is received on account within a discount period?
18. What accounts are affected, and how, when Supergolf receives cash within a discount period for a sale of clothing on account?
19. Why does Supergolf record credit card sales and cash sales as one transaction?
20. What is the source document for recording cash and credit card sales?
21. What accounts are affected, and how, by a cash and credit card sales transaction involving sales from Supergolf's clothing and equipment departments?
22. Why is a check mark placed in the Post. Ref. column of the cash receipts journal for a cash and credit card sale transaction?
23. How often does Supergolf post amounts recorded in the cash receipts journal's Accounts Receivable Credit column?
24. Why do businesses post transactions affecting vendor and customer accounts frequently during the month?
25. What is the recommended order in which to post journals?

CASES FOR MANAGEMENT DECISION

CASE 1 D'Angelos sells a complete line of men's clothing. The accounting records are not kept on a departmental basis. The manager suggests to the accountant that the accounting records be reorganized on a departmental basis. The accountant feels that the line of merchandise sold is so closely related that organizing the accounting records on a departmental basis would not be worth the extra time and effort. Do you agree with the manager or the accountant? Why?

CASE 2 Executive Office Products specializes in office furniture, office machines, and office supplies. All accounting records are kept on a departmental basis. When merchandise is returned by a customer or an allowance is granted, a journal entry is made debiting the appropriate sales account and crediting Accounts Receivable and the customer account. Do you agree or disagree with this accounting procedure? Why?

CASE 3 Migliori Enterprises, Inc., sells a complete line of interior decorating products. To encourage early payment for sales on account, a sales discount is granted. When cash is received on account within a discount period, a sales discount amount and a sales tax on the discount amount are deducted from the invoice amount. The manager suggests that the business not record any sales tax for sales on account at the time of sale. Sales tax would only be recorded at the end of the fiscal period or when sales tax is due. The manager feels that this procedure would be easier and take less time because a sales tax would not need to be figured each time a sales discount is figured. The accountant disagrees with the manager's suggestion. With whom do you agree? Why?

APPLICATION PROBLEMS

PROBLEM 3-1 Journalizing and posting departmental sales on account and sales returns and allowances

Decorating Center, Inc., has two departments: Wallpaper and Paint. The ledgers are given in the working papers accompanying this textbook. The balances are recorded as of September 1 of the current year.

Instructions: 1. Record the following selected transactions on page 9 of a sales journal and page 6 of a sales returns and allowances journal. Source documents are abbreviated as follows: credit memorandum, CM; sales invoice, S.

Sept. 1. Sold wallpaper on account to Molly Dean, $125.00, plus sales tax, $6.25. S142.
    3. Sold paint on account to Judy O'Bryan, $320.00, plus sales tax, $16.00. S143.
    3. Granted credit to Molly Dean for unused wallpaper returned, $30.00, plus sales tax, $1.50, from S142. CM24.
    5. Sold paint on account to Bruce Byers, $415.00, plus sales tax, $20.75. S144.
    8. Sold wallpaper on account to Molly Dean, $88.00, plus sales tax, $4.40. S145.
  12. Granted credit to Bruce Byers for unused paint returned, $75.00, plus sales tax, $3.75, from S144. CM25.
  15. Sold paint on account to Kathy Angell, $135.00, plus sales tax, $6.75. S146.
  17. Granted credit to Molly Dean for defective wallpaper returned, $28.00, plus sales tax, $1.40, from S145. CM26.
  20. Sold wallpaper on account to Lyle Sanders, $65.00, plus sales tax, $3.25. S147.
  23. Sold wallpaper on account to Jess Watts, $98.00, plus sales tax, $4.90. S148.
  26. Granted credit to Lyle Sanders for unused wallpaper returned, $23.00, plus sales tax, $1.15, from S147. CM27.
  27. Sold wallpaper on account to Bruce Byers, $145.00, plus sales tax, $7.25. S149.
  29. Sold paint on account to Jefferson School District, $265.00. No sales tax. S150.
  30. Sold wallpaper on account to Judy O'Bryan, $385.00, plus sales tax, $19.25. S151.

2. Post individual items from the sales journal and sales returns and allowances journal.
3. Prove and rule the sales journal. Post the totals.
4. Prove and rule the sales returns and allowances journal. Post the totals.

PROBLEM 3-2 Figuring sales tax, sales discounts, and amounts due

Rivero's, Inc., a departmentalized merchandising business, charges a 5% sales tax on all sales. A 2% sales discount is granted to customers for early payment of their accounts. The following selected sales on account are paid within the discount period.

Sale No.	Sales Amount
83	$1,050.00
84	930.00
85	1,250.00
86	720.00
87	380.00
88	840.00
89	1,160.00
90	280.00

Instructions: Use a form similar to the one below. Figure and record the following amounts: sales tax amount, Column 3; amount due before discount, Column 4; sales discount amount, Column 5; sales tax amount on discount, Column 6; amount due after discount, Column 7.

1	2	3	4	5	6	7
Sale No.	Sales Amount	Sales Tax Amount	Amount Due Before Discount	Sales Discount Amount	Sales Tax Amount On Discount	Amount Due After Discount
83	$1,050.00	$52.50	$1,102.50	$21.00	$1.05	$1,080.45

PROBLEM 3-3   Journalizing and posting departmental cash receipts

Ranch Wear, Inc., has two departments: Boots and Coats. The ledgers are given in the working papers accompanying this textbook. The balances are recorded as of November 1 of the current year.

Instructions: 1. Record the following selected transactions for November of the current year. Use page 13 of a cash receipts journal. A 5% sales tax is charged on all sales. A 2% sales discount is granted to customers for early payment of their accounts. Source documents are abbreviated as follows: receipt, R; cash register tape, T.

Nov. 1. Received on account from Mary Hyde, $884.94, covering S102 for coats ($860.00 plus sales tax, $43.00) less 2% discount, $17.20, and less sales tax, $0.86. R87.

  2. Received on account from Roger Cantrell, $267.54, covering S103 for boots ($260.00 plus sales tax, $13.00) less 2% discount, $5.20, and less sales tax, $0.26. R88.

  5. Recorded cash and credit card sales for November 1-5: boots, $3,620.00; coats, $4,130.00; plus sales tax, $387.50. T5.

  8. Received on account from Teri Miceli, $391.02, covering S104 for a coat ($380.00 plus sales tax, $19.00) less 2% discount, $7.60, and less sales tax, $0.38. R89.

  10. Received on account from Gene Tate, $436.30, covering S105 for boots ($424.00 plus sales tax, $21.20) less 2% discount, $8.48, and less sales tax, $0.42. R90.

  12. Recorded cash and credit card sales for November 7-12: boots, $4,680.00; coats, $5,120.00; plus sales tax, $490.00. T12.

  15. Received on account from Greg Payne, $185.22, covering S106 for boots ($180.00 plus sales tax, $9.00) less 2% discount, $3.60, and less sales tax, $0.18. R91.

  19. Recorded cash and credit card sales for November 14-19: boots, $4,510.00; coats, $5,230.00; plus sales tax, $487.00. T19.

  22. Received on account from Peggy Allison, $275.77, covering S107 for boots ($268.00 plus sales tax, $13.40) less 2% discount, $5.36, and less sales tax, $0.27. R92.

25. Received on account from Teri Miceli, $596.82, covering S108 for a coat ($580.00 plus sales tax, $29.00) less 2% discount, $11.60, and less sales tax, $0.58. R93.
26. Recorded cash and credit card sales for November 21-26: boots, $4,750.00; coats, $5,490.00; plus sales tax, $512.00. T26.
29. Received on account from Greg Payne, $257.25, covering S109 for boots ($250.00 plus sales tax, $12.50) less 2% discount, $5.00, and less sales tax, $0.25. R94.
30. Recorded cash and credit card sales for November 27-30: boots, $2,370.00; coats, $2,740.00; plus sales tax, $255.50. T30.

2. Post individual items from the cash receipts journal.
3. Prove the cash receipts journal.
4. Prove cash. The balance on the last check stub is $53,596.86. Additional information is given below.

Cash on hand at the beginning of the month $43,840.00
Cash paid during the month 38,310.00

5. Rule the cash receipts journal. Post the totals.

ENRICHMENT PROBLEMS

MASTERY PROBLEM 3-M   Journalizing departmental sales, sales returns and allowances, and cash receipts

Wilderness, Inc., has two departments: Camping Gear and Hiking Gear. A 5% sales tax is charged on all sales. A 2% sales discount is granted to customers for early payment of their accounts.

Instructions: 1. Record the following selected transactions for June of the current year. Use page 10 of a sales journal, page 5 of a sales returns and allowances journal, and page 14 of a cash receipts journal. Source documents are abbreviated as follows: credit memorandum, CM; receipt, R; sales invoice, S; cash register tape, T.

June 1. Sold camping gear on account to Steve Leny, $560.00, plus sales tax. S134.
   3. Sold camping gear on account to Celia Perez, $430.00, plus sales tax. S135.
   4. Received on account from William Hodges, covering S132 for hiking gear ($360.00 plus sales tax) less discount and less sales tax. R83.
   4. Recorded cash and credit card sales for June 1-4: camping gear, $3,280.00; hiking gear, $3,520.00; plus sales tax. T4.
   6. Granted credit to Celia Perez for defective camping gear returned, $92.00, plus sales tax, from S135. CM28.
   8. Received on account from Norma Howard, covering S131 for camping gear ($609.00 plus sales tax) less discount and less sales tax. R84.
   9. Received on account from Celia Perez, covering S133 for hiking gear ($399.00 plus sales tax) less discount and less sales tax. R85.
   11. Received on account from Steve Leny, covering S134 for camping gear ($560.00 plus sales tax) less discount and less sales tax. R86.
   11. Sold camping gear on account to Paul DeBra, $840.00, plus sales tax. S136.
   11. Recorded cash and credit card sales for June 6-11: camping gear, $4,720.00; hiking gear, $5,030.00; plus sales tax. T11.
   13. Received on account from Celia Perez, covering S135 for camping gear ($430.00 plus sales tax) less CM28 ($92.00 plus sales tax) less discount and less sales tax. R87.

· 15. Sold hiking gear on account to Linda Barr, $428.00, plus sales tax. S137.

17. Sold camping gear on account to Norma Howard, $240.00, plus sales tax. S138.

18. Recorded cash and credit card sales for June 13-18: camping gear, $5,130.00; hiking gear, $4,980.00; plus sales tax. T18.

21. Granted credit to Linda Barr for defective hiking gear returned, $67.00, plus sales tax, from S137. CM29.

21. Received on account from Paul DeBra, covering S136 for camping gear ($840.00 plus sales tax) less discount and less sales tax. R88.

25. Received on account from Linda Barr, covering S137 for hiking gear ($428.00 plus sales tax) less CM29 ($67.00 plus sales tax) less discount and less sales tax. R89.

25. Recorded cash and credit card sales for June 20-25: camping gear, $4,750.00; hiking gear, $4,910.00; plus sales tax. T25.

27. Received on account from Norma Howard, covering S138 for camping gear ($240.00 plus sales tax) less discount and less sales tax. R90.

28. Sold hiking gear on account to Alpine Schools, $760.00; no sales tax. S139.

30. Recorded cash and credit card sales for June 27-30: camping gear, $2,480.00; hiking gear, $2,610.00; plus sales tax. T30.

2. Prove and rule the sales journal and the sales returns and allowances journal.

3. Prove the cash receipts journal.

4. Prove cash. The balance on the last check stub is $52,614.14. Additional information is given below.

Cash on hand at the beginning of the month	$36,940.00
Cash paid during the month	31,620.86

5. Rule the cash receipts journal.

CHALLENGE PROBLEM 3-C Journalizing departmental sales, sales returns and allowances, and cash receipts

Assume that Wilderness, Inc., the business described in Mastery Problem 3-M, is located in a state that does not charge a retail sales tax. Also, assume that Wilderness allows customers a 1% discount to encourage early payment. The journals with the proper headings are given in the working papers.

Instructions: 1. Record the transactions given in Mastery Problem 3-M without sales tax. Use page 13 of a sales journal, page 4 of a sales returns and allowances journal, and page 14 of a cash receipts journal.

2. Prove and rule the journals.

4 Figuring and Recording Departmental Payroll Data

ENABLING PERFORMANCE TASKS

After studying Chapter 4, you will be able to:
a. Define accounting terms related to departmental payroll systems.
b. Identify accounting concepts and practices related to departmental payroll systems.
c. Complete payroll records.
d. Record a payroll.

Total operating expenses for most businesses include large payments for employee services and related taxes. The money paid for an employee's services is called a salary. The period covered by a salary payment is called a pay period. The total amount paid to all employees for a pay period is called a payroll. Taxes based on the payroll of a business are called payroll taxes. Payroll expenses are reported as separate items because they represent a business activity with dollar amounts large enough to affect business decisions. Therefore, all payroll expenses are reported as separate items in accounting records and financial statements. (CONCEPT: Materiality)

An employer is required by federal, state, and local laws to keep accurate payroll records for the business and for each individual employee. Both employees and employer must pay certain payroll taxes. Employers are required to withhold certain payroll taxes from an employee's salary each pay period. Periodically, employers must pay government agencies all payroll taxes withheld from employees' salaries as well as the employer's payroll taxes. A business must also provide a yearly report to each employee showing the total salary earned and the total taxes withheld. Therefore, a business must keep records of each employee's earnings, amounts withheld, and net amount paid. Payroll records also must show the total amount of payroll taxes that a business must pay.

Payroll information a business must keep and report is specified by federal, state, and local governments. However, the payroll system used by individual businesses may differ. A business protects itself by keeping complete and accurate payroll records showing all required information.

EMPLOYEE BENEFITS

Payments to employees for nonworking hours and to insurance and retirement programs are called employee benefits. Employee benefits are provided by most businesses as a reward for continuous service. These benefits generally include vacation time, sick leave time, and personal leave time with pay after a period of continuous employment. Employee benefits may also include payments by the employer for medical insurance and retirement. The number and type of employee benefits vary among businesses. Regardless of the type and number of employee benefits, records must be maintained of each employee's benefits earned, used, and available. Supergolf has three employee benefits. (1) Vacation time. (2) Sick leave time. (3) Personal leave time. The time available to Supergolf's employees is outlined in the schedule shown in Illustration 4-1.

SUPERGOLF Employee Benefits Schedule				
	1	2	3	4
Benefits	Earned After 12 Months	Biweekly After 12 Months	Minimum Time Blocks	Maximum Carry Over
Vacation time hours	40	4	4	120
Sick leave time hours......	0	2	1	80
Personal leave time hours..	0	1	1	24

Illustration 4-1
Employee benefits
schedule

Vacation time

Supergolf's employees are entitled to one week (40 hours) of paid vacation time after completing one full year of employment. Beginning with the second year of employment, employees earn four paid vacation hours for each biweekly pay period of at least 80 hours. Beginning in the second year of employment, employees may take vacation time in blocks of hours. Vacation time may be taken in blocks of at least four hours each or up to the maximum number of hours accumulated. Employees who do not use their full number of paid vacation hours in one year may carry over the unused hours to the following year. Each employee may accumulate up to three weeks (120 hours) of paid vacation time.

Sick leave time

Beginning with the second year of employment, Supergolf's employees are allowed two paid sick leave hours for each biweekly pay period of at least 80 hours. Sick leave time must be taken in blocks of at least one hour each or up to the maximum number of hours accumulated. Sick leave time may accumulate up to a maximum of 80 hours.

Personal leave time

Supergolf's employees are allowed one paid personal leave hour for each biweekly pay period of at least 80 hours beginning with the second year of employment. Personal leave time is to be used for required time away from a business for personal reasons. Personal leave activities might include such items as conducting personal business or taking a child to a doctor. Personal leave time must be taken in blocks of at least one hour at a time and cannot exceed eight hours at a time. Personal leave time may accumulate up to a maximum of 24 hours.

EMPLOYEE EARNINGS

An employee's pay rate is usually stated as a rate per hour, day, week, month, or year. Pay is sometimes based on pieces produced per unit of time, such as number of pieces produced per hour.

Supergolf has a biweekly pay period of 80 hours. The basic salary may be supplemented by other types of earnings. For example, in addition to a basic biweekly salary, an employee may receive commissions, cost-of-living adjustments, a share of profits, or a bonus.

Supergolf has three types of employee earnings. First, an hourly salary is paid biweekly to salesclerks and accounting department employees. Second, a biweekly salary is paid to each of the two department supervisors and the store manager. Third, a monthly commission is also paid to each of the department supervisors.

FIGURING A DEPARTMENTAL PAYROLL

Supergolf's payroll system shows the amount of employee benefits, payroll expense, and withholdings for each employee and each department.

Benefits authorization

A benefits authorization form is used to record and authorize employee benefits. Supergolf pays employee benefits biweekly on 80 hours of continuous work. Employee benefits are not paid for hours in excess of 80 per pay period. Salesclerks and accounting department employees must have their employee benefits authorized by their department supervisor. Department supervisors must have their employee benefits authorized by the store manager.

Employee benefits are recorded in the Hours Avail. column of a benefits authorization form. Each employee's authorization form with the available hours recorded is forwarded to the appropriate department supervisor at the beginning of each pay period. Benefits authorizations for the department supervisors are sent to the store manager. A department supervisor or manager records employee benefits hours used on the benefits authorization form as they are used during each pay period. Vicki Aron's benefits authorization form, completed by department supervisor Barbara Carew for the pay period ended July 2, 1988, is shown in Illustration 4-2.

		BENEFITS AUTHORIZATION													
EMPLOYEE NO. 7		EMPLOYEE Vicki J. Aron													
PAY PERIOD ENDED 7-2-88		DEPARTMENT Clothing													
	HOURS AVAIL.	M	T	W	T	F	S	M	T	W	T	F	S	HOURS USED
VACATION	34			8										8
SICK LEAVE	40							4						4
PERSONAL LEAVE	24										1			1

Barbara A. Carew   7-2-88

MANAGER (only if needed)   DEPARTMENT SUPERVISOR   DATE

Illustration 4-2
Benefits authorization

Ms. Aron's benefits authorization shows the hours available at the beginning of the pay period. The form also shows the authorized vacation, sick leave, and personal leave time used during the pay period. Eight hours of vacation time were used on Wednesday of the first week. Four hours of sick leave time were used on Monday and one hour of personal leave time was used on Thursday of the second week. The department supervisor signs and forwards the benefits authorization to the accounting department.

Benefits record

Detailed information about each employee's benefits is brought together in a benefits record. A benefits record is used to summarize total benefits earned, used, and available at the end of each pay period.

Supergolf keeps its benefits records on printed sheets. One sheet is used for each employee. Each sheet covers a calendar year. Since a biweekly payroll system has 26 pay periods in a calendar year, Supergolf's benefits record has 26 lines. One line is used to summarize employee benefits for each pay period. Accumulated employee benefits available at the end of one calendar year are brought forward and recorded on the next year's benefits record. Vicki Aron's benefits record for 1988 is shown in Illustration 4-3.

BENEFITS RECORD

EMPLOYEE NO. 7   EMPLOYEE NAME Vicki J. Aron   DEPARTMENT Clothing

DATE OF INITIAL EMPLOYMENT April 6, 1981   YEAR 1988

		1	2	3	4	5	6	7	8	9	10	11	12
		VACATION TIME				SICK LEAVE TIME				PERSONAL LEAVE TIME			
PAY PERIOD ENDED		BEGIN. HOURS AVAIL.	HOURS EARNED	HOURS USED	ACC. HOURS AVAIL.	BEGIN. HOURS AVAIL.	HOURS EARNED	HOURS USED	ACC. HOURS AVAIL.	BEGIN. HOURS AVAIL.	HOURS EARNED	HOURS USED	ACC. HOURS AVAIL.
1	1-2	74	4	8	70	28	2	0	30	23	1	0	24
2	1-16	70	4	0	74	30	2	4	28	24	1	4	21
3	1-30	74	4	0	78	28	2	0	30	21	1	0	22
4	2-13	78	4	0	82	30	2	2	30	22	1	2	21
5	2-27	82	4	0	86	30	2	0	32	21	1	0	22
6	3-12	86	4	80	10	32	2	0	34	22	1	0	23
7	3-26	10	4	0	14	34	2	0	36	23	1	0	24
8	4-9	14	4	0	18	36	2	8	30	24	1	2	23
9	4-23	18	4	0	22	30	2	0	32	23	1	0	24
10	5-7	22	4	0	26	32	2	0	34	24	1	0	25
11	5-21	26	4	4	26	34	2	0	36	25	1	0	26
12	6-4	26	4	0	30	36	2	0	38	26	1	4	23
13	6-18	30	4	0	34	38	2	0	40	23	1	0	24
14	7-2	34	4	8	30	40	2	4	38	24	1	1	24
15													

Illustration 4-3
Benefits record

For the first 1988 pay period ended January 2, Vicki Aron's accumulated hours available from the last pay period of 1987 are entered in the Begin. Hours Avail. columns, columns 1, 5, and 9. Accumulated vacation time hours available, 74, are taken from column 4 of the 1987 benefits record. These hours are entered on line 1 in the Vacation Time Begin. Hours Avail. column, column 1, of the 1988 benefits record. The accumulated sick leave time hours, 28, are taken from column 8 of the 1987 benefits record. These hours are entered on line 1 in the Sick Leave Time Begin. Hours Avail. column, column 5, of the 1988 benefits record. The accumulated personal leave time hours, 23, are taken from column 12 of the 1987 benefits record. These hours are entered on line 1 in the Personal Leave Time Begin. Hours

Avail. column, column 9, of the 1988 benefits record. Beginning hours available *plus* hours earned *minus* hours used *equals* the accumulated hours available at the end of a pay period. For example, the vacation time accumulated hours available for the pay period ended January 2 are figured as shown below.

Beginning Vacation Hours Available		Vacation Hours Earned during Pay Period		Vacation Hours Used		Accumulated Vacation Hours Available
74	+	4	–	8	=	70

The hours available at the end of one pay period are carried forward as the beginning hours available for the next pay period. For example, 70 vacation hours are available after the pay period ended January 2. The number of hours, 70, is carried forward on the benefits record, line 2, column 1, as the next period's beginning vacation hours. Sick leave time and personal leave time are recorded in the same way.

After each employee's benefits record is completed, the employee benefits hours available are recorded on each employee's benefits authorization form. The accounting department sends the benefits authorizations to the appropriate department supervisor or manager for use during the next pay period. The accounting department also records employee benefits on employees' time cards.

Payroll time card

Supergolf is open for business six days a week from 9:00 A.M. until 6:00 P.M. However, employees usually work only a five-day week of 40 hours. Days worked during a week vary so that enough employees are available for each of the six days the business is open. For example, one employee may work Monday through Friday while another employee may work Tuesday through Saturday.

Supergolf's salesclerks and accounting employees are paid an hourly salary biweekly for the two regular 40-hour work weeks. All time worked in excess of eight hours in any one day is considered overtime. Employees are paid 1.5 times the regular hourly rate for overtime hours. Supergolf uses a time clock to record regular and overtime hours worked by each employee paid an hourly salary.

In Supergolf's time-clock system, a payroll time card is inserted in the time clock each time an employee arrives for work and leaves work. A time clock records the time on a payroll time card when a card is inserted.

Vicki Aron's time card for the pay period ended July 2, 1988, is shown in Illustration 4-4.

The time card shows that Ms. Aron had a total of 80 *regular* hours for the biweekly pay period. Her lunch period is from 1 to 2 P.M. daily. Her time

NAME	Vicki J. Aron						
DEPARTMENT	Clothing						
EMPLOYEE NO.	7						
PAY PERIOD ENDED	7-2-88						

MORNING		AFTERNOON		OVERTIME		HOURS	
IN	OUT	IN	OUT	IN	OUT	REG	OT
≥ 9:00	≥ 1:01	≥ 2:00	≥ 6:03	≥ 7:00	≥ 8:01	8	1
⊢ 8:58	⊢ 1:00	⊢ 1:59	⊢ 6:00			8	
						V8	
⊢ 8:59	⊢ 1:02	⊢ 2:01	⊢ 6:00			8	
⊢ 9:00	⊢ 1:00	⊢ 2:00	⊢ 6:01			8	
≥ 8:57	≥ 1:00					4S4	
⊢ 8:59	⊢12:58	⊢ 2:00	⊢ 6:00			8	
≥ 9:01	≥ 1:02	≥ 2:00	≥ 6:02			8	
⊢ 9:03	⊢12:59	⊢ 3:01	⊢ 6:00			7P1	
⊢ 9:00	⊢ 1:01	⊢ 2:00	⊢ 6:01	⊢ 6:29	⊢ 9:31	8	3

	HOURS	RATE	AMOUNT
REGULAR	80	6.00	480.00
OVERTIME	4	9.00	36.00
TOTAL HOURS	84	TOTAL EARNINGS	516.00

Illustration 4-4
Payroll time card

card also shows that she worked 4 *overtime* hours: 1 hour on Monday of the first week and 3 hours on Friday of the second week.

At the end of the biweekly pay period, the authorized employee benefit hours are entered on the payroll time cards. The employee benefits hours are shown by the first letter of the benefit written next to the hours. Ms. Aron's time card, Illustration 4-4, shows *V8* written in the Hours Reg column for Wednesday of the first week. Ms. Aron gets credit for eight regular hours for the day even though the hours represented vacation time. *S4* is written next to the 4 hours of regular hours worked on Monday of the second week to show that 4 hours were used for sick leave time. *P1* is written next to the 7 hours of regular time worked on Thursday of the second week to show that 1 hour was used for personal leave time.

The number of hours for Ms. Aron is determined to be 84. Using the 84 hours, Ms. Aron's biweekly earnings are figured. Ms. Aron's regular salary is $480.00 (80 hours × $6.00 per hour). Ms. Aron's overtime pay is $36.00 (4 hours × $6.00 × 1.5). The regular salary, $480.00, plus the overtime salary, $36.00, equals the total earnings, $516.00.

Commissions record

Supervisors for each of the two departments — clothing and equipment — are paid a regular biweekly salary. They are not paid for overtime hours. To pay for supervisory duties and to encourage efforts to increase sales, the supervisors are also paid a 1% commission on the department's monthly net sales. The store manager is paid a regular biweekly salary and receives no salary for overtime hours. The store manager however normally receives an annual bonus based on the sales record for both departments.

Commissions for the previous month's net sales are included with the first biweekly pay period of a month. A commissions record is used to record the data necessary to figure each department supervisor's commission. Supergolf's commissions record for Barbara Carew, clothing department supervisor, is shown in Illustration 4-5.

General information is recorded at the top of the form. The sales on account for June, *$8,890.65*, are obtained from the sales journal, Illustration 3-4, Chapter 3. The cash and credit card sales for June, *$23,520.00*, are obtained from the cash receipts journal, Illustration 3-6, Chapter 3. The sales discounts for June, *$127.00*, are also obtained from the cash receipts journal, Illustration 3-6. The sales returns and allowances for June, *$380.00*, are obtained from the sales returns and allowances journal,

COMMISSIONS RECORD

Employee No. __3__   Employee Name __Barbara A. Carew__
Commission __1%__   Month __June__   Year __1988__
Dept. __Clothing__   Regular Biweekly Salary __$450.00__

Sales
  Sales on Account... $ 8,890.65
  Cash and Credit Card Sales.............................. 23,520.00
  Total Sales.. $32,410.65
  Less: Sales Discounts................. $ 127.00
    Sales Returns
    and Allowances 380.00   507.00
  Net Sales... $31,903.65
  Commission on Net Sales................................. $ 319.04

Illustration 4-5
Commissions record

Illustration 3-5, Chapter 3. Commission on net sales for Barbara Carew is figured below.

Net Sales	×	Commission Rate	=	Commission on Net Sales
$31,903.65	×	1%	=	$319.04

Payroll deductions

Supergolf is required by law to withhold two federal taxes from each employee's pay: income withholding tax and FICA tax. FICA tax is also known as social security tax. FICA are the initials for the Federal Insurance Contributions Act.

Some cities and states also require that employers deduct amounts from employees' earnings for income and other taxes. Laws for handling state, city, and county taxes vary.

Some businesses also have other deductions from employees' earnings for life insurance, hospital insurance, pension plans, and savings deposits. Supergolf makes deductions from its employees' pay for federal income tax, state income tax, FICA tax, life insurance, and hospital insurance.

COMPLETING PAYROLL RECORDS

A business must complete a number of payroll records in order to provide the payroll information required by governmental agencies.

Preparing a payroll register

A business form on which all payroll information is recorded is called a payroll register. A payroll register summarizes the payroll for one pay period and shows amounts earned, amounts withheld, and cash paid out for all employees.

Supergolf prepares a separate payroll register for each biweekly payroll. Supergolf's payroll register for the biweekly pay period ended July 2, 1988, is shown in Illustration 4-6.

Entering basic employee data in a payroll register. The last day of the biweekly payroll period, July 2, 1988, is entered at the top of the payroll register. The date of payment, July 9, 1988, is also entered at the top of the payroll register. The time between the end of a pay period and the date of payment is needed to prepare the payroll records and payroll checks. Employee No., Name, Marital Status, and No. of Allowances are taken from personnel records kept for each employee. The payroll register, Illustration 4-6, line 1, columns 1–4, shows the basic employee data for Vicki Aron.

> For each person supported, including the employee, an employee is entitled to a reduction in the amount on which income tax is figured. A deduction from total earnings for each person legally supported by a taxpayer is called a withholding allowance.

Entering data from time cards in a payroll register. The time card, Illustration 4-4, shows the hours worked and earnings for Vicki Aron. This payroll information is entered in the payroll register on the line with the employee's name. The payroll register, line 1, columns 5–9, shows the information from Vicki Aron's time card.

Entering data from commissions records in a payroll register. The commissions record, Illustration 4-5, shows information about Barbara Carew's

PAY PERIOD ENDED *July 2, 1988*   PAYROLL REGISTER

	EMPL. NO.	EMPLOYEE'S NAME	MARITAL STATUS	NO. OF ALLOW- ANCES	TOTAL HOURS	EARNINGS REGULAR	OVERTIME	COMMIS- SION	TOTAL	
1	7	Aron, Vicki J.	M	3	84	48000	3600		51600	1
2	10	Carew, Barbara A.	S	1	—	45000		31904	76904	2
3	16	Cole, David M.	M	2	82	44000	1650		45650	3
4	9	Esch, Carl L.	S	1	80	46400			46400	4
5	15	Felice, Jeff R.	M	2	—	60000			60000	5
6	11	Fye, Amy L.	M	3	83	44800	2520		47320	6
7	18	Hanes, Linda C.	M	2	80	48000			48000	7
8	19	Irwin, Glenda S.	M	2	81	48000	900		48900	8
9	21	Letson, Thelma M.	S	2	80	46400			46400	9
10	14	Lewis, Kent J.	M	3	—	40000		35526	75526	10
15	8	Ryan, Janice P.	S	1	82	46400	1740		48140	15
16		Totals				709000	19410	67430	795840	16
17										17

Illustration 4-6
Payroll register
(left side)

commission for June, 1988. Department supervisors do not account for their hourly time on a time card. A line is therefore drawn through the Total Hours column, column 5, as shown on line 2 of the payroll register. Each department supervisor's salary remains the same for each biweekly pay period. Therefore, the salary amount is recorded in the Regular Earnings column, column 6. Commissions from the commissions records are entered in the Commission Earnings column, column 8. Regular Earnings, column 6, and Commission Earnings, column 8, are added together to determine Total Earnings for the biweekly pay period.

Entering departmental and administrative salaries in a payroll register. Time cards and commissions records show the department to be charged for each employee's total earnings. Total earnings are entered in columns 10 or 11 of the payroll register according to the department in which the employee works. Salaries of non-sales employees, such as accounting department employees, are entered in the Admin. Salaries column, column 12. The store manager's salary is also entered in column 12 on line 5.

The payroll register, line 1, column 10, shows that Vicki Aron's salary is charged to the clothing department. The entry on line 4, column 11, shows that Carl Esch's salary is charged to the equipment department.

Entering deductions for employees' federal income tax. The federal income tax amount to be withheld from each employee's total earnings is determined from withholding tables furnished by the federal government. Partial federal income tax tables for biweekly payroll periods are shown in Illustration 4-7.

			PAYROLL REGISTER							
DATE OF PAYMENT July 9, 1988										
DEPARTMENT		ADMIN. SALARIES	DEDUCTIONS					PAID		
CLOTHING	EQUIPMENT		FEDERAL INCOME TAX	STATE INCOME TAX	FICA TAX	OTHER	TOTAL	NET PAY	CK. NO.	
51600			3700	2580	3612 H	L 1280 2800	13972	37628	246	1
76904			12000	3845	5383 H	1600	22828	54076	247	2
		45650	3400	2283	3196 H	2800	11679	33971	248	3
	46400		5500	2320	3248 H	L 1280 1600	13948	32452	249	4
		60000	5800	3000	4200 H	L 1280 2800	17080	42920	250	5
	47320		3100	2366	3312 H	2800	11578	35742	251	6
	48000		4000	2400	3360 H	L 1280 2800	13840	34160	252	7
48900			4000	2445	3423 H	2800	12668	36232	253	8
		46400	4800	2320	3248 H	2800	13168	33232	254	9
	75526		7500	3776	5287 H	L 1280 2800	20643	54883	255	10
48140			5900	2405	3370 H	1600	13275	34865	260	15
369504	274286	152050	76700	39792	55709 H	L 6400 36000	214601	581239		16

Illustration 4-6
Payroll register
(right side)

BIWEEKLY Payroll Period — Employee NOT MARRIED

At least	But less than	0	1	2	3	4	5	6	7	8	9	10 or more
And the wages are-		And the number of withholding allowances claimed is—										
		The amount of income tax to be withheld shall be—										
$440	$460	$59	$51	$45	$38	$32	$26	$20	$14	$9	$4	$0
460	480	62	55	48	41	35	29	23	17	12	7	2
480	500	66	59	51	45	38	32	26	20	14	9	4
500	520	70	62	55	48	41	35	29	23	17	12	7
520	540	74	66	59	51	45	38	32	26	20	14	9
540	560	78	70	62	55	48	41	35	29	23	17	12
560	580	82	74	66	59	51	45	38	32	26	20	14
580	600	87	78	70	62	55	48	41	35	29	23	17
600	620	92	82	74	66	59	51	45	38	32	26	20
620	640	96	87	78	70	62	55	48	41	35	29	23
640	660	101	92	82	74	66	59	51	45	38	32	26
660	680	105	96	87	78	70	62	55	48	41	35	29
680	700	110	101	92	82	74	66	59	51	45	38	32
700	720	115	105	96	87	78	70	62	55	48	41	35
720	740	120	110	101	92	82	74	66	59	51	45	38
740	760	126	115	105	96	87	78	70	62	55	48	41
760	780	131	120	110	101	92	82	74	66	59	51	45
780	800	136	126	115	105	96	87	78	70	62	55	48
800	820	141	131	120	110	101	92	82	74	66	59	51
820	840	146	136	126	115	105	96	87	78	70	62	55

BIWEEKLY Payroll Period — Employee MARRIED

At least	But less than	0	1	2	3	4	5	6	7	8	9	10 or more
And the wages are-		And the number of withholding allowances claimed is—										
		The amount of income tax to be withheld shall be—										
$380	$400	$37	$31	$26	$20	$15	$10	$6	$2	$0	$0	$0
400	420	40	34	29	23	18	13	8	4	0	0	0
420	440	43	37	31	26	20	15	10	6	2	0	0
440	460	46	40	34	29	23	18	13	8	4	0	0
460	480	49	43	37	31	26	20	15	10	6	2	0
480	500	52	46	40	34	29	23	18	13	8	4	0
500	520	55	49	43	37	31	26	20	15	10	6	2
520	540	58	52	46	40	34	29	23	18	13	8	4
540	560	62	55	49	43	37	31	26	20	15	10	6
560	580	65	58	52	46	40	34	29	23	18	13	8
580	600	68	62	55	49	43	37	31	26	20	15	10
600	620	71	65	58	52	46	40	34	29	23	18	13
620	640	75	68	62	55	49	43	37	31	26	20	15
640	660	79	71	65	58	52	46	40	34	29	23	18
660	680	82	75	68	62	55	49	43	37	31	26	20
680	700	86	79	71	65	58	52	46	40	34	29	23
700	720	89	82	75	68	62	55	49	43	37	31	26
720	740	93	86	79	71	65	58	52	46	40	34	29
740	760	97	89	82	75	68	62	55	49	43	37	31
760	780	100	93	86	79	71	65	58	52	46	40	34

Illustration 4-7
Section of income tax
withholding tables for
biweekly pay period

Tax regulations change from time to time. Regulations used in this textbook are those in effect at the time this book was written.

An employee's total earnings, marital status, and number of allowances claimed determines the federal income tax amount to be withheld. For example, Vicki Aron's total earnings for the biweekly pay period ended July 2, 1988, are $516.00. Vicki is married and claims 3 allowances. The two columns at the left of the tax table for married persons show ranges of earnings amounts. The total earnings amount, $516.00, is in the range of "at least 500 but less than 520." The withholding amount, $37.00, is found on the same line in the column at the right with a 3 at the top. The federal income tax deduction, *$37.00*, is recorded in the payroll register, line 1, column 13.

Entering deductions for employees' state income tax. The state in which Supergolf operates has an income tax on the total earnings of its residents.

The state income tax amount to be withheld from employees' earnings is usually determined from withholding tables furnished by the state. Ms. Aron's state income tax deduction, *$25.80*, is entered in the payroll register, line 1, column 14.

Entering deductions for employees' FICA tax. The FICA tax is based on employee earnings paid in a calendar year. Congress sets the tax base and the tax rates for FICA tax. An act of Congress can change the base and rate at any time.

> Accounting procedures involved are the same regardless of changes in tax bases and tax rates. Therefore, a FICA tax rate of 7% on a maximum annual salary of $45,000.00 is assumed for all payroll calculations in this textbook.

Vicki Aron's FICA tax deduction for the biweekly pay period ended July 2, 1988, is figured as shown below.

Total Earnings	×	**FICA Tax Rate**	=	**FICA Tax Deduction**
$516.00	×	7%	=	$36.12

Ms. Aron's FICA tax deduction, *$36.12*, is recorded in the payroll register on line 1, column 15.

Entering employees' other deductions. Besides income taxes and FICA tax, some employees have two other deductions.

1. *Life insurance.* This deduction is $12.80 per biweekly pay period for employees desiring life insurance. Not all employees have life insurance premiums deducted from their earnings. The amount for life insurance is written in the payroll register, column 16. The deduction is identified by writing the letter *L* in front of the amount.
2. *Hospital insurance.* This deduction is $16.00 per biweekly pay period for each insured single employee claiming one allowance. The deduction is $28.00 for each married employee and also for each single employee claiming more than one dependent. The deduction for hospital insurance is written in the payroll register, column 16. The hospital insurance deduction is identified by writing the letter *H* in front of the amount.

Ms. Aron's deductions for life insurance, *L 12.80*, and hospital insurance, *H 28.00*, are entered in the payroll register, line 1, column 16.

Figuring employees' net pay

After all deductions are entered in the payroll register, the amounts for deductions are added and the total is written in column 17. The net amount to be paid is then figured by subtracting the total deductions, column 17, from total earnings, column 9. The net pay for Vicki Aron is figured below.

Total Earnings **(column 9)**	−	**Total Deductions** **(column 17)**	=	**Net Pay** **(column 18)**
$516.00	−	$139.72	=	$376.28

Ms. Aron's net pay amount, *$376.28*, is entered in the payroll register, line 1, column 18.

Proving a payroll register's accuracy

When the net pay has been entered for all employees, each payroll register amount column is totaled. The Total Deductions column is subtracted from the Total Earnings column. The result should equal the total of the Net Pay column. If the totals do not agree, the errors must be found and corrected. Proving the accuracy of Supergolf's payroll register for pay period ended July 2, 1988, is shown below.

Total Earnings (column 9)	−	Total Deductions (column 17)	=	Net Pay (column 18)
$7,958.40	−	$2,146.01	=	$5,812.39

The net pay, $5,812.39, figured above is the same as the total for column 18, Net Pay. The payroll register is proved. After the payroll register is proved, double lines are ruled below all amount column totals.

Preparing an employee's earnings record

A business must send a quarterly report to federal and state governments showing employees' taxable earnings and taxes withheld from employees' earnings. Detailed information about each employee's earnings is brought together in a single record for each employee. A business form showing details of all items affecting payments made to an employee is called an employee's earnings record. An employee's total earnings and deductions for each pay period are summarized on one line of the employee's earnings record. Supergolf prepares an earnings record for each employee each quarter.

Supergolf keeps its employee's earnings records on printed cards. One card is used for each quarter of the year. Vicki Aron's earnings record for the third quarter of 1988 is shown in Illustration 4-8.

Illustration 4-8
Employee's earnings
record

EARNINGS RECORD FOR QUARTER ENDED *Sept. 30, 1988*

EMPLOYEE NO. *7* NAME *Aron, Vicki J.* SOCIAL SECURITY NO. *512-36-7216*
MARITAL STATUS *m* WITHHOLDING ALLOWANCES *3* HOURLY RATE *$6.00* SALARY
DEPARTMENT *Clothing* POSITION *Salesclerk*

1	2	3	4	5	6	7	8	9	10
PAY PERIOD		TOTAL EARNINGS	DEDUCTIONS					NET PAY	ACCUMULATED EARNINGS
NO.	ENDED		FEDERAL INCOME TAX	STATE INCOME TAX	FICA TAX	OTHER	TOTAL		
									634000
1	7/2	51600	3700	2580	3612	L 1280 H 2800	13972	37628	685600
2									
3									

The biweekly pay period ended July 2, 1988, is the first pay period of the third quarter ended September 30. Vicki Aron's salary and deductions are shown in the first entry on her earnings record.

Information needed to complete the amount columns of an employee's earnings record is obtained from amount columns of a payroll register. Ms. Aron's payroll information is obtained from the payroll register, Illustration 4-6, line 1. This payroll information is recorded in the amount columns of Ms. Aron's earnings record.

The Accumulated Earnings column of the employee's earnings record shows the accumulated earnings since the beginning of the fiscal year. Accumulated earnings are often referred to as year-to-date earnings. Year-to-date earnings are needed for each employee because certain payroll taxes do not apply after an employee's earnings reach a specified amount. For example, employers pay federal and state unemployment taxes only on the first $7,000.00 of each employee's earnings during a calender year. FICA taxes also are paid only on a maximum amount determined by law.

The first entry in the Accumulated Earnings column, $6,340.00, is Ms. Aron's accumulated earnings for the first two quarters ended June 30, 1988. The total earnings for the pay period ended July 2, 1988, $516.00, are added to the accumulated earnings to get the new accumulated earnings to date. The new accumulated earnings amount, *$6,856.00,* is entered on the same line as the other payroll information for the pay period ended July 2, 1988.

PAYING A PAYROLL

Supergolf pays its employees biweekly by check. A special payroll bank account and special payroll checks are used.

Payroll bank account

After a biweekly payroll register has been completed, a check is written payable to Payroll for the total net amount owed to employees. This check is deposited in a special payroll bank account against which payroll checks are written for individual employees' net pay.

The payroll bank account does not appear in the general ledger or on the chart of accounts. The amount of the biweekly deposit to the payroll account equals exactly the sum of the biweekly salary payments. The special payroll account balance therefore is reduced to zero as soon as all employees have cashed their payroll checks. Because the special payroll bank account has a balance only until all payroll checks are cashed, no special account is needed in the general ledger.

Automatic check deposit

Employees may authorize an employer to deposit payroll checks in specified banks. The procedure of depositing payroll checks directly to an

employee's checking or savings account in a specified bank is called automatic check deposit. The use of automatic check deposit for payroll does
not change the accounting procedures for recording payroll.

RECORDING A PAYROLL

A business' payroll register contains the information needed to prepare
a payroll check.

Journalizing a payroll payment

The source document for journalizing a payroll payment is the check
stub of the check written for the net payroll amount. *(CONCEPT: Objective
Evidence)*

Salary Expense — Clothing	
3,695.04	

Salary Expense — Equipment	
2,742.86	

Salary Expense — Administrative	
1,520.50	

Employees Income Tax Payable — Federal	
	767.00

Employees Income Tax Payable — State	
	397.92

FICA Tax Payable	
	557.09

Hospital Insurance Premiums Payable	
	360.00

Life Insurance Premiums Payable	
	64.00

Cash	
	5,812.39

July 9, 1988.
Paid biweekly payroll: clothing, $3,695.04; equipment, $2,742.86; administrative, $1,520.50 (less deductions: employees' income tax — federal, $767.00; employees' income tax — state, $397.92; FICA tax, $557.09; hospital insurance, $360.00; life insurance, $64.00); total, $5,812.39. Check No. 426.

The department and administrative salaries for the
pay period are the totals of columns 10–12 of the payroll
register, Illustration 4-6. The deductions are the totals of
columns 13–16 of the payroll register. The total net amount
paid to all employees for the pay period is the total of
column 18 of the payroll register.

The analysis of this payroll transaction is shown in the T
accounts. Salary Expense — Clothing is increased by a $3,695.04
debit. Salary Expense — Equipment is increased by a $2,742.86 debit.
Salary Expense — Administrative is increased by a $1,520.50
debit. Employees Income Tax Payable — Federal is increased by a
$767.00 credit. Employees Income Tax Payable — State is increased
by a $397.92 credit. FICA Tax Payable is increased by a $557.09
credit. Hospital Insurance Premiums Payable is increased by a
$360.00 credit. Life Insurance Premiums Payable is increased by a
$64.00 credit. Cash is decreased by a $5,812.39 credit.

The entry for Supergolf's payroll payment on July 9,
1988, is shown on lines 1–8 of the cash payments journal,
Illustration 4-9.

Journalizing an employer's payroll taxes

Most employers have three separate payroll taxes. (1) Employer's FICA
tax. (2) Federal unemployment tax. (3) State unemployment tax.

	DATE	ACCOUNT TITLE	CK. NO.	POST. REF.	GENERAL DEBIT	GENERAL CREDIT	ACCOUNTS PAYABLE DEBIT	PURCH. DISCOUNT CR. CLOTHING	PURCH. DISCOUNT CR. EQUIPMENT	CASH CREDIT	
										CASH PAYMENTS JOURNAL PAGE *13*	
1	1988 July 9	Salary Expense – Clothing	426		3 695 04					5 812 39	1
2		Salary Expense – Equip.			2 742 86						2
3		Salary Expense – Admin.			1 520 50						3
4		Emp. Inc. Tax Pay. – Fed.				767 00					4
5		Emp. Inc. Tax Pay. – State				397 92					5
6		FICA Tax Payable				557 09					6
7		Hosp. Ins. Premiums Pay.				360 00					7
8		Life Ins. Premiums Pay.				64 00					8
15	28	Emp. Inc. Tax Pay. – Fed.	433		1 520 40					3 730 90	15
16		FICA Tax Payable			2 210 50						16
17	29	Unemploy. Tax Pay. – Fed.	434		290 48					290 48	17
18	29	Unemploy. Tax Pay. – State	435		1 960 71					1 960 71	18
19											19
20											20

Unemployment taxes are used to pay qualified workers cash benefits for limited periods of unemployment.

Illustration 4-9 Payroll payment entry

Employees in a few states also have deductions from their earnings for state unemployment tax. Employees do not pay federal unemployment tax.

An employer's payroll taxes expense is based on a percentage of employee earnings. The employer's FICA tax is figured at the same rate and on the same earnings used in figuring the FICA tax for employees. The federal unemployment tax is 6.2% on the first $7,000.00 earned by each employee. An employer generally can deduct from federal unemployment payments the amounts paid to state unemployment funds. This deduction cannot be more than 5.4% of taxable earnings. The effective federal unemployment tax rate in most states is therefore .8% on the first $7,000.00 earned by each employee. (Federal 6.2% − deductible for state 5.4% = 0.8%.) All of the unemployment tax on the first $7,000.00 of salary is paid by the employer.

None of Supergolf's employees has earned $7,000.00 by the pay period ended July 2, 1988. Therefore, Supergolf's federal unemployment tax is 0.8% of $7,958.40 total earnings, or $63.67. Supergolf's state unemployment tax is 5.4% of $7,958.40 total earnings, or $429.75.

Jeff Felice, manager, would have earned over $7,000.00 by July 2, 1988, had he worked since the beginning of the year. However, he started work at Supergolf on March 1, 1988.

The source document for recording an employer's payroll taxes is a memorandum. *(CONCEPT: Objective Evidence)*

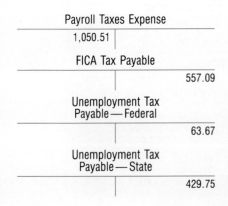

July 9, 1988.
Recorded payroll taxes expense for the biweekly pay period ended July 2, 1988: FICA tax payable, $557.09; unemployment tax payable — federal, $63.67; unemployment tax payable — state, $429.75; total, $1,050.51. Memorandum No. 42.

The analysis of this transaction is shown in the T accounts. Payroll Taxes Expense is increased by a $1,050.51 debit. FICA Tax Payable is increased by a $557.09 credit. Unemployment Tax Payable — Federal is increased by a $63.67 credit. Unemployment Tax Payable — State is increased by a $429.75 credit.

The entry to record the employer's payroll taxes for the pay period ended July 2 and paid on July 9 is shown on lines 1–5 of the general journal, Illustration 4-10.

Illustration 4-10
Employer's payroll
taxes entry

	DATE	ACCOUNT TITLE	POST. REF.	DEBIT	CREDIT	
1	1988 July 9	Payroll Taxes Expense		1 05051		1
2		FICA Tax Payable			557 09	2
3		Unemploy. Tax Pay. - Fed.			63 67	3
4		Unemploy. Tax Pay. - State			429 75	4
5		M42				5
6						6

GENERAL JOURNAL   PAGE 10

PAYING PAYROLL TAXES LIABILITIES

Employers must pay to federal, state, and local governments all payroll taxes withheld from employees' earnings as well as the employer's payroll taxes. The frequency of payments is determined by the amount owed.

Journalizing federal income tax and FICA tax payment

If the amount owed is less than $500.00 a quarter, payment is due at the end of the quarter. If the amount owed is between $500.00 and $3,000.00 by the end of any month, payment is due by the 15th of the following month. If the amount owed is $3,000.00 or more within a month, payment is due three banking days following specified payment periods. The federal government identifies eight specified payment periods in which unpaid taxes of $3,000.00 or more are due. The eight specified payment periods are the 3rd, 7th, 11th, 15th, 19th, 22nd, 25th, and the last day of each month.

At the end of Supergolf's second biweekly pay period ended July 16 and paid on July 23, 1988, federal payroll taxes liabilities for the month exceed

$3,000.00. Payment therefore must be made three banking days following the July 25 specified payment period, or July 28. The source document for a federal income tax and FICA tax payment is a check stub. *(CONCEPT: Objective Evidence)*

> *July 28, 1988.*
> *Paid June liabilities for employees' federal income tax, $1,520.40, and FICA tax, $2,210.50; total, $3,730.90. Check No. 433.*

The analysis of this transaction is shown in the T accounts. Employees Income Tax Payable—Federal is decreased by a $1,520.40 debit. FICA Tax Payable is decreased by a $2,210.50 debit. This FICA tax amount includes both the amounts withheld from employees and the employer's share. Cash is decreased by a $3,730.90 credit.

Employees Income Tax Payable—Federal	
1,520.40	

FICA Tax Payable	
2,210.50	

Cash	
	3,730.90

The entry for payment of these liabilities is shown on lines 15 and 16 of the cash payments journal, Illustration 4-9.

Supergolf's liability for state income tax withholding is paid at the end of each quarter.

Journalizing federal unemployment tax payment

If the annual federal unemployment tax is $100.00 or less, payment is due annually by January 31 of the following year. If the annual tax is over $100.00, quarterly payments are required in the month following the end of the quarter.

Supergolf's federal unemployment tax for the second quarter of 1988 is $290.48. Payment is required during the first month of the following quarter, July, 1988. The source document for a federal unemployment tax payment is a check stub. *(CONCEPT: Objective Evidence)*

> *July 29, 1988.*
> *Paid liability for second quarter federal unemployment tax, $290.48. Check No. 434.*

The analysis of this transaction is shown in the T accounts. Unemployment Tax Payable—Federal is decreased by a $290.48 debit. Cash is decreased by a $290.48 credit.

Unemployment Tax Payable—Federal	
290.48	

Cash	
	290.48

The entry for payment of the federal unemployment tax is shown on line 17 of the cash payments journal, Illustration 4-9.

Journalizing state unemployment tax payment

Requirements for paying state unemployment taxes vary. Usually, employers are required to pay the state unemployment tax during the month following each calendar quarter.

Supergolf's state unemployment tax for the second quarter of 1988 is $1,960.71. The source document for a state unemployment tax payment is a check stub. (*CONCEPT: Objective Evidence*)

July 29, 1988.
Paid liability for second quarter state unemployment tax, $1,960.71.
Check No. 435.

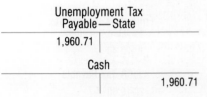

The analysis of this transaction is shown in the T accounts. Unemployment Tax Payable—State is decreased by a $1,960.71 debit. Cash is decreased by a $1,960.71 credit.

The entry for payment of this liability is shown on line 18 of the cash payments journal, Illustration 4-9.

ACCOUNTING TERMS

What is the meaning of each of the following?

1. salary
2. pay period
3. payroll
4. payroll taxes
5. employee benefits
6. payroll register
7. withholding allowance
8. employee's earnings record
9. automatic check deposit

QUESTIONS FOR INDIVIDUAL STUDY

1. Why are payroll expenses reported as separate items in accounting records and financial statements?

2. Reporting payroll expenses as separate items in accounting records and financial statements is an application of which accounting concept?

3. Who requires that payroll information be kept and reported for each employee and the business?

4. Why are employee benefits provided by most businesses?

5. What are Supergolf's three employee benefits?

6. On what basis might employee earnings be figured?

7. An employee's salary may be supplemented by what other types of earnings?

8. What are the three types of employee earnings paid by Supergolf?

9. How does Supergolf record regular and overtime hours worked for each employee?

10. When are commissions paid to Supergolf's department supervisors?

11. What are the two federal taxes that are withheld from an employee's pay?

12. Why do the payroll date and the date of payment differ on Supergolf's payroll register?

13. How does Supergolf determine the federal income tax to be withheld from each employee's pay?

14. Who sets the tax base and the tax rates for FICA tax?

15. How many employee's earnings records does Supergolf use for each employee?

16. Where is the information obtained for completing an employee's earnings record?

17. Using a check stub as the source document for a payroll payment is an application of which accounting concept?

18. What three separate payroll taxes do most employers have?

19. How is an employer's FICA tax figured?

20. What is the source document for recording an employer's payroll taxes entry?

21. What accounts are affected, and how, by a federal unemployment tax payment?

CASES FOR MANAGEMENT DECISION

CASE 1 Fashion Corner keeps its accounting records on a departmental basis. All general ledger accounts that affect gross profit on sales are identified by department. However, the operating expenses connected with sales are not kept on a departmental basis. As the salary expense is the largest single selling expense, the accounting department recommends that the business consider setting up special salary expense accounts for each of the sales departments. The store manager disagrees with the recommendation because salesclerks do not work solely in individual departments. The store manager feels that it would not be feasible to identify salary ex-

penses by department. Therefore, the decision was made to continue using one salary expense account for all departments. Do you agree or disagree with the decision? Why?

CASE 2 Supergolf uses one account, Payroll Taxes Expense, in which to record all of the expenses for FICA tax, federal unemployment tax, and state unemployment tax. Micromart uses three expense accounts — FICA Tax Expense, Federal Unemployment Tax Expense, and State Unemployment Tax Expense — when recording the business' three payroll tax expenses. Which system of recording taxes is more desirable? Explain your answer.

APPLICATION PROBLEMS

PROBLEM 4-1   Preparing a benefits record

Plouff's provides the same employee benefits as those described for Supergolf in this chapter.

Instructions: Prepare Rose Doyle's benefits record for the first four biweekly pay periods of the current year. Information needed to complete the record is below.

Employee Name: Rose M. Doyle		Department: Women's Shoes			
Date of Initial Employment: November 1, 1986		Employee No.: 14			
Pay Period	Regular Hours	Employee Benefits Available		Employee Benefits Used	
1/2	80	V63	S72	P16	V8	S0	P4
1/16	80	_____	_____	_____	V0	S4	P2
1/30	80	_____	_____	_____	V16	S0	P0
2/13	80	_____	_____	_____	V0	S2	P3
V = Vacation time; S = Sick leave time; P = Personal leave time					

PROBLEM 4-2   Figuring employees' earnings

The information below is taken from the time cards for each employee.

Employee Number	Hours Worked Regular	Overtime	Regular Rate
1	80	4	$7.50
2	80	2	6.00
3	80	0	8.25
4	80	3	7.00
5	80	1	8.50

Instructions: Use a form similar to the one below. For each employee, figure the amount of regular, overtime, and total earnings. Overtime hours are paid at 1.5 times the regular rate. The amounts figured for Employee No. 1 are given as an example.

Employee Number	Hours Worked		Regular Rate	Earnings		Total Earnings
	Regular	Overtime		Regular	Overtime	
1	80	4	$7.50	$600.00	$45.00	$645.00

PROBLEM 4-3 Recording employee benefits and figuring earnings on time cards

Kenchen's has two departments: Furniture and Hardware. A biweekly payroll system of 26 pay periods per year is used. Salesclerks and employees in the accounting department are paid on an hourly basis and receive 1.5 times the regular hourly pay rate for all hours worked over 80 each pay period. A time card is used for hourly employees to record hours worked.

Kenchen's provides the same employee benefits as those described for Supergolf in this chapter. The employee benefits provided are shown in Illustration 4-1. A benefits authorization form like the one shown in Illustration 4-2 is also used.

Time cards and benefits authorization forms for selected employees of Kenchen's are provided in the working papers. The time cards and employee benefits authorizations are for the biweekly pay period ended March 12 of the current year.

Instructions: 1. Prepare an employee benefits record for each employee.
2. Record employee benefits hours on time cards for each employee.
3. Figure regular, overtime, and total hours worked by each employee on the time cards.
4. Complete each time card by figuring regular, overtime, and total earnings.

The time cards prepared in this problem are needed to complete Problem 4-5.

PROBLEM 4-4 Preparing departmental commissions records

Kenchen's employs a departmental supervisor for each of its two departments. Departmental supervisors are paid a biweekly salary and receive monthly commissions of 1% of net sales. Commissions are paid for the previous month in the first pay period of the current month. Data from the accounting records for the month ended February 29 of the current year are below.

    a. Furniture department: sales on account, $7,623.40; cash and credit card sales, $12,936.20; sales discounts, $138.40; sales returns and allowances, $709.80.
    b. Hardware department: sales on account, $6,930.10; cash and credit card sales, $14,730.60; sales discounts, $122.70; sales returns and allowances, $1,318.50.

Instructions: Prepare a commissions record for each departmental supervisor given below similar to the one in this chapter. Use February of the current year as the date.

    a. Furniture department
        Employee name: Mary A. Brady
        Employee number: 9
        Regular salary: $540.00

    b. Hardware department
        Employee name: Paul T. Burke
        Employee number: 14
        Regular salary: $520.00

The commissions records prepared in this problem are needed to complete Problem 4-5.

PROBLEM 4-5   Completing a payroll register

The time cards prepared in Problem 4-3 and the commissions records prepared in Problem 4-4 are needed to complete this problem.

Kenchen's partially completed payroll register for the pay period ended March 12 is provided in the working papers. Additional data needed to complete the payroll register are below.

    a. A deduction is to be made from each employee's pay for federal income tax. Use the appropriate income tax withholding tables shown in Illustration 4-7.

    b. A deduction of 5% is to be made from each employee's pay for state income tax.

    c. A deduction of 7% is to be made from each employee's pay for FICA tax.

    d. All employees have dental insurance, $9.40, and hospital insurance, $13.20, deducted from their pay each biweekly pay period. These deductions are to be recorded in the Other Deductions column of the payroll register. The letter D is to be written in front of the dental insurance deduction. The letter H is to be written in front of the hospital insurance deduction. Both the dental and hospital insurance deductions are written on one line of the payroll register for each employee.

Instructions: Complete the payroll register for the pay period ended March 12 and paid on March 19 of the current year.

The payroll register prepared in Problem 4-5 is needed to complete Problems 4-6 and 4-7.

PROBLEM 4-6   Completing an employee's earnings record

The payroll register prepared in Problem 4-5 is needed to complete this problem.

A partially completed employee's earnings record for each of Kenchen's employees is provided in the working papers.

Instructions: Complete the employee's earnings record for each employee. This pay period is the sixth of the first quarter of the current year.

PROBLEM 4-7   Paying a departmental payroll

The payroll register prepared in Problem 4-5 is needed to complete this problem.

Instructions: 1. Record the March 19 payroll payment on page 15 of a cash payments journal. The source document is Check No. 463.

    2. Record the employer's payroll taxes on page 8 of a general journal. Use March 19 of the current year as the date. The source document is Memorandum No. 41. Employer tax rates are: FICA, 7%; federal unemployment, 0.8%; state unemployment, 5.4%.

PROBLEM 4-8   Figuring and paying payroll taxes liabilities

Payroll data for McCalister's for the first quarter of the current year are below. Employer tax rates are: FICA, 7%; federal unemployment, 0.8%; state unemployment, 5.4%.

Payroll Month	Total Earnings	FICA Tax Withheld	Federal Income Tax Withheld
March	$ 8,986.00	$629.02	$993.88
First Quarter	26,962.30	—	—

Instructions: 1. Figure the liability for federal income tax and FICA tax withheld, plus the employer's liability for FICA tax. Record the payment of federal income tax withholding and FICA tax on page 11 of a cash payments journal. The payment is made on April 15 using Check No. 462 as the source document.

2. Figure the federal unemployment tax liability for the first quarter. Record the payment on page 13 of a cash payments journal. The payment is made on April 30 using Check No. 515 as the source document.

3. Figure the state unemployment tax liability for the first quarter. Record the payment on page 13 of a cash payments journal. The payment is made on April 30 using Check No. 516 as the source document.

ENRICHMENT PROBLEMS

MASTERY PROBLEM 4-M   Completing payroll records; paying payroll; and recording taxes

Ochoa Music Mart has two departments: Records and Tapes. A biweekly payroll system of 26 pay periods per year is used. Salesclerks and employees in the accounting department are paid on an hourly basis and receive 1.5 times the regular hourly pay rate for all hours worked over 80 each pay period. A time card is used for hourly employees to record hours worked.

Department supervisors are paid a biweekly salary and receive monthly commissions of 1% of net sales. Commissions are paid for the previous month in the first pay period of the next month.

Ochoa Music Mart provides the same employee benefits as those described for Supergolf in this chapter. The employee benefits provided are in the employee benefits schedule shown in Illustration 4-1. A benefits authorization form like the one shown in Illustration 4-2 is also used.

Ochoa Music Mart's partially completed payroll records for selected employees are provided in the working papers. The payroll records are for the pay period ended February 13 and paid on February 20 of the current year.

Instructions: 1. Complete the benefits record for each employee and record employee benefits hours used on the time cards.

2. Figure regular, overtime, and total hours worked by each employee.

3. Complete each time card by figuring regular, overtime, and total earnings.

4. Complete the commissions record for each departmental supervisor. Data from the accounting records for the month ended January 31 of the current year are below.

   a. Records department: sales on account, $5,334.60; cash and credit card sales, $7,922.10; sales discounts, $92.40; sales returns and allowances, $312.20.
   b. Tapes department: sales on account, $5,668.90; cash and credit card sales, $8,375.30; sales discounts, $101.70; sales returns and allowances, $288.60.

5. Complete the payroll register for the pay period ended February 13 and paid February 20 of the current year. Additional data needed to complete the payroll register are below.

   a. A deduction is to be made from each employee's pay for federal income tax. Use the appropriate income tax withholding tables shown in Illustration 4-7.
   b. A deduction of 5% is to be made from each employee's pay for state income tax.
   c. A deduction of 7% is to be made from each employee's pay for FICA tax.
   d. All employees have life insurance, $8.20, and hospital insurance, $14.80, deducted from their pay each biweekly pay period. The letter L is to be written in front of the life insurance deduction. The letter H is to be written in front of the hospital insurance deduction.

6. Complete the employee's earnings record for each employee. This pay period is the fourth of the first quarter of the current year.

7. Record the February 20 payroll payment on page 9 of a cash payments journal. The source document is Check No. 143.

8. Record the employer's payroll taxes on page 5 of a general journal. Use February 20 of the current year as the date. The source document is Memorandum No. 14. Employer tax rates are: FICA, 7%; federal unemployment, 0.8%; state unemployment, 5.4%. The employee's FICA tax withheld and the employer's share of FICA tax will not be equal due to rounding differences.

CHALLENGE PROBLEM 4-C   Preparing a benefits record

Walden's uses a semimonthly payroll system. Three employee benefits are provided. (1) Vacation time. (2) Sick leave time. (3) Personal leave time. The time available is outlined in Walden's employee benefits schedule shown below.

Walden's Employee Benefits				
Benefits	Earned After 12 Months	Semimonthly After 12 Months	Minimum Time Blocks	Maximum Carry Over
Vacation time hours	40	3 1/3	4	120
Sick leave time hours	0	1 2/3	1	80
Personal leave time hours . .	0	1	1	24

Instructions: Prepare Alice Dotson's benefits record for the first four semimonthly pay periods of the current year using the employee benefits schedule shown above. Information needed to complete the record is below.

Employee Name: Alice K. Dotson Date of Initial Employment: June 5, 1985					Department: Women's Wear Employee No.: 7		
Pay Period	Regular Hours	Employee Benefits Available			Employee Benefits Used		
1/15	80	V35 1/3	S28 2/3	P18	V0	S4	P2
1/31	80	_____	_____	_____	V4	S0	P3
2/15	80	_____	_____	_____	V8	S8	P0
2/29	80	_____	_____	_____	V0	S0	P2
V = Vacation time; S = Sick leave time; P = Personal leave time							

5 Financial Reporting for a Departmentalized Business

ENABLING PERFORMANCE TASKS

After studying Chapter 5, you will be able to:

a. Define accounting terms related to financial reporting for a departmentalized business.

b. Identify accounting concepts and practices related to financial reporting for a departmentalized business.

c. Complete selected interim and end-of-fiscal-period work for a departmentalized business.

d. Analyze financial statements through selected performance ratios.

Valuable financial information is included in a business' ledgers. To be useful for management decision making however the information must be summarized and reported in the form of financial statements. Businesses usually summarize and report ledger information periodically. Because businesses must prepare tax reports at least once a year, businesses summarize and report accounting information at least once a year. Some businesses however summarize and report ledger information more frequently in order to analyze business operations more often. The length of time for which a business analyzes financial information is called a fiscal period. (*CONCEPT: Accounting Period Cycle*) Businesses may use fiscal periods of one month, three months, six months, or twelve months. Each business decides what fiscal period best meets the needs of that particular business. Supergolf uses a calendar-year fiscal period.

A departmentalized business prepares the same financial statements in the same form as a nondepartmentalized business. In addition, a departmentalized business usually prepares reports about how well each department is doing. A statement prepared at the end of a fiscal period showing the gross profit for each department is called a departmental statement of gross profit.

A departmental statement of gross profit provides a manager with information about revenue and costs for each department. A review of this information may show a need to (a) change merchandise selling prices, (b) change suppliers of merchandise, (c) change or add products, or (d) discontinue a department.

INTERIM DEPARTMENTAL STATEMENT OF GROSS PROFIT

Gross profit information reflects changes between costs and selling prices. A departmental statement of gross profit also provides information that can be used to quickly determine potential profits. Therefore, a departmental statement of gross profit is often prepared at the end of each month even though the fiscal period is for more than one month. A statement showing gross profit for each department for a portion of a fiscal period is called an interim departmental statement of gross profit. Supergolf prepares monthly interim departmental statements of gross profit.

Determining ending inventory value

To prepare an interim departmental statement of gross profit, both beginning and ending inventory values are needed. The ending inventory for one month is also the beginning inventory for the next month.

Two principal methods are used to determine actual quantities of merchandise on hand. Merchandise inventory determined by counting, weighing, or measuring items of merchandise on hand is called a periodic inventory. A periodic inventory is sometimes known as a physical inventory. Merchandise inventory determined by keeping a continuous record of increases, decreases, and balance on hand is called a perpetual inventory. A perpetual inventory is sometimes known as a book inventory.

A merchandise inventory value is relatively easy to determine at any time when a perpetual inventory is kept. However, keeping a perpetual inventory may not be practical for a merchandising business with numerous items of merchandise. For a periodic inventory, a physical count of merchandise is made. However, a monthly periodic inventory may not be practical. When a perpetual inventory is not kept and a monthly periodic inventory is not practical, merchandise inventory may be estimated. Estimating inventory by using previous years' percentage of gross profit on operations is called the gross profit method of estimating an inventory.

Estimating ending inventory value

Because of the numerous items of merchandise, Supergolf determines its monthly ending inventory by using the gross profit method of estimating an inventory. A printed estimated merchandise inventory sheet is used to record the necessary data.

The clothing department's estimated inventory sheet prepared on June 30, 1988, is shown in Illustration 5–1.

ESTIMATED MERCHANDISE INVENTORY SHEET
Gross Profit Method

Department _Clothing_   Date _6-30-88_

1	Beginning inventory, January 1	$184,334.61
2	Net purchases to date	56,550.10
3	Merchandise available for sale	$240,884.71
4	Net sales to date	$185,848.80
5	Less estimated gross profit (Net sales × Estimated gross profit **45** %)	83,631.96
6	Estimated cost of merchandise sold	102,216.84
7	Estimated ending inventory	$138,667.87

Illustration 5-1
Estimated merchandise
inventory sheet

Supergolf's estimated merchandise inventory sheet is prepared as described below.

Line 1: The beginning inventory, January 1, is obtained from the general ledger. The balance of Merchandise Inventory—Clothing, $184,334.61, is the actual merchandise inventory on hand at the beginning of the fiscal period. The amount is the result of the periodic inventory count from December 31, 1987.

> Even when estimated inventory methods are used, a periodic inventory is usually taken at least once a year.

Line 2: The net purchases to date, $56,550.10, is obtained from general ledger accounts. The amount is figured as below.

Purchases—Clothing	$59,430.60
Less Purchases Returns and Allowances—Clothing	1,790.30
	$57,640.30
Less Purchases Discount—Clothing	1,090.20
Equals net purchases to date (January 1-June 30)	$56,550.10

Line 3: The merchandise available for sale, $240,884.71, is figured by adding lines 1 and 2.

Line 4: The net sales to date, $185,848.80, is obtained from general ledger accounts. The amount is figured as below.

Sales—Clothing	$188,640.20
Less Sales Returns and Allowances—Clothing	2,010.80
	$186,629.40
Less Sales Discount—Clothing	780.60
Equals net sales to date (January 1-June 30)	$185,848.80

Line 5: The estimated gross profit, $83,631.96, is figured by multiplying the amount on line 4 by 45%. The percentage used is a gross profit estimate based on records of previous years' operations.

Line 6: The estimated cost of merchandise sold, $102,216.84, is figured by subtracting the amount on line 5 from the amount on line 4.

Line 7: The estimated ending inventory, $138,667.87, is figured by subtracting the amount on line 6 from the amount on line 3 ($240,884.71 minus $102,216.84 equals $138,667.87). The clothing department's June 30, 1988, estimated merchandise inventory, $138,667.87, is used on the interim departmental statement of gross profit. The same procedure is used to figure the equipment department's estimated ending merchandise inventory.

Preparing an interim departmental statement of gross profit

Supergolf's interim departmental statement of gross profit for the month ended June 30, 1988, is shown in Illustration 5-2.

Supergolf Interim Departmental Statement of Gross Profit For Month Ended June 30, 1988							
	Clothing	*% of Net Sales	Equipment	*% of Net Sales	Total	*% of Net Sales
Operating Revenue:						
Net Sales............	$31,903.65	100.0	$35,526.30	100.0	$67,429.95	100.0
Cost of Merchandise Sold:						
Est. Mdse. Inv., June 1 .	$146,048.42		$141,555.80		$287,604.22	
Net Purchases.........	9,902.40		17,061.50		26,963.90	
Mdse. Available for Sale .	$155,950.82		$158,617.30		$314,568.12	
Less Est. End. Inv.,						
June 30	138,667.87		139,321.50		277,989.37	
Cost of Merchandise Sold		17,282.95	54.2	19,295.80	54.3	36,578.75	54.2
Gross Profit on Operations		$14,620.70	45.8	$16,230.50	45.7	$30,851.20	45.8

*Rounded to nearest 0.1%

Data are organized into three sections. (1) Operating Revenue. (2) Cost of Merchandise Sold. (3) Gross Profit on Operations. The beginning inventory for each department is the estimated ending inventory from the interim departmental statement of gross profit for the month ended May 31, 1988.

Illustration 5-2
Interim departmental
statement of gross profit

Analyzing an interim departmental statement of gross profit

To help a manager analyze financial information, relationships between items in a financial statement are figured. The percentage relationship between one financial statement item and the total that includes that item is called a component percentage. The relationship between each item and net sales may be shown in a separate column on a financial statement. Four basic components are included in every sales dollar. (1) Cost of merchandise sold. (2) Gross profit on operations. (3) Operating expenses. (4) Net income.

A comparison between two numbers showing how many times one number exceeds the other is called a ratio. A ratio may be expressed as a stated ratio, a percentage ratio, or a fraction ratio. Supergolf figures monthly the percentage ratio of cost of merchandise sold and gross profit on operations to net sales.

Stated ratios and fraction ratios are described in Chapter 19.

Cost of merchandise sold. Because the cost of merchandise sold is a significant cost, management attempts to keep this cost as low as possible. Supergolf's interim departmental statement of gross profit, Illustration 5-2, shows that the ratio of total cost of merchandise sold to total net sales is 54.2%. This percentage ratio is determined as figured below.

Total Cost of Merchandise Sold	÷	Total Net Sales	=	Ratio of Total Cost of Merchandise Sold to Total Net Sales
$36,578.75	÷	$67,429.95	=	54.2%

A percentage ratio of cost of merchandise sold to net sales is also figured for each department.

Gross profit on operations. The excess of net sales over cost of merchandise sold is gross profit on operations. Gross profit on operations must be large enough to cover total operating expenses and produce a net income. Analysis of the interim departmental statement of gross profit shows that the ratio of total gross profit on operations to total net sales is 45.8%. This percentage ratio is determined as figured below.

Total Gross Profit on Operations	÷	Total Net Sales	=	Ratio of Total Gross Profit on Operations to Total Net Sales
$30,851.20	÷	$67,429.95	=	45.8%

A percentage ratio of gross profit on operations to net sales is also figured for each department.

The percentage ratios of operating expenses and net income to net sales, the third and fourth components in each sales dollar, are figured and analyzed at the end of each fiscal period.

Determining acceptable levels of performance. For ratios to be useful, a business must know acceptable levels of performance. To determine acceptable levels of performance, businesses generally make comparisons with previous performance and with industry performance standards that are published by industry organizations. Based on these sources, Supergolf determines that an acceptable ratio of departmental and total cost of merchandise sold to net sales should not be more than 55%. Supergolf further determines that an acceptable ratio of departmental and total gross profit on operations to net sales should not be less than 45%.

An analysis of the interim departmental statement of gross profit for the month ended June 30, 1988, indicates acceptable levels of performance. The ratio of total cost of merchandise sold to net sales, 54.2%, is not more than 55%. The ratio of total gross profit on operations to net sales, 45.8%, is not less than 45%. The ratios of cost of merchandise sold and gross profit on operations to net sales for each department also indicate acceptable levels of performance.

PROVING ACCURACY OF POSTING TO SUBSIDIARY LEDGERS

Supergolf prepares a report showing the total of all accounts receivable ledger accounts. A listing of customer accounts, account balances, and total amount due from all customers is called a schedule of accounts receivable. The total on a schedule of accounts receivable must equal the balance of the general ledger controlling account, Accounts Receivable. Supergolf's schedule of accounts receivable is shown in Illustration 5-3.

Supergolf Schedule of Accounts Receivable June 30, 1988	
Larry Bissell	$ 1,650.60
Easy-Golf	644.70
Alex Grant	892.50
Greenview Golf League	1,785.00
Marsha Kraft	245.70
Parkside Golf Club	1,391.25
Stuart Schools	875.25
Helene Vega	3,675.00
David Weir	2,695.00
Total Accounts Receivable	$13,855.00

Illustration 5-3
Schedule of accounts receivable

Supergolf also prepares a report showing the total of all accounts payable ledger accounts. A listing of vendor accounts, account balances, and total amount due all vendors is called a schedule of accounts payable. The total on a schedule of accounts payable must equal the balance of the controlling account, Accounts Payable. Supergolf's schedule of accounts payable is shown in Illustration 5-4.

The balances of both controlling accounts, Accounts Receivable and Accounts Payable, agree with the totals shown on the two schedules. Therefore, posting to subsidiary ledgers is assumed to be correct.

Supergolf

Schedule of Accounts Payable
June 30, 1988

Classic Golf Supply...	$ 6,360.60
Ecolo-Golf Co...	8,920.00
Golf Pride Apparel..	1,290.00
Keno Golf Products...	1,514.30
Nova Golf Carts..	10,840.00
Turfco, Inc..	3,610.40
Universal Golf Supply...	625.00
Total Accounts Payable.......................................	$33,160.30

Illustration 5-4
Schedule of accounts
payable

WORK SHEET FOR A DEPARTMENTALIZED BUSINESS

If debits equal credits in journals, and if posting is done correctly, debits will equal credits in a general ledger. A proof of the equality of debits and credits in a general ledger is called a trial balance.

A trial balance is most often prepared as part of the end-of-fiscal-period activities. Another of these activities is the completion of a work sheet. A columnar accounting form on which the financial condition of a business is summarized is called a work sheet.

Supergolf completes the end-of-fiscal-period work as of December 31 each year. (CONCEPT: *Accounting Period Cycle*)

Trial balance on a departmental work sheet

A trial balance is prepared in a work sheet's Trial Balance columns. General ledger accounts are listed in the account title column in the same order in which they appear in the general ledger. All accounts are listed regardless of whether there is a balance or not. Supergolf's trial balance for the year ended December 31, 1988, is on the work sheet shown in Illustration 5-5.

After all general ledger accounts and balances have been entered, the Trial Balance columns are totaled and checked for equality. The two column totals, $1,272,352.71, are the same. The Trial Balance columns are ruled as shown on line 56 of the work sheet.

Adjustments on a departmental work sheet

Some general ledger accounts are not up to date. For example, bad debts expense has not been recorded. The entries needed to bring accounts up to date are planned in the work sheet's adjustments columns.

Bad debts expense adjustment. Merchandise is sometimes sold on account to customers who later are unable to pay the amounts owed. Amounts that cannot be collected from customers are business expenses.

Accurate financial reporting requires that expenses be recorded in the fiscal period in which the expenses contribute to earning revenue. *(CONCEPT: Matching Expenses with Revenue)*

Supergolf has found from past experience that approximately 1% of sales on account will be uncollectible. Sales on account for 1988 were $215,940.00. The estimated bad debts expense is $2,159.40 ($215,940.00 times .01).

Four questions are asked in analyzing the bad debts expense adjustment.

1. What is the balance of the bad debts expense account?. . . . .   Zero
2. What should the balance be for this account? $2,159.40
3. What must be done to correct the account balance? Increase   2,159.40
4. What adjusting entry is made?
   Debit Bad Debts Expense. 2,159.40
   Credit Allowance for Uncollectible Accounts. 2,159.40

The analysis of the adjustment for the bad debts expense is shown in the T accounts. Bad Debts Expense is increased by a $2,159.40 debit. Allowance for Uncollectible Accounts, a contra asset account, is increased by a $2,159.40 credit. The Allowance for Uncollectible Accounts balance represents the total estimated amount that Supergolf believes will not be collected from accounts receivable. This estimated amount is not deducted from the Accounts Receivable balance until Supergolf knows for sure which customers will not pay. The estimated bad debts amount therefore is recorded in a separate account titled Allowance for Uncollectible Accounts.

Bad Debts Expense	
(a) 2,159.40	

Allowance for Uncollectible Accounts	
	Bal. 240.60
	(a) 2,159.40

Entries related to bad debts expense are described in Chapter 9.

The bad debts expense adjustment is recorded on the work sheet, lines 4 and 47, Illustration 5-5. The adjustment is labeled *(a)* because it is the first adjustment recorded.

Merchandise inventory adjustments. Supergolf's merchandise inventory — clothing account balance on January 1, 1988, is $184,334.61. The merchandise inventory — equipment account balance on January 1, 1988, is $197,844.60. The two account balances on December 31, the end of the fiscal year, are the same amounts, $184,334.61 and $197,844.60. The two accounts have not changed during the year because purchases and sales transactions have not been recorded in the two inventory accounts.

Two income summary accounts, temporary capital accounts, are used as companion accounts to adjust the two merchandise inventory accounts at the end of a fiscal period.

The actual count of merchandise on December 31, 1988, shows that the clothing merchandise inventory is valued at $202,855.00. An adjustment is needed to bring the clothing merchandise inventory account up to date.

Four questions are asked in analyzing the clothing merchandise inventory adjustment.

Supergolf
Work Sheet
For Year Ended December 31, 1988

| | TRIAL BALANCE | | ADJUSTMENTS | | INCOME STATEMENT | | BALANCE SHEET | |
ACCOUNT TITLE	DEBIT	CREDIT	DEBIT	CREDIT	DEBIT	CREDIT	DEBIT	CREDIT
1 Cash	5054000						5054000	
2 Petty Cash	50000						50000	
3 Accounts Receivable	1385500						1385500	
4 Allow. for Uncoll. Accts.		24060		(a)215940				240000
5 Mdse. Inv. – Clothing	18433461		(b)1852039				20285500	
6 Mdse. Inv. – Equipment	19784460			(c)936000			18848460	
7 Supplies – Office	1260000			(d)990000			270000	
8 Supplies – Store	1443000			(e)784000			659000	
9 Prepaid Insurance	980000			(f)560000			420000	
10 Office Equipment	1680000						1680000	
11 Accum. Depr. – Office Equip.		592000		(g)148000				740000
12 Store Equipment	3890000						3890000	
13 Accum. Depr. – Store Equip.		1800000		(h)300000				2100000
14 Accounts Payable		3316030						3316030
15 Employ. Inc. Tax Pay. – Fed.		168075						168075
16 Employ. Inc. Tax Pay. – State		98000						98000
17 Federal Inc. Tax Pay.				(i)327216				327216
18 FICA Tax Payable		236070						236070
19 Sales Tax Payable		339690						339690
20 Unemploy. Tax Pay. – Fed.		2360						2360
21 Unemploy. Tax Pay. – State		15930						15930
22 Hosp. Ins. Premiums Pay.		108000						108000
23 Life Ins. Premiums Pay		19200						19200
24 Capital Stock		35000000						35000000
25 Retained Earnings		4121050						4121050

	Trial Balance Debit	Trial Balance Credit	Adjustments Debit	Adjustments Credit	Income Statement Debit	Income Statement Credit
26 Income Summary—Clothing			(c)936000		936000	
27 Income Summary—Equip.			(b)1852039			1852039
28 Income Summary—General						
29 Sales—Clothing		35001676				35001676
30 Sales—Equipment		43835780				43835780
31 Sales Ret. & Allow.—Clothing	432000				432000	
32 Sales Ret. & Allow.—Equip.	631230				631230	
33 Sales Discount—Clothing	147030				147030	
34 Sales Discount—Equip.	214080				214080	
35 Purchases—Clothing	21083320				21083320	
36 Purchases—Equipment	23573970				23573970	
37 Purch. Ret. & Allow.—Clothing		368000				368000
38 Purch. Ret. & Allow.—Equip.		1350000				1350000
39 Purch. Discount—Clothing		378320				378320
40 Purch. Discount—Equip.		461030				461030
41 Advertising Expense	431000				431000	
42 Credit Card Fee Expense	492000				492000	
43 Depr. Exp.—Store Equip.			(a)300000		300000	
44 Salary Expense—Clothing	9064020				9064020	
45 Salary Expense—Equipment	7220080				7220080	
46 Supplies Expense—Store			(c)784000		784000	
47 Bad Debts Expense			(e)215940		215940	
48 Depr. Exp.—Office Equip.			(g)148000		148000	
49 Insurance Expense			(b)560000		560000	
50 Miscellaneous Expense	541000				541000	
51 Payroll Taxes Expense	2136040				2136040	
52 Rent Expense	1800000				1800000	
53 Salary Expense—Admin.	4355308				4355308	
54 Supplies Expense—Office			(d)990000		990000	
55 Federal Income Tax	1156000		(f)327216		1483216	
56	127235271	127235271	6113195	6113195	77536006	83246845
57 Net Inc. after Fed. Inc. Tax					5710839	
58					83246845	83246845

Illustration 5-5
Departmental work sheet

1. What is the balance of the merchandise
    inventory — clothing account? $184,334.61
2. What should the balance be for this account? 202,855.00
3. What must be done to correct the account
    balance? .... Increase   18,520.39
4. What adjusting entry is made?
        Debit Merchandise Inventory — Clothing................   18,520.39
        Credit Income Summary — Clothing 18,520.39

Merchandise Inventory — Clothing

Bal. 184,334.61	
(b) 18,520.39	

Income Summary — Clothing

	(b) 18,520.39

The analysis of the merchandise inventory — clothing adjustment is shown in the T accounts.

The ending clothing inventory, $202,855.00, is $18,520.39 larger than the inventory account's current balance, $184,334.61. Therefore, Merchandise Inventory — Clothing is increased by a $18,520.39 debit. Income Summary — Clothing is increased by a $18,520.39 credit. The balance of Merchandise Inventory — Clothing after this adjustment, $202,855.00, is equal to the actual inventory. The account is up to date.

A similar adjustment is made for Merchandise Inventory — Equipment, using Income Summary — Equipment as the companion account. However, the ending equipment inventory is smaller than the inventory account's current balance. The inventory account balance must be decreased. Therefore, Income Summary — Equipment is debited and Merchandise Inventory — Equipment is credited.

The two inventory adjustments are entered on the work sheet, lines 5, 6, 26, and 27, Illustration 5-5. The Merchandise Inventory — Clothing adjustment is labeled (b). The Merchandise Inventory — Equipment adjustment is labeled (c).

Supplies inventory adjustments. Supergolf's supplies — office account balance on December 31, 1988, is $12,600.00. The supplies — store account balance is $14,430.00. These account balances include two items. (1) The account balances on January 1, 1988. (2) The cost of supplies bought during the year. The account balances do not reflect the value of any supplies used during the year, an operating expense.

The actual count of supplies on December 31, 1988, shows that the office supplies inventory is valued at $2,700.00. The difference between the December 31 account balance, $12,600.00, and the ending inventory value, $2,700.00, is the amount of office supplies used during the fiscal year, $9,900.00. An adjustment is needed to bring the office supplies inventory account up to date. (CONCEPT: Matching Expenses with Revenue)

Four questions are asked in analyzing the office supplies inventory adjustment.

1. What is the balance of the supplies — office account? $12,600.00
2. What should the balance be for this account? 2,700.00
3. What must be done to correct the account
    balance? ....Decrease   9,900.00

4. What adjusting entry is made?
  Debit Supplies Expense — Office .... $ 9,900.00
  Credit Supplies — Office 9,900.00

The analysis of the office supplies inventory adjustment is shown in the T accounts. Supplies Expense — Office is increased by a $9,900.00 debit. Supplies — Office is decreased by a $9,900.00 credit. The balance of Supplies — Office after this adjustment, $2,700.00, is equal to the actual inventory. The account is up to date.

Supplies Expense — Office	
(d) 9,900.00	

Supplies — Office	
Bal. 12,600.00	(d) 9,900.00

A similar adjustment is made for Supplies — Store inventory.

The two supplies adjustments are entered on the work sheet, lines 7, 8, 46, and 54, Illustration 5-5. The Supplies — Office adjustment is labeled (d). The Supplies — Store adjustment is labeled (e).

Prepaid insurance adjustment. The prepaid insurance account balance on line 9 of the work sheet's trial balance, Illustration 5-5, is $9,800.00. This balance includes two items. (1) The account balance on January 1, 1988. (2) The value of insurance premiums paid during the year. The account balance does not reflect the value of any insurance used during the year, an operating expense.

On December 31, 1988, Supergolf determines that the amount of unexpired prepaid insurance is $4,200.00. The difference between the December 31 account balance, $9,800.00, and the unexpired prepaid insurance value, $4,200.00, is the amount of insurance used during the year, $5,600.00. An adjustment is needed to bring the prepaid insurance account up to date. (CONCEPT: Matching Expenses with Revenue)

Four questions are asked in analyzing the prepaid insurance adjustment.

1. What is the balance of the prepaid insurance account? $9,800.00
2. What should the balance be for this account? 4,200.00
3. What must be done to correct the account
 balance? ....Decrease 5,600.00
4. What adjusting entry is made?
  Debit Insurance Expense 5,600.00
  Credit Prepaid Insurance 5,600.00

The analysis of the adjustment needed to bring the prepaid insurance account up to date is shown in the T accounts. Insurance Expense is increased by a $5,600.00 debit. Prepaid Insurance is decreased by a $5,600.00 credit. The balance of Prepaid Insurance after this adjustment, $4,200.00, is equal to the actual unexpired prepaid insurance. The account is up to date.

Insurance Expense	
(f) 5,600.00	

Prepaid Insurance	
Bal. 9,800.00	(f) 5,600.00

The Prepaid Insurance adjustment is entered on the work sheet, lines 9 and 49, Illustration 5-5. The adjustment is labeled (f).

Depreciation expense adjustments. Assets which will be used for a number of years in the operation of a business are called plant assets. Plant assets are not bought for purposes of resale to customers in the normal course of business. Plant assets decrease in value because of use and because of the passage of time as they become older and new models become available. The portion of a plant asset's cost transferred to an expense account in each fiscal period during a plant asset's useful life is called depreciation. The decrease in the value of equipment because of use and passage of time is an operating expense. *(CONCEPT: Matching Expenses with Revenue)* The amount of depreciation is an estimate. The actual decrease in equipment value is not known until equipment is disposed of or sold. For this reason, the *estimated* depreciation is recorded in a separate contra asset account for each type of equipment.

Figuring the amount of depreciation is described more fully in Chapter 10.

Supergolf estimates that the yearly depreciation on office equipment is $1,480.00. An adjustment is needed to bring the depreciation expense — office equipment account up to date.

Four questions are asked in analyzing the depreciation expense — office equipment adjustment.

1. What is the balance of the depreciation expense — office equipment account? .... Zero
2. What should the balance be for this account? $1,480.00
3. What must be done to correct the account balance? .... Increase 1,480.00
4. What adjusting entry is made?
   Debit Depreciation Expense — Office Equipment............ 1,480.00
   Credit Accumulated Depreciation — Office Equipment 1,480.00

Depreciation Expense — Office Equipment

(g) 1,480.00	

Accumulated Depreciation — Office Equipment

	Bal. 5,920.00
	(g) 1,480.00

An analysis of the depreciation expense — office equipment adjustment is shown in the T accounts. Depreciation Expense — Office Equipment is increased by a $1,480.00 debit. Accumulated Depreciation — Office Equipment is increased by a $1,480.00 credit.

A similar adjustment is made for Depreciation Expense — Store Equipment.

The two depreciation adjustments are entered on the work sheet, lines 11, 13, 43, and 48. The Depreciation Expense — Office Equipment adjustment is labeled *(g)*. The Depreciation Expense — Store Equipment adjustment is labeled *(h)*.

Federal income tax adjustment. Corporations anticipating federal income taxes of $40.00 or more are required to estimate their annual tax. The estimated tax is paid in quarterly installments in April, June, September, and December. Even though a corporation pays a quarterly estimated tax, the actual income tax must be figured at the end of each fiscal year.

Supergolf estimated $11,560.00 federal income tax for 1988. Each quarterly income tax payment is recorded in a cash payments journal as a debit to Federal Income Tax and a credit to Cash. Supergolf determines at the end of the fiscal year that the federal income tax is $14,832.16. An adjustment is needed to bring the federal income tax account up to date.

Four questions are asked in analyzing the federal income tax adjustment.

1. What is the balance of the federal income tax account?.... $11,560.00
2. What should the balance be for this account? 14,832.16
3. What must be done to correct the account
    balance? .... Increase   3,272.16
4. What adjusting entry is made?
         Debit Federal Income Tax............................   3,272.16
         Credit Federal Income Tax Payable 3,272.16

An analysis of the federal income tax adjustment is shown in the T accounts. Federal Income Tax is increased by a $3,272.16 debit. Federal Income Tax Payable is increased by a $3,272.16 credit.

The Federal Income Tax adjustment is entered on the work sheet, lines 17 and 55. The adjustment is labeled (*i*).

Federal Income Tax		
Bal.	11,560.00	
(i)	3,272.16	

Federal Income Tax Payable		
		(i) 3,272.16

> Figuring federal income tax at the end of a fiscal period is described in more detail in Chapter 15.

Debits must equal credits in a work sheet's Adjustments columns. After all adjustments have been entered on a work sheet, the Adjustments columns are totaled and checked for equality. The two column totals, $61,131.95, are the same. The work sheet's Adjustments columns are ruled as shown on line 56 of the work sheet, Illustration 5–5.

Work sheet's Balance Sheet columns

The asset, liability, and stockholders' equity account balances are extended to a work sheet's Balance Sheet columns. For those accounts affected by adjustments, new balances are figured and extended. For example, Allowance for Uncollectible Accounts, line 4 of the work sheet, Illustration 5–5, has a Trial Balance Credit balance of $240.60. The Adjustments Credit column amount of $2,159.40 makes the new account balance $2,400.00 ($240.60 plus $2,159.40). The new credit balance, *$2,400.00*, is extended to the Balance Sheet Credit column.

The two Balance Sheet columns are totaled. These two totals are out of balance by the amount of change in stockholders' equity resulting from a net income or a net loss. Supergolf's two balance sheet column totals are on line 56 of the work sheet.

Work sheet's Income Statement columns

The balances of all revenue, cost, and expense accounts are extended to a work sheet's Income Statement columns. The amounts in the Adjustments columns for Income Summary—Clothing and Income Summary—Equipment are also extended to the Income Statement columns. This procedure is shown on Supergolf's work sheet, lines 26 and 27, Illustration 5–5. The two Income Statement columns are totaled. These two totals are out of balance by the amount of change in stockholders' equity resulting from a net income or net loss. Supergolf's two Income Statement column totals are on line 56 of the work sheet.

Net income on a work sheet

The difference between a work sheet's two Income Statement column totals is the net income or net loss for a fiscal period. If the credit column total is larger than the debit column total, the difference is the increase in stockholders' equity resulting from a net income. If the debit column total is larger than the credit column total, the difference is a decrease in stockholders' equity resulting from a net loss.

Supergolf's two Income Statement column totals result in a net income as figured below.

Income Statement Credit column total (line 56)	$832,468.45
Less Income Statement Debit column total (line 56). . . .	775,360.06
Equals net income for the fiscal period	$ 57,108.39

The net income, $57,108.39, is written under the work sheet's Income Statement Debit column total, line 57, to make the two Income Statement columns balance. The words *Net Income after Fed. Inc. Tax* are written in the Account Title column on the same line.

The difference between a work sheet's two Balance Sheet column totals is the net income or net loss for a fiscal period. If the debit column total is larger than the credit column total, the difference is an increase in stockholders' equity resulting from a net income. If the credit column total exceeds the debit column total, the difference is a decrease in stockholders' equity resulting from a net loss.

Supergolf's net income, $57,108.39, is written under the work sheet's Balance Sheet Credit column total, line 57, to make the two Balance Sheet columns balance.

> When a net loss occurs, the net loss amount is written on a work sheet in the Income Statement Credit and Balance Sheet Debit columns.

After the net income amount is written in the two work sheet columns, the last four columns are totaled again. These new totals are shown on line 58, Illustration 5–5. The totals for each pair of columns must be the same. The two Income Statement totals are the same, $832,468.45. The two Balance Sheet totals are the same, $525,424.60. If the totals of each pair of columns are equal, the work sheet is assumed to be correct.

When the same net income or net loss amount makes the Income Statement columns and Balance Sheet columns balance, the work sheet is ruled as shown on line 58. If columns do not balance, errors must be found and corrected before final ruling is done.

FINANCIAL STATEMENTS FOR A DEPARTMENTALIZED BUSINESS

Financial statements are prepared to report a business' financial progress and condition. (*CONCEPT: Adequate Disclosure*) Supergolf prepares four important financial statements at the end of the annual fiscal period. (*CONCEPT: Accounting Period Cycle*) (1) Departmental statement of gross profit. (2) Income statement. (3) Statement of stockholders' equity. (4) Balance sheet. In preparing financial statements, Supergolf applies accounting principles the same way from one accounting period to the next. (*CONCEPT: Consistent Reporting*)

Departmental statement of gross profit

Supergolf's departmental statement of gross profit for the fiscal year ended December 31, 1988, is shown in Illustration 5-6.

	Clothing	*% of Net Sales	Equipment	*% of Net Sales	Total	*% of Net Sales
Supergolf **Departmental Statement of Gross Profit** **For Year Ended December 31, 1988**						
Operating Revenue:						
Net Sales............	$344,226.46	100.0	$429,904.70	100.0	$774,131.16	100.0
Cost of Merchandise Sold:						
Mdse. Inventory, Jan. 1.	$184,334.61		$197,844.60		$382,179.21	
Net Purchases.........	203,370.00		217,629.40		420,999.40	
Mdse. Available for Sale.	$387,704.61		$415,474.00		$803,178.61	
Less Ending Inv., Dec. 31	202,855.00		188,484.60		391,339.60	
Cost of Mdse. Sold.....		184,849.61	53.7	226,989.40	52.8	411,839.01	53.2
Gross Profit on Operations	$159,376.85	46.3	$202,915.30	47.2	$362,292.15	46.8

*Rounded to nearest 0.1%

The departmental statement of gross profit prepared at the end of a fiscal period is similar to the monthly interim departmental statement of gross profit. However, monthly interim departmental statements of gross profit use estimated ending inventories. The annual departmental statement of gross profit uses the actual ending periodic inventories.

Illustration 5-6
Departmental statement of gross profit

Data needed to complete the departmental statement of gross profit are taken from the work sheet's Trial Balance, Income Statement, and Balance Sheet columns.

Supergolf analyzes the annual departmental statement of gross profit in the same way as the interim departmental statement of gross profit. Percentage ratios of the total cost of merchandise sold and gross profit on operations to net sales are figured. The same percentage ratios are also figured for each department.

Supergolf uses the same performance standards for the annual departmental statement of gross profit as for the interim departmental statement of gross profit. The ratio of total cost of merchandise sold to total net sales should be not more than 55%. The ratio of total gross profit on operations to total net sales should be not less than 45%. The same performance standards are used for each department.

An analysis of the annual departmental statement of gross profit indicates acceptable levels of performance. The ratio of total cost of merchandise sold to total net sales, 53.2%, is not more than 55%. The ratio of total gross profit on operations to total net sales, 46.8%, is not less than 45%. The ratios of cost of merchandise sold and gross profit on operations to net sales for each department also indicate acceptable levels of performance.

Income statement

A financial statement showing the revenue and expenses for a fiscal period is called an income statement. An income statement reports financial progress of a business for a fiscal period. Supergolf's income statement for the annual fiscal period ended December 31, 1988, is shown in Illustration 5-7.

The data used to prepare Supergolf's income statement are obtained from the work sheet's Trial Balance, Income Statement, and Balance Sheet columns.

Besides analyzing the ratios of cost of merchandise sold and gross profit on operations to net sales for a fiscal year, Supergolf also analyzes the percentage ratios of total operating expenses and net income to net sales. Comparisons with previous performance and with industry performance standards that are published by industry organizations are used to determine acceptable levels of performance. From these sources, Supergolf determines acceptable percentage ratios for the end of the fiscal period. (1) Cost of merchandise sold, not more than 55% of net sales. (2) Gross profit on operations, not less than 45% of net sales. (3) Total operating expenses, not more than 38% of net sales. (4) Net income, not less than 7% of net sales. The percentage ratios of cost of merchandise sold, gross profit on operations, total operating expenses, and net income to net sales are shown in a separate column on the income statement. The percentage ratios of total gross profit on operations and total cost of merchandise sold to net sales are obtained from the departmental statement of gross profit. The ratio of total operating expenses to net sales is determined as figured below.

Total Operating Expenses	÷	Net Sales	=	Ratio of Total Operating Expenses to Net Sales
$290,351.60	÷	$774,131.16	=	37.5%

Supergolf
Income Statement
For Year Ended December 31, 1988

				*% of Net Sales
Operating Revenue:				
Sales....................................			$788,374.56	
Less: Sales Returns & Allowances.........		$ 10,632.30		
Sales Discount....................		3,611.10	14,243.40	
Net Sales.............................			$774,131.16	100.0
Cost of Merchandise Sold:				
Merchandise Inventory, Jan. 1, 1988			$382,179.21	
Purchases		$446,572.90		
Less: Purchases Returns & Allowances	$17,180.00			
Purchases Discount	8,393.50	25,573.50		
Net Purchases			420,999.40	
Total Cost of Mdse. Avail. for Sale.........			$803,178.61	
Less Mdse. Inventory, Dec. 31, 1988.......			391,339.60	
Cost of Merchandise Sold			411,839.01	53.2
Gross Profit on Operations			$362,292.15	46.8
Operating Expenses:				
Selling Expenses:				
Advertising Expense....................		$ 4,310.00		
Credit Card Fee Expense		4,920.00		
Depreciation Expense—Store Equip......		3,000.00		
Salary Expense—Clothing		90,640.20		
Salary Expense—Equipment............		72,200.80		
Supplies Expense—Store...............		7,840.00		
Total Selling Expenses..................			$182,911.00	
Administrative Expenses:				
Bad Debts Expense		$ 2,159.40		
Depreciation Expense—Office Equip.		1,480.00		
Insurance Expense		5,600.00		
Miscellaneous Expense		5,410.00		
Payroll Taxes Expense..................		21,360.40		
Rent Expense.........................		18,000.00		
Salary Expense—Administrative.........		43,530.80		
Supplies Expense—Office		9,900.00		
Total Administrative Expenses			107,440.60	
Total Operating Expenses			290,351.60	37.5
Net Income before Federal Income Tax......			$ 71,940.55	
Less Federal Income Tax.................			14,832.16	
Net Income after Federal Income Tax			$ 57,108.39	7.4

*Rounded to nearest 0.1%

The ratio of net income after federal income tax to net sales is determined as figured below.

Illustration 5-7
Income statement

Net Income	÷	Net Sales	=	Ratio of Net Income to Net Sales
$57,108.39	÷	$774,131.16	=	7.4%

An analysis of Supergolf's income statement ended December 31, 1988, indicates acceptable levels of performance. The ratio of cost of merchandise sold to net sales, 53.2%, is acceptable based on the performance standard of not more than 55% of net sales. The ratio of gross profit on operations to net sales, 46.8%, is acceptable based on the performance standard of not less than 45% of net sales. The ratio of total operating expenses to net sales, 37.5%, is acceptable based on the performance standard of not more than 38% of net sales. The ratio of net income to net sales, 7.4%, is acceptable based on the performance standard of not less than 7% of net sales.

Statement of stockholders' equity

A financial statement that shows changes in a corporation's ownership for a fiscal period is called a statement of stockholders' equity. Supergolf's statement of stockholders' equity for the fiscal year ended December 31, 1988, is shown in Illustration 5-8.

Supergolf Statement of Stockholders' Equity For Year Ended December 31, 1988		
Capital Stock:		
$175 Per Share		
January 1, 1988, 2,000 Shares Issued	$350,000.00	
Issued during 1988, None..	-0-	
Balance, December 31, 1988, 2,000 Shares Issued........................		$350,000.00
Retained Earnings:		
January 1, 1988	$ 41,210.50	
Plus Net Income for 1988...	57,108.39	
Balance, December 31, 1988...		98,318.89
Total Stockholders' Equity, December 31, 1988		$448,318.89

Illustration 5-8
Statement of
stockholders' equity

A statement of stockholders' equity contains two major sections. (1) Capital Stock. Total shares of ownership in a corporation are known as capital stock. (2) Retained Earnings. An amount earned by a corporation and not yet distributed to stockholders is called retained earnings.

The first section shows that Supergolf started the fiscal year, January 1, 1988, with $350,000.00 capital stock. This capital stock consisted of 2,000 shares of stock issued prior to January 1, 1988. During 1988, Supergolf did not issue any additional stock. Thus, at the end of the fiscal year, Supergolf still had $350,000.00 capital stock. This information is obtained from the previous year's statement of stockholders' equity and the capital stock account.

The second section of Supergolf's statement of stockholders' equity shows that the business started the fiscal year, January 1, 1988, with

$41,210.50 retained earnings. This amount represents previous years' earnings that have been kept in the business. For the fiscal year ended December 31, 1988, Supergolf earned net income of $57,108.39. This amount is obtained from line 57 of the work sheet, Illustration 5-5. The net income, $57,108.39, is added to the January 1, 1988, balance of Retained Earnings, $41,210.50, to obtain the December 31, 1988, balance, $98,318.89. Supergolf's capital stock, $350,000.00, plus retained earnings, $98,318.89, equals total stockholders' equity on December 31, 1988, $448,318.89.

Balance sheet

A financial statement that reports assets, liabilities, and stockholders' equity on a specific date is called a balance sheet. A balance sheet reports a business' financial condition on a specific date. Supergolf's balance sheet for the yearly fiscal period ended December 31, 1988, is shown in Illustration 5-9, page 98.

Data used in preparing a balance sheet are obtained from two sources. (1) Work sheet Balance Sheet columns. (2) Statement of Stockholders' Equity. On a balance sheet the total assets must equal the total liabilities plus stockholders' equity. Supergolf's balance sheet, Illustration 5-9, has total assets of $494,624.60, and total liabilities and stockholders' equity of the same amount. Because the two amounts are the same, Supergolf's balance sheet is in balance and assumed to be correct.

DEPARTMENTAL ADJUSTING AND CLOSING ENTRIES

Account balances are changed only by posting journal entries. Journal entries made to bring general ledger accounts up to date are called adjusting entries. At the end of a fiscal period, the temporary capital account balances are transferred to an income summary account. This procedure summarizes in one account the effect of operating the business. Journal entries used to prepare temporary capital accounts for a new fiscal period are called closing entries.

Adjusting entries

Supergolf's adjusting entries made on December 31, 1988, are shown in Illustration 5-10, page 99.

Supergolf uses information in the work sheet's Adjustments columns, Illustration 5-5, as the source of adjusting entries.

The words *Adjusting Entries* are written on line 1 in the Account Title column. This statement identifies a group of adjusting entries. Therefore,

Supergolf
Balance Sheet
December 31, 1988

ASSETS

Current Assets:
Cash		$ 50,540.00
Petty Cash		500.00
Accounts Receivable	$13,855.00	
Less Allowance for Uncollectible Accounts	2,400.00	11,455.00
Merchandise Inventory — Clothing		202,855.00
Merchandise Inventory — Equipment		188,484.60
Supplies — Office		2,700.00
Supplies — Store		6,590.00
Prepaid Insurance		4,200.00
Total Current Assets		$467,324.60

Plant Assets:
Office Equipment	$16,800.00	
Less Accumulated Depreciation — Office Equipment	7,400.00	$ 9,400.00
Store Equipment	$38,900.00	
Less Accumulated Depreciation — Store Equipment	21,000.00	17,900.00
Total Plant Assets		27,300.00
Total Assets		$494,624.60

LIABILITIES

Current Liabilities:
Accounts Payable	$ 33,160.30
Employees Income Tax Payable — Federal	1,680.75
Employees Income Tax Payable — State	980.00
Federal Income Tax Payable	3,272.16
FICA Tax Payable	2,360.70
Sales Tax Payable	3,396.90
Unemployment Tax Payable — Federal	23.60
Unemployment Tax Payable — State	159.30
Hospital Insurance Premiums Payable	1,080.00
Life Insurance Premiums Payable	192.00
Total Current Liabilities	$ 46,305.71

STOCKHOLDERS' EQUITY

Capital Stock	$350,000.00
Retained Earnings	98,318.89
Total Stockholders' Equity	448,318.89
Total Liabilities and Stockholders' Equity	$494,624.60

Illustration 5-9
Balance sheet

a source document or explanation is not written for each individual adjusting entry.

After the adjusting entries are posted, general ledger accounts will have up-to-date balances as of December 31, 1988.

	DATE	ACCOUNT TITLE	POST. REF.	DEBIT	CREDIT	
		GENERAL JOURNAL		PAGE 8		
1		Adjusting Entries				1
2	1988 Dec. 31	Bad Debts Expense		2 1 5 9 40		2
3		Allow. for Uncoll. Accts.			2 1 5 9 40	3
4	31	Merchandise Inv. - Clothing		18 5 2 0 39		4
5		Income Summary - Clothing			18 5 2 0 39	5
6	31	Income Summary - Equip.		9 3 6 0 00		6
7		Merchandise Inv. - Equip.			9 3 6 0 00	7
8	31	Supplies Expense - Office		9 9 0 0 00		8
9		Supplies - Office			9 9 0 0 00	9
10	31	Supplies Expense - Store		7 8 4 0 00		10
11		Supplies - Store			7 8 4 0 00	11
12	31	Insurance Expense		5 6 0 0 00		12
13		Prepaid Insurance			5 6 0 0 00	13
14	31	Depr. Exp. - Office Equip.		1 4 8 0 00		14
15		Accum. Depr. - Office Equip.			1 4 8 0 00	15
16	31	Depr. Exp. - Store Equip.		3 0 0 0 00		16
17		Accum. Depr. - Store Equip.			3 0 0 0 00	17
18	31	Federal Income Tax		3 2 7 2 16		18
19		Federal Income Tax Pay.			3 2 7 2 16	19
20						20
21						21

Illustration 5-10
Adjusting entries

Closing entries

Supergolf's closing entries made on December 31, 1988, are shown in Illustration 5-11.

Information needed for closing entries is obtained from the work sheet's Income Statement columns. Supergolf records three closing entries to prepare the general ledger for the next fiscal period.

1. Close separate departmental income summary accounts with credit balances and sales, contra cost, and other income accounts by transferring their balances to Income Summary — General. This combined entry is in the general journal, lines 1-9, Illustration 5-11.

2. Close separate departmental income summary accounts with debit balances and contra sales, cost, and expense accounts by transferring their balances to Income Summary — General. This combined entry is in the general journal, lines 10-32, Illustration 5-11.

3. Close Income Summary — General by transferring its balance to the retained earnings account. The income summary — general account balance is equal to the net income (or net loss) for a fiscal period. This entry is in the general journal, lines 33 and 34, Illustration 5-11.

	DATE	ACCOUNT TITLE	POST. REF.	DEBIT	CREDIT	
		GENERAL JOURNAL			PAGE 9	
1		Closing Entries				1
2	1988 Dec. 31	Income Summary – Clothing		1852039		2
3		Sales – Clothing		35001676		3
4		Sales – Equipment		43835780		4
5		Purch. Ret. & Allow. – Clothing		368000		5
6		Purch. Ret. & Allow. – Equipment		1350000		6
7		Purch. Discount – Clothing		378320		7
8		Purch. Discount – Equipment		461030		8
9		Income Summary – General			83246845	9
10	31	Income Summary – General		77536006		10
11		Income Summary – Equip.			936000	11
12		Sales Ret. & Allow. – Clothing			432000	12
13		Sales Ret. & Allow. – Equipment			631230	13
14		Sales Discount – Clothing			147030	14
15		Sales Discount – Equipment			214080	15
16		Purchases – Clothing			21083320	16
17		Purchases – Equipment			23573970	17
18		Advertising Expense			431000	18
19		Credit Card Fee Expense			492000	19
20		Depr. Exp. – Store Equip.			300000	20
21		Salary Expense – Clothing			9064020	21
22		Salary Expense – Equipment			7220080	22
23		Supplies Expense – Store			784000	23
24		Bad Debts Expense			215940	24
25		Depr. Exp. – Office Equip.			148000	25
26		Insurance Expense			560000	26
27		Miscellaneous Expense			541000	27
28		Payroll Taxes Expense			2136040	28
29		Rent Expense			1800000	29
30		Salary Expense – Admin.			4353080	30
31		Supplies Expense – Office			990000	31
32		Federal Income Tax			1483216	32
33	31	Income Summary – General		5710839		33
34		Retained Earnings			5710839	34

Illustration 5-11
Closing entries

After closing entries are posted, all temporary capital accounts have zero balances and are prepared for a new fiscal period.

DEPARTMENTAL POST-CLOSING TRIAL BALANCE

Debits must always equal credits in general ledger accounts. The trial balance recorded on the work sheet, Illustration 5-5, proves that debits do equal credits before adjusting and closing entries are posted. After adjusting and closing entries are posted, equality of general ledger debits and credits is proved again. This procedure assures that the equality of debits and credits has been maintained in preparation for a new fiscal period.

A trial balance prepared after the closing entries are posted is called a post-closing trial balance. Supergolf's post-closing trial balance prepared on December 31, 1988, is shown in Illustration 5-12.

Supergolf Post-Closing Trial Balance December 31, 1988		
Cash	$ 50,540.00	
Petty Cash	500.00	
Accounts Receivable	13,855.00	
Allowance for Uncollectible Accounts		$ 2,400.00
Merchandise Inventory — Clothing	202,855.00	
Merchandise Inventory — Equipment	188,484.60	
Supplies — Office	2,700.00	
Supplies — Store	6,590.00	
Prepaid Insurance	4,200.00	
Office Equipment	16,800.00	
Accumulated Depreciation — Office Equipment		7,400.00
Store Equipment	38,900.00	
Accumulated Depreciation — Store Equipment		21,000.00
Accounts Payable		33,160.30
Employees Income Tax Payable — Federal		1,680.75
Employees Income Tax Payable — State		980.00
Federal Income Tax Payable		3,272.16
FICA Tax Payable		2,360.70
Sales Tax Payable		3,396.90
Unemployment Tax Payable — Federal		23.60
Unemployment Tax Payable — State		159.30
Hospital Insurance Premiums Payable		1,080.00
Life Insurance Premiums Payable		192.00
Capital Stock		350,000.00
Retained Earnings		98,318.89
	$525,424.60	$525,424.60

Illustration 5-12
Post-closing trial balance

The total of debit balances, $525,424.60, is the same as the total of credit balances. The equality of general ledger debits and credits is proved. Supergolf's general ledger is ready for the next fiscal period.

SUMMARY OF ACCOUNTING CYCLE

Accounting procedures used by Supergolf, a departmentalized merchandising business, are described in Chapters 2 through 5. The procedures used for the fiscal year ended December 31, 1988, are followed each year. The series of accounting activities included in recording financial information for a fiscal period is called an accounting cycle. Accounting cycle procedures provide information for preparing interim and end-of-fiscal-period financial statements. (*CONCEPT: Accounting Period Cycle.*) Supergolf's complete accounting cycle is shown in Illustration 5-13.

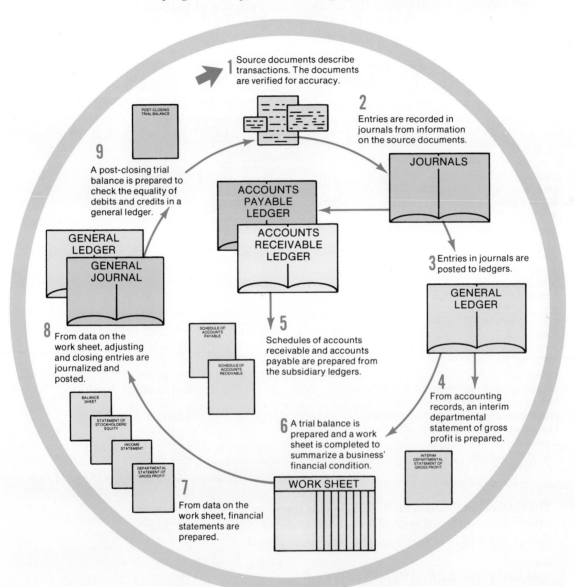

1 Source documents describe transactions. The documents are verified for accuracy.

2 Entries are recorded in journals from information on the source documents.

9 A post-closing trial balance is prepared to check the equality of debits and credits in a general ledger.

POST-CLOSING TRIAL BALANCE

JOURNALS

ACCOUNTS PAYABLE LEDGER

ACCOUNTS RECEIVABLE LEDGER

3 Entries in journals are posted to ledgers.

GENERAL LEDGER

GENERAL JOURNAL

8 From data on the work sheet, adjusting and closing entries are journalized and posted.

GENERAL LEDGER

5 Schedules of accounts receivable and accounts payable are prepared from the subsidiary ledgers.

SCHEDULE OF ACCOUNTS PAYABLE

SCHEDULE OF ACCOUNTS RECEIVABLE

4 From accounting records, an interim departmental statement of gross profit is prepared.

INTERIM DEPARTMENTAL STATEMENT OF GROSS PROFIT

6 A trial balance is prepared and a work sheet is completed to summarize a business' financial condition.

BALANCE SHEET

STATEMENT OF STOCKHOLDERS' EQUITY

INCOME STATEMENT

DEPARTMENTAL STATEMENT OF GROSS PROFIT

7 From data on the work sheet, financial statements are prepared.

WORK SHEET

Illustration 5-13
Accounting cycle

An accounting cycle begins with source documents proving that transactions did occur. (*CONCEPT: Objective Evidence*) Supergolf's fiscal year cycle includes preparation of a monthly interim departmental statement of gross profit. An interim departmental statement of gross profit provides management with information about how each department is doing. A

cycle also includes preparation of financial statements at the end of a fiscal period to give a complete and accurate picture of a business' financial operations. (*CONCEPT: Adequate Disclosure*) An accounting cycle is completed when the general ledger is proved by a post-closing trial balance.

ACCOUNTING TERMS

What is the meaning of each of the following?

1. fiscal period
2. departmental statement of gross profit
3. interim departmental statement of gross profit
4. periodic inventory
5. perpetual inventory
6. gross profit method of estimating an inventory
7. component percentage
8. ratio
9. schedule of accounts receivable
10. schedule of accounts payable
11. trial balance
12. work sheet
13. plant assets
14. depreciation
15. income statement
16. statement of stockholders' equity
17. retained earnings
18. balance sheet
19. adjusting entries
20. closing entries
21. post-closing trial balance
22. accounting cycle

QUESTIONS FOR INDIVIDUAL STUDY

1. Why is one year a common length of time for summarizing and reporting accounting information?
2. Using a calendar year for a fiscal period is an application of which accounting concept?
3. What additional information beyond regular financial statements does a departmentalized business provide management?
4. What possible changes might a manager make after reviewing the gross profit for each department?
5. How often is an interim departmental statement of gross profit generally prepared?
6. What are the two principal methods for determining quantities of merchandise on hand?
7. How does a business determine an ending inventory when neither a periodic inventory is taken nor a perpetual inventory is kept?
8. How does Supergolf determine its ending inventory at the end of each month?
9. How does Supergolf determine the beginning inventory when preparing an interim departmental statement of gross profit?
10. What information is used to determine an estimated gross profit percentage?
11. What four basic components are included in every sales dollar?
12. How large must gross profit on operations be?
13. An adjustment to bring the bad debts expense account up to date at the end of a fiscal period is an application of which accounting concept?
14. How many income summary accounts does Supergolf use to adjust the merchandise inventory accounts?
15. Preparing financial statements to report the financial progress and condition of a business is an application of which accounting concept?
16. What four financial statements does Supergolf prepare at the end of its fiscal period?
17. Applying accounting principles the same way from one accounting period to the next is an application of which accounting concept?
18. What is the major difference between the

two departmental statements of gross profit prepared by Supergolf?

19. Where does Supergolf obtain the data needed to prepare a departmental statement of gross profit?

20. What are the two major sections of a statement of stockholders' equity?

21. Where is information needed for adjusting entries obtained?

22. Where is information needed for closing entries obtained?

23. What are the three closing entries recorded by Supergolf to prepare the general ledger for the next fiscal year?

CASES FOR MANAGEMENT DECISION

CASE 1 Financial information for Watney's for the month ended August 31 of the current year is listed below.

Beginning inventory,
    January 1 . . . .$108,000.00
Net purchases, January 1 to
    August 31 . . . .   52,500.00
Net sales, January 1 to
    August 31 . . . .   76,800.00

You are asked to report the estimated ending inventory on August 31 using the gross profit method for estimating an inventory. What will you report?

CASE 2 Jackson Supply is a departmentalized business. An interim departmental statement of gross profit is prepared monthly. A departmental statement of gross profit is prepared at the end of each yearly fiscal period. The manager suggests that the accountant extend the statements of gross profit by including a division of all expenses by department. The accountant indicates that the time required to divide the expenses by department would not add significantly to the information available for decision making. Do you agree or disagree with the accountant? Why?

CASE 3 Morgan Sporting Goods recently changed its accounting system to provide information for each of its departments. The chart of accounts includes separate departmental accounts for merchandise inventory, operating revenue, and cost accounts. Operating expenses are not departmentalized. One income summary account will be used for adjusting and closing entries. Will the departmentalized accounting system developed provide the information needed to review how well each department is doing? Do you have any suggestions for improvement?

APPLICATION PROBLEMS

PROBLEM 5-1   Estimating ending merchandise inventory

Chaney's Beachwear has two departments: Men's Wear and Women's Wear. Data obtained from the accounting records on January 31 of the current year are below.

	Men's Wear	Women's Wear
Beginning inventory, January 1	$148,000.00	$153,000.00
Net purchases to date	14,300.00	15,100.00
Net sales to date	49,200.00	53,400.00
Gross profit on operations (percentage based on records of previous years' operations)		45% of sales

Instructions: Prepare an estimated merchandise inventory sheet for each department similar to the one in this chapter. Use January 31 of the current year as the date.

PROBLEM 5-2 Figuring percentage ratios of cost of merchandise sold and gross profit on operations to net sales

Data from the interim departmental statements of gross profit for six businesses are below.

Business	Component	Amount
1	Total Net Sales Total Cost of Merchandise Sold Total Gross Profit on Operations	$100,000.00 60,000.00 40,000.00
2	Total Net Sales Total Cost of Merchandise Sold Total Gross Profit on Operations	$150,000.00 80,000.00 70,000.00
3	Total Net Sales Total Cost of Merchandise Sold Total Gross Profit on Operations	$130,000.00 60,000.00 70,000.00
4	Total Net Sales Total Cost of Merchandise Sold Total Gross Profit on Operations	$180,000.00 100,000.00 80,000.00
5	Total Net Sales Total Cost of Merchandise Sold Total Gross Profit on Operations	$160,000.00 85,000.00 75,000.00
6	Total Net Sales Total Cost of Merchandise Sold Total Gross Profit on Operations	$220,000.00 115,000.00 105,000.00

Use a form similar to the one below.

1	2	3	4
Business	Component	Amount	Percentage Ratio
1	Total Net Sales Total Cost of Merchandise Sold Total Gross Profit on Operations	$100,000.00 60,000.00 40,000.00	100.0% 60.0% 40.0%

Instructions: Figure percentage ratios of total cost of merchandise sold and total gross profit on operations to total net sales for each business. Round percentage computations to the nearest 0.1%. Enter the percentage ratios in column 4. The percentage ratios for Business 1 are given as examples.

PROBLEM 5-3 Preparing an interim departmental statement of gross profit; figuring and recording percentage ratios

Motor Sports has two departments: Cycles and Mopeds. The following data were obtained from the accounting records on March 31 of the current year.

	Cycles	Mopeds
Beginning inventory, January 1	$193,300.00	$167,500.00
Estimated beginning inventory, March 1	168,442.00	146,218.80
Net purchases to date	29,200.00	24,840.00
Net sales to date ....'.....	97,200.00	93,800.00
Net purchases for March...........................	16,871.50	9,978.40
Net sales for March	36,500.00	34,600.00
Gross profit on operations (percentage based on records of previous years' operations)		40% of sales

Instructions: 1. Prepare an estimated merchandise inventory sheet for each department similar to the one in this chapter. Use March 31 of the current year as the date.

2. Prepare an interim departmental statement of gross profit for the month ended March 31 of the current year. Figure and enter departmental and total percentage ratios of cost of merchandise sold and gross profit on operations to net sales. Round percentage computations to the nearest 0.1%.

PROBLEM 5-4   Preparing subsidiary schedules

Gombosky's vendor and customer accounts and balances on December 31 of the current year are below.

Vendor	Account Balance	Customer	Account Balance
Acton, Inc.	$2,350.40	Mary Barnas	$1,210.20
Doyle Associates	1,620.30	Teresa Conroy	820.70
Huertas Supply	936.80	Paul DeYoung	726.10
J & M Enterprises	1,262.50	John Klem	1,304.20
Tafoya Products	826.10	Irma Musgrove	619.60
Veloz Associates	2,370.60	Alex Vail	1,926.40

Instructions: 1. Prepare a schedule of accounts payable for December 31 of the current year. Compare the schedule total with the balance, $9,366.70, of the general ledger controlling account Accounts Payable. If the totals are not the same, find and correct the errors.

2. Prepare a schedule of accounts receivable for December 31 of the current year. Compare the schedule total with the balance, $6,607.20, of the general ledger controlling account Accounts Receivable. If the totals are not the same, find and correct the errors.

PROBLEM 5-5   Figuring and analyzing ratios of total operating expenses to net sales

Data obtained from the income statements of six businesses are below.

Business	Net Sales	Total Operating Expenses	Performance Standard— Not more than:
1	$150,000.00	$45,000.00	32.0%
2	130,300.00	36,500.00	26.0%
3	175,500.00	51,750.00	30.0%
4	145,600.00	35,930.00	25.0%
5	185,300.00	58,250.00	30.0%
6	165,900.00	44,980.00	28.0%

Use a form similar to the one below.

1	2	3	4	5	6
Business	Net Sales	Total Operating Expenses	Performance Standard— Not more than:	Percentage Ratio	Performance Level
1	$150,000.00	$45,000.00	32.0%	30.0%	A

Instructions: 1. Figure the percentage ratio of total operating expenses to net sales for each business. Round percentage computations to the nearest 0.1%. Enter the percentage ratios in column 5.

2. Determine the performance level for each business by comparing the percentage ratio with the performance standard. If the performance level is acceptable, write an A in column 6. If the performance level is unacceptable, write a U in column 6. The percentage ratio and performance level for Business 1 are given as examples.

PROBLEM 5-6 Figuring and analyzing percentage ratios of net income to net sales

Data obtained from the income statements of six businesses are below.

Business	Net Sales	Net Income	Performance Standard— Not less than:
1	$145,200.00	$15,130.00	10.0%
2	193,100.00	24,150.00	12.0%
3	161,750.00	10,820.00	8.0%
4	138,920.00	13,940.00	9.0%
5	174,600.00	8,200.00	6.0%
6	159,820.00	19,350.00	11.0%

Use a form similar to the one below.

1	2	3	4	5	6
Business	Net Sales	Net Income	Performance Standard— Not less than:	Percentage Ratio	Performance Level
1	$145,200.00	$15,130.00	10.0%	10.4%	A

Instructions: 1. Figure the percentage ratio of net income to net sales for each business. Round percentage computations to the nearest 0.1%. Enter the percentage ratio in column 5.

2. Determine the performance level by comparing the percentage ratio with the performance standard. If the performance level is acceptable, write an A in column 6. If the performance level is unacceptable, write a U in column 6. The percentage ratio and performance level for Business 1 are given as examples.

PROBLEM 5-7   Completing end-of-fiscal-period work for a departmentalized business

Superior Floor Covering has two departments: Carpeting and Linoleum. The general ledger accounts and their balances are recorded on a work sheet in the working papers accompanying this textbook.

Instructions: 1. Complete Superior's departmental work sheet for the year ended December 31 of the current year. The adjustment information for December 31 is below.

Bad debts expense	$ 2,259.10
Merchandise inventory—carpeting	173,450.80
Merchandise inventory—linoleum	168,820.10
Office supplies inventory	4,930.60
Store supplies inventory	5,720.40
Value of prepaid insurance	4,600.00
Depreciation expense—office equipment	1,280.00
Depreciation expense—store equipment	2,800.00
Federal income tax for the year	15,351.45

2. Prepare a departmental statement of gross profit for the year ended December 31 of the current year. Figure and record percentage ratios of cost of merchandise sold and gross profit on operations to net sales. Round percentage computations to the nearest 0.1%.

3. Prepare an income statement for the year ended December 31 of the current year. Record the percentage ratios of cost of merchandise sold and gross profit on operations to net sales from the departmental statement of gross profit. Figure and record the percentage ratio of total operating expenses to net sales. Figure and record the percentage ratio of net income to net sales. Round percentage computations to the nearest 0.1%.

4. Prepare a statement of stockholders' equity for the year ended December 31 of the current year. Additional information is below.

January 1 balance of capital stock account	$200,000.00
(2,000 shares at $100.00 per share)	
No additional capital stock issued.	

5. Prepare a balance sheet.

6. Record adjusting and closing entries on pages 15 and 16 of a general journal.

ENRICHMENT PROBLEMS

MASTERY PROBLEM 5-M   Completing end-of-fiscal-period work for a departmentalized business

Worley's has two departments: Appliances and Furniture. The general ledger accounts and their balances are recorded on a work sheet in the working papers accompanying this textbook.

Instructions: 1. Complete Worley's departmental work sheet for the year ended December 31 of the current year. The adjustment information for December 31 is as follows.

Bad debts expense	$ 1,970.40
Merchandise inventory—appliances	205,380.20
Merchandise inventory—furniture	236,520.80
Office supplies inventory	3,710.30
Store supplies inventory	4,220.50

Value of prepaid insurance	$ 3,800.00
Depreciation expense—office equipment	1,200.00
Depreciation expense—store equipment	2,600.00
Federal income tax for the year	15,393.00

2. Prepare a departmental statement of gross profit for the year ended December 31 of the current year. Figure and record the percentage ratios of cost of merchandise sold and gross profit on operations to net sales. Round percentage computations to the nearest 0.1%.

3. Prepare an income statement for the year ended December 31 of the current year. Record the percentage ratios of cost of merchandise sold and gross profit on operations to net sales from the departmental statement of gross profit. Figure and record the percentage ratio of total operating expenses to net sales. Figure and record the percentage ratio of net income to net sales. Round percentage computations to the nearest 0.1%.

4. Prepare a statement of stockholders' equity for the year ended December 31 of the current year. Additional information is below.

January 1 balance of capital stock account	$300,000.00
(1,500 shares at $200.00 per share)	
No additional stock issued.	

5. Prepare a balance sheet.

6. Record adjusting and closing entries on pages 18 and 19 of a general journal.

CHALLENGE PROBLEM 5-C Estimating value of merchandise destroyed by fire

The entire inventory of Meir's Sport Center was destroyed by fire on March 13. From the accounting records that were not destroyed by the fire, the following data were obtained.

Beginning inventory, January 1	$318,520.30
Net purchases to date	42,100.00
Net sales to date	93,610.40

In a special sale held in January, the sales amount was $27,460.00. The average gross profit on the merchandise sold during the sale was 10% of sales. The sales balance was made with a gross profit of 40% on net sales.

Instructions: Prepare an estimated merchandise inventory sheet similar to the one in this chapter to estimate the value of the merchandise destroyed by the fire. Use March 13 of the current year as the date.

Reinforcement Activity 1
Processing and Reporting Departmentalized Accounting Data

This activity reinforces selected learnings from Part 2, Chapters 2 through 5. The complete accounting cycle is for a departmentalized merchandising business organized as a corporation.

ARTISTRY, INC.

Artistry, Inc. has two departments: Art Equipment and Art Supplies. Artistry is open for business Monday through Saturday. A monthly rent is paid on the building. The business owns the office and store equipment.

Artistry sells art equipment and art supplies to individuals and schools. Cash sales and sales on account are made. The business uses a national credit card service in addition to its own company credit card.

Artistry's fiscal year is January 1 through December 31. During the fiscal year, a monthly interim departmental statement of gross profit is prepared.

Artistry uses the chart of accounts shown on the following page. The journals and ledgers used by Artistry are similar to those illustrated in Part 2. The journal and ledger forms are provided in the working papers accompanying this textbook. Beginning balances have been recorded in the ledgers.

Preparing an interim departmental statement of gross profit

Artistry prepares an interim departmental statement of gross profit each month. The following data are obtained from the accounting records at the end of November of the current year.

	Art Equipment	Art Supplies
Beginning inventory, January 1	$163,164.20	$146,840.30
Estimated beginning inventory, November 1	176,561.55	152,699.90
Net purchases to date	133,339.60	129,949.20
Net sales to date	213,679.55	219,670.40
Net purchases for November	12,250.20	13,410.58
Net sales for November	18,480.60	19,240.30
Gross profit on operations (percentage based on records of previous years' operations)		45% of sales

Instructions: 1. Use the gross profit method of estimating an inventory to prepare an estimated merchandise inventory sheet for each department for November of the current year.

2. Prepare an interim departmental statement of gross profit for the month ended November 30 of the current year. Figure and enter departmental and total percentage ratios of cost of merchan-

ARTISTRY, INC.
General Ledger Chart of Accounts

Balance Sheet Accounts

(1000) ASSETS

1100	Current Assets
1105	Cash
1110	Petty Cash
1115	Accounts Receivable
1120	Allowance for Uncollectible Accounts
1125-1	Merchandise Inventory—Art Equipment
1125-2	Merchandise Inventory—Art Supplies
1130	Supplies—Office
1135	Supplies—Store
1140	Prepaid Insurance
1200	Plant Assets
1205	Office Equipment
1210	Accumulated Depreciation—Office Equipment
1215	Store Equipment
1220	Accumulated Depreciation—Store Equipment

(2000) LIABILITIES

2105	Accounts Payable
2110	Employees Income Tax Payable—Federal
2115	Employees Income Tax Payable—State
2120	Federal Income Tax Payable
2125	FICA Tax Payable
2130	Sales Tax Payable
2135	Unemployment Tax Payable—Federal
2140	Unemployment Tax Payable—State
2145	Hospital Insurance Premiums Payable
2150	Life insurance Premiums Payable

(3000) STOCKHOLDERS' EQUITY

3105	Capital Stock
3110	Retained Earnings
3115-1	Income Summary—Art Equipment
3115-2	Income Summary—Art Supplies
3120	Income Summary—General

Income Statement Accounts

(4000) OPERATING REVENUE

4105-1	Sales—Art Equipment
4105-2	Sales—Art Supplies
4110-1	Sales Returns and Allowances—Art Equipment
4110-2	Sales Returns and Allowances—Art Supplies
4115-1	Sales Discount—Art Equipment
4115-2	Sales Discount—Art Supplies

(5000) COST OF MERCHANDISE

5105-1	Purchases—Art Equipment
5105-2	Purchases—Art Supplies
5110-1	Purchases Returns and Allowances—Art Equipment
5110-2	Purchases Returns and Allowances—Art Supplies
5115-1	Purchases Discount—Art Equipment
5115-2	Purchases Discount—Art Supplies

(6000) OPERATING EXPENSES

6100	Selling Expenses
6105	Advertising Expense
6110	Credit Card Fee Expense
6115	Depreciation Expense—Store Equipment
6120-1	Salary Expense—Art Equipment
6120-2	Salary Expense—Art Supplies
6125	Supplies Expense—Store
6200	Administrative Expenses
6205	Bad Debts Expense
6210	Depreciation Expense—Office Equipment
6215	Insurance Expense
6220	Miscellaneous Expense
6225	Payroll Taxes Expense
6230	Rent Expense
6235	Salary Expense—Administrative
6240	Supplies Expense—Office

(7000) INCOME TAX

7105	Federal Income Tax

Subsidiary Ledgers Charts of Accounts

Accounts Receivable Ledger

110	Marie Akels
120	Milton Betka
130	Teresa Davis
140	Bruce Foltz
150	Gifford Public Schools
160	Barbara Judge
170	Janice Kemp
180	David Ling
190	Reed Public Schools

Accounts Payable Ledger

210	Apcoa Art Supplies
220	CMB Distributors
230	Grandeau Products
240	H & R Crafts
250	Milano Art Supply
260	Olympic Crafts, Inc.
270	Shapiro Art Supplies

dise sold and gross profit on operations to net sales. Round percentage computations to the nearest 0.1%

Recording a corporation's transactions

Instructions: 3. Record the following selected transactions for December of the current year. A 5% sales tax is charged on all sales to individuals. No sales tax is charged on sales to schools. A 2% sales discount is granted to customers for early payment of their accounts. All purchases on account are subject to a 2% discount if payment is made within the discount period. Source documents are abbreviated as follows: check, C; credit memorandum, CM; debit memorandum, DM; memorandum, M; purchase invoice, P; receipt, R; sales invoice, S; cash register tape, T.

Dec. 1. Paid monthly payroll: art equipment, $4,522.20; art supplies, $4,310.40; administrative, $2,630.25 (less deductions: employees' income tax—federal, $1,283.60; employees' income tax—state, $573.14; FICA tax, $802.40; hospital insurance, $840.00; life insurance, $104.00). C340.

   1. Recorded payroll taxes expense for monthly pay period ended November 30: FICA tax payable, $802.40; unemployment tax payable—federal, $20.90; unemployment tax payable—state, $141.08. M40.

   1. Paid December rent, $1,200.00. C341.

   2. Bought office supplies for cash, $135.00. C342.

   2. Granted credit to Gifford Public Schools for defective art supplies returned, $250.00, from S94. CM31.

   2. Purchased art equipment on account from Olympic Crafts, Inc., $1,933.00. P115.

   3. Granted credit to Barbara Judge for defective art equipment returned, $75.00, plus sales tax, from S95. CM32.

   3. Recorded cash and credit card sales for December 1–3: art equipment, $1,978.00; art supplies, $1,588.50; plus sales tax. T3.

   Posting. Post the items that are to be posted individually. Post from the journals in this order: sales journal, sales returns and allowances journal, purchases journal, purchases returns and allowances journal, general journal, cash receipts journal, cash payments journal.

   5. Returned defective art equipment to H & R Crafts, $1,435.00, from P112. DM58.

   5. Sold art equipment on account to Milton Betka, $880.00, plus sales tax. S97.

   5. Received on account from Teresa Davis, covering S92 for art supplies ($480.00 plus sales tax) less discount and less sales tax. R139.

   6. Paid on account to CMB Distributors, covering P111 for art equipment, $2,230.10, less discount. C343.

   7. Paid on account to H & R Crafts, covering P112 for art equipment, $5,430.15, less DM58 for $1,435.00 and less discount. C344.

   7. Returned defective art equipment to Olympic Crafts, Inc., $300.00, from P115. DM59.

   8. Received on account from Gifford Public Schools, covering S94 for art supplies, $6,240.20, less CM31 for $250.00 and less discount. R140.

   8. Received on account from Barbara Judge, covering S95 for art equipment ($250.00 plus sales tax) less CM32 ($75.00 plus sales tax) less discount and less sales tax. R141.

   8. Received on account from Reed Public Schools, covering S96 for art equipment, $9,581.50, less discount. R142.

   8. Paid on account to Milano Art Supply, covering P113 for art supplies, $565.40, less discount. C345.

   9. Paid on account to Olympic Crafts, Inc., covering P114 for art equipment, $4,920.20, less discount. C346.

9. Granted credit to Milton Betka for defective art equipment returned, $100.00, plus sales tax, from S97. CM33.
10. Recorded cash and credit card sales for December 5–10: art equipment, $3,946.50; art supplies, $3,150.00; plus sales tax. T10.
    Posting. Post the items that are to be posted individually.
12. Paid on account to Olympic Crafts, Inc., covering P115 for art equipment, $1,933.00, less DM59 for $300.00 and less discount. C347.
13. Sold art supplies on account to Marie Akels, $450.00, plus sales tax. S98.
15. Paid November liabilities for employees' federal income tax, $1,240.80, and FICA tax, $1,582.90. C348.
15. Paid quarterly federal income tax estimate, $1,250.00. C349. (Debit Federal Income Tax; credit Cash.)
15. Received on account from Milton Betka, covering S97 for art equipment ($880.00 plus sales tax) less CM33 ($100.00 plus sales tax) less discount and less sales tax. R143.
17. Recorded cash and credit card sales for December 12-17: art equipment, $3,820.60; art supplies, $3,240.50; plus sales tax. T17.
    Posting. Post the items that are to be posted individually.
22. Sold art supplies on account to Reed Public Schools, $4,750.00; no sales tax. S99.
22. Purchased art supplies on account from Shapiro Art Supplies, $1,647.00. P116.
22. Purchased art supplies on account from Apcoa Art Supplies, $1,278.50. P117.
23. Sold art equipment on account to Bruce Foltz, $1,720.00, plus sales tax. S100.
23. Sold art supplies on account to Janice Kemp, $920.00, plus sales tax. S101.
23. Received on account from Marie Akels, covering S98 for art supplies ($450.00 plus sales tax) less discount and less sales tax. R144.
24. Replenished petty cash. Charge the following accounts: Supplies—Store, $145.00; Advertising Expense, $160.00; Miscellaneous Expense, $110.00. C350.
24. Purchased art equipment on account from CMB Distributors, $1,500.00. P118.
24. Recorded cash and credit card sales for December 19-24: art equipment, $4,160.10; art supplies, $3,420.50; plus sales tax. T24.
    Posting. Post the items that are to be posted individually.
26. Sold art supplies on account to David Ling, $540.00, plus sales tax. S102.
26. Returned defective art supplies to Apcoa Art Supplies, $265.00, from P117. DM60.
27. Purchased art equipment on account from Milano Art Equipment, $2,540.50. P119.
27. Purchased art supplies on account from Grandeau Products, $3,240.00. P120.
28. Sold art equipment on account to David Ling, $650.00, plus sales tax. S103.

4. Prepare a bank statement reconciliation for December 29 of the current year. The bank statement is dated December 28. The following information is needed.

Bank statement balance, December 28	$51,513.56
Bank service charge for December	11.40
Bank credit card charge for December	354.20
Balance on Check Stub No. 350	55,350.09
Outstanding deposit, December 29	7,959.63
Outstanding checks: Nos. 348, 349, 350	

5. Record the following selected transactions for December of the current year.

Dec. 30. Recorded bank service charge, $11.40. M41.
30. Recorded bank credit card charge, $354.20. M42.
31. Granted credit to Reed Public Schools for defective art supplies returned, $1,500.00, from S99. CM34.

31. Sold art equipment on account to Gifford Public Schools, $6,200.00; no sales tax. S104.
31. Recorded cash and credit card sales for December 26–31: art equipment, $3,580.40; art supplies, $2,480.00; plus sales tax. T31.
    Posting. Post the items that are to be posted individually.

Completing journals

Instructions: 6. Prove and rule the sales journal and the sales returns and allowances journal. Post the totals of the special columns.

7. Prove and rule the purchases journal and the purchases returns and allowances journal. Post the totals of the special columns.

8. Prove the cash receipts journal and the cash payments journal.

9. Prove cash. The balance on Check Stub No. 351 is $61,347.91.

10. Rule the cash receipts journal. Post the totals of the special columns.

11. Rule the cash payments journal. Post the totals of the special columns.

Completing end-of-fiscal-period work

Instructions: 12. Prepare a schedule of accounts receivable and a schedule of accounts payable for December 31 of the current year. Compare each schedule total with the balance of the controlling account in the general ledger. The total and the balance should be the same.

13. Prepare a trial balance on a work sheet for the year ended December 31 of the current year.

14. Complete the work sheet. The following information is needed for adjustments.

Bad debts expense	$ 920.00
Merchandise inventory—art equipment, December 31	174,469.25
Merchandise inventory—art supplies, December 31	151,439.85
Office supplies inventory, December 31..........................	4,635.00
Store supplies inventory, December 31	3,960.00
Value of prepaid insurance, December 31	4,400.00
Depreciation expense—office equipment..........................	870.00
Depreciation expense—store equipment	940.00
Federal income tax for the year................................	5,322.40

15. Prepare a departmental statement of gross profit for the year ended December 31 of the current year. Figure and record the percentage ratios of cost of merchandise sold and gross profit on operations to net sales. Round percentage computations to the nearest 0.1%.

16. Prepare an income statement for the year ended December 31 of the current year. Record the percentage ratios of cost of merchandise sold and gross profit on operations to net sales from the departmental statement of gross profit. Figure and record the percentage ratios of total operating expenses and net income after federal income tax to net sales. Round percentage computations to the nearest 0.1%.

17. Prepare a statement of stockholders' equity for the year ended December 31 of the current year. The following additional information is needed.

January 1 balance of capital stock account	$300,000.00
(3,000 shares at $100.00 per share)	
No additional stock issued.	

18. Prepare a balance sheet for December 31 of the current year.

19. Record the adjusting entries on page 8 of a general journal. Post the adjusting entries.

20. Record the closing entries on page 9 of a general journal. Post the closing entries.

21. Prepare a post-closing trial balance.

OAKHILL FURNITURE INC.
A BUSINESS SIMULATION

Oakhill Furniture, Inc., is a departmentalized merchandising business organized as a corporation. This business simulation covers the realistic transactions completed by Oakhill Furniture, Inc., which has two departments: furniture and accessories. The activities included in the accounting cycle for Oakhill Furniture, Inc., are listed below. This simulation is available from the publisher.

Activities in Oakhill Furniture, Inc.

1. Recording selected transactions in special journals and a general journal.
2. Figuring and recording departmental payroll data.
3. Preparing a bank statement reconciliation.
4. Posting items to be posted individually to a general ledger and subsidiary ledgers.
5. Proving and ruling the journals.
6. Posting column totals to a general ledger.
7. Preparing schedules of accounts receivable and accounts payable.
8. Preparing a trial balance on a work sheet.
9. Planning adjustments and completing a work sheet.
10. Preparing financial statements.
11. Recording and posting adjusting entries.
12. Recording and posting closing entries.
13. Preparing a post-closing trial balance.

3
Automated Accounting

GENERAL BEHAVIORAL GOALS

1. Know accounting terminology related to an automated departmentalized accounting system for a merchandising business organized as a corporation.
2. Understand accounting concepts and practices related to an automated departmentalized accounting system for a merchandising business organized as a corporation.
3. Demonstrate accounting procedures used in an automated departmentalized accounting system for a merchandising business organized as a corporation.

COMPUTEX
General Ledger Chart of Accounts

Balance Sheet Accounts

(1000) ASSETS

1100	Current Assets
1105	Cash
1110	Petty Cash
1115	Accounts Receivable
1120	Allowance for Uncollectible Accounts
1125-1	Merchandise Inventory — Hardware
1125-2	Merchandise Inventory — Software
1130	Supplies — Office
1135	Supplies — Store
1140	Prepaid Insurance
1200	Plant Assets
1205	Computer Equipment
1210	Accumulated Depreciation — Computer Equipment
1215	Office Equipment
1220	Accumulated Depreciation — Office Equipment
1225	Store Equipment
1230	Accumulated Depreciation — Store Equipment

(2000) LIABILITIES

2105	Accounts Payable
2110	Employees Income Tax Payable — Federal
2115	Employees Income Tax Payable — State
2120	Federal Income Tax Payable
2125	FICA Tax Payable
2130	Sales Tax Payable
2135	Unemployment Tax Payable — Federal
2140	Unemployment Tax Payable — State
2145	Hospital Insurance Premiums Payable
2150	Life Insurance Premiums Payable
2155	Dividends Payable

(3000) STOCKHOLDERS' EQUITY

3105	Capital Stock
3110	Retained Earnings
3115	Dividends
3120-1	Income Summary — Hardware
3120-2	Income Summary — Software

Income Statement Accounts

(4000) OPERATING REVENUE

4105-1	Sales — Hardware
4105-2	Sales — Software
4110-1	Sales Returns and Allowances — Hardware
4110-2	Sales Returns and Allowances — Software
4115-1	Sales Discount — Hardware
4115-2	Sales Discount — Software

(5000) COST OF MERCHANDISE

5105-1	Purchases — Hardware
5105-2	Purchases — Software
5110-1	Purchases Returns and Allowances — Hardware
5110-2	Purchases Returns and Allowances — Software
5115-1	Purchases Discount — Hardware
5115-2	Purchases Discount — Software

(6000) OPERATING EXPENSES

6100	Selling Expenses
6105	Advertising Expense
6108	Credit Card Fee Expense
6110	Depreciation Expense — Store Equipment
6115-1	Salary Expense — Hardware
6115-2	Salary Expense — Software
6120	Supplies Expense — Store
6200	Administrative Expenses
6205	Bad Debts Expense
6210	Depreciation Expense — Computer Equipment
6215	Depreciation Expense — Office Equipment
6218	Equipment Repair Expense
6220	Insurance Expense
6225	Miscellaneous Expense
6230	Payroll Taxes Expense
6235	Rent Expense
6240	Salary Expense — Administrative
6245	Supplies Expense — Office

(9000) INCOME TAX

9105	Federal Income Tax

Subsidiary Ledgers

Customer List

110	Mary Abler
115	Charles Baxter
120	Joan Daly
130	Gator Furniture Co.
140	Martha Seger
150	Taft Sporting Goods
160	Hubert Verrico

Vendor List

210	Abbott Software Company
215	Computer Products, Inc.
220	Gardner Office Supplies
230	International Computers
240	Martin's Office Products
245	Star Software, Inc.
250	United Computer Systems

The chart of accounts for Computex is illustrated above for
ready reference as you study Part 3 of this textbook.

6 An Automated Accounting System for a Departmentalized Business

ENABLING PERFORMANCE TASKS

After studying Chapter 6, you will be able to:

a. Define accounting terms related to an automated departmentalized accounting system.
b. Identify accounting concepts and practices related to chart of accounts file maintenance activities for an automated departmentalized merchandising business.
c. Prepare a file maintenance input form to add and delete accounts for an automated departmentalized merchandising business.
d. Prepare a journal entries input form to divide an account balance.

Financial information is needed to make decisions about a business' operations. Accounting records therefore must include data that are current, accurate, and complete. Working with data according to precise instructions is called processing. Producing financial information requires an organized set of recording and reporting procedures.

The recording and reporting of financial information in an accounting system may be by hand or by machine. An accounting system in which data are recorded and reported mostly by hand is called manual accounting. Supergolf, the business described in Part 2, uses manual accounting. An accounting system in which data are recorded and reported mostly by using automated machines is called automated accounting. Some procedures are also done by hand in an automated accounting system. Regardless of the accounting system used, accounting concepts are the same and are applied in the same way in each accounting period. (CONCEPT: Consistent Reporting)

COMPUTER INFORMATION SYSTEM

A machine that accepts data, applies procedures, and produces results according to stored instructions is called a computer. Both large and small businesses use computers. A system using a computer to process data is called a computer information system.

Choosing a computer for a computer information system

The three types of computers currently used in computer information systems are (1) mainframe computers, (2) minicomputers, and (3) microcomputers.

A large-sized computer with the greatest computing speed, largest storage capacity, and the most powerful processing capability is called a mainframe computer. Businesses that need to process large amounts of data at very fast processing speeds often choose a mainframe computer.

A medium-sized computer with intermediate computing speed, storage capacity, and processing capability is called a minicomputer. Businesses with less data to be processed and less need for processing speed than businesses using a mainframe computer often choose a minicomputer.

A small-sized computer with the slowest computing speed, smallest storage capacity, and the least processing capability is called a microcomputer. Businesses with limited data to be processed and with a need for processing speed greater than can be achieved with manual methods often choose a microcomputer.

Designing computer instructions for a computer information system

Processing data by computer requires step-by-step instructions for doing each job within an information system. A set of instructions followed by a computer to process data is called a computer program. A person who prepares a computer program is called a computer programmer.

Several computer programs are generally needed for a complete information system. Programs used to direct the operations of a computer are called software. Software prepared to tell the computer how to operate itself is called systems software. A computer cannot operate without systems software. Therefore, systems software is usually supplied by the computer manufacturer. Software prepared to direct the operations of a computer for specific applications is called applications software. Applications software is generally prepared by businesses that develop software for resale to computer users. Software designed to process accounting data is an example of applications software.

Processing data in a computer information system

A computer information system includes both human and computer functions.

Human functions. Human functions consist of gathering and arranging original data for entry into the computer, and using the processed data for decision making.

Computer functions. Computer functions consist of input, processing, storage, and output. Each computer function requires a separate computer unit. Computer units are called hardware.

Data put into a computer are called input. A common input unit is a computer keyboard. Entering data on a computer keyboard is called key-entering. Each character key-entered is displayed on a television-like screen often referred to as a computer monitor.

Working with data according to precise instructions is known as processing. Processing is performed by a central processing unit (CPU). A CPU is used to perform three distinct tasks. (1) Control all computer units. (2) Store computer instructions and data to be processed. (3) Process stored data.

Filing or holding data until needed is called storage. A CPU has limited space for internal data storage. Therefore, secondary storage units are usually attached to a CPU. Data are then transferred to a CPU from secondary storage as needed during processing. A magnetic disk is the most widely used secondary storage. A flexible magnetic disk commonly used as secondary storage for microcomputers is called a diskette. A diskette is also known as a floppy disk.

Information produced by a computer is called output. Computer output in printed, human-readable form is called a printout. A computer information system is shown in Illustration 6-1.

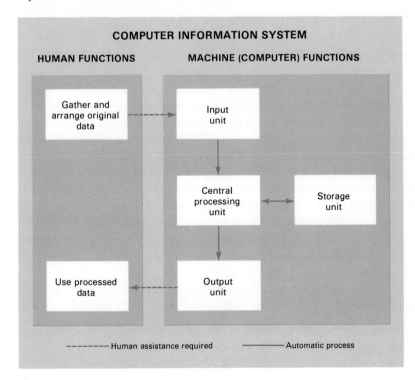

Illustration 6-1
Computer information
system

AUTOMATED ACCOUNTING SYSTEM

Automated accounting is a specialized computer information system designed to process accounting data. Automated accounting is based on the same accounting concepts as manual accounting. Likewise, an accounting cycle is the same in both automated accounting and manual accounting. Only the procedures differ. In automated accounting, a computer does the routine and repetitive accounting activities. Automated accounting requires the same human and computer functions as any computer information system.

Computex, a merchandising business organized as a corporation, sells computer hardware and computer software. However, Computex does not use a departmental accounting system at the present time. The business' financial information is recorded and reported separately from the stockholders' personal financial information. *(CONCEPT: Business Entity)* Computex's accounting records and financial statements are designed as though the business will continue indefinitely. *(CONCEPT: Going Concern)*

Computex uses an automated accounting system. A microcomputer, with associated systems software and applications software, is used to process the business' accounting data. Computex uses a monthly fiscal period. *(CONCEPT: Accounting Period Cycle)*

General ledger file maintenance

Automated accounting uses the same general ledger account titles as manual accounting. General ledger accounts are numbered in the same way for both manual and automated accounting. The numbering system used must meet three needs. (1) A separate numeric listing must be provided for each ledger division. (2) A predesigned arrangement of numbers must be provided within each ledger division. (3) Enough account number digits must be provided to allow the addition of new accounts. The procedure for arranging accounts in a ledger, selecting account numbers, and keeping records current is called file maintenance.

Each business numbers its accounts according to its particular needs. Computex uses a four-digit numbering system for general ledger accounts with each account number initially assigned sequentially by 5's. Assigning account numbers by 5's allows adding new accounts easily. New accounts can be added between existing account numbers without renumbering all accounts.

In automated accounting, all general ledger data are stored on secondary storage. Computex's microcomputer uses a diskette for secondary storage.

Adding a new general ledger account. A numbering system must contain enough digits to allow addition of new accounts without changing the numbers of existing accounts. A new account is assigned the unused middle number between two existing accounts. When no exact middle number is available, the nearest *even whole* number is used.

On June 1, 1988, Computex needs to add a new account, Credit Card Fee Expense, between the two existing accounts Advertising Expense, 6105, and Depreciation Expense—Store, 6110. The unused middle number between 6105 and 6110 is 6107.5. The number 6107.5 contains 5 digits and cannot be assigned in a four-digit numbering system. Therefore, account number 6108, the nearest *even whole* number is used. The new account, Credit Card Fee Expense, is placed in the general ledger as shown below.

6105 Advertising Expense (existing account)
6108 CREDIT CARD FEE EXPENSE (new account)
6110 Depreciation Expense—Store (existing account)

In automated accounting, file maintenance activities for a general ledger include recording additions and deletions on a general ledger file maintenance input form. The entry to add the new account Credit Card Fee Expense is on line 1 of the general ledger file maintenance input form shown in Illustration 6-2.

RUN DATE _06/01/88_ MM DD YY		GENERAL LEDGER FILE MAINTENANCE Input Form	
	1	**2**	
	ACCOUNT NUMBER	ACCOUNT TITLE	
1	6108	Credit Card Fee Expense	1
2	6250	(Delete)	2

Illustration 6-2
Entries for general ledger
file maintenance

The date to be printed on reports prepared by a computer is called the run date. The run date, *06/01/88,* is written in the space provided at the top of the form. The new account number, *6108,* is recorded in the Account Number column. The new account title, Credit Card Fee Expense, is entered in the Account Title column.

If an additional account is added between account number 6105 and 6108, the nearest middle unused *even whole* number is 6106. If no even whole number is available for assignment, the remaining unused *odd whole* number is assigned. If accounts have been assigned account numbers 6106 and 6108, the remaining unused *odd whole* number is 6107.

New accounts that are added after the last account in a division are assigned the next number in sequence. Life Insurance Premiums Payable, 2150, is the last existing account in the liabilities division. If Computex decides to add a new account after the last existing account in the liabilities division, the new account would be assigned number 2155.

Deleting a general ledger account. When an account is no longer needed, the account is removed from the general ledger chart of accounts.

The account number is then available for a new general ledger account. On June 1, 1988, the beginning of a new monthly fiscal period, Computex decides to delete the account Utilities Expense, 6250. The utilities expense account has a zero balance due to the closing entries completed on May 31, 1988.

Computex's applications software does not allow the deletion of an account with a balance. If an account balance exists, the balance must be transferred to another account. Dividing and transferring an account balance is described later in this chapter.

The entry to delete the account Utilities Expense is on line 2 of the general ledger file maintenance input form shown in Illustration 6-2.

The account number to be deleted, *6250,* is recorded in the Account Number column. The word *(Delete)* is written in the Account Title column. A word which is not an account title and is not to be key-entered is placed in parentheses.

Processing general ledger file maintenance data. A keyboard entry tells the computer that general ledger file maintenance is needed. Spaces for entering file maintenance data are then displayed on the computer monitor. General ledger file maintenance data are key-entered as shown for the new account Credit Card Fee Expense in Illustration 6-3.

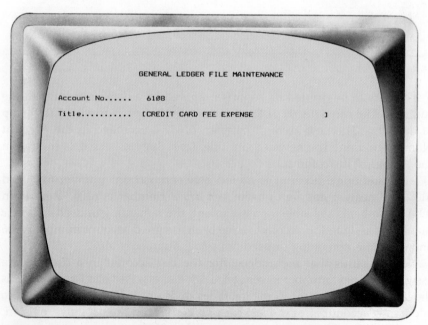

GENERAL LEDGER FILE MAINTENANCE

Account No......   6108

Title..........   [CREDIT CARD FEE EXPENSE   ]

Illustration 6-3
Computer monitor display
for general ledger file
maintenance

Data on each line of the file maintenance input form are key-entered. After all entries have been key-entered and processed, a chart of accounts is printed. A partial chart of accounts is shown in Illustration 6-4.

```
 RUN DATE 06/01/88                         COMPUTEX
                              GENERAL LEDGER CHART OF ACCOUNTS

 ----------------------------------------------
 ACCOUNT                          ACCOUNT
 NUMBER   CLASSIFICATION          TITLE
 ----------------------------------------------
 EXPENSES
 6105     SELLING EXPENSES        ADVERTISING EXPENSE
 6108                             CREDIT CARD FEE EXPENSE
 6110                             DEPRECIATION EXPENSE--STORE EQUIPMENT
 6115                             SALARY EXPENSE
 6120                             SUPPLIES EXPENSE--STORE
 6205     ADMIN. EXPENSES         BAD DEBTS EXPENSE
 6210                             DEPRECIATION EXPENSE--COMPUTER EQUIP.
 6215                             DEPRECIATION EXPENSE--OFFICE EQUIP.
 6218                             EQUIPMENT REPAIR EXPENSE
 6220                             INSURANCE EXPENSE
 6225                             MISCELLANEOUS EXPENSE
 6230                             PAYROLL TAXES EXPENSE
 6235                             RENT EXPENSE
 6240                             SALARY EXPENSE--ADMINISTRATIVE
 6245                             SUPPLIES EXPENSE--OFFICE
 INCOME TAX
 9105                             FEDERAL INCOME TAX
```

The general ledger file maintenance input form, Illustration 6-2, is used to check that the changes have been made on the chart of accounts.

Illustration 6-4
Partial chart of accounts

Subsidiary ledger file maintenance

Automated accounting uses the same subsidiary ledgers as manual accounting. An accounts payable ledger contains accounts for all vendors to whom money is owed. An accounts receivable ledger contains accounts for all customers purchasing merchandise on account.

Accounts in subsidiary ledgers are numbered in the same way for both manual and automated accounting. The numbering system used for subsidiary ledger accounts must meet the same three needs as for general ledger accounts. Each business numbers accounts in its subsidiary ledgers according to its particular needs. Computex uses a three-digit numbering system for its subsidiary ledger accounts. Computex's subsidiary ledgers generally require more file maintenance than a general ledger. Therefore, subsidiary ledger account numbers are assigned by 10's to provide more numbers for adding new accounts between existing accounts.

In automated accounting, all subsidiary ledger data are stored on secondary storage. Computex's microcomputer uses a diskette for secondary storage.

Adding a new subsidiary ledger account. The procedure for adding a new account to a subsidiary ledger is the same as for a general ledger. A new account to be added between two existing accounts is assigned the unused middle number. When no exact middle number is available, the nearest *even whole* number is used.

A new vendor account, Computer Products, Inc., is added to Computex's accounts payable ledger on June 1, 1988. The proper alphabetic position of this account is between the accounts of Abbott Software Company, 210, and Gardner Office Supplies, 220. The unused middle number, 215, is assigned to the account of Computer Products, Inc., as shown below.

> 210 Abbott Software Company (existing account)
> 215 COMPUTER PRODUCTS, INC. (new account)
> 220 Gardner Office Supplies (existing account)

A new customer account, Charles Baxter, is also added to Computex's accounts receivable ledger on June 1, 1988. The proper alphabetic position of this account is between the accounts of Mary Abler, 110, and Joan Daly, 120. The unused middle number, 115, is assigned to the account of Charles Baxter as shown below.

> 110 Mary Abler (existing account)
> 115 CHARLES BAXTER (new account)
> 120 Joan Daly (existing account)

In automated accounting, file maintenance activities for subsidiary ledgers include recording additions and deletions on file maintenance input forms. A vendor file maintenance input form is used to enter additions and deletions for an accounts payable ledger. A customer file maintenance input form is used to enter additions and deletions for an accounts receivable ledger. The steps in completing file maintenance input forms for subsidiary ledgers are similar to the steps used for completing a general ledger file maintenance input form. Adding the account Computer Products, Inc., to the accounts payable ledger is shown on line 1 of the vendor file maintenance input form in Illustration 6-5.

Illustration 6-5
Entries for vendor file
maintenance

	VENDOR FILE MAINTENANCE Input Form	
RUN DATE 06/01/88 MM DD YY		
1	2	
VENDOR NUMBER	VENDOR NAME	
1 215	Computer Products, Inc.	1
2 290	(Delete)	2
3		3
4		4

Deleting a subsidiary ledger account. When an account is no longer needed, the account is removed from the subsidiary ledger. The account number is then available for a new subsidiary ledger account.

Deleting vendor account 290 on June 1, 1988, is shown on line 2 of the vendor file maintenance input form in Illustration 6-5.

Processing subsidiary ledger file maintenance data. A keyboard entry tells the computer that either vendor or customer file maintenance is needed. Spaces for entering file maintenance data are then displayed on the computer monitor. Vendor file maintenance data are key-entered as shown for the new account Computer Products, Inc., in Illustration 6-6.

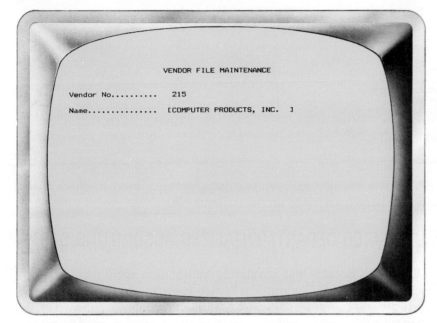

```
                    VENDOR FILE MAINTENANCE

     Vendor No..........   215

     Name...............   [COMPUTER PRODUCTS, INC.   ]
```

Illustration 6-6
Computer monitor display for vendor file maintenance

Data on each line of the file maintenance input form are key-entered. After all entries have been key-entered and processed, a vendor list is printed. Computex's vendor list is shown in Illustration 6-7.

```
   RUN DATE 06/01/88                    COMPUTEX
                                       VENDOR LIST

   ----------------
   VENDOR    VENDOR
   NUMBER    NAME
   ----------------
   210       ABBOTT SOFTWARE COMPANY
   215       COMPUTER PRODUCTS, INC.
   220       GARDNER OFFICE SUPPLIES
   230       INTERNATIONAL COMPUTERS
   240       MARTIN'S OFFICE PRODUCTS
   245       STAR SOFTWARE, INC.
   250       UNITED COMPUTER SYSTEMS
```

Illustration 6-7
Vendor list

The vendor file maintenance input form, Illustration 6-5, is used to check that the changes have been made on the vendor list.

The customer file maintenance form is similar to the vendor file maintenance form. Only the column headings differ. Data on each line are key-entered. After all file maintenance entries have been key-entered and processed, a customer list is printed. Computex's customer list is shown in Illustration 6-8.

```
RUN DATE 06/01/88                    COMPUTEX
                                  CUSTOMER LIST

     -------------------
     CUSTOMER   CUSTOMER
     NUMBER     NAME
     -------------------
      110       MARY ABLER
      115       CHARLES BAXTER
      120       JOAN DALY
      130       GATOR FURNITURE CO.
      140       MARTHA SEGER
      150       TAFT SPORTING GOODS
      160       HUBERT VERRICO
```

Illustration 6-8
Customer list

The customer file maintenance input form is used to check that the changes have been made on the customer list.

AUTOMATED DEPARTMENTALIZED ACCOUNTING SYSTEM

Computex decides that accounting information about each phase of its business is needed. Computex sells two types of merchandise: computer hardware and computer software. Computex's current automated accounting system does not provide information about which type of merchandise produces more profit. On July 1, 1988, Computex decides to organize its accounting information into two departments: hardware and software.

An accounting system showing accounting information for two or more departments is known as a departmentalized accounting system. In a departmentalized accounting system, a number of separate departmental accounts are needed in the general ledger.

Determining departmental accounts needed

In a departmentalized accounting system, gross profit is figured for each department. Therefore, all accounts used to figure gross profit must be departmentalized. These accounts include all revenue, contra revenue, merchandise inventory, cost accounts, and contra cost accounts. Separate income summary accounts must also be provided in order to bring merchandise inventory accounts up to date at the end of a fiscal period.

The income summary—general account used in a manual departmentalized accounting system to close departmental income summary accounts is not needed in an automated accounting system. The applications computer software contains instructions to close the departmental income summary accounts directly to the retained earnings account.

Separate departmental salary accounts are also needed to separate salaries for the two departments. Computex's separate departmental accounts are shown in the chart of accounts, page 118. The accounts for the hardware department are indicated by a −1 after the account number. The accounts for the software department are indicated by a −2 after the account number.

Adding departmental accounts

When Computex changes to an automated departmentalized accounting system on July 1, 1988, file maintenance is required to add the new departmental accounts. A general ledger file maintenance input form is used to enter the new departmental accounts. The entries to add the departmental accounts are shown on the general ledger file maintenance input form in Illustration 6-9.

	ACCOUNT NUMBER	ACCOUNT TITLE	
		GENERAL LEDGER FILE MAINTENANCE Input Form	
	RUN DATE 07/01/88 MM DD YY		
1	1125 − 1	Merchandise Inventory − Hardware	1
2	1125 − 2	Merchandise Inventory − Software	2
3	3120 − 1	Income Summary − Hardware	3
4	3120 − 2	Income Summary − Software	4
5	4105 − 1	Sales − Hardware	5
6	4105 − 2	Sales − Software	6
7	4110 − 1	Sales Returns and Allow. − Hardware	7
8	4110 − 2	Sales Returns and Allow. − Software	8
9	4115 − 1	Sales Discount − Hardware	9
10	4115 − 2	Sales Discount − Software	10
11	5105 − 1	Purchases − Hardware	11
12	5105 − 2	Purchases − Software	12
13	5110 − 1	Purchases Returns and Allow. − Hardware	13
14	5110 − 2	Purchases Returns and Allow. − Software	14
15	5115 − 1	Purchases Discount − Hardware	15
16	5115 − 2	Purchases Discount − Software	16
17	6115 − 1	Salary Expense − Hardware	17
18	6115 − 2	Salary Expense − Software	18
19			19

Illustration 6-9
Entries for general ledger file maintenance to add departmental accounts

Processing file maintenance data to add departmental accounts

A keyboard entry tells the computer that general ledger file maintenance is needed. Spaces for entering general ledger file maintenance data are then displayed on the computer monitor.

Data on each line of the file maintenance input form are key-entered. After all entries have been key-entered and processed, a chart of accounts is printed. A partial chart of accounts with departmental accounts added is shown in Illustration 6-10.

```
RUN DATE 07/01/88                        COMPUTEX
                              GENERAL LEDGER CHART OF ACCOUNTS

      ------------------------------------------
      ACCOUNT                          ACCOUNT
      NUMBER   CLASSIFICATION          TITLE
      ------------------------------------------
      ASSETS

      1125                             MERCHANDISE INVENTORY
      1125-1                           MERCHANDISE INVENTORY--HARDWARE
      1125-2                           MERCHANDISE INVENTORY--SOFTWARE

      STOCKHOLDERS' EQUITY

      3120                             INCOME SUMMARY
      3120-1                           INCOME SUMMARY--HARDWARE
      3120-2                           INCOME SUMMARY--SOFTWARE
      SALES
      4105                             SALES
      4105-1                           SALES--HARDWARE
      4105-2                           SALES--SOFTWARE
      4110                             SALES RETURNS AND ALLOWANCES
      4110-1                           SALES RETURNS AND ALLOW.--HARDWARE
      4110-2                           SALES RETURNS AND ALLOW.--SOFTWARE
      4115                             SALES DISCOUNT
      4115-1                           SALES DISCOUNT--HARDWARE
      4115-2                           SALES DISCOUNT--SOFTWARE
      COST OF MERCHANDISE
      5105                             PURCHASES
      5105-1                           PURCHASES--HARDWARE
      5105-2                           PURCHASES--SOFTWARE
      5110                             PURCHASES RETURNS AND ALLOWANCES
      5110-1                           PURCHASES RETURNS AND ALLOW.--HARDWARE
      5110-2                           PURCHASES RETURNS AND ALLOW.--SOFTWARE
      5115                             PURCHASES DISCOUNT
      5115-1                           PURCHASES DISCOUNT--HARDWARE
      5115-2                           PURCHASES DISCOUNT--SOFTWARE
      EXPENSES

      6115                             SALARY EXPENSE
      6115-1                           SALARY EXPENSE--HARDWARE
      6115-2                           SALARY EXPENSE--SOFTWARE
```

Illustration 6-10
Partial chart of accounts
with departmental
accounts added

The general ledger file maintenance input form, Illustration 6-9, is used to check that the changes have been made on the chart of accounts.

Dividing an account balance

The post-closing trial balance printed on June 30, 1988, is used to determine which account balances need to be divided between departmental accounts on July 1. Computex determines that the merchandise inventory account is the only account with a balance to be divided between the two departmental merchandise inventory accounts. Other departmental accounts have zero balances resulting from the closing entries at the end of the previous fiscal period.

The periodic inventory taken at the close of the previous fiscal period, June 30, 1988, is examined to determine the merchandise inventory amounts to be used for each department. Computex determines that the merchandise inventory account balance, $426,830.50, should be divided as follows.

Merchandise Inventory — Hardware	$323,465.00
Merchandise Inventory — Software	103,365.50
Total merchandise inventory	$426,830.50

Journalizing an entry to divide an account balance

Computex uses a journal entries input form to record all journal entries. A memorandum is the source document used to record an entry to divide an account balance. *(CONCEPT: Objective Evidence)*

The analysis of the journal entry to divide the merchandise inventory account balance is shown in the T accounts. Merchandise Inventory — Hardware is debited for $323,465.00. Merchandise Inventory — Software is debited for $103,365.50. Merchandise Inventory is credited for $426,830.50 to reduce the account balance to zero.

GENERAL LEDGER

Merchandise Inventory — Hardware

323,465.00 |

Merchandise Inventory — Software

103,365.50 |

Merchandise Inventory

Bal.   426,830.50 | 426,830.50

The entry to record the division of the merchandise inventory account balance is shown on the journal entries input form in Illustration 6-11.

BATCH NO.	1		JOURNAL ENTRIES Input Form		PAGE 1 OF 1 PAGES	
RUN DATE 07/01/88 MM DD YY						
1 DAY	2 DOC. NO.	3 VENDOR/ CUSTOMER NO.	4 GENERAL LEDGER ACCT. NO.	5 DEBIT	6 CREDIT	
01	M38		1125-1	323465 00		1
			1125-2	103365 50		2
			1125		426830 50	3
			PAGE TOTALS			
			BATCH TOTALS	426830 50	426830 50	

Illustration 6-11
Entries to divide an account balance

The number assigned to a group of journal entries is called a batch number. Batch numbers are assigned sequentially. As the journal entry to divide an account balance is the first journal entry of a new fiscal period, batch number 1 is assigned. Each page of journal entries to be processed by a computer is identified by a page number.

The batch number, *1*, and the run date, *07/01/88*, are recorded in the spaces provided at the top of the form. The page number for the first page of the batch, *1*, is recorded in the space provided at the top of the form. The total number of pages is entered after the entire batch has been recorded.

The day, *01*, is entered in the Day column, line 1. The document number, *M38*, is entered in the Doc. No. column. Since this entry does not involve an entry to a subsidiary ledger, the Vendor/Customer No. column is left blank. The account number for Merchandise Inventory—Hardware, *1125-1*, is written in the General Ledger Acct. No. column. The amount debited to Merchandise Inventory—Hardware, *$323,465.00*, is recorded in the Debit column.

On line 2, the Day, Doc. No., and Vendor/Customer No. columns are left blank. These data are recorded only once for each complete transaction. The account number for Merchandise Inventory—Software, *1125-2*, is written in the General Ledger Acct. No. column. The amount debited to Merchandise Inventory—Software, *$103,365.50*, is recorded in the Debit column.

On line 3, the nondepartmental merchandise inventory account number, *1125*, is written in the General Ledger Acct. No. column. The amount credited to Merchandise Inventory, *$426,830.50*, is recorded in the Credit column. This entry closes the nondepartmental merchandise inventory account.

After the journal entry to divide the balance of the merchandise inventory account has been recorded, the Debit and Credit columns are totaled. The totals are recorded on the Batch Totals line at the bottom of the journal entries input form.

> When more than one page is used to record a batch of journal entries, totals for each page including the last page are recorded on the Page Totals line at the bottom of the form. After all journal entries and page totals have been recorded, each set of page totals is then added. The total debits and total credits for all journal entries in the batch are recorded on the last page on the Batch Totals line. This procedure is illustrated in Chapter 7.

The two totals recorded at the bottom of the journal entries input form are compared to assure equality of debits and credits. As the two totals are the same, $426,830.50, the entries on the input form are assumed to be correct.

The final step is to record the number of pages in the batch, *1*, in the space provided at the top of the form.

> If two pages had been required for the batch, the first page would be numbered page 1 of 2 pages. The second page would be numbered page 2 of 2 pages. This page numbering method helps keep all pages together in sequence and helps assure that all pages have been accounted for.

Processing a journal entry to divide an account balance

In manual accounting, a journal entry is recorded in a journal and posted to accounts stored in a ledger. In Computex's automated departmentalized accounting system, a journal entry is key-entered and posted to accounts stored on a diskette.

A keyboard entry tells the computer that a journal entry is to be recorded. Spaces for entering journal entry data are displayed on the computer monitor. Journal entry data are key-entered as shown in Illustration 6-12.

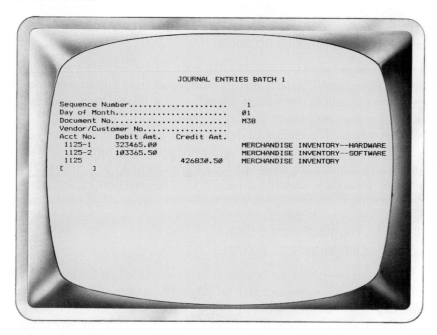

Illustration 6-12
Computer monitor display for a journal entry

After the journal entry to divide an account balance has been key-entered and posted, a journal entries report is printed. Computex's journal entries report for the division of an account balance is shown in Illustration 6-13.

Illustration 6-13
Journal entries report for the division of an account balance

```
  RUN DATE Ø7/Ø1/88                     COMPUTEX
                           JOURNAL ENTRIES BATCH NUMBER 1


    ---------------------------------------------------------------------------
    SEQ.                DOCUMENT    VENDOR/
    NO.     DAY         NUMBER      CUSTOMER                    DEBIT        CREDIT
    ---------------------------------------------------------------------------
    ØØ1     Ø1          M38
            1125-1      MERCHANDISE INVENTORY--HARDWARE        323465.ØØ
            1125-2      MERCHANDISE INVENTORY--SOFTWARE        1Ø3365.5Ø
            1125        MERCHANDISE INVENTORY                               426830.5Ø
                                                              ------------  ------------
                        TOTALS                                 426830.5Ø    426830.5Ø
                                                              ============  ============
                        IN BALANCE
```

The journal entries report is checked for accuracy by comparing the totals on the report with the batch totals on the last page of the journal entries input form. If the totals are not the same, the error must be found and corrected. The computer assigns a sequence number to each transaction entered so that each transaction may be identified if corrections are needed. If the totals are the same, the entry to divide an account balance is assumed to be correct.

Deleting nondepartmental accounts

After all departmental accounts have been added and after any account balances have been divided, related nondepartmental accounts must be deleted. For example, Merchandise Inventory is the related nondepartmental account for the Merchandise Inventory—Hardware and Merchandise Inventory—Software accounts. The entries to delete the nondepartmental accounts are recorded on a general ledger file maintenance input form. The account number and *(Delete)* are recorded for each account to be deleted. This is the same procedure described earlier for the deletion of any general ledger account.

Processing file maintenance data to delete nondepartmental accounts

A keyboard entry tells the computer that general ledger file maintenance is needed. Spaces for entering general ledger file maintenance data are then displayed on the computer monitor.

Data on each line of the file maintenance input form are key-entered. After all entries have been key-entered and processed, a chart of accounts is printed. The general ledger file maintenance input form is used to check that the changes have been made on the chart of accounts. The chart of accounts with departmental accounts added and related nondepartmental accounts deleted is shown on page 118.

ACCOUNTING TERMS

What is the meaning of each of the following?

1. processing
2. manual accounting
3. automated accounting
4. computer
5. computer information system
6. mainframe computer
7. minicomputer
8. microcomputer
9. computer program
10. computer programmer
11. software
12. systems software
13. applications software
14. hardware
15. input
16. key-entering
17. storage
18. diskette
19. output
20. printout
21. file maintenance
22. run date
23. batch number

QUESTIONS FOR INDIVIDUAL STUDY

1. Applying accounting concepts in the same way in each accounting period is an application of which accounting concept?
2. What are the three types of computers currently used in a computer information system?
3. What type of computer would a business with a need for intermediate computing speed, storage capacity, and processing capability likely choose?
4. Who usually supplies systems software?
5. What is one example of applications software?
6. What are the two human functions in a computer information system?
7. What are the three distinct tasks performed by a central processing unit (CPU)?
8. What type of computer does Computex use?
9. Using a monthly fiscal period to report financial data is an application of which accounting concept?
10. What are the three needs that must be met by a numbering system?
11. What type of secondary storage does Computex's computer use?
12. When no exact middle number is available for assignment to a new account, what number is used?
13. How is the accuracy of a chart of accounts determined?
14. Why does Computex assign subsidiary ledger account numbers by 10's when general ledger account numbers are assigned by 5's?
15. What accounts must be departmentalized in order to figure gross profit by department?
16. How does Computex determine the balances for the two merchandise inventory accounts?
17. What type of form does Computex use to record journal entries?

CASES FOR MANAGEMENT DECISION

CASE 1 Schafer's, Inc., a merchandising business, sells paint and wallpaper. The business uses an automated nondepartmentalized accounting system. The accountant recommends that the accounting records be departmentalized to provide information about which phase of the business produces more profit. The recommendation is that merchandise inventory and all revenue and cost accounts be identified by department. The store manager agrees with the recommendation to departmentalize some of the accounting records. However, the manager feels that departmentalizing the revenue and cost accounts would be sufficient to determine how each department is contributing to the total net income of the business. The manager does not feel maintaining separate merchandise inventory accounts would be worth the extra time and effort. Do you agree with the recommendation of the accountant or the manager? Why?

CASE 2 Delio Golf Center has two departments: Golf Clothing and Golf Equipment. The business uses an automated departmentalized accounting system similar to the one used by Computex in this chapter. A decision has been made to open an additional store in a shopping center. Changes in the accounting system needed to record and report accounting data for both stores are being considered. The accountant recommends that the existing numbering system for the chart of accounts be expanded to identify each store. The manager disagrees with the recommendation. The manager suggests that the new store should have a separate accounting system. The same chart of accounts would be used in both stores. The same financial statements would also be prepared for both stores. Do you agree with the recommendation of the accountant or the manager? Why?

APPLICATION PROBLEMS

PROBLEM 6-1   Performing file maintenance activities; adding and deleting general ledger accounts

The following is a partial general ledger chart of accounts.

6110	Advertising Expense	6218	Electricity Expense
6112	Depreciation Expense— Store Equipment	6220	Miscellaneous Expense
		6225	Rent Expense
6210	Bad Debts Expense	6230	Supplies Expense—Office
6215	Depreciation Expense— Office Equipment	6235	Telephone Expense

Accounts Added	**Accounts Deleted**
Credit Card Fee Expense	Advertising Expense
Depreciation Expense—Computer Equipment	Electricity Expense
	Telephone Expense
Salary Expense—Administrative	

Instructions: Assign account numbers to the new accounts using the unused middle number method. Prepare a general ledger file maintenance input form to add and delete the accounts. Use October 1 of the current year as the run date. Use Computex's chart of accounts at the beginning of this part as a guide for the location of the new accounts.

PROBLEM 6-2   Performing file maintenance activities; adding and deleting subsidiary ledger accounts

The following is a partial customer list.

110	Cindy Allore	150	Tami Karr
120	Richard Beard	155	Wayne Keifer
130	John Berti	160	Lori McAllister
135	Diane Devoe	170	Dwight Richardson
140	Marcia Hillman	180	Larry Whitehouse

Accounts Added	**Accounts Deleted**
Thomas Arthur	Richard Beard
Valerie Clevinger	Marcia Hillman
Joseph Voison	Lori McAllister

Instructions: Assign account numbers to the new accounts using the unused middle number method. Prepare a customer file maintenance input form to add and delete the accounts. Use March 1 of the current year as the run date.

PROBLEM 6-3   Performing file maintenance activities; adding departmentalized accounts and dividing an account balance

The following is a partial general ledger chart of accounts.

1125	Merchandise Inventory	5105	Purchases
3120	Income Summary	5110	Purchases Returns and Allowances
4105	Sales		
4110	Sales Returns and Allowances	5115	Purchases Discount
4115	Sales Discount	6120	Salary Expense

Instructions: 1. Prepare a general ledger file maintenance input form to departmentalize the accounts into two departments: Hardware and Plumbing. Use Computex's chart of accounts as a guide for adding new departmental accounts. Use June 1 of the current year as the run date.

2. Prepare a journal entries input form to divide the merchandise inventory account balance, $336,483.50, between the two departmental inventory accounts. The division of the merchandise inventory account balance is as follows: Hardware, $172,640.00; Plumbing, $163,843.50. The remaining departmental accounts have zero balances because June 1 is the start of a new fiscal period. Use June 1 of the current year as the run date. Batch No. 1. Memorandum No. 32.

3. Prepare a general ledger file maintenance input form to delete the related nondepartmental accounts. Use June 1 of the current year as the run date.

ENRICHMENT PROBLEMS

MASTERY PROBLEM 6-M   Performing file maintenance activities

The following is a partial general ledger chart of accounts for Imperial Shoes.

1105 Cash	5105 Purchases
1110 Accounts Receivable	5110 Purchases Returns and
1120 Merchandise Inventory	Allowances
2145 Hospital Insurance	5115 Purchases Discount
Premiums Payable	6105 Advertising Expense
3120 Income Summary	6110 Depreciation Expense—
4105 Sales	Store Equipment
4110 Sales Returns and Allowances	6115 Salary Expense
4115 Sales Discount	6245 Utilities Expense

Accounts Added	**Account Deleted**
Petty Cash	Utilities Expense
Credit Card Fee Expense	

Accounts Departmentalized	
Merchandise Inventory	Purchases
Income Summary	Purchases Returns and Allowances
Sales	Purchases Discount
Sales Returns and Allowances	Salary Expense
Sales Discount	

Instructions: 1. Prepare a general ledger file maintenance input form to add, delete, and departmentalize the appropriate accounts. Imperial Shoes will have two departments: Men's Shoes and Women's Shoes. Use July 1 of the current year as the run date. Use Computex's chart of accounts as a guide for adding and departmentalizing general ledger accounts.

2. Prepare a journal entries input form to divide the merchandise inventory balance, $326,840.50, between the two departmental merchandise inventory accounts. The division of the account balance is as follows: Men's Shoes, $146,740.50; Women's Shoes, $180,100.00. The remaining departmental accounts have zero balances because July 1 is the start of a new monthly fiscal period. Use July 1 of the current year as the run date. Batch No. 1. Memorandum No. 43.

3. Prepare a general ledger file maintenance input form to delete the related nondepartmental accounts. Use July 1 of the current year as the run date.

4. Prepare a customer file maintenance input form to add and delete the appropriate accounts from the following customer list. Use July 1 of the current year as the run date.

Partial Customer List

125 Norman Aziala	150 Charles Lorenz
130 Susan Deni	160 Roger Theisen
140 Linda Gibson	170 Debbie Ulrich

Accounts Added	**Accounts Deleted**
John Desai	Norman Aziala
Phyllis Mayan	Debbie Ulrich

CHALLENGE PROBLEM 6-C   Performing vendor file maintenance activities

The following is the vendor list for Adkins Decorating.

210 Astro Paint, Inc.	260 Modern Paint Products
220 Atlas Paint Supply	265 Renaus Wallcovering Studio
225 Balboa's Wallcovering	270 Stokes Paint Distributors
230 Casas Paint Products	275 Tower Paint Mfg.
240 D & J Paint Co.	278 Vilaso Store Supplies
248 Julian Wallpaper, Inc.	280 Wallcovering Outlet
250 Kaiser Office Supplies	290 World Wide Wallcovering

Accounts Deleted	**Accounts Added**
Atlas Paint Supply	Austin Store Supplies
Balboa's Wallcovering	Colburn Paint, Inc.
Julian Wallpaper, Inc.	Garrett Wallcovering
Vilaso Store Supplies	Tabor Wallpaper Co.

Instructions: Prepare a vendor file maintenance input form to delete and add the appropriate accounts. Use November 1 of the current year as the run date.

Computer Application 1
Automated Accounting Cycle for a
Departmentalized Business: Performing
File Maintenance Activities

The general ledger file maintenance input forms, customer file maintenance input form, and the journal entries input form completed in Mastery Problem 6-M, Chapter 6, are needed to complete Computer Application 1.

Imperial Shoes completed the input forms for departmentalizing its automated accounting system. Computer Application 1 provides for the use of a microcomputer to input and process the data from the completed forms. Chapter 6 describes the manual and computer operations required to departmentalize an automated accounting system.

Reports may be displayed or printed by the computer. If a printer is available with the computer being used, select the *Print* option when given the choice of displaying or printing reports. If a printer is not available, select the *Display* option. When the *Display* option is selected, the report will be displayed on the computer monitor.

COMPUTER APPLICATION PROBLEM

COMPUTER APPLICATION PROBLEM 1 Performing file maintenance activities

Instructions: 1. Load the Systems Selection Menu from the *Advanced Automated Accounting* diskette according to the instructions for the computer being used. Select Problem CA-1. The general ledger chart of accounts, customer list, and opening balances are stored on the template diskette.

2. Key-enter the file maintenance data from the general ledger file maintenance input form completed in Mastery Problem 6-M, Instruction 1.

3. Display/Print the revised chart of accounts.

4. Key-enter the journal entry from the journal entries input form completed in Mastery Problem 6-M, Instruction 2.

5. Display/Print the journal entries report. Check the accuracy by comparing the report totals with the totals on the input form.

6. Key-enter the file maintenance data from the general ledger file maintenance input form completed in Mastery Problem 6-M, Instruction 3.

7. Display/Print the revised chart of accounts.

8. Key-enter the file maintenance data from the customer file maintenance input form completed in Mastery Problem 6-M, Instruction 4.

9. Display/Print the revised customer list.

7 Recording and Posting Business Transactions in an Automated Accounting System

ENABLING PERFORMANCE TASKS

After studying Chapter 7, you will be able to:

a. Identify accounting concepts and practices related to recording and posting departmentalized business transactions in an automated accounting system.

b. Record business transactions for a departmentalized automated accounting system.

An accounting system may be either manual or automated. An automated accounting system uses a computer to perform the routine and repetitive accounting activities. Computex, a merchandising business, uses an automated accounting system. Chapter 6 describes file maintenance procedures needed to departmentalize Computex's automated accounting system. Chapter 7 describes Computex's procedures for recording and processing departmentalized business transactions.

ANALYZING, RECORDING, AND POSTING BUSINESS TRANSACTIONS

Analyzing transactions into debit and credit parts is required in both manual and automated accounting. In manual accounting, the debit and credit parts of a transaction are recorded in a journal. Periodically, transaction data are posted to a general ledger. In automated accounting, the debit and credit parts of a transaction are recorded on a journal entries input form. Periodically, transaction data are key-entered into the computer and automatically posted to a general ledger stored on secondary storage.

Computex uses a one-month fiscal period. (CONCEPT: Accounting Period Cycle) Computex records daily all transaction data on a journal entries input form. Transaction data recorded on the journal entries input form are key-entered and processed weekly.

DEPARTMENTAL PURCHASES

Computex uses a separate purchases account for each of its two departments, hardware and software.

Purchases on account

July 1, 1988.
Purchased hardware on account from Computer Products, Inc., $13,475.50.
Purchase Invoice No. 267.

In the general ledger, Purchases—Hardware is increased by a $13,475.50 debit. Accounts Payable is increased by a $13,475.50 credit. In the accounts payable subsidiary ledger, the vendor account, Computer Products, Inc., is increased by a $13,475.50 credit.

This transaction is recorded on lines 1 and 2 of the journal entries input form shown in Illustration 7-1.

Illustration 7-1
Journal entries input form
with purchases
transactions recorded

						JOURNAL ENTRIES				
BATCH NO. 2						Input Form		PAGE 1 OF ___ PAGES		
RUN DATE 07/02/88 MM DD YY										
1	2	3		4		5		6		
DAY	DOC. NO.	VENDOR/ CUSTOMER NO.		GENERAL LEDGER ACCT. NO.		DEBIT		CREDIT		
01	P267	215		5105-1		13475 50				1
				2105				13475 50		2
01	DM25	245		2105		250 00				3
				5110-2				250 00		4
										5

Batch No. 1 was assigned to the journal entries input form dividing the merchandise inventory account in Chapter 6. Therefore, the transactions entered on this new journal entries input form are assigned Batch No. 2. Also, the run date on which data from this journal entries input form will be key-entered and processed is July 2, 1988.

The batch number, *2*, the run date, *07/02/88*, and the page number for the first page of the batch, *1*, are written in the spaces provided at the top of the journal entries input form. The total number of pages is recorded after the entire batch has been recorded.

The day, *01*, is recorded in the Day column, line 1. The document number, *P267*, is entered in the Doc. No. column. The vendor number, *215*, is recorded in the Vendor/Customer No. column. The account number for Purchases—Hardware, *5105-1*, is written in the General Ledger Acct. No.

column. The amount debited to Purchases—Hardware, *$13,475.50*, is recorded in the Debit column.

On line 2, the Day, Doc. No., and Vendor/Customer No. columns are left blank. These data are recorded only once for each complete transaction. The account number for Accounts Payable, *2105*, is written in the General Ledger Acct. No. column. The amount credited to Accounts Payable, *$13,475.50*, is recorded in the Credit column.

Purchases returns and allowances

July 1, 1988.
Returned defective software to Star Software, Inc., $250.00, from Purchase Invoice No. 262. Debit Memorandum No. 25.

In the general ledger, Accounts Payable is decreased by a $250.00 debit. Purchases Returns and Allowances—Software is increased by a $250.00 credit. In the accounts payable subsidiary ledger, the vendor account, Star Software, Inc., is decreased by a $250.00 debit.

This transaction is recorded on lines 3 and 4 of the journal entries input form shown in Illustration 7-1.

The day, *01*, is written in the Day column, line 3. The document number, *DM25*, is recorded in the Doc. No. column. The vendor number, *245*, is entered in the Vendor/Customer No. column. The account number for Accounts Payable, *2105*, is written in the General Ledger Acct. No. column. The amount debited to Accounts Payable, *$250.00*, is recorded in the Debit column. On line 4, the account number for Purchases Returns and Allowances—Software, *5110-2*, and the credit amount, *$250.00*, are recorded.

DEPARTMENTAL CASH PAYMENTS

Computex makes most cash payments by check. Therefore, check stubs are the source documents for most cash payments. *(CONCEPT: Objective Evidence)*

Cash payment for a payroll

July 1, 1988.
Paid semimonthly payroll: hardware, $3,690.00; software, $3,200.00; administrative, $1,810.00 (less deductions: employees' income tax—federal, $860.20; employees' income tax—state, $496.30; FICA tax, $609.00; hospital insurance, $162.00; life insurance, $120.00); total, $6,452.50. Check No. 246.

Salary Expense—Hardware is increased by a $3,690.00 debit. Salary Expense—Software is increased by a $3,200.00 debit. Salary Expense—Administrative is increased by a $1,810.00 debit. Employees Income Tax Payable—Federal is increased by a $860.20 credit. Employees Income Tax Payable—State is increased by a $496.30 credit. FICA Tax Payable is increased by a $609.00 credit. Hospital Insurance

Premiums Payable is increased by a $162.00 credit. Life Insurance Premiums Payable is increased by a $120.00 credit. Cash is decreased by a $6,452.50 credit.

This transaction is recorded on lines 5 through 13 of the journal entries input form shown in Illustration 7-2.

BATCH NO. 2		JOURNAL ENTRIES			
RUN DATE 07/02/88 MM DD YY		Input Form		PAGE 1 OF ____ PAGES	
1	2	3	4	5	6
DAY	DOC. NO.	VENDOR/ CUSTOMER NO.	GENERAL LEDGER ACCT. NO.	DEBIT	CREDIT
5	01 C246		6115-1	3690 00	
6			6115-2	3200 00	
7			6240	1810 00	
8			2110		860 20
9			2115		496 30
10			2125		609 00
11			2145		162 00
12			2150		120 00
13			1105		6452 50
14	01 C247	250	2105	7690 00	
15			1105		7536 20
16			5115-1		153 80
17	01 C248		1130	87 50	
18			1105		87 50
19	01 C249		6235	1600 00	
20			1105		1600 00
21	02 C250		1130	113 60	
22			1135	88 40	
23			6105	118 70	
24			6225	89 50	
25			1105		410 20

Illustration 7-2
Journal entries input form with cash payments recorded

The day, *01*, is written in the Day column, line 5. The document number, *C246*, is recorded in the Doc. No. column. The account number for Salary Expense—Hardware, *6115-1*, is entered in the General Ledger Acct. No. column. The amount debited to Salary Expense—Hardware, *$3,690.00*, is written in the Debit column.

On line 6, the account number for Salary Expense—Software, *6115-2*, and the debit amount, *$3,200.00*, are recorded. The account number for Salary Expense—Administrative, *6240*, and the amount debited, *$1,810.00*, are written on line 7. The account number for Employees Income Tax Payable—Federal, *2110*, and the amount credited, *$860.20*, are entered on line 8. On line 9, the account number for Employees Income Tax Payable—State, *2115*, and the amount credited, *$496.30*, are recorded. The account number for FICA Tax Payable, *2125*, and the amount credited, *$609.00*, are entered on line 10. The account number for Hospital Insurance Premiums Payable, *2145*, and the amount credited, *$162.00*, are written on line 11. On line 12, the account number for Life Insurance Premiums Payable, *2150*, and the amount credited, *$120.00*, are recorded. On line 13, the account number for Cash, *1105*, and the amount credited, *$6,452.50*, are entered.

Cash payment on account

July 1, 1988.
Paid on account to United Computer Systems, $7,536.20, covering Purchase Invoice No. 261 for hardware, $7,690.00, less 2% discount, $153.80. Check No. 247.

In the general ledger, Accounts Payable is decreased by a $7,690.00 debit. Cash is decreased by a $7,536.20 credit. Purchases Discount — Hardware is increased by a $153.80 credit. In the accounts payable subsidiary ledger, the vendor account, United Computer Systems, is decreased by a $7,690.00 debit.

This transaction is recorded on lines 14 through 16 of the journal entries input form shown in Illustration 7-2.

The day, *01*, is written in the Day column, line 14. The document number, *C247*, is entered in the Doc. No. column. The vendor number, *250*, is recorded in the Vendor/Customer No. column. The account number for Accounts Payable, *2105*, is written in the General Ledger Acct. No. column. The amount debited to Accounts Payable, *$7,690.00*, is entered in the Debit column.

On line 15, the account number for Cash, *1105*, and the amount credited, *$7,536.20*, are recorded. The account number for Purchases Discount — Hardware, *5115-1*, and the amount credited, *$153.80*, are entered on line 16.

Cash payment for supplies

July 1, 1988.
Bought office supplies for cash, $87.50. Check No. 248.

Supplies — Office is increased by an $87.50 debit. Cash is decreased by an $87.50 credit.

This transaction is recorded on lines 17 and 18 of the journal entries input form shown in Illustration 7-2.

The day, *01*, is written in the Day column, line 17. The document number, *C248*, is entered in the Doc. No. column. This transaction does not involve an entry to a subsidiary ledger. Therefore, the Vendor/Customer No. column is left blank. The account number for Supplies — Office, *1130*, is recorded in the General Ledger Acct. No. column. The amount debited to Supplies — Office, *$87.50*, is written in the Debit column. On line 18, the account number for Cash, *1105*, and the amount credited, *$87.50*, are recorded.

Cash payment for an expense

July 1, 1988.
Paid July rent, $1,600.00. Check No. 249.

Rent Expense is increased by a $1,600.00 debit. Cash is decreased by a $1,600.00 credit.

This transaction is recorded on lines 19 and 20 of the journal entries input form shown in Illustration 7-2.

The day, *01*, is written in the Day column, line 19. The document number, *C249*, is recorded in the Doc. No. column. The account number for Rent Expense, *6235*, is entered in the General Ledger Acct. No. column. The amount debited to Rent Expense, *$1,600.00*, is written in the Debit column. On line 20, the account number for Cash, *1105*, and the amount credited, *$1,600.00*, are recorded.

Cash payment to replenish petty cash

July 2, 1988.
Replenished petty cash. Charge the following accounts: Supplies—Office, $113.60; Supplies—Store, $88.40; Advertising Expense, $118.70; Miscellaneous Expense, $89.50; total, $410.20. Check No. 250.

Supplies—Office is increased by a $113.60 debit. Supplies—Store is increased by an $88.40 debit. Advertising Expense is increased by a $118.70 debit. Miscellaneous Expense is increased by an $89.50 debit. Cash is decreased by a $410.20 credit, the total amount needed to replenish petty cash.

This transaction is recorded on lines 21 through 25 of the journal entries input form shown in Illustration 7-2.

The day, *02*, is written in the Day column, line 21. The document number, *C250*, is recorded in the Doc. No. column. The account number for Supplies—Office, *1130*, is entered in the General Ledger Acct. No. column. The amount debited to Supplies—Office, *$113.60*, is written in the Debit column.

On line 22, the account number for Supplies—Store, *1135*, and the amount debited, *$88.40*, are recorded. The account number for Advertising Expense, *6105*, and the amount debited, *$118.70*, are written on line 23. The account number for Miscellaneous Expense, *6225*, and the amount debited, *$89.50*, are entered on line 24. On line 25, the account number for Cash, *1105*, and the amount credited, *$410.20*, are recorded.

COMPLETING A PAGE OF JOURNAL ENTRIES

Each journal entries input form has 25 lines. When the 25 lines have been used to record journal entries, the Debit and Credit columns are totaled. The totals are written in the space provided at the bottom of the journal entries input form as shown in Illustration 7-3.

	BATCH NO. 2		JOURNAL ENTRIES				
	RUN DATE 07/02/88		Input Form		PAGE 1 OF ___ PAGES		
	MM DD YY						

1	2	3	4	5	6
DAY	DOC. NO.	VENDOR/ CUSTOMER NO.	GENERAL LEDGER ACCT. NO.	DEBIT	CREDIT
25			1105		410 20	25
			PAGE TOTALS	32213 20	32213 20
			BATCH TOTALS		

Illustration 7-3
Journal entries input form
with page totals recorded

The two totals are compared to assure equality of debits and credits. As the two totals, $32,213.20, are the same, the journal entries on page 1 of Batch No. 2 are assumed to be correct.

In order to prove equality of debits and credits for each page of journal entries, no partial entries are recorded on a page. For example, if a journal entry will not fit in the remaining lines on a page, the complete entry is recorded on the next page. Therefore, some lines may be blank on individual pages of journal entries.

DEPARTMENTAL SALES

Departmental sales are recorded at time of sale, regardless of when payment is received. *(CONCEPT: Realization of Revenue)* Computex uses a separate sales account for each of its two departments, hardware and software.

Sales on account

July 2.
Sold hardware on account to Charles Baxter, $1,250.00, plus sales tax, $62.50; total, $1,312.50. Sales Invoice No. 88.

In the general ledger, Accounts Receivable is increased by a $1,312.50 debit. Sales Tax Payable is increased by a $62.50 credit. Sales—Hardware is increased by a $1,250.00 credit. In the accounts receivable subsidiary ledger, the customer account, Charles Baxter, is increased by a $1,312.50 debit.

This transaction is recorded on lines 1 through 3 of the journal entries input form shown in Illustration 7-4.

The batch number, 2, the run date, 07/02/88, and the page number, 2, are written in the space provided at the top of the journal entries input form.

The day, 02, is written in the Day column, line 1. The document number, S88, is entered in the Doc. No. column. The customer number, 115, is recorded in the Vendor/Customer No. column. The account number for Accounts Receivable, 1115, is written in the General Ledger Acct. No.

BATCH NO. [2]			JOURNAL ENTRIES			
RUN DATE _07/02/88_			Input Form	PAGE _2_ OF ____ PAGES		
MM DD YY						

1	2	3	4	5	6	
DAY	DOC. NO.	VENDOR/ CUSTOMER NO.	GENERAL LEDGER ACCT. NO.	DEBIT	CREDIT	
1. 02	588	115	1115	1312 50		1
2.			2130		62 50	2
3.			4105-1		1250 00	3
4. 02	CM38	150	2130	44 75		4
5.			4110-2	895 00		5
6.			1115		939 75	6
7.						7

Illustration 7-4
Journal entries input form
with sales transactions
recorded

column. The amount debited to Accounts Receivable, *$1,312.50*, is entered in the Debit column.

On line 2, the account number for Sales Tax Payable, *2130*, and the amount credited, *$62.50*, are recorded. The account number for Sales—Hardware, *4105-1*, and the amount credited, *$1,250.00*, are entered on line 3.

Sales returns and allowances

July 2, 1988.
Granted credit to Taft Sporting Goods for software returned, $895.00, plus sales tax, $44.75, from Sales Invoice No. 85; total, $939.75. Credit Memorandum No. 38.

In the general ledger, Sales Tax Payable is decreased by a $44.75 debit. Sales Returns and Allowances—Software is increased by an $895.00 debit. Accounts Receivable is decreased by a $939.75 credit. In the accounts receivable ledger, the customer account, Taft Sporting Goods, is decreased by a $939.75 credit.

This transaction is recorded on lines 4 through 6 of the journal entries input form shown in Illustration 7-4.

The day, *02*, is written in the Day column, line 4. The document number, *CM38*, is recorded in the Doc. No. column. The customer number, *150*, is entered in the Vendor/Customer No. column. The account number for Sales Tax Payable, *2130*, is written in the General Ledger Acct. No. column. The amount debited to Sales Tax Payable, *$44.75*, is recorded in the Debit column.

On line 5, the account number for Sales Returns and Allowances—Software, *4110-2*, and the amount debited, *$895.00*, are entered. The account number for Accounts Receivable, *1115*, and the amount credited, *$939.75*, are written on line 6.

DEPARTMENTAL CASH RECEIPTS

Most of Computex's cash receipts are from cash received on account and cash and credit card sales.

Cash received on account

July 2, 1988.
Received on account from Gator Furniture Co., $1,893.36, covering Sales Invoice No. 86 for hardware, $1,932.00 ($1,840.00 plus sales tax, $92.00) less 2% discount, $36.80, and less sales tax, $1.84. Receipt No. 79.

In the general ledger, Cash is increased by a $1,893.36 debit. Sales Tax Payable is decreased by a $1.84 debit. Sales Discount—Hardware is increased by a $36.80 debit. Accounts Receivable is decreased by a $1,932.00 credit. In the accounts receivable subsidiary ledger, the customer account, Gator Furniture Co., is decreased by a $1,932.00 credit.

This transaction is recorded on lines 7 through 10 of the journal entries input form shown in Illustration 7-5.

BATCH NO. **2**

RUN DATE **07/02/88**
MM DD YY

JOURNAL ENTRIES
Input Form

PAGE **2** OF _____ PAGES

	DAY	DOC. NO.	VENDOR/ CUSTOMER NO.	GENERAL LEDGER ACCT. NO.	DEBIT	CREDIT	
7	02	R79	130	1105	1893 36		7
8				2130	1 84		8
9				4115-1	36 80		9
10				1115		1932 00	10
11	02	T2		1105	10710 00		11
12				2130		510 00	12
13				4105-1		7840 00	13
14				4105-2		2360 00	14
15							15

Illustration 7-5
Journal entries input form with cash receipts transactions recorded

The day, *02*, is written in the Day column, line 7. The document number, *R79*, is recorded in the Doc. No. column. The customer number, *130*, is entered in the Vendor/Customer No. column. The account number for Cash, *1105*, is written in the General Ledger Acct. No. column. The amount debited to Cash, *$1,893.36*, is recorded in the Debit column.

On line 8, the account number for Sales Tax Payable, *2130*, and the amount debited, *$1.84*, are entered. The account number for Sales Discount—Hardware, *4115-1*, and the amount debited, *$36.80*, are written on line 9. The account number for Accounts Receivable, *1115*, and the amount credited, *$1,932.00*, are recorded on line 10.

Cash and credit card sales

July 2, 1988.
Recorded cash and credit card sales for July 1 and 2: hardware, $7,840.00; software, $2,360.00; plus sales tax, $510.00; total, $10,710.00. Cash Register Tape No. 2.

Cash is increased by a $10,710.00 debit. Sales Tax Payable is increased by a $510.00 credit. Sales—Hardware is increased by a $7,840.00 credit. Sales—Software is increased by a $2,360.00 credit.

This transaction is recorded on lines 11 through 14 of the journal entries input form shown in Illustration 7-5.

The day, *02*, is written in the Day column, line 11. The document number, *T2*, is recorded in the Doc. No. column. The account number for Cash, *1105*, is entered in the General Ledger Acct. No. column. The amount debited to Cash, *$10,710.00*, is written in the Debit column.

On line 12, the account number for Sales Tax Payable, *2130*, and the amount credited, *$510.00*, are recorded. The account number for Sales—Hardware, *4105-1*, and the amount credited, *$7,840.00*, are entered on line 13. The account number for Sales—Software, *4105-2*, and the amount credited, *$2,360.00*, are written on line 14.

COMPLETING A BATCH OF JOURNAL ENTRIES

After all weekly transactions have been recorded, Computex totals the Debit and Credit columns of the last page of journal entries. The totals are recorded in the space provided at the bottom of the journal entries input form. The two totals are then compared to assure equality of debits and credits. As the two totals are the same, $14,894.25, the entries on page 2 of Batch No. 2 are assumed to be correct.

After proving equality of debits and credits for the last page of journal entries, total debits and total credits for each page are added. These totals, $47,107.45, are recorded as Batch Totals in the space provided on the last page of journal entries. The number of pages in the batch, 2, is recorded in the space provided at the top of each input form. The bottom of the journal entries input form for the last page of Batch No. 2 is shown in Illustration 7-6.

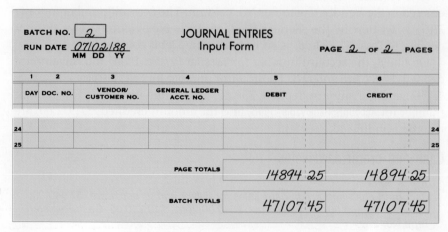

Illustration 7-6
Journal entries input form
with page totals and
batch totals recorded

PROCESSING DATA FROM A JOURNAL ENTRIES INPUT FORM

A keyboard entry tells the computer that a journal entry is to be recorded. Spaces for entering data from a journal entries input form are displayed on the computer monitor. Journal entry data are then key-entered one line at a time.

After all lines on the input forms have been key-entered and processed, a journal entries report is prepared as shown in Illustration 7-7.

Illustration 7-7
Journal entries report

```
RUN DATE 07/02/88                      COMPUTEX
                          JOURNAL ENTRIES BATCH NUMBER 2

-----------------------------------------------------------------------
  SEQ.              DOCUMENT    VENDOR/
  NO.    DAY        NUMBER      CUSTOMER                   DEBIT      CREDIT
-----------------------------------------------------------------------
  002    01         P267        215
         5105-1     PURCHASES--HARDWARE                  13475.50
         2105       ACCOUNTS PAYABLE                                13475.50

  003    01         DM25        245
         2105       ACCOUNTS PAYABLE                       250.00
         5110-2     PURCHASES RETURNS AND ALLOW.--SOFTWARE            250.00

  004    01         C246
         6115-1     SALARY EXPENSE--HARDWARE              3690.00
         6115-2     SALARY EXPENSE--SOFTWARE              3200.00
         6240       SALARY EXPENSE--ADMINISTRATIVE        1810.00
         2110       EMPLOYEES INCOME TAX PAYABLE--FED.                860.20
         2115       EMPLOYEES INCOME TAX PAYABLE--STATE               496.30
         2125       FICA TAX PAYABLE                                  609.00
         2145       HOSPITAL INSURANCE PREMIUMS PAYABLE               162.00
         2150       LIFE INSURANCE PREMIUMS PAYABLE                   120.00
         1105       CASH                                             6452.50

  005    01         C247        250
         2105       ACCOUNTS PAYABLE                      7690.00
         1105       CASH                                             7536.20
         5115-1     PURCHASES DISCOUNT--HARDWARE                      153.80


  009    02         S88         115
         1115       ACCOUNTS RECEIVABLE                   1312.50
         2130       SALES TAX PAYABLE                                 62.50
         4105-1     SALES--HARDWARE                                 1250.00

  010    02         CM38        150
         2130       SALES TAX PAYABLE                       44.75
         4110-2     SALES RETURNS AND ALLOW.--SOFTWARE      895.00
         1115       ACCOUNTS RECEIVABLE                               939.75

  011    02         R79         130
         1105       CASH                                  1893.36
         2130       SALES TAX PAYABLE                         1.84
         4115-1     SALES DISCOUNT--HARDWARE                 36.80
         1115       ACCOUNTS RECEIVABLE                              1932.00

  012    02         T2
         1105       CASH                                 10710.00
         2130       SALES TAX PAYABLE                                 510.00
         4105-1     SALES--HARDWARE                                  7840.00
         4105-2     SALES--SOFTWARE                                  2360.00
                                                         ------------ ------------
                    TOTALS                               47107.45    47107.45

                                                         ============ ============
           IN BALANCE
```

A journal entries report is checked for accuracy by comparing the report totals, $47,107.45, with the batch totals on the last page of the journal entries input form, $47,107.45. As the totals are the same, the journal entries report is assumed to be correct.

QUESTIONS FOR INDIVIDUAL STUDY

1. What are the major differences in the recording and posting procedures between a manual and an automated accounting system?
2. What accounts are affected, and how, by a departmental purchase on account?
3. When is the total number of pages recorded on a journal entries input form?
4. What accounts are affected, and how, by a departmental purchases return or allowance?
5. What accounts are affected, and how, by a departmental cash payment on account?
6. What accounts are affected, and how, by a cash payment for office supplies?
7. What accounts are affected, and how, by a cash payment for an expense?
8. Why are no partial entries recorded on a

page of journal entries input form?
9. Always recording sales at the time of sale, regardless of when payment is received, is an application of which accounting concept?
10. What accounts are affected, and how, by a departmental sale on account?
11. What accounts are affected, and how, by a departmental sales return or allowance?
12. What accounts are affected, and how, by a departmental cash receipt on account?
13. What accounts are affected, and how, by departmental cash and credit card sales?
14. Why are the two totals recorded at the bottom of a journal entries input form compared?
15. How is a journal entries report checked for accuracy?

CASE FOR MANAGEMENT DECISION

CASE 1 Soundcenter sells a complete line of records and tapes. Soundcenter uses an automated departmentalized accounting system. All transactions are recorded on a journal entries input form similar to the one used by Computex in this chapter. The manager suggests that the journal entries input form be redesigned to more closely match the special journal used in manual accounting. The manager feels that the input form would be easier to read if an account title column and special amount columns were included. The accountant disagrees with the manager's suggestion. With whom do you agree? Why?

APPLICATION PROBLEMS

PROBLEM 7-1   Recording departmental purchases on account and purchases returns and allowances

Garcia's Western Fashions, Inc., has two departments: Boots and Coats. A partial general ledger chart of accounts and a partial vendor list are given on the following page.

General Ledger Chart of Accounts	Vendor List

General Ledger Chart of Accounts

2105 Accounts Payable
5105-1 Purchases—Boots
5105-2 Purchases—Coats
5110-1 Purchases Returns and
       Allowances—Boots
5110-2 Purchases Returns and
       Allowances—Coats

Vendor List

210 Antonio Footwear, Inc.
215 Carthage Leather Co.
220 R & R Western Wear
230 Western Apparel, Inc.
240 Yates Western Footwear

Instructions: 1. Record the following selected transactions on a journal entries input form. Use August 6 of the current year as the run date. Batch No. 1. Source documents are abbreviated as follows: debit memorandum, DM; purchase invoice, P.

Aug. 1. Purchased coats on account from R & R Western Wear, $1,250.00. P182.
    1. Purchased boots on account from Yates Western Footwear, $1,635.00. P183.
    2. Purchased boots on account from Antonio Footwear, Inc., $860.00. P184.
    3. Returned defective coats to Western Apparel, Inc., $427.00, from P176. DM26.
    3. Purchased coats on account from Carthage Leather Co., $1,480.00. P185.
    4. Returned defective boots to Antonio Footwear, Inc., $216.00, from P179. DM27.
    5. Returned defective coats to R & R Western Wear, $346.00, from P182. DM28.
    5. Purchased boots on account from Yates Western Footwear, $735.00. P186.
    6. Returned defective boots to Antonio Footwear, Inc., $135.00, from P184. DM29.

  2. Total the Debit and Credit columns. Prove the equality of debits and credits.

PROBLEM 7-2 Recording departmental cash payments

Broden Computers, Inc., has two departments: Hardware and Software. A partial general ledger chart of accounts and a partial vendor list are given below.

General Ledger Chart of Accounts	Vendor List

General Ledger Chart of Accounts

1105 Cash
1135 Supplies—Store
2105 Accounts Payable
2110 Employees Income Tax
       Payable—Federal
2115 Employees Income Tax
       Payable—State
2125 FICA Tax Payable
2145 Hospital Insurance Premiums
       Payable
2150 Life Insurance Premiums
       Payable
5115-1 Purchases Discount—Hardware
5115-2 Purchases Discount—Software
6105 Advertising Expense
6115-1 Salary Expense—Hardware
6115-2 Salary Expense—Software
6225 Miscellaneous Expense
6240 Salary Expense—Administrative

Vendor List

210 Bentley Computer Products
220 Computer Software, Inc.
225 Kramer Computers
230 United Software
240 Wesley Computing, Inc.

Instructions: 1. Record the following selected transactions on a journal entries input form. A 2% purchases discount is allowed for prompt payment. Use October 15 of the current year as the run date. Batch No. 2. Source documents are abbreviated as follows: check, C; debit memorandum, DM; purchase invoice, P.

Oct. 10. Paid for advertising, $138.00. C221.
  10. Paid on account to United Software, $1,225.00, covering P188 for software, $1,250.00, less 2% discount, $25.00. C222.
  11. Paid on account to Bentley Computer Products, $8,192.80, covering P189 for hardware, $8,360.00, less 2% discount, $167.20. C223.
  12. Bought store supplies for cash, $115.00. C224.
  12. Paid on account to Computer Software, Inc., $637.00, covering P190 for software, $650.00, less 2% discount, $13.00. C225.
  13. Paid on account to Kramer Computers, $9,643.20, covering P191 for hardware, $9,840.00, less 2% discount, $196.80. C226.
  14. Paid miscellaneous expense, $88.00. C227.
  15. Replenished petty cash. Charge the following accounts: Supplies—Store, $110.00; Advertising Expense, $93.00; Miscellaneous Expense, $101.00; total, $304.00. C228.
  15. Paid on account to Wesley Computing, Inc., $12,877.20, covering P192 for hardware, $13,640.00, less DM31, $500.00, and less 2% discount, $262.80. C229.

2. Total the Debit and Credit columns. Prove the equality of debits and credits.
3. Continue recording the following Batch No. 2 transactions on a journal entries input form.

Oct. 15. Paid semimonthly payroll: hardware, $3,820.00; software, $3,580.00; administrative, $2,040.00 (less deductions: employees' income tax—federal, $1,260.30; employees' income tax—state, $506.20; FICA tax, $660.80; hospital insurance, $192.00; life insurance, $136.00); total, $6,684.70. C230.
  15. Bought store supplies for cash, $93.00. C231.

4. Total the Debit and Credit columns. Prove the equality of debits and credits.

PROBLEM 7-3   Recording departmental sales on account and sales returns and allowances

Quality Office Products has two departments: Furniture and Typewriters. A partial general ledger chart of accounts and a partial customer list are given below.

General Ledger Chart of Accounts		Customer List	
1115	Accounts Receivable	110	Marion Aden
2130	Sales Tax Payable	120	Bonita Caldwell
4105-1	Sales—Furniture	130	William Geyer
4105-2	Sales—Typewriters	135	Jennie Miles
4110-1	Sales Returns and Allowances—Furniture	140	Larry Tipson
4110-2	Sales Returns and Allowances—Typewriters		

Instructions: 1. Record the following selected transactions on a journal entries input form. A 5% sales tax is charged on all sales. Use March 19 of the current year as the run date. Batch No. 3. Source documents are abbreviated as follows: credit memorandum, CM; sales invoice, S.

Mar. 14. Sold furniture on account to William Geyer, $380.00, plus sales tax, $19.00. S138.
  14. Sold furniture on account to Jennie Miles, $1,240.00, plus sales tax, $62.00. S139.
  15. Granted credit to Marion Aden for a typewriter returned, $280.00, plus sales tax, $14.00, from S134. CM27.
  16. Sold a typewriter on account to Bonita Caldwell, $650.00, plus sales tax, $32.50. S140.
  16. Sold furniture on account to Larry Tipson, $185.00, plus sales tax, $9.25. S141.

17. Granted credit to Jennie Miles for furniture returned, $225.00, plus sales tax, $11.25, from S139. CM28.
18. Granted credit to William Geyer for furniture returned, $150.00, plus sales tax, $7.50, from S138. CM29.
19. Sold a typewriter on account to Marion Aden, $750.00, plus sales tax, $37.50. S142.

2. Total the Debit and Credit columns. Prove the equality of debits and credits.

PROBLEM 7-4   Recording departmental cash receipts

Schaefer's Floor Covering, Inc., has two departments: Carpet and Linoleum. A partial general ledger chart of accounts and a partial customer list are given below.

General Ledger Chart of Accounts	Customer List
1105 Cash	110 Laurie Ames
1115 Accounts Receivable	115 David Coyne
2130 Sales Tax Payable	120 Bertha Gomez
4105-1 Sales — Carpet	130 Ronald Price
4105-2 Sales — Linoleum	
4115-1 Sales Discount — Carpet	
4115-2 Sales Discount — Linoleum	

Instructions: 1. Record the following selected transactions on a journal entries input form. Use February 6 of the current year as the run date. Batch No. 1. A 5% sales tax is charged on all sales. A 2% sales discount is granted to customers for early payment of their accounts. Source documents are abbreviated as follows: credit memorandum, CM; receipt, R; sales invoice, S; cash register tape, T.

Feb. 1. Received on account from Ronald Price, $1,646.40, covering S82 for carpet ($1,600.00 plus sales tax, $80.00) less 2% discount, $32.00, and less sales tax, $1.60. R45.
  1. Received on account from Bertha Gomez, $2,469.60, covering S85 for carpet ($2,400.00 plus sales tax, $120.00) less 2% discount, $48.00, and less sales tax, $2.40. R46.
  2. Received on account from Laurie Ames, $987.84, covering S83 for linoleum ($960.00 plus sales tax, $48.00) less 2% discount, $19.20, and less sales tax, $0.96. R47.
  4. Received on account from David Coyne, $1,378.86, covering S84 for linoleum ($1,340.00 plus sales tax, $67.00) less 2% discount, $26.80, and less sales tax, $1.34. R48.
  5. Received on account from Bertha Gomez, $3,045.84, covering S86 for carpet ($3,260.00 plus sales tax, $163.00) less CM22 ($300.00 plus sales tax, $15.00), less 2% discount, $59.20, and less sales tax, $2.96. R49.
  6. Recorded cash and credit card sales for February 1–6: carpet, $4,620.00; linoleum, $3,360.00; plus sales tax, $399.00. T6.

2. Total the Debit and Credit columns. Prove the equality of debits and credits.

ENRICHMENT PROBLEMS

MASTERY PROBLEM 7-M   Recording departmental business transactions

Pelican Marine, Inc., has two departments: Boats and Motors. A 2% purchases discount is allowed for prompt payment. A 5% sales tax is charged on all sales. A 2% sales discount is granted to customers for early payment of their accounts. A partial general ledger chart of accounts, and partial customer and vendor lists are given on the following page.

General Ledger Chart of Accounts

1105	Cash	4110-2	Sales Returns and
1115	Accounts Receivable		Allowances—Motors
1135	Supplies—Store	4115-1	Sales Discount—Boats
2105	Accounts Payable	4115-2	Sales Discount—Motors
2110	Employees Income Tax	5105-1	Purchases—Boats
	Payable—Federal	5105-2	Purchases—Motors
2115	Employees Income Tax	5110-1	Purchases Returns and
	Payable—State		Allowances—Boats
2125	FICA Tax Payable	5110-2	Purchases Returns and
2130	Sales Tax Payable		Allowances—Motors
2145	Hospital Insurance Premiums	5115-1	Purchases Discount—Boats
	Payable	5115-2	Purchases Discount—Motors
2150	Life Insurance Premiums	6105	Advertising Expense
	Payable	6115-1	Salary Expense—Boats
4105-1	Sales—Boats	6115-2	Salary Expense—Motors
4105-2	Sales—Motors	6225	Miscellaneous Expense
4110-1	Sales Returns and	6235	Rent Expense
	Allowances—Boats	6240	Salary Expense—Administrative

Customer List		Vendor List	
110	Deborah Aneed	210	Anchor Boats, Inc.
120	George Bland	220	Condor Enterprises
130	Lori Devine	230	Donzi Boats
140	Ricardo Loseth	240	Portman Motors, Inc.
150	Wendy Therman	250	Sear-Gear Co.

Instructions: 1. Record the following selected transactions on journal entries input forms. Use November 5 of the current year as the run date. Batch No. 1. Source documents are abbreviated as follows: check, C; credit memorandum, CM; debit memorandum, DM; purchase invoice, P; receipt, R; sales invoice, S; and cash register tape, T.

Nov. 1. Paid November rent, $1,200.00. C310.
   1. Paid semimonthly payroll: boats, $3,160.00; motors, $3,380.00; administrative, $2,190.00 (less deductions: employees' income tax—federal, $760.20; employees' income tax—state, $374.20; FICA tax, $611.10; hospital insurance, $148.00; life insurance, $102.00); total, $6,734.50. C311.
   1. Purchased boats on account from Donzi Boats, $3,860.00. P140.
   1. Purchased motors on account from Sear-Gear Co., $4,620.00. P141.
   2. Returned defective motor to Portman Motors, Inc., $1,275.00, from P138. DM22.
   2. Sold boats on account to Lori Devine, $850.00, plus sales tax, $42.50. S246.
   2. Paid on account to Condor Enterprises, $1,646.40, covering P135 for a motor, $1,680.00, less 2% discount, $33.60. C312.
   2. Bought store supplies for cash, $86.00. C313.
   3. Sold a motor on account to Ricardo Loseth, $1,120.00, plus sales tax, $56.00. S247.
   3. Received on account from Deborah Aneed, $2,932.65, covering S240 for a boat ($2,850.00 plus sales tax, $142.50) less 2% discount, $57.00, and less sales tax, $2.85. R209.
   4. Granted credit to Lori Devine for boat returned, $100.00, plus sales tax, $5.00, from S246. CM19.
   5. Recorded cash and credit card sales for November 1–5: boats, $16,520.00; motors, $11,850.00; plus sales tax, $1,418.50. T5.

2. Total the Debit and Credit columns. Prove the equality of debits and credits.

3. Record the following selected transactions on a journal entries input form. Use November 12 of the current year as the run date. Batch No. 2.

Nov. 7. Purchased motors on account from Portman Motors, Inc., $14,920.00. P142.

9. Returned defective boat to Donzi Boats, $1,150.00, from P140. DM23.

10. Replenished petty cash. Charge the following accounts: Supplies—Store, $135.00; Advertising Expense, $93.00; Miscellaneous Expense, $86.00; total, $314.00. C314.

11. Paid on account to Donzi Boats, $2,655.80, covering P140 for boats, $3,860.00, less DM23, $1,150.00, and less 2% discount, $54.20. C315.

11. Paid on account to Sear-Gear Co., $4,527.60, covering P141 for motors, $4,620.00, less 2% discount, $92.40. C316.

12. Received on account from Lori Devine, $771.75, covering S246 for boats ($850.00 plus sales tax, $42.50) less CM19 ($100.00 plus sales tax, $5.00), less 2% discount, $15.00, and less sales tax, $0.75. R210.

12. Recorded cash and credit card sales for November 7–12: boats, $14,920.00; motors, $9,850.00; plus sales tax, $1,238.50. T12.

4. Total the Debit and Credit columns. Prove the equality of debits and credits.

CHALLENGE PROBLEM 7-C   Recording departmental business transactions

Zicaro's Home Center has two departments: Hardware and Plumbing. A 2% purchases discount is allowed for prompt payment. A 5% sales tax is charged on all sales. A 2% sales discount is granted to customers for early payment of their accounts. A partial general ledger chart of accounts, and partial customer and vendor lists are given below.

General Ledger Chart of Accounts

1105	Cash	4115-1	Sales Discount—Hardware
1115	Accounts Receivable	4115-2	Sales Discount—Plumbing
2105	Accounts Payable	5105-1	Purchases—Hardware
2130	Sales Tax Payable	5105-2	Purchases—Plumbing
4105-1	Sales—Hardware	5110-1	Purchases Returns and
4105-2	Sales—Plumbing		Allowances—Hardware
4110-1	Sales Returns and	5110-2	Purchases Returns and
	Allowances—Hardware		Allowances—Plumbing
4110-2	Sales Returns and	5115-1	Purchases Discount—Hardware
	Allowances—Plumbing	5115-2	Purchases Discount—Plumbing

Customer List

110	Mark Benrod
120	Melody Gardy
130	Frank Wells

Vendor List

210	Ace Plumbing Supplies
220	Dependable Hardware Co.
230	Gilco Hardware Products

Instructions: 1. Record the following selected transactions on a journal entries input form. Use August 27 of the current year as the run date. Batch No. 4. Source documents are abbreviated as follows: check, C; credit memorandum, CM; debit memorandum, DM; and receipt, R.

Aug. 22. Returned defective hardware to Dependable Hardware Co., $776.00. DM38.

23. Paid on account to Ace Plumbing Supplies, covering P118 for plumbing, $1,235.00, less discount. C273.

24. Granted credit to Melody Gardy for plumbing returned, $50.00, plus sales tax, from S195. CM27.

25. Received on account from Mark Benrod, covering S193 for hardware ($720.00 plus sales tax) less discount, and less sales tax. R152.
26. Received on account from Frank Wells, covering S190 for plumbing ($950.00 plus sales tax) less CM26 ($150.00 plus sales tax), less discount, and less sales tax. R153.
27. Paid on account to Gilco Hardware Products, covering P119 for hardware, $2,150.00, less DM36, $325.00, and less discount. C274.

2. Total the Debit and Credit columns. Prove the equality of debits and credits.

Computer Application 2
Automated Accounting Cycle for a Departmentalized Business: Recording and Posting Business Transactions

The journal entries input forms completed in Mastery Problem 7-M, Chapter 7, are needed to complete Computer Application 2.

Pelican Marine, Inc., completed the journal entries input forms needed to record business transactions for its automated departmentalized accounting system. Computer Application 2 provides for the use of a microcomputer to input and process the data from the completed forms. Chapter 7 describes the manual and computer operations required to record and process business transactions in an automated departmentalized accounting system.

COMPUTER APPLICATION PROBLEM

COMPUTER APPLICATION PROBLEM 2   Recording and posting business transactions

Instructions: 1. Load the Systems Selection Menu from the *Advanced Automated Accounting* diskette according to the instructions for the computer being used. Select Problem CA-2. The general ledger chart of accounts, vendor and customer lists, and opening balances are stored on the template diskette.

2. Key-enter the journal entries from the journal entries input forms completed in Mastery Problem 7-M, Batch No. 1.

3. Display/Print the journal entries report for Batch No. 1. Check the accuracy by comparing the report totals with the totals on the input form.

4. Key-enter the journal entries from the journal entries input form completed in Mastery Problem 7-M, Batch No. 2.

5. Display/Print the journal entries report for Batch No. 2. Check the accuracy by comparing the report totals with the totals on the input form.

8 End-of-Fiscal-Period Work in an Automated Accounting System

ENABLING PERFORMANCE TASKS

After studying Chapter 8, you will be able to:

a. Identify accounting concepts and practices related to end-of-fiscal-period work in an automated departmentalized accounting system.
b. Plan adjusting entries needed to update general ledger account balances.
c. Record adjusting entries on a journal entries input form.

The general ledger stored on secondary storage in an automated accounting system contains valuable decision-making data. To be useful however these data must be summarized and reported in the form of financial statements. Financial statements must contain all pertinent information essential for a reader's understanding of a business' financial status. *(CONCEPT: Adequate Disclosure)*

PREPARING END-OF-FISCAL-PERIOD REPORTS IN AN AUTOMATED ACCOUNTING SYSTEM

In manual accounting, end-of-fiscal-period reports are prepared from data stored in general and subsidiary ledgers as described in Chapter 5 for Supergolf. In automated accounting, end-of-fiscal-period reports are prepared by a computer using instructions in computer software. Keyboard entries tell the computer which reports to print. The run date used for all end-of-fiscal-period reports is the ending date of the fiscal period.

PROCESSING A TRIAL BALANCE

A trial balance is prepared to prove the equality of debits and credits in the general ledger and to use for planning adjustments. Computex's trial balance for July 31, 1988, is shown in Illustration 8-1. Debits equal credits on the trial balance. Therefore, Computex's general ledger is in balance and assumed to be correct.

Illustration 8-1
Trial balance

```
RUN DATE 07/31/88                    COMPUTEX
                                   TRIAL BALANCE
-----------------------------------------------------------------------
ACCOUNT      ACCOUNT
NUMBER       TITLE                                  DEBIT        CREDIT
-----------------------------------------------------------------------
1105         CASH                                 71602.70
1110         PETTY CASH                             600.00
1115         ACCOUNTS RECEIVABLE                  23067.90
1120         ALLOWANCE FOR UNCOLLECTIBLE ACCOUNTS                110.30
1125-1       MERCHANDISE INVENTORY--HARDWARE     323465.00
1125-2       MERCHANDISE INVENTORY--SOFTWARE     103365.50
1130         SUPPLIES--OFFICE                     11260.40
1135         SUPPLIES--STORE                      11420.30
1140         PREPAID INSURANCE                     3600.00
1205         COMPUTER EQUIPMENT                   18320.00
1210         ACCUM. DEPR.--COMPUTER EQUIPMENT                  1800.00
1215         OFFICE EQUIPMENT                     22640.00
1220         ACCUM. DEPR.--OFFICE EQUIPMENT                   10940.00
1225         STORE EQUIPMENT                      28920.00
1230         ACCUM. DEPR.--STORE EQUIPMENT                     9620.00
2105         ACCOUNTS PAYABLE                                 26608.90
2110         EMPLOYEES INCOME TAX PAYABLE--FED.                1630.40
2115         EMPLOYEES INCOME TAX PAYABLE--STATE                980.20
2125         FICA TAX PAYABLE                                  2424.80
2130         SALES TAX PAYABLE                                 3773.90
2135         UNEMPLOYMENT TAX PAYABLE--FEDERAL                  138.50
2140         UNEMPLOYMENT TAX PAYABLE--STATE                    935.25
2145         HOSPITAL INSURANCE PREMIUMS PAYABLE                324.00
2150         LIFE INSURANCE PREMIUMS PAYABLE                    240.00
3105         CAPITAL STOCK                                   400000.00
3110         RETAINED EARNINGS                               141830.50
4105-1       SALES--HARDWARE                                  51860.60
4105-2       SALES--SOFTWARE                                  27750.30
4110-1       SALES RETURNS AND ALLOW.--HARDWARE    2340.10
4110-2       SALES RETURNS AND ALLOW.--SOFTWARE     920.30
4115-1       SALES DISCOUNT--HARDWARE               580.40
4115-2       SALES DISCOUNT--SOFTWARE               310.00
5105-1       PURCHASES--HARDWARE                  28820.70
5105-2       PURCHASES--SOFTWARE                  11580.80
5110-1       PURCHASES RETURNS AND ALLOW.--HARDWARE            2710.10
5110-2       PURCHASES RETURNS AND ALLOW.--SOFTWARE           1140.60
5115-1       PURCHASES DISCOUNT--HARDWARE                      510.40
5115-2       PURCHASES DISCOUNT--SOFTWARE                      223.80
6105         ADVERTISING EXPENSE                    436.10
6108         CREDIT CARD FEE EXPENSE                630.00
6115-1       SALARY EXPENSE--HARDWARE              7500.00
6115-2       SALARY EXPENSE--SOFTWARE             6200.00
6225         MISCELLANEOUS EXPENSE                  465.30
6230         PAYROLL TAXES EXPENSE                 2286.15
6235         RENT EXPENSE                          1600.00
6240         SALARY EXPENSE--ADMINISTRATIVE        3620.00
                                                 ------------  ------------
             TOTALS                              685551.65     685551.65
                                                 ============  ============
```

PROCESSING SUBSIDIARY LEDGER SCHEDULES

Computex prepares subsidiary ledger schedules at the end of each fiscal period. These schedules are prepared to prove the accuracy of vendor and customer accounts and the controlling accounts in the general ledger.

Computex's schedule of accounts payable on July 31, 1988, is shown in Illustration 8-2.

```
RUN DATE 07/31/88                     COMPUTEX
                            SCHEDULE OF ACCOUNTS PAYABLE


        -----------------------------------------------------------

         VENDOR    VENDOR
         NUMBER    NAME                              AMOUNT
        -----------------------------------------------------------
          210      ABBOTT SOFTWARE COMPANY           4370.60
          215      COMPUTER PRODUCTS, INC.           3000.00
          220      GARDNER OFFICE SUPPLIES            460.10
          230      INTERNATIONAL COMPUTERS           6340.50
          240      MARTIN'S OFFICE PRODUCTS           327.40
          245      STAR SOFTWARE, INC.               1600.00
          250      UNITED COMPUTER SYSTEMS          10510.30
                                                   ---------
                   TOTAL ACCOUNTS PAYABLE          26608.90
                                                   =========
```

Illustration 8-2
Schedule of accounts
payable

The schedule of accounts payable total must equal the balance of the general ledger controlling account, Accounts Payable. The balance of Accounts Payable on the trial balance and the total of the schedule of accounts payable are the same, $26,608.90. Therefore, the schedule of accounts payable is assumed to be correct.

Computex's schedule of accounts receivable on July 31, 1988, is shown in Illustration 8-3.

The schedule of accounts receivable total must equal the balance of the general ledger controlling account, Accounts Receivable. The balance of Accounts Receivable on the trial balance and the total of the schedule of accounts receivable are the same, $23,067.90. Therefore, the schedule of accounts receivable is assumed to be correct.

```
RUN DATE 07/31/88                         COMPUTEX
                              SCHEDULE OF ACCOUNTS RECEIVABLE

      --------------------------------------------------------------
      CUSTOMER    CUSTOMER
      NUMBER      NAME                               AMOUNT
      --------------------------------------------------------------
       110        MARY ABLER                        3360.00
       115        CHARLES BAXTER                      945.00
       120        JOAN DALY                          1968.75
       130        GATOR FURNITURE CO.               10101.00
       140        MARTHA SEGER                       1323.55
       150        TAFT SPORTING GOODS                1200.40
       160        HUBERT VERRICO                     4169.20
                                                 --------------
                  TOTAL ACCOUNTS RECEIVABLE        23067.90
                                                 ==============
```

Illustration 8-3
Schedule of accounts
receivable

UPDATING GENERAL LEDGER ACCOUNTS

At the end of a fiscal period, some general ledger accounts do not contain up-to-date balances. Adjusting entries are made to bring these general ledger account balances up to date.

Recording adjusting entries

Computex plans needed adjustments using the trial balance. Computex analyzes adjusting entries in the same way as described in Chapter 5. The adjusting entries are recorded on a journal entries input form.

Batch No. 1 was used to record the division of the merchandise inventory account balance as described in Chapter 6. Batch Nos. 2 through 6 were used to record weekly transactions as described in Chapter 7. Therefore, the next consecutive batch number, 7, is used to record the adjusting entries.

Bad debts expense adjustment. Computex estimates that the bad debts expense for the monthly fiscal period ended July 31, 1988, is $461.35. *(CONCEPT: Matching Expenses with Revenue)* Bad Debts Expense is increased by a $461.35 debit. Allowance for Uncollectible Accounts, a contra asset account, is increased by a $461.35 credit. This adjusting entry is on lines 1 and 2 of the journal entries input form shown in Illustration 8-4.

	BATCH NO. 7			JOURNAL ENTRIES		
	RUN DATE 07/31 /88			Input Form	PAGE 1 OF 1 PAGES	
	MM DD YY					

	1	2	3	4	5	6	
	DAY	DOC. NO.	VENDOR/ CUSTOMER NO.	GENERAL LEDGER ACCT. NO.	DEBIT	CREDIT	
1	31	Adj.Ent.		6205	461 35		1
2				1120		461 35	2
3				3120-1	2540 30		3
4				1125-1		2540 30	4
5				3120-2	3441 40		5
6				1125-2		3441 40	6
7				6245	580 50		7
8				1130		580 50	8
9				6120	740 00		9
10				1135		740 00	10
11				6220	360 00		11
12				1140		360 00	12
13				6210	200 00		13
14				1210		200 00	14
15				6215	330 00		15
16				1220		330 00	16
17				6110	300 00		17
18				1230		300 00	18
19				9105	1812 50		19
20				2120		1812 50	20
25							25
				PAGE TOTALS			
				BATCH TOTALS	10766 05	10766 05	

Illustration 8-4
Journal entries input form with adjusting entries recorded

The batch number, 7, the run date, 07/31/88, and the page number, 1, are written in the spaces provided at the top of the journal entries input form.

The day, 31, is recorded in the Day column, line 1. The day is recorded only on the first line for a group of adjusting entries. The abbreviation for adjusting entries, Adj. Ent., is recorded in the Doc. No. column. The abbreviation is recorded only on the first line for a group of adjusting entries. The Vendor/Customer No. column is left blank for adjusting entries. The account number for Bad Debts Expense, 6205, is entered in the General Ledger Acct. No. column. The amount debited to Bad Debts Expense, $461.35, is written in the Debit column.

On line 2, the account number for Allowance for Uncollectible Accounts, *1120*, is written in the General Ledger Acct. No. column. The amount credited to Allowance for Uncollectible Accounts, *$461.35*, is recorded in the Credit column.

Merchandise inventory adjustments. Computex uses two income summary accounts to adjust the two merchandise inventory accounts at the end of a fiscal period. The adjusting entries for the merchandise inventory accounts are shown on lines 3 through 6, Illustration 8-4.

The merchandise inventory — hardware account balance shown on the trial balance, Illustration 8-1, is $323,465.00. The estimated value of the hardware merchandise on July 31, 1988, is $320,924.70.

Income Summary — Hardware is debited for $2,540.30. Merchandise Inventory — Hardware is decreased by a $2,540.30 credit. This adjusting entry is on lines 3 and 4.

The merchandise inventory — software account balance shown on the trial balance is $103,365.50. The estimated value of the software merchandise on July 31, 1988, is $99,924.10.

Income Summary — Software is debited for $3,441.40. Merchandise Inventory — Software is decreased by a $3,441.40 credit. This adjusting entry is on lines 5 and 6.

Supplies inventory adjustments. Before adjustments, a supplies account balance includes (a) the beginning account balance, and (b) the cost of supplies bought during the fiscal period. A supplies account balance must be adjusted to reflect the value of any supplies used, an operating expense, during a fiscal period. *(CONCEPT: Matching Expenses with Revenue)* The adjusting entries for the supplies accounts are shown on lines 7 through 10, Illustration 8-4.

The supplies — office account balance shown on the trial balance, Illustration 8-1, is $11,260.40. The value of office supplies on hand on July 31, 1988, is $10,679.90.

Supplies Expense — Office is increased by a $580.50 debit. Supplies — Office is decreased by a $580.50 credit. This adjusting entry is on lines 7 and 8.

The supplies — store account balance shown on the trial balance is $11,420.30. The value of store supplies on hand on July 31, 1988, is $10,680.30.

Supplies Expense — Store is increased by a $740.00 debit. Supplies — Store is decreased by a $740.00 credit. This adjusting entry is on lines 9 and 10.

Prepaid insurance adjustment. Before adjustments, a prepaid insurance account balance includes (a) the beginning account balance, and (b) the value of insurance premiums paid during the fiscal period. The account balance must be adjusted to reflect the value of insurance used during the fiscal period. *(CONCEPT: Matching Expenses with Revenue)*

The prepaid insurance account balance shown on the trial balance, Illustration 8-1, is $3,600.00. Computex determines that on July 31, 1988, the amount of unexpired prepaid insurance is $3,240.00. The difference between these two amounts, $360.00, is the insurance expense for the fiscal period.

Insurance Expense is increased by a $360.00 debit. Prepaid Insurance is decreased by a $360.00 credit. This adjusting entry is on lines 11 and 12, Illustration 8-4.

Depreciation expense adjustments. Computex's estimated monthly depreciation expenses are: computer equipment, $200.00; office equipment, $330.00; store equipment, $300.00. The adjusting entries for depreciation expense are shown on lines 13 through 18, Illustration 8-4.

Depreciation Expense—Computer Equipment is increased by a $200.00 debit. Accumulated Depreciation—Computer Equipment is increased by a $200.00 credit. This adjusting entry is on lines 13 and 14.

Depreciation Expense—Office Equipment is increased by a $330.00 debit. Accumulated Depreciation—Office Equipment is increased by a $330.00 credit. This adjusting entry is on lines 15 and 16.

Depreciation Expense—Store Equipment is increased by a $300.00 debit. Accumulated Depreciation—Store Equipment is increased by a $300.00 credit. This adjusting entry is on lines 17 and 18.

Federal income tax adjustment. An adjustment is needed at the end of each monthly fiscal period to record the estimated monthly federal income tax. Computex estimates that the federal income tax amount for the month is $1,812.50.

Federal Income Tax is increased by a $1,812.50 debit. Federal Income Tax Payable is increased by a $1,812.50 credit. This adjusting entry is on lines 19 and 20, Illustration 8-4.

After all adjusting entries have been recorded, Computex totals the Debit and Credit columns. As the adjusting entries are recorded on a single page, the totals are recorded as Batch Totals in the space provided at the bottom of the journal entries input form.

The two totals are compared to assure the equality of debits and credits. Because the two totals are the same, $10,766.05, the adjusting entries on the input form are assumed to be correct. The number of pages in the batch, 1, is recorded in the space provided at the top of the input form.

Processing adjusting entries

A keyboard entry tells the computer that a journal entry is to be recorded. Spaces for entering data from a journal entries input form are displayed on the computer monitor. After all lines on the input form have been key-entered and processed, a journal entries report is printed. The journal entries report for Computex's adjusting entries is shown in Illustration 8-5.

```
RUN DATE 07/31/88                    COMPUTEX
                          JOURNAL ENTRIES BATCH NUMBER 7
--------------------------------------------------------------------------------
SEQ.            DOCUMENT    VENDOR/
NO.    DAY      NUMBER      CUSTOMER                     DEBIT         CREDIT
--------------------------------------------------------------------------------
060    31       ADJ.ENT.
       6205     BAD DEBTS EXPENSE                        461.35
       1120     ALLOWANCE FOR UNCOLLECTIBLE ACCOUNTS                    461.35
       3120-1   INCOME SUMMARY--HARDWARE               2540.30
       1125-1   MERCHANDISE INVENTORY--HARDWARE                       2540.30
       3120-2   INCOME SUMMARY--SOFTWARE               3441.40
       1125-2   MERCHANDISE INVENTORY--SOFTWARE                       3441.40
       6245     SUPPLIES EXPENSE--OFFICE                580.50
       1130     SUPPLIES--OFFICE                                       580.50
       6120     SUPPLIES EXPENSE--STORE                 740.00
       1135     SUPPLIES--STORE                                        740.00

061    31       ADJ.ENT.
       6220     INSURANCE EXPENSE                       360.00
       1140     PREPAID INSURANCE                                      360.00
       6210     DEPRECIATION EXPENSE--COMPUTER EQUIP.   200.00
       1210     ACCUM. DEPR.--COMPUTER EQUIPMENT                       200.00
       6215     DEPRECIATION EXPENSE--OFFICE EQUIP.     330.00
       1220     ACCUM. DEPR.--OFFICE EQUIPMENT                         330.00
       6110     DEPRECIATION EXPENSE--STORE EQUIPMENT   300.00
       1230     ACCUM. DEPR.--STORE EQUIPMENT                          300.00
       9105     FEDERAL INCOME TAX                     1812.50
       2120     FEDERAL INCOME TAX PAYABLE                            1812.50
                                                     ------------  ------------
                TOTALS                                 10766.05      10766.05

                                                     ============  ============
                IN BALANCE
```

A journal entries report is checked for accuracy by comparing the report totals, $10,766.05, with the totals on the journal entries input form, $10,766.05. As the totals are the same, the journal entries report for adjusting entries is assumed to be correct.

Illustration 8-5
Journal entries report for adjusting entries

PROCESSING FINANCIAL STATEMENTS

After the adjusting entries have been key-entered and processed, Computex uses the computer to prepare financial statements.

Departmental statements of gross profit

Computex's departmental statements of gross profit for the month ended July 31, 1988, are shown in Illustration 8-6.

```
                              COMPUTEX
                 DEPARTMENT 1 STATEMENT OF GROSS PROFIT
                      FOR MONTH ENDED 07/31/88
                                                              % OF NET
      S A L E S                                                SALES
      ---------                                                --------

      SALES--HARDWARE                            51860.60
      SALES RETURNS AND ALLOW.--HARDWARE         -2340.10
      SALES DISCOUNT--HARDWARE                    -580.40
                                                ------------
      NET SALES                                              48940.10    100

      C O S T   O F   M D S E .   S O L D
      ------------------------------------------
      BEGINNING INVENTORY                       323465.00
      PURCHASES--HARDWARE                        28820.70
      PURCHASES RETURNS AND ALLOW.--HARDWARE     -2710.10
      PURCHASES DISCOUNT--HARDWARE                -510.40
                                                ------------
      MDSE. AVAILABLE FOR SALE                  349065.20
      LESS ENDING INVENTORY                     320924.70
                                                ------------
      COST OF MDSE. SOLD                                     28140.50    57.5
                                                            ------------
      GROSS PROFIT ON OPERATIONS                            20799.60    42.5
                                                            ============
```

```
                              COMPUTEX
                 DEPARTMENT 2 STATEMENT OF GROSS PROFIT
                      FOR MONTH ENDED 07/31/88
                                                              % OF NET
      S A L E S                                                SALES
      ---------                                                --------

      SALES--SOFTWARE                            27750.30
      SALES RETURNS AND ALLOW.--SOFTWARE          -920.30
      SALES DISCOUNT--SOFTWARE                    -310.00
                                                ------------
      NET SALES                                              26520.00    100

      C O S T   O F   M D S E .   S O L D
      ------------------------------------------
      BEGINNING INVENTORY                       103365.50
      PURCHASES--SOFTWARE                         11580.80
      PURCHASES RETURNS AND ALLOW.--SOFTWARE     -1140.60
      PURCHASES DISCOUNT--SOFTWARE                -223.80
                                                ------------
      MDSE. AVAILABLE FOR SALE                  113581.90
      LESS ENDING INVENTORY                      99924.10
                                                ------------
      COST OF MDSE. SOLD                                     13657.80    51.5
                                                            ------------
      GROSS PROFIT ON OPERATIONS                            12862.20    48.5
                                                            ============
```

Illustration 8-6
Departmental statements of gross profit

The computer figures and prints the same percentage ratios for analyzing a departmental statement of gross profit as those described for Supergolf in Chapter 5. Computex makes comparisons with previous performance and with industry standards published by industry organizations and arrives at the following departmental performance standards.

	Hardware	Software
Ratio of cost of merchandise sold to net sales, not *more* than.....................	58%	54%
Ratio of gross profit on operations to net sales, not *less* than......................	42%	46%

An analysis of the departmental statements of gross profit indicates acceptable levels of performance for both departments. The ratios of cost of merchandise sold to net sales are not more than the acceptable performance standards for either department. The ratios of gross profit on operations to net sales are not less than the acceptable performance standards for both departments.

Income statement

An income statement for a departmentalized business combines the amounts reported on departmental statements of gross profit. Computex's income statement for the month ended July 31, 1988, is shown in Illustration 8-7.

The computer figures and prints the same percentage ratios for analyzing an income statement as those described for Supergolf in Chapter 5. Acceptable levels of performance are determined by making comparisons with previous performance and with industry standards that are published by industry organizations. Based on these comparisons, Computex uses the following performance standards.

Ratio of cost of merchandise sold to net sales, not *more* than...	60%
Ratio of gross profit on operations to net sales, not *less* than..	40%
Ratio of total operating expenses to net sales, not *more* than...	35%
Ratio of net income after federal income tax to net sales, not *less* than..	6%

An analysis of Computex's income statement indicates acceptable levels of performance for all percentage ratios. The cost of merchandise sold and total operating expenses are not more than the acceptable performance standards. The gross profit on operations and net income after federal income tax are not less than the acceptable performance standards.

```
                          COMPUTEX
                      INCOME STATEMENT
                  FOR MONTH ENDED 07/31/88
                                                         % OF NET

      S A L E S                                          SALES
      ---------                                          --------

      SALES--HARDWARE                      51860.60
      SALES--SOFTWARE                      27750.30
      SALES RETURNS AND ALLOW.--HARDWARE    -2340.10
      SALES RETURNS AND ALLOW.--SOFTWARE     -920.30
      SALES DISCOUNT--HARDWARE               -580.40
      SALES DISCOUNT--SOFTWARE               -310.00
                                           ------------
      NET SALES                                         75460.10    100

      C O S T   O F   M D S E .   S O L D
      -----------------------------------------

      BEGINNING INVENTORY                 426830.50
      PURCHASES--HARDWARE                  28820.70
      PURCHASES--SOFTWARE                  11580.80
      PURCHASES RETURNS AND ALLOW.--HARDWARE  -2710.10
      PURCHASES RETURNS AND ALLOW.--SOFTWARE  -1140.60
      PURCHASES DISCOUNT--HARDWARE           -510.40
      PURCHASES DISCOUNT--SOFTWARE           -223.80
                                           ------------
      MDSE. AVAILABLE FOR SALE            462647.10
      LESS ENDING INVENTORY               420848.80
                                           ------------
      COST OF MDSE. SOLD                                41798.30    55.4
                                                        ------------
      GROSS PROFIT ON OPERATIONS                        33661.80    44.6

      O P E R A T I N G   E X P E N S E S
      ---------------------------------------
      ADVERTISING EXPENSE                    436.10
      CREDIT CARD FEE EXPENSE                630.00
      DEPRECIATION EXPENSE--STORE EQUIPMENT  300.00
      SALARY EXPENSE--HARDWARE              7500.00
      SALARY EXPENSE--SOFTWARE             6200.00
      SUPPLIES EXPENSE--STORE                740.00
                                           ------------
      TOTAL SELLING EXPENSES              15806.10

      BAD DEBTS EXPENSE                      461.35
      DEPRECIATION EXPENSE--COMPUTER EQUIP.  200.00
      DEPRECIATION EXPENSE--OFFICE EQUIP.    330.00
      INSURANCE EXPENSE                      360.00
      MISCELLANEOUS EXPENSE                  465.30
      PAYROLL TAXES EXPENSE                 2286.15
      RENT EXPENSE                          1600.00
      SALARY EXPENSE--ADMINISTRATIVE        3620.00
      SUPPLIES EXPENSE--OFFICE               580.50
                                           ------------
      TOTAL ADMIN. EXPENSES                9903.30
                                           ------------
      TOTAL OPERATING EXPENSES                          25709.40    34.1
                                                        ------------
      NET INCOME BEFORE INCOME TAX                       7952.40

      I N C O M E   T A X
      ---------------------
      FEDERAL INCOME TAX                    1812.50
                                           ------------
      NET INCOME AFTER INCOME TAX                        6139.90     8.1
                                                        ============
```

Illustration 8-7   Income statement

Balance sheet

In Supergolf's manual accounting system, Part 2, detailed information about owner's equity is reported in a statement of stockholders' equity. In Computex's automated accounting system, summary information about stockholders' equity is reported on the balance sheet. Computex's balance sheet on July 31, 1988, is shown in Illustration 8-8.

Illustration 8-8
Balance sheet

```
                        COMPUTEX
                      BALANCE SHEET
                        07/31/88

     A S S E T S
     ------------
     CURRENT ASSETS
     CASH                                    71602.70
     PETTY CASH                                600.00
     ACCOUNTS RECEIVABLE                     23067.90
     ALLOWANCE FOR UNCOLLECTIBLE ACCOUNTS     -571.65
     MERCHANDISE INVENTORY--HARDWARE        320924.70
     MERCHANDISE INVENTORY--SOFTWARE         99924.10
     SUPPLIES--OFFICE                        10679.90
     SUPPLIES--STORE                         10680.30
     PREPAID INSURANCE                        3240.00
                                           ------------
     TOTAL CURRENT ASSETS                   540147.95

     PLANT ASSETS
     COMPUTER EQUIPMENT                       18320.00
     ACCUM. DEPR.--COMPUTER EQUIPMENT        -2000.00
     OFFICE EQUIPMENT                         22640.00
     ACCUM. DEPR.--OFFICE EQUIPMENT         -11270.00
     STORE EQUIPMENT                          28920.00
     ACCUM. DEPR.--STORE EQUIPMENT           -9920.00
                                           ------------
     TOTAL PLANT ASSETS                      46690.00

                                           ------------
     TOTAL ASSETS                                       586837.95
                                                      ============
     L I A B I L I T I E S
     ----------------------
     ACCOUNTS PAYABLE                        26608.90
     EMPLOYEES INCOME TAX PAYABLE--FED.       1630.40
     EMPLOYEES INCOME TAX PAYABLE--STATE       980.20
     FEDERAL INCOME TAX PAYABLE               1812.50
     FICA TAX PAYABLE                         2424.80
     SALES TAX PAYABLE                        3773.00
     UNEMPLOYMENT TAX PAYABLE--FEDERAL         138.50
     UNEMPLOYMENT TAX PAYABLE--STATE           935.25
     HOSPITAL INSURANCE PREMIUMS PAYABLE       324.00
     LIFE INSURANCE PREMIUMS PAYABLE           240.00
                                           ------------
     TOTAL LIABILITIES                                   38867.55

     S T O C K H O L D E R S '   E Q U I T Y
     ----------------------------------------
     CAPITAL STOCK                          400000.00
     RETAINED EARNINGS                      141830.50
     NET INCOME                               6139.90
                                           ------------
     TOTAL STOCKHOLDERS' EQUITY                         547970.40
                                                      ------------
     TOTAL LIABILITIES & EQUITY                         586837.95
                                                      ============
```

PREPARING A GENERAL LEDGER FOR A NEW FISCAL PERIOD

Revenue and expense accounts must have zero balances at the beginning of each fiscal period. Therefore, closing entries must be made to prepare temporary accounts for a new fiscal period.

Closing temporary accounts

In manual accounting, closing entries are manually recorded in a journal and posted to general ledger accounts. In Computex's automated accounting system, the computer software contains instructions for closing entries. A keyboard entry is made to tell the computer to close the temporary accounts in the general ledger stored on secondary storage. Computex closes all temporary accounts at the end of each monthly fiscal period. (CONCEPT: Accounting Period Cycle) No journal entries need to be key-entered. Therefore, no journal entries report is printed.

Post-closing trial balance

General ledger accounts must always have equal debits and credits. Computex's trial balance, Illustration 8-1, proves that debits equal credits before adjusting and closing entries are posted.

After the temporary capital accounts are closed, equality of general ledger debits and credits is proved again. A keyboard entry is made to tell the computer to print a post-closing trial balance. Computex's post-closing trial balance prepared on July 31, 1988, is shown in Illustration 8-9.

The total of the debit account balances is the same as the total of the credit account balances, $610,599.60. The equality of general ledger debits and credits is proved. Computex's general ledger is ready for the next fiscal period.

QUESTIONS FOR INDIVIDUAL STUDY

1. Reporting all information essential for a reader's understanding of a business' financial status on financial statements is an application of which accounting concept?
2. How are end-of-fiscal-period reports prepared in an automated accounting system?
3. What run date is used on all end-of-fiscal-period reports?
4. Why is a trial balance prepared in an au-

tomated accounting system?
5. Why are subsidiary schedules prepared in an automated accounting system?
6. On what form are adjusting entries recorded?
7. How is a journal entries report checked for accuracy?
8. How does Computex determine acceptable levels of performance for each of its departments?
9. Computex's analysis of the departmental

```
RUN DATE 07/31/88                      COMPUTEX
                              POST-CLOSING TRIAL BALANCE
-----------------------------------------------------------------------------
ACCOUNT      ACCOUNT
NUMBER       TITLE                                      DEBIT          CREDIT
-----------------------------------------------------------------------------
1105         CASH                                    71602.70
1110         PETTY CASH                                600.00
1115         ACCOUNTS RECEIVABLE                     23067.90
1120         ALLOWANCE FOR UNCOLLECTIBLE ACCOUNTS                      571.65
1125-1       MERCHANDISE INVENTORY--HARDWARE        320924.70
1125-2       MERCHANDISE INVENTORY--SOFTWARE         99924.10
1130         SUPPLIES--OFFICE                        10679.90
1135         SUPPLIES--STORE                         10680.30
1140         PREPAID INSURANCE                        3240.00
1205         COMPUTER EQUIPMENT                       18320.00
1210         ACCUM. DEPR.--COMPUTER EQUIPMENT                         2000.00
1215         OFFICE EQUIPMENT                        22640.00
1220         ACCUM. DEPR.--OFFICE EQUIPMENT                          11270.00
1225         STORE EQUIPMENT                         28920.00
1230         ACCUM. DEPR.--STORE EQUIPMENT                            9920.00
2105         ACCOUNTS PAYABLE                                        26608.90
2110         EMPLOYEES INCOME TAX PAYABLE--FED.                       1630.40
2115         EMPLOYEES INCOME TAX PAYABLE--STATE                       980.20
2120         FEDERAL INCOME TAX PAYABLE                               1812.50
2125         FICA TAX PAYABLE                                         2424.80
2130         SALES TAX PAYABLE                                        3773.00
2135         UNEMPLOYMENT TAX PAYABLE--FEDERAL                         138.50
2140         UNEMPLOYMENT TAX PAYABLE--STATE                          935.25
2145         HOSPITAL INSURANCE PREMIUMS PAYABLE                       324.00
2150         LIFE INSURANCE PREMIUMS PAYABLE                          240.00
3105         CAPITAL STOCK                                          400000.00
3110         RETAINED EARNINGS                                      147970.40
                                                    ------------    ------------
             TOTALS                                 610599.60       610599.60
                                                    ============    ============
```

Illustration 8-9
Post-closing trial balance

statements of gross profit for the month ended July 31, 1988, indicated acceptable levels of performance for both departments. Why?

10. Was Computex's ratio of total operating expenses to net sales acceptable or unacceptable? Why?

11. How is information about stockholders' equity reported in Computex's automated accounting system?

12. In Computex's automated accounting system, how are closing entries recorded and processed?

13. How often are temporary accounts closed?

14. Why is a post-closing trial balance prepared in an automated accounting system?

CASE FOR MANAGEMENT DECISION

CASE 1 Westlawn Department Store uses an automated departmentalized accounting system. Reports similar to those prepared by Computex in this chapter are prepared at the end of each fiscal period. The manager feels that closing entries should be recorded and key-entered to assure that temporary accounts are closed properly. The manager is concerned about possible computer or software failure which could result in not having equality of debits and credits in the general ledger to start a new fiscal period. The accountant disagrees with the manager's suggestion. The accountant feels that the time saved by having the computer do the closing entries is worth a possible computer or software failure. Further, the accountant feels the post-closing trial balance prepared by the computer provides an accuracy check on the closing process performed by the computer. Do you agree with the manager or the accountant? Why?

APPLICATION PROBLEM

PROBLEM 8-1   Recording adjusting entries on a journal entries input form

Broden Office Products has two departments: Furniture and Supplies. The following general ledger accounts need adjustment at the end of the fiscal period.

Account Number	Account Title	Account Balance
1120	Allowance for Uncollectible Accounts	$ 269.40
1125-1	Merchandise Inventory — Furniture	178,450.30
1125-2	Merchandise Inventory — Supplies	163,947.20
1130	Supplies — Office	9,230.80
1135	Supplies — Store	8,739.20
1140	Prepaid Insurance.....................................	2,925.00
1210	Accumulated Depreciation — Computer Equipment	2,940.00
1220	Accumulated Depreciation — Office Equipment	9,200.00
1230	Accumulated Depreciation — Store Equipment..............	12,500.00
2120	Federal Income Tax Payable	—
3120-1	Income Summary — Furniture..........................	—
3120-2	Income Summary — Supplies............................	—
6110	Depreciation Expense — Store Equipment.................	—
6120	Supplies Expense — Store	—
6205	Bad Debts Expense	—
6210	Depreciation Expense — Computer Equipment.............	—

Account Number	Account Title	Account Balance
6215	Depreciation Expense—Office Equipment	—
6220	Insurance Expense..	—
6245	Supplies Expense—Office	—
9105	Federal Income Tax	—

Adjustment information, October 31

Bad debts expense	$ 1,250.20
Merchandise inventory—furniture....................................	182,530.20
Merchandise inventory—supplies....................................	158,820.70
Office supplies inventory.......................................	8,470.10
Store supplies inventory	7,230.50
Value of prepaid insurance......................................	2,600.00
Depreciation expense—computer equipment	350.00
Depreciation expense—office equipment............................	420.00
Depreciation expense—store equipment	380.00
Federal income tax...	1,280.00

Instructions: 1. Record the adjusting entries on a journal entries input form. Use October 31 of the current year as the run date. Batch No. 5.

2. Total and prove the Debit and Credit columns.

ENRICHMENT PROBLEMS

MASTERY PROBLEM 8-M   Recording adjusting entries on a journal entries input form

MicroPlus, Inc., has two departments: Hardware and Software. The following general ledger accounts need adjustment at the end of the fiscal period.

Account Number	Account Title	Account Balance
1120	Allowance for Uncollectible Accounts	$ 140.20
1125-1	Merchandise Inventory—Hardware	296,850.30
1125-2	Merchandise Inventory—Software	116,240.20
1130	Supplies—Office	11,420.00
1135	Supplies—Store.......................................	11,910.40
1140	Prepaid Insurance......................................	3,500.00
1210	Accumulated Depreciation—Computer Equipment.........	2,200.00
1220	Accumulated Depreciation—Office Equipment	9,640.60
1230	Accumulated Depreciation—Store Equipment.............	10,130.00
2120	Federal Income Tax Payable	—
3120-1	Income Summary—Hardware............................	—
3120-2	Income Summary—Software...........................	—
6110	Depreciation Expense—Store Equipment.................	—
6120	Supplies Expense—Store	—
6205	Bad Debts Expense	—
6210	Depreciation Expense—Computer Equipment.............	—
6215	Depreciation Expense—Office Equipment	—
6220	Insurance Expense.....................................	—
6245	Supplies Expense—Office	—
9105	Federal Income Tax	—

Adjustment information, July 31

Bad debts expense	$ 436.75
Merchandise inventory—hardware...............................	294,935.60
Merchandise inventory—software	118,610.30
Office supplies inventory..	10,810.40
Store supplies inventory	11,260.20
Value of prepaid insurance......................................	3,150.00
Depreciation expense—computer equipment	410.00
Depreciation expense—office equipment.........................	360.00
Depreciation expense—store equipment	340.00
Federal income tax..	1,320.00

Instructions: 1. Record the adjusting entries on a journal entries input form. Use July 31 of the current year as the run date. Batch No. 5.

2. Total and prove the Debit and Credit columns.

CHALLENGE PROBLEM 8-C   Recording adjusting entries on a journal entries input form

Noveltex, Inc., has two departments: Cards and Gifts. The following general ledger accounts need adjustment at the end of the fiscal period.

Account Number	Account Title	Account Balance
1120	Allowance for Uncollectible Accounts	$ 182.20
1125-1	Merchandise Inventory—Cards.........................	133,252.40
1125-2	Merchandise Inventory—Gifts	164,320.10
1130	Supplies—Office	8,350.20
1135	Supplies—Store.......................................	9,120.80
1140	Prepaid Insurance.....................................	2,250.00
1210	Accumulated Depreciation—Computer Equipment.........	2,740.00
1220	Accumulated Depreciation—Office Equipment	8,700.00
1230	Accumulated Depreciation—Store Equipment.............	10,600.00
2120	Federal Income Tax Payable	—
3120-1	Income Summary—Cards	—
3120-2	Income Summary—Gifts	—
6110	Depreciation Expense—Store Equipment.................	—
6120	Supplies Expense—Store	—
6205	Bad Debts Expense	—
6210	Depreciation Expense—Computer Equipment.............	—
6215	Depreciation Expense—Office Equipment	—
6220	Insurance Expense....................................	—
6245	Supplies Expense—Office	—
9105	Federal Income Tax	—

Adjustment information, April 30

Bad debts expense	$ 387.20
Merchandise inventory—cards	135,420.60
Merchandise inventory—gifts	167,140.10
Office supplies inventory...	7,620.50
Store supplies inventory	8,740.30
Value of prepaid insurance.......................................	2,000.00
Depreciation expense—computer equipment	380.00
Depreciation expense—office equipment...........................	420.00
Depreciation expense—store equipment	340.00
Federal income tax...	1,260.00

Instructions: 1. Record the adjusting entries on a journal entries input form. Use April 30 of the current year as the run date. Batch No. 5.

    2. Total and prove the Debit and Credit columns.

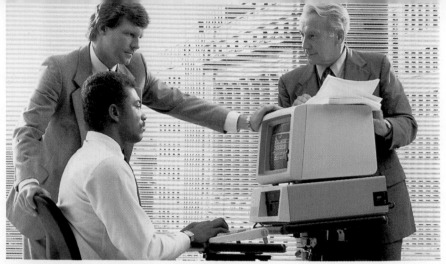

Computer Application 3
Automated Accounting Cycle for a Departmentalized Business: Completing End-of-Fiscal-Period Work

The journal entries input form completed in Mastery Problem 8-M, Chapter 8, is needed to complete Computer Application 3.

MicroPlus, Inc., completed the journal entries input form needed to record adjusting entries for its automated departmentalized accounting system. Computer Application 3 provides for the use of a microcomputer to input and process the data from the completed form and prepare end-of-fiscal-period reports. Chapter 8 describes the manual and computer operations required to record and process adjusting entries and prepare end-of-fiscal-period reports.

COMPUTER APPLICATION PROBLEM

COMPUTER APPLICATION PROBLEM 3   Completing end-of-fiscal-period work

Instructions: 1. Load the Systems Selection Menu from the *Advanced Automated Accounting* diskette according to the instructions for the computer being used. Select Problem CA-3. The general ledger chart of accounts, vendor and customer lists, and end-of-fiscal-period account balances are stored on the template diskette.

2. Display/Print the trial balance.

3. Display/Print the schedule of accounts payable. Check the accuracy of the schedule by comparing the schedule total with the balance of the general ledger controlling account on the trial balance.

4. Display/Print the schedule of accounts receivable. Check the accuracy of the schedule by comparing the schedule total with the balance of the general ledger controlling account on the trial balance.

5. Key-enter adjustment data from the journal entries input form completed in Mastery Problem 8-M.

6. Display/Print the journal entries report. Check the accuracy by comparing the report totals with the totals on the input form.

7. Display/Print the departmental statement of gross profit for Department 1.

8. Display/Print the departmental statement of gross profit for Department 2.

9. Display/Print the income statement.

10. Display/Print the balance sheet.

11. Close the general ledger.

12. Display/Print the post-closing trial balance.

4

General Accounting Adjustments

GENERAL BEHAVIORAL GOALS

1. Know accounting terminology related to general accounting adjustments.
2. Understand accounting concepts and practices related to general accounting adjustments.
3. Demonstrate accounting procedures for general accounting adjustments.

THE GALLERY, INC.
Chart of Accounts

Balance Sheet Accounts

(1000) ASSETS

1100	Current Assets
1105	Cash
1110	Petty Cash
1115	Notes Receivable
1120	Interest Receivable
1125	Accounts Receivable
1130	Allowance for Uncollectible Accounts
1135	Merchandise Inventory
1140	Supplies — Sales
1145	Supplies — Warehouse
1150	Supplies — Administrative
1155	Prepaid Insurance
1160	Prepaid Interest
1200	Plant Assets
1205	Equipment — Store
1210	Accumulated Depreciation — Store Equipment
1215	Equipment — Warehouse
1220	Accumulated Depreciation — Warehouse Equipment
1225	Equipment — Office
1230	Accumulated Depreciation — Office Equipment
1235	Building
1240	Accumulated Depreciation — Building
1245	Land

(2000) LIABILITIES

2100	Current Liabilities
2105	Notes Payable
2110	Interest Payable
2115	Accounts Payable
2120	Employees Income Tax Payable
2125	Federal Income Tax Payable
2130	FICA Tax Payable
2135	Salaries Payable
2140	Sales Tax Payable
2145	Unearned Rent
2150	Unemployment Tax Payable — Federal
2155	Unemployment Tax Payable — State
2200	Long-Term Liability
2205	Mortgage Payable

(3000) STOCKHOLDERS' EQUITY

3105	Capital Stock
3110	Retained Earnings
3115	Income Summary

Income Statement Accounts

(4000) OPERATING REVENUE

4105	Sales
4110	Sales Returns and Allowances
4115	Sales Discount

(5000) COST OF MERCHANDISE

5105	Purchases
5110	Purchases Returns and Allowances
5115	Purchases Discount

(6000) OPERATING EXPENSES

6100	Selling Expenses
6105	Advertising Expense
6110	Credit Card Fee Expense
6115	Depreciation Expense — Store Equipment
6120	Miscellaneous Expense — Sales
6125	Salary Expense — Sales
6130	Supplies Expense — Sales
6200	Warehouse Expenses
6205	Depreciation Expense — Warehouse Equipment
6210	Miscellaneous Expense — Warehouse
6215	Salary Expense — Warehouse
6220	Supplies Expense — Warehouse
6300	Administrative Expenses
6305	Bad Debts Expense
6310	Depreciation Expense — Building
6315	Depreciation Expense — Office Equipment
6320	Insurance Expense
6325	Miscellaneous Expense — Administrative
6330	Payroll Taxes Expense
6335	Property Tax Expense
6340	Salary Expense — Administrative
6345	Supplies Expense — Administrative

(7000) OTHER REVENUE

7105	Gain on Plant Assets
7110	Interest Income
7115	Rent Income

(8000) OTHER EXPENSES

8105	Interest Expense
8110	Loss on Plant Assets

(9000) INCOME TAX

9105	Federal Income Tax

The chart of accounts for The Gallery, Inc., is illustrated above
for ready reference as you study Part 4 of this textbook.

9 Accounting for Uncollectible Accounts

ENABLING PERFORMANCE TASKS

After studying Chapter 9, you will be able to:
a. Define accounting terms related to uncollectible accounts.
b. Identify accounting concepts and practices related to uncollectible accounts.
c. Analyze and record entries for writing off uncollectible accounts.
d. Figure and analyze accounts receivable turnover ratios.

Selling merchandise on credit is a major strength in the American economy. Most businesses today sell on credit to some customers. However, businesses try to avoid selling to customers who might not pay what is owed. Therefore, businesses should investigate each new customer's credit rating before selling merchandise on account.

Regardless of the care taken in granting credit, some customers will not pay for a variety of reasons. Some customers cannot pay because of personal financial reasons. A few customers do not pay because of oversight. Accounts receivable that cannot be collected are called uncollectible accounts. Uncollectible accounts are sometimes known as bad debts.

When a sale on account is made to a customer, the amount is recorded in a general ledger account titled Accounts Receivable. The amount remains recorded in this asset account until paid or until specifically known to be uncollectible.

When a customer account is known to be uncollectible, the account is no longer an asset. An uncollectible account should be canceled and removed from the business' assets. Canceling the balance of a customer account because the customer does not pay is called writing off an account.

DIRECT WRITE-OFF METHOD OF RECORDING BAD DEBTS EXPENSE

An amount owed by a specific customer is part of the accounts receivable account balance until paid or until written off as uncollectible. An uncollectible account is closed by transferring the balance to a general ledger account titled Bad Debts Expense.

Garment Center does alteration work on clothing for its customers. The business has few sales on account. Therefore, the business has a small number of accounts receivable and few of these accounts become uncollectible. Therefore, Garment Center records bad debts expense only when a specific account is actually known to be uncollectible. Recording bad debts expense only when an amount is actually known to be uncollectible is called the direct write-off method of recording bad debts.

Writing off an uncollectible account—direct write-off method

On November 15, 1988, Garment Center learned that Jane Norwell is unable to pay her account. Garment Center decides that Miss Norwell's account is uncollectible.

GENERAL LEDGER
Bad Debts Expense

| Write off | 40.00 | |

Accounts Receivable

| | | Write off | 40.00 |

ACCOUNTS RECEIVABLE LEDGER
Jane Norwell

| Balance | 40.00 | Write off | 40.00 |

November 15, 1988.
Wrote off past due account of Jane Norwell as uncollectible, $40.00. Memorandum No. 21.

The analysis of this transaction is shown in the T accounts. In the general ledger, Bad Debts Expense is increased by a $40.00 debit. Accounts Receivable is decreased by a $40.00 credit. In the accounts receivable ledger, Jane Norwell's account is decreased by a $40.00 credit.

The general journal entry to record this transaction is shown in Illustration 9-1.

Illustration 9-1
Entry to write off an uncollectible account—direct write-off method

	DATE	ACCOUNT TITLE	POST. REF.	DEBIT	CREDIT	
1	1988 Nov. 15	Bad Debts Expense		4000		1
2		Accts. Rec. / Jane Norwell	✓		4000	2
3		M21				3

GENERAL JOURNAL   PAGE 14

After this entry is recorded and posted, Jane Norwell's account has a zero balance. Also, the balance of Accounts Receivable no longer includes the $40.00 as part of the business' assets.

Collecting a written-off account—direct write-off method

Sometimes a customer's written-off account is later collected. When the account is written off, the balance is recorded as an expense. When the account is later collected, the amount is recorded as other revenue.

January 21, 1989.
Received full payment for Jane Norwell's account, previously written off as uncollectible, $40.00. Memorandum No. 54 and Receipt No. 49.

Garment Center needs a complete record of accounts receivable. Therefore, when a previously written-off account is collected, two actions are needed. (1) The customer account is reopened. (2) The receipt of cash is recorded. There are two source documents for this transaction. One source document, a memorandum, is for the entry to reopen the customer account. The other source document, a receipt, is for the receipt of cash on account from the customer. *(CONCEPT: Objective Evidence)*

The analysis of the entry to reopen a customer account is shown in the T accounts. In the general ledger, Accounts Receivable is increased by a $40.00 debit. Bad Debts Collected is increased by a $40.00 credit. In the accounts receivable ledger, Jane Norwell's account is increased by a $40.00 debit.

The bad debts collected account is closed to Income Summary at the end of a fiscal period. The account is reported on an income statement as part of Other Revenue.

The general journal entry to reopen Miss Norwell's account is shown in Illustration 9-2.

GENERAL LEDGER
Accounts Receivable

Reopen	40.00	Write off	40.00

Bad Debts Collected

		Reopen	40.00

ACCOUNTS RECEIVABLE LEDGER
Jane Norwell

Balance	40.00	Write off	40.00
Reopen	40.00		

	GENERAL JOURNAL			PAGE *16*	
DATE	ACCOUNT TITLE	POST. REF.	DEBIT	CREDIT	
21	Accts. Rec. / Jane Norwell	✓	40 00		
	Bad Debts Collected			40 00	
	M54				

Illustration 9-2
Entry to reopen an account previously written off as uncollectible

The analysis of the entry for the receipt of cash on account from Miss Norwell is shown in the T accounts. In the general ledger, Cash is increased by a $40.00 debit. Accounts Receivable is decreased by a $40.00 credit. In the accounts receivable ledger, the customer account is decreased by a $40.00 credit.

The entry to record this transaction in a cash receipts journal is shown in Illustration 9-3.

After both these entries are recorded and posted, Jane Norwell's account shows a complete history.

1. A $40.00 debit balance resulting from a sale on account.
2. A $40.00 credit when the account was written off as uncollectible.
3. A $40.00 debit when the account was reopened.
4. A $40.00 credit when cash was received on account.

GENERAL LEDGER
Cash

Received	40.00	

Accounts Receivable

Reopen	40.00	Write off	40.00
		Received	40.00

ACCOUNTS RECEIVABLE LEDGER
Jane Norwell

Balance	40.00	Write off	40.00
Reopen	40.00	Received	40.00

	CASH RECEIPTS JOURNAL									PAGE 4	
				1	2	3	4	5	6	7	8
DATE	ACCOUNT TITLE	DOC. NO.	POST. REF.	GENERAL		ACCOUNTS RECEIVABLE CREDIT	SALES CREDIT	SALES TAX PAYABLE		SALES DISCOUNT DEBIT	CASH DEBIT
				DEBIT	CREDIT			DEBIT	CREDIT		
21	*Jane Norwell*	R49				4000					4000

Illustration 9-3
Entry to record cash
received for an account
previously written off as
uncollectible

ALLOWANCE METHOD OF RECORDING BAD DEBTS EXPENSE

Some businesses use the direct write-off method and record bad debts expense only when a specific customer account is determined to be uncollectible. However, when the direct write-off method is used, the expense may be recorded in a fiscal period different than the fiscal period of the sale. Bad debts expense should be recorded in the same fiscal period in which the sales revenue is received. *(CONCEPT: Matching Expenses with Revenue)*

At the time sales on account are made, a business has no way of knowing for sure which customer will not pay an amount due. Therefore, an estimate is made based on past history of bad debts expense for a business. Crediting the estimated value of uncollectible accounts to a contra account is called the allowance method of recording losses from uncollectible accounts. Two methods are commonly used to estimate bad debts expense. (1) Percentage of sales method. (2) Percentage of accounts receivable method.

The *percentage of sales method* assumes that a percentage of each sales dollar will become a bad debt. Therefore, emphasis is placed on estimating a percentage of sales that will not be collected. This estimated amount is charged to Bad Debts Expense. There are two variations of this method. (1) Estimating bad debts expense by using a percentage of net sales. (2) Estimating bad debts expense by using a percentage of total sales on account.

The *percentage of accounts receivable method* assumes that a percentage of the accounts receivable account balance is bad debts. Therefore, emphasis is placed on estimating a percentage of accounts receivable that will not be collected. An amount that will bring the balance of Allowance for Uncollectible Accounts up to the estimated amount is recorded in that account. There are two variations of this method. (1) Estimating the amount of uncollectible accounts by aging accounts receivable. (2) Estimating the amount of uncollectible accounts by using a percentage of the accounts receivable account balance.

Estimating bad debts expense by using a percentage of net sales

Past experience of Movers, Inc., indicates that approximately 0.5% of net sales will prove to be uncollectible. On December 31, 1988, Movers figures its estimated bad debts expense as shown below.

Total Sales	−	Sales Returns and Allowances	−	Sales Discount	=	Net Sales
$113,897.55	−	$756.29	−	$655.51	=	$112,485.75

Net Sales	×	Percentage	=	Estimated Addition to Allowance for Uncollectible Accounts
$112,485.75	×	0.5%	=	$562.43

Movers estimates that of the $112,485.75 net sales in 1988, $562.43 eventually will prove to be uncollectible. The adjusting entry made at the end of the fiscal period affects two accounts: Bad Debts Expense and Allowance for Uncollectible Accounts. Movers does not know yet which customer accounts in the accounts receivable ledger will become uncollectible. Therefore, the amount cannot be recorded directly in accounts receivable.

The analysis for this adjustment is shown in the T accounts. Bad Debts Expense is increased by a $562.43 debit. The contra asset account Allowance for Uncollectible Accounts is increased by a $562.43 credit.

Before the adjustment is made, Movers' general ledger shows Allowance for Uncollectible Accounts with a $25.87 credit balance. This balance is what remains of estimates made in previous fiscal periods but not yet specifically identified by customer. The balance of the allowance account after the adjustment is $588.30 ($25.87 *plus* $562.43).

Bad Debts Expense	
Adjustment 562.43	

Allowance for Uncollectible Accounts	
	Balance 25.87
	Adjustment 562.43

This adjustment for bad debts expense is entered on a work sheet as shown in Illustration 9-4.

Movers, Inc.
Work Sheet
For Year Ended December 31, 1988

ACCOUNT TITLE	TRIAL BALANCE DEBIT	TRIAL BALANCE CREDIT	ADJUSTMENTS DEBIT	ADJUSTMENTS CREDIT	INCOME STATEMENT DEBIT	INCOME STATEMENT CREDIT	BALANCE SHEET DEBIT	BALANCE SHEET CREDIT	
4 *Allow. for Uncoll. Accts.*		2587		(a) 56243					4
49 *Bad Debts Expense*			(a) 56243						49

The credit amount of adjustment (*a*), $562.43, is recorded in the Adjustments Credit column on line with the account title Allowance for Uncollectible Accounts. The corresponding debit, $562.43, is recorded in the Adjustments Debit column on line with the account title Bad Debts Expense.

Illustration 9-4
Adjustment for bad debts expense on a work sheet

Estimating bad debts expense by using a percentage of total sales on account

Penrod, Inc., bases its estimate of bad debts expense on a percentage of total sales on account. Penrod's past records show that approximately 1% of total sales on account during a fiscal period will become uncollectible. During 1988, the business had total sales on account of $116,603.91. Penrod estimates that 1% of the total sales on account, $1,166.04, will eventually prove uncollectible. The business figures its bad debts expense as shown below.

Total Sales On Account	×	Percentage	=	Estimated Addition to Allowance for Uncollectible Accounts
$116,603.91	×	1%	=	$1,166.04

The adjustment is analyzed in the T accounts. Bad Debts Expense is increased by a $1,166.04 debit. Allowance for Uncollectible Accounts is increased by a $1,166.04 credit.

Bad Debts Expense

Adjustment 1,166.04	

Allowance for Uncollectible Accounts

	Balance 293.66
	Adjustment 1,166.04

The allowance account's previous balance, $293.66, is the estimated uncollectible amount recorded in previous fiscal periods but not yet actually written off. The new balance of the allowance account is $1,459.70 (previous balance, $293.66, *plus* adjustment, $1,166.04).

The balance of Allowance for Uncollectible Accounts may increase from year to year. If the increase is large, this may indicate that an incorrect percentage is being used to figure the uncollectible amount. When this occurs, a new percentage should be figured based on actual experience for the past two or three years.

Regardless of the method used to figure the amount, the adjustment is entered on a work sheet in the same way as previously described. The same two general ledger accounts are affected, Allowance for Uncollectible Accounts and Bad Debts Expense.

Estimating the balance of Allowance for Uncollectible Accounts by aging accounts receivable

Analyzing accounts receivable according to when they are due is called aging accounts receivable. Thermal, Inc., ages accounts receivable at the end of each fiscal period to provide information for the bad debts expense adjustment. Thermal sells on terms of 2/10, n/30. Thermal expects customers to pay in full within 30 days. If cash has not been received within 30 days, reminders are mailed to the customers. If cash has not been received after 60 days, special attempts are made to collect the amount due. If an amount has not been collected from a customer after 90 days, the business stops selling on account to that customer until collection has been made. Also, after an account is 90 days or more overdue, the business notifies the local credit bureau which adds the information to its files.

Thermal's schedule of accounts receivable by age, December 31, 1988, is shown in Illustration 9-5.

Customer	Account Balance	Not Yet Due	Days Account Balance Past Due			
			1-30	31-60	61-90	Over 90
LuAnn Astor	$ 835.51	$ 835.51				
Mary Dunkirk	32.58		$ 32.58			
Fred Phillips	199.55					199.55
Kathy Quay	138.00	100.00	38.00			
Thomas Yost	33.67				33.67	
Totals	$12,991.97	$8,834.08	$3,052.90	$649.54	$138.45	$317.00
Percentages	—	0.1%	0.2%	0.4%	10.0%	80.0%

Illustration 9-5
Schedule of accounts receivable by age

Based on past records, Thermal determines that a percentage of each accounts receivable age group will become uncollectible in the future. For example, as shown in Illustration 9-5, 0.4% of the accounts receivable overdue 31-60 days will probably become uncollectible. Also, 80% of the accounts overdue more than 90 days probably will become uncollectible.

Using these percentages, Thermal figures the total amount of estimated uncollectible accounts receivable as shown in Illustration 9-6.

Age Group	Amount	Percentage	Uncollectible
Not yet due	$ 8,834.08	0.1%	$ 8.83
1-30 days	3,052.90	0.2%	6.11
31-60 days	649.54	0.4%	2.60
61-90 days	138.45	10.0%	13.85
Over 90 days	317.00	80.0%	253.60
Totals	$12,991.97	—	$284.99

Illustration 9-6
Estimating the balance of Allowance for Uncollectible Accounts by aging accounts receivable

Of the total accounts receivable on December 31, 1988, $12,991.97, the business estimates that $284.99 will prove to be uncollectible in the future.

Thermal's general ledger shows that Allowance for Uncollectible Accounts has a $60.78 credit balance. This balance is what remains of estimates made in previous fiscal periods but not yet specifically identified by customer name. However, the current balance for the allowance account should be $284.99. The additional amount to be recorded is figured as shown below.

Estimated Balance of Allowance for Uncollectible Accounts		Current Balance of Allowance Account		Estimated Addition to Allowance for Uncollectible Accounts
$284.99	—	$60.78	=	$224.21

Bad Debts Expense

Adjustment 224.21	

Allowance for Uncollectible Accounts

	Balance 60.78
	Adjustment 224.21

The analysis of this adjustment for bad debts expense is shown in the T accounts. Bad Debts Expense is increased by a $224.21 debit. Allowance for Uncollectible Accounts is increased by a $224.21 credit. The new balance of the allowance account is $284.99 ($60.78 *plus* $224.21).

The aging accounts receivable method is based on amounts still owed by customers at the time the bad debts expense is estimated. Many businesses do not use the aging method because of the additional work required in analyzing accounts receivable for the aging schedule. However, with the increased availability of computers to make the calculations, more businesses can use the aging method.

Estimating the balance of Allowance for Uncollectible Accounts by using a percentage of the accounts receivable account balance

The Gallery, Inc., organized as a corporation, is a merchandising business that sells furniture. Gallery expects to make money and continue in business indefinitely. *(CONCEPT: Going Concern)* Gallery estimates its amount of bad debts expense by using a percentage of the accounts receivable account balance at the end of a fiscal period. This method assumes that a percentage of the current amount still to be collected from customers will prove to be uncollectible.

On December 31, 1988, Gallery's accounts receivable account balance is $47,462.79. Gallery's past experience indicates that approximately 3% of the accounts receivable account balance will be uncollectible. The estimated addition to the balance of Allowance for Uncollectible Accounts is figured as shown below.

Balance of Accounts Receivable Account	×	Percentage	=	Estimated Balance of Allowance for Uncollectible Accounts
$47,462.79	×	3%	=	$1,423.88

Estimated Balance of Allowance for Uncollectible Accounts	−	Current Balance of Allowance Account	=	Estimated Addition to Allowance for Uncollectible Accounts
$1,423.88	−	$54.34	=	$1,369.54

Bad Debts Expense

Adjustment 1,369.54	

Allowance for Uncollectible Accounts

	Balance 54.34
	Adjustment 1,369.54

The analysis of this adjustment is shown in the T accounts. Bad Debts Expense is increased by a $1,369.54 debit. Allowance for Uncollectible Accounts is increased by a $1,369.54 credit. The new balance of the allowance account is $1,423.88 ($54.34 *plus* $1,369.54).

Writing off an uncollectible account—allowance method

The procedures for writing off an account are the same regardless of the allowance method used to figure the estimated bad debts expense. When a specific customer account is known to be uncollectible, the account balance is written off. Gallery determines that Carla Reins will not pay the amount she owes, $32.80. The balance is no longer *estimated* to be uncollectible, it is *actually determined* to be uncollectible.

> January 5, 1989.
> Wrote off past due account of Carla Reins as uncollectible, $32.80. Memorandum No. 71.

The analysis of this transaction is shown in the T accounts. In the general ledger, Allowance for Uncollectible Accounts is decreased by a $32.80 debit. Accounts Receivable is decreased by a $32.80 credit. In the subsidiary ledger, the customer account is also decreased by a $32.80 credit. After this entry is posted, Carla Reins' account has a zero balance.

In a previous fiscal period, an adjusting entry was recorded for estimated bad debts expense resulting in an Allowance for Uncollectible Accounts balance of $1,423.88. This balance is the estimated amount of uncollectible accounts. The $32.80 debit entry in this account removes an amount that is no longer estimated, but is actual.

GENERAL LEDGER
Allowance for Uncollectible Accounts

Write off	32.80	Balance	1,423.88

Accounts Receivable

Balance	47,462.79	Write off	32.80

ACCOUNTS RECEIVABLE LEDGER
Carla Reins

Balance	32.80	Write off	32.80

> Bad Debts Expense is not affected when a business writes off an account using the allowance method. The expense is recorded in an adjusting entry at the end of a previous fiscal period.

The general journal entry to write off an uncollectible account is the same regardless of the allowance method used to figure the estimated amount. The general journal entry made by Gallery on January 5 is shown in Illustration 9-7.

	GENERAL JOURNAL			PAGE 1		
DATE	ACCOUNT TITLE	POST. REF.	DEBIT	CREDIT		
5	Allow. for Uncoll. Accts.		3280			4
	Accts. Rec./Carla Reins	✓		3280		5
	M71					6

Illustration 9-7
Entry to write off an uncollectible account—allowance method

The aging accounts receivable method and the percentage of the accounts receivable account balance method are similar. Both methods are based on *actual* amounts owed by customers at the end of a fiscal period. Gallery uses the percentage of the accounts receivable account balance method because it is the more easily figured of the two methods.

Collecting a written-off account—allowance method

During the next year, Gallery receives a check in full payment of the amount owed by Carla Reins. The account was written off on January 5, 1989. The records must show that Ms. Reins' account actually was collected. Ms. Reins' account should show a complete history of her credit dealings with Gallery. The account is reopened to reverse the previous entry that wrote off the account when it was thought to be uncollectible.

GENERAL LEDGER
Accounts Receivable

Balance	47,462.79	Write off	32.80
Reopen	32.80		

Allowance for Uncollectible Accounts

Write off	32.80	Balance	1,423.88
		Reopen	32.80

ACCOUNTS RECEIVABLE LEDGER
Carla Reins

Balance	32.80	Write off	32.80
Reopen	32.80		

April 5, 1990.
Received full payment for Carla Reins' account, previously written off as uncollectible, $32.80. Memorandum No. 92 and Receipt No. 280.

The analysis of this transaction is shown in the T accounts. In the general ledger, Accounts Receivable is increased by a $32.80 debit. Allowance for Uncollectible Accounts is increased by a $32.80 credit. In the accounts receivable ledger, Carla Reins' account is increased by a $32.80 debit. The accounts now appear as they were before Ms. Reins' account was written off as uncollectible.

The general journal entry to record this entry is shown in Illustration 9-8.

GENERAL JOURNAL PAGE 4

	DATE	ACCOUNT TITLE	POST. REF.	DEBIT	CREDIT	
1	1990 Apr. 5	Accts. Rec. / Carla Reins	✓	32 80		1
2		Allow. for Uncoll. Accts.			32 80	2
3		M92				3
4						4

Illustration 9-8
Entry to reopen an account previously written off as uncollectible

GENERAL LEDGER
Cash

Received	32.80		

Accounts Receivable

Balance	47,462.79	Write off	32.80
Reopen	32.80	Received	32.80

ACCOUNTS RECEIVABLE LEDGER
Carla Reins

Balance	32.80	Write off	32.80
Reopen	32.80	Received	32.80

After Carla Reins' account is reopened, an entry is made to record the cash received on account. The analysis of this part of the transaction is shown in the T accounts.

In the general ledger, Cash is increased by a $32.80 debit. Accounts Receivable is decreased by a $32.80 credit. In the accounts receivable ledger, Carla Reins' account is also decreased by a $32.80 credit.

The entry to record this transaction is similar to the entry shown in Illustration 9-3.

ACCOUNTS RECEIVABLE TURNOVER RATIO

Gallery needs cash to purchase additional merchandise to sell to customers and to pay for operating expenses. If amounts due from customers are not collected promptly, too large a share of the business' assets are in accounts receivable and not immediately usable. Any business selling on account needs prompt collection from credit customers.

Gallery needs to know how promptly customers are making payments on account. If the customers are not paying promptly, the business will adopt new procedures to speed collections. One means of analyzing a business' collection efficiency is to figure the accounts receivable turnover ratio. The number of times the average amount of accounts receivable is collected annually is called the accounts receivable turnover ratio.

Some businesses figure an accounts receivable turnover ratio monthly. With monthly rates, a business can take steps at the end of each month to improve collection practices. However, most businesses find that an annual ratio is sufficient. The annual ratio is used to revise collection policies for the next fiscal year.

Figuring the accounts receivable turnover ratio

The difference between the balance of Accounts Receivable and the estimated uncollectible accounts is called the book value of accounts receivable. Gallery figures its book value of accounts receivable as shown below.

Total Accounts Receivable	−	Estimated Uncollectible Accounts	=	Book Value of Accounts Receivable
$47,462.79	−	$1,423.88	=	$46,038.91

The accounts receivable turnover ratio is figured by dividing sales on account by the average book value of accounts receivable. Gallery figures its 1988 accounts receivable turnover ratio as shown below.

Beginning Book Value of Accounts Receivable	+	Ending Book Value of Accounts Receivable	÷	2	=	Average Book Value of Accounts Receivable
($46,912.31	+	$46,038.91)	÷	2	=	$46,475.61

Net Sales on Account	÷	Average Book Value of Accounts Receivable	=	Accounts Receivable Turnover Ratio
$330,312.85	÷	$46,475.61	=	7.1 times

An accounts receivable turnover ratio of 7.1 times means that Gallery turns over (or collects) its average accounts receivable about seven times a year.

Gallery sells on account to customers on terms of n/30. These terms mean that Gallery expects customers to pay amounts owed within 30 days. The expected accounts receivable turnover ratio is 12.0 times, or one-twelfth of a year (30 days). This expected number of days for payment is figured as follows.

$$
\begin{array}{ccccc}
\textbf{Days in} & \div & \textbf{Expected} & = & \textbf{Expected Average} \\
\textbf{Year} & & \textbf{Accounts Receivable} & & \textbf{Number of Days} \\
& & \textbf{Turnover Ratio} & & \textbf{for Payment} \\
365 & \div & 12.0 & = & 30
\end{array}
$$

Gallery figures its actual number of days for payment as shown below.

$$
\begin{array}{ccccc}
\textbf{Days in} & \div & \textbf{Accounts Receivable} & = & \textbf{Actual Average Number} \\
\textbf{Year} & & \textbf{Turnover Ratio} & & \textbf{of Days for Payment} \\
365 & \div & 7.1 & = & 51
\end{array}
$$

Gallery's customers are taking an average of about 51 days to pay their accounts in full.

Analyzing accounts receivable turnover ratios

Most of Gallery's customers do pay their accounts, but they take much longer than the expected 30 days. Gallery's accounts receivable turnover ratios and collection periods for the past several years are shown below.

The Gallery, Inc. — Accounts Receivable Turnover Ratios							
Years	1982	1983	1984	1985	1986	1987	1988
Ratio	6.3	6.4	6.0	6.4	6.8	6.8	7.1
Days for Payment	58	57	61	57	54	54	51

From 1982 to 1988, the accounts receivable turnover ratio has risen from 6.3 to 7.1 times. In 1982, customers took an average of 58 days to pay their accounts in full. In 1988, customers are taking an average of 51 days to pay their accounts in full, seven fewer days than in 1982. However, the 1988 turnover ratio, 7.1 times, is still much lower than the expected rate of 12.

With the exception of 1984, the turnover ratio has been steadily increasing. On the average, customers have been paying their accounts in full in a fewer number of days each year. Gallery wants this favorable trend to continue.

Gallery needs to plan additional ways to encourage customers to pay their accounts in less time. The goal is to have a turnover ratio of 12 times as compared to the present rate of 7.1. The business might take several steps to create a more favorable accounts receivable turnover ratio.

1. Send statements of account to customers more often, including a request for prompt payment.
2. Do not sell on account to any customer who has an account for which payment is overdue more than 30 days.
3. Encourage more cash sales and fewer sales on account.
4. Conduct a more rigorous credit check on new customers before extending credit to them.

Sometimes a demand for quicker payment can result in loss of business. Some customers might start buying from competitors. A business must weigh a change in credit policies with the effect the change will have on total sales.

ACCOUNTING TERMS

What is the meaning of each of the following?

1. uncollectible accounts
2. writing off an account
3. direct write-off method of recording bad debts
4. allowance method of recording losses from uncollectible accounts
5. aging accounts receivable
6. accounts receivable turnover ratio
7. book value of accounts receivable

QUESTIONS FOR INDIVIDUAL STUDY

1. Why should the amount of an uncollectible account be removed from a business' assets?
2. In the direct write-off method, what is done with the amount of an uncollectible account?
3. When an account is written off in the direct write-off method, which general ledger accounts are affected, and how?
4. When using the direct write-off method, if an account is reopened because payment is received, which general ledger accounts are affected, and how?
5. When cash is received for an account previously written off as uncollectible, why is the customer account reopened?
6. Using the allowance method of recording bad debts expense is an application of which accounting concept?
7. What are the four methods described in this text that might be used to figure the estimated amount of bad debts expense for a fiscal period?
8. What is the formula for estimating bad debts expense based on net sales?
9. When using the allowance method of figuring bad debts expense, what general ledger accounts are affected. and how?
10. If the allowance for uncollectible accounts account balance increases from year to year, what is the probable cause?
11. Why is the aging accounts receivable method of figuring the amount of bad debts expense not more popularly used?
12. When using the allowance method to write off an account, which general ledger accounts are affected, and how?
13. When using the allowance method, if an account is reopened because payment is received, which general ledger accounts are affected, and how?
14. Why do most businesses want prompt payment from customers?
15. What is the formula for figuring average book value of accounts receivable?
16. What is the formula for figuring the accounts receivable turnover ratio?
17. If a business desires an accounts receivable turnover ratio of 12 times and actually has a turnover ratio of 6 times, how can this be interpreted?
18. How can a business decide if an accounts receivable turnover ratio of 6 times is acceptable or not?

CASES FOR MANAGEMENT DECISION

CASE 1 Waterburg, Inc., sells merchandise for cash and on account. The business uses the direct write-off method of recording bad debts expense. For the past two years, the amount of uncollectible accounts written off each year has been about 1% of the net sales on account. Net sales on account last year were $316,228.00. An accountant has recommended that the business change to the allowance method of recording bad debts expense. However, management is reluctant to accept the recommendation because the business has used the direct write-off method for a long time and personnel fully understand it. What do you recommend and why?

CASE 2 As a reaction to the situation described in Case 1, one of the business' managers recommends that the problem be eliminated completely. The business should sell only for cash and not sell on account. What is your opinion of this recommendation? Explain your answer.

CASE 3 The following entries were made in each of the years shown. What effect will the entries in each of these years have on the business' financial statements?

1987   Adjusting entry; debit Bad Debts Expense, credit Allowance for Uncollectible Accounts, $2,000.00.

1988   Wrote off George Grover's account as uncollectible, $450.00.

1989   Reopened George Grover's account; received payment in full for the account, $450.00.

APPLICATION PROBLEMS

PROBLEM 9-1   Recording bad debts expense — direct write-off method

Park, Inc., uses the direct write-off method of recording bad debts expense. Selected transactions for the corporation's current year are given below.

Instructions: Record the following transactions. Use page 12 of a general journal and page 10 of a cash receipts journal similar to those shown in this chapter. Source documents are abbreviated as follows: memorandum, M; receipt, R.

Jan. 20. Wrote off past due account of Beth Quincy as uncollectible, $165.48. M15.

Feb. 15. Wrote off past due account of Edward Day as uncollectible, $52.00. M21.

Apr. 10. Received full payment for Louise May's account, previously written off as uncollectible, $168.43. M34 and R89.

June 14. Wrote off past due account of Charles Wagoner as uncollectible, $89.97. M68.

Oct.   5. Received full payment for Beth Quincy's account, previously written off as uncollectible, $165.48. M104 and R135.

Nov.   1. Received payment for Baker Olds' account, previously written off as uncollectible, $217.53. M127 and R139.

PROBLEM 9-2   Estimating amount of bad debts expense by using a percentage of net sales — allowance method

Maxors, Inc., has the following general ledger account balances on December 31 of the current year, before adjusting entries are recorded.

Accounts Receivable	$ 23,731.39
Allowance for Uncollectible Accounts	427.16
Sales	246,900.13
Sales Returns and Allowances	1,082.14
Sales Discount	1,496.90

Instructions: 1. Figure the estimated amount for the bad debts expense adjusting entry on December 31. The corporation estimates that the amount of bad debts expense is equal to 0.5% of net sales.

2. Record the adjusting entry for bad debts expense on page 7 of a general journal. Use December 31 of the current year as the date.

PROBLEM 9-3   Estimating amount of bad debts expense by using a percentage of total sales on account—allowance method

Bangor, Inc., has a total of $168,717.32 in sales on account for the current year. The corporation estimates that bad debts expense each year is equal to 1% of sales on account.

Instructions: 1. Figure the amount of bad debts expense for the year's adjusting entry.

2. Record the adjusting entry for bad debts expense on page 5 of a general journal. Use December 31 of the current year as the date.

PROBLEM 9-4   Estimating the balance of Allowance for Uncollectible Accounts by aging accounts receivable—allowance method

The following information has been obtained from the records of Klear, Inc.

Customer	Account Balance	Not Yet Due	Days Account Balance Past Due			
			1-30	31-60	61-90	Over 90
Ed Ball	$ 418.28	$ 418.28				
Carol Kane	321.75		$ 321.75			
Henry Overbeck	530.99	400.00	30.99			
Myrtle Phelps	120.84					120.84
Totals	$13,662.05	$9,619.18	$1,254.83	$862.57	$1,574.57	$350.90
Percentages	—	0.1%	0.2%	0.3%	0.8%	50.0%

The balance of Allowance for Uncollectible Accounts on December 31 before adjusting entries are recorded is $43.24.

Instructions: 1. Figure the estimated balance of Allowance for Uncollectible Accounts. Prepare a list of estimated uncollectible amounts in each age group similar to the list in Illustration 9-6.

2. Record the adjusting entry for bad debts expense on page 30 of a general journal. Use December 31 of the current year as the date.

PROBLEM 9-5   Estimating the balance of Allowance for Uncollectible Accounts by using a percentage of the accounts receivable account balance—allowance method

Use the information given in Problem 9-4.

Instructions: 1. Figure the estimated balance of Allowance for Uncollectible Accounts. Klear, Inc., estimates that 2% of the accounts receivable account balance will become uncollectible in the future.

2. Record the adjusting entry for bad debts expense on page 17 of a general journal. Use December 31 of the current year as the date.

PROBLEM 9-6   Writing off uncollectible accounts—allowance method

The following selected transactions were completed by Tableware, Inc., during the current year. Tableware uses the allowance method of recording bad debts expense.

Instructions: Record the following transactions. Use page 14 of a general journal. The source document is abbreviated as memorandum, M.

Feb. 11. Wrote off past due account of Wilbur Mason as uncollectible, $57.00. M12.
Apr. 15. Wrote off past due account of Mabel Bloom as uncollectible, $129.58. M21.
July 20. Wrote off past due account of Dan Hilyard as uncollectible, $27.50. M39.
Oct. 10. Wrote off past due account of LuAnn Boyd as uncollectible, $48.13. M61.

PROBLEM 9-7   Recording the receipt of cash for written-off accounts — allowance method

Selected transactions completed by Tableware, Inc., during the current year are given below.

Instructions: Record the following transactions. Use page 15 of a general journal and page 20 of a cash receipts journal. Source documents are abbreviated as follows: memorandum, M; receipt, R.

Apr. 2. Received full payment for Wilbur Mason's account, previously written off as un-
          collectible, $57.00. M17 and R43.
May 14. Received full payment for Mabel Bloom's account, previously written off as uncollectible,
          $129.58. M25 and R47.
Dec. 5. Received full payment for LuAnn Boyd's account, previously written off as uncollectible,
          $48.13. M81 and R103.

PROBLEM 9-8   Figuring accounts receivable turnover ratios

Information about four businesses for the current year is given below.

Business	For Current Year			Last Year's Turnover Ratio
	Beginning Book Value of Accounts Receivable	Ending Book Value of Accounts Receivable	Net Sales on Account	
A	$ 17,201.18	$ 15,820.93	$ 113,320.36	8.0
B	27,160.52	27,320.42	130,754.25	6.0
C	34,058.33	29,725.77	158,648.50	5.0
D	106,432.28	127,718.74	1,301,322.50	9.0

Instructions: 1. For each business, figure the accounts receivable turnover ratio for the current year.
    2. Answer the questions below.
      a. Which business had the best turnover ratio last year? This current year?
      b. Which business had the worst turnover ratio last year? This current year?
      c. Which business had the greatest amount of improvement in the turnover ratio from last
         year to this year?
      d. Which business had the least amount of improvement in its turnover ratio from last year
         to this year?

ENRICHMENT PROBLEMS

MASTERY PROBLEM 9-M   Recording transactions for uncollectible accounts — allowance method

The following selected transactions for Norwood, Inc., were completed during the current year.

Instructions: 1. Record the following transactions. Use page 19 of a general journal and page 30 of a cash receipts journal. Source documents are abbreviated as follows: memorandum, M; receipt, R.

Jan. 9. Wrote off past due account of Joan Mueller as uncollectible, $534.65. M20.
Mar. 4. Wrote off past due account of James York as uncollectible, $782.50. M29.
Mar. 28. Received full payment for Joan Mueller's account, previously written off as uncollectible, $534.65. M40 and R24.
June 20. Wrote off past due account of Alice Armbruster as uncollectible, $617.16. M58.
Oct. 7. Wrote off past due account of Martha Hoggenboom as uncollectible, $808.15. M74.
Dec. 11. Received full payment for James York's account, previously written off as uncollectible, $782.50. M82 and R92.

2. Continue using page 19 of the general journal. Record the adjusting entry needed for bad debts expense. Use December 31 of the current year as the date. Selected account balances for Norwood, Inc., are given below before adjustments on December 31 of the current year.

Accounts Receivable	$ 20,171.68
Sales	280,065.10
Sales Returns and Allowances	919.82
Sales Discount	1,605.70

Norwood uses the percentage of net sales method. The percentage is 1%.

3. If all the entries recorded in the general journal and cash receipts journal were posted, including the adjusting entry, what would be the new balance of Allowance for Uncollectible Accounts? The January 1 balance of Allowance for Uncollectible Accounts, before the transactions for the year were recorded, was $1,463.89.

CHALLENGE PROBLEM 9-C   Estimating and recording bad debts expense by aging accounts receivable — allowance method

Use the information given in Mastery Problem 9-M. A partial schedule of accounts receivable by age is given below.

Customer	Account Balance	Not Yet Due	Days Account Balance Past Due			
			1-30	31-60	61-90	Over 90
Totals	$20,171.68	$15,234.64	$1,307.65	$898.90	$1,640.87	$1,089.62
Percentages	—	0.2%	0.6%	1.0%	7.0%	60.0%

Instructions: 1. Record the transactions given in Problem 9-M. Use page 26 of a general journal and page 35 of a cash receipts journal.

2. Continue using page 26 of the general journal. Record the adjusting entry for bad debts expense. Estimate the balance of Allowance for Uncollectible Accounts by using the partial schedule of accounts receivable by age given above. Use December 31 of the current year as the date. The January 1 balance of Allowance for Uncollectible Accounts, before the transactions for the year were recorded, was $1,463.89.

10 Accounting for Plant Assets

ENABLING PERFORMANCE TASKS

After studying Chapter 10, you will be able to:
a. Define accounting terms related to plant assets.
b. Identify accounting concepts and practices related to plant assets.
c. Record information on plant asset records.
d. Figure plant asset depreciation.
e. Record entries for buying and disposing of plant assets.
f. Record entries for estimated depreciation.
g. Figure and record property tax expense.

Current assets, such as accounts receivable and supplies, are converted to cash or used up in a short period of time, usually within a year. Some assets, such as equipment, buildings, and land, are not used up or converted to cash within a year. Assets which will be used for a number of years in the operation of a business are known as plant assets. Plant assets are also known as fixed assets or long-term assets.

An office equipment business may sell such things as desks, chairs, file cabinets, and typewriters. These items are for sale to customers and are not used in the operation of the business. Therefore, equipment purchased for sale to customers is classified as merchandise rather than as plant assets.

PLANT ASSET RECORD

A business keeps a separate record of each plant asset owned. An accounting form on which a business records information about each plant asset is called a plant asset record. Gallery uses a printed card as its plant asset record. The plant asset record is shown in Illustration 10-1.

Gallery's plant asset record has three sections. Section 1 is prepared when a plant asset is bought. Information in this section shows whether the plant asset is for use in the store, office, or warehouse. Also included is a

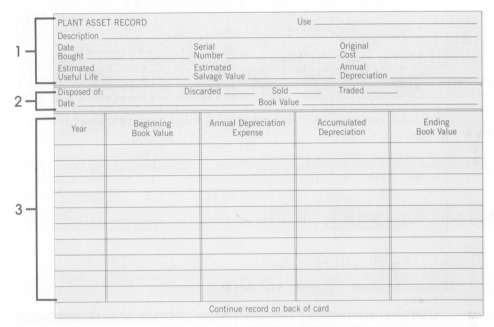

PLANT ASSET RECORD   Use _____
Description _____
Date   Serial   Original
Bought _____   Number _____   Cost _____
Estimated   Estimated   Annual
Useful Life _____   Salvage Value _____ Depreciation _____

Disposed of: Discarded _____   Sold _____   Traded _____
Date _____ Book Value _____

Year	Beginning Book Value	Annual Depreciation Expense	Accumulated Depreciation	Ending Book Value

Continue record on back of card

description, the date on which bought, its serial number, and information needed to figure annual depreciation for the plant asset. Section 2 provides space for recording disposition of the plant asset. Section 3 provides space for recording annual depreciation.

Illustration 10-1
Plant asset record

Figuring depreciation and disposing of plant assets are described later in this chapter.

BUYING PLANT ASSETS

When a plant asset is bought, a journal entry is recorded and information is placed on a plant asset record.

Buying a plant asset for cash

Gallery needs a new typewriter. Because the typewriter is to be used in the office, the plant asset is classified as office equipment.

Gallery has three kinds of plant assets. Separate general ledger accounts are used for office equipment, store equipment, and warehouse equipment.

January 2, 1989.
Paid cash for new typewriter, $680.00. Check No. 62.

The analysis of this transaction is shown in the T accounts. Equipment—Office is increased by a $680.00 debit. Cash is decreased by a $680.00 credit.

The entry to record this transaction in a cash payments journal is shown in Illustration 10-2.

Equipment—Office	
680.00	

Cash	
	680.00

CASH PAYMENTS JOURNAL									PAGE /	
					1	2	3	4	5	
DATE	ACCOUNT TITLE	CHECK No.	POST. REF.	GENERAL		ACCOUNTS PAYABLE DEBIT	PURCHASES DISCOUNT CREDIT	CASH CREDIT		
				DEBIT	CREDIT					
1989 Jan. 2	Equipment—Office	62		680.00				680.00		1
										2

A plant asset record is also prepared for this new plant asset as shown in Illustration 10-3.

PLANT ASSET RECORD		Use ___Office___
Description __Typewriter__		
Date Bought __January 2, 1989__	Serial Number ___X3492D194___	Original Cost ___$680.00___
Estimated Useful Life __5 years__	Estimated Salvage Value __$130.00__	Annual Depreciation __$110.00__
Disposed of: Date _____	Discarded _____ Sold _____ Book Value _____	Traded _____
Year	Beginning Book Value	Annual Depreciation Expense	Accumulated Depreciation	Ending Book Value

The plant asset record is filed alphabetically along with all the other plant asset records for office equipment.

Buying a plant asset on account

Not all plant assets are bought for cash. Gallery sometimes buys a plant asset on one date and pays for it on a later date.

GENERAL LEDGER

Equipment — Office

695.00 |

Accounts Payable

| 695.00

ACCOUNTS PAYABLE LEDGER

Royalty Company

| 695.00

January 2, 1989.
Bought office paper shredder on account from Royalty Company: cost, $695.00. Memorandum No. 70.

The analysis of this transaction is shown in the T accounts. In the general ledger, Equipment—Office is increased by a $695.00 debit. Accounts Payable is increased by a $695.00 credit. In the accounts payable ledger, the vendor account, Royalty Company, is also increased by a $695.00 credit.

The general journal entry for this transaction is shown in Illustration 10-4.

GENERAL JOURNAL				PAGE /	
DATE	ACCOUNT TITLE	POST. REF.	DEBIT	CREDIT	
1989 Jan. 2	Equipment —Office		695.00		1
	Accts. Pay./Royalty Co.	✓		695.00	2
	M70				3

This transaction does not involve the purchase of merchandise. Therefore, the entry is *not* recorded in a purchases journal.

The procedure for preparing the shredder's plant asset record is similar to the procedure previously described for a typewriter.

FIGURING DEPRECIATION USING THE STRAIGHT-LINE METHOD

Plant assets may wear out, may no longer be needed in a business' operations, or may become outdated when new models are available. For these reasons, plant assets decrease in value from one year to the next. For example, Gallery's paper shredder is worth $695.00 on January 2, 1989, the day it was bought. However, at the end of 1989, the shredder is not worth that much. The value will decrease because of use. The portion of a plant asset's cost transferred to an expense account in each fiscal period during a plant asset's useful life is known as depreciation. (CONCEPT: *Matching Expenses with Revenue*)

Land, because of its permanent nature, is not subject to depreciation. Increases or decreases in land value are usually recorded only when land is sold or otherwise disposed of.

Three factors are used to figure a plant asset's annual depreciation.

1. Original cost.
2. Estimated salvage value.
3. Estimated useful life.

Plant assets' original cost

The total costs paid to make a plant asset usable to a business are called original cost. These costs include the purchase price, delivery costs, and any necessary installation costs. For example, the cost of electrical wiring for store counter lights is part of the original cost of a new store counter. (CONCEPT: *Historical Cost*) The original cost of a plant asset minus the accumulated depreciation is called the book value of a plant asset.

Plant assets' salvage value

When plant assets are disposed of, often some part of the original cost value still remains. When a plant asset is bought, only an estimate of the final value can be made. The amount an owner expects to receive when a plant asset is removed from use is called the estimated salvage value. Salvage value is also known as residual value, scrap value, or trade-in value.

Until a plant asset is disposed of, most businesses have difficulty determining a plant asset's *exact* salvage value. Thus, until actually disposed of, a plant asset's salvage value can only be *estimated*. Because salvage value is used to figure a plant asset's annual depreciation, the most accurate estimate possible is made when a plant asset is bought.

Plant assets' useful life

The number of years a plant asset is expected to be productive for a business is called the estimated useful life. A plant asset's useful life differs from one situation to another. A personal car may last from five to seven years. The same model car used as a taxi may last for only one year.

Businesses most often use past experience as the basis for estimating a plant asset's useful life. If a typewriter usually lasts five years for a specific business, then five years is the estimated useful life of new typewriters for that business. Sometimes however a business has difficulty estimating a plant asset's useful life. The Internal Revenue Service issues guidelines which give useful life for many plant assets. Businesses often use these guidelines to assure that depreciation figures are within current tax regulations.

Straight-line method of figuring depreciation

Charging an *equal* amount of depreciation expense for a plant asset each fiscal period is called the straight-line method of figuring depreciation. Gallery uses the straight-line method.

Other methods of figuring depreciation are described later in this chapter. Regardless of the method used, the accounts debited and credited for depreciation are the same.

Gallery buys a paper shredder on January 2, 1989, for $695.00. Estimated salvage value is $125.00. Estimated useful life is five years. Annual depreciation is figured as shown below.

Original Cost	–	Estimated Salvage Value	=	Estimated Total Depreciation
$695.00	–	$125.00	=	$570.00

Estimated Total Depreciation	÷	Estimated Useful Life	=	Estimated Annual Depreciation
$570.00	÷	5	=	$114.00

Estimated annual depreciation also may be figured by an annual percentage rate. In the above example, the plant asset has an estimated useful life of five years. Therefore the annual depreciation rate is 20% (100% *divided by* 5 *equals* .20 or 20%). Estimated total depreciation, $570.00, *times* depreciation rate, 20%, *equals* estimated annual depreciation, $114.00.

Most plant assets have a salvage value at the end of their useful lives. However, if a plant asset wears out completely, there is no salvage value, and total depreciation would be the same as the original cost.

Depreciation for part of a year

A calendar month is the smallest unit of time used when figuring depreciation. A plant asset may be placed in service at a date other than the first day of a fiscal period. In such cases, depreciation is figured to the nearest first of a month. For example, a plant asset is bought on June 8, 1989. For purposes of figuring depreciation, the plant asset is assumed to have been placed in service on June 1, the nearest first of a month. Depreciation is figured for seven months, June through December, 1989. Another plant asset is bought on June 17, 1989. The plant asset is assumed to have been placed in service on July 1. Depreciation is figured for six months, July through December.

Annual depreciation over the useful life of a plant asset is shown in Illustration 10-5.

Plant asset: Cabinet
Original cost: $500.00
Estimated salvage value: $100.00
Estimated useful life: 5 years
Estimated annual depreciation: $80.00

Year	Beginning Book Value	Annual Depreciation	Accumulated Depreciation	Ending Book Value
1	$500.00	$80.00	$ 80.00	$420.00
2	420.00	80.00	160.00	340.00
3	340.00	80.00	240.00	260.00
4	260.00	80.00	320.00	180.00
5	180.00	80.00	400.00	100.00

Illustration 10-5
Annual depreciation for a plant asset using the straight-line method

The ending book value for one year is the beginning book value for the next year. At the end of the third year, the cabinet described in Illustration 10-5 has a book value of $260.00.

At the end of the fifth year, the ending book value is equal to the estimated salvage value, $100.00. Even if a plant asset is used longer than its estimated useful life, depreciation is not recorded once the book value equals the estimated salvage value.

RECORDING DEPRECIATION

Gallery records estimated annual depreciation in two places for each plant asset. (1) On the plant asset record. (2) As part of adjusting entries which are posted to general ledger accounts.

Recording estimated annual depreciation on a plant asset record

On December 31, 1989, Gallery records the estimated annual depreciation on each plant asset record. This information is placed on a plant asset record as shown in Illustration 10-6.

In section 3 of the plant asset record, the year is recorded in the Year column. The ending book value for the previous year is recorded in the

PLANT ASSET RECORD				Use _Office_	

Description __Paper Shredder__

Date Bought _January 2, 1989_	Serial Number __S15534__	Original Cost __$695.00__
Estimated Useful Life __5 years__	Estimated Salvage Value __$125.00__	Annual Depreciation __$114.00__

Disposed of: Discarded _____   Sold _____   Traded _____
Date _____ Book Value _____

Year	Beginning Book Value	Annual Depreciation Expense	Accumulated Depreciation	Ending Book Value
1989	$695.00	$114.00	$114.00	$581.00

Illustration 10-6
Depreciation recorded on
a plant asset record

Beginning Book Value column. In this case there is no previous ending book value because this plant asset is first put in service during 1989. Therefore, the original cost value, *$695.00*, is written in the Beginning Book Value column. The depreciation for the plant asset is recorded in the Annual Depreciation Expense column. The new amount of accumulated depreciation is recorded in the Accumulated Depreciation column. A new book value is figured and recorded in the Ending Book Value column.

Gallery follows the same procedures in recording depreciation information on all plant asset records.

Recording estimated annual depreciation in a general journal

After estimated depreciation is recorded on the plant asset records, depreciation amounts for the year are totaled. For example, Gallery totals annual depreciation recorded on December 31, 1989, for all office equipment plant asset records. The total for all office equipment depreciation is $10,571.00. At the end of a fiscal period, estimated depreciation on office equipment is recorded as part of the business' adjusting entries.

Depreciation Expense — Office Equipment

Adjusting	10,571.00	

Accumulated Depreciation — Office Equipment

	Balance	38,434.00
	Adjusting	10,571.00

The analysis of this adjusting entry is shown in the T accounts. Depreciation Expense — Office Equipment is increased by a $10,571.00 debit. Accumulated Depreciation — Office Equipment is increased by a $10,571.00 credit.

The adjusting entry for office equipment depreciation expense is shown in Illustration 10-7.

GENERAL JOURNAL					PAGE _13_
DATE	ACCOUNT TITLE	POST. REF.	DEBIT	CREDIT	
	Adjusting Entries				1
31	*Depr. Exp. — Office Equip.*		10571 00		22
	Accum. Depr. — Office Equip.			10571 00	23
					24

Illustration 10-7
Adjusting entry for office
equipment depreciation
expense

A similar depreciation expense adjusting entry is recorded for store equipment, warehouse equipment, and building.

DISPOSING OF PLANT ASSETS

Gallery usually disposes of plant assets in one of three ways.

1. The plant asset is discarded because no useful life remains.
2. The plant asset is sold because it is no longer needed even though it might still be usable.
3. The plant asset is traded for another plant asset of the same kind.

Discarding a plant asset with no book value

If a plant asset's total accumulated depreciation is equal to the original cost value, the plant asset has no book value. Gallery discards a storage cabinet that has no book value.

January 5, 1989.
Discarded storage cabinet bought in January, 1984: cost, $175.00; total accumulated depreciation recorded to December 31, 1988, $175.00. Memorandum No. 72.

The analysis of this transaction is shown in the T accounts. Accumulated Depreciation—Office Equipment is decreased by a $175.00 debit. This debit cancels the total depreciation recorded for the cabinet. Equipment—Office is decreased by a $175.00 credit. This credit cancels the original cost, $175.00, recorded when the cabinet was bought. When this entry is recorded and posted, all amounts for the discarded cabinet are removed from the two accounts. The general journal entry for this transaction is shown in Illustration 10-8.

Accumulated Depreciation—
Office Equipment

Discarded	175.00	Balance	175.00

Equipment—Office

Cost	175.00	Discarded	175.00

		GENERAL JOURNAL			PAGE /	
	DATE	ACCOUNT TITLE	POST. REF.	DEBIT	CREDIT	
7	5	Accum. Depr. – Office Equip.		1 75 00		7
8		Equipment – Office			1 75 00	8
9		M 72				9
10						10

Illustration 10-8
Entry to record discarding a plant asset with no ending book value

A notation is made in section 2 of the plant asset record for this plant asset as shown in Illustration 10-9.

The date on which the cabinet is discarded, *January 5, 1989,* is written in the space for the disposition date. The book value at the time the cabinet is discarded, *None,* is written in the space for disposition book value.

PLANT ASSET RECORD		Use __Office__		

Description __Storage Cabinet__

Date Bought __January 3, 1984__ Serial Number __None__ Original Cost __$175.00__

Estimated Useful Life __5 years__ Estimated Salvage Value __None__ Annual Depreciation __$35.00__

Disposed of: _____ Discarded __X__ Sold _____ Traded _____
Date __January 5, 1989__ Book Value __None__

Year	Beginning Book Value	Annual Depreciation Expense	Accumulated Depreciation	Ending Book Value
1984	$175.00	$35.00	$ 35.00	$140.00
1985	140.00	35.00	70.00	105.00
1986	105.00	35.00	105.00	70.00
1987	70.00	35.00	140.00	35.00
1988	35.00	35.00	175.00	---

Continue record on back of card

Illustration 10-9
Notation on plant asset record showing discarding of a plant asset

Discarding a plant asset with a book value

Gallery discards a table that is damaged beyond repair. The table still has a book value.

June 30, 1989.
Discarded office table bought in June, 1985: cost, $200.00; total accumulated depreciation recorded to December 31, 1988, $140.00. Memorandum No. 92.

Depreciation for part of a year. A plant asset may be disposed of at any time during its useful life. When a plant asset is disposed of, its depreciation from the beginning of the current fiscal year to date of disposal is recorded. For example, adjusting entries for depreciation expense were last recorded on December 31, 1988. The table is discarded on June 30, 1989. Before entries are made for the disposal of the table, six months' depreciation must be recorded. The six months' depreciation is for the period from January 1 to June 30, 1989. The estimated annual depreciation for the table is $40.00.

The analysis of this entry is shown in the T accounts. Depreciation Expense — Office Equipment is increased by a $20.00 debit. Accumulated Depreciation — Office Equipment is increased by a $20.00 credit.

Depreciation Expense — Office Equipment	
Add. depr. 20.00	

Accumulated Depreciation — Office Equipment	
	Balance 140.00
	Add depr. 20.00

The entry to record the six months' depreciation is shown on lines 4–6 of the general journal in Illustration 10-10.

A notation is made in section 3 of the plant asset record for this table.

GENERAL JOURNAL					PAGE 6
DATE	ACCOUNT TITLE	POST. REF.	DEBIT	CREDIT	
30	Depr. Exp. — Office Equip.		20 00		4
	Accum. Depr. — Office Equip.			20 00	5
	M92				6
30	Accum. Depr. — Office Equip.		160 00		7
	Loss on Plant Assets		40 00		8
	Equipment — Office			200 00	9
	M92				10

Illustration 10-10
Entries to record depreciation for part of a year and discard a plant asset with book value

Entry to discard a plant asset with book value. After the partial year's depreciation is recorded, an entry is made for discarding the table. Discarding a plant asset with a book value is a loss to the business. The amount of the loss on the table is figured as shown below.

Original Cost	−	Total Accumulated Depreciation	=	Plant Asset Book Value
$200.00	−	$160.00	=	$40.00

The analysis of this transaction is shown in the T accounts. Accumulated Depreciation.— Office Equipment is decreased by a $160.00 debit. Loss on Plant Assets is increased by a $40.00 debit. Equipment — Office is decreased by a $200.00 credit.

Accumulated Depreciation — Office Equipment			
Discarded	160.00	Balance	140.00
		Add. depr.	20.00

Loss on Plant Assets		
Discarded	40.00	

Equipment — Office		
Cost	200.00	Discarded	200.00

Losses from discarding plant assets are not regular operating expenses. Therefore, Loss on Plant Assets is classified as an other expense account as shown in Gallery's chart of accounts.

The entry to record this transaction is shown on lines 7–10 of the general journal, Illustration 10-10. A notation is made in section 2 of the plant asset record for this office table.

Selling a plant asset for less than book value

Gallery decides that a typewriter bought in 1986 is no longer needed. Gallery sells the typewriter to an employee.

January 4, 1989.
Received $185.00 for typewriter bought in 1985: cost, $600.00; total accumulated depreciation recorded to December 31, 1988, $400.00. Receipt No. 60.

The amount of the loss is figured as shown below.

Original Cost	−	Total Accumulated Depreciation	−	Cash Received	=	Loss on Plant Asset
$600.00	−	$400.00	−	$185.00	=	$15.00

Estimated annual depreciation is used to figure a plant asset's book value. Therefore, until a plant asset is disposed of, the plant asset's book value is also an *estimated* amount. When a plant asset is sold, the amount received is the plant asset's *actual* value. As previously described, the typewriter sold by Gallery has an estimated book value of $200.00 on January 4, 1989. However, the *actual* value is the amount of cash received for the typewriter, $185.00. The actual value is $15.00 less than the estimated book value.

The analysis of this transaction is shown in the T accounts. Cash is increased by a $185.00 debit. Accumulated Depreciation—Office Equipment is decreased by a $400.00 debit. Loss on Plant Assets is increased by a $15.00 debit. Equipment—Office is decreased by a $600.00 credit.

The entry to record this transaction in a cash receipts journal is shown in Illustration 10-11.

Cash	
Sold 185.00	

Accumulated Depreciation— Office Equipment	
Sold 400.00	Balance 400.00

Loss on Plant Assets	
Sold 15.00	

Equipment—Office	
Cost 600.00	Sold 600.00

CASH RECEIPTS JOURNAL   PAGE 1

					GENERAL		ACCOUNTS RECEIVABLE CREDIT	SALES CREDIT	SALES TAX PAYABLE		SALES DISCOUNT DEBIT	CASH DEBIT	
	DATE	ACCOUNT TITLE	DOC. NO.	POST. REF.	DEBIT	CREDIT			DEBIT	CREDIT			
1	1989 Jan. 4	Accum. Depr.—Office Equip.	R60		40000								1
2		Loss on Plant Assets			1500							18500	2
3		Equipment—Office				60000							3
4													4

Illustration 10-11
Entry to record selling a plant asset for less than book value

A notation is made in section 2 of the plant asset record for this typewriter.

Selling a plant asset for more than book value

Gallery sells a warehouse cart for more than its estimated book value. The source documents for this transaction are a memorandum, detailing the need for an additional three months' depreciation, and a receipt. (CONCEPT: *Objective Evidence*)

March 31, 1989.
Received $700.00 for warehouse cart bought in January, 1983: cost, $1,500.00; total accumulated depreciation recorded to December 31, 1988, $840.00. Memorandum No. 99 and Receipt No. 75.

Depreciation Expense— Warehouse Equipment	
Add. depr. 35.00	

Accumulated Depreciation— Warehouse Equipment	
	Balance 840.00
	Add. depr. 35.00

Depreciation for part of a year. Estimated annual depreciation for the cart is $140.00. Depreciation for 3 months, one-fourth of a year, equals $35.00. The analysis of this entry is shown in the T accounts.

Depreciation Expense—Warehouse Equipment is increased by a $35.00 debit. Accumulated Depreciation—Warehouse Equipment is increased by a $35.00 credit.

This entry is similar to the entry on lines 4–6 of the general journal, Illustration 10-10. A notation is made in section 3 of the plant asset record for this cart.

Entry to record selling a plant asset for more than book value. After depreciation is recorded for part of a year, an entry is made for the sale of the plant asset.

The analysis of this transaction is shown in the T accounts. Cash is increased by a $700.00 debit. Accumulated Depreciation— Warehouse Equipment is decreased by an $875.00 debit. Equipment—Warehouse is decreased by a $1,500.00 credit. Gain on Plant Assets is increased by a $75.00 credit. The amount of the gain is figured as shown below.

Cash	
Sold 700.00	

Accumulated Depreciation—Warehouse Equipment	
Sold 875.00	Balance 840.00
	Add. depr. 35.00

Equipment—Warehouse	
Cost 1,500.00	Sold 1,500.00

Gain on Plant Assets	
	Sold 75.00

Original Cost	−	Total Accumulated Depreciation	−	Cash Received	=	Gain on Plant Asset
$1,500.00	−	$875.00	−	$700.00	=	$75.00

A gain from the sale of plant assets is not operating revenue. Therefore, Gain on Plant Assets is classified as an other revenue account as shown in Gallery's chart of accounts.

The entry to record this transaction in a cash receipts journal is shown in Illustration 10-12.

CASH RECEIPTS JOURNAL PAGE 3

		DATE	ACCOUNT TITLE	DOC. NO.	POST. REF.	GENERAL DEBIT	GENERAL CREDIT	ACCOUNTS RECEIVABLE CREDIT	SALES CREDIT	SALES TAX PAYABLE DEBIT	SALES TAX PAYABLE CREDIT	SALES DISCOUNT DEBIT	CASH DEBIT	
21		31	Accum. Depr. Warehouse Equip.	R75		875 00							700 00	21
22			Equipment—Warehouse				1500 00							22
23			Gain on Plant Assets				75 00							23
24														24

A notation is made in section 2 of the plant asset record for this cart.

Trading a plant asset

Businesses often buy a new plant asset paying for it with cash and trading in a similar plant asset. For example, Gallery needs a new store counter. The vendor agrees to take an old store counter in trade. The source documents for this transaction are a memorandum and a check stub. (CONCEPT: Objective Evidence)

Illustration 10-12
Entry to record selling a plant asset for more than book value

June 27, 1989.
Paid cash, $850.00, plus old store counter, for new store counter: cost of old counter, $1,000.00; total accumulated depreciation recorded to December 31, 1988, $720.00. Memorandum No. 130 and Check No. 154.

Depreciation Expense—Store Equipment

Add. depr.	45.00	

Accumulated Depreciation— Store Equipment

	Balance	720.00
	Add. depr.	45.00

Recording depreciation for part of a year. Additional depreciation for the six months of 1989 is first recorded. The analysis of this transaction is shown in the T accounts.

Depreciation Expense—Store Equipment is increased by a $45.00 debit. Accumulated Depreciation—Store Equipment is increased by a $45.00 credit. The entry to record the additional depreciation is similar to the one shown on lines 4–6 of the general journal, Illustration 10-10. A notation is made in section 3 of the plant asset record for the old counter.

Recording trade-in of old plant asset for a new plant asset. The Internal Revenue Service does not allow a loss or gain on plant assets traded for similar plant assets. The new plant asset's original cost equals the cash *actually* paid plus the book value of the traded item. *(CONCEPT: Historical Cost)* The original cost of the new counter is figured below.

Old Counter Original Cost	–	Total Accumulated Depreciation	=	Old Counter Ending Book Value
$1,000.00	–	$765.00	=	$235.00

Old Counter Ending Book Value	+	Cash Paid	=	New Counter Original Cost
$235.00	+	$850.00	=	$1,085.00

Equipment—Store

Cost	1,000.00	Trade in	1,000.00
Trade in	1,085.00		

Accumulated Depreciation— Store Equipment

Trade in	765.00	Balance	720.00
		Add. depr.	45.00

Cash

		Trade in	850.00

The analysis of this transaction is shown in the T accounts. Equipment—Store is decreased by a $1,000.00 credit, the original cost of the old counter. Equipment—Store is also increased by a $1,085.00 debit, the original cost of the new counter. Accumulated Depreciation—Store Equipment is decreased by a $765.00 debit, total depreciation recorded to date on the traded item. Cash is decreased by a $850.00 credit.

The entry to record trading the old counter for the new counter is shown in Illustration 10-13.

A notation is made in section 2 of the old counter's plant asset record. A new plant asset record is prepared for the new counter.

CASH PAYMENTS JOURNAL   PAGE 6

	DATE	ACCOUNT TITLE	CHECK NO.	POST. REF.	GENERAL DEBIT	GENERAL CREDIT	ACCOUNTS PAYABLE DEBIT	PURCHASES DISCOUNT CREDIT	CASH CREDIT	
18	27	Equipment – Store	154		1085 00				850 00	18
19		Accum. Depr. – Store Equip.			765 00					19
20		Equipment – Store				1000 00				20

Illustration 10-13
Entry to record trading one plant asset for another plant asset of the same kind

Disposing of buildings

Entries to record discarding (tearing down) or selling buildings are handled the same as for any other plant asset. Buildings are seldom traded for new buildings. But, if a building is traded for another building, the entry is the same as for other plant assets.

Disposing of land

Land is considered to be a permanent plant asset. Therefore, the useful life is not estimated, and annual depreciation is not recorded for land. The book value of land is the original cost. *(CONCEPT: Historical Cost)*

Land is seldom discarded (abandoned). Usually land is sold at the same time as the buildings on the land are sold. Any gain or loss on the disposal of land is recorded at the time the land is disposed of.

When land is sold, Cash is debited and Land is credited. Any gain or loss from the sale of land is recorded in either Gain on Plant Assets or Loss on Plant Assets.

OTHER METHODS OF FIGURING DEPRECIATION

Gallery uses the straight-line method of figuring depreciation. An equal amount of depreciation is recorded each year during a plant asset's useful life.

Many plant assets depreciate more in the early years of useful life than in later years. For example, an automobile's market price will decrease more the first year of service than in later years. Therefore, charging more depreciation in a plant asset's early years may be more accurate than charging the same amount each year. Three methods other than the straight-line method of figuring depreciation may be used.

1. Declining-balance method of figuring depreciation.
2. Sum-of-the-years-digits method of figuring depreciation.
3. Production-unit method of figuring depreciation.

Regardless of the method used to figure the amount of depreciation, the general ledger accounts affected are the same.

Declining-balance method of figuring depreciation

Multiplying the book value at the end of each fiscal period by a constant depreciation rate is called the declining-balance method of figuring depreciation. Although the rate is the same each year, the book value declines from one year to the next because of the increasing accumulated depreciation. The greatest book value exists during the first year. Therefore, the greatest depreciation is recorded in the first year. Because the smallest book value exists during the last year, the least depreciation is recorded in the last year.

The declining-balance depreciation rate is greater than the straight-line rate. Because of the ease in figuring, many businesses use a declining-balance rate that is twice the straight-line rate. For example, if a plant asset has an estimated useful life of 5 years, then the declining-balance rate is figured as shown below.

Total Depreciation	÷	Estimated Years of Useful Life	=	Straight-Line Rate
100%	÷	5	=	20%

Straight-Line Rate	×	2	=	Declining-Balance Rate
20%	×	2	=	40%

Depreciation figured using both the declining-balance and the straight-line methods is shown in Illustration 10-14.

Plant asset: Cash Register					
Original cost: $2,000.00					
Estimated salvage value: $175.00					
Estimated useful life: 5 years					
	Straight-Line Method			Declining-Balance Method		
Year	Beg. Book Value	Annual Depr.	End. Book Value	Beg. Book Value	Annual Depr.	End. Book Value
1	$2,000.00	$ 365.00	$1,635.00	$2,000.00	$ 800.00	$1,200.00
2	1,635.00	365.00	1,270.00	1,200.00	480.00	720.00
3	1,270.00	365.00	905.00	720.00	288.00	432.00
4	905.00	365.00	540.00	432.00	172.80	259.20
5	540.00	365.00	175.00	259.20	84.20	175.00
Total Depr.	—	$1,825.00	—	—	$1,825.00	—

Illustration 10-14
Comparison of two methods of figuring annual depreciation for the same plant asset

When using the declining-balance method, the annual depreciation amount is figured using the beginning book value for each year. More depreciation is recorded in a plant asset's earlier years. The annual depreciation for the first year using the declining-balance method is figured as shown below.

Beginning Book Value	×	Rate	=	Annual Depreciation
$2,000.00	×	40%	=	$800.00

The ending book value for the first year is figured as shown below.

Beginning Book Value	−	Annual Depreciation	=	Ending Book Value
$2,000.00	−	$800.00	=	$1,200.00

The ending book value for one year is the beginning book value for the next year.

When using the declining-balance method, a different amount of depreciation is recorded each year. Also, special care must be taken in figuring depreciation for the last year of useful life. A plant asset is never depreciated below its estimated salvage value. Therefore, in the last year, only enough depreciation expense is recorded to reduce the plant asset's book value to salvage value. For example, in Illustration 10-14, depreciation in the fifth year is $84.20 and the ending book value is $175.00.

When using the straight-line method, the same amount, $365.00, is recorded as the annual depreciation for each year of the plant asset's useful life. The straight-line method results in a book value equal to salvage value at the end of the last year of useful life. The straight-line method is easier to figure than the declining-balance method.

Sum-of-the-years-digits method of figuring depreciation

Another method of figuring depreciation is based on a fraction derived from the years' digits for the useful life of a plant asset. Using fractions based on years of a plant asset's useful life is called the sum-of-the-years-digits method of figuring depreciation. The fractions are determined as shown below for the plant asset in Illustration 10-14.

Years' Digits	Fraction
1	5/15
2	4/15
3	3/15
4	2/15
5	1/15
Total 15	

The years' digits are added $(1 + 2 + 3 + 4 + 5 = 15)$. Then, using the sum of the years' digits, a fraction is created for each year with the years' digits in reverse order. Year 1 has a fraction of 5/15. Year 5 has a fraction of 1/15.

The first year's depreciation and ending book value are figured as shown below.

Original Cost	–	Estimated Salvage Value	=	Total Estimated Depreciation
$2,000.00	–	$175.00	=	$1,825.00

Total Estimated Depreciation	×	Year's Fraction	=	Estimated Annual Depreciation
$1,825.00	×	5/15	=	$608.33

Each year's annual depreciation is figured by multiplying the total estimated depreciation times that year's fraction. The sum-of-the-years-digits method results in a last year ending book value equal to the plant asset's salvage value. The depreciation is figured using the year's fractions as shown in Illustration 10-15.

Plant asset: Cash Register
Original cost: $2,000.00
Estimated salvage value: $175.00
Estimated total depreciation: $1,825.00
Estimated useful life: 5 years

Year	Fraction	×	Total Depreciation	=	Year's Annual Depreciation
1	5/15		$1,825.00		$ 608.33
2	4/15		1,825.00		486.67
3	3/15		1,825.00		365.00
4	2/15		1,825.00		243.33
5	1/15		1,825.00		121.67
Total	—		—		$1,825.00

Illustration 10-15
Figuring depreciation using the sum-of-the-years-digits method

Comparison of three methods of figuring depreciation

A comparison of three methods of figuring depreciation is shown in Illustration 10-16.

Plant asset: Cash Register
Original cost: $2,000.00
Estimated salvage value: $175.00
Estimated useful life: 5 years

Year	Straight-Line Method	Declining-Balance Method	Sum-of-the-Years-Digits Method
1	$ 365.00	$ 800.00	$ 608.33
2	365.00	480.00	486.67
3	365.00	288.00	365.00
4	365.00	172.80	243.33
5	365.00	84.20	121.67
Totals	$1,825.00	$1,825.00	$1,825.00
Ending Book Value	$ 175.00	$ 175.00	$ 175.00

Illustration 10-16
Comparison of three methods of figuring annual depreciation for the same plant asset

The straight-line method is relatively easy to figure. The total depreciation for the five years is $1,825.00. However, the same depreciation amount is recorded for each of the five years of estimated life.

The declining-balance method is relatively easy to figure. Also, this method records a greater depreciation amount in the early years than is true of the straight-line method.

The sum-of-the-years-digits method is not as easy to use as the straight-line or declining-balance methods. However, this method also records a greater depreciation amount in the early years than is true of the straight-line method.

Production-unit method of figuring depreciation

Sometimes a plant asset's useful life depends on how much the asset is used. For example, an automobile will wear out faster if driven 80,000 miles rather than 60,000 miles a year. Figuring estimated annual depreciation based on the amount of production expected from a plant asset is called the production-unit method of figuring depreciation.

Muldooney Delivery Service owns a small truck. The truck's original cost is $12,000.00, estimated salvage value is $2,000.00, and estimated useful life is 80,000 miles. The truck's depreciation rate is figured as shown below.

Original Cost	−	Estimated Salvage Value	=	Estimated Total Depreciation
$12,000.00	−	$2,000.00	=	$10,000.00

Estimated Total Depreciation	÷	Estimated Useful Life	=	Estimated Depreciation Per Mile Driven
$10,000.00	÷	80,000 miles	=	$0.125

The truck's annual depreciation during its useful life is shown in Illustration 10-17.

Plant asset: Truck
Original cost: $12,000.00
Estimated salvage value: $2,000.00
Estimated useful life: 80,000 miles
Estimated total depreciation: $10,000.00
Depreciation rate: $0.125 per mile driven

Year	Beginning Book Value	Miles Driven	Annual Depreciation	Ending Book Value
1	$12,000.00	8,000	$1,000.00	$11,000.00
2	11,000.00	21,000	2,625.00	8,375.00
3	8,375.00	23,000	2,875.00	5,500.00
4	5,500.00	20,000	2,500.00	3,000.00
5	3,000.00	5,000	625.00	2,375.00
Totals	—	77,000	$9,625.00	—

Illustration 10-17
Annual depreciation for a plant asset using production-unit method

Estimated annual depreciation for the first year is figured as shown below.

Total Miles Driven	×	Depreciation Rate	=	Estimated Annual Depreciation
8,000	×	$0.125	=	$1,000.00

Estimated depreciation for each year of the truck's estimated useful life is figured at 12.5 cents per mile driven. As shown in Illustration 10-17, the truck's total depreciation at the end of five years is $9,625.00.

DEPLETION

Some plant assets decrease in value because part of the plant asset is physically removed in the operation of a business. For example, a lumber business owns land on which there are many trees. The business removes the trees to use for lumber. The land with the trees still growing on it is more valuable than the land after the trees have been removed. The decrease in a plant asset's value because of the removal of a natural resource is called depletion.

MacPherson Company owns land on which a coal mine is located. The land with the coal has an original cost of $100,000.00. The company's experts estimate that the land contains 40,000 tons of recoverable coal. Also, after the coal is removed, the estimated value of the remaining land is $25,000.00. Therefore, each ton of coal taken from the land decreases the land's value by $1.875. Figuring the depletion rate is shown below.

Original Cost		Estimated Salvage Value		Estimated Total Value of Coal
$100,000.00	−	$25,000.00	=	$75,000.00

Estimated Total Value of Coal		Estimated Tons of Recoverable Coal		Depletion Rate Per Ton of Coal
$75,000.00	÷	40,000	=	$1.875

In the first year of operation, the business removed 7,000 tons of coal. The depletion for the first year is $13,125.00 (tons removed, 7,000, *times* depletion rate, $1.875, *equals* depletion, $13,125.00).

MacPherson uses general ledger accounts titled Mine, Accumulated Depletion—Mine, and Depletion Expense—Mine. To record depletion, Accumulated Depletion—Mine is credited and Depletion Expense—Mine is debited. Entries are similar to those for depreciation of other plant assets.

FIGURING AND PAYING PROPERTY TAX

For tax purposes, state and federal governments define two kinds of property: real and personal. Land and anything attached to the land is called real property. Real property is sometimes known as real estate. All property not classified as real property is called personal property. For tax purposes, these definitions apply whether the property is owned by a business or an individual.

Figuring assessed value of property

An asset's value determined by tax authorities for the purpose of figuring taxes is called the assessed value. Assessed value is usually based on the judgment of persons known as assessors. Assessors are elected by citizens or are specially trained employees of a governmental unit.

The assessed value of an asset may not be the same as the book value on the business' or individual's records. The assessed value is assigned to an asset for tax purposes only. Often the assessed value is only a part of the true value of the asset. However, many persons and businesses use the assessed value to estimate the market value of an asset.

Figuring property tax on plant assets

Most governmental units with taxing power have a tax based on the value of real property. The real property tax is used on buildings and land. Some governmental units also tax personal property, such as cars, boats, trailers, and airplanes.

A governmental taxing unit determines a tax rate to use in figuring taxes. The tax rate is multiplied by an asset's *assessed* value. The assessed value is not the book value recorded on a business' records.

Gallery's buildings and land have been assessed for a total of $55,000.00. The city tax rate is 5%. Gallery's annual property tax is figured as shown below.

Assessed Value	×	Tax Rate	=	Annual Property Tax
$55,000.00	×	5%	=	$2,750.00

Gallery is required to pay property tax in two installments. On May 1 and November 1 of each year, Gallery must pay the city $1,375.00 (annual tax, $2,750.00, *divided by* 2 *equals* each installment, $1,375.00).

Paying property tax on plant assets

On May 1, 1989, Gallery pays the first installment of its property tax.

May 1, 1989.
Paid first installment of property tax, $1,375.00. Check No. 122.

The analysis of this transaction is shown in the T accounts. Property Tax Expense is increased by a $1,375.00 debit. Cash is decreased by a $1,375.00 credit.

Property Tax Expense	
1,375.00	

Cash	
	1,375.00

The entry to pay property tax is shown in Illustration 10-18.

Payment of all assessed taxes is necessary if a firm is to continue in business. Therefore, Gallery classifies property tax as an operating expense.

DATE		ACCOUNT TITLE	CHECK NO.	POST. REF.	GENERAL		ACCOUNTS PAYABLE DEBIT	PURCHASES DISCOUNT CREDIT	CASH CREDIT
					DEBIT	CREDIT			
1989 may	1	Property Tax Expense	122		137500				137500

CASH PAYMENTS JOURNAL   PAGE 5

Illustration 10-18
Entry to record paying
property tax

ACCOUNTING TERMS

What is the meaning of each of the following?

1. plant asset record
2. original cost
3. book value of a plant asset
4. estimated salvage value
5. estimated useful life
6. straight-line method of figuring depreciation
7. declining-balance method of figuring depreciation
8. sum-of-the-years-digits method of figuring depreciation
9. production-unit method of figuring depreciation
10. depletion
11. real property
12. personal property
13. assessed value

QUESTIONS FOR INDIVIDUAL STUDY

1. What are some examples of plant assets?
2. What two general ledger accounts are affected, and how, by a transaction to buy office equipment for cash?
3. What two general ledger accounts are affected, and how, by a transaction to buy office equipment on account?
4. Why is a transaction to buy office equipment on account *not* recorded in the purchases journal?
5. Why do plant assets decrease in value each year?
6. Recording annual depreciation for plant assets is an application of which accounting concept?
7. Why is annual depreciation *not* recorded for land?
8. What three factors are used in figuring a plant asset's estimated annual depreciation?
9. When using the straight-line method, what are the two formulas used to figure a plant asset's estimated annual depreciation?
10. What is the smallest unit of time used when figuring depreciation?
11. In what two places does Gallery record annual depreciation for each plant asset?
12. What are the three ways Gallery might dispose of a plant asset?
13. What accounts are affected, and how, when office equipment with no remaining book value is discarded?
14. What does Gallery do with plant asset records for plant assets that have been discarded, sold, or traded?
15. A business sold a plant asset on March 31 of the current year. What entry may need to be recorded before the entry is made for the sale of this plant asset?
16. What accounts are affected, and how, when office equipment with some remaining book value is discarded?
17. What accounts are affected, and how, when office equipment is sold for cash less than its book value?
18. What accounts are affected, and how, when warehouse equipment is sold for cash greater than the remaining book value?
19. Which accounts are affected, and how, when cash and old store equipment are

given for new store equipment?

20. In Question 19, what is the formula for figuring the new equipment's original cost?

21. How do the straight-line, declining-balance, and sum-of-the-years-digits methods of figuring depreciation compare?

22. What is the basis for the production-unit method of figuring depreciation?

23. How does a mining company figure the amount of depletion for a year?

24. What accounts are affected, and how, by an entry to pay property tax?

CASES FOR MANAGEMENT DECISION

CASE 1 A corporation's plant assets include office equipment, a building, and the land on which the building is located. The corporation's general ledger includes a single account titled Plant Assets and a single account titled Accumulated Depreciation — Plant Assets. The corporation's accountant suggests that the plant asset account be divided into three accounts titled Office Equipment, Building, and Land. The corporation's president does not think this is a good idea. With whom do you agree and why?

CASE 2 A corporation owns land on which there is both an active coal mine and timber. The corporation also owns an office building and the land on which it is located. The corporation uses three plant asset accounts: 1. Land and Buildings (depreciation figured using the straight-line method). 2. Timber (depreciation figured using the declining-balance method). 3. Coal Mine (depreciation figured using the declining-balance method). Do you agree with the accounting procedures being used? Explain your answers.

APPLICATION PROBLEMS

PROBLEM 10-1   Recording the buying of plant assets

Selected transactions completed by Mendowser, Inc., during 1985 are given below.

Instructions: 1. Record the following transactions. Use page 3 of a general journal and page 5 of a cash payments journal. Source documents are abbreviated as follows: check, C; memorandum, M.

Jan. 2, 1985. Paid cash for office file cabinet: cost, $300.00; estimated salvage value, $50.00; estimated useful life, 5 years; Serial No., FC2467. C130.

Jan. 3, 1985. Bought on account from Doarn, Inc., office typewriter: cost, $350.00; estimated salvage value, none; estimated useful life, 5 years; Serial No., X4672Y101. M11.

Mar. 31, 1985. Bought on account from Bessler, Inc., hand truck for warehouse: cost, $100.00; estimated salvage value, $25.00; estimated useful life, 5 years; Serial No., 23D4689. M24.

May 1, 1985. Paid cash for used truck to be used between warehouses: cost, $8,500.00; estimated salvage value, $1,000.00; estimated useful life, 5 years; Serial No., 45J3257XF29. C210.

July 1, 1985. Paid cash for store shelving: cost, $500.00; estimated salvage value, $25.00; estimated useful life, 10 years; Serial No., none. C250.

2. Complete section 1 of a plant asset record similar to the one in Illustration 10-1 for each plant asset. Leave the line for annual depreciation blank.

The plant asset records used in Problem 10-1 are needed to complete Problems 10-2, 10-3, and 10-4.

PROBLEM 10-2   Figuring depreciation using the straight-line method

The plant asset records used in Problem 10-1 are needed to complete Problem 10-2.

Instructions: Use the plant asset records completed in Problem 10-1. Complete a depreciation table similar to Illustration 10-5 for each of the plant assets bought by Mendowser, Inc. Record the annual depreciation in section 1 of the plant asset records.

The depreciation tables completed in Problem 10-2 are needed to complete Problem 10-3.

PROBLEM 10-3   Recording estimated annual depreciation

The plant asset records used in Problem 10-1 and the depreciation tables completed in Problem 10-2 are needed to complete Problem 10-3.

Instructions: 1. Use page 12 of a general journal and the depreciation tables prepared in Problem 10-2. Record the three adjusting entries for office, warehouse, and store depreciation expense for the first year. Use December 31, 1985, as the date.

    2. Use the plant asset records prepared in Problem 10-1. For each plant asset, record depreciation for 1985 in section 3 of the record.

    3. Record the three adjusting entries for the second year. Use December 31, 1986, as the date.

    4. For each plant asset, record depreciation in section 3 of the plant asset record for 1986, 1987, and 1988.

The plant asset records used in Problem 10-3 are needed to complete Problem 10-4.

PROBLEM 10-4   Recording transactions for disposing of plant assets

The plant asset records used in Problem 10-3 are needed to complete Problem 10-4.

Mendowser, Inc., completed the selected transactions given below. Use the appropriate plant asset records from Problem 10-3 for additional information needed. Use page 1 of a general journal, page 4 of a cash receipts journal, and page 5 of a cash payments journal. Source documents are abbreviated as follows: check, C; memorandum, M; receipt, R.

Jan. 21, 1989. Discarded office typewriter bought on January 3, 1985. Accumulated depreciation to December 31, 1988, $280.00. M522.

Jan. 28, 1989. Discarded file cabinet bought on January 2, 1985. Accumulated depreciation to December 31, 1988, $200.00. M523.

Mar. 29, 1990. Received $10.00 for hand truck bought on March 31, 1985. Accumulated depreciation to December 31, 1989, $71.25. M575 and R645.

Dec. 31, 1990. Received $250.00 for shelving bought on July 1, 1985. Accumulated depreciation to December 31, 1989, $213.75. M631 and R733.

Dec. 31, 1990. Paid cash, $8,000.00, plus old truck bought on May 1, 1985, for new truck. Accumulated depreciation recorded to December 31, 1989, $7,000.00. M632 and C815.

Instructions: 1. For each transaction in 1989, do the following.

a. Record an entry for additional depreciation if needed.

b. Record an entry to dispose of the plant asset.

c. Make appropriate notations in the plant asset record.

    2. Complete each plant asset record for the year.

    3. Repeat instructions 1 and 2 for 1990.

PROBLEM 10-5   Figuring depreciation using the straight-line, declining-balance, and sum-of-the-years-digits methods

On December 31 of 1988, the records of Palley, Inc., show the following information about an office desk the business owns.

Date bought	Jan. 1, 1988
Original cost..	$3,200.00
Estimated salvage value	200.00
Estimated useful life	4 years

Instructions: Prepare a table similar to Illustration 10-16 showing depreciation figured using the straight-line, declining-balance, and sum-of-the-years-digits methods.

PROBLEM 10-6   Figuring depreciation using the production-unit method

The records of Metzger, Inc., show the following information about a truck the business owns.

Truck Date bought: January 1, 1985 Original cost: $9,000.00 Estimated rate of depreciation per mile driven: $0.14 Estimated salvage value: $1,000.00	
Year	**Miles Driven**
1985	10,500
1986	11,300
1987	9,900
1988	11,500
1989	12,200

Instructions: Prepare a depreciation table similar to Illustration 10-17 for this truck.

PROBLEM 10-7   Figuring depletion

The records of Personna, Inc., show the following information on December 31, 1989, about a coal mine the business owns.

Mine Date bought: May 3, 1985 Original cost: $35,000.00 Estimated rate of depletion per ton of coal mined: $0.80 Estimated salvage value: $1,000.00	
Year	**Tons of Coal Mined**
1985	8,000
1986	7,400
1987	9,000
1988	10,500
1989	7,200

Instructions: Prepare a depletion table similar to Illustration 10-17.

PROBLEM 10-8   Figuring and recording property tax

Deliveries, Inc., has real property with an assessed value of $300,000.00. The tax rate in the city where the property is located is 4.5% of assessed value. Property tax is paid in two installments.

Instructions: 1. Figure Deliveries' total annual property tax for the current year.

2. Record the first property tax payment on February 1 of the current year. Use page 5 of a cash payments journal. Check No. 124.

ENRICHMENT PROBLEMS

MASTERY PROBLEM 10-M   Recording transactions for plant assets

The plant asset records for Wheeler, Inc., are given in the working papers accompanying this textbook. The business uses the straight-line method of figuring depreciation expense. The selected transactions given below were completed during 1988. All equipment is office equipment.

Instructions: 1. Record the following transactions. Record an entry for additional depreciation if needed. Use page 22 of a general journal, page 44 of a cash receipts journal, and page 40 of a cash payments journal. Source documents are abbreviated as follows: check, C; memorandum, M; receipt, R.

Jan.   2. Paid cash for new typewriter: cost, $1,400.00; estimated salvage value, $400.00; estimated useful life, 5 years; Serial No. SD345J267. C122.

Jan.   2. Discarded office desk, Serial No. D3481, bought on January 5, 1983. M47.

Mar. 29. Discarded office table, Serial No. T3929, bought on March 29, 1983. M52.

Mar. 30. Received $100.00 for typewriter, Serial No. TM48194H32, bought on April 6, 1982. M54 and R191.

June 29. Received $150.00 for filing cabinet, Serial No. FC125, bought on June 28, 1979. M62 and R224.

July   2. Paid cash, $500.00, plus old copying machine, Serial No. C56M203, for new copying machine: estimated salvage value of new machine, $100.00; estimated useful life of new machine, 5 years; Serial No. of new machine, C35194. M70 and C239.

2. Make needed notations on plant asset records or prepare new records.

CHALLENGE PROBLEM 10-C   Recording transactions for plant assets

Milltown, Inc., completed the selected transactions given below. Milltown uses the straight-line method of figuring depreciation expense.

Instructions: Record the following transactions. Use page 2 of a general journal, page 3 of a cash receipts journal, and page 4 of a cash payments journal. Source documents are abbreviated as follows: check, C; memorandum, M; receipt, R.

Jan.   3, 1985. Paid cash for new office typewriter: cost, $500.00; estimated salvage value, $100.00; estimated useful life, 8 years; Serial No., T45M3409. C130.

Mar.   1, 1985. Paid cash for office desk: cost, $500.00; estimated salvage value, $150.00; estimated useful life, 5 years; Serial No., D345. C190.

June 30, 1985. Paid cash for office chair: cost, $100.00; estimated salvage value, $10.00; estimated useful life, 5 years; Serial No., none. C200.

July   1, 1985. Paid cash for delivery truck: cost, $10,000.00; estimated salvage value, $1,000.00; estimated useful life, 5 years; Serial No., 345X32LD54. C220.

Jan.   2, 1987. Paid cash, $300.00, plus old typewriter, Serial No. T45M3409, bought in 1985, for
                 new typewriter: estimated salvage value of new typewriter, $100.00; estimated
                 useful life, 5 years; Serial No. of new typewriter, T64M4391. C300.
July   1, 1987. Discarded office chair bought on June 30, 1985. M66.
Sept. 1, 1987. Paid cash, $5,000.00, plus old delivery truck, Serial No. 345X32LD54, for new
                 delivery truck: estimated salvage value of new truck, $2,000.00; estimated useful
                 life of new truck, 5 years; Serial No. of new truck, 432XY30LE25. M70 and C310.
Dec. 31, 1987. Received $350.00 for office desk bought on March 1, 1985. M81 and R146.

Computer Application 4
Preparing Depreciation Schedules

Both manual and automated methods may be used to figure depreciation on plant assets and prepare depreciation schedules. Gallery, the business described in Part 4, uses manual methods to figure depreciation and prepare depreciation schedules. Computer Application 4 provides for the use of a microcomputer to input plant asset data, figure depreciation, and print depreciation schedules. Depreciation may be figured and schedules prepared for the straight-line, declining-balance, and sum-of-the-years-digits methods. Computer Application 4 contains instructions for using a microcomputer to solve Problem 10-5, Chapter 10.

COMPUTER APPLICATION PROBLEM

COMPUTER APPLICATION PROBLEM 4   Preparing depreciation schedules

Instructions: 1. Load the Systems Selection Menu from the *Advanced Automated Accounting* diskette according to the instructions for the computer being used. Select Problem CA-4. The company name and run date are stored on the template diskette.

2. Key-enter the data about Palley's office desk given in the text for Problem 10-5 for the straight-line method.

3. Display/Print a depreciation schedule for the straight-line method.

4. Key-enter the data about Palley's office desk given in the text for Problem 10-5 for the declining-balance method.

5. Display/Print a depreciation schedule for the declining-balance method.

6. Key-enter the data about Palley's office desk given in the text for Problem 10-5 for the sum-of-the-years-digits method.

7. Display/Print a depreciation schedule for the sum-of-the-years-digits method.

11 Accounting for Notes Payable, Prepaid Expenses, and Accrued Expenses

ENABLING PERFORMANCE TASKS

After studying Chapter 11, you will be able to:
a. Define accounting terms related to notes payable, prepaid expenses, and accrued expenses.
b. Identify accounting concepts and practices related to notes payable, prepaid expenses, and accrued expenses.
c. Record transactions for notes payable.
d. Analyze and record adjusting entries related to prepaid and accrued expenses.
e. Analyze and record reversing entries related to prepaid and accrued expenses.

Accounting records must show all information needed to prepare a business' financial statements. (CONCEPT: *Adequate Disclosure*) Businesses often have financial activities which require special accounting procedures. Some businesses may need to borrow money. Quite often a business' pay period does not end on the same day as the end of a fiscal period. Some salary may be owed to employees but will not be paid until the next fiscal period. An expense owed but not yet paid must be recorded during the fiscal period in which incurred. (CONCEPT: *Matching Expenses with Revenue*)

NOTES PAYABLE AND INTEREST EXPENSE

A written and signed promise to pay a sum of money is called a promissory note. A promissory note that a business issues to a creditor is called a note payable. The day a note is issued is called the date of a note. The original amount of a note is called the principal of a note. The date a note is due is called the maturity date of a note. An amount paid for the use of money is called interest.

Issuing notes payable

Gallery occasionally borrows money from a bank. The bank accepts a note from Gallery as evidence of the debt. The source document for issuing a note payable is a copy of the note payable. *(CONCEPT: Objective Evidence)*

March 2, 1989.
Issued a 6-month, 15% note payable to First Trust Bank, $1,200.00. Note Payable No. 6.

The percentage of the principal that is paid for use of the money is called the interest rate of a note. The interest rate for Note Payable No. 6 is 15%.

The analysis of this transaction to issue a note payable is shown in the T accounts.

Cash is increased by a $1,200.00 debit, the amount received from the bank for Note Payable No. 6. Notes Payable is increased by a $1,200.00 credit.

Gallery's cash receipts journal entry to record issuing this note payable is shown in Illustration 11-1.

Cash	
1,200.00	

Notes Payable	
	1,200.00

CASH RECEIPTS JOURNAL   PAGE 3

	DATE	ACCOUNT TITLE	DOC. NO.	POST. REF.	GENERAL DEBIT	GENERAL CREDIT	ACCOUNTS RECEIVABLE CREDIT	SALES CREDIT	SALES TAX PAYABLE DEBIT	SALES TAX PAYABLE CREDIT	SALES DISCOUNT DEBIT	CASH DEBIT	
1	1989 Mar. 2	Notes Payable	NP6			1 2000 0						1 2000 0	1
2													2

Illustration 11-1
Entry for issuing a note payable for cash

Figuring a note's maturity date and interest

The length of time between the issuance and maturity date of a note may be expressed in months or in days. For example, the time for Gallery's Note Payable No. 6 is six months. A note's time may also be stated in days.

Figuring a note's maturity date with the time stated in months. The maturity date for Note Payable No. 6 is figured as shown below.

Time	Number of Months
March 2 to April 2	1
April 2 to May 2	1
May 2 to June 2	1
June 2 to July 2	1
July 2 to August 2	1
August 2 to September 2	1
Total number of months	6

From a date in one month to the same date in the next month is counted as one month. For example, from March 2 to April 2 is counted as one month. The maturity date for Note Payable No. 6, a 6-month note, is September 2.

Figuring a note's interest with the time stated in months. When the time of a note is stated in months, 12 months are used in the interest formula. The interest for Gallery's Note Payable No. 6 is figured as shown below.

Principal	×	Interest Rate	×	Fraction of a Year	=	Interest for Six Months
$1,200.00	×	15%	×	$\frac{6}{12}$	=	$90.00

The fraction of a year is composed of two numbers. The top number, 6, is the time of the note. The bottom number, 12, is the number of months in a year. The total interest on Note Payable No. 6 is $90.00.

Figuring a note's maturity date with the time stated in days. On March 2, Olan Company issued a note payable with the time stated in days.

March 2, 1989.
Issued a 180-day, 15% note payable to American National Bank, $1,200.00.
Note Payable No. 3.

As previously described, Gallery figures the maturity date by even months for Note Payable No. 6. Thus, from March 2 to September 2 is an even six months. However, when a note's time is stated in days, the actual days are counted. The maturity date for Olan's Note Payable No. 3 is figured as shown below.

Time	Number of Days
March 2 to March 31	29
April 1 to April 30	30
May 1 to May 31	31
June 1 to June 30	30
July 1 to July 31	31
August 1 to August 29	29
Total number of days	180

From March 2 to March 31 is 29 days because the date on which a note is issued is not counted. Only 29 days are counted in August to make a total of 180. The maturity date for Note Payable No. 3, a 180-day note, is August 29.

Figuring a note's interest with the time stated in days. When the time of a note is stated in days, the interest is figured using 365 days in a year. The interest on Olan's Note Payable No. 3 is figured as shown below.

Principal	×	Interest Rate	×	Fraction of a Year	=	Interest for 180 Days
$1,200.00	×	15%	×	$\frac{180}{365}$	=	$88.77

The fraction of a year is composed of two numbers. The top number, 180, is the time of the note. The bottom number, 365, is the total number of days in a year.

In the two examples, interest for Gallery's 15%, 6-month note is $90.00, and interest for Olan's 15%, 180-day note is $88.77.

Paying a note payable

September 2, 1989.
Paid First Trust Bank $1,290.00 for Note Payable No. 6, $1,200.00, plus interest, $90.00. Check No. 359.

Notes Payable	
1,200.00	Balance 1,200.00

Interest Expense	
90.00	

Cash	
	1,290.00

The analysis of this transaction is shown in the T accounts. Notes Payable is decreased by a $1,200.00 debit, the note's principal amount. The $1,200.00 debit cancels the $1,200.00 credit recorded at the time the note was issued. Interest Expense is increased by a $90.00 debit, Gallery's interest expense for use of the bank's money for six months. Cash is decreased by a $1,290.00 credit, the total cash paid.

Gallery's cash payments journal entry to record payment of this note payable is shown in Illustration 11-2.

CASH PAYMENTS JOURNAL   PAGE 12

	DATE	ACCOUNT TITLE	CHECK No.	POST. REF.	GENERAL DEBIT	GENERAL CREDIT	ACCOUNTS PAYABLE DEBIT	PURCHASES DISCOUNT CREDIT	CASH CREDIT	
1	1989 Sept. 2	Notes Payable	359		1 200 00				1 290 00	1
2		Interest Expense			90 00					2
3										3
4										4

Illustration 11-2
Entry for payment of a
note payable

Interest Expense is listed as an Other Expense on Gallery's chart of accounts.

Discounting a note payable

Some businesses are required to pay interest in advance when borrowing money from a bank. The interest is deducted in advance from the amount borrowed. A note on which interest is paid in advance is called a *discounted note*. Interest collected in advance on a note is called a *bank discount*. The amount received for a note after the bank discount has been deducted is called *proceeds*.

December 1, 1989.
Discounted at 15% at State Street Bank a 60-day note, $1,000.00; discount, $24.66; proceeds, $975.34. Note Payable No. 10.

Gallery figures the note's discount as shown below.

Principal	×	Interest Rate	×	Fraction of a Year	=	Bank Discount
$1,000.00	×	15%	×	$\frac{60}{365}$	=	$24.66

Gallery figures the note's proceeds as shown below.

Principal   –   **Bank Discount**   =   **Proceeds**
$1,000.00   – $24.66   = $975.34

When the note is discounted at the bank, Gallery receives cash equal to the proceeds, $975.34. The analysis of this transaction is shown in the T accounts.

Cash is increased by a $975.34 debit, the proceeds from the note. Interest Expense is increased by a $24.66 debit, the amount of the bank discount. Notes Payable is increased by a $1,000.00 credit, the principal of the note.

Cash	
Proceeds 975.34	

Interest Expense	
Discount 24.66	

Notes Payable	
	Principal 1,000.00

Gallery's cash receipts journal entry to record the discounting of this note payable is shown in Illustration 11-3.

CASH RECEIPTS JOURNAL   PAGE 24

	DATE	ACCOUNT TITLE	DOC. NO.	POST. REF.	GENERAL DEBIT	GENERAL CREDIT	ACCOUNTS RECEIVABLE CREDIT	SALES CREDIT	SALES TAX PAYABLE DEBIT	SALES TAX PAYABLE CREDIT	SALES DISCOUNT DEBIT	CASH DEBIT	
1	1989 Dec. 1	Interest Expense	NP10		2466							97534	1
2		Notes Payable				100000							2
3													3
4													4
5													5

PREPAID EXPENSES

Illustration 11-3
Entry to record discounting a note payable

Expenses paid in one fiscal period but not reported as expenses until a later fiscal period are called prepaid expenses. Prepaid expenses include such items as supplies, prepaid insurance, and interest on discounted notes payable. Only that portion of prepaid expenses that has been used in the current fiscal period should be reported as an expense in that fiscal period. (CONCEPT: *Matching Expenses with Revenue*) Prepaid expenses may be recorded initially as assets or as expenses. Supergolf, described in Part 2, records supplies and prepaid insurance initially as assets. Gallery records prepaid expenses initially as expenses.

Prepaid expense amounts are assets until actually used. For example, Gallery has a quantity of sales supplies on hand on any given day during the year. These sales supplies could be sold and thus converted into cash, an asset. The amount recorded in Supplies Expense—Sales is a mixture of expense (already used) and asset (not yet used). An adjusting entry could be made each day to separate the expense from the asset portion of this account's balance. However, as a practical accounting procedure, an adjusting entry is made only when financial statements need to be prepared. (CONCEPT: *Adequate Disclosure*)

Recording information about supplies

When Supergolf, described in Part 2, buys office supplies, the asset Supplies — Office is debited and Cash is credited. However, when Gallery buys sales supplies, Supplies Expense — Sales is debited and Cash is credited. Both Supergolf and Gallery record adjusting entries for supplies at the end of a fiscal period. The adjusting entries are made so that the prepaid expenses actually used during a fiscal period are reported as expenses. (*CONCEPT: Matching Expenses with Revenue*)

Supergolf's and Gallery's two related supplies accounts before adjustments are made at the end of a fiscal period are shown in the T accounts.

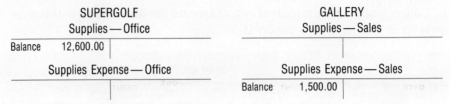

Supergolf recorded the prepaid supplies initially in the asset account Supplies — Office. The $12,600.00 debit balance is the beginning inventory of supplies plus the total value of all office supplies bought during the fiscal period. Nothing has been recorded in Supergolf's office supplies expense account during the fiscal period.

Gallery records prepaid supplies initially in Supplies Expense — Sales. The $1,500.00 debit balance is the beginning sales supplies inventory plus the total value of all sales supplies bought during the fiscal period. Nothing has been recorded in Gallery's sales supplies account during the fiscal period.

Adjusting entry for supplies. As described in Chapter 5, Supergolf determines that the office supplies inventory is $2,700.00 and the office supplies expense for the fiscal period is $9,900.00. On December 31, 1989, Gallery determines that the sales supplies ending inventory is $500.00.

The analysis of the adjusting entries for supplies are shown in the T accounts.

SUPERGOLF		GALLERY	
Supplies — Office		**Supplies — Sales**	
Balance 12,600.00	Adjusting 9,900.00	Adjusting 500.00	
Supplies Expense — Office		**Supplies Expense — Sales**	
Adjusting 9,900.00		Balance 1,500.00	Adjusting 500.00

For Supergolf's accounts, Supplies — Office is decreased by a $9,900.00 credit. The new balance of this account, $2,700.00, is the ending office supplies inventory on December 31, 1988. Supplies Expense — Office is increased by a $9,900.00 debit. The new balance of this account, $9,900.00, is the supplies expense for 1988.

For Gallery's accounts, Supplies — Sales is increased by a $500.00 debit. The new balance of this account, $500.00, is the ending sales supplies inventory on December 31, 1989. Supplies Expense — Sales is decreased by a $500.00 credit. The new balance of this account, $1,000.00, is the sales supplies expense for 1989.

Although Supergolf and Gallery use different procedures, both correctly separate and record the asset and expense portions of supplies costs.

Supergolf's general journal adjusting entry for office supplies is shown on lines 8 and 9 of Illustration 5-10, Chapter 5. Gallery's general journal adjusting entry for sales supplies is shown on lines 8 and 9 of Illustration 11-4.

	DATE	ACCOUNT TITLE	POST. REF.	DEBIT	CREDIT	
		GENERAL JOURNAL			PAGE *13*	
1		*Adjusting Entries*				1
8	31	*Supplies — Sales*		50000		8
9		*Supplies Expense — Sales*			50000	9
10	31	*Supplies — Warehouse*		29750		10
11		*Supplies Expense — Warehouse*			29750	11
12	31	*Supplies — Administrative*		22294		12
13		*Supplies Expense — Admin.*			22294	13
14						14

Illustration 11-4
Adjusting entry for supplies recorded initially as an expense

Gallery makes a similar adjusting entry for Supplies Expense — Warehouse and Supplies Expense — Administrative as shown on lines 10–13 of Illustration 11-4.

Closing entry for supplies expense. To prepare a general ledger for the next fiscal period, closing entries are recorded and posted. The effect of closing entries on Supergolf's and Gallery's supplies expense accounts is shown in the T accounts.

SUPERGOLF		GALLERY	
Income Summary		Income Summary	
Closing 9,900.00		Closing 1,000.00	
Supplies Expense — Office		Supplies Expense — Sales	
Adjusting 9,900.00	Closing 9,900.00	Balance 1,500.00	Adjusting 500.00
			Closing 1,000.00

The other supplies expense accounts are also closed as part of the closing entries for both Supergolf and Gallery.

Need for reversing entries. After the closing entries have been posted, Supergolf's general ledger accounts are ready for the next fiscal period.

However, Gallery's general ledger accounts are not ready for the next fiscal period.

Gallery initially records the value of all supplies bought in an expense account. On December 31, 1989, the value of Gallery's sales supplies inventory, $500.00, is the debit balance of Supplies—Sales. On January 1, 1990, the $500.00 should be a debit in Supplies Expense—Sales. Then the $500.00 debit can be added to the value of sales supplies bought during 1990.

Some businesses that record prepaid items initially as expenses reverse the adjusting entries for prepaid expenses at the beginning of each fiscal period. An entry made at the beginning of one fiscal period to reverse an adjusting entry made in the previous fiscal period is called a reversing entry.

Supergolf records supplies initially as assets, and does not record reversing entries. The office supplies inventory, December 31, 1988, $2,700.00, is in the account where it can be added to the value of supplies bought in 1989.

Gallery records supplies initially as expenses, and does need to record reversing entries. Accountants use a rule of thumb to determine if a reversing entry is needed. A reversing entry is needed for an adjusting entry that creates a balance in an asset or a liability account which previously had a zero balance.

Reversing entry for supplies expense. Because Gallery's adjusting entry for sales supplies created a balance in Supplies—Sales, a reversing entry is needed. The analysis of Gallery's reversing entry for sales supplies expense is shown in the T accounts.

Supplies Expense—Sales is increased by a $500.00 debit. Supplies—Sales is decreased by a $500.00 credit. The balance of Supplies—Sales is zero as it was before the adjusting entry.

Gallery's reversing entries for the supplies expense accounts are shown in Illustration 11-5. These reversing entries are the opposite of the adjusting entries shown in Illustration 11-4.

Supplies Expense — Sales			
Balance	1,500.00	Adjusting	500.00
Reversing	500.00	Closing	1,000.00

Supplies — Sales			
Adjusting	500.00	Reversing	500.00

GENERAL JOURNAL				PAGE 1	
DATE	ACCOUNT TITLE	POST. REF.	DEBIT	CREDIT	
	Reversing Entries				1
1	*Supplies Expense—Sales*		500 00		4
	Supplies—Sales			500 00	5
1	*Supplies Expense—Warehouse*		297 50		6
	Supplies—Warehouse			297 50	7
1	*Supplies Expense—Admin.*		222 94		8
	Supplies—Administrative			222 94	9

Illustration 11-5
Reversing entries for
supplies recorded initially
as an expense

Recording information about prepaid insurance

Supergolf, described in Part 2, initially records prepaid insurance premiums as an asset. Supergolf's general journal adjusting entry for insurance expense is shown on lines 12 and 13, Illustration 5-10, Chapter 5.

Gallery initially records prepaid insurance premiums as expenses. When Gallery pays insurance premiums, Cash is credited and Insurance Expense is debited.

Adjusting entry for prepaid insurance. The value of Gallery's unused insurance premiums on December 31 is $200.00. The analysis for this adjusting entry is shown in the T accounts.

Prepaid Insurance is increased by a $200.00 debit. The new balance of this account, $200.00, is the value of unused insurance premiums at the end of the fiscal period. Insurance Expense is decreased by a $200.00 credit. The new balance of this account, $600.00, is the value of insurance expense for the fiscal period.

Prepaid Insurance		
Adjusting	200.00	

Insurance Expense			
Balance	800.00	Adjusting	200.00

Gallery's general journal adjusting entry for prepaid insurance is shown in Illustration 11-6.

	GENERAL JOURNAL			PAGE 13	
DATE	ACCOUNT TITLE	POST. REF.	DEBIT	CREDIT	
1	*Adjusting Entries*				1
14	31 Prepaid Insurance		20000		14
15	Insurance Expense			20000	15
16					16
17					17
18					18
19					19

Illustration 11-6
Adjusting entry for prepaid insurance

Closing entry for insurance expense. Insurance Expense is closed as part of Gallery's closing entries. The effect of this closing entry on the insurance expense account is shown in the T accounts.

Income Summary		
Closing	600.00	

Insurance Expense			
Balance	800.00	Adjusting	200.00
		Closing	600.00

Reversing entry for insurance expense. Supergolf, described in Part 2, does not need to record a reversing entry for insurance expense. However, Gallery's adjusting entry for insurance expense, described in this chapter, created a balance in the asset account, Prepaid Insurance. Therefore, on January 1, 1990, Gallery does need a reversing entry for insurance expense. The analysis of Gallery's reversing entry for insurance expense is shown in the T accounts.

Insurance Expense

Balance	800.00	Adjusting	200.00
Reversing	200.00	Closing	600.00

Prepaid Insurance

Adjusting	200.00	Reversing	200.00

Insurance Expense is increased by a $200.00 debit. The new balance of this account, $200.00, now can be added to the value of insurance premiums paid during 1990. Prepaid Insurance is decreased by a $200.00 credit. The new balance of this account is zero.

Gallery's general journal reversing entry for insurance expense is shown in Illustration 11-7.

	GENERAL JOURNAL				PAGE /
	DATE	ACCOUNT TITLE	POST. REF.	DEBIT	CREDIT
1		*Reversing Entries*			
10	/	*Insurance Expense*		200 00	
11		*Prepaid Insurance*			200 00
12					
13					

Illustration 11-7
Reversing entry for insurance expense

Recording information about prepaid interest

Gallery records prepaid interest initially as an expense. When Gallery discounted Note Payable No. 10, the discount, $24.66, was debited to Interest Expense.

Adjusting entry for prepaid interest. Note Payable No. 10 has existed from December 1 to December 31, 1989. On December 31, only 30 days of Gallery's prepaid interest expense has been earned by the bank during 1989. The remaining 30 days' interest is still prepaid.

The interest for 30 days is figured as shown below.

Principal	×	Interest Rate	×	Fraction of a Year	=	Interest for 30 Days
$1,000.00	×	15%	×	$\frac{30}{365}$	=	$12.33

Prepaid Interest

Adjusting	12.33	

Interest Expense

Balance	139.32	Adjusting	12.33

The analysis of this adjusting entry is shown in the T accounts. Prepaid Interest is increased by a $12.33 debit. The new balance of this account, $12.33, is the value of the remaining prepaid interest on Note Payable No. 10. Interest Expense is decreased by a $12.33 credit. The new balance of this account, $126.99, includes the interest expense on Note Payable No. 10 for 1989. (CONCEPT: *Matching Expenses with Revenue*)

Gallery's general journal adjusting entry for prepaid interest is shown in Illustration 11-8.

DATE	ACCOUNT TITLE	POST. REF.	DEBIT	CREDIT	
	Adjusting Entries				1
31	*Prepaid Interest*		1233		16
	Interest Expense			1233	17
					18
					19
					20

GENERAL JOURNAL   PAGE *13*

Illustration 11-8
Adjusting entry for prepaid interest

Closing entry for interest expense. Interest Expense is closed as part of Gallery's closing entries. The effect of this closing entry for Interest Expense is described later in this chapter.

Reversing entry for interest expense. Gallery's asset Prepaid Interest had no balance previous to the adjusting entries. Therefore, on January 1, 1990, Gallery does need a reversing entry for interest expense. The analysis of Gallery's reversing entry for interest expense is shown in the T accounts.

Interest Expense is increased by a $12.33 debit. The new balance of this account, $12.33, now can be added to payments for additional prepaid interest during 1990. Prepaid Interest is decreased by a $12.33 credit. The new balance of this account is zero.

The $2.05 debit in Interest Expense is for an adjusting entry described later in this chapter.

Interest Expense			
Balance	139.32	Adjusting	12.33
Adjusting	2.05	Closing	129.04
Reversing	12.33		

Prepaid Interest			
Adjusting	12.33	Reversing	12.33

Gallery's general journal reversing entry for interest expense is shown in Illustration 11-9.

DATE	ACCOUNT TITLE	POST. REF.	DEBIT	CREDIT	
	Reversing Entries				1
1	*Interest Expense*		1233		12
	Prepaid Interest			1233	13
					14
					15
					16
					17

GENERAL JOURNAL   PAGE *1*

Illustration 11-9
Reversing entry for interest expense

ACCRUED EXPENSES

Expenses incurred in one fiscal period but not paid until a later fiscal period are called accrued expenses. In any specific fiscal period, Gallery may have four kinds of accrued expenses. (1) Accrued interest expense. (2) Accrued salary expense. (3) Accrued employer's payroll taxes expense. (4) Accrued federal income tax.

Recording information about accrued interest expense

On December 31, 1989, Gallery has two notes payable. (1) Note Payable No. 10, dated December 1, 1989; a discounted note on which interest is prepaid. (2) Note Payable No. 11, $500.00, 60 days, 10%, dated December 16; a note on which interest has accrued.

Adjusting entry for accrued interest expense. On December 31, Gallery owes 15 days accrued interest on Note Payable No. 11. The accrued interest expense for this note should be reported in the 1989 fiscal period. *(CONCEPT: Matching Expenses with Revenue)* The accrued interest is figured as shown below.

Principal	×	Interest Rate	×	Fraction of a Year	=	Interest Expense
$500.00	×	10%	×	$\frac{15}{365}$	=	$2.05

Interest Expense			
Balance	139.32	Adjusting	12.33
Adjusting	2.05		

Interest Payable			
		Adjusting	2.05

The analysis of this adjusting entry is shown in the T accounts. Interest Expense is increased by a $2.05 debit, the interest expense for Note Payable No. 11 for the 1989 fiscal period. Interest Payable is increased by a $2.05 credit, the interest owed on Note Payable No. 11 at the end of the fiscal period.

The $12.33 credit in Interest Expense is the adjusting entry for prepaid interest described earlier in this chapter.

Gallery's general journal adjusting entry for accrued interest expense is shown in Illustration 11-10.

	GENERAL JOURNAL		PAGE 13	
DATE	ACCOUNT TITLE	POST. REF.	DEBIT	CREDIT
	Adjusting Entries			
31	Interest Expense		205	
	Interest Payable			205

Illustration 11-10
Adjusting entry for
accrued interest expense

Closing entry for interest expense. Interest expense is closed as part of Gallery's closing entries. The effect of closing entries on the interest expense account is shown in the T accounts.

Income Summary	
Closing 129.04	

Interest Expense	
Balance 139.32	Adjusting 12.33
Adjusting 2.05	Closing 129.04

Reversing entry for accrued interest expense. Gallery's adjusting entries for accrued expenses create balances in asset or liability accounts. Therefore, Gallery's adjusting entries for accrued expenses are reversed on January 1 of the next fiscal period.

The analysis of Gallery's reversing entry for accrued interest expense is shown in the T accounts.

Interest Payable	
Reversing 2.05	Adjusting 2.05

Two reversing entries affect Interest Expense. One is for accrued interest, $2.05, page 238. The other is for prepaid interest, $12.33, described earlier in this chapter.

Interest Expense	
Balance 139.32	Adjusting 12.33
Adjusting 2.05	Closing 129.04
Reversing 12.33	Reversing 2.05

Gallery's reversing entry for accrued interest expense is shown in Illustration 11-11.

	GENERAL JOURNAL			PAGE /	
DATE	ACCOUNT TITLE	POST. REF.	DEBIT	CREDIT	
1	*Reversing Entries*				1
14	1 *Interest Payable*		2 05		14
15	*Interest Expense*			2 05	15

Illustration 11-11
Reversing entry for accrued interest expense

When Note Payable No. 11 is paid on February 14, 1990, the interest expense is $8.22. The total interest should be divided between the two fiscal periods as shown below.

Interest Expense Recorded in 1989	+	Interest Expense to be Recorded in 1990	=	Total Interest Expense for Note Payable No. 11
$2.05	+	$6.17	=	$8.22

With a reversing entry, the analysis of a transaction to pay Note Payable No. 11 is shown in the T accounts.

Notes Payable is decreased by a $500.00 debit. Interest Expense is increased by an $8.22 debit. The $8.22 debit in Interest Expense is offset by the $2.05 credit. The difference, $6.17, is the 1990 interest expense on Note Payable No. 11. Cash is decreased by a $508.22 credit.

Without a reversing entry, $2.05 of the interest would be reported twice. The $2.05 amount is recorded once as an adjusting entry in 1989. The amount is recorded a second

Notes Payable	
Payment 500.00	Balance 500.00

Interest Payable	
Reversing 2.05	Adjusting 2.05

Interest Expense	
Payment 8.22	Reversing 2.05

Cash	
	Payment 508.22

time as part of the $8.22 debit in 1990 when the note is paid. The analysis of an entry to pay Note Payable No. 11 without reversing entries is shown in the T accounts.

Notes Payable			
Payment	500.00	Balance	500.00

Interest Payable			
		Adjusting	2.05

Interest Expense			
Payment	8.22		

Cash			
		Payment	508.22

The entry to pay Note Payable No. 11 affects the accounts in the same way as previously described. However, the result in Interest Expense is different. Before the payment is recorded, Interest Expense has a zero balance because of the closing entries on December 31, 1989. Interest Expense is increased by an $8.22 debit. There is no offsetting credit from a reversing entry. Therefore, the amount charged in 1990 is $8.22 instead of $6.17. Also, the $2.05 credit in Interest Payable still remains as a liability after the payment is recorded.

The double charge might be avoided if accounting personnel are careful to divide the interest amount when the note is paid. The part of the interest chargeable to 1989, $2.05, is recorded as a debit in Interest Payable. The part chargeable to 1990, $6.17, is recorded as a debit in Interest Expense. The analysis of an entry to split the interest is shown in the T accounts.

Notes Payable			
Payment	500.00	Balance	500.00

Interest Payable			
Payment	2.05	Adjusting	2.05

Interest Expense			
Payment	6.17		

Cash			
		Payment	508.22

Notes Payable is decreased by a $500.00 debit. Interest Payable is decreased by a $2.05 debit. The new balance of this liability account is zero as it was before the adjustment. Interest Expense is increased with a $6.17 debit, the 1990 interest on Note Payable No. 11. Cash is decreased with a $508.22 credit.

Although the entry described above could be used to divide the interest between fiscal periods, Gallery prefers to use reversing entries. Gallery's accounting personnel do not have to remember to check an entry each time a note is paid to determine if interest should be divided.

Recording information about accrued salary expense

Gallery pays its employees each Friday for the time worked during the previous week. For example, on Friday, December 29, 1989, all employees are paid for the time they worked during the week ended on Friday, December 22, 1989. The employees do not work on Saturday or Sunday. Therefore, at the end of the 1989 fiscal period, Gallery has accrued salary expense for five days from December 25 to December 29.

Adjusting entry for accrued salary expense. On December 31, 1989, Gallery owes but has not paid the employees for Monday through Friday of the previous week. On Friday, January 5, the employees will receive a paycheck that includes five days' pay from the previous fiscal period. On December 31, even though the employees have not been paid, salaries for five days are reported as a 1989 expense. (CONCEPT: *Matching Expenses with Revenue*) The financial statements must show all the business expenses for a fiscal period. (CONCEPT: *Adequate Disclosure*)

The salaries that Gallery owes on December 31, 1989, are listed below.

Sales salaries owed.................................... $800.00
Warehouse salaries owed 400.00
Administrative salaries owed......................... 650.00

The analysis of the adjusting entry for accrued salary expense is shown in the T accounts.

Salary Expense—Sales is increased by a $800.00 debit, the portion of the accrued salaries applicable to sales. Salary Expense—Warehouse is increased by a $400.00 debit, the portion of the accrued salaries applicable to the warehouse. Salary Expense—Administrative is increased by a $650.00 debit, the portion of the accrued salaries applicable to administration. Salaries Payable is increased by a $1,850.00 credit, the total accrued salaries owed to employees on December 31, 1989.

Gallery's general journal adjusting entry for accrued salary expense is shown in Illustration 11-12.

Salary Expense—Sales

| Balance | 42,075.00 | |
| Adjusting | 800.00 | |

Salary Expense—Warehouse

| Balance | 21,037.50 | |
| Adjusting | 400.00 | |

Salary Expense—Administrative

| Balance | 35,062.50 | |
| Adjusting | 650.00 | |

Salaries Payable

| | | Adjusting | 1,850.00 |

GENERAL JOURNAL				PAGE *13*	
DATE	ACCOUNT TITLE	POST. REF.	DEBIT	CREDIT	
1	*Adjusting Entries*				1
28	*31 Salary Expense – Sales*		*80000*		28
29	*Salary Expense – Warehouse*		*40000*		29
30	*Salary Expense – Administrative*		*65000*		30
31	*Salaries Payable*			*185000*	31
32					32
33					33
34					34
35					35
36					36
37					37
38					38

Illustration 11-12
Adjusting entry for
accrued salary expense

Closing entry for salary expense. The effect of closing entries on the salary expense accounts is shown in the T accounts.

Income Summary

| Closing | 100,025.00 | |

Salary Expense—Warehouse

| Balance | 21,037.50 | Closing | 21,437.50 |
| Adjusting | 400.00 | | |

Salary Expense—Sales

| Balance | 42,075.00 | Closing | 42,875.00 |
| Adjusting | 800.00 | | |

Salary Expense—Administrative

| Balance | 35,062.50 | Closing | 35,712.50 |
| Adjusting | 650.00 | | |

Salaries Payable

| Reversing | 1,850.00 | Adjusting | 1,850.00 |

Salary Expense — Sales

| Balance | 42,075.00 | Closing | 42,875.00 |
| Adjusting | 800.00 | Reversing | 800.00 |

Salary Expense — Warehouse

| Balance | 21,037.50 | Closing | 21,437.50 |
| Adjusting | 400.00 | Reversing | 400.00 |

Salary Expense — Administrative

| Balance | 35,062.50 | Closing | 35,712.50 |
| Adjusting | 650.00 | Reversing | 650.00 |

Reversing entry for accrued salary expense. The analysis of Gallery's reversing entry for accrued salary expense, January 1, 1990, is shown in the T accounts.

Salaries Payable is decreased by a $1,850.00 debit. Salary Expense — Sales is decreased by a $800.00 credit. Salary Expense — Warehouse is decreased by a $400.00 credit. Salary Expense — Administrative is decreased by a $650.00 credit. The three expense accounts have contra balances after the reversing entry. When the payroll is paid in January, 1990, a portion of the amount debited in each account is offset by the credit contra balance.

Gallery's general journal reversing entry for accrued salary expense is shown in Illustration 11-13.

	GENERAL JOURNAL			PAGE 1	
DATE	ACCOUNT TITLE	POST. REF.	DEBIT	CREDIT	
	Reversing Entries				1
16	1 Salaries Payable		1 850 00		16
17	Salary Expense – Sales			800 00	17
18	Salary Expense – Warehouse			400 00	18
19	Salary Expense – Admin.			650 00	19
20					20

Illustration 11-13
Reversing entry for accrued salary expense

Recording information about accrued employer's payroll taxes expense

Employer's payroll taxes for accrued salaries must be recorded at the end of a fiscal period. Gallery has three employer's payroll taxes: (1) FICA tax, (2) federal unemployment tax, and (3) state unemployment tax.

Adjusting entry for accrued employer's payroll taxes expense. Gallery's accrued employer's payroll taxes are figured as shown below.

Tax	Taxable Accrued Salary ×	Tax Rate =	Accrued Employer's Payroll Tax Expense
FICA	$1,850.00	7.0%	$129.50
Federal Unemployment	365.00	0.8%	2.92
State Unemployment	365.00	5.4%	19.71
Total	—	—	$152.13

The taxable salaries for FICA and unemployment taxes are different. Only $365.00 of the $1,850.00 accrued salary is subject to unemployment taxes.

The analysis of Gallery's adjusting entry for accrued employer's payroll taxes expense is shown in the T accounts.

Payroll Taxes Expense			Unemployment Tax Payable — Federal		
Balance	9,032.10			Balance	30.00
Adjusting	152.13			Adjusting	2.92

FICA Tax Payable			Unemployment Tax Payable — State		
		Balance	269.50		Balance	207.90
		Adjusting	129.50		Adjusting	19.71

Payroll Taxes Expense is increased by a $152.13 debit. FICA Tax Payable is increased by a $129.50 credit. Unemployment Tax Payable — Federal is increased by a $2.92 credit. Unemployment Tax Payable — State is increased by a $19.71 credit.

Gallery's adjusting entry for accrued employer's payroll taxes expense is shown in Illustration 11-14.

	DATE	ACCOUNT TITLE	POST. REF.	DEBIT	CREDIT	
		GENERAL JOURNAL			PAGE 13	
1		*Adjusting Entries*				1
32	31	Payroll Taxes Expense		15213		32
33		FICA Tax Payable			12950	33
34		Unemploy. Tax Pay.—Federal			292	34
35		Unemploy. Tax Pay.—State			1971	35
36						36
37						37

Illustration 11-14
Adjusting entry for accrued employer's payroll taxes expense

Closing entry for employer's payroll taxes expense. The effect of Gallery's closing entry on the payroll taxes expense account is shown in the T accounts.

Income Summary			Payroll Taxes Expense		
Closing	9,184.23		Balance	9,032.10	Closing	9,184.23
			Adjusting	152.13		

Reversing entry for accrued employer's payroll taxes expense. The analysis of the reversing entry for Gallery's accrued employer's payroll taxes expense is shown in the T accounts.

FICA Tax Payable			Unemployment Tax Payable — State		
Reversing	129.50	Balance	269.50	Reversing	19.71	Balance	207.90
		Adjusting	129.50			Adjusting	19.71

Unemployment Tax Payable — Federal			Payroll Taxes Expense		
Reversing	2.92	Balance	30.00	Balance	9,032.10	Closing	9,184.23
		Adjusting	2.92	Adjusting	152.13	Reversing	152.13

Gallery's general journal reversing entry for accrued employer's payroll taxes expense is shown in Illustration 11-15.

	GENERAL JOURNAL			PAGE /	
DATE	ACCOUNT TITLE	POST. REF.	DEBIT	CREDIT	
1	*Reversing Entries*				1
20	1	*FICA Tax Payable*		129 50		20
21		*Unemploy. Tax Pay.—Federal*		2 92		21
22		*Unemploy. Tax Pay.—State*		19 71		22
23		*Payroll Taxes Expense*			152 13	23
24						24
25						25
26						26
27						27
28						28

Illustration 11-15
Reversing entry for accrued employer's payroll taxes expense

Reporting information about a corporation's accrued federal income tax

Corporations must pay federal income tax on net income. At the beginning of each year, Gallery makes an estimate of its federal income tax. The estimated amount is paid in four quarterly payments. At the end of a year, Gallery figures its actual income tax for the year. Any unpaid federal income tax is an accrued expense for which an adjusting entry is made.

Adjusting entry for accrued federal income tax. On December 31, 1989, Gallery's records show that four quarterly income tax payments have been made in 1989 for a total of $8,000.00. On December 31, 1989, Gallery figures that its actual income tax is $10,000.00. Thus, the accrued federal income tax remaining to be paid is $2,000.00 (total tax, $10,000.00, minus amount paid, $8,000.00).

How information on a work sheet is used to figure the amount of accrued federal income tax is described in Chapter 15.

The effect of this adjusting entry is shown in the T accounts. Federal Income Tax is increased by a $2,000.00 debit. Federal Income Tax Payable is increased by a $2,000.00 credit.

Federal Income Tax	
Balance	8,000.00
Adjusting	2,000.00

Federal Income Tax Payable	
	Adjusting 2,000.00

Federal Income Tax Payable is a current liability account. Federal Income Tax is in a general ledger division titled Income Tax. These accounts are shown on Gallery's chart of accounts.

The entry to record accrued federal income tax is shown in Illustration 11-16.

GENERAL JOURNAL					PAGE *13*	
DATE	ACCOUNT TITLE	POST. REF.	DEBIT	CREDIT		
	Adjusting Entries					1
38	*31*	*Federal Income Tax*		2 000 00		38
39		*Federal Income Tax Payable*			2 000 00	39
40						40

Illustration 11-16
Adjusting entry for accrued federal income tax

Closing entry for federal income tax. The effect of Gallery's closing entry on the federal income tax account is shown in the T accounts.

Income Summary			Federal Income Tax		
Closing	10,000.00		Balance	8,000.00	Closing 10,000.00
			Adjusting	2,000.00	

Reversing entry for accrued federal income tax. The analysis of the reversing entry for Gallery's accrued federal income tax is shown in the T accounts.

Federal Income Tax Payable is decreased by a $2,000.00 debit. The new balance of this account is zero as it was before the adjustment. Federal Income Tax is decreased by a $2,000.00 credit. The account's contra balance, $2,000.00, will be offset by a $2,000.00 debit when the final $2,000.00 payment for 1989 federal income tax is made in 1990. Thus, the payment is made in 1990, but the expense is reported in the 1989 fiscal year. (CONCEPT: *Matching Expenses with Revenue*)

Federal Income Tax Payable		
Reversing	2,000.00	Adjusting 2,000.00

Federal Income Tax		
Balance	8,000.00	Closing 10,000.00
Adjusting	2,000.00	Reversing 2,000.00

Gallery's reversing entry for accrued federal income tax is shown in Illustration 11-17.

GENERAL JOURNAL					PAGE *1*	
DATE	ACCOUNT TITLE	POST. REF.	DEBIT	CREDIT		
	Reversing Entries					1
26	*1*	*Federal Income Tax Payable*		2 000 00		26
27		*Federal Income Tax*			2 000 00	27
28						28

Illustration 11-17
Reversing entry for accrued federal income tax

SUMMARY

A summary of the adjusting and reversing entries described in this chapter is given in Illustration 11-18.

Item	Adjusting Entry		Reversing Entry	
	Account Debited	Account Credited	Account Debited	Account Credited
Supergolf's prepaid items recorded initially as assets: Supplies Insurance	Supplies Expense Insurance Expense	Supplies Prepaid Insurance	no reversing entry made no reversing entry made	
Gallery's prepaid items recorded initially as expenses: Supplies Insurance Interest	Supplies Prepaid Insurance Prepaid Interest	Supplies Expense Insurance Expense Interest Expense	Supplies Expense Insurance Expense Interest Expense	Supplies Prepaid Insurance Prepaid Interest
Gallery's accrued items: Interest Salaries Employer's Payroll Taxes	Interest Expense Salary Expense Payroll Taxes Expense	Interest Payable Salaries Payable FICA Tax Payable Unemployment Tax Payable — Federal Unemployment Tax Payable — State	Interest Payable Salaries Payable FICA Tax Payable Unemployment Tax Payable — Federal Unemployment Tax Payable — State	Interest Expense Salary Expense Payroll Taxes Expense
Federal Income Tax	Federal Income Tax	Federal Income Tax Payable	Federal Income Tax Payable	Federal Income Tax

Illustration 11-18
Summary of adjusting and reversing entries for
prepaid and accrued expenses

ACCOUNTING TERMS

What is the meaning of each of the following?

1. promissory note
2. note payable
3. date of a note
4. principal of a note
5. maturity date of a note

6. interest
7. interest rate of a note
8. discounted note
9. bank discount

10. proceeds
11. prepaid expenses
12. reversing entry
13. accrued expenses

QUESTIONS FOR INDIVIDUAL STUDY

1. What general ledger accounts are affected, and how, when a note payable is issued for cash?
2. What is the formula Gallery uses to figure interest on notes?
3. Which general ledger accounts are affected, and how, when Gallery pays a note payable plus interest?

4. Which general ledger accounts are affected, and how, when Gallery records a discounted note payable?

5. Which general ledger accounts are affected, and how, when Gallery buys sales supplies for cash?

6. Recording an adjusting entry for prepaid expenses is an application of which accounting concept?

7. Why is an adjusting entry made for supplies at the end of a fiscal period?

8. What rule of thumb can accountants use to determine if reversing entries are needed?

9. Which accounts are affected and how by Gallery's reversing entry for sales supplies expense?

10. Which accounts are affected, and how, by Gallery's reversing entry for insurance expense?

11. Which accounts are affected, and how, by Gallery's adjusting entry for prepaid interest?

12. Which accounts are affected, and how, by Gallery's reversing entry for interest expense?

13. As described in this chapter, what four kinds of accrued expenses might Gallery have at the end of a fiscal period?

14. Which accounts are affected, and how, by Gallery's adjusting entry for accrued interest expense?

15. Which accounts are affected, and how, by Gallery's reversing entry for accrued interest expense?

16. Which general ledger accounts are affected, and how, by Gallery's adjusting entry for accrued salary expense?

17. Which accounts are affected, and how, by Gallery's reversing entry for accrued salary expense?

18. Which accounts are affected, and how, by Gallery's adjusting entry for accrued employer's payroll taxes expense?

19. Which accounts are affected, and how, by Gallery's reversing entry for accrued employer's payroll taxes expense?

20. Which accounts are affected, and how, by Gallery's reversing entry for accrued federal income tax?

CASES FOR MANAGEMENT DECISION

CASE 1 Betsy Becker owns a small business. At the end of each month, Mrs. Becker's business borrows money from a bank and uses the proceeds to pay all outstanding accounts payable. The business discounts a 15-day, 15% note payable for each loan. Each month to date, Betsy Becker's business has been able to pay the notes payable when due. Mrs. Becker uses this procedure to maintain good credit ratings with vendors. Is Mrs. Becker's reasoning sound? Explain your answer.

CASE 2 Jerry Odman owns and operates Odman, Inc. The business needs to borrow $5,000.00. First State Bank will lend the money on a 3-month, 12% note with the note plus interest due on the maturity date. Citizens National Bank will discount a note at 12% for 3 months. Which would be better for Odman's? Explain your answer.

CASE 3 The Dalby Corporation records buying of supplies by debiting Supplies. The business also records payments for insurance by debiting Insurance Expense. Is this acceptable accounting procedure? Explain your answer.

CASE 4 Jose Santez, owner and manager of Santez, Inc., does not record adjusting or reversing entries for accrued payroll. Mr. Santez says that the matter is taken care of when the first payroll is recorded in the next month. The CPA who advises Mr. Santez suggests that the adjusting and reversing entries should be made. He states that omission of these entries affects the information reported on the business' financial statements. With whom do you agree? Explain your answer.

APPLICATION PROBLEMS

PROBLEM 11-1   Recording the issuing, discounting, and paying of notes payable

Wilmindon, Inc., completed the selected transactions given below during the current year.

Instructions: 1. Figure the maturity dates for each of the three notes. Source documents are abbreviated as follows: check, C; note payable, NP.

Aug. 1.   Issued a 3-month, 10% note to Fifth State Bank, $1,000.00. NP1.
Sept. 2. Discounted at 10% at First State Bank a 60-day note, $1,000.00; discount, $16.44; proceeds, $983.56. NP2.
Oct. 1.   Issued a 60-day, 10% note to Main Industrial Bank, $500.00. NP3.

   2. Figure the total amount of interest due at maturity for each of the three notes.
   3. Record the transactions on page 8 of a cash receipts journal.
   4. Record the following transactions on page 10 of a cash payments journal. Use the maturity dates figured in Instruction 1, and the interest amounts figured in Instruction 2.

     Paid Fifth State Bank $1,000.00 principal plus interest due on NP1. C45.
     Paid First State Bank $1,000.00 principal plus interest due on NP2. C52.
     Paid Main Industrial Bank $500.00 principal plus interest due on NP3. C59.

PROBLEM 11-2   Recording adjusting entries and reversing entries for prepaid expenses recorded initially as expenses

The following information is from the records of Drisdale, Inc., on December 31 of the current year before adjusting entries are recorded.

    General ledger account balances:
       Supplies Expense—Sales, debit $2,200.00
       Supplies Expense—Administrative, debit.........................   1,000.00
       Insurance Expense, debit 2,900.00
       Interest Expense, debit 26.53
       Notes Payable, credit...   1,000.00
         (Discounted at 10% the 60-day Note
         Payable No. 4 issued December 1.)
    Inventories, December 31:
       Sales supplies..   870.00
       Administrative supplies 250.00
       Unused insurance premiums 720.00

Instructions: 1. Record the adjusting entries for supplies and insurance on page 10 of a general journal. Use December 31 of the current year as the date.
   2. Continue using page 10 of the general journal. Figure the amount of prepaid interest on Note Payable No. 4 as of December 31 of the current year. Record the adjusting entry for prepaid interest on Note Payable No. 4.
   3. Record the needed reversing entries on page 1 of a general journal. Use January 1 of the next year as the date.

PROBLEM 11-3   Recording adjusting and reversing entries for accrued expenses

The following information is from the records of Northeastern, Inc., as of December 31 of the current year before adjusting entries are recorded.

Accrued interest on notes payable .... $ 4.15
Accrued payroll:
    Sales salaries 400.00
    Administrative salaries....................................... 500.00
Accrued employer's payroll taxes:
    FICA tax 63.00
    Federal unemployment tax 7.20
    State unemployment tax 48.60
Accrued federal income tax 1,000.00

Instructions: 1. Record the adjusting entries for each of the following: accrued interest, accrued payroll, accrued employer's payroll taxes, accrued federal income tax. Use page 8 of a general journal. Use December 31 of the current year as the date.

2. Record the needed reversing entries on page 1 of a general journal. Use January 1 of the next year as the date.

ENRICHMENT PROBLEMS

MASTERY PROBLEM 11-M **Recording adjusting and reversing entries for prepaid expenses recorded initially as expenses and for accrued expenses**

Willart, Inc., completed the following selected transactions during the current year. Willart records prepaid expenses initially as expenses. Source documents are abbreviated as follows: check, C; note payable, NP.

July 1. Issued a 2-month, 15% note to Centerville Trust Bank, $500.00. NP1.
Sept. 1. Paid Centerville Trust Bank $512.50 for NP1, $500.00, plus interest, $12.50. C105.
Oct. 31. Issued a 3-month, 10% note to Centerville State Bank, $1,000.00. NP2.
Nov. 1. Issued a 90-day, 10% note to Centerville Trust Bank, $1,500.00. NP3.
Dec. 1. Discounted at 10% at Centerville State Bank a 60-day note, $800.00; discount, $13.15; proceeds, $786.85. NP4.

Instructions: 1. Figure the maturity dates for Notes Payable Nos. 2, 3, and 4.

2. Record the transactions on page 4 of a cash receipts journal and page 5 of a cash payments journal.

3. Record the adjusting entries for prepaid and accrued expenses on page 3 of a general journal. Use December 31 of the current year as the date. The following information is from the business' records on December 31 of the current year before adjusting entries are recorded.

General ledger account balances:
    Supplies Expense — Sales .... $ 500.00
    Supplies Expense — Administrative 300.00
    Insurance Expense.. 800.00
    Notes Payable.. 3,000.00
Inventories, December 31:
    Sales supplies... 200.00
    Administrative supplies 100.00
    Unused insurance premiums 250.00
    Remaining prepaid interest................................... 6.58
Accrued interest on notes payable 41.33
Accrued payroll:
    Sales salaries 315.00
    Administrative salaries....................................... 250.00

Accrued employer's payroll taxes:	
FICA tax	$ 39.55
Federal unemployment tax	2.83
State unemployment tax	36.74
Accrued federal income tax	700.00

4. Record the needed reversing entries on page 1 of a general journal. Use January 1 of the next year as the date.

CHALLENGE PROBLEM 11-C   Recording adjusting entries for prepaid expenses recorded initially as assets and adjusting and reversing entries for accrued expenses

Monahan, Inc., completed the following selected transactions during the current year. Monahan records prepaid expenses initially as assets. Source documents are abbreviated as follows: check, C; note payable, NP.

Aug. 1. Issued a 3-month, 10% note to Findley State Bank, $1,000.00. NP3.
Sept. 30. Issued a 6-month, 12% note to First Bank and Trust Company, $1,500.00. NP4.
Nov. 1. Paid Findley State Bank $1,025.00 for NP3, $1,000.00, plus interest, $25.00. C95.
Nov. 30. Discounted at 10% at Findley State Bank a 90-day note, $400.00; discount, $9.86; proceeds, $390.14. NP5.

Instructions: 1. Figure the maturity dates for Notes Payable Nos. 4 and 5.

2. Record the transactions on page 12 of a cash receipts journal and page 11 of a cash payments journal.

3. Record the adjusting entries for prepaid and accrued items on page 7 of a general journal. Use December 31 of the current year as the date. The following information is from the business' records on December 31 of the current year before adjusting entries are recorded.

General ledger account balances:	
Supplies — Sales	$600.00
Supplies — Administrative	500.00
Prepaid Insurance	900.00
Prepaid Interest	34.86
Inventories, December 31:	
Sales supplies	250.00
Administrative supplies	200.00
Unused insurance premiums	550.00
Remaining prepaid interest	6.46
Accrued interest on notes payable	45.37
Accrued payroll:	
Sales salaries	425.00
Administrative salaries	355.00
Accrued employer's payroll taxes:	
FICA tax	54.60
Federal unemployment tax	3.90
State unemployment tax	43.68
Accrued federal income tax	900.00

4. Record the needed reversing entries on page 1 of a general journal. Use January 1 of the next year as the date.

12 Accounting for Notes Receivable, Unearned Revenue, and Accrued Revenue

ENABLING PERFORMANCE TASKS

After studying Chapter 12, you will be able to:
a. Define accounting terms related to notes receivable, unearned revenue, and accrued revenue.
b. Identify accounting concepts and practices related to notes receivable, unearned revenue, and accrued revenue.
c. Analyze and record entries for notes receivable.
d. Analyze and record adjusting and reversing entries for unearned revenue and accrued revenue.

   Financial statements must show all information about notes receivable and revenue. *(CONCEPT: Adequate Disclosure)* Accounting for these items often requires special procedures.

   Rent income is usually received in advance. If all the revenue from rent is not earned at the end of a fiscal period, an adjustment is made to separate and record unearned rent. Some businesses accept notes from customers who want an extension of time in which to pay. An adjustment for interest income that is earned but not yet received may have to be made. The revenue earned during a fiscal period must be recorded during that fiscal period. *(CONCEPT: Matching Expenses with Revenue)*

NOTES RECEIVABLE AND INTEREST INCOME

   Promissory notes that a business accepts from customers are called notes receivable. Most notes receivable are accepted from customers who need an extension of time in which to pay.

Accepting a note receivable

The source document for a transaction to accept a note is a copy of the note receivable. *(CONCEPT: Objective Evidence)*

November 3, 1989.
Received a 30-day, 12% note receivable from Don Jacobson for an extension of time on his account, $200.00. Note Receivable No. 11.

GENERAL LEDGER	
Notes Receivable	
200.00	

Accounts Receivable	
	200.00

ACCOUNTS RECEIVABLE LEDGER	
Don Jacobson	
Balance 200.00	200.00

The analysis of this transaction is shown in the T accounts. In the general ledger, Notes Receivable is increased by a $200.00 debit. Accounts Receivable is decreased by a $200.00 credit. The amount to be received has been changed from an account receivable to a note receivable. In the accounts receivable ledger, the customer account, Don Jacobson, is also decreased by a $200.00 credit.

The entry to record this transaction is shown in Illustration 12-1.

GENERAL JOURNAL						PAGE //
	DATE	ACCOUNT TITLE	POST. REF.	DEBIT	CREDIT	
1	1989 nov. 3	Notes Receivable		200 00		1
2		Accts. Rec. / Don Jacobson	✓		200 00	2
3		NR11				3
4						4
5						5

Illustration 12-1
Entry to record accepting
a note receivable

Recording cash received for a note receivable

December 3, 1989.
Received from Don Jacobson $201.97 in settlement of Note Receivable No. 11, $200.00, plus interest, $1.97; total, $201.97. Receipt No. 300.

Interest on Note Receivable No. 11 is figured as shown below.

Principal	×	Interest Rate	×	Fraction of a Year	=	Interest for 30 Days
$200.00	×	12%	×	$\frac{30}{365}$	=	$1.97

Cash	
201.97	

Notes Receivable	
Balance 200.00	200.00

Interest Income	
	1.97

The analysis of this transaction is shown in the T accounts. Cash is increased by a $201.97 debit, the amount of cash received for the note plus interest. Notes Receivable is decreased by a $200.00 credit, the note's principal. This credit cancels the $200.00 debit recorded when the note was received. Interest Income is increased by a $1.97 credit, the interest received on the note.

Interest Income is classified as an other revenue account as shown on Gallery's chart of accounts.

The entry to record this transaction is shown in Illustration 12-2.

				GENERAL		ACCOUNTS RECEIVABLE CREDIT	SALES CREDIT	SALES TAX PAYABLE		SALES DISCOUNT DEBIT	CASH DEBIT	
DATE	ACCOUNT TITLE	DOC. NO.	POST. REF.	DEBIT	CREDIT			DEBIT	CREDIT			
9	3 Notes Receivable	R300			20000						20197	9
10	Interest Income				197							10
11												11
12												12
13												13
14												14

CASH RECEIPTS JOURNAL — PAGE 24

Recording a dishonored note receivable

Illustration 12-2
Entry to record receipt of cash for a note receivable

A note that is not paid when due is called a dishonored note. The notes receivable account balance should include only the value of notes receivable that a business expects to collect. Otherwise Notes Receivable will be reported incorrectly on a balance sheet. *(CONCEPT: Adequate Disclosure)*

June 1, 1989.
Rebecca Sills dishonored Note Receivable No. 8 due today: principal, $150.00; interest, $3.70; total, $153.70. Memorandum No. 120.

On June 1, the maturity date of Note Receivable No. 8, Miss Sills owes the principal, $150.00, plus interest, $3.70. Miss Sills fails to pay a total debt of $153.70. Although the note is dishonored, Miss Sills still owes the money to Gallery. Therefore, the total amount owed, $153.70, must appear in the business' records.

This entry for a dishonored note receivable does not cancel the debt. The debt is transferred to Accounts Receivable and carried on the records until Miss Sills pays the amount, or her account is declared uncollectible.

The analysis of this transaction is shown in the T accounts. In the general ledger, Accounts Receivable is increased by a $153.70 debit, the total amount owed by Miss Sills. Notes Receivable is decreased by a $150.00 credit, the principal of the dishonored note. Interest Income is increased by a $3.70 credit, the amount of interest earned to maturity on Note Receivable No. 8. In the accounts receivable ledger, the account for Rebecca Sills is increased by a $153.70 debit.

The entry to record this transaction is shown in Illustration 12-3.

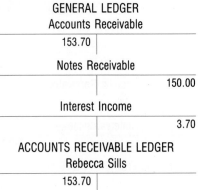

GENERAL LEDGER
Accounts Receivable

| 153.70 | |

Notes Receivable

| | 150.00 |

Interest Income

| | 3.70 |

ACCOUNTS RECEIVABLE LEDGER
Rebecca Sills

| 153.70 | |

Illustration 12-3
Entry to record a
dishonored note
receivable

GENERAL JOURNAL					PAGE 6	
DATE	ACCOUNT TITLE	POST. REF.	DEBIT	CREDIT		
1989 June 1	Accts. Rec./Rebecca Sills	✓	15370			1
	Notes Receivable			15000		2
	Interest Income			370		3
	M120					4

Recording cash received for a dishonored note receivable

Sometimes payment may be received on a previously dishonored note. When this happens, additional interest is charged from maturity date to payment date.

September 30, 1989.
Received from Rebecca Sills for dishonored Note Receivable No. 8: principal, $153.70, plus additional interest, $5.10; total, $158.80. Receipt No. 201.

The additional days for which interest is owed are figured as shown below.

Time	Number of Days
June 1 to June 30	29
July 1 to July 31	31
August 1 to August 31	31
September 1 to September 30	30
Total number of days	121

The interest due is figured as shown below.

Principal	×	Interest Rate	×	Fraction of a Year	=	Additional Interest
$153.70	×	10%	×	$\frac{121}{365}$	=	$5.10

The additional interest is based on the total debt owed on the date the note is dishonored, $153.70. The time begins when the note is dishonored, June 1, 1989, and ends on the day cash is received from Miss Sills, September 30, 1989.

The analysis of this transaction is shown in the T accounts. In the general ledger, Cash is increased by a $158.80 debit. This amount is the total received from Miss Sills for the dishonored note receivable plus additional interest. Accounts Receivable is decreased by a $153.70 credit. This amount is the debt before additional interest is added. Interest Income is increased by a $5.10 credit, the additional interest owed from June 1 to September 30. In the accounts receivable ledger, the customer account, Rebecca Sills, is decreased by a $153.70 credit.

GENERAL LEDGER

Cash

158.80	

Accounts Receivable

Balance	153.70	153.70

Interest Income

	5.10

ACCOUNTS RECEIVABLE LEDGER

Rebecca Sills

Balance	153.70	153.70

The entry to record this transaction is shown in Illustration 12-4.

				GENERAL		ACCOUNTS RECEIVABLE CREDIT	SALES CREDIT	SALES TAX PAYABLE		SALES DISCOUNT DEBIT	CASH DEBIT	
DATE	ACCOUNT TITLE	DOC. NO.	POST. REF.	DEBIT	CREDIT			DEBIT	CREDIT			
1989 Sept. 30	Rebecca Sills	R201				153 70					158 80	1
	Interest Income				5 10							2

CASH RECEIPTS JOURNAL PAGE *18*

Illustration 12-4
Entry to record cash
received for a dishonored
note receivable

UNEARNED REVENUE

Some revenue is received during a fiscal period, but is not actually earned until the next fiscal period. Revenue received in one fiscal period but not earned until the next fiscal period is called unearned revenue.

Unearned revenue may be recorded initially as a liability or as revenue. Beck, Inc., rents part of a building to Wiltshire, Inc., and initially records the unearned revenue as a liability. Beck prefers to delay recording unearned revenue as revenue until it is actually earned as the space is used. Gallery also rents out part of its building and initially records the unearned revenue as revenue.

Recording unearned revenue initially either as a liability or as revenue is acceptable accounting practice. Gallery prefers recording unearned revenue as revenue because the unearned revenue eventually will become revenue as the building space is used.

Comparison of adjusting entry for unearned revenue recorded initially as a liability and initially as revenue

Beck receives rent, $6,600.00, for three months in advance.

December 1, 1989.
Received three months' rent in advance from Wiltshire, Inc., $6,600.00. Receipt No. 220.

Gallery also receives rent, $6,600.00, for three months in advance.

December 1, 1989.
Received three months' rent in advance from Speedy Mail Service, $6,600.00. Receipt No. 294.

The analysis of these transactions for both Beck and Gallery is shown in the T accounts. Beck records prepaid revenue initially as a liability. Gallery records prepaid revenue initially as revenue.

BECK				GALLERY		
Cash				Cash		
6,600.00				6,600.00		

Unearned Rent				Rent Income		
	Balance	24,200.00			Balance	24,200.00
		6,600.00				6,600.00

Beck's balance in Unearned Rent, $24,200.00, is the rent revenue for eleven months, January 1 to November 30, 1989. On December 1, Cash is increased by a $6,600.00 debit, and Unearned Rent is increased by a $6,600.00 credit for three months' rent.

Gallery's balance in Rent Income, $24,200.00, is the rent revenue for eleven months, January 1 to November 30, 1989. On December 1, Cash is increased by a $6,600.00 debit, and Rent Income is increased by a $6,600.00 credit for three months' rent.

Only that part of rent actually earned should be recorded as revenue in a fiscal period. An adjusting entry is needed to separate the earned and unearned portions of the rent received in advance.

For Beck, on December 31, 1989, one of the three months' rent has been earned, and two months' rent is unearned. Therefore, two-thirds of the rent received in advance is still unearned. The same is true for Gallery. The amount of unearned rent is figured as shown below.

Rent Received in Advance	×	Fraction Still Unearned	=	Unearned Rent
$6,600.00	×	$\frac{2}{3}$	=	$4,400.00

Total Rent Received	−	Unearned Rent	=	1989 Rent Revenue
$30,800.00	−	$4,400.00	=	$26,400.00

The analysis of the adjusting entries for unearned rent revenue is shown in the T accounts.

BECK				GALLERY		
Unearned Rent				Unearned Rent		
Adjusting	26,400.00	Balance	30,800.00		Adjusting	4,400.00

Rent Income				Rent Income		
	Adjusting	26,400.00		Adjusting	4,400.00	Balance	30,800.00

Beck's liability account, Unearned Rent, is decreased by a $26,400.00 debit. The new balance of this account, $4,400.00, is the remaining unearned rent at the end of 1989. The revenue account, Rent Income, is increased by a $26,400.00 credit. The new balance of this account, $26,400.00, is Beck's 1989 rent revenue.

Gallery's liability account, Unearned Rent, is increased by a $4,400.00 credit. The new balance of this account, $4,400.00, is the remaining unearned rent at the end of 1989. The revenue account, Rent Income, is decreased by a $4,400.00 debit. The new balance of Rent Income, $26,400.00, is Gallery's 1989 rent revenue.

Unearned Rent is classified as a Current Liability and Rent Income is classified as Other Revenue as shown on Gallery's chart of accounts.

Gallery's adjusting entry for unearned rent revenue is shown in Illustration 12-5.

	DATE	ACCOUNT TITLE	POST. REF.	DEBIT	CREDIT	
		GENERAL JOURNAL			PAGE /3	
1		*Adjusting Entries*				1
36	31	*Rent Income*		4 400 00		36
37		*Unearned Rent*			4 400 00	37
38						38

Illustration 12-5
Adjusting entry for unearned rent revenue

Closing entry for unearned revenue

On December 31, 1989, Rent Income is closed as part of both Beck's and Gallery's closing entries. The effect of the closing entries on Rent Income is shown in the T accounts.

BECK
Rent Income

Closing	26,400.00	Adjusting	26,400.00

Income Summary

		Closing	26,400.00

GALLERY
Rent Income

Adjusting	4,400.00	Balance	30,800.00
Closing	26,400.00		

Income Summary

		Closing	26,400.00

In Beck's closing entry, Rent Income is decreased and closed by a $26,400.00 debit. Income Summary is affected by a $26,400.00 credit. In Gallery's closing entry, Rent Income is also decreased and closed by a $26,400.00 debit and Income Summary is affected by a $26,400.00 credit.

Reversing entry for unearned revenue

Reversing entries for prepaid and accrued expenses were described in Chapter 11. Reversing entries for unearned revenue are made for the same reasons as for the prepaid expenses, to avoid recording some amounts twice. Beck's adjusting entry for unearned rent *did not* create a balance in the liability account. Therefore, Beck does not need to make a reversing entry.

Gallery's adjusting entry did create a balance in the liability account, Unearned Rent. Therefore, Gallery *does need* to make a reversing entry for unearned rent on January 1, 1990. After the closing entries are recorded and posted on December 31, 1989, Rent Income has a zero balance. A reversing entry is recorded on January 1, 1990. The analysis of this reversing entry is shown in the T accounts.

Unearned Rent is decreased by a $4,400.00 debit. The new balance of Unearned Rent is zero as it was before the adjusting entry. Rent Income is increased by a $4,400.00 credit. On January 1, 1990, after the reversing entry is posted, Rent Income has a $4,400.00 credit balance. The remaining rent received in advance, $4,400.00, is part of the rent revenue for 1990.

Unearned Rent			
Reversing	4,400.00	Adjusting	4,400.00

Rent Income			
Adjusting	4,400.00	Balance	30,800.00
Closing	26,400.00	Reversing	4,400.00

The reversing entry for unearned rent revenue is shown in Illustration 12-6.

GENERAL JOURNAL

	DATE	ACCOUNT TITLE	POST. REF.	DEBIT	CREDIT	
1		*Reversing Entries*				1
24	*1*	*Unearned Rent*		440000		24
25		*Rent Income*			440000	25
26						26
27						27
28						28

PAGE *1*

Illustration 12-6
Reversing entry for
unearned rent revenue

ACCRUED REVENUE

Revenue earned in one fiscal period but not received until a later fiscal period is called accrued revenue. For example, a business accepts a 30-day note on December 15, 1989. During December, the business earns interest for 16 days. However, the business will not receive any of the interest until the note's maturity in January, 1990. Interest for the first 16 days must be recorded in 1989. (CONCEPT: *Matching Expenses with Revenue*)

Figuring accrued interest income

On December 31, 1989, Gallery's records show that the business has two notes receivable still on hand.

Note Receivable No. 12. Date, December 1, 1989; principal, $400.00; interest rate, 10%; time, 60 days.

Note Receivable No. 13. Date, December 16, 1989; principal, $600.00; interest rate, 10%; time, 30 days.

Accrued interest on the two notes is figured as shown below.

Note	Principal	×	Interest Rate	×	Fraction of a Year	=	Accrued Interest Income
12	$400.00	×	10%	×	$\dfrac{30}{365}$	=	$3.29
13	600.00	×	10%	×	$\dfrac{15}{365}$	=	2.47

Total accrued interest income, December 31, 1989........ $5.76

Adjusting entry for accrued interest income

The analysis of Gallery's adjusting entry for accrued interest income is shown in the T accounts. Interest Receivable is increased by a $5.76 debit. Interest Income is increased by a $5.76 credit.

Interest Receivable is classified as a Current Asset as shown on Gallery's chart of accounts.

Interest Receivable	
Adjusting 5.76	

Interest Income	
	Balance 62.48
	Adjusting 5.76

The adjusting entry for accrued interest income is shown in Illustration 12-7.

	DATE	ACCOUNT TITLE	POST. REF.	DEBIT	CREDIT	
1		*Adjusting Entries*				1
2	*1989 Dec. 31*	*Interest Receivable*		5 76		2
3		*Interest Income*			5 76	3
4						4
5						5

GENERAL JOURNAL — PAGE 13

Illustration 12-7
Adjusting entry for accrued interest income

Closing entry for interest income

The effect of Gallery's closing entries on Interest Income is shown in the T accounts.

Interest Income	
Closing 68.24	Balance 62.48
	Adjusting 5.76

Income Summary	
	Closing 68.24

Reversing entry for accrued interest income

Interest Income has a zero balance after closing entries are recorded and posted on December 31, 1989. However, the adjusting entry for accrued interest income created a balance in the asset Interest Receivable. Therefore, Gallery needs a reversing entry on January 1, 1990, for accrued interest income. The analysis of this reversing entry is shown in the T accounts.

Interest Income			
Closing	68.24	Balance	62.48
Reversing	5.76	Adjusting	5.76

Interest Receivable			
Adjusting	5.76	Reversing	5.76

Interest Income is decreased by a $5.76 debit. The new debit balance of Interest Income is $5.76. Interest Receivable is decreased by a $5.76 credit. The new balance of Interest Receivable is zero as it was before the adjusting entry.

This reversing entry is shown in Illustration 12-8.

Illustration 12-8
Reversing entry for
accrued interest income

		GENERAL JOURNAL		PAGE /	
DATE		ACCOUNT TITLE	POST. REF.	DEBIT	CREDIT
		Reversing Entries			
1990 Jan.	1	Interest Income		576	
		Interest Receivable			576

SUMMARY

A summary of the adjusting and reversing entries described in this chapter is shown in Illustration 12-9.

Item	Adjusting Entry		Reversing Entry	
	Account Debited	Account Credited	Account Debited	Account Credited
Unearned revenue recorded initially as a liability:				
Rent Income	Unearned Rent	Rent Income	no reversing entry made	
Unearned revenue recorded initially as revenue:				
Rent Income	Rent Income	Unearned Rent	Unearned Rent	Rent Income
Accrued revenue:				
Interest Income	Interest Receivable	Interest Income	Interest Income	Interest Receivable

Illustration 12-9
Summary of adjusting and reversing entries for
unearned and accrued revenue

ACCOUNTING TERMS

What is the meaning of each of the following?

1. notes receivable

2. dishonored note

3. unearned revenue

4. accrued revenue

QUESTIONS FOR INDIVIDUAL STUDY

1. Assuring that financial statements show all information about notes receivable and revenue is an application of which accounting concept?

2. Why might a business accept a note receivable from a customer?
3. What accounts are affected, and how, by an entry to accept a note receivable?
4. What accounts are affected, and how, when cash is received in settlement of a note receivable plus interest?
5. What happens to the debt on Gallery's records when a note receivable is dishonored?
6. What accounts are affected, and how, by an entry to record a dishonored note?
7. What accounts are affected, and how, when cash is received for a dishonored note receivable?
8. What accounts are affected, and how, when Gallery receives rent in advance?
9. What accounts are affected, and how, in recording Gallery's adjusting entry for unearned rent?
10. What accounts are affected, and how, by a reversing entry for unearned rent?
11. What accounts are affected, and how, by an adjusting entry for accrued interest income?
12. What accounts are affected, and how, by a reversing entry for accrued interest income?

CASES FOR MANAGEMENT DECISION

CASE 1 Mason, Inc., received a 60-day, 12%, $500.00 note receivable from a customer. The customer dishonored the note at maturity. The accounting clerk recorded the dishonored note receivable by debiting Accounts Receivable and crediting Notes Receivable for the amount owed at maturity, $509.86. 30 days later, the customer paid $514.89 for the dishonored note. The accounting clerk recorded this amount by debiting Cash and crediting Notes Receivable. Mason's bookkeeper checked the work and decided that the entries were both incorrect. Are the entries incorrect? Explain your answer.

CASE 2 At the beginning of December, Maxby Rentals receives three months' rent in advance. On December 31, Maxby's does *not* make an adjusting entry for unearned rent. What effect will this have on the firm's financial statements?

CASE 3 The Sweet Shop's accounting personnel claim that they have never made reversing entries at the end of any fiscal period. Under what circumstances could this be true and still result in correct records?

APPLICATION PROBLEMS

PROBLEM 12-1   Recording entries for notes receivable

Best, Inc., completed the following selected transactions during the current year.

Instructions: Record the following transactions. Use page 1 of a general journal and page 3 of a cash receipts journal. Source documents are abbreviated as follows: memorandum, M; note receivable, NR; receipt, R.

Aug. 1. Received a 60-day, 10% note receivable from Moses Williams for an extension of time on his account, $100.00. NR1.
Aug. 1. Received a 2-month, 12% note receivable from Gary Byrd for an extension of time on his account, $200.00. NR2.
Sept. 30. Moses Williams dishonored NR1 due today: principal, $100.00; interest, $1.64. M12.

Oct.	1.	Received a 2-month, 10% note receivable from Melinda Cruz for an extension of time on her account, $500.00. NR3.
Oct.	1.	Received from Gary Byrd in settlement of NR2, $200.00, plus interest, $4.00. R10.
Dec.	1.	Received from Moses Williams for dishonored NR1: principal, $101.64, plus additional interest, $1.73. R32.
Dec.	1.	Received from Melinda Cruz in settlement of NR3, $500.00, plus interest, $8.33. R33.

PROBLEM 12-2 Recording adjusting and reversing entries for unearned revenue

The information below is from the records of Boots, Inc., on December 31 of the current year before adjustments are recorded. Boots records unearned revenue initially as revenue.

General ledger account balances:

Unearned Rent	zero
Rent Income	$24,000.00

Information for adjustment:

December 31, rent still unearned	$ 2,000.00

Instructions: 1. Record the adjusting entry for unearned rent. Use page 4 of a general journal. Use December 31 of the current year as the date.

2. Continue using page 4 of the general journal. Record the reversing entry for unearned rent. Use January 1 of the next year as the date.

PROBLEM 12-3 Recording adjusting and reversing entries for accrued revenue

On December 31 of the current year, Wilson, Inc., has two notes receivable.

Note Receivable No. 1. Date, November 1 of the current year; principal, $100.00; interest rate, 10%; time, 90 days.

Note Receivable No. 2. Date, December 1 of the current year; principal, $200.00; interest rate, 10%; time, 60 days.

Instructions: 1. Figure the accrued interest on Notes Receivable Nos. 1 and 2 as of December 31 of the current year.

2. Record the adjusting entry for accrued interest income. Use page 1 of a general journal. Use December 31 of the current year as the date.

3. Continue using page 1 of the general journal. Record the reversing entry for accrued interest income. Use January 1 of the next year as the date.

ENRICHMENT PROBLEMS

MASTERY PROBLEM 12-M Recording entries for notes receivable, unearned revenue, and accrued revenue

Sorstat, Inc., completed the following transactions during the current year. Sorstat records prepaid and unearned items initially as expenses and revenue.

Instructions: 1. Record the following transactions. Use page 3 of a general journal and page 4 of a cash receipts journal. Source documents are abbreviated as follows: memorandum, M; note receivable, NR; receipt, R.

July   1. Received a 90-day, 10% note receivable from Thomas Carlson for an extension of time on his account, $200.00. NR12.

July   5. Received a 3-month, 12% note receivable from John Westmore for an extension of time on his account, $200.00. NR13.

Sept. 29. Thomas Carlson dishonored NR12 due today: principal, $200.00; interest $4.93. M32.

Oct.   5. Received from John Westmore in settlement of NR13: $200.00, plus interest, $6.00. R65.

Nov.   1. Received three months' rent in advance from Maldon, Inc., $1,200.00. R70.

Dec.   1. Received from Thomas Carlson for dishonored NR12: principal, $204.93, plus additional interest, $3.54. R81.

2. Continue using page 3 of the general journal. Record the needed adjusting entries using the information below. Use December 31 of the current year as the date.

Accrued interest on notes receivable, December 31 .... $ 10.24
Rent received in advance and still unearned 400.00

3. Record the needed reversing entries. Use page 4 of a general journal. Use January 1 of the next year as the date.

CHALLENGE PROBLEM 12-C Recording entries for notes receivable, unearned revenue, and accrued revenue

Wischer, Inc., completed the transactions given below during the current year. Wischer records prepaid and unearned items initially as expenses and revenue.

Instructions: 1. Record the following transactions. Figure amounts as needed for each transaction. Use page 4 of a general journal and page 7 of a cash receipts journal. Source documents are abbreviated as follows: memorandum, M; note receivable, NR; receipt, R.

July   1. Received a 90-day, 14% note receivable from Susan Bradley for an extension of time on her account, $400.00. NR26.

Aug.   1. Received a 60-day, 12% note receivable from Donald Murdock for an extension of time on his account, $500.00. NR27.

Sept. 29. Susan Bradley dishonored NR26 due today. M45.

Sept. 30. Received cash from Donald Murdock in settlement of NR27. R70.

Nov. 15. Received cash from Susan Bradley for dishonored NR26. R85.

Dec.   1. Received a 90-day, 10% note receivable from Janet Vincent for an extension of time on her account, $300.00. NR28.

Dec.   1. Received three months' rent in advance from Lawson, Inc., $2,100.00. R97.

2. Continue using page 4 of the general journal. Record the adjusting entries for the following items. Use December 31 of the current year as the date.

a. Accrued interest income. Figure the accrued interest for Note Receivable No. 28.

b. Unearned rent revenue. Figure the unearned portion of the rent received in advance from Lawson, Inc.

3. Record the needed reversing entries. Use page 5 of a general journal. Use January 1 of the next year as the date.

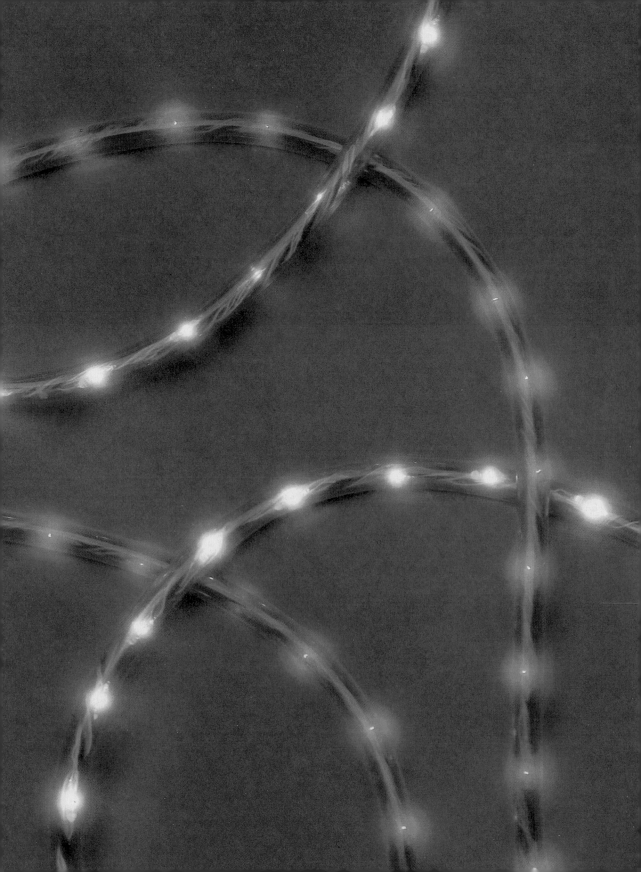

5
Corporation Accounting

GENERAL BEHAVIORAL GOALS

1. Know accounting terminology related to a corporation.
2. Understand accounting concepts and practices related to a corporation.
3. Demonstrate accounting procedures unique to a corporation.

AQUAPRO, INC.
Chart of Accounts

Balance Sheet Accounts

(1000) ASSETS

__1100   Current Assets__

1105	Cash
1110	Petty Cash
1115	Notes Receivable
1120	Interest Receivable
1125	Accounts Receivable
1130	Allowance for Uncollectible Accounts
1135	Subscriptions Receivable
1140	Merchandise Inventory
1145	Supplies — Sales
1150	Supplies — Delivery
1155	Supplies — Administrative
1160	Prepaid Insurance
1165	Prepaid Interest

__1200   Long-Term Investment__

1205	Bond Sinking Fund

__1300   Plant Assets__

1305	Store Equipment
1310	Accumulated Depreciation — Store Equipment
1315	Delivery Equipment
1320	Accumulated Depreciation — Delivery Equipment
1325	Office Equipment
1330	Accumulated Depreciation — Office Equipment
1335	Building
1340	Accumulated Depreciation — Building
1345	Land

__1400   Intangible Asset__

1405	Organization Costs

(2000) LIABILITIES

__2100   Current Liabilities__

2105	Notes Payable
2110	Interest Payable
2115	Accounts Payable
2120	Employees Income Tax Payable
2125	Federal Income Tax Payable
2130	FICA Tax Payable
2135	Salaries Payable
2140	Sales Tax Payable
2145	Unemployment Tax Payable — Federal
2150	Unemployment Tax Payable — State
2155	Hospital Insurance Premiums Payable
2160	Dividends Payable

__2200   Long-Term Liability__

2205	Bonds Payable

(3000) STOCKHOLDERS' EQUITY

3105	Capital Stock — Common
3110	Stock Subscribed — Common
3115	Capital Stock — Preferred
3120	Stock Subscribed — Preferred
3125	Paid-in Capital in Excess of Par/Stated Value
3130	Discount on Sale of Capital Stock
3135	Treasury Stock
3140	Paid-in Capital from Sale of Treasury Stock
3145	Retained Earnings
3150	Dividends — Common Stock
3155	Dividends — Preferred Stock
3160	Income Summary

Income Statement Accounts

(4000) OPERATING REVENUE

4105	Sales
4110	Sales Returns and Allowances
4115	Sales Discount

(5000) COST OF MERCHANDISE

5105	Purchases
5110	Purchases Returns and Allowances
5115	Purchases Discount

(6000) OPERATING EXPENSES

__6100   Selling Expenses__

6105	Advertising Expense
6110	Credit Card Fee Expense
6115	Depreciation Expense — Store Equipment
6120	Miscellaneous Expense — Sales
6125	Salary Expense — Sales
6130	Supplies Expense — Sales

__6200   Delivery Expenses__

6205	Depreciation Expense — Delivery Equipment
6210	Miscellaneous Expense — Delivery
6215	Salary Expense — Delivery
6220	Supplies Expense — Delivery

__6300   Administrative Expenses__

6305	Bad Debts Expense
6310	Depreciation Expense — Office Equipment
6315	Depreciation Expense — Building
6320	Insurance Expense
6325	Miscellaneous Expense — Administrative
6330	Payroll Taxes Expense
6335	Property Tax Expense
6340	Salary Expense — Administrative
6345	Supplies Expense — Administrative
6350	Utilities Expense

(7000) OTHER REVENUE

7105	Gain on Plant Assets
7110	Interest Income

(8000) OTHER EXPENSES

8105	Interest Expense
8110	Loss on Plant Assets
8115	Organization Expense

(9000) INCOME TAX

9105	Federal Income Tax

The chart of accounts for AquaPro, Inc., is illustrated above for
ready reference as you study Part 5 of this textbook.

13 Organizational Structure of a Corporation

ENABLING PERFORMANCE TASKS

After studying Chapter 13, you will be able to:
a. Define accounting terms related to corporate accounting.
b. Identify accounting concepts and practices related to corporate accounting.
c. Figure dividends for a corporation.
d. Record transactions for starting a corporation.
e. Prepare a balance sheet for a newly formed corporation.

A business may be organized by law to exist separately and apart from its owners. An organization with the legal rights of a person and which may be owned by many persons is known as a corporation. *(CONCEPT: Business Entity)* Corporations differ from other forms of businesses principally in the nature of ownership and management.

NATURE OF A CORPORATION

A corporation's ownership is divided into units. Each unit of ownership in a corporation is known as a share of stock. Total shares of ownership in a corporation is known as capital stock. An owner of one or more shares of a corporation is known as a stockholder.

A corporation may have many owners. A large number of owners could have difficulty participating in a business' management. Therefore, the owners elect a small group to represent their combined interests and to be responsible for a corporation's management. A group of persons elected by the stockholders to manage a corporation is called a board of directors. A board of directors determines corporate policies and selects corporate officers to supervise the day-to-day management of the corporation.

Legal requirements for forming a corporation

Individuals wishing to form a corporation must submit an application to the designated officials of the state in which the company is to be incorporated. A written application requesting permission to form a corporation is called the articles of incorporation. Some applications are submitted to the federal government, but most applications are submitted to a state government.

When the application is approved, a corporation comes into existence. The approved articles of incorporation are called a charter. A charter is sometimes known as a certificate of incorporation.

AquaPro, Inc., is a corporation selling scuba diving equipment and accessories for personal and professional use. The articles of incorporation submitted for AquaPro, Inc., are shown in Illustration 13-1.

Illustration 13-1
Articles of Incorporation
(page 1)

ARTICLES OF INCORPORATION
OF
AQUAPRO, INC.

We, the undersigned, for the purpose of forming a corporation for profit under the laws of the State of Florida, hereby adopt the following Articles of Incorporation:

Article I - Name

The name of this corporation is AquaPro, Inc.

Article II - Nature of Business

This corporation may engage in any activity or business permitted under the laws of the United States and of the State of Florida.

Article III - Capital Stock

The maximum authorized capital stock is:

Common stock: 100,000 shares; $10.00 stated-value.
Preferred stock: 50,000 shares; 9%; $100.00 par-value; noncumulative; nonparticipating.

Article IV - Initial Capital

The amount of capital with which this corporation will begin business is not less than Five Hundred Thousand Dollars ($500,000.00).

Article V - Term of Existence

This corporation shall have perpetual existence.

Article VI - Address

The present address of the principal office of this corporation is 2309 Anderson Road, Miami, Florida.
The Board of Directors may from time to time move the corporation's principal office to another place in the State of Florida.

Article VII - Directors

The number of directors of this corporation shall be determined in accordance with the by-laws, but the number shall never be less than three.

Article VIII - Initial Directors

The names and addresses of the members of the first Board of Directors of this corporation are:

Ruth R. Miguel	2309 Anderson Road	Miami, Florida
Andrus M. Miguel	2309 Anderson Road	Miami, Florida
Betty L. Andrews	14239 S.W. 43rd Street	Miami, Florida
Leon T. Franklin	3104 S.W. 50th Street	Miami, Florida
Brian J. Mitchell	21910 Sunrise Drive	Miami, Florida

AquaPro is organized as a corporation to sell scuba and diving equipment. However, in the articles of incorporation, Article II, the nature of the business is described in broad, general terms. With this broad purpose, AquaPro may expand into other kinds of business activities without applying for a new charter.

Rights of stockholders

Most stockholders have four basic rights.

1. The right to vote at stockholders' meetings unless an exception is made for a particular class of stock.

Illustration 13-1
Articles of Incorporation
(page 2)

Article IX - Incorporators and Initial Subscribers

The names and addresses of the persons signing these articles of incorporation as incorporators and as initial subscribers for stock are:

Ruth R. Miguel	2309 Anderson Road	Miami, Florida
Andrus M. Miguel	2309 Anderson Road	Miami, Florida
Betty L. Andrews	14239 S.W. 43rd Street	Miami, Florida
Leon T. Franklin	3104 S.W. 50th Street	Miami, Florida
Brian J. Mitchell	21910 Sunrise Drive	Miami, Florida

Article X - Beginning of Corporate Existence

Corporate existence shall begin when these articles of incorporation have been filed with and approved by the State of Florida and all filing fees and taxes have been paid.

Article XI - Amendments

This corporation reserves the right to amend or repeal any provisions contained in these articles of incorporation, or any amendment thereto, and any right conferred upon the stockholders is subject to this reservation.

IN WITNESS WHEREOF, we have executed and acknowledged these articles of incorporation this 12th day of December, 1987.

Ruth R. Miguel   *Leon T. Franklin*

Andrus M. Miguel   *Brian J. Mitchell*

Betty L. Andrews

STATE OF FLORIDA)
COUNTY OF DADE) ss:

Before me, an officer duly authorized in the State and County aforesaid, to take acknowledgments, personally appeared Ruth R. Miguel, Andrus M. Miguel, Betty L. Andrews, Leon T. Franklin, and Brian J. Mitchell, to me known to be the persons described in and who executed the foregoing instrument, and they acknowledged before me that they executed the same.

WITNESS my hand and official seal in the County and State aforesaid, this 12th day of December, 1987.

Wilma B. Schuman
Notary Public, State of Florida

(SEAL)

My commission expires June 30, 1989

2. The right to share in a corporation's earnings.
3. The right to maintain the same percentage of ownership in a corporation. If additional stock is issued, existing stockholders have first choice to buy additional shares to maintain their same percentage of ownership.
4. The right to share in the distribution of a corporation's assets if a corporation ceases operations and sells all its assets.

CAPITAL STOCK AND DIVIDENDS OF A CORPORATION

Corporations may issue two kinds of stock: common and preferred. Stock that does not give stockholders any special preferences is called common stock. Stock that gives stockholders preference in earnings and other rights is called preferred stock. AquaPro is authorized to issue both common and preferred stock as described in Article III, Illustration 13-1.

Value of stock

Shares of stock are frequently assigned a value. A value assigned to a share of stock and printed on the stock certificate is called the par value. A share of stock that has an authorized value printed on the stock certificate is called par-value stock.

A share of stock that has no authorized value printed on the stock certificate is called no-par-value stock. Some states require that no-par-value stock be assigned a stated or specific value. No-par-value stock that is assigned a value by a corporation is called stated-value stock. Stated-value stock is similar to par-value stock except that the value is not printed on the stock certificates.

Common stock

If a corporation issues only one kind of stock, that stock is common stock. If a corporation issues only common stock, the common stockholders are entitled to all distributed earnings. Earnings distributed to stockholders are called dividends. In most corporations, only owners of common stock have a right to vote on matters brought before the stockholders. AquaPro is authorized to issue no-par-value common stock with a stated value of $10.00.

Preferred stock

To attract more investors, a corporation may offer preferred stock with preferences in some of the basic stockholders' rights. Preferred stockholders usually do not have voting rights and cannot influence when and how much is paid in dividends. Therefore, a typical preference given to preferred stockholders is to receive dividends before common stockholders. Preferred stock dividends may be stated as a percentage of par value or as an amount per share.

Several kinds of preferred stock may be issued and each may have different preferences. Four kinds of preferred stock are described below.

Cumulative preferred stock. Preferred stock with a provision that unpaid dividends will accumulate from one year to another is called cumulative preferred stock. For example, during 1988, Sailing, Inc., voted $48,000.00 for dividends. The corporation has outstanding 1,000 shares of 10%, $100.00 par-value cumulative preferred stock, total value of $100,000.00. The corporation also has outstanding 20,000 shares of $10.00 stated-value common stock, total value of $200,000.00. Sailing figures its 1988 dividends as follows.

Value of Outstanding Preferred Stock	×	Dividend Rate	=	Annual Preferred Dividend Amount
$100,000.00	×	10%	=	$10,000.00

Total Available for Dividends	−	Preferred Dividend Amount	=	Amount Available for Common Dividends
$48,000.00	−	$10,000.00	=	$38,000.00

In 1989, Sailing voted only $8,000.00 for dividends. The 1989 dividends are figured as follows.

Value of Outstanding Preferred Stock	×	Dividend Rate	=	Annual Preferred Dividend Amount
$100,000.00	×	10%	=	$10,000.00

Total Available for Dividends	−	Preferred Dividend Amount	=	Unpaid Preferred Dividend Amount	=	Amount Available for Common Dividends
$8,000.00	−	$10,000.00	=	$2,000.00	=	zero

A sufficient amount is not voted in 1989 to pay the full $10,000.00 (10%) preferred dividend. Therefore, no dividend is paid to common stockholders.

Sailing must pay the remaining 2% dividend to preferred stockholders during 1989 before any dividends can be paid to common stockholders. If the remaining 2% dividend is *not* paid during 1989, then in 1990 preferred stock must receive a 12% dividend before common stock receives any dividends. This 12% consists of the 1989 remaining 2% plus 10% for 1990.

Noncumulative preferred stock. Preferred stock for which unpaid dividends do not accumulate from one year to another is called noncumulative preferred stock. If the full preferred dividend is not voted during a fiscal year, the difference does not have to be declared and paid in future years. For example, during 1988, Ace Motors, Inc., has $8,000.00 available for dividends. The corporation has outstanding 1,000 shares of 10%, $100.00 par-value noncumulative preferred stock. The corporation also has outstanding 20,000 shares of $10.00 stated-value common stock. Ace Motors figures its 1988 dividends as follows.

Value of Outstanding Preferred Stock	×	Dividend Rate	=	Annual Preferred Dividend Amount
$100,000.00	×	10%	=	$10,000.00

Total Available for Dividends	−	Preferred Dividend Amount	=	Unpaid Preferred Dividend Amount	=	Amount Available for Common Dividends
$8,000.00	−	$10,000.00	=	$2,000.00	=	zero

Even though a full 10% is not paid to Ace Motors' preferred stockholders in 1988, the difference, 2%, is not carried over to future years. In 1989, Ace Motors votes $12,000.00 for dividends. The 1989 dividends are figured as follows.

Value of Outstanding Preferred Stock	×	Dividend Rate	=	Annual Preferred Dividend Amount
$100,000.00	×	10%	=	$10,000.00

Total Available for Dividends	−	Preferred Dividend Amount	=	Amount Available for Common Dividends
$12,000.00	−	$10,000.00	=	$2,000.00

Participating preferred stock. Preferred stock with a right to share with common stock in dividends above a stated percentage or amount is called participating preferred stock. For example, in 1988, BayTours, Inc., votes $48,000.00 for dividends. BayTours has outstanding 1,000 shares of 10%, $100.00 par-value participating preferred stock, and 20,000 shares of $10.00 stated-value common stock. Preferred stock participates with common at an equal rate after 10% of stated or par value has been paid on each kind of stock. BayTours figures its 1988 dividends as follows.

	Value of Outstanding Stock	×	Dividend Rate	=	Initial Dividends
Preferred	$100,000.00	×	10%	=	$10,000.00
Common	200,000.00	×	10%	=	20,000.00
Totals	$300,000.00				$30,000.00

Total Available for Dividends	−	Total Initial Dividends	=	Participating Dividends
$48,000.00	−	$30,000.00	=	$18,000.00

Participating Dividends	÷	Total Value of Outstanding Stock	=	Participating Dividend Rate
$18,000.00	÷	$300,000.00	=	6%

	Value of Outstanding Stock	×	Participating Rate	=	Participating Dividends
Preferred	$100,000.00	×	6%	=	$ 6,000.00
Common	$200,000.00	×	6%	=	12,000.00

The following is a summary of BayTours' 1988 dividends.

		Amount	Rate
Preferred stock:	Initial dividends	$10,000.00	10%
	Participating dividends............	6,000.00	6%
	Total	$16,000.00	16%
Common stock:	Initial dividends	$20,000.00	10%
	Participating dividends............	12,000.00	6%
	Total	$32,000.00	16%

In 1989, BayTours votes $20,000.00 for dividends. The 1989 dividends are figured as follows.

Value of Outstanding Preferred Stock	×	Dividend Rate	=	Initial Preferred Dividends
$100,000.00	×	10%	=	$10,000.00

Total Available for Dividends	−	Initial Preferred Dividends	=	Amount Available for Common Dividends
$20,000.00	−	$10,000.00	=	$10,000.00

Common Dividends Amount	÷	Value of Outstanding Common Stock	=	Common Dividend Rate
$10,000.00	÷	$200,000.00	=	5%

The following is a summary of BayTours' 1989 dividends.

	Amount	Rate
Preferred stock initial dividends....................	$10,000.00	10%
Common stock dividends	$10,000.00	5%

The preferred stock receives the full stated 10%. Common stock receives only 5%, which is not equal to the stated 10%. Therefore, a participating dividend is not paid in 1989.

Nonparticipating preferred stock. Preferred stock with no right to share with common stock in dividends above a stated percentage or amount is called nonparticipating preferred stock. All of the dividend amount in excess of the amount needed to pay dividends to preferred stock is used for common stock dividends. For example, during 1988, Coastal, Inc., votes $40,000.00 for dividends. Coastal has 1,000 shares of 10%, $100.00 par-value nonparticipating preferred stock, and 20,000 shares of $10.00 stated-value common stock. Coastal figures its 1988 dividends as follows.

Value of Outstanding Preferred Stock	×	Dividend Rate	=	Annual Preferred Dividend Amount
$100,000.00	×	10%	=	$10,000.00

Total Available for Dividends	−	Preferred Dividend Amount	=	Amount Available for Common Dividends
$40,000.00	−	$10,000.00	=	$30,000.00

In 1989, Coastal votes $9,000.00 for dividends. The dividends are figured as follows.

Value of Outstanding Preferred Stock	×	Dividend Rate	=	Annual Preferred Dividend Amount
$100,000.00	×	10%	=	$10,000.00

Total Available for Dividends	–	Preferred Dividend Amount	=	Unpaid Preferred Dividend Amount	=	Amount Available for Common Dividends
$9,000.00	–	$10,000.00	=	$1,000.00	=	zero

Coastal is unable to pay a full $10,000.00 preferred dividend. Therefore, no common dividend is paid. Unless Coastal's preferred stockholders are paid a total of $10,000.00 in any year, the common stockholders do not receive dividends.

Cumulative and participating features of preferred stock are desirable to stockholders. However, every preferred stockholder gain comes at the expense of common stockholders. For example, if preferred stockholders have a participating right in dividends, then common stockholders give up a right to some dividends. A few corporations may give voting rights to some kinds of preferred stock. If this situation occurs, then common stockholders' voting influence is less because more shares have voting rights. No stockholder is entitled to dividends until a corporation's board of directors votes to pay dividends.

The number of preferred stock preferences normally is determined by demand for the stock and the corporation's need for additional capital. When demand for a corporation's preferred stock is low, more preferences are often added to preferred stock being issued.

AquaPro is authorized to issue 9%, $100.00 par-value noncumulative nonparticipating preferred stock as described in Article III, Illustration 13-1.

Figuring and paying dividends for AquaPro is described in Chapter 15.

TRANSACTIONS WHEN STARTING A CORPORATION

AquaPro's articles of incorporation, Illustration 13-1, were approved by the State of Florida on December 26, 1987. The resulting charter was received by the corporation on December 31, 1987. The charter is AquaPro's legal approval to begin transacting business in the name of the corporation. The corporation needs assets to operate. The initial capital is obtained by selling stock to the incorporators.

Capital accounts of a corporation

Because of the potential number of owners, a corporation does not keep a separate capital account for each stockholder. Instead, a single, summary general ledger capital account is kept for each kind of stock issued. When a corporation issues only common stock, the value of all stock issued is recorded in a single capital stock account. When a corporation issues both common and preferred stock, separate capital stock accounts are used for common and preferred stock.

A corporation's net income is recorded in a capital account titled Retained Earnings. Using this account keeps the net income separate from the recorded values of issued capital stock. A net income is credited and a net loss is debited to Retained Earnings. A debit balance in Retained Earnings is often referred to as a deficit.

Each of AquaPro's incorporators agrees to buy 10,000 shares of common stock when the corporation is formed. Thus, a total of 50,000 shares of common stock, stated value $10.00, is issued for a total of $500,000.00.

Issuing capital stock when forming a corporation

The newly authorized corporation, AquaPro, Inc., receives $500,000.00 in cash for which it issues 50,000 shares of common stock to the five incorporators.

January 2, 1988.
Received from five incorporators for 50,000 shares of $10.00 stated-value common stock, $500,000.00. Receipt Nos. 1–5.

The analysis of this transaction is shown in the T accounts. Cash is debited for $500,000.00. Capital Stock—Common is credited for $500,000.00, the value of the issued common stock.

The entry to record this transaction is shown in Illustration 13-2.

Cash	
500,000.00	

Capital Stock—Common	
	500,000.00

					CASH RECEIPTS JOURNAL								PAGE *1*	
					1	2	3	4	5	6		7	8	
DATE	ACCOUNT TITLE	DOC. NO.	POST. REF.	GENERAL		ACCOUNTS RECEIVABLE CREDIT	SALES CREDIT	SALES TAX PAYABLE		SALES DISCOUNT DEBIT	CASH DEBIT	
				DEBIT	CREDIT			DEBIT	CREDIT			
1988 Jan. 2	Capital Stock—Common	R1-5			500000000						500000000	1
												2

Corporate records of stock issued

Written evidence of the number of shares each stockholder owns in a corporation is called a stock certificate. A corporation issues a stock certificate when full payment is received for stock. A stock certificate usually contains the issue date, certificate number, number of shares, and name of the stockholder.

A record is also kept of stock issued to each stockholder. Some corporations handle the issuing and transferring of stock certificates as well as

Illustration 13-2
Entry to record cash received for common stock

the record of stock ownership. Many corporations however engage a transfer agent, such as a bank, to issue certificates and keep stock ownership records.

Subscribing for capital stock

Corporations frequently contract with investors for the sale of capital stock with payment to be received at a later date. Future payment for the stock may be made all at one time or on an installment plan. Entering into an agreement with a corporation to buy capital stock and pay at a later date is called subscribing for capital stock.

Recording a stock subscription. On January 2, 1988, Elaine Underwood subscribed for 1,000 shares of AquaPro's common stock at $10.00 a share. She agreed to pay $5,000.00 on February 1, 1988, and $5,000.00 not later than March 1, 1988.

January 2, 1988.
Received a subscription from Elaine Underwood for 1,000 shares of $10.00 stated-value common stock, $10,000.00. Memorandum No. 1.

Subscriptions Receivable	
10,000.00	

Stock Subscribed — Common	
	10,000.00

The analysis of this transaction is shown in the T accounts. Subscriptions Receivable is debited for $10,000.00. The asset account Subscriptions Receivable shows the unpaid amount of all subscriptions. Stock Subscribed — Common is credited for $10,000.00. The capital account Stock Subscribed — Common shows the total amount of stock subscribed but not issued. This capital account is used because stock certificates are issued only when the stock is fully paid for. The amounts are recorded in Capital Stock — Common only when stock is fully paid for and stock certificates are issued.

The entry to record this transaction is shown in Illustration 13-3.

Illustration 13-3
Entry to record a stock subscription

	DATE		ACCOUNT TITLE	POST. REF.	DEBIT	CREDIT	
1	*1988 Jan.*	*2*	*Subscriptions Receivable*		*10 000 00*		1
2			*Stock Subscribed – Common*			*10 000 00*	2
3			*M 1*				3
4							4

GENERAL JOURNAL   PAGE *1*

Recording cash received for a stock subscription. On February 1, 1988, AquaPro receives cash from Elaine Underwood for half of her stock subscription.

February 1, 1988.
Received from Elaine Underwood in partial payment of stock subscription, $5,000.00. Receipt No. 6.

The analysis of this transaction is shown in the T accounts. Cash is debited for $5,000.00. Subscriptions Receivable is credited for $5,000.00. The new balance of this account, $5,000.00, is the amount still owed by Miss Underwood for her stock subscription.

The entry to record this transaction is shown in Illustration 13-4.

Cash	
5,000.00	

Subscriptions Receivable	
Balance 10,000.00	5,000.00

CASH RECEIPTS JOURNAL   PAGE 2

	DATE	ACCOUNT TITLE	DOC. NO.	POST. REF.	GENERAL DEBIT	GENERAL CREDIT	ACCOUNTS RECEIVABLE CREDIT	SALES CREDIT	SALES TAX PAYABLE DEBIT	SALES TAX PAYABLE CREDIT	SALES DISCOUNT DEBIT	CASH DEBIT	
1	1988 Feb. 1	Subscriptions Rec.	R6			5 000 00						5 000 00	1
2													2
3													3

A similar entry is made on March 1 when Miss Underwood pays the second installment of the stock subscription as shown in the T accounts.

Illustration 13-4
Entry to record cash received for a stock subscription

Cash	
Feb. 1 5,000.00	
Mar. 1 5,000.00	

Subscriptions Receivable	
Balance 10,000.00	Feb. 1 5,000.00
	Mar. 1 5,000.00

Recording issuance of stock previously subscribed. When a stock subscription is fully paid for, a stock certificate is issued to the stockholder.

March 1, 1988.
Issued Stock Certificate No. 6 to Elaine Underwood for 1,000 shares of $10.00 stated-value common stock. Memorandum No. 29.

The analysis of this transaction is shown in the T accounts. Stock Subscribed—Common is debited for $10,000.00. Capital Stock—Common is credited for $10,000.00. The new balance of this account, $510,000.00, is the value of all common stock issued by AquaPro.

The entry to record the issuance of stock to Miss Underwood is shown in Illustration 13-5.

Stock Subscribed—Common	
10,000.00	Balance 10,000.00

Capital Stock—Common	
	Balance 500,000.00
	10,000.00

GENERAL JOURNAL   PAGE 3

	DATE	ACCOUNT TITLE	POST. REF.	DEBIT	CREDIT	
1	1988 Mar. 1	Stock Subscribed — Common		10 000 00		1
2		Capital Stock — Common			10 000 00	2
3		M29				3
4						4
5						5

Illustration 13-5
Entry to record issuance of stock previously subscribed

ORGANIZATION COSTS OF A CORPORATION

Fees and other expenses of organizing a corporation are called organization costs. Organization costs may include the following items.

1. An incorporation fee paid to the state when the articles of incorporation are submitted.
2. Attorney's fees for legal services during the process of incorporation.
3. Other incidental expenses incurred prior to receiving a charter.

A corporation cannot be formed without organization costs. Until a charter is received, a corporation does not exist to pay the organization costs. Therefore, one of the incorporators usually agrees to pay these costs until the charter is granted. After a charter is received, a corporation usually reimburses incorporators for the organization costs.

If substantial organization costs were recorded as an expense in a corporation's first year, net income could be reduced unreasonably during that first year. Furthermore, benefits derived from these expenditures extend over many years. Therefore, these costs are recorded in an asset account, Organization Costs, until charged as an expense. Adjusting entries to record portions of the organization costs as an expense each year are described in Chapter 15. (CONCEPT: *Matching Expenses with Revenue*) Assets of a non-physical nature that have value for a business are called intangible assets.

Ruth Miguel agrees to pay the organization costs for AquaPro until its charter is received. On January 2, 1988, Mrs. Miguel submits a statement of organization costs, $1,200.00, that she incurred prior to the receipt of the charter.

> January 2, 1988.
> Paid to Ruth Miguel as reimbursement for organization costs, $1,200.00. Check No. 1.

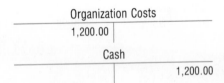

Organization Costs

| 1,200.00 | |

Cash

| | 1,200.00 |

The analysis of this transaction is shown in the T accounts. Organization Costs is debited for $1,200.00. Cash is credited for $1,200.00.

The entry to record this transaction is shown in Illustration 13-6.

					GENERAL		ACCOUNTS PAYABLE DEBIT	PURCHASES DISCOUNT CREDIT	CASH CREDIT	
	DATE	ACCOUNT TITLE	CHECK NO.	POST. REF.	DEBIT	CREDIT				
1	1988 Jan. 2	Organization Costs	1		1 200 00				1 200 00	1
2										2
3										3

CASH PAYMENTS JOURNAL   PAGE 1

Illustration 13-6
Entry to record payment of organization costs

BALANCE SHEET OF A NEWLY FORMED CORPORATION

AquaPro's balance sheet at the end of business on January 2, 1988, is shown in Illustration 13-7.

AquaPro, Inc.
Balance Sheet
January 2, 1988

ASSETS

Current Assets:		
Cash..	$498,800.00	
Subscriptions Receivable	10,000.00	
Total Current Assets		$508,800.00
Intangible Asset:		
Organization Costs.......................................		1,200.00
Total Assets		$510,000.00

STOCKHOLDERS' EQUITY

Paid-in Capital:		
Capital Stock—Common (50,000 shares, $10.00 stated value)	$500,000.00	
Stock Subscribed—Common (1,000 shares)................	10,000.00	
Total Paid-in Capital.......................................		$510,000.00
Total Stockholders' Equity..................................		$510,000.00

Illustration 13-7
Balance sheet of a corporation

The heading, Intangible Asset, is listed on the balance sheet as the last subdivision in the assets section. If a corporation has long-term investments and plant assets, these would be shown on a balance sheet before intangible assets.

AquaPro's cash on hand, January 2, is the original $500,000.00 paid by the incorporators *minus* the $1,200.00 paid for organization costs. The subscriptions receivable on January 2 is the amount due from Elaine Underwood.

Paid-in capital is a subdivision of the stockholders' equity section of a balance sheet. AquaPro's paid-in capital on January 2 consists of $500,000.00 in issued common stock plus $10,000.00 in common stock subscribed. On this date, AquaPro has not issued any preferred stock. Therefore, no value for preferred stock is shown on the balance sheet.

ACCOUNTING TERMS

What is the meaning of each of the following?

1. board of directors
2. articles of incorporation
3. charter
4. common stock
5. preferred stock
6. par value
7. par-value stock
8. no-par-value stock

9. stated-value stock
10. dividends
11. cumulative
    preferred stock
12. noncumulative
    preferred stock

13. participating
    preferred stock
14. nonparticipating
    preferred stock
15. stock certificate

16. subscribing for
    capital stock
17. organization costs
18. intangible assets

QUESTIONS FOR INDIVIDUAL STUDY

1. What are the responsibilities of a corporation's board of directors?
2. What must individuals do who wish to form a corporation?
3. When does a corporation actually come into existence?
4. What four basic rights do stockholders usually have?
5. What are the two basic kinds of stock a corporation might issue?
6. What are the differences between cumulative and noncumulative stock?
7. What are the differences between participating and nonparticipating stock?
8. What usually determines the number of preferences given to preferred stock?
9. In place of a general ledger capital account for each owner, how does a corporation show stock ownership?
10. What is the title of a corporation's capital account showing how much net income is kept in the business?
11. How are the initial capital and assets of a corporation obtained?

12. What accounts are affected, and how, when common stock is initially sold and issued to a corporation's incorporators?
13. What accounts are affected, and how, when a corporation receives a subscription for common stock?
14. What accounts are affected, and how, when a corporation receives cash in payment of a stock subscription?
15. What accounts are affected, and how, when a corporation issues common stock previously subscribed?
16. Using adjusting entries to record portions of a corporation's organization costs as an expense is an application of which accounting concept?
17. What accounts are affected, and how, when a corporation reimburses an incorporator for the costs of organizing a corporation?
18. Where on a corporation's balance sheet is the Intangible Asset subdivision placed?

CASES FOR MANAGEMENT DECISION

CASE 1 Martha Retinger is considering whether she should buy stock as an investment. She asks you whether it would be better to buy common stock or preferred stock. How would you answer her? Explain your suggestions.

CASE 2 Paul Hinton has inherited some money and is investigating the possibility of investing some of it in stock. He asks you which of the following preferred stock would be best. (1) Cumulative, nonparticipating. (2) Noncumulative, participating. (3) Cumulative, participating. (4) Noncumulative, non-

participating. What would you tell Mr. Hinton? Explain your answer?

CASE 3 Don and Edith Mercer currently own all the issued common stock, $100,000.00, in a newly formed corporation, Mercer, Inc. No preferred stock has been issued. They both decide that the corporation needs $25,000.00 additional capital. They decide to sell additional stock. Mr. Mercer suggests that the corporation sell more common stock. Mrs. Mercer suggests that the corporation sell preferred stock. With whom do you agree? Explain your answer.

APPLICATION PROBLEMS

PROBLEM 13-1   Figuring dividends of corporations

Each of the following corporations has outstanding 6,000 shares of 10%, $100.00 par-value preferred stock and 20,000 shares of $10.00 stated-value common stock.

Corp.	Classification of Preferred Stock	Amount voted for dividends in		
		1987	1988	1989
A	Noncumulative, nonparticipating	$50,000.00	$70,000.00	$90,000.00
B	Cumulative, nonparticipating	50,000.00	70,000.00	90,000.00
C	Noncumulative, participating	50,000.00	70,000.00	90,000.00
D	Cumulative, participating	50,000.00	70,000.00	90,000.00

Instructions: For each corporation's preferred and common stock, figure the amount of dividends to be paid each year.

PROBLEM 13-2   Recording transactions for starting a corporation

Kingston Corporation received its charter on January 2 of the current year. The corporation is authorized to issue 50,000 shares of $15.00 stated-value common stock.

Instructions: Record the following selected transactions on page 1 of a cash receipts journal and page 1 of a general journal. Source documents are abbreviated as follows: memorandum, M; receipt, R.

Jan. 2. Received from three incorporators for 22,500 shares of $15.00 stated-value common stock, $337,500.00. R1-3.
Jan. 5. Received a subscription from Eva Reitez for 500 shares of $15.00 stated-value common stock, $7,500.00. M2.
Jan. 10. Received from Eva Reitez in payment of stock subscription, $7,500.00. R4.
Jan. 10. Issued Stock Certificate No. 4 to Eva Reitez for 500 shares of $15.00 stated-value common stock, $7,500.00. M3.

PROBLEM 13-3   Recording transactions for starting a corporation

Welbourne Corporation received its charter on January 3 of the current year. The corporation is authorized to issue 75,000 shares of $10.00 stated-value common stock and 50,000 shares of 10%, $100.00 par-value preferred stock.

Instructions: 1. Record the following selected transactions on page 1 of a cash receipts journal, page 1 of a cash payments journal, and page 1 of a general journal. Source documents are abbreviated as follows: check, C; memorandum, M; receipt, R.

Jan. 3. Received from three incorporators for 24,000 shares of $10.00 stated-value common stock, $240,000.00. R1-3.
Jan. 3. Paid to Matthew Hanks as reimbursement for organization costs, $1,000.00. C1.
Jan. 5. Received a subscription from Alice Baker for 600 shares of $10.00 stated-value common stock, $6,000.00. M1.

Jan. 10. Received a subscription from Mary Bush for 10,000 shares of $10.00 stated-value common stock, $100,000.00. M2.

Feb. 1. Received from Alice Baker in payment of stock subscription, $6,000.00. R4.

Feb. 1. Issued Stock Certificate No. 4 to Alice Baker for 600 shares of $10.00 stated-value common stock, $6,000.00. M3.

Feb. 1. Received from Mary Bush in partial payment of stock subscription, $50,000.00. R5.

Feb. 15. Received a subscription from Thomas Mayer for 300 shares of $10.00 stated-value common stock, $3,000.00. M4.

Mar. 1. Received from Mary Bush in final payment of stock subscription, $50,000.00. R6.

Mar. 1. Issued Stock Certificate No. 5. to Mary Bush for 10,000 shares of $10.00 stated-value common stock. M5.

2. Prepare a balance sheet for Welbourne Corporation as of March 2 of the current year.

ENRICHMENT PROBLEMS

MASTERY PROBLEM 13-M   Recording transactions for starting a corporation

Bauyo, Inc., received its charter on August 1 of the current year. The corporation is authorized to issue 75,000 shares of $15.00 stated-value common stock and 25,000 shares of 10%, $100.00 par-value noncumulative participating preferred stock.

Instructions: 1. Record the following selected transactions on page 1 of a cash receipts journal, page 1 of a cash payments journal, and page 1 of a general journal. Source documents are abbreviated as follows: check, C; memorandum, M; receipt, R.

Aug. 2. Received from three incorporators for 50,000 shares of $15.00 stated-value common stock, $750,000.00. R1-3.

Aug. 2. Paid to Jake Harmon as reimbursement for organization costs, $1,500.00. C1.

Aug. 6. Received a subscription from Rebecca Vale for 500 shares of $15.00 stated-value common stock, $7,500.00. M1.

Aug. 21. Received a subscription from Angie Better for 1,000 shares of $15.00 stated-value common stock, $15,000.00. M2.

Sept. 10. Received from Rebecca Vale in payment of stock subscription, $7,500.00. R4.

Sept. 10. Issued Stock Certificate No. 4 to Rebecca Vale for 500 shares of $15.00 stated-value common stock, $7,500.00. M3.

Oct. 1. Received from Angie Better in partial payment of stock subscription, $7,500.00. R5.

Oct. 15. Received a subscription from Nancy Ayers for 2,000 shares of $15.00 stated-value common stock, $30,000.00. M4.

Nov. 1. Received from Angie Better in final payment of stock subscription, $7,500.00. R6.

Nov. 1. Issued Stock Certificate No. 5 to Angie Better for 1,000 shares of $15.00 stated-value common stock, $15,000.00. M5.

2. Prepare a balance sheet for Bauyo, Inc., as of November 2 of the current year.

3. At the end of the following year, Bauyo has outstanding 53,500 shares of common stock and 1,000 shares of preferred stock. At the end of the fiscal year, the corporation's board of directors votes $25,000.00 to be used as dividends. Figure the total amount of dividends for preferred stock and for common stock.

CHALLENGE PROBLEM 13-C Figuring dividends for a corporation

Keiting, Inc., has the following outstanding stock.

10,000 shares of $10.00 stated-value common stock.
2,000 shares of 9%, $100.00 par-value cumulative participating preferred stock.

The corporation's board of directors votes the following dividends for each year shown.

Year	Amount voted for dividends	Year	Amount voted for dividends
1984	$18,000.00	1987	12,000.00
1985	15,000.00	1988	17,000.00
1986	33,000.00	1989	37,000.00

Instructions: 1. For each year, figure the total amount of dividends to be paid to both common and preferred stockholders.

2. Figure the percentage of total par or stated value that the dividends were for each year for both common and preferred stock.

14 Acquiring Additional Capital for a Corporation

ENABLING PERFORMANCE TASKS

After studying Chapter 14, you will be able to:
a. Define accounting terms related to acquiring capital for a corporation.
b. Identify accounting concepts and practices related to acquiring capital for a corporation.
c. Analyze and record entries for issuing additional capital stock.
d. Analyze and record entries for buying and selling treasury stock.
e. Analyze and record entries for bonds payable.

Capital for a corporation is usually acquired in one of three ways. (1) Stock is sold to investors. (2) Part of the net income is retained in the business. (3) Money is borrowed.

CAPITAL STOCK

A corporation usually requests authority to issue more shares of stock than it expects to sell to initial subscribers. As the need arises for more capital, a corporation can issue some of the remaining authorized stock. For example, AquaPro is authorized by its charter to issue a total of 100,000 shares of common stock and 50,000 shares of preferred stock. *(CONCEPT: Business Entity)* However, AquaPro initially issued only 51,000 shares of common stock as described in Chapter 13. As additional capital is needed, AquaPro may sell some of the remaining shares of common or some shares of preferred stock.

Issuing preferred stock at par value

AquaPro decides that additional capital is needed, and that stock will be issued to raise the additional capital. Michael Landers pays par value,

$100.00, for 700 shares of preferred stock. The amounts to be recorded are figured as follows.

No. of Shares	×	Par Value per Share	=	Total Par Value
700	×	$100.00	=	$70,000.00

March 1, 1989.
Received from Michael Landers for 700 shares of $100.00 par-value preferred stock at $100.00 per share, $70,000.00. Receipt No. 17.

The analysis of this transaction is shown in the T accounts. Cash is debited for $70,000.00. Capital Stock—Preferred is credited for $70,000.00.

The entry to record this transaction is shown in Illustration 14-1.

Cash

70,000.00	

Capital Stock—Preferred

	70,000.00

CASH RECEIPTS JOURNAL   PAGE 3

	DATE	ACCOUNT TITLE	DOC. NO.	POST. REF.	GENERAL DEBIT	GENERAL CREDIT	ACCOUNTS RECEIVABLE CREDIT	SALES CREDIT	SALES TAX PAYABLE DEBIT	SALES TAX PAYABLE CREDIT	SALES DISCOUNT DEBIT	CASH DEBIT	
1	1989 Mar. 1	Capital Stock—											1
2		Preferred	R17			7000000						7000000	2
3													3
4													4

A stock certificate is issued to Mr. Landers.

Issuing preferred stock for more than par value

Sometimes preferred stock is issued for more than its par value. AquaPro sells 200 shares of preferred stock at $125.00 per share to Tony Ursler. The amounts to be recorded for the 200 shares of preferred stock are figured as follows.

	No. of Shares	×	Value per Share	=	Value
Total received	200	×	$125.00	=	$25,000.00
Par value	200	×	100.00	=	20,000.00
Amount received in excess of par value					$ 5,000.00

April 2, 1989.
Received from Tony Ursler for 200 shares of $100.00 par-value preferred stock at $125.00 per share, $25,000.00. Receipt No. 27.

The analysis of this transaction is shown in the T accounts. Cash is debited for $25,000.00, the total amount received. Capital Stock—Preferred is credited for $20,000.00, the total par value of the preferred stock issued. Paid-in Capital in Excess of Par/Stated Value is credited for $5,000.00, the amount received in excess of the par value.

Illustration 14-1
Entry to record issuing preferred stock at par value

Cash

25,000.00	

Capital Stock—Preferred

	Balance	70,000.00
		20,000.00

Paid-in Capital in Excess of Par/Stated Value

	5,000.00

The entry to record this transaction is shown in Illustration 14-2.

CASH RECEIPTS JOURNAL

PAGE 4

DATE	ACCOUNT TITLE	DOC. No.	POST. REF.	GENERAL DEBIT	GENERAL CREDIT	ACCOUNTS RECEIVABLE CREDIT	SALES CREDIT	SALES TAX PAYABLE DEBIT	SALES TAX PAYABLE CREDIT	SALES DISCOUNT DEBIT	CASH DEBIT	
1989 Apr. 2	Capital Stock —											1
	Preferred	R27			2000000						2500000	2
	Paid-in Capital											3
	in Excess of											4
	Par/Stated Value				500000							5
												6
												7
												8
												9
												10
												11

Illustration 14-2
Entry to record issuing preferred stock for more than par value

Issuing preferred stock for less than par value

An amount less than par or stated value at which capital stock is sold is called a discount on capital stock. The legal treatment of discounts on capital stock varies from state to state. In some states, a stockholder may be liable for the amount of discount on par-value stock if a corporation is unable to pay creditors. In other states, a stockholder is not liable for the amount of the discount.

AquaPro sells 1,000 shares of $100.00 par-value preferred stock to Naomi Tudor at a price of $90.00 per share. The amounts involved in the transaction are figured as follows.

	No. of Shares	×	Value per Share	=	Value
Par value	1,000	×	$100.00	=	$100,000.00
Total received	1,000	×	90.00	=	90,000.00
Total discount					$ 10,000.00

September 9, 1989.
Received from Naomi Tudor for 1,000 shares of $100.00 par-value preferred stock at $90.00 per share, $90,000.00. Receipt No. 80.

Cash	
90,000.00	

Discount on Sale of Capital Stock	
10,000.00	

Capital Stock — Preferred	
	Balance 90,000.00
	100,000.00

The analysis of this transaction is shown in the T accounts. Cash is debited for $90,000.00, the amount of cash received for the 1,000 shares of preferred stock. Discount on Sale of Capital Stock is debited for $10,000.00, the discount amount. Capital Stock—Preferred is credited for $100,000.00, the par value of the 1,000 shares of preferred stock.

The entry to record this transaction is shown in Illustration 14-3.

			DATE	ACCOUNT TITLE	DOC. NO.	POST. REF.	GENERAL DEBIT	GENERAL CREDIT	ACCOUNTS RECEIVABLE CREDIT	SALES CREDIT	SALES TAX PAYABLE DEBIT	SALES TAX PAYABLE CREDIT	SALES DISCOUNT DEBIT	CASH DEBIT		

CASH RECEIPTS JOURNAL   PAGE 9

8	9 Discount on Sale										8
9	of Capital Stock	R80	100000					900000	9
10	Capital Stock —								10
11	Preferred			1000000					11
12									12

Issuing preferred stock for assets other than cash

Occasionally corporations issue capital stock in exchange for assets other than cash. When other assets are used to pay for capital stock, the investor and corporation must agree upon the value of the other assets. AquaPro issues 100 shares of preferred stock to Jon Oldermeir in exchange for office equipment.

The office equipment is accepted in full payment of the 100 shares of preferred stock. The agreed upon total value of the equipment is $10,000.00. Therefore, the equipment fully pays for the 100 shares of preferred stock.

October 3, 1989.
Received office equipment from Jon Oldermeir at an agreed value of $10,000.00 for 100 shares of $100.00 par-value preferred stock. Memorandum No. 35.

The analysis of this transaction is shown in the T accounts. Office Equipment is debited for $10,000.00. Capital Stock—Preferred is credited for $10,000.00.

The entry to record this transaction is shown in Illustration 14-4.

Illustration 14-3
Entry to record issuing preferred stock for less than par value

Office Equipment	
10,000.00	

Capital Stock — Preferred	
	Balance 190,000.00
	10,000.00

	DATE	ACCOUNT TITLE	POST. REF.	DEBIT	CREDIT	
	GENERAL JOURNAL			PAGE 10		
1	1989 Oct. 3	Office Equipment		100000		1
2		Capital Stock — Preferred			1000000	2
3		M35				3

Illustration 14-4
Entry to record issuing preferred stock for assets other than cash

Issuing common stock with no par value

Common stock often has no par value assigned to it or printed on the stock certificates. However, some corporations assign a value to common stock for purposes of recording its value. With no-par-value stock, the entire amount paid by an investor is recorded in the capital stock account. Massin, Inc., sells no-par-value common stock.

June 8, 1989.
Received from Nancy Draw for 100 shares of no-par-value common stock at
$11.00 per share, $1,100.00. Receipt No. 24.

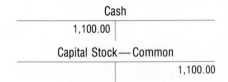

Cash
| 1,100.00 |

Capital Stock — Common
| | 1,100.00 |

The analysis of this transaction is shown in the T accounts. Cash is debited for $1,100.00, the total amount received. Capital Stock—Common is credited for $1,100.00, the total amount received for the 100 shares of stock.

The entry to record this transaction is shown in Illustration 14-5.

	DATE	ACCOUNT TITLE	DOC. NO.	POST. REF.	GENERAL DEBIT	GENERAL CREDIT	ACCOUNTS RECEIVABLE CREDIT	SALES CREDIT	SALES TAX PAYABLE DEBIT	SALES TAX PAYABLE CREDIT	SALES DISCOUNT DEBIT	CASH DEBIT	
12	8	Capital Stock —											12
13		Common	R24			110000						110000	13
14													14
15													15
16													16
17													17
18													18

CASH RECEIPTS JOURNAL   PAGE 6

Illustration 14-5
Entry to record issuing no-par-value common stock

AquaPro's common stock is no-par-value stock. However, AquaPro assigns a stated value to the stock. No-par-value common stock with a stated value is recorded using the same procedures as par-value preferred stock. An entry for issuing common stock at stated value is shown in Illustration 13-2, Chapter 13.

Issuing common stock for less than stated value

AquaPro's common stock account balance should include only the stated value of all common stock issued. AquaPro's management has not sold any common stock at a discount.

Patte, Inc., issues common stock at a discount.

March 1, 1989.
Received from May Marcelli for 700 shares of $10.00 stated-value common
stock at $9.00 per share, $6,300.00. Receipt No. 184.

Cash
| 6,300.00 |

Discount on Sale of Capital Stock
| 700.00 |

Capital Stock — Common
| | 7,000.00 |

The analysis of this transaction is shown in the T accounts. Cash is debited for $6,300.00, the total amount received. Discount on Sale of Capital Stock is debited for $700.00, the discount on the stock sold. Capital Stock—Common is credited for $7,000.00, the stated value of the 700 shares of common stock.

The entry to record Patte's transaction is shown in Illustration 14-6.

CASH RECEIPTS JOURNAL										PAGE 4	
				1	2	3	4	5	6	7	8
DATE	ACCOUNT TITLE	DOC. NO.	POST. REF.	GENERAL		ACCOUNTS RECEIVABLE CREDIT	SALES CREDIT	SALES TAX PAYABLE		SALES DISCOUNT DEBIT	CASH DEBIT
				DEBIT	CREDIT			DEBIT	CREDIT		
8	1 Discount on Sale										8
9	of Capital Stock	R184		70000							630000 9
10	Capital Stock —										10
11	Common				700000						11
12											12

Issuing common stock for more than stated value

AquaPro sells 100 shares of common stock to Eleanor Nichols for $11.00 a share. The amounts involved in this sale of common stock are figured as follows.

Illustration 14-6
Entry to record issuing common stock for less than stated value

	No. of Shares	×	Value per Share	=	Value
Total received	100	×	$11.00	=	$1,100.00
Stated value	100	×	10.00	=	1,000.00
Amount received in excess of stated value					$ 100.00

September 5, 1989.
Received from Eleanor Nichols for 100 shares of $10.00 stated-value common stock at $11.00 per share, $1,100.00. Receipt No. 78.

The analysis of this transaction is shown in the T accounts. Cash is debited for $1,100.00, the total amount received. Capital Stock—Common is credited for $1,000.00, the total stated value of the 100 shares. Paid-in Capital in Excess of Par/Stated Value is credited for $100.00, the amount received in excess of the stated value.

The entry to record this transaction is shown in Illustration 14-7.

Cash

1,100.00 |

Capital Stock — Common

| Balance 510,000.00
| 1,000.00

Paid-in Capital in Excess of Par/Stated Value

| Balance 5,000.00
| 100.00

CASH RECEIPTS JOURNAL										PAGE 9	
				1	2	3	4	5	6	7	8
DATE	ACCOUNT TITLE	DOC. NO.	POST. REF.	GENERAL		ACCOUNTS RECEIVABLE CREDIT	SALES CREDIT	SALES TAX PAYABLE		SALES DISCOUNT DEBIT	CASH DEBIT
				DEBIT	CREDIT			DEBIT	CREDIT		
1	1989 Sept. 5 Capital Stock —										1
2	Common	R78			100000						110000 2
3	Paid-in Capital										3
4	in Excess of										4
5	Par / Stated Value				10000						5
6											6
7											7

Illustration 14-7
Entry to record issuing common stock for more than stated value

TREASURY STOCK

A corporation's own stock that has been issued and reacquired is called treasury stock. When a corporation buys treasury stock, the number of shares outstanding is reduced. However, treasury stock is still considered to be issued stock. A corporation usually intends to use the treasury stock for a specific purpose. For example, a corporation may acquire treasury stock to be given to employees as bonus payments.

Treasury stock is not an asset of a corporation. Since treasury stock is not owned by a stockholder, no one has voting rights. Dividends are not paid for the stock as long as the treasury stock is held by the issuing corporation. Once treasury stock is given or sold to a stockholder, it ceases to be treasury stock and is again capital stock outstanding.

Buying treasury stock

A corporation records treasury stock at the price paid regardless of the stock's par or stated value. *(CONCEPT: Historical Cost)*

October 30, 1989.
Paid to Elaine Underwood for 600 shares of $10.00 stated-value common stock at $12.00 per share, $7,200.00. Check No. 93.

Treasury Stock	
7,200.00	

Cash	
	7,200.00

The analysis of this transaction is shown in the T accounts. Treasury Stock is debited for $7,200.00, the amount paid for the 600 shares of treasury stock. Cash is credited for $7,200.00.

Capital stock accounts have normal credit balances. Treasury Stock is a contra capital stock account and therefore has a normal debit balance.

The entry to record this transaction is shown in Illustration 14-8.

					GENERAL		ACCOUNTS PAYABLE	PURCHASES DISCOUNT	CASH
	DATE	ACCOUNT TITLE	CHECK NO.	POST. REF.	DEBIT	CREDIT	DEBIT	CREDIT	CREDIT
1	1989 Oct. 30	Treasury Stock	93		7200 00				7200 00
2									

CASH PAYMENTS JOURNAL   PAGE *10*

Illustration 14-8
Entry to record buying treasury stock

Selling treasury stock for original cost

AquaPro sells some of its treasury stock at the $12.00 original cost.

November 10, 1989.
Received from Harry Goode for 10 shares of treasury stock at $12.00 per share, $120.00. Treasury stock was bought on October 30, 1989, at $12.00 per share. Receipt No. 100.

Cash	
120.00	

Treasury Stock	
Balance 7,200.00	120.00

The analysis of this transaction is shown in the T accounts. Cash is debited for $120.00. Treasury Stock is credited for $120.00.

The entry to record this transaction is shown in Illustration 14-9.

	DATE	ACCOUNT TITLE	DOC. NO.	POST. REF.	GENERAL DEBIT	GENERAL CREDIT	ACCOUNTS RECEIVABLE CREDIT	SALES CREDIT	SALES TAX PAYABLE DEBIT	SALES TAX PAYABLE CREDIT	SALES DISCOUNT DEBIT	CASH DEBIT	
1	1989 Nov. 10	Treasury Stock	R100			1 2000						1 2000	1
2													2
3													3

CASH RECEIPTS JOURNAL — PAGE 10

Selling treasury stock for more than original cost

AquaPro sells 200 shares of treasury stock to Mary Long for $15.00 per share. The amounts involved in this transaction are figured as follows.

Illustration 14-9
Entry to record selling treasury stock for original cost

	No. of Shares	×	Value per Share	=	Value
Total received	200	×	$15.00	=	$3,000.00
Original cost	200	×	12.00	=	2,400.00
Amount received in excess of original cost					$ 600.00

November 20, 1989.
Received from Mary Long for 200 shares of treasury stock at $15.00 per share, $3,000.00. Treasury stock was bought on October 30, 1989, at $12.00 per share. Receipt No. 103.

The analysis of this transaction is shown in the T accounts. Cash is debited for $3,000.00, the total amount received from the sale of the treasury stock. Treasury Stock is credited for $2,400.00, the original cost of the 200 shares of treasury stock. Paid-in Capital from Sale of Treasury Stock is credited for $600.00, the amount received in excess of the treasury stock's original cost.

The entry to record this transaction is shown in Illustration 14-10.

Cash

| 3,000.00 | |

Treasury Stock

| Balance 7,080.00 | 2,400.00 |

Paid-in Capital from Sale of Treasury Stock

| | 600.00 |

	DATE	ACCOUNT TITLE	DOC. NO.	POST. REF.	GENERAL DEBIT	GENERAL CREDIT	ACCOUNTS RECEIVABLE CREDIT	SALES CREDIT	SALES TAX PAYABLE DEBIT	SALES TAX PAYABLE CREDIT	SALES DISCOUNT DEBIT	CASH DEBIT	
8	20	Treasury Stock	R103			2 40000						3 00000	8
9		Paid-in Capital											9
10		from Sale of											10
11		Treasury Stock				6 0000							11
12													12
13													13

CASH RECEIPTS JOURNAL — PAGE 11

Illustration 14-10
Entry to record selling treasury stock for more than original cost

Selling treasury stock for less than original cost

On December 13, 1989, AquaPro sells 100 shares of treasury stock to Gerald Rooney for $10.00 per share. The amounts involved in this transaction are figured as follows.

	No. of Shares	×	Value per Share	=	Value
Original cost	100	×	$12.00	=	$1,200.00
Total Received	100	×	10.00	=	1,000.00
Amount received less than original cost					$ 200.00

December 13, 1989.
Received from Gerald Rooney for 100 shares of treasury stock at $10.00 per share, $1,000.00. Treasury stock was bought October 30, 1989, at $12.00 per share. Receipt No. 137.

Cash	
1,000.00	

Paid-in Capital from Sale of Treasury Stock	
200.00	Balance 600.00

Treasury Stock	
Balance 4,680.00	1,200.00

The analysis of this transaction is shown in the T accounts. Cash is debited for $1,000.00, the total amount of cash received. Paid-in Capital from Sale of Treasury Stock is debited for $200.00, the amount received less than the treasury stock's original cost. Treasury Stock is credited for $1,200.00, the original cost.

The entry for this transaction is shown in Illustration 14-11.

						CASH RECEIPTS JOURNAL						PAGE 12	
						1	2	3	4	5	6	7	8
	DATE	ACCOUNT TITLE	DOC. NO.	POST. REF.	GENERAL DEBIT	GENERAL CREDIT	ACCOUNTS RECEIVABLE CREDIT	SALES CREDIT	SALES TAX PAYABLE DEBIT	SALES TAX PAYABLE CREDIT	SALES DISCOUNT DEBIT	CASH DEBIT	
10	13	Paid-in Capital											10
11		from Sale of											11
12		Treasury Stock	R137		20000							100000	12
13		Treasury Stock				120000							13
14													14
15													15

Illustration 14-11
Entry to record selling treasury stock for less than original cost

When treasury stock transactions occur, no entry is made in Capital Stock — Common or Capital Stock — Preferred. Treasury stock is considered to be issued stock. The difference between the balances of the capital stock accounts and the treasury stock account is the value of outstanding stock. After the entry on December 13 to sell treasury stock, the number of Aqua-Pro's outstanding shares of capital stock is figured as follows.

	No. of Shares Issued	−	No. of Shares of Treasury Stock	=	No. of Shares Outstanding
Common	51,100	−	290	=	50,810
Preferred	2,000	−	0	=	2,000

CORPORATE BONDS PAYABLE

A business' management may find that needed capital for expansion could be obtained from retained net income during the next five to ten years. However, the business may need the additional capital immediately. A corporation's board of directors must decide whether to raise the needed capital by selling additional stock or borrowing the money.

An advantage of selling stock is that the additional capital becomes part of a corporation's permanent capital. Permanent capital does not have to be returned to stockholders in the near future. Another advantage is that dividends do not have to be paid to stockholders unless the earnings are sufficient to warrant such payments. A disadvantage of selling more stock to raise additional capital is that the ownership is spread over more shares and more owners.

An advantage of borrowing the additional capital is that stockholders' equity is not spread over additional shares of stock. A disadvantage is that interest must be paid on the loan, which decreases the net income. This decrease in net income may also decrease the amount available for dividends.

Large loans are sometimes difficult to obtain for short periods of time or from one bank or one individual. Therefore, corporations frequently borrow the needed capital with the provision that the loan is due several years in the future. The loan can be paid out of future earnings accumulated over several years.

A printed, long-term promise to pay a specified amount on a specified date, and to pay interest at stated intervals is called a bond. Bonds are similar to notes payable because they are both written promises to pay. However, most notes payable are for one year or less while bonds generally run for a long period of time, such as 5, 10, or 20 years.

All the bonds representing the total amount of a loan are called a bond issue. A corporation usually sells an entire bond issue to a securities dealer who sells individual bonds to the public.

Issuing bonds

On July 1, 1988, AquaPro decides to borrow $200,000.00 to expand its building. AquaPro issues 200, 12%, $1,000.00 par-value bonds. The bonds are scheduled to mature in 10 years, on July 1, 1998. Annual interest on the bonds is to be paid on July 1 of each year. The bond issue is sold at par value to a securities dealer.

July 1, 1988.
Received for the face value of a 10-year, 12%, $1,000.00 par-value bond issue,
$200,000.00. Receipt No. 57.

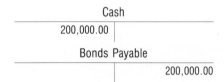

Cash
| 200,000.00 | |

Bonds Payable
| | 200,000.00 |

The analysis of this transaction is shown in the T accounts. Cash is debited for $200,000.00. Bonds Payable is credited for $200,000.00.

The entry to record this transaction is shown in Illustration 14-12.

					GENERAL		ACCOUNTS RECEIVABLE CREDIT	SALES CREDIT	SALES TAX PAYABLE		SALES DISCOUNT DEBIT	CASH DEBIT	
	DATE	ACCOUNT TITLE	DOC. NO.	POST. REF.	DEBIT	CREDIT			DEBIT	CREDIT			
1	1988 July 1	Bonds Payable		R57		200000 00						200000 00	1
2													2
3													3

CASH RECEIPTS JOURNAL — PAGE 7

Illustration 14-12
Entry to record issuing bonds

Paying interest on bonds

A year's interest is paid to each bondholder on July 1 of each year until the bond's maturity date. A person or institution, usually a bank, who is given legal authorization to administer property for the benefit of property owners is called a trustee. AquaPro pays the interest amount to a bond trustee who in turn handles the details of paying each individual bondholder.

The 1989 annual interest on the bond issue is figured as follows.

Balance Owed on Bond Issue	×	Bond Interest Rate	=	1989 Annual Interest
$200,000.00	×	12%	=	$24,000.00

July 1, 1989.
Paid to bond trustee for annual interest on bond issue, $24,000.00. Check No. 361.

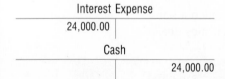

Interest Expense
| 24,000.00 | |

Cash
| | 24,000.00 |

The analysis of this transaction is shown in the T accounts. Interest Expense is debited for $24,000.00. Cash is credited for $24,000.00.

The entry to record this transaction is shown in Illustration 14-13.

					GENERAL		ACCOUNTS PAYABLE DEBIT	PURCHASES DISCOUNT CREDIT	CASH CREDIT	
	DATE	ACCOUNT TITLE	CHECK NO.	POST. REF.	DEBIT	CREDIT				
1	1989 July 1	Interest Expense	361		24000 00				24000 00	1
2										2
3										3

CASH PAYMENTS JOURNAL — PAGE 8

Illustration 14-13
Entry to record paying interest on bonds

Depositing cash in a bond sinking fund

Because bondholders want assurance that a bond issue will be paid at maturity, AquaPro annually deposits money with the bond trustee. An amount set aside to pay a bond issue when due is called a bond sinking fund. The bond sinking fund is increased each year by $20,000.00, an amount equal to one-tenth of the total principal. On the bond issue's maturity date, a total of $200,000.00 will be available in the bond sinking fund to pay the bondholders.

Instead of paying $200,000.00 from a single year's earnings, AquaPro spreads the amount over the ten years that the bond issue is outstanding. Recognizing a portion of an expense or amount owed in each of several years is called amortization. Annually depositing a portion of a bond issue's principal with a trustee is a form of amortization.

July 1, 1989.
Paid to bond trustee for annual deposit to bond sinking fund, $20,000.00.
Check No. 362.

The analysis of this transaction is shown in the T accounts. Bond Sinking Fund is debited for $20,000.00. Cash is credited for $20,000.00.

The entry to record this transaction is shown in Illustration 14-14.

Bond Sinking Fund	
20,000.00	

Cash	
	20,000.00

			CASH PAYMENTS JOURNAL				PAGE 8	
				1	2	3	4	5
DATE	ACCOUNT TITLE	CHECK No.	POST. REF.	GENERAL DEBIT	GENERAL CREDIT	ACCOUNTS PAYABLE DEBIT	PURCHASES DISCOUNT CREDIT	CASH CREDIT
1 Bond Sinking Fund		*362*		*2000000*				*2000000*

Illustration 14-14
Entry to record depositing cash in a bond sinking fund

A bond sinking fund is an asset to AquaPro until the trustee makes payment to the bondholders. The bond trustee invests the sinking fund. The interest earned each year reduces the deposit that AquaPro must make in that year. For example, the trustee reports to AquaPro in 1990 that the sinking fund investment earned $1,600.00. Therefore, on July 1, 1990, AquaPro pays only $18,400.00 to the sinking fund trustee. This amount is figured as shown below.

Amount of Increase in Sinking Fund		Interest Earned During Year		1990 Amount to Be Deposited
$20,000.00	−	$1,600.00	=	$18,400.00

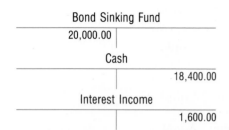

Bond Sinking Fund

| 20,000.00 | |

Cash

| | 18,400.00 |

Interest Income

| | 1,600.00 |

July 1, 1990.
Paid to bond trustee, $18,400.00, and recorded interest earned on bond sinking fund, $1,600.00. Check No. 569.

The analysis of this transaction is shown in the T accounts. Bond Sinking Fund is debited for $20,000.00. Cash is credited for $18,400.00, the actual amount deposited. Interest Income is credited for $1,600.00, the amount of interest earned.

The entry to record this transaction is shown in Illustration 14-15.

					GENERAL		ACCOUNTS PAYABLE DEBIT	PURCHASES DISCOUNT CREDIT	CASH CREDIT	
	DATE	ACCOUNT TITLE	CHECK NO.	POST. REF.	DEBIT	CREDIT				
1	1990 July 1	Bond Sinking Fund	569		2000000				1840000	1
2		Interest Income				160000				2
3										3

CASH PAYMENTS JOURNAL PAGE 9

Illustration 14-15
Entry to record annual interest earned on and deposit to a bond sinking fund

As the bond sinking fund balance increases, the amount of interest earned in a year usually will increase. Thus, the amount AquaPro must deposit each year will decrease.

Retiring a bond issue

When AquaPro's bonds are due on July 1, 1998, the bond trustee uses the bond sinking fund to pay the bondholders. Paying the amounts owed to bondholders for a bond issue is called retiring a bond issue.

July 1, 1998.
Received notice from bond trustee that bond issue was retired using bond sinking fund, $200,000.00. Memorandum No. 562.

Bonds Payable

| Retired | 200,000.00 | Balance | 200,000.00 |

Bond Sinking Fund

| Balance | 200,000.00 | Retired | 200,000.00 |

The analysis of this transaction is shown in the T accounts. Bonds Payable is debited for $200,000.00, the total amount of the bond issue. Bond Sinking Fund is credited for $200,000.00, the amount in the fund used to retire the bond issue. After this entry is posted, both Bonds Payable and Bond Sinking Fund will have zero balances.

The entry to record this transaction is shown in Illustration 14-16.

GENERAL JOURNAL PAGE 20

	DATE	ACCOUNT TITLE	POST. REF.	DEBIT	CREDIT	
1	1998 July 1	Bonds Payable		200 00000		1
2		Bond Sinking Fund			20000000	2
3		M562				3

Illustration 14-16
Entry to record retiring a bond issue

All of AquaPro's bond issue matures on July 1, 1998. Bonds that all mature on the same date are called term bonds. AquaPro's bonds are term bonds. Sometimes portions of a bond issue mature on different dates. Portions of a bond issue that mature on different dates are called serial bonds. For example, a 10-year bond issue with one-tenth of the bonds maturing every year is a serial bond issue. An advantage of serial bonds is that interest does not have to be paid on the total bond issue for the total 10 years.

COMPARISON OF CAPITAL STOCK AND BONDS AS A SOURCE OF CORPORATE CAPITAL

A comparison of capital stock and bonds as a source of corporate capital is shown in Illustration 14-17.

Capital Stock	Bonds
1. Stockholders are corporate owners.	1. Bondholders are corporate creditors.
2. Capital Stock is a stockholders' equity account.	2. Bonds Payable is a liability account.
3. Stockholders have a secondary claim against corporate assets.	3. Bondholders have a primary, or first claim, against corporate assets.
4. Dividends are paid to stockholders out of corporate net income.	4. Interest paid to bondholders is a corporate expense.
5. Dividends are not fixed costs; dividends do not have to be paid if net income is insufficient.	5. Interest on bonds is a fixed expense; the expense must be paid when due; payment does not depend on amount of net income.
6. Amount received from sale of stock is relatively permanent capital; amount invested by stockholders does not have to be returned to them in foreseeable future.	6. Amount received from sale of bonds is not permanent; amount invested by bondholders must be returned to them on bonds' maturity date.

Illustration 14-17
Comparison of capital stock and bonds as a source of corporate capital

ACCOUNTING TERMS

What is the meaning of each of the following?

1. discount on capital stock
2. treasury stock
3. bond
4. bond issue

5. trustee
6. bond sinking fund
7. amortization

8. retiring a bond issue
9. term bonds
10. serial bonds

QUESTIONS FOR INDIVIDUAL STUDY

1. In what three ways might a corporation acquire capital?
2. Why might a corporation obtain authorization for more shares of stock than will be issued when the corporation is first formed?
3. What accounts are affected, and how, when AquaPro receives cash for preferred stock sold at par value?
4. What accounts are affected, and how, when AquaPro receives cash for preferred stock sold for more than par value?
5. What accounts are affected, and how, when AquaPro receives cash for preferred stock sold for less than par value?
6. What accounts are affected, and how, when AquaPro receives cash for common stock sold for more than stated value?
7. When a corporation records treasury stock at the price paid regardless of the stock's par or stated value, which accounting concept is being applied?
8. What accounts are affected, and how, when a corporation buys its own stock?
9. What accounts are affected, and how, when treasury stock is sold for more than

its original cost?
10. What accounts are affected, and how, when treasury stock is sold for less than its original cost?
11. What are two advantages in raising needed capital by selling stock?
12. What is an advantage in raising additional capital by borrowing?
13. What is a disadvantage of borrowing additional capital?
14. What accounts are affected, and how, when bonds are sold by a corporation?
15. What accounts are affected, and how, when a corporation pays interest to a bond trustee?
16. What accounts are affected, and how, when a corporation deposits cash with a trustee for the first payment of a bond issue's principal?
17. What accounts are affected, and how, when a corporation deposits cash with a trustee for partial payment of a bond issue's principal, and interest has been earned on the bond sinking fund?
18. What accounts are affected, and how, when a corporation's bond issue is retired?

CASES FOR MANAGEMENT DECISION

CASE 1 Edna Mallory pays $110,000.00 for 1,000 shares of $100.00 stated-value common stock of Weildun, Inc. A year later, Mrs. Mallory sells the 1,000 shares of stock to Max Dubroit for a total of $120,000.00. Mr. Dubroit sends a notice to Weildun so that ownership can be changed on the corporation's stock records. An accounting clerk at Weildun is not sure what journal entry should be made so that the business' general ledger will reflect the correct information. What advice would you give the accounting clerk?

CASE 2 Diving, Inc., estimates that with an additional $300,000.00 capital with which

to expand the business, an additional $40,000.00 in net income can be earned. The board of directors is considering three alternatives for acquiring the additional capital. (1) Issue 300, 10-year, 10%, $1,000.00 face value bonds. (2) Sell 6,000 shares of 10%, $50.00 par-value cumulative preferred stock. (3) Sell 1,500 shares of $200.00 stated-value common stock. The corporation has been paying an annual $16.00 per share dividend on common stock. The corporation's average tax rate on net income is 21%. What factors should you advise the corporation to consider before deciding on which alternative to use?

APPLICATION PROBLEMS

PROBLEM 14-1   Recording capital stock transactions

Holding, Inc., is authorized to issue 100,000 shares of $10.00 stated-value common stock, and 10,000 shares of 10%, $100.00 par-value preferred stock. Holding has 25,000 shares of common stock outstanding.

Instructions: Record the following selected transactions completed by Holding during the current year. Use page 15 of a cash receipts journal and page 3 of a general journal. Source documents are abbreviated as follows: memorandum, M; receipt, R.

Jan. 6. Received from Oliver Renfrew for 500 shares of $10.00 stated-value common stock at $10.00 per share, $5,000.00. R400.

Mar. 13. Received from Wanda Sears for 150 shares of $10.00 stated-value common stock at $9.00 per share, $1,350.00. R482.

Apr. 15. Received from Dan Findlay for 400 shares of $100.00 par-value preferred stock at $100.00 per share, $40,000.00. R518.

June 5. Received from John Wong for 500 shares of $100.00 par-value preferred stock at $90.00 per share, $45,000.00. R601.

July 1. Received office equipment from Maria Vallejos at an agreed value of $12,500.00 for 125 shares of $100.00 par-value preferred stock. M48.

PROBLEM 14-2   Recording treasury stock transactions

Gates, Inc., is authorized to issue 75,000 shares of $10.00 stated-value common stock. Gates has 50,000 shares of stock outstanding.

Instructions: Record the following selected transactions completed by Gates in the current year. Use page 6 of a cash receipts journal and page 9 of a cash payments journal. Source documents are abbreviated as follows: check, C; receipt, R.

Jan. 21. Paid to William Cast for 325 shares of $10.00 stated-value common stock at $10.00 per share, $3,250.00. C100.

Jan. 31. Received from Erin Hall for 225 shares of treasury stock at $10.00 per share, $2,250.00. Treasury stock was bought on January 21 for $10.00 per share. R115.

Mar. 22. Paid to Elliott Lawrence for 750 shares of $10.00 stated-value common stock at $11.00 per share, $8,250.00. C138.

Apr. 15. Received from Sharon Upton for 100 shares of treasury stock at $12.00 per share, $1,200.00. Treasury stock was bought on January 21 for $10.00 per share. R151.

July 30. Received from Mike Malley for 300 shares of treasury stock at $10.00 per share, $3,000.00. Treasury stock was bought on March 22 for $11.00 per share. R203.

PROBLEM 14-3   Recording bonds payable transactions

On January 1, 1989, Bellweather, Inc., received cash, $100,000.00, for a bond issue. The bond agreement provides that a bond sinking fund is to be increased by $5,000.00 every six months for the next ten years.

Instructions: Record the following selected transactions using page 3 of a cash receipts journal, page 2 of a cash payments journal, and page 1 of a general journal. Source documents are abbreviated as follows: check, C; memorandum, M; receipt, R.

Jan.   1, 1989.   Received for the face value of a 10-year, 9%, $1,000.00 par-value bond issue, $100,000.00. R104.
June 30, 1989.   Paid to bond trustee for semiannual interest on bond issue, $4,500.00. C300.
June 30, 1989.   Paid to bond trustee for semiannual deposit to bond sinking fund, $5,000.00. C301.
Dec. 31, 1989.   Paid to bond trustee semiannual interest on bond issue, $4,500.00. C504.
Dec. 31, 1989.   Paid to bond trustee for semiannual deposit to bond sinking fund, $5,000.00, less interest earned on bond sinking fund, $400.00. C505.
Jan.   1, 1999.   Received notice from bond trustee that bond issue was retired using bond sinking fund, $100,000.00. M159.

ENRICHMENT PROBLEMS

MASTERY PROBLEM 14-M   Recording transactions for stocks and bonds

Blatt, Inc., is authorized to issue 40,000 shares of $20.00 stated-value common stock, and 40,000 shares of 10%, $200.00 par-value preferred stock.

Instructions: Record the following selected transactions using page 3 of a cash receipts journal, page 2 of a cash payments journal, and page 1 of a general journal. Source documents are abbreviated as follows: check, C; memorandum, M; receipt, R.

Jan.   1, 1989.   Received for the face value of a 10-year, 9%, $1,000.00 par-value bond issue, $100,000.00. R204.
Jan.   6, 1989.   Received from Leo Blake for 500 shares of $20.00 stated-value common stock at $20.00 per share, $10,000.00. R210.
Jan. 21, 1989.   Paid to Laura Sennett for 425 shares of $20.00 stated-value common stock at $20.00 per share, $8,500.00. C100.
Jan. 31, 1989.   Received from Eric Allen for 225 shares of treasury stock at $20.00 per share, $4,500.00. Treasury stock was bought on January 21 at $20.00 per share. R215.
Mar. 13, 1989.   Received from Ruth Garnett for 150 shares of $20.00 stated-value common stock at $22.00 per share, $3,300.00. R220.
Mar. 22, 1989.   Paid to Lawrence Hopkins for 750 shares of $20.00 stated-value common stock at $21.00 per share, $15,750.00. C138.
Apr. 15, 1989.   Received from Peter Rauch for 100 shares of treasury stock at $22.00 per share, $2,200.00. Treasury stock was bought on January 21 at $20.00 per share. R231.
Apr. 15, 1989.   Received from Patrick Emery for 400 shares of $200.00 par-value preferred stock at $195.00 per share, $78,000.00. R232.
June 5, 1989.   Received from Lucille Haney for 500 shares of $200.00 par-value preferred stock at $200.00 per share, $100,000.00. R307.
June 30, 1989.   Paid to bond trustee for semiannual interest on bond issue, $4,500.00. C200.
June 30, 1989.   Paid to bond trustee for semiannual deposit to bond sinking fund, $5,000.00. C201.
July   1, 1989.   Received office equipment from Jane Bradley at an agreed value of $25,000.00 for 125 shares of $200.00 par-value preferred stock. M98.
July 30, 1989.   Received from Loretta Schnell for 300 shares of treasury stock at $20.00 per share, $6,000.00. One hundred shares of treasury stock were bought on January 21 at $20.00 per share. Two hundred shares were bought on March 22 at $21.00 per share. R353.
Dec. 31, 1989.   Paid to bond trustee for semiannual interest on bond issue, $4,500.00. C504.

Dec. 31, 1989. Paid to bond trustee for semiannual deposit to bond sinking fund, $5,000.00, less interest earned on bond sinking fund, $400.00. C505.

Jan. 1, 1999. Received notice from bond trustee that bond issue was retired using bond sinking fund, $100,000.00. M381.

CHALLENGE PROBLEM 14-C   Recording transactions for stocks and bonds

MacLeon, Inc., is authorized to issue 100,000 shares of $10.00 stated-value common stock and 25,000 shares of 9%, $100.00 par-value preferred stock. On January 1, 1989, MacLeon has the following outstanding stock: common stock, 40,000 shares; preferred stock, 10,000 shares.

Provisions of a bond issue, January 2, 1989, include (a) interest on the bond issue is to be paid on June 30 and December 31 of each year, and (b) MacLeon must assure an increase of $15,000.00 in a bond sinking fund on June 30 and December 31 of each year.

Instructions: Record the following selected transactions using page 3 of a cash receipts journal, page 2 of a cash payments journal, and page 1 of a general journal. Source documents are abbreviated as follows: check, C; memorandum, M; receipt, R.

Jan. 2, 1989. Received for the face value of a 10-year, 8%, $1,000.00 par-value bond issue, $300,000.00. R251.

Jan. 24, 1989. Received from Rachel Gordon for 1,500 shares of common stock, $18,000.00. R264.

Feb. 5, 1989. Paid to Henry Eiler for 1,000 shares of $10.00 stated-value common stock, $12,000.00. C233.

Feb. 20, 1989. Received from Nelly Baker for 500 shares of preferred stock, $50,000.00. R305.

Mar. 14, 1989. Received office equipment from Angela Kopson at an agreed value of $7,000.00 for 700 shares of common stock. M195.

May 26, 1989. Received from Harold Day for 200 shares of treasury stock, $2,400.00. Treasury stock was bought on February 5. R410.

June 30, 1989. Paid to bond trustee for semiannual interest on bonds payable. C389.

June 30, 1989. Paid to bond trustee for semiannual deposit to bond sinking fund, $15,000.00. C390.

July 10, 1989. Received from Susan Rahls for 300 shares of preferred stock, $29,700.00. R487.

Sept. 18, 1989. Received from Kenneth Oberman for 250 shares of treasury stock, $3,750.00. Treasury stock was bought on February 5. R561.

Oct. 14, 1989. Received from Gerald Mansk for 150 shares of preferred stock, $14,850.00. R600.

Dec. 31, 1989. Paid to bond trustee for semiannual interest on bonds payable. C634.

Dec. 31, 1989. Paid to bond trustee for semiannual deposit to bond sinking fund. Interest earned on money in sinking fund since last payment on June 30, $2,200.00. C635.

Jan. 2, 1999. Received notice from bond trustee that bond issue was retired using bond sinking fund. M428.

15 Financial Analysis and Reporting for a Corporation

ENABLING PERFORMANCE TASKS

After studying Chapter 15, you will be able to:
a. Define accounting terms related to financial analysis and reporting for a corporation.
b. Identify accounting concepts and practices related to financial analysis and reporting for a corporation.
c. Complete selected end-of-fiscal-period work for a corporation.
d. Record entries for declaring and paying dividends for a corporation.
e. Make selected analysis of financial statements for a corporation.

A corporation's board of directors and officers need financial information as a basis for making sound management decisions. The directors also need the information to determine whether or not to distribute earnings to stockholders. Stockholders and other potential investors need the information to determine if they will continue or begin investing in the corporation. Creditors need the information to determine if the corporation will be able to meet its credit obligations. *(CONCEPT: Adequate Disclosure)*

DIVIDENDS

As part of a corporation's closing entries, net income after federal income tax is credited to an account titled Retained Earnings. Rather than distribute all net income to owners, corporations may retain a portion to finance future business expansion and improvement. However, most corporations distribute some of the earnings to stockholders.

Corporate earnings distributed to stockholders are known as dividends. Action of a board of directors to distribute a portion of corporate earnings to stockholders on a specific date is called declaring a dividend. The board determines when and what amount of the retained earnings will be distributed. A corporation has no obligation to distribute money to stockholders until the board of directors has declared a dividend.

Three important dates are involved in distributing a dividend.

1. *Date of declaration.* The date on which a board of directors votes to distribute a dividend is called the date of declaration.
2. *Date of record.* The date that determines which stockholders are to receive dividends is called the date of record. Stockholders may buy and sell stock at any time. However, only persons listed as stockholders on the date of record will receive dividends.
3. *Date of payment.* The date on which dividends are actually to be paid to stockholders is called the date of payment. Ordinarily the date of payment is several weeks after the date of record. Thus, a corporation has time to determine who is entitled to receive dividends and to prepare dividend checks for mailing on the date of payment.

Transactions are recorded in a corporation's accounts on two of the three dates: (1) date of declaration, and (2) date of payment.

Declaring a dividend

When a board of directors declares a dividend, the corporation is obligated to pay the dividend. A liability is therefore incurred by the corporation and must be recorded.

November 1, 1989.
AquaPro's board of directors voted to declare dividends on preferred stock, $18,000.00, and common stock, $45,729.00; date of record, December 1, 1989; date of payment, January 15, 1990. Memorandum No. 42.

Dividends — Common Stock	
45,729.00	

Dividends — Preferred Stock	
18,000.00	

Dividends Payable	
	63,729.00

The analysis of this transaction is shown in the T accounts. Dividends — Common Stock is debited for $45,729.00. Dividends — Preferred Stock is debited for $18,000.00. Dividends Payable is credited for $63,729.00.

The entry to record this transaction is shown in Illustration 15-1.

	DATE		ACCOUNT TITLE	POST. REF.	DEBIT	CREDIT	
1	1989 Nov.	1	Dividends — Common Stock		4572900		1
2			Dividends — Preferred Stock		1800000		2
3			Dividends Payable			6372900	3
4			M42				4
5							5

GENERAL JOURNAL   PAGE 11

Illustration 15-1
Entry to record declaring a dividend

Paying a dividend

On January 15, 1990, AquaPro issues a single check for the total amount of the dividends to be paid. The single check is deposited in a special dividend checking account. A separate check for each eligible stockholder is written against the special checking account. This procedure avoids a large number of entries in AquaPro's cash payments journal. The special dividend checking account also reserves cash specifically for paying the dividends.

AquaPro's dividend check is given to an agent who handles the details of preparing and mailing stockholders' checks. AquaPro's agent is the bank where the corporation has its checking account.

January 15, 1990.
Paid the dividends declared November 1, 1989, $63,729.00.
Check No. 352.

Dividends Payable

| 63,729.00 | Balance | 63,729.00 |

Cash

| | 63,729.00 |

The analysis of this transaction is shown in the T accounts. Dividends Payable is debited and Cash is credited for $63,729.00.

The entry to record this transaction is shown in Illustration 15-2.

			CHECK No.	POST. REF.	GENERAL		ACCOUNTS PAYABLE DEBIT	PURCHASES DISCOUNT CREDIT	CASH CREDIT	
	DATE	ACCOUNT TITLE			DEBIT	CREDIT				
18	15	Dividends Payable	352		63 72 9 00				63 72 9 00	18
19										19

CASH PAYMENTS JOURNAL   PAGE /

Illustration 15-2
Entry to record paying a dividend

CORPORATE WORK SHEET

AquaPro's end-of-fiscal-period work includes preparation of a work sheet and financial statements. The corporation also analyzes selected information on the financial statements. The analysis helps interested persons better understand the information reported. AquaPro's work sheet for the fiscal year ended December 31, 1989, is shown in Illustration 15-3.

Planning adjustments on a corporate work sheet

Adjustments on AquaPro's work sheet are similar to those described for Gallery in Part 4. AquaPro also records adjustments for organization expense and federal income tax.

Organization expense adjustment. Corporate organization costs are recorded as intangible assets. However, over a period of time, a business will have difficulty determining an intangible asset's continuing value.

Therefore, most corporations do not carry organization costs indefinitely as an asset. Internal Revenue Service tax regulations provide that organization costs may be amortized as expenses over a period from five to forty years. AquaPro uses a five-year amortization schedule.

AquaPro incurred total organization costs of $1,200.00. One-fifth of this amount, $240.00, is to be amortized in each of the first five years. In each of the years 1988 and 1989, $240.00 was amortized as an expense. The analysis of the 1989 adjustment is shown in the T accounts.

Organization Expense is debited for $240.00. Organization Costs is credited for $240.00. The new balance of Organization Costs, $720.00, is the amount to be amortized in the next three years.

The adjustment for organization expense is shown on AquaPro's work sheet, lines 24 and 80, Illustration 15-3.

Organization Expense		
1989	240.00	

Organization Costs		
Balance	1,200.00	1988 240.00
		1989 240.00

Federal income tax adjustment. At the beginning of 1989, AquaPro estimates its annual net income, and figures its *estimated* 1989 federal income tax, $36,000.00. AquaPro then pays the estimated tax to the federal government in four equal installments of $9,000.00 each. As of December 31, 1989, AquaPro figures its *actual* 1989 federal income tax to determine if accrued income tax is due. An adjustment is planned on the work sheet for the accrued tax.

The following steps are used to figure the total amount of federal income tax and the amount of adjustment needed on the work sheet.

1 Complete the work sheet's Adjustments columns except for the federal income tax adjustment. Do not total the Adjustments columns at this time.

2 Extend all amounts, except the balances of Federal Income Tax Payable and Federal Income Tax, to the work sheet's Income Statement and Balance Sheet columns.

3 Figure the work sheet's Income Statement column totals using an adding machine. Do not record the column totals on the work sheet. Figure the difference between the two totals. The difference is the net income before federal income tax. AquaPro's net income before federal income tax is figured as follows.

Income Statement Credit Column Total	−	Income Statement Debit Column Total	=	Net Income before Federal Income Tax
$914,269.14	−	$785,347.19	=	$128,921.95

4 Figure the amount of federal income tax using a tax rate table furnished by the Internal Revenue Service. AquaPro's actual federal income tax for 1989 is $39,054.10.

Tax rate tables showing income tax rates for corporations are distributed by the Internal Revenue Service. Each corporation should check a current

Aqua-Pro, Inc.
Work Sheet
For Year Ended December 31, 1989

| | TRIAL BALANCE | | ADJUSTMENTS | | INCOME STATEMENT | | BALANCE SHEET | |
ACCOUNT TITLE	DEBIT	CREDIT	DEBIT	CREDIT	DEBIT	CREDIT	DEBIT	CREDIT
1 Cash	171,478.15						171,478.15	
2 Petty Cash	500.00						500.00	
3 Notes Receivable	5,000.00						5,000.00	
4 Interest Receivable			(a) 49.32				49.32	
5 Accounts Receivable	143,470.93						143,470.93	
6 Allow. for Uncoll. Accts.		420.13		(b) 7,099.91				7,520.04
7 Subscriptions Receivable								
8 Merchandise Inventory	240,119.50			(c) 831.58			239,287.92	
9 Supplies — Sales	13,445.42			(d) 7,859.35			5,586.07	
10 Supplies — Delivery	17,023.84			(e) 12,140.25			4,883.59	
11 Supplies — Administrative	23,369.81			(f) 18,916.40			4,453.41	
12 Prepaid Insurance	18,890.00			(g) 6,217.00			12,673.00	
13 Prepaid Interest			(h) 8.88				8.88	
14 Bond Sinking Fund	20,000.00						20,000.00	
15 Store Equipment	141,862.45						141,862.45	
16 Accum. Depr. — Store Equip.		14,327.45		(i) 17,704.20				32,031.65
17 Delivery Equipment	128,102.10						128,102.10	
18 Accum. Depr. — Delivery Equip.		7,817.10		(j) 12,561.35				20,378.45
19 Office Equipment	63,464.50						63,464.50	
20 Accum. Depr. — Office Equip.		6,114.50		(k) 13,396.13				19,510.63
21 Building	135,000.00						135,000.00	
22 Accum. Depr. — Building		15,000.00		(l) 2,500.00				17,500.00
23 Land	100,000.00						100,000.00	
24 Organization Costs	9,600.00			(m) 2,400.00			7,200.00	
25 Notes Payable		15,000.00						15,000.00
26 Interest Payable				(n) 12,005.92				12,005.92
27 Accounts Payable		14,142.00						14,142.00
28 Employ. Income Tax Pay.		1,188.70						1,188.70
29 Federal Income Tax Pay.				(o) 3,054.10				3,054.10
30 FICA Tax Payable		695.64		(p) 81.83				777.47
31 Salaries Tax Payable				(q) 1,169.13				1,169.13
32 Sales Tax Payable		2,066.04						2,066.04
33 Unemploy. Tax Pay. — Federal		79.50		(p) 9.35				88.85
34 Unemploy. Tax Pay. — State		536.63		(p) 63.13				599.76
35 Hosp. Ins. Premiums Pay.		406.00						406.00
36 Dividends Payable		63,729.00						63,729.00
37 Bonds Payable		200,000.00						200,000.00
38 Capital Stock — Common		200,000.00						200,000.00
39 Stock Subscribed — Common		51,100.00						51,100.00
40 Capital Stock — Preferred		200,000.00						200,000.00

Account							
Stock Subscribed—Preferred							
P'd. in Cap. in Ex. of Par/Stated Value	510000						510000
Disc. on Sale of Capital Stock	1000000					1000000	
Treasury Stock	348000					348000	
P'd. in Cap. from Sale of Tr. Stock	40000						40000
Retained Earnings	6244153						6244153
Dividends—Common Stock	4572900					4572900	
Dividends—Preferred Stock	1800000					1800000	
Income Summary			(c) 8315 8		8315 8		
Sales	90370769					90370769	
Sales Returns & Allow.	284255			284255			
Sales Discount	218642			218642			
Purchases	42953648			42953648			
Purchases Returns & Allow.	273000				273000		
Purchases Discount	719035				719035		
Advertising Expense	1093200			1093200			
Credit Card Fee Expense	1229859			1229859			
Depr. Exp.—Store Equip.			(a) 1770420	1770420			
Miscellaneous Exp.—Sales	535000			535000			
Salary Expense—Sales	6512600		(b) 63849	6576449			
Supplies Expense—Sales			(f) 785935	785935			
Depr. Exp.—Delivery Equip.			(i) 1256135	1256135			
Miscellaneous Exp.—Delivery	1391000			1391000			
Salary Expense—Delivery	2905050		(g) 28480	2933530			
Supplies Expense—Delivery			(j) 1214025	1214025			
Bad Debts Expense			(h) 709991	709991			
Depr. Exp.—Office Equip.			(k) 1339613	1339613			
Depr. Exp.—Building			(l) 250000	250000			
Insurance Expense			(e) 621700	621700			
Miscellaneous Exp.—Admin.	1520575			1520575			
Payroll Taxes Expense	1574127		(p) 15431	1589558			
Property Tax Expense	750000			750000			
Salary Expense—Admin.	2507555		(o) 24584	2532139			
Supplies Expense—Admin.			(d) 1891640	1891640			
Utilities Expense	2562725			2562725			
Gain on Plant Assets					(q) 4932		4932
Interest Income		59178					64110
Interest Expense	1217818		(m) 800592	2417522			
Loss on Plant Assets			(a) 888	888			
Organization Expense			(m) 24000	24000			
Federal Income Tax	3600000		(p) 305410	3905410			
	200845624	200845624	11590783	11590783	82440129	91426914	125374932
Net Inc. after Fed. Inc. Tax					8986785		8986785
					91426914	91426914	125374932

Illustration 15-3 Corporate work sheet

table to find the applicable rates. Corporation rates current when this text was written were used to figure AquaPro's federal income taxes.

5 Figure the amount of accrued federal income tax.

Actual Tax	–	Tax Already Paid	=	Accrued Federal Income Tax
$39,054.10	–	$36,000.00	=	$3,054.10

The tax already paid, $36,000.00, is the balance of Federal Income Tax as shown in the work sheet's Trial Balance columns, line 81.

6 Record the accrued federal income tax adjustment in the work sheet's Adjustments columns. This adjustment is shown on lines 29 and 81 of the work sheet.

7 Extend the new balance of Federal Income Tax Payable, $3,054.10, to the Balance Sheet Credit column. Extend the new balance of Federal Income Tax, $39,054.10, to the Income Statement Debit column.

Completing a corporate work sheet

The work sheet's Adjustments, Income Statement, and Balance Sheet columns are totaled and the work sheet is completed as shown on lines 82–84.

CORPORATE INCOME STATEMENT

AquaPro prepares three important financial statements. (1) Income statement. (2) Statement of stockholders' equity. (3) Balance sheet. (CONCEPT: Adequate Disclosure)

Preparing a corporate income statement

Federal income tax represents a large portion of a corporation's net income before income tax is paid. Therefore, both net income before and after federal income tax has been deducted are shown on a corporate income statement. This method of reporting shows how much of a business' income is used to pay federal income tax.

AquaPro's income statement is shown in Illustration 15-4.

Analyzing a corporate income statement

AquaPro analyzes seven items related to information on an income statement. (1) Ratio of cost of merchandise sold to net sales. (2) Ratio of gross profit to net sales. (3) Ratio of total operating expenses to net sales. (4) Ratio of net income before federal income tax to net sales. (5) Ratio of federal income tax to net sales. (6) Ratio of net income after federal income tax to net sales. (7) Earnings per share.

AquaPro, Inc.
Income Statement
For Year Ended December 31, 1989

				*% of Net Sales
Operating Revenue:				
Sales		$903,707.69		
Less: Sales Returns & Allowances	$ 2,842.55			
Sales Discount	2,186.42	5,028.97		
Net Sales			$898,678.72	100.0
Cost of Merchandise Sold:				
Merchandise Inventory, Jan. 1, 1989		$240,119.50		
Purchases	$429,536.48			
Less: Purchases Returns & Allowances	$2,730.00			
Purchases Discount	7,190.35	9,920.35		
Net Purchases		419,616.13		
Total Cost of Mdse. Avail. for Sale		$659,735.63		
Less Mdse. Inventory, Dec. 31, 1989		239,287.92		
Cost of Merchandise Sold			420,447.71	46.8
Gross Profit on Operations			$478,231.01	53.2
Operating Expenses:				
Selling Expenses:				
Advertising Expense	$ 10,932.00			
Credit Card Fee Expense	12,298.59			
Depreciation Expense — Store Equip.	17,704.20			
Miscellaneous Expense — Sales	5,350.00			
Salary Expense — Sales	65,764.49			
Supplies Expense — Sales	7,859.35			
Total Selling Expenses		$119,908.63		
Delivery Expenses:				
Depreciation Expense — Delivery Equip.	$ 12,561.35			
Miscellaneous Expense — Delivery	13,910.00			
Salary Expense — Delivery	29,335.30			
Supplies Expense — Delivery	12,140.25			
Total Delivery Expenses		67,946.90		
Administrative Expenses:				
Bad Debts Expense	$ 7,099.91			
Depreciation Expense — Office Equip.	13,396.13			
Depreciation Expense — Building	2,500.00			
Insurance Expense	6,217.00			
Miscellaneous Expense — Administrative	15,205.75			
Payroll Taxes Expense	15,895.58			
Property Tax Expense	7,500.00			
Salary Expense — Administrative	25,321.39			
Supplies Expense — Administrative	18,916.40			
Utilities Expense	25,627.25			
Total Administrative Expenses		137,679.41		
Total Operating Expenses			325,534.94	36.2
Income from Operations			$152,696.07	
Other Revenue:				
Interest Income		$ 641.10		
Other Expenses:				
Interest Expense	$ 24,175.22			
Organization Expense	240.00			
Total Other Expenses		24,415.22		
Net Deduction			23,774.12	
Net Income before Federal Income Tax			$128,921.95	14.3
Less Federal Income Tax			39,054.10	4.3
Net Income after Federal Income Tax			$ 89,867.85	10.0

*Rounded to nearest 0.1%.

Illustration 15-4   Corporate income statement

Ratio of cost of merchandise sold to net sales. This ratio is figured as follows.

Cost of Merchandise Sold	÷	Net Sales	=	Ratio of Cost of Merchandise Sold to Net Sales
$420,447.71	÷	$898,678.72	=	46.8%

The ratio, 46.8%, means that for each dollar of net sales, $0.468 is paid for the merchandise sold. For businesses similar to AquaPro, a ratio of cost of merchandise sold to net sales between 45–50% is considered acceptable. AquaPro's ratio is in the acceptable range.

Ratio of gross profit to net sales. This ratio is figured as follows.

Gross Profit	÷	Net Sales	=	Ratio of Gross Profit to Net Sales
$478,231.01	÷	$898,678.72	=	53.2%

The ratio, 53.2%, means that for each dollar of net sales, the corporation earns $0.532 in gross profit. Businesses similar to AquaPro consider between 50–55% an acceptable ratio. Therefore, AquaPro's ratio is in the acceptable range.

Ratio of total operating expenses to net sales. This ratio is figured as follows.

Total Operating Expenses	÷	Net Sales	=	Ratio of Total Operating Expenses to Net Sales
$325,534.94	÷	$898,678.72	=	36.2%

The ratio, 36.2%, means that for each dollar of net sales, the corporation paid $0.362 for operating expenses. Businesses similar to AquaPro consider between 30–40% an acceptable ratio. Therefore, AquaPro's ratio is in the acceptable range.

Ratio of net income before federal income tax to net sales. This ratio is figured as follows.

Net Income before Federal Income Tax	÷	Net Sales	=	Ratio of Net Income before Federal Income Tax to Net Sales
$128,921.95	÷	$898,678.72	=	14.3%

The ratio, 14.3%, means that for each dollar of net sales, the corporation earns net income of $0.143 before income tax. Businesses similar to Aqua-Pro consider a ratio of net income before federal income tax between 10–25% as acceptable. AquaPro's ratio is within this acceptable range.

Ratio of federal income tax to net sales. This ratio is figured as follows.

Federal Income Tax	÷	Net Sales	=	Ratio of Federal Income Tax to Net Sales
$39,054.10	÷	$898,678.72	=	4.3%

The ratio, 4.3%, means that for each dollar of net sales, the corporation paid $0.043 for federal income tax. Businesses similar to AquaPro find that an acceptable ratio is between 4–5%. AquaPro's ratio is within the acceptable range.

Ratio of net income after federal income tax to net sales. This ratio is figured as follows.

Net Income after Federal Income Tax	÷	Net Sales	=	Ratio of Net Income after Federal Income Tax to Net Sales
$89,867.85	÷	$898,678.72	=	10.0%

The ratio, 10.0%, means that for each dollar of net sales, AquaPro earns $0.10 after federal income taxes are paid. For businesses similar to AquaPro, a ratio of net income after federal income tax to net sales between 10–15% is considered acceptable. AquaPro's ratio is just within the acceptable range.

Earnings per share. The total earnings for outstanding preferred stock, equal to the 9% dividend specified on the stock certificates, is figured as follows.

Total Par Value	×	Dividend Rate	=	Preferred Stock's Share of Net Income
$200,000.00	×	9%	=	$18,000.00

The total share of net income for common stock is the remainder of the net income after the preferred stock's share is deducted.

Total Net Income	−	Preferred Stock's Share of Net Income	=	Common Stock's Share of Net Income
$89,867.85	−	$18,000.00	=	$71,867.85

The amount of net income belonging to a single share of stock is called earnings per share. Earnings per share is figured on the number of shares outstanding. For example, AquaPro has 51,100 shares of common stock issued. However, 290 of these shares are treasury stock, and therefore not outstanding stock. AquaPro has 50,810 shares of outstanding common stock (51,100 shares − 290 shares = 50,810).

For the year ended December 31, 1989, AquaPro's earnings per share is figured as follows.

	Share of Net Income	÷	Shares of Stock Outstanding	=	Earnings Per Share
Preferred	$18,000.00	÷	2,000	=	$9.00
Common	71,867.85	÷	50,810	=	1.41
Total	$89,867.85				

Businesses similar to AquaPro consider earnings per share between $1.30 and $2.00 on common stock to be acceptable. AquaPro's earnings per share for common stock is in the acceptable range.

CORPORATE STATEMENT OF STOCKHOLDERS' EQUITY

A statement of stockholders' equity shows changes occurring in the stockholders' equity during a fiscal period.

Preparing a corporate statement of stockholders' equity

AquaPro's statement of stockholders' equity has two major sections: (1) Paid-in Capital, and (2) Retained Earnings. AquaPro's statement of stockholders' equity, prepared on December 31, 1989, is shown in Illustration 15-5.

AquaPro, Inc.
Statement of Stockholders' Equity
For Year Ended December 31, 1989

Paid-in Capital:			
Common Stock, $10.00 Per Share:			
January 1, 1989, 51,000 Shares Issued..................	$510,000.00		
Issued during 1989, 100 Shares.........................	1,000.00		
Balance, December 31, 1989, 51,100 Shares Issued		$511,000.00	
Preferred Stock, $100.00 Per Share:			
January 1, 1989, No Shares Issued	-0-		
Issued during 1989, 2,000 Shares.......................	$200,000.00		
Balance, December 31, 1989, 2,000 Shares Issued		200,000.00	
Total Value of Capital Stock Issued			$711,000.00
Additional Paid-in Capital:			
Paid-in Capital in Excess of Par/Stated Value..............	$ 5,100.00		
Paid-in Capital from Sale of Treasury Stock	400.00	$ 5,500.00	
Less Discount on Sale of Capital Stock		10,000.00	
Total Additional Paid-in Capital...........................			(4,500.00)
Total Paid-in Capital......................................			$706,500.00
Retained Earnings:			
January 1, 1989		$ 62,441.53	
Net Income after Federal Income Tax for 1989	$ 89,867.85		
Less Dividends Declared	63,729.00		
Net Increase during 1989................................		26,138.85	
Balance, December 31, 1989..............................			88,580.38
Total Paid-in Capital and Retained Earnings.................			$795,080.38
Less Treasury Stock, 290 Shares of Common Stock,			
December 31, 1989			3,480.00
Total Stockholders' Equity, December 31, 1989			$791,600.38

Illustration 15-5
Corporate statement of
stockholders' equity

Some businesses prepare a statement of retained earnings instead of a statement of stockholders' equity. A statement of retained earnings includes only information about the changes in retained earnings during a fiscal period. The remainder of the information about changes in paid-in capital is placed on the corporation's balance sheet. However, AquaPro prepares a statement of stockholders' equity so that all the information need not be placed on the balance sheet.

During 1989, AquaPro issued 100 shares of common stock and 2,000 shares of preferred stock. As of December 31, 1989, AquaPro has issued $511,000.00 in common stock and $200,000.00 in preferred stock for a total stock issue of $711,000.00. AquaPro also has $3,480.00 in treasury stock. Therefore, the total stock outstanding is $707,520.00. The total stockholders' equity, $791,600.38, is shown on the last line of the statement of stockholders' equity.

Analyzing a corporate statement of stockholders' equity

AquaPro analyzes three items related to information on its statement of stockholders' equity. (1) Equity per share. (2) Market value per share. (3) Price-earnings ratio.

Equity per share. The amount of total stockholders' equity belonging to a single share of stock is called equity per share. The equity per share for AquaPro's preferred and common stock is figured as follows.

	Total Stockholders' Equity	÷	Shares of Capital Stock Outstanding	=	Equity Per Share
Preferred	$200,000.00	÷	2,000	=	$100.00
Common	591,600.38	÷	50,810	=	11.64
Total	$791,600.38				

The equity of preferred stock is equal to its total par value, $200,000.00, or $100.00 per share. The remainder of the total stockholders' equity is the equity of the common stock, $591,600.38, or $11.64 per share. Most businesses consider common stock equity at least equal to its stated value to be acceptable. AquaPro's common stock equity per share is greater than stated value and is acceptable.

Market value per share. The price at which a share of stock may be sold on the stock market is called market value. The market value is determined by how much a buyer is willing to pay for the stock. Therefore, market price is established by investors' buying and selling the corporation's stock on the stock market. If a business is profitable and pays adequate dividends, investors often will offer to pay a market price higher than the stock's par or stated value. If a business is not profitable, or does not pay regular dividends, investors often will offer to pay a market price lower than the stock's par or stated value.

Stock is recorded on a corporation's records at the par or stated value. A stock's market value is not recorded on corporate records.

Price-earnings ratio. The relationship between a stock's market value per share and earnings per share is called the price-earnings ratio. Investors usually want to buy stock in companies that are earning a reasonable amount of net income. One way to determine if a company is earning a reasonable amount of net income is to figure the price-earnings ratio. The ratio is then compared to standards for similar companies.

AquaPro's 1989 earnings per share is $10.00 for preferred stock and $1.41 for common stock as previously described. Using stock market reports on December 31, 1989, the price-earnings ratio for common stock is figured as follows.

Market Price Per Share	÷	Earnings Per Share	=	Price-Earnings Ratio
$11.00	÷	$1.41	=	7.8 times

The common stock price-earnings ratio, 7.8 times, means that the stock is selling for 7.8 times its share of the earnings. For businesses similar to AquaPro, a common stock price-earnings ratio between 6.0 and 10.0 times is considered acceptable. AquaPro's price-earnings ratio for common stock is acceptable.

CORPORATE BALANCE SHEET

A corporate balance sheet reports assets, liabilities, and stockholders' equity on a specific date.

Preparing a corporate balance sheet

AquaPro's December 31, 1989, balance sheet is shown in Illustration 15-6. AquaPro's balance sheet is similar to the one described for Gallery in Chapter 12. However, AquaPro includes two additional accounts: Bond Sinking Fund and Organization Costs. Bond Sinking Fund is listed in the balance sheet's Assets section under the heading Long-Term Investment. Organization Costs is listed in the Assets section under the heading Intangible Asset.

Only the total stockholders' equity obtained from the stockholders' equity statement are included under the heading Stockholders' Equity. If more detail is needed, AquaPro's statement of stockholders' equity can be read.

Analyzing a corporate balance sheet

AquaPro figures three ratios based on information from its balance sheet items. (1) Accounts receivable turnover ratio. (2) Rate earned on average stockholders' equity. (3) Rate earned on average total assets.

AquaPro, Inc.
Balance Sheet
December 31, 1989

ASSETS

Current Assets:			
Cash		$171,478.15	
Petty Cash		500.00	
Notes Receivable		5,000.00	
Interest Receivable		49.32	
Accounts Receivable	$143,470.93		
Less Allowance for Uncollectible Accounts	7,520.04	135,950.89	
Merchandise Inventory		239,287.92	
Supplies — Sales		5,586.07	
Supplies — Delivery		4,883.59	
Supplies — Administrative		4,453.41	
Prepaid Insurance		12,673.00	
Prepaid Interest		8.88	
Total Current Assets			$ 579,871.23
Long-Term Investment:			
Bond Sinking Fund			20,000.00
Plant Assets:			
Store Equipment	$141,862.45		
Less Accumulated Depreciation — Store Equipment	32,031.65	$109,830.80	
Delivery Equipment	$128,102.10		
Less Accumulated Depreciation — Delivery Equipment	20,378.45	107,723.65	
Office Equipment	$ 63,464.50		
Less Accumulated Depreciation — Office Equipment	19,510.63	43,953.87	
Building	$135,000.00		
Less Accumulated Depreciation — Building	17,500.00	117,500.00	
Land		100,000.00	
Total Plant Assets			479,008.32
Intangible Asset:			
Organization Costs			720.00
Total Assets			$1,079,599.55

LIABILITIES

Current Liabilities:			
Notes Payable		$ 1,500.00	
Interest Payable		12,005.92	
Accounts Payable		1,414.20	
Employees Income Tax Payable		1,188.70	
Federal Income Tax Payable		3,054.10	
FICA Tax Payable		777.47	
Salaries Payable		1,169.13	
Sales Tax Payable		2,066.04	
Unemployment Tax Payable — Federal		88.85	
Unemployment Tax Payable — State		599.76	
Hospital Insurance Premiums Payable		406.00	
Dividends Payable		63,729.00	
Total Current Liabilities			$ 87,999.17
Long-Term Liability:			
Bonds Payable			200,000.00
Total Liabilities			$ 287,999.17

STOCKHOLDERS' EQUITY

Total Stockholders' Equity	791,600.38
Total Liabilities and Stockholders' Equity	$1,079,599.55

Illustration 15-6   Corporate balance sheet

Accounts receivable turnover ratio. AquaPro figures this ratio as follows.

1 Figure the average book value of accounts receivable.

Accounts Receivable Beginning Balance		Allowance for Uncollectible Accounts		Beginning Book Value
$80,560.50	−	$7,009.91	=	$73,550.59

Accounts Receivable Ending Balance		Allowance for Uncollectible Accounts		Ending Book Value
$143,470.93	−	$7,520.04	=	$135,950.89

Beginning Book Value of Accounts Receivable		Ending Book Value of Accounts Receivable				Average Book Value of Accounts Receivable
($73,550.59	+	$135,950.89)	÷	2	=	$104,750.74

2 Figure the accounts receivable turnover ratio.

Net Sales on Account		Average Book Value of Accounts Receivable		Accounts Receivable Turnover Ratio
$587,410.00	÷	$104,750.74	=	5.6 times

3 Figure the average number of days for payment.

Days in Year		Accounts Receivable Turnover Ratio		Average Number of Days for Payment
365	÷	5.6	=	65.2

AquaPro sells on terms of n/30. Therefore, AquaPro expects payment within 30 days. The expected accounts receivable turnover ratio is 12.2 times, or one-twelfth of a year (30 days). AquaPro's average number of days for payment, 65.2, are greater than the expected level of 30 days. Therefore, AquaPro's accounts receivable turnover ratio, 5.6, is unacceptable. AquaPro needs to consider ways to encourage customers to pay their accounts within the credit period of n/30.

Rate earned on average stockholders' equity. The relationship between net income and the average stockholders' equity is called the rate earned on average stockholders' equity. AquaPro figures the rate earned on average stockholders' equity as follows.

January 1 Stockholders' Equity		December 31 Stockholders' Equity				Average Stockholders' Equity
($768,941.53	+	$791,600.38)	÷	2	=	$780,270.96

Net Income after Federal Income Tax		Average Stockholders' Equity		Rate Earned on Average Stockholders' Equity
$89,867.85	÷	$780,270.96	=	11.5%

For each dollar stockholders have invested, AquaPro is earning $0.115 in net income. The best investment is in a corporation with the highest rate earned on average stockholders' equity. For example, Muldore, Inc., has a rate earned on average stockholders' equity of 9.6% compared to AquaPro's rate of 11.5%. *Based on this one analysis,* if an investor has a choice, Aqua-Pro's stock is a better investment than Muldore's.

Rate earned on average total assets. The relationship between net income and average total assets is called rate earned on average total assets. AquaPro figures this rate as follows.

$$
\left(\begin{array}{c} \text{January 1} \\ \text{Total Assets} \end{array} + \begin{array}{c} \text{December 31} \\ \text{Total Assets} \end{array}\right) \div 2 = \begin{array}{c} \text{Average} \\ \text{Total Assets} \end{array}
$$

$$
(\$911,947.62 \quad + \quad \$1,079,599.55) \div 2 = \$995,773.59
$$

Net Income after Federal Income Tax	÷	Average Total Assets	=	Rate Earned on Average Total Assets
$89,867.85	÷	$995,773.59	=	9.0%

For each dollar of assets owned by the corporation, the business has earnings of $0.09 after the federal income tax is paid. Information published by trade organizations shows that businesses similar to AquaPro tend to have a rate earned on average total assets between 8.0% and 10.0%. Aqua-Pro's rate, 9.0%, is acceptable.

Other methods of analyzing corporate financial statement items are described in Chapter 19.

OTHER END-OF-FISCAL-PERIOD WORK

In addition to a work sheet and financial statements, AquaPro also prepares adjusting entries, closing entries, a post-closing trial balance, and reversing entries.

Corporate adjusting entries

AquaPro's December 31, 1989, adjusting entries are shown in Illustration 15-7, page 318.

Corporate closing entries

AquaPro records four closing entries at the end of a fiscal period.

1. Close income statement accounts with credit balances to Income Summary.
2. Close income statement accounts with debit balances to Income Summary.
3. Close Income Summary and record net income or net loss in Retained Earnings.
4. Close the dividends accounts to Retained Earnings.

AquaPro's December 31, 1989, closing entries are shown in Illustration 15-8, page 319.

	DATE	ACCOUNT TITLE	POST. REF.	DEBIT	CREDIT	
		Adjusting Entries				1
2	1989 Dec. 31	Interest Receivable		4932		2
3		Interest Income			4932	3
4	31	Bad Debts Expense		709991		4
5		Allow. for Uncoll. Accts.			709991	5
6	31	Income Summary		83158		6
7		Merchandise Inventory			83158	7
8	31	Supplies Expense – Sales		785935		8
9		Supplies – Sales			785935	9
10	31	Supplies Expense – Delivery		1214025		10
11		Supplies – Delivery			1214025	11
12	31	Supplies Expense – Admin.		1891640		12
13		Supplies – Administrative			1891640	13
14	31	Insurance Expense		621700		14
15		Prepaid Insurance			621700	15
16	31	Prepaid Interest		888		16
17		Interest Expense			888	17
18	31	Depr. Exp. – Store Equip.		1770420		18
19		Accum. Depr. – Store Equip.			1770420	19
20	31	Depr. Exp. – Delivery Equip.		1256135		20
21		Accum. Depr. – Delivery Equip.			1256135	21
22	31	Depr. Exp. – Office Equip.		1339613		22
23		Accum. Depr. – Office Equip.			1339613	23
24	31	Depr. Exp. – Building		250000		24
25		Accum. Depr. – Building			250000	25
26	31	Organization Expense		24000		26
27		Organization Costs			24000	27
28	31	Interest Expense		1200592		28
29		Interest Payable			1200592	29
30	31	Salary Expense – Sales		63849		30
31		Salary Expense – Delivery		28480		31
32		Salary Expense – Admin.		24584		32
33		Salaries Payable			116913	33
34	31	Payroll Taxes Expense		15431		34
35		FICA Tax Payable			8183	35
36		Unemploy. Tax Pay. – Federal			935	36
37		Unemploy. Tax Pay. – State			6313	37
38	31	Federal Income Tax		305410		38
39		Federal Income Tax Payable			305410	39

GENERAL JOURNAL   PAGE 13

Illustration 15-7
Corporate adjusting
entries

	DATE		ACCOUNT TITLE	POST. REF.	DEBIT	CREDIT	
1	1989		*Closing Entries*				1
2	Dec.	31	Sales		90370769		2
3			Purchases Returns & Allow.		273000		3
4			Purchases Discount		719035		4
5			Interest Income		64110		5
6			Income Summary			91426914	6
7		31	Income Summary		82356971		7
8			Sales Returns & Allow.			284255	8
9			Sales Discount			218642	9
10			Purchases			42953648	10
11			Advertising Expense			1093200	11
12			Credit Card Fee Expense			1229859	12
13			Depr. Exp. – Store Equip.			1770420	13
14			Misc. Exp. – Sales			535000	14
15			Salary Exp. – Sales			6576449	15
16			Supplies Exp. – Sales			785935	16
17			Depr. Exp. – Delivery Equip.			1256135	17
18			Misc. Exp. – Delivery			1391000	18
19			Salary Exp. – Delivery			2933530	19
20			Supplies Exp. – Delivery			1214025	20
21			Bad Debts Expense			709991	21
22			Depr. Exp. – Office Equip.			1339613	22
23			Depr. Exp. – Building			250000	23
24			Insurance Expense			621700	24
25			Misc. Exp. – Admin.			1520575	25
26			Payroll Taxes Expense			1589558	26
27			Property Tax Expense			750000	27
28			Salary Exp. – Admin.			2532139	28
29			Supplies Exp. – Admin.			1891640	29
30			Utilities Expense			2562725	30
31			Interest Expense			2417522	31
32			Organization Expense			24000	32
33			Federal Income Tax			3905410	33
34		31	Income Summary		8986785		34
35			Retained Earnings			8986785	35
36		31	Retained Earnings		6372900		36
37			Dividends – Common Stock			4572900	37
38			Dividends – Preferred Stock			1800000	38
39							39
40							40
41							41
42							42
43							43

GENERAL JOURNAL PAGE 14

Illustration 15-8
Corporate closing entries

AquaPro's first three closing entries on lines 2–35 are similar to those described for Supergolf in Chapter 5. The fourth closing entry on lines 36–38 closes AquaPro's two dividends accounts.

The debit balance of Dividends—Common Stock plus the debit balance of Dividends—Preferred Stock equals the total amount of dividends declared during the fiscal period. Since dividends decrease the earnings retained in the corporation, the dividends accounts are closed to Retained Earnings. After the closing entry for the dividends accounts is posted, Dividends—Common Stock and Dividends—Preferred Stock have zero balances. The total amount of dividends declared during the year, $63,729.00, has been recorded as a debit in Retained Earnings.

Corporate post-closing trial balance

AquaPro's December 31, 1989, post-closing trial balance is shown in Illustration 15-9, page 321.

Corporate reversing entries

If an adjusting entry creates a balance in an asset or liability account, AquaPro reverses the adjusting entry. AquaPro's reversing entries, made on January 1, 1990, are shown in Illustration 15-10.

	DATE	ACCOUNT TITLE	POST. REF.	DEBIT	CREDIT	
		GENERAL JOURNAL			PAGE 1	
1	1990	Reversing Entries				1
2	Jan. 1	Interest Income		4932		2
3		Interest Receivable			4932	3
4	1	Interest Expense		888		4
5		Prepaid Interest			888	5
6	1	Interest Payable		120059		6
7		Interest Expense			120059	7
8	1	Salaries Payable		116913		8
9		Salary Exp. – Sales			63849	9
10		Salary Exp. – Delivery			28480	10
11		Salary Exp. – Administrative			24584	11
12	1	FICA Tax Payable		8183		12
13		Unemploy. Tax Pay. – Federal		935		13
14		Unemploy. Tax Pay. – State		6313		14
15		Payroll Taxes Expense			15431	15
16	1	Federal Income Tax Payable		305410		16
17		Federal Income Tax			305410	17
18						18
19						19

Illustration 15-10
Corporate reversing entries

AquaPro, Inc.
Post-Closing Trial Balance
December 31, 1989

Cash	$ 171,478.15	
Petty Cash	500.00	
Notes Receivable	5,000.00	
Interest Receivable	49.32	
Accounts Receivable	143,470.93	
Allowance for Uncollectible Accounts		$ 7,520.04
Merchandise Inventory	239,287.92	
Supplies — Sales	5,586.07	
Supplies — Delivery	4,883.59	
Supplies — Administrative	4,453.41	
Prepaid Insurance	12,673.00	
Prepaid Interest	8.88	
Bond Sinking Fund	20,000.00	
Store Equipment	141,862.45	
Accumulated Depreciation — Store Equipment		32,031.65
Delivery Equipment	128,102.10	
Accumulated Depreciation — Delivery Equipment		20,378.45
Office Equipment	63,464.50	
Accumulated Depreciation — Office Equipment		19,510.63
Building	135,000.00	
Accumulated Depreciation — Building		17,500.00
Land	100,000.00	
Organization Costs	720.00	
Notes Payable		1,500.00
Interest Payable		12,005.92
Accounts Payable		1,414.20
Employees Income Tax Payable		1,188.70
Federal Income Tax Payable		3,054.10
FICA Tax Payable		777.47
Salaries Payable		1,169.13
Sales Tax Payable		2,066.04
Unemployment Tax Payable — Federal		88.85
Unemployment Tax Payable — State		599.76
Hospital Insurance Premiums Payable		406.00
Dividends Payable		63,729.00
Bonds Payable		200,000.00
Capital Stock — Common		511,000.00
Capital Stock — Preferred		200,000.00
Paid-in Capital in Excess of Par/Stated Value		5,100.00
Discount on Sale of Capital Stock	10,000.00	
Treasury Stock	3,480.00	
Paid-in Capital from Sale of Treasury Stock		400.00
Retained Earnings		88,580.38
	$1,190,020.32	$1,190,020.32

Illustration 15-9
Corporate post-closing
trial balance

CORPORATE FEDERAL INCOME TAX RETURN

AquaPro must file a federal income tax return and pay income taxes. Page 1 of AquaPro's Form 1120, U.S. Corporation Income Tax Return for 1989, is shown in Illustration 15-11.

ACCOUNTING TERMS

What is the meaning of each of the following?

1. declaring a dividend
2. date of declaration
3. date of record
4. date of payment
5. earnings per share
6. equity per share
7. market value
8. price-earnings ratio
9. rate earned on average stockholders' equity
10. rate earned on average total assets

QUESTIONS FOR INDIVIDUAL STUDY

1. Reporting information for the use of stockholders, investors, and creditors is an application of which accounting concept?
2. What accounts are affected, and how, by an entry to record the declaration of dividends for both common and preferred stock?
3. What accounts are affected, and how, by an entry to record payment of dividends for common and preferred stock?
4. What accounts are affected, and how, by AquaPro's adjustment for organization expense?
5. What accounts are affected, and how, by AquaPro's adjustment for federal income tax?
6. What is the formula for figuring the ratio of cost of merchandise sold to net sales?
7. What is the formula for figuring the ratio of gross profit to net sales?
8. What is the formula for figuring the ratio of net income before federal income tax to net sales?
9. What is the formula for figuring the ratio of federal income tax to net sales?
10. What is the formula for figuring the ratio of net income after federal income tax to net sales?
11. What is the formula for figuring a corporation's earnings per share?
12. What is the formula for figuring a corporation's equity per share?
13. What determines the market price of a corporation's stock?
14. What is the formula for figuring the price-earnings ratio?
15. What is the formula for figuring the accounts receivable turnover ratio?
16. What is the formula for figuring the rate earned on average stockholders' equity?
17. What is the formula for figuring the rate earned on average total assets?
18. What guide does AquaPro use in determining if a reversing entry should be recorded?
19. What form is used by AquaPro to report annual income for federal income tax purposes?

Form **1120**

Department of the Treasury
Internal Revenue Service

U.S. Corporation Income Tax Return

For calendar 1989 or tax year beginning .... 1989, ending .... 19 ....
► For Paperwork Reduction Act Notice, see page 1 of the instructions.

OMB No. 1545-0123

Check if a—
A Consolidated return ☐
B Personal Holding Co. ☐
C Business Code No. (See the list in the Instructions)
5995

Use IRS label. Otherwise please print or type.

Name
AquaPro, Inc.

Number and street
2309 Anderson Road

City or town, state, and ZIP code
Miami, Florida 33149-6419

D Employer Identification number
74-1334457

E Date incorporated
December 26, 1987

F Total assets (see Specific Instructions)

Dollars | Cents
1,079,599|55

G Check box if there has been a change in address from the previous year . . . . ► ☐ $

				Dollars	Cents
Income	1 a Gross receipts or sales 901,521.27 b Less returns and allowances 2,842.55 Balance ►	1c		898,678	72
	2 Cost of goods sold and/or operations (Schedule A)	2		420,447	71
	3 Gross profit (line 1c less line 2)	3		478,231	01
	4 Dividends (Schedule C)	4		-0-	
	5 Interest	5		641	10
	6 Gross rents	6		-0-	
	7 Gross royalties	7		-0-	
	8 Capital gain net income (attach separate Schedule D)	8		-0-	
	9 Net gain or (loss) from Form 4797, line 17, Part II (attach Form 4797) . . .	9		-0-	
	10 Other income (see instructions—attach schedule)	10		-0-	
	11 TOTAL income—Add lines 3 through 10 and enter here . . . . ►	11		478,872	11
Deductions	12 Compensation of officers (Schedule E)	12		30,105	30
	13 a Salaries and wages 90,315.88 b Less jobs credit -0- Balance ►	13c		90,315	88
	14 Repairs	14		-0-	
	15 Bad debts (Schedule F if reserve method is used)	15		7,099	91
	16 Rents	16		-0-	
	17 Taxes	17		23,395	58
	18 Interest	18		24,175	22
	19 Contributions (see instructions for 10% limitation)	19		-0-	
	20 Depreciation (attach Form 4562) 20 46,161 68				
	21 Less depreciation claimed in Schedule A and elsewhere on return . 21a -0-	21b		46,161	68
	22 Depletion	22		-0-	
	23 Advertising	23		10,932	00
	24 Pension, profit-sharing, etc. plans	24		-0-	
	25 Employee benefit programs	25		-0-	
	26 Other deductions (attach schedule)	26		7,764	59
	27 TOTAL deductions—Add lines 12 through 26 and enter here . . . . . ►	27		349,950	16
	28 Taxable income before net operating loss deduction and special deductions (line 11 less line 27) .	28		128,921	95
	29 Less: a Net operating loss deduction (see instructions) . . . . . 29a -0-				
	b Special deductions (Schedule C) . . . . 29b -0-	29c		-0-	
Tax and Payments	30 Taxable income (line 28 less line 29c)	30		128,921	95
	31 TOTAL TAX (Schedule J)	31		39,054	10
	32 **Payments:**				
	a 1988 overpayment allowed as a credit . . . -0-				
	b 1989 estimated tax payments 36,000 00				
	c Less 1989 refund applied for on Form 4466 . . (-0-) 36,000 00				
	d Tax deposited with Form 7004 . . . . -0-				
	e Credit from regulated investment companies (attach Form 2439) . . -0-				
	f Credit for Federal tax on gasoline and special fuels (attach Form 4136) . -0-	32		36,000	00
	33 Enter any **PENALTY** for underpayment of estimated tax—check ► ☐ if Form 2220 is attached	33		-0-	
	34 **TAX DUE**—If the total of lines 31 and 33 is larger than line 32, enter AMOUNT OWED	34		3,054	10
	35 **OVERPAYMENT**—If line 32 is larger than the total of lines 31 and 33, enter AMOUNT OVERPAID	35			
	36 Enter amount of line 35 you want: Credited to 1990 estimated tax ► Refunded ►	36			

Please Sign Here

Under penalties of perjury, I declare that I have examined this return, including accompanying schedules and statements, and to the best of my knowledge and belief, it is true, correct, and complete. Declaration of preparer (other than taxpayer) is based on all information of which preparer has any knowledge.

► *Betty L. Andrews* 3/15/90 ► Treasurer
Signature of officer Date Title

Paid Preparer's Use Only

Preparer's signature ► Date Check if self-employed ► ☐ Preparer's social security number

Firm's name (or yours, if self-employed) and address ► E.I. No. ► ZIP code ►

Illustration 15-11
Form 1120, U.S. Corporation Income Tax Return

CASES FOR MANAGEMENT DECISION

CASE 1 Dorothy Ursula considers investing in some corporate stock. She has narrowed the choice to the stock of two companies. The following is a summary of information about the two corporations' stock. Which corporation's stock do you suggest Miss Ursula buy? Explain your answer.

	Corp. A	Corp. B
Market price per share.....	$50.00	$25.00
Equity per share.	30.00	70.00
Earnings per share........	15.40	13.00
Price-earnings ratio.........	3.25 times	1.92 times

CASE 2 A corporation president suggests to the accounting department that the statement of stockholders' equity be dropped from the end-of-fiscal-period work. The president's reason is that the same information is reported on the corporation's balance sheet. The accounting department wants to continue using the statement. Which would you recommend? Why?

CASE 3 James DeGorde has $10,000.00 in a bank savings account which is earning 6% interest. He is thinking of investing the money in stock that has a stated value and a current market price of $100.00 per share. For the past three years the stock dividends have amounted to $9.00 per share per year. Mr. DeGorde asks your advice. What would you recommend? Explain your answer.

APPLICATION PROBLEMS

PROBLEM 15-1   Recording entries for corporate dividends

Lighting, Inc., completed the following selected transactions.

Instructions: Record the transactions using page 10 of a general journal and page 13 of a cash payments journal. Source documents are abbreviated as follows: check, C; memorandum, M.

Nov. 25, 1989. Lighting's board of directors voted to declare dividends on preferred stock, $10,000.00, and common stock, $23,000.00; date of record, December 31, 1989; date of payment, February 1, 1990. M65.

Feb. 1, 1990. Paid the dividends declared November 25, 1989, $33,000.00. C139.

PROBLEM 15-2   Preparing a corporate work sheet

The general ledger account titles and balances for Tolton, Inc., are recorded on a work sheet in the working papers accompanying this textbook.

Instructions: Complete the work sheet for December 31 of the current year. The following additional information is needed.

Accrued interest income	$ 10.17
Bad debts expense	1,264.05
Inventories, December 31:	
Merchandise inventory	51,450.23
Sales supplies	1,202.70
Delivery supplies	1,052.95
Administrative supplies...	959.85
Value of prepaid insurance..	1,436.58
Prepaid interest expense	1.85

Depreciation expense:
Store equipment.. $1,294.57
Delivery equipment 2,753.16
Office equipment 3,018.64
Building 1,450.00
Organization expense 50.00
Accrued interest expense 4,002.57
Accrued salaries:
Sales 153.97
Delivery 68.51
Administrative... 593.49
Accrued payroll taxes:
FICA tax payable.. 57.12
Unemployment tax payable—federal 6.53
Unemployment tax payable—state 44.06
Accrued federal income tax 41.52

The work sheet prepared in this problem is needed to complete Problems 15-3, 15-4, 15-5, and 15-6.

PROBLEM 15-3   Preparing a corporate income statement

The work sheet prepared in Problem 15-2 is needed to complete this problem.

Instructions: 1. Prepare an income statement for the year ended December 31 of the current year.

2. As part of the income statement figure the following items. (a) Ratio of cost of merchandise sold to net sales. (b) Ratio of gross profit to net sales. (c) Ratio of total operating expenses to net sales. (d) Ratio of net income before federal income tax to net sales. (e) Ratio of federal income tax to net sales. (f) Ratio of net income after federal income tax to net sales. (g) Earnings per share. Tolton has 10,900 shares of $10.00 stated-value common stock issued and 420 shares of $100.00 par-value preferred stock issued. Treasury stock consists of 70 shares of common stock. The dividend rate on preferred stock is 10%.

PROBLEM 15-4   Preparing a corporate statement of stockholders' equity

The work sheet prepared in Problem 15-2 is needed to complete this problem.

Instructions: 1. Prepare a statement of stockholders' equity for the year ended December 31 of the current year. Use the following additional information.

	January 1 Balance	Issued During the Year	December 31 Balance
Common stock:			
No. of shares	10,000	900	10,900
Amount........................	$100,000.00	$ 9,000.00	$109,000.00
Preferred stock:			
No. of shares	320	100	420
Amount........................	$ 32,000.00	$10,000.00	$ 42,000.00

Treasury stock consists of 70 shares of common stock.
The January 1 balance of Retained Earnings was $13,411.26.

2. Figure the following items. (a) Equity per share of stock. (b) Price-earnings ratio. The market price of common stock on December 31 is $11.00.

The statement of stockholders' equity prepared in this problem is needed to complete Problem 15-5.

PROBLEM 15-5   Preparing a corporate balance sheet

The work sheet prepared in Problem 15-2 and the statement of stockholders' equity prepared in Problem 15-4 are needed to complete this problem.

Instructions: 1. Prepare a balance sheet for December 31 of the current year.

2. Figure the following items. (a) Rate earned on average stockholders' equity. Total stockholders' equity on January 1 was $143,951.26. (b) Rate earned on average total assets. Total assets on January 1 were $233,699.75.

PROBLEM 15-6   Completing other end-of-fiscal-period work

The work sheet prepared in Problem 15-2 is needed to complete this problem.

Instructions: 1. Record the adjusting entries on pages 12 and 13 of a general journal.

2. Prepare page 1 of a Form 1120, U.S. Corporation Income Tax Return. The following additional information is needed.

> Business Code No., 5995
> Employer identification number, 65-0243548.
> Date incorporated, January 2, 19--.
> Address: 952 South Liberty Road, Salem, Oregon 97302-6438
> Compensation of officers, $6,609.02.

3. Record the closing entries on pages 14 and 15 of a general journal.

4. Record the reversing entries. Continue to use page 15 of the general journal. Use January 1 of the year following the current year as the date.

ENRICHMENT PROBLEMS

MASTERY PROBLEM 15-M   End-of-fiscal-period work for a corporation

The general ledger account titles and balances for Wescox, Inc., are recorded on a work sheet in the working papers accompanying this textbook.

Instructions: 1. Complete the work sheet for December 31, 1989. The following additional information is needed.

Accrued interest income	$ 17.18
Bad debts expense	2,134.41
Inventories, December 31:	
Merchandise inventory	86,876.38
Sales supplies	2,030.82
Delivery supplies	1,777.97
Administrative supplies	1,620.75
Value of prepaid insurance	2,425.73
Prepaid interest expense	3.12
Depreciation expense:	
Store equipment	5,097.14
Delivery equipment	4,648.86
Office equipment	2,185.95
Building	2,400.00

Organization expense	$	75.00
Accrued interest expense		7,004.34
Accrued salaries:		
Sales		259.98
Delivery		115.67
Administrative		1,002.13
Accrued payroll taxes:		
FICA tax payable		96.45
Unemployment tax payable — federal		11.02
Unemployment tax payable — state		74.40
Accrued federal income tax		24.37

2. Prepare an income statement for the year ended December 31, 1989. As part of the income statement figure the following items. (a) Ratio of cost of merchandise sold to net sales. (b) Ratio of gross profit to net sales. (c) Ratio of total operating expenses to net sales. (d) Ratio of net income before federal income tax to net sales. (e) Ratio of federal income tax to net sales. (f) Ratio of net income after federal income tax to net sales. (g) Earnings per share. Wescox has 18,400 shares of $10.00 stated-value common stock issued and 720 shares of $100.00 par-value preferred stock issued. Treasury stock consists of 120 shares of common stock. The dividend rate on preferred stock is 10%.

3. Prepare a statement of stockholders' equity for the year ended December 31, 1989. Use the following additional information.

	January 1 Balance	Issued During the Year	December 31 Balance
Common stock:			
No. of shares	18,000	400	18,400
Amount	$180,000.00	$ 4,000.00	$184,000.00
Preferred stock:			
No. of shares	600	120	720
Amount	$ 60,000.00	$12,000.00	$ 72,000.00

The January 1 balance of Retained Earnings was $22,645.60

4. Figure the following items based on information on the statement of stockholders' equity. (a) Equity per share of stock. (b) Price-earnings ratio. The market price of common stock on December 31 is $10.00.

5. Prepare a balance sheet for December 31, 1989.

6. Figure the following items based on information from the balance sheet. (a) Rate earned on average stockholders' equity. Total stockholders' equity on January 1 was $260,485.60. (b) Rate earned on average total assets. Total assets on January 1 were $347,548.29.

7. Record the adjusting entries on pages 12 and 13 of a general journal.

8. Record the closing entries on pages 14 and 15 of a general journal.

9. Record the reversing entries. Continue to use page 15 of the general journal. Use January 1, 1990, as the date.

10. Record the following selected transactions on page 17 of a general journal and page 21 of a cash payments journal. Source documents are abbreviated as follows: check, C; memorandum, M.

Nov. 24, 1990. Wescox's board of directors voted to declare dividends on preferred stock, $7,200.00, and common stock, $24,437.50; date of record, December 31, 1990; date of payment, February 1, 1991. M72.

Feb. 1, 1991. Paid the dividends declared November 24, 1990, $31,637.50. C164.

CHALLENGE PROBLEM 15-C   End-of-fiscal-period work for a corporation

The general ledger account titles and balances for Knoll, Inc., are recorded on a work sheet in the working papers accompanying this textbook.

Instructions: 1. Complete the work sheet for December 31 of the current year. The following additional information is needed.

Accrued interest income	$ 10.31
Bad debts expense	1,280.65
Inventories, December 31:	
Merchandise inventory	67,287.92
Sales supplies	1,218.49
Delivery supplies	1,066.78
Administrative supplies	972.45
Value of prepaid insurance	1,455.44
Prepaid interest expense	1.87
Depreciation expense:	
Store equipment	1,311.57
Delivery equipment	2,789.31
Office equipment	3,058.28
Building	1,450.00
Organization expense	50.00
Accrued interest expense	4,002.64
Accrued salaries:	
Sales	155.99
Delivery	69.40
Administrative	601.28
Accrued payroll taxes:	
FICA tax payable	57.87
Unemployment tax payable—federal	6.61
Unemployment tax payable—state	44.64

Federal income tax for the year is figured at the following rates:
15% of the first $25,000.00 net income before taxes.
18% of the next $25,000.00 net income before taxes.
30% of the next $25,000.00 net income before taxes.
40% of the next $25,000.00 net income before taxes.
46% of the net income before taxes above $100,000.00.

2. Prepare an income statement for the year ended December 31 of the current year. As part of the income statement figure the following items. (a) Ratio of cost of merchandise sold to net sales. (b) Ratio of gross profit to net sales. (c) Ratio of total operating expenses to net sales. (d) Ratio of net income before federal income tax to net sales. (e) Ratio of federal income tax to net sales. (f) Ratio of net income after federal income tax to net sales. (g) Earnings per share. Knoll has 11,000 shares of $10.00 stated-value common stock issued and 430 shares of $100.00 par-value preferred stock issued. Treasury stock consists of 70 shares of common stock. The dividend rate on preferred stock is 10%.

3. Prepare a statement of stockholders' equity for the year ended December 31 of the current year. Account balances on January 1 were: Capital Stock—Common (10,000 shares), $100,000.00; Capital Stock—Preferred (300 shares), $30,000.00; Retained Earnings, $13,587.36. Treasury stock consists of 70 shares of common stock.

4. Figure the following items based on the statement of stockholders' equity. (a) Equity per share of stock. (b) Price-earnings ratio. The market price of common stock on December 31 is $9.75.

5. Prepare a balance sheet for December 31 of the current year.

6. Figure the following items based on information from the balance sheet. (a) Rate earned on average stockholders' equity. Total stockholders' equity on January 1 was $142,127.36. (b) Rate earned on average total assets. Total assets on January 1 were $199,116.94.

7. Record the adjusting entries on pages 12 and 13 of a general journal.

8. Record the closing entries on pages 14 and 15 of a general journal.

9. Record the reversing entries. Continue to use page 15 of the general journal. Use January 1 of the year following the current year as the date.

Reinforcement Activity 2

Recording Selected Accounting Transactions and Completing End-of-Fiscal-Period Work for a Corporation

This activity reinforces selected learnings from Parts 4 and 5, Chapters 9 through 15.

EASTLAND, INC.

The accounting activities are for Eastland, Inc., a merchandising business organized as a corporation. Eastland sells lumber and related products to building contractors, homeowners, and other consumers. Eastland's fiscal year is from January 1 through December 31.

PART A: RECORDING SELECTED TRANSACTIONS FOR A CORPORATION

In Part A of this reinforcement activity, selected transactions for Eastland, Inc., completed during December of the current year, are journalized.

Eastland uses the chart of accounts shown on the following page. The journals used by Eastland are similar to those illustrated in Parts 4 and 5.

Journalizing selected transactions

Instructions: 1. Record the following selected transactions completed by Eastland during December of the current year. Use a cash receipts journal, a cash payments journal, and a general journal similar to those used in Chapter 10. Eastland records prepaid interest expense initially as an expense. Other prepaid and unearned items are recorded initially as assets and liabilities. Source documents are abbreviated as follows: check, C; memorandum, M; note payable, NP; note receivable, NR; receipt, R.

Dec. 1. Eastland's board of directors voted to declare dividends on preferred stock, $2,020.00, and common stock, $5,890.00; date of record, December 5; date of payment, December 30. M21.

1. Wrote off past due account of Jane Gerard as uncollectible, $166.50. M22.

1. Received three months' rent in advance from Westflake, Inc., $1,800.00. R126.

1. Discarded a store fixture: cost, $200.00; total accumulated depreciation to December 31 of last year, $163.33; additional depreciation for the current year, $36.67. M23.

1. Received a subscription from Myra Delmont for 30 shares of $100.00 par-value preferred stock, $3,000.00. M24.

2. Paid cash for a new office typewriter, $755.00. C296.

EASTLAND, INC.
Chart of Accounts

Balance Sheet Accounts

(1000) ASSETS

1100	Current Assets
1105	Cash
1110	Petty Cash
1115	Notes Receivable
1120	Interest Receivable
1125	Accounts Receivable
1130	Allowance for Uncollectible Accounts
1135	Subscriptions Receivable
1140	Merchandise Inventory
1145	Supplies — Sales
1150	Supplies — Administrative
1155	Prepaid Insurance
1160	Prepaid Interest
1200	Long-Term Investment
1205	Bond Sinking Fund
1300	Plant Assets
1305	Store Equipment
1310	Accumulated Depreciation — Store Equipment
1315	Office Equipment
1320	Accumulated Depreciation — Office Equipment
1325	Building
1330	Accumulated Depreciation — Building
1335	Land
1400	Intangible Asset
1405	Organization Costs

(2000) LIABILITIES

2100	Current Liabilities
2105	Notes Payable
2110	Interest Payable
2115	Accounts Payable
2120	Employees Income Tax Payable
2125	Federal Income Tax Payable
2130	FICA Tax Payable
2135	Salaries Payable
2140	Sales Tax Payable
2145	Unearned Rent
2150	Unemployment Tax Payable — Federal
2155	Unemployment Tax Payable — State
2160	Hospital Insurance Premiums Payable
2165	Dividends Payable
2200	Long-Term Liability
2205	Bonds Payable

(3000) STOCKHOLDERS' EQUITY

3105	Capital Stock — Common
3110	Stock Subscribed — Common
3115	Capital Stock — Preferred
3120	Stock Subscribed — Preferred
3125	Paid-in Capital in Excess of Par/Stated Value
3130	Treasury Stock
3135	Paid-in Capital from Sale of Treasury Stock
3140	Retained Earnings
3145	Dividends — Common Stock
3150	Dividends — Preferred Stock
3155	Income Summary

Income Statement Accounts

(4000) OPERATING REVENUE

4105	Sales
4110	Sales Returns and Allowances
4115	Sales Discount

(5000) COST OF MERCHANDISE

5105	Purchases
5110	Purchases Returns and Allowances
5115	Purchases Discount

(6000) OPERATING EXPENSES

6100	Selling Expenses
6105	Advertising Expense
6110	Credit Card Fee Expense
6115	Depreciation Expense — Store Equipment
6120	Miscellaneous Expense — Sales
6125	Salary Expense — Sales
6130	Supplies Expense — Sales
6200	Administrative Expenses
6205	Bad Debts Expense
6210	Depreciation Expense — Office Equipment
6215	Depreciation Expense — Building
6220	Insurance Expense
6225	Miscellaneous Expense — Administrative
6230	Payroll Taxes Expense
6235	Property Tax Expense
6240	Salary Expense — Administrative
6245	Supplies Expense — Administrative
6250	Utilities Expense

(7000) OTHER REVENUE

7105	Gain on Plant Assets
7110	Interest Income
7115	Rent Income

(8000) OTHER EXPENSES

8105	Interest Expense
8110	Loss on Plant Assets
8115	Organization Expense

(9000) INCOME TAX

9105	Federal Income Tax

4. Rick Plunkett dishonored NR4 due today: principal, $150.00; interest, $3.70. M25.
4. Discarded an office table: cost, $250.00; total accumulated depreciation to December 31 of last year, $150.00; additional depreciation for the current year, $50.00. M26.
4. Received a 60-day, 10% note receivable from Alice Wendson for an extension of time on her account, $500.00. NR5.
5. Issued a 6-month, 10% note payable to First Trust Bank, $2,000.00. NP6.
5. Paid to bond trustee for annual interest on bond issue, $24,000.00. C297.
5. Paid to bond trustee for annual deposit to bond sinking fund, $20,000.00, less interest earned on bond sinking fund, $1,600.00. C298.
6. Received from Jane Miller for 700 shares of $10.00 stated-value common stock at $11.00 per share, $7,700.00. R134.
7. Received from David Jones in settlement of NR1: $150.00, plus interest, $2.47. R136.
11. Received $70.00 for an office typewriter: cost, $700.00; total accumulated depreciation to December 31 of last year, $500.00; additional depreciation for the current year, $100.00. M28 and R138.
11. Paid to Lois Breize for 60 shares of $10.00 stated-value common stock at $9.00 per share, $540.00. C302.
12. Paid First Trust Bank $306.00 for NP4, $300.00, plus interest, $6.00. C303.
13. Received from John Mikey for 200 shares of $10.00 stated-value common stock at $10.00 per share, $2,000.00. R140.
14. Received from Allison Mickleson in settlement of NR2: $247.50, plus interest, $4.07. R141.
16. Paid First National Bank $1,016.44 for NP3, $1,000.00, plus interest, $16.44. C309.
19. Received an office copier from J. Oldy at an agreed value of $1,000.00 for 10 shares of $100.00 par-value preferred stock. M30.
20. Received full payment for Jane Gerard's account, previously written off as uncollectible, $166.50. M31 and R143.
21. Paid cash, $800.00, plus an old office typewriter, for a new typewriter: cost of old typewriter, $1,000.00; total accumulated depreciation to December 31 of last year, $720.00; additional depreciation for the current year, $90.00. M32 and C315.
27. Discounted at 12% at First National Bank a 60-day note, $5,000.00; discount, $98.63; proceeds, $4,901.37. NP7.
28. Received from John Relway for 10 shares of treasury stock at $13.00 per share, $130.00. Treasury stock was bought on December 11 at $9.00 per share. R146.
29. Received $800.00 for an old cash register used in sales: cost, $1,600.00; total accumulated depreciation to December 31 of last year, $896.00; additional depreciation for the current year, $144.00. M36 and R147.
29. Received from Rick Plunkett for dishonored NR4: principal, $153.70, plus additional interest, $1.05. R148.
29. Received from Myra Delmont in payment of stock subscription, $3,000.00. Issued Stock Certificate No. 14 for 30 shares of $100.00 par-value preferred stock. M37 and R149.
30. Paid the dividends declared December 1, $7,910.00. C319.

2. Prove and rule the cash receipts and cash payments journals.

PART B: COMPLETING END-OF-FISCAL-PERIOD WORK

In Part B, Eastland's end-of-fiscal-period work is completed. This work is similar to activities described in Chapter 15. The December 31 trial balance is recorded on a work sheet in the working papers accompanying this textbook.

Instructions: 3. Complete the work sheet for December 31 of the current year. Use the following information for adjustments.

Accrued interest income	$ 3.70
Bad debts expense	223.47
Inventories, December 31:	
Merchandise inventory.	141,318.63
Sales supplies	1,417.85
Administrative supplies	730.00
Value of prepaid insurance	970.00
Prepaid interest expense	92.06
Depreciation expense:	
Store equipment	8,300.00
Office equipment.	1,150.00
Building.	1,500.00
Organization expense	300.00
Accrued interest expense	2,025.00
Accrued salaries:	
Sales	3,232.04
Administrative	716.50
Accrued payroll taxes:	
FICA tax payable	276.40
Unemployment tax payable — federal.	15.79
Unemployment tax payable — state	106.58
Rent received in advance and still unearned	1,200.00
Accrued federal income tax	896.87

4. Prepare an income statement for the year ended December 31 of the current year. As part of the income statement figure the following items. (a) Ratio of cost of merchandise sold to net sales. (b) Ratio of gross profit to net sales. (c) Ratio of total operating expenses to net sales. (d) Ratio of net income before federal income tax to net sales. (e) Ratio of federal income tax to net sales. (f) Ratio of net income after federal income tax to net sales. (g) Earnings per share. Eastland has 12,680 shares of $10.00 stated-value common stock issued and 444 shares of $100.00 par-value preferred stock issued. Treasury stock consists of 50 shares of common stock. The dividend rate on the preferred stock is 10%. There are 12,630 shares of common stock outstanding.

5. Prepare a statement of stockholders' equity for the year ended December 31 of the current year. Use the following additional information.

	January 1 Balance	Issued During the Year	December 31 Balance
Common stock:			
No. of shares	11,780	900	12,680
Amount.	$117,800.00	$9,000.00	$126,800.00
Preferred stock:			
No. of shares	404	40	444
Amount.	$ 40,400.00	$4,000.00	$ 44,400.00
Treasury stock (common stock):			
No. of shares	0	50	50
Amount	0	$ 450.00	$ 450.00

The January 1 balance of Retained Earnings was $23,759.39.

6. Figure the following items based on information on the statement of stockholders' equity. (a) Equity per share of stock. (b) Price-earnings ratio. The market price of common stock on December 31 of the current year is $10.00.

7. Prepare a balance sheet for December 31 of the current year.

8. Figure the following items based on information from the balance sheet. (a) Rate earned on average stockholders' equity. Total stockholders' equity on January 1 of the current year was $182,759.39. (b) Rate earned on average total assets. Total assets on January 1 of the current year were $399,822.40. (c) Accounts receivable turnover ratio. Account balances on January 1 of the current year were as follows. Accounts Receivable, $27,614.63; Allowance for Uncollectible Accounts, $436.04. The total net sales on account for the year were $234,436.51. (d) Average number of days for payment.

9. Record the adjusting entries on pages 13 and 14 of a general journal.

10. Record the closing entries on pages 14 and 15 of a general journal.

11. Record the reversing entries. Continue to use page 15 of the general journal. Use January 1 of the year following the current year as the date.

Computer Application 5
Automated Accounting Cycle
for a Corporation: Completing
End-of-Fiscal-Period Work

Manual accounting procedures for completing end-of-fiscal-period work for a corporation are described in Chapter 15. Computer Application 5 provides for the use of a microcomputer to complete end-of-fiscal-period work for a corporation. Computer Application 5 contains instructions for using a microcomputer to solve Mastery Problem 15-M, Chapter 15.

COMPUTER APPLICATION PROBLEM

COMPUTER APPLICATION PROBLEM 5 Completing end-of-fiscal-period work

Instructions: 1. Load the Systems Selection Menu from the *Advanced Automated Accounting* diskette according to the instructions for the computer being used. Select Problem CA-5. The general ledger chart of accounts and current balances have been entered and stored on the template diskette.

2. Display/Print the trial balance.

3. Refer to Mastery Problem 15-M, Chapter 15, Instruction 1. Record the adjusting entries on journal entries input forms. Use December 31, 1989, as the run date. Batch No. 54. Write ADJ.ENT. in the Doc. No. column, line 1. Account numbers needed are given on the following page.

4. Key-enter adjustment data from the completed journal entries input forms.

5. Display/Print the journal entries report for adjusting entries. Check the accuracy by comparing the report totals with the batch totals on the input form.

6. Display/Print the income statement.

7. Display/Print the balance sheet.

8. Close the general ledger.

9. Refer to Problem 15-M, Instruction 9. Record the reversing entries on a journal entries input form. Use January 1,1990, as the run date. Batch No. 1. Write REV.ENT. in the Doc. No. column, line 1.

Acct. No.	Account Title	Acct. No.	Account Title
1105	Cash	6115	Depr. Exp. — Store Equip.
1120	Interest Receivable	6125	Salary Expense — Sales
1130	Allow. for Uncoll. Accts.	6130	Supplies Expense — Sales
1135	Merchandise Inventory	6205	Depr. Exp. — Delivery Equip.
	(balance, $87,146.53)	6215	Salary Expense — Delivery
1140	Supplies — Sales	6220	Supplies Expense — Delivery
	(balance, $4,893.53)	6305	Bad Debts Expense
1145	Supplies — Delivery	6310	Depr. Exp. — Office Equip.
	(balance, $6,195.01)	6315	Depr. Exp. — Building
1150	Supplies — Administrative	6320	Insurance Expense
	(balance, $8,485.59)	6330	Payroll Taxes Expense
1155	Prepaid Insurance	6340	Salary Expense — Admin.
	(balance, $6,871.77)	6345	Supplies Expense — Admin.
1160	Prepaid Interest	7105	Interest Income
1310	Accum. Depr. — Store Equip.	8105	Interest Expense
1320	Accum. Depr. — Delivery Equip.	8110	Organization Expense
1330	Accum. Depr. — Office Equip.	9105	Federal Income Tax
1340	Accum. Depr. — Building		
1405	Organization Costs		
2110	Interest Payable		
2125	Federal Income Tax Payable		
2130	FICA Tax Payable		
2135	Salaries Payable		
2145	Unemployment Tax Payable — Federal		
2150	Unemployment Tax Payable — State		
2160	Dividends Payable		
3140	Dividends — Common Stock		
3145	Dividends — Preferred Stock		
3150	Income Summary		

10. Key-enter the data from the journal entries input form.

11. Display/Print the journal entries report for reversing entries. Check the accuracy of the report.

12. Refer to Problem 15-M, Instruction 10. Record the November 24, 1990, declaration of dividends on a journal entries input form. Use November 24, 1990, as the run date. Batch No. 49.

13. Key-enter the data from the journal entries input form.

14. Display/Print the journal entries report for the declaration of dividends. Check the accuracy of the report.

15. Refer to Problem 15-M, Instruction 10. Record the February 1, 1991, payment of dividends declared on a journal entries input form. Use February 2, 1991, as the run date. Batch No. 6.

16. Key-enter the data from the journal entries input form.

17. Display/Print the journal entries report for the payment of dividends declared. Check the accuracy of the report.

GreenGrow, Inc., is a merchandising business organized as a corporation. This business simulation covers the realistic transactions completed by GreenGrow, Inc., which sells garden equipment. The activities included in the accounting cycle for GreenGrow, Inc., are listed below. This simulation is available from the publisher.

Activities in GreenGrow, Inc.

1. Recording selected transactions in special journals and a general journal.
2. Posting items to be posted individually to a general ledger and subsidiary ledgers.
3. Proving and ruling the journals.
4. Posting column totals to a general ledger.
5. Preparing schedules of accounts receivable and accounts payable.
6. Preparing a trial balance on a work sheet.
7. Planning adjustments and completing a work sheet.
8. Preparing financial statements.
9. Recording and posting adjusting entries.
10. Recording and posting closing entries.
11. Preparing a post-closing trial balance.

6
Management Accounting

GENERAL BEHAVIORAL GOALS

1. Know accounting terminology related to management accounting for a corporation.
2. Understand accounting concepts and practices related to management accounting for a corporation.
3. Demonstrate management accounting procedures for a corporation.

SUNTROL, INC.
Chart of Accounts

Balance Sheet Accounts

(1000) ASSETS

1100 Current Assets

1105	Cash
1110	Petty Cash
1115	Notes Receivable
1120	Interest Receivable
1125	Accounts Receivable
1130	Allowance for Uncollectible Accounts
1135	Merchandise Inventory
1140	Supplies — Sales
1145	Supplies — Office
1150	Prepaid Insurance

1200 Plant Assets

1205	Equipment — Delivery
1210	Accumulated Depreciation — Delivery Equipment
1215	Equipment — Office
1220	Accumulated Depreciation — Office Equipment
1225	Equipment — Warehouse
1230	Accumulated Depreciation — Warehouse Equipment

(2000) LIABILITIES

2100 Current Liabilities

2105	Notes Payable
2110	Interest Payable
2115	Accounts Payable
2120	Employees Income Tax Payable
2125	Federal Income Tax Payable
2130	FICA Tax Payable
2135	Sales Tax Payable
2140	Unemployment Tax Payable — Federal
2145	Unemployment Tax Payable — State
2150	Dividends Payable

2200 Long-Term Liability

2205	Mortgage Payable

(3000) CAPITAL

3105	Capital Stock
3110	Retained Earnings
3115	Dividends
3120	Income Summary

Income Statement Accounts

(4000) OPERATING REVENUE

4105	Sales
4110	Sales Returns and Allowances
4115	Sales Discount

(5000) COST OF MERCHANDISE

5105	Purchases
5110	Purchases Returns and Allowances
5115	Purchases Discount

(6000) OPERATING EXPENSES

6100 Selling Expenses

6105	Advertising Expense
6110	Delivery Expense
6115	Depreciation Expense — Delivery Equipment
6120	Depreciation Expense — Warehouse Equipment
6125	Miscellaneous Expense — Sales
6130	Salary Expense — Commissions
6135	Salary Expense — Regular
6140	Supplies Expense — Sales

6200 Administrative Expenses

6205	Bad Debts Expense
6210	Depreciation Expense — Office Equipment
6215	Insurance Expense
6220	Miscellaneous Expense — Administrative
6225	Payroll Taxes Expense
6230	Rent Expense
6235	Salary Expense — Administrative
6240	Supplies Expense — Office
6245	Utilities Expense

(7000) OTHER REVENUE

7105	Gain on Plant Assets
7110	Interest Income

(8000) OTHER EXPENSES

8105	Interest Expense
8110	Loss on Plant Assets

(9000) INCOME TAX

9105	Federal Income Tax

The chart of accounts for Suntrol, Inc., is illustrated above for ready reference as you study Part 6 of this textbook.

16 Inventory Planning and Valuation

ENABLING PERFORMANCE TASKS

After studying Chapter 16, you will be able to:
a. Define accounting terms related to planning and valuing inventory.
b. Identify accounting concepts and practices related to planning, counting, and valuing inventory.
c. Value a merchandise inventory using selected costing methods.
d. Estimate a merchandise inventory using selected estimating methods.
e. Figure merchandise inventory turnover ratio and average number of days' sales in merchandise inventory.

A merchandising business must have appropriate merchandise on hand. A merchandising business with merchandise on hand that customers do not want will make few sales. The planning for and valuing of the merchandise on hand is important to a merchandising business.

NATURE OF MERCHANDISE INVENTORY

Merchandise is continually being purchased and sold. The actual merchandise inventory changes from day to day. The flow of inventory costs through a business' records is shown in Illustration 16-1.

The cost of the merchandise available for sale consists of two elements.

1. The value of the beginning merchandise inventory.
2. The value of the net purchases added to the inventory during the fiscal period.

At the end of each fiscal period, the cost of the merchandise available for sale is divided into two parts.

3. The value of the ending merchandise inventory. The ending merchandise inventory represents a *current* asset value that will be charged as costs in *future* fiscal periods.

Illustration 16-1
Flow of inventory costs
through a business'
records

4. The cost of the merchandise sold during the *current* fiscal period. This cost materially affects the amount of net income reported for the fiscal period. *(CONCEPT: Adequate Disclosure)*

Effect of errors in valuing an inventory

The value of both beginning and ending merchandise inventory affects items on an income statement, a statement of stockholders' equity, and a balance sheet. The effect is shown in Illustration 16-2.

Reports and Items Affected	If Ending Inventory is	
	Understated	Overstated
Income Statement:		
Cost of Merchandise Sold	Overstated	Understated
Gross Profit................................	Understated	Overstated
Net Income	Understated	Overstated
Statement of Stockholders' Equity:		
Net Income	Understated	Overstated
Retained Earnings...........................	Understated	Overstated
Stockholders' Equity	Understated	Overstated
Balance Sheet:		
Merchandise Inventory	Understated	Overstated
Total Assets	Understated	Overstated
Stockholders' Equity	Understated	Overstated

Illustration 16-2
Effect of errors in valuing
merchandise inventory

An accurate merchandise inventory value must be determined to adequately report the progress and condition of a merchandising business. *(CONCEPT: Adequate Disclosure)* If the inventory is understated, the net income will be understated. As a result, total assets and total stockholders' equity will be understated. If the inventory is overstated, the reverse will be true, and additional income tax must be paid on the overstated income. In neither situation will accurate information be reported on financial statements. *(CONCEPT: Adequate Disclosure)*

Costs to include in an inventory's value

The value placed on a merchandise inventory should include two costs.

1. The price paid to vendors for the merchandise. The price paid includes the purchase invoice amount less discounts, returns, and allowances granted by the vendors.
2. The costs involved in getting the merchandise to the place of business and ready for sale. This cost includes transportation charges paid by the buyer.

Goods to include in an inventory's count

Typically, a business counts as part of its inventory all merchandise for sale legally owned by the business. When title to goods passes to the buyer, the goods become part of the buyer's inventory regardless of where the goods are physically located.

Goods in transit. A vendor's terms of sale may include the provision *FOB shipping point.* FOB is an abbreviation for the phrase Free On Board. FOB shipping point means that the buyer pays the transportation charges. Under FOB shipping point terms, the title to the goods passes to the buyer as soon as the vendor delivers the goods to a transportation business. These goods in transit, but not yet received by the buyer, are part of the *buyer's* inventory.

If the terms of sale are *FOB destination,* the vendor pays the transportation charges. Title to these goods passes to the buyer when the goods are received by the buyer. These goods in transit, but not yet received by the buyer, are part of the *vendor's* inventory.

Goods on consignment. Goods which are given to a business to sell, but for which title to the goods remains with the vendor, are called a consignment. The person or business who receives goods on consignment is called the consignee. The person who gives goods on consignment is called the consignor.

The consignee agrees to receive, care for, and attempt to sell the consigned goods. If the goods are sold, the consignee deducts a commission from the sale amount, and the remainder is sent to the consignor. In a consignment, title to the goods does not pass to the consignee. The goods on consignment are part of the consignor's inventory.

A consignee agrees to give goods on consignment due care and to make adequate attempts to sell the goods. Therefore, a consignee has implied liabilities if anything should happen to the goods before they are sold. A consignee often reports the value of consigned goods as an attachment or footnote to the business' balance sheet.

Many methods may be used to place a value on merchandise inventory. A specific business usually uses a method that best matches a fiscal period's revenue and costs for that business. *(CONCEPT: Matching Expenses with Revenue)*

INVENTORY COUNT

Valuing an inventory starts with determining the number of each item on hand. Sometimes the number on hand is obtained by physically counting the individual items. Sometimes the number on hand is obtained by keeping a continuous record showing the number purchased and sold for each merchandise item.

Perpetual inventory

Merchandise inventory determined by keeping a continuous record of increases, decreases, and balance on hand is known as a perpetual inventory. Suntrol, Inc., sells custom-made louvered window blinds and keeps a perpetual inventory of parts and finished blinds.

A perpetual inventory provides day-to-day records about the quantity of merchandise on hand. Based on the records, management knows when the inventory is low and additional merchandise should be ordered. A record is kept of the number on hand, purchases, and sales of each kind of merchandise. A form used to show kind of merchandise, quantity received, quantity sold, and balance on hand is called a stock record. A file of stock records for all merchandise on hand is called a stock ledger.

In addition to other information on a stock record, a notation is made of the minimum balance at which a reorder is to be placed. For example, Suntrol determines that four weeks is required to order and to receive a shipment of window brackets from a vendor. Suntrol also determines that in a four week period, an average of 400 window brackets will be used. Therefore, Suntrol has established 400 as the minimum balance before a reorder is sent to a vendor. Each reorder is to be for 2,000 items.

Suntrol's stock record card for window brackets is shown in Illustration 16-3.

On January 1, 1989, the corporation had 1,200 window brackets on hand as shown in column 7 of the stock record card. On January 31, 380 window brackets are issued to installers to use with louvered blinds sold to customers. This decrease is recorded on the stock record card as shown in columns 4–6. On February 28, another 440 brackets are issued. After the decrease on February 28, Suntrol had 380 brackets remaining as shown in column 7. That number on hand, 380, is below the minimum count of 400. Therefore, on February 28 a purchase order for 2,000 brackets is prepared and sent to a vendor. On March 20, another 100 brackets are used, and the balance is reduced to 280.

STOCK RECORD						
Description *Window brackets*					Stock No. *B452*	
Reorder *2,000*		Minimum *400*			Location *Bin 56*	
1	2	3	4	5	6	7
INCREASES			DECREASES			BALANCE
Date	Purchase Invoice No.	Quantity	Date	Sales Invoice No.	Quantity	Quantity
1989 *Jan. 1*						*1,200*
			Jan. 31	*254*	*380*	*820*
			Feb. 28	*519*	*440*	*380*
			Mar. 20	*713*	*100*	*280*
Mar. 30	*147*	*2,000*				*2,280*
			Dec. 15	*1845*	*200*	*1,200*

Illustration 16-3
Stock record card

On March 30, 2,000 brackets are received from the vendor and recorded on the stock record card as shown in columns 1–3. The new balance of brackets on hand, 2,280, is recorded in column 7.

On December 31, 1989, when a merchandise inventory count is needed, Suntrol uses the last amount shown in column 7 of each stock record card. For example, in Illustration 16-3 the December 31 inventory count for window brackets is 1,200.

> Cost (or purchase) prices change from time to time. Therefore, Suntrol does not record cost prices on stock record cards. When needed, cost prices are obtained from copies of purchase invoices.

Periodic inventory

Merchandise inventory determined by counting, weighing, or measuring merchandise on hand is known as a periodic inventory. The counting, weighing, or measuring of items on hand for a periodic inventory is known as "taking an inventory." For businesses with a large quantity of merchandise on hand, taking a merchandise inventory count is expensive. For this reason, businesses usually take a periodic merchandise inventory only once each fiscal period.

When only a periodic inventory is used, a business must check carefully each day to determine if the quantity of any inventory item is low. However, the low quantity of a merchandise item can be overlooked. When this happens, the business may not have the merchandise when customers want it. For this reason, Suntrol uses a perpetual inventory method. Errors can occur however even when a perpetual inventory method is used. Suntrol therefore takes a periodic inventory once each year to check the accuracy of the perpetual inventory.

In taking a periodic inventory, Suntrol uses an inventory record as shown in Illustration 16-4.

	INVENTORY RECORD			
Date November 30, 1989				
1	2	3	4	5
Stock Number	Description	On Hand	Unit Cost	Total Cost
S351	Window brackets	50	1.00	50.00
S352	Window brackets	100	.75	75.00
	Total			57,960.00

Illustration 16-4
Inventory record

The inventory record is completed in five steps.

1 The stock numbers and descriptions are recorded on the form in columns 1 and 2. The data are obtained from sales records.

2 The actual count of items on hand is written in column 3.

3 The cost per item is recorded in column 4. The data are obtained from purchase invoices.

4 The total cost for each item is figured and recorded in column 5. Total cost for each item is figured by multiplying the unit cost, column 4, by the number of items on hand, column 3.

5 Column 5 is totaled. The total of column 5, $57,960.00, is the total value of the ending merchandise inventory.

The periodic inventory count is compared to the perpetual inventory, and any differences are adjusted on the stock record cards.

INVENTORY VALUE

Once Suntrol takes a periodic inventory, a dollar cost is determined for each item. *(CONCEPT: Unit of Measurement)* The unit costs are obtained from purchase invoices. For example, in Illustration 16-4 the 50 S351 window brackets have a unit cost of $1.00 and a total cost of $50.00. The 100 S352 window brackets have a unit cost of $0.75 and a total value of $75.00. Different methods exist for selecting the value to use for inventory items.

Fifo method

Charging the cost of merchandise purchased first to the cost of merchandise sold first is called the first-in, first-out inventory costing method. *Fifo* is an abbreviation for first in, first out. The fifo method of determining the value of merchandise on hand assumes that the merchandise purchased first (first in) is the merchandise sold first (first out). Thus, the fifo method uses the most recent purchase prices. For example, Suntrol has an inventory of 150 yards of blue pull cording. If Suntrol used the fifo method, the cording would be valued as shown in Illustration 16-5.

Fifo Inventory Costing Method				
Purchase			Ending Inventory	
Date	Quantity (yards)	Unit Price	Quantity (yards)	Value
May, 1989	100	$1.90	0	0.00
October, 1989	100	2.00	50	$100.00
November, 1989 . . .	100	2.25	100	225.00
Totals			150	$325.00

Illustration 16-5
Inventory values figured using the fifo method

Of the 150 yards of cording on hand, 100 yards are assumed to be from the most recent purchase, November, 1989, at $2.25 per yard. The remaining 50 yards are assumed to have been purchased on the next most recent date, October, 1989, at $2.00 per yard. None is considered part of the 100 yards purchased on the earliest date, May, 1989, at $1.90 per yard. The total value, using the fifo method, is $325.00. The cording purchased in May is the *first in*. Therefore, the business assumes that the cording purchased in May is also the *first out,* or first sold.

Lifo method

Charging the cost of merchandise purchased last to the cost of merchandise sold first is called the last-in, first-out inventory costing method. *Lifo* is an abbreviation for last in, first out. The lifo method of determining the value of merchandise on hand assumes that the merchandise purchased *last* (last in) is the merchandise sold *first* (first out). Thus, the lifo method uses the earliest purchase prices. If Suntrol used the lifo method, the 150 yards of blue pull cording would be valued as shown in Illustration 16-6.

Of the 150 yards currently on hand, 100 yards are assumed to have been purchased on the earliest date, May, 1989, at $1.90 per yard. The remaining 50 yards are assumed to have been purchased on the next earliest date, October, 1989, at $2.00 per yard. None is considered to be part of the 100 yards purchased on the most recent date, November, 1989, at $2.25 per yard. The total value, using the lifo method, is $290.00. The cording purchased in November is the *last in*. Therefore, the business assumes that the cording purchased in November is also the *first out,* or first sold.

Lifo Inventory Costing Method				
Purchase			Ending Inventory	
Date	Quantity (yards)	Unit Price	Quantity (yards)	Value
May, 1989	100	$1.90	100	$190.00
October, 1989	100	2.00	50	100.00
November, 1989 . . .	100	2.25	0	0.00
Totals			150	$290.00

Illustration 16-6
Inventory values figured using the lifo method

Weighted-average method

Charging the average cost of beginning inventory plus merchandise purchased during a fiscal period to the cost of merchandise sold is called the weighted-average inventory costing method. This method is based on the assumption that the value is an average of the price paid for similar items purchased during the accounting period. If Suntrol used the weighted-average method, the value of the 150 yards of blue pull cording would be figured as shown in Illustration 16-7.

Weighted-Average Inventory Costing Method Quantity on Hand, 150 yards			
Purchase			Cost Value
Date	Quantity (yards)	Unit Price	
May, 1989	100	$1.90	$190.00
October, 1989	100	2.00	200.00
November, 1989	100	2.25	225.00
Totals	300		$615.00

Total Cost Value		Total Quantity Purchased		Average Cost per Yard
$615.00	÷	300	=	$2.05

Average Cost per Yard		Quantity on Hand		Ending Inventory Value
$2.05	×	150 yards	=	$307.50

Illustration 16-7
Inventory values figured using the weighted-average method

The 150 yards of cording currently on hand are assumed to have been purchased at an average cost of $2.05 per yard. Therefore, the total value, using the weighted-average method, is $307.50.

Valuing inventory during periods of changing prices

In the situations for valuing inventory previously described in this chapter, prices increased from $1.90 to $2.25 per yard. Sometimes prices decrease and the results change when using the previously described inventory costing methods.

Valuing inventory during a period of increasing prices. Three ways of valuing an inventory of 150 yards of blue pull cording during a period of increasing prices are summarized in Illustration 16-8.

Summary of Three Methods of Valuing Inventory of 150 Yards of Blue Pull Cording during a Period of Increasing Prices						Weighted-Average Method
Purchase		Fifo Method		Lifo Method		
Date	Cost	Quantity	Value	Quantity	Value	
May, 1989	$1.90	0	0.00	100	$190.00	Average Cost $2.05
Oct., 1989	2.00	50	$100.00	50	100.00	
Nov., 1989	2.25	100	225.00	0	0.00	
Totals		150	$325.00	150	$290.00	$307.50

The value of the ending inventory affects the cost of merchandise sold amount on an income statement. The higher the ending inventory, the lower the cost of merchandise sold amount, and vice versa. Therefore, during a period of *increasing prices,* the fifo method usually will result in the lowest cost of merchandise sold. The lifo method usually will result in the highest cost of merchandise sold.

The higher the cost of merchandise sold, the lower the net income reported on financial statements, and vice versa. Therefore, during a period of *increasing prices,* the fifo method usually will result in the highest reported net income. The lifo method usually will result in the lowest reported net income.

Valuing inventory during a period of decreasing prices. If Suntrol valued its inventory during a period of decreasing prices, the three inventory costing methods would be summarized as shown in Illustration 16-9.

Illustration 16-8
Summary of three methods of valuing inventory during periods of increasing prices

Illustration 16-9
Summary of three methods of valuing inventory during periods of decreasing prices

Summary of Three Methods of Valuing Inventory of 150 Yards of Blue Pull Cording during a Period of Decreasing Prices						Weighted-Average Method
Purchase		Fifo Method		Lifo Method		
Date	Cost	Quantity	Value	Quantity	Value	
May, 1989	$2.25	0	0.00	100	$225.00	Average Cost $2.05
Oct., 1989	2.00	50	$100.00	50	100.00	
Nov., 1989	1.90	100	190.00	0	0.00	
Totals		150	$290.00	150	$325.00	$307.50

During a period of *decreasing prices,* as shown in Illustration 16-9, the fifo method usually results in the lowest merchandise inventory value. This lower inventory value results in a higher cost of merchandise sold and a lower net income. During a period of *decreasing prices,* the lifo method usually results in the highest merchandise inventory value. This higher inventory value results in a lower cost of merchandise sold and a higher net income.

A comparison of three methods of valuing inventory during periods of increasing or decreasing prices is shown in Illustration 16-10.

Comparison of Three Methods of Valuing Inventory during Periods of Increasing or Decreasing Prices			
Prices are	Total Inventory Value Using		
	Fifo Method	Lifo Method	Weighted-Average Method
Increasing	$325.00	$290.00	$307.50
Decreasing	$290.00	$325.00	$307.50

Illustration 16-10
Comparison of three
methods of valuing
inventory

Each business selects the method of valuing merchandise inventory that best fits that business' policies and goals. Businesses select one method of valuing merchandise inventory and use it for a number of years. In this way, the information on a series of financial statements can be compared easily. *(CONCEPT: Consistent Reporting)* Suntrol uses the weighted-average method because that is the easiest to figure with the kind of merchandise being sold.

LOWER OF COST OR MARKET METHOD

Charging the lower of cost or market price to the ending merchandise inventory is called the lower of cost or market inventory costing method. When merchandise is purchased, the value is recorded at cost price. *(CONCEPT: Historical Cost)* If the cost price is higher than the market price at the end of a fiscal period, the inventory is reduced to the market price. However, if the purchase or cost price is lower than the market price, the inventory is maintained at the cost price.

Two amounts are needed to apply the lower of cost or market method. (1) The value of the inventory using the fifo, lifo, or weighted-average method. (2) The current market price of the inventory. These two amounts are then compared, and the lower of the two is used to value the inventory. For example, Suntrol uses the weighted-average method of costing an inventory. The weighted-average cost and the current market price for 150 yards of blue pull cording are shown in Illustration 16-11. The weighted-average cost is $307.50 and the current market price is $300.00. In the lower of cost or market method, the market price of the blue pull cording is lower than the weighted average cost. Therefore the cording is valued at the market price of $300.00.

Lower of Cost or Market Inventory Costing Method			
Costing Method	Cost Price	Market Price (150 yards × $2.00 current market price)	Lower of Cost or Market
Weighted-Average	$307.50	$300.00	$300.00
Fifo	325.00	300.00	300.00
Lifo	290.00	300.00	290.00

If Suntrol used the fifo method, the fifo cost would be $325.00. The $300.00 market price is lower than the fifo cost, so the market price would be used instead of the fifo cost. If Suntrol used the lifo method, the lifo cost would be $290.00. The lifo cost is lower than the market price, so the lifo cost would be used to value the inventory.

Illustration 16-11
Inventory values using lower of cost or market method

ESTIMATED MERCHANDISE INVENTORY VALUE

A business that prepares monthly interim financial statements needs a value for monthly ending merchandise inventory. But, taking a monthly periodic inventory is usually too expensive to be worthwhile. Therefore, monthly ending inventories may be estimated.

Two methods that may be used to estimate an ending merchandise inventory are (1) gross profit method, and (2) retail method.

Gross profit method

Estimating ending merchandise inventory by using previous years' percentage of gross profit on operations is known as the gross profit method of estimating inventory. The gross profit method of estimating inventory is based on the assumption that a continuing relationship exists between gross profit and net sales. Based on experience in previous fiscal periods, a gross profit to net sales percentage is figured.

Suntrol's estimated ending merchandise inventory on November 30, 1989, using the gross profit method, is figured as shown in Illustration 16-12.

1 January 1 beginning inventory, $55,890.00, line 1, is obtained from the merchandise inventory account in the general ledger.

Illustration 16-12
Estimating ending
merchandise inventory
using the gross profit
method

ESTIMATED MERCHANDISE INVENTORY SHEET
Gross Profit Method

Company _Suntrol, Inc._   Date _11-30-89_

1	Beginning inventory, January 1		$ 55,890.00
2	Net purchases to date		664,010.00
3	Merchandise available for sale		$ 719,900.00
4	Net sales to date	$1,425,000.00	
5	Less estimated gross profit (Net sales × Estimated gross profit 53.54%)	762,945.00	
6	Estimated cost of merchandise sold		662,055.00
7	Estimated ending inventory		$ 57,845.00

2 Net purchases to date, $664,010.00, line 2, is obtained from the purchases, purchases returns and allowances, and purchases discount accounts in the general ledger.

3 Merchandise available for sale, $719,900.00, line 3, is figured by adding the amounts on lines 1 and 2.

4 Net sales to date, $1,425,000.00, line 4, is obtained from the sales, sales returns and allowances, and sales discount accounts in the general ledger.

5 Estimated gross profit, $762,945.00, line 5, is figured by multiplying the amount on line 4 by 53.54%. The percentage, 53.54%, is an average of the gross profit percentages from Suntrol's income statements for the past three years.

6 Estimated cost of merchandise sold, $662,055.00, line 6, is figured by subtracting the amount on line 5 from the amount on line 4.

7 Estimated ending inventory, $57,845.00, line 7, is figured by subtracting the amount on line 6 from the amount on line 3.

An ending merchandise inventory figured using the gross profit method is an estimate and the amount may not be absolutely accurate. However, when preparing monthly interim financial statements the estimated amount is sufficiently accurate without taking a periodic inventory.

Retail method

Estimating inventory value by using a percentage based on both cost and retail prices is called the retail method of estimating inventory. To use the retail method, separate records must be kept of both cost price and retail price for net purchases, net sales, and beginning merchandise inventory.

An estimated ending merchandise inventory, using the retail method, is figured for Bolin, Inc., as shown in Illustration 16-13.

ESTIMATED MERCHANDISE INVENTORY SHEET
Retail Method

Company _Bolin, Inc._ _____ Date _12-31-89_

		Cost	Retail
1	Beginning inventory, January 1	$ _296,500.00_	$ _462,630.68_
2	Net purchases to date...	_171,828.35_	_268,104.77_
3	Merchandise available for sale................................	$ _468,328.35_	$ _730,735.45_
4	Less net sales to date..		_264,841.67_
5	Estimated ending inventory at retail........................		$ _465,893.78_
6	Estimated ending inventory at cost (Inventory at Retail × percentage _64.1_ %)..............	$ _298,637.91_	

Illustration 16-13
Estimating ending merchandise inventory using the retail method

1 January 1 beginning inventory at cost, $296,500.00, line 1, is obtained from the merchandise inventory account in the general ledger. Beginning inventory at retail, $462,630.68, is obtained from the separate record of retail prices.

2 Net purchases to date at cost, $171,828.35, line 2, is obtained from the purchases, purchases returns and allowances, and purchases discount accounts in the general ledger. Net purchases to date at retail, $268,104.77, is obtained from the separate record of retail prices.

3 Merchandise available for sale at cost, $468,328.35, and at retail, $730,735.45, line 3, is figured by adding lines 1 and 2.

4 Net sales to date at retail, $264,841.67, line 4, is obtained from the sales, sales returns and allowances, and sales discount accounts in the general ledger.

5 Estimated ending inventory at retail, $465,893.78, line 5, is figured by subtracting line 4 from line 3.

6 Estimated ending inventory at cost, $298,637.91, line 6, is figured by multiplying the amount on line 5 by 64.1%. The percentage of merchandise available for sale at cost to merchandise available for sale at retail, 64.1%, is figured from the amounts on line 3.

Merchandise Available for Sale at Cost		Merchandise Available for Sale at Retail		Percentage
$468,328.35	÷	$730,735.45	=	64.1%

Many businesses needing to estimate ending merchandise inventory use the previously described gross profit method. The gross profit method does not require that separate records be kept at cost and retail prices as is true of the retail method. Suntrol uses a perpetual inventory. Therefore, monthly ending inventories are available from the stock record cards without estimating or taking a monthly inventory.

MERCHANDISE INVENTORY TURNOVER

The more rapidly a business sells merchandise, the more chance a business has of making a satisfactory net income. For example, more revenue results from selling 100 square feet of blinds per day than from selling 50 square feet per day. Two measures of the speed with which merchandise inventory is sold are (1) merchandise inventory turnover ratio, and (2) average number of days' sales in merchandise inventory.

Merchandise inventory turnover ratio

The number of times the average amount of merchandise inventory is sold during a specific period of time is called the merchandise inventory turnover ratio. A merchandise inventory turnover ratio expresses a relationship between an average inventory and the cost of merchandise sold. Merchandise inventory represents a large investment for most merchandising businesses. Therefore, a low turnover ratio usually indicates a low return on investment.

Suntrol figures its merchandise inventory turnover ratio for December, 1989, as shown below.

/December 1 Merchandise Inventory		December 31\ Merchandise Inventory /	÷	2	=	Average Merchandise Inventory
($55,200.00	+	$57,960.00)	÷	2	=	$56,580.00

Cost of Merchandise Sold		Average Merchandise Inventory	=	Merchandise Inventory Turnover Ratio
$53,437.00	÷	$56,580.00	=	.94 times

A merchandise inventory turnover ratio of .94 times means that the business sold a little less than one average inventory during the month of December.

Suntrol's merchandise inventory turnover ratio for all of 1989 is figured as follows.

/January 1 Merchandise Inventory		December 31\ Merchandise Inventory /	÷	2	=	1989 Average Merchandise Inventory
($55,890.00	+	$57,960.00)	÷	2	=	$56,925.00

Cost of Merchandise Sold	÷	1989 Average Merchandise Inventory	=	1989 Merchandise Inventory Turnover Ratio
$662,055.00	÷	$56,925.00	=	11.6 times

An 11.6 merchandise inventory turnover ratio means that the business sold the average merchandise inventory 11.6 times during 1989. Suntrol compares its merchandise inventory turnover ratio with those published by national trade associations. Businesses similar to Suntrol have an average merchandise inventory turnover ratio of 8.0 times. Suntrol's turnover ratio of 11.6 is acceptable.

> A merchandise inventory ratio of 11.6 times is unusually high for most businesses. Suntrol does exceptionally well to achieve this ratio.

Average number of days' sales in merchandise inventory

The period of time needed to sell an average amount of merchandise inventory is called the average number of days' sales in merchandise inventory. The average number of days' sales in merchandise inventory based on an 11.6 times ratio is figured as follows.

Days in Year	÷	Merchandise Inventory Turnover Ratio	=	Average Number of Days' Sales in Merchandise Inventory
365	÷	11.6	=	31.5 days

An average of 31.5 days means that an average inventory tends to be sold once every 31.5 days. Published averages from trade associations show that businesses similar to Suntrol have an average number of days' sales in merchandise inventory of 45.6 days. Suntrol's average of 31.5 is satisfactory.

The higher the number of days in merchandise inventory, the longer merchandise tends to remain unsold. A business can reduce the merchandise inventory turnover ratio and the number of days' sales in merchandise inventory by reducing the size of the inventory kept on hand. However, a lower inventory level may not meet the demands of customers. A business also can improve its turnover ratio and the number of days' sales in merchandise inventory by increasing the amount of merchandise sold during a month or a year.

ACCOUNTING TERMS

What is the meaning of each of the following?

1. consignment
2. consignee
3. consignor
4. stock record
5. stock ledger
6. first-in, first-out inventory costing method
7. last-in, first-out inventory costing method
8. weighted-average inventory costing method
9. lower of cost or market inventory costing method
10. retail method of estimating inventory
11. merchandise inventory turnover ratio
12. average number of days' sales in merchandise inventory

QUESTIONS FOR INDIVIDUAL STUDY

1. What two elements make up the cost of the merchandise available for sale?
2. Into what parts is the cost of merchandise available for sale divided at the end of a fiscal period?
3. What items on financial statements are affected, and how, when an ending merchandise inventory is overstated?
4. Being sure that inventories are correctly valued so that no errors from this source occur on financial statements is an application of which accounting concept?
5. What two costs go into the value placed on a merchandise inventory?
6. Who has title to goods that are in transit with terms of FOB shipping point?
7. Who has title to goods that are in transit with terms of FOB destination?
8. Who has title to goods that are on consignment?
9. Choosing a method of valuing inventories is based on an application of which accounting concept?
10. How does Suntrol know when to reorder an inventory item?
11. How can the number of items on hand be determined when a perpetual inventory is kept?
12. Why do businesses with large merchandise inventories usually take a periodic inventory only once each fiscal period?
13. How will errors in a perpetual inventory be discovered?
14. Where does Suntrol obtain the cost prices for items listed on an inventory record?
15. Which merchandise is assumed to be sold first when a business uses the fifo method?
16. Which merchandise is assumed to be sold first when a business uses the lifo method?
17. What is the formula for figuring the average cost per unit of merchandise when the weighted-average method is used?
18. During a period of increasing prices, which method of valuing inventories usually gives the highest inventory value?
19. During a period of decreasing prices, which method of valuing inventories usually gives the highest inventory value?
20. Why might a business use the gross profit method instead of the retail method to estimate monthly ending inventory?
21. What can be interpreted from a merchandise inventory turnover ratio of 5 times?

CASES FOR MANAGEMENT DECISION

CASE 1 Mendozer, Inc., keeps a perpetual merchandise inventory. A new member of the board of directors notices that two employees work full time keeping the inventory records. The director suggests that the corporation stop using the perpetual inventory system and take a periodic inventory once a year when information is needed for financial statements. The director also suggests that the salaries saved by eliminating the positions of the two inventory employees will be more than the cost of an annual periodic inventory. What is your opinion of this suggestion? Explain your answer.

CASE 2 Power, Inc., sells many different kinds of replacement parts for hydraulic power units. The corporation takes a periodic inventory once every three months for use in preparing quarterly financial statements. A newly employed accountant suggests that the corporation change over to a perpetual inventory. What would you recommend? Explain your recommendation.

CASE 3 For the past ten years, during a period of high inflation and increasing prices, Shenley, Inc., has been using the fifo method. For the past two years however prices have stopped increasing and the trend in the current year is toward decreasing prices. Shenley's new accountant suggests that the corporation change to the lifo inventory costing method. What do you recommend? Explain your answer.

APPLICATION PROBLEMS

PROBLEM 16-1   Keeping perpetual inventory records

Howarty, Inc., keeps a perpetual merchandise inventory.

Instructions: 1. Use stock records similar to the one described in this chapter. Complete the heading for each of the following two inventory items. Also, record the balance on May 1 of the current year for each item.

> Beige lamp shades; Stock No. S51; reorder, 20; minimum, 5; location, Bin 12; number on hand, May 1, 11.

> Brown electric cords; Stock No. C10; reorder, 25; minimum, 5; location, Bin 40; number on hand, May 1, 15.

2. Record on the stock records the merchandise items received and issued during May of the current year.

May   4. Issued 4 lamp shades, S21.
     6. Issued 5 electric cords, S22.
   12. Issued 6 cords, S23.
   13. Issued 2 shades, S24.
   15. Received 20 shades, P16.
   17. Issued 10 shades, S25.
   18. Received 25 cords, P17.
   20. Issued 10 cords, S26.
   21. Issued 10 shades, S27.
   21. Issued 15 cords, S28.
   25. Issued 5 shades, S29.
   26. Issued 3 cords, S30.
   30. Received 20 shades, P18.
   31. Received 25 cords, P19.

PROBLEM 16-2   Valuing inventory using fifo, lifo, and weighted-average methods

Montinani, Inc., takes a periodic inventory on December 31 of the current year. The following information is obtained from Montinani's records.

Stock No.	January 1 Inventory		First Purchase		Second Purchase		Third Purchase		Fourth Purchase		December 31 Inventory
	No.	Cost	No.	Cost	No.	Cost	No.	Cost	No.	Cost	
A15	10	$5.00	10	$6.00	10	$7.00	10	$8.00	10	$6.00	30
B10	12	4.00	5	4.00	5	6.00	10	5.00	5	4.00	20
C8	6	9.00	10	9.00	10	8.00	10	7.00	10	6.00	35
D23	5	6.00	5	6.00	5	6.00	5	5.00	5	5.00	15
E30	15	3.00	10	4.00	10	5.00	10	3.00	10	2.00	45

Instructions: 1. Use a form similar to the one on the following page. Figure the inventory values using the fifo, lifo, and weighted-average inventory costing methods. The amounts for Stock No. A15 are shown as an example.

Stock No.	Dec. 31 Inventory	Inventory Costing Method					
		Fifo		Lifo		Weighted-Average	
		Unit Cost	Value	Unit Cost	Value	Unit Cost	Value
A15	30	10 @ $6.00 10 @ 8.00 10 @ 7.00	$210.00	10 @ $5.00 10 @ 6.00 10 @ 7.00	$180.00	30 @ $6.40	$192.00
B10							
Total Values							

2. Total the three Value columns.

3. Which of the three methods of costing inventory results in the highest inventory value for Montinani, Inc.? Which results in the lowest inventory value?

PROBLEM 16-3   Valuing inventory using lower of cost or market method

Softside, Inc., obtained the following information from its records on December 31 of the current year.

Stock No.	Inventory	Cost	Market
N50	20	$ 3.25	$ 3.50
P23	35	2.00	1.75
R10	5	19.00	20.00
T55	11	8.00	9.00
V2	8	17.00	15.00
W16	3	25.00	25.00
X58	15	12.00	10.00

Instructions: 1. Use a form similar to the one below. Figure the inventory value for each item of merchandise using the lower of cost or market inventory costing method. The values for Stock No. N50 are given as an example.

Stock No.	Inventory	Price to Use		Total Value
		Cost	Market	
N50	20	$3.25		$65.00
Total				

2. Total the Total Value column.

PROBLEM 16-4   Estimating ending merchandise inventory

The following information is obtained from the records of two corporations.

Item	Miley, Inc.		Dowsage, Inc.	
	Cost	Retail	Cost	Retail
Beginning inventory . . .	$16,200.00	$34,885.00	$ 37,200.00	$ 80,106.00
Net purchases to date .	65,100.00	99,265.00	108,600.00	165,594.00
Net sales to date	81,900.00	94,550.00	141,000.00	142,833.00
Gross profit percentage	30%		40%	

Instructions: 1. Figure the estimated ending inventory for the two corporations using the gross profit method of costing inventory. Use August 31 of the current year as the date.

2. Figure the estimated ending inventory for the two corporations using the retail method of costing inventory.

PROBLEM 16-5 Figuring merchandise inventory turnover ratio and average number of days' sales in merchandise inventory

Selected information for three corporations is given below.

Item	Corporation		
	A	B	C
Beginning merchandise inventory .	$ 49,200.00	$ 50,000.00	$ 52,100.00
Ending merchandise inventory	53,000.00	49,300.00	47,500.00
Cost of merchandise sold	480,700.00	422,100.00	525,600.00

Instructions: 1. For each corporation, figure the merchandise inventory turnover ratio.

2. For each corporation, figure the average number of days' sales in merchandise inventory.

3. Which corporation has the best merchandise inventory turnover ratio?

ENRICHMENT PROBLEMS

MASTERY PROBLEM 16-M Valuing merchandise inventory; figuring merchandise inventory turnover ratio and average number of days' sales in merchandise inventory

On December 31 of the current year, Bandee, Inc., takes a periodic inventory. The following selected information is obtained from Bandee's records.

Stock No.	January 1 Inventory		First Purchase		Second Purchase		December 31 Inventory	Market Price
	No.	Cost	No.	Cost	No.	Cost		
G25	14	$ 7.00	15	$ 8.00	15	$ 9.00	25	$ 9.00
J15	16	5.00	10	5.00	10	8.00	30	7.00
K10	8	12.00	15	11.00	15	11.00	25	10.00
M35	7	8.00	7	8.00	7	8.00	10	8.00
N52	5	4.00	10	6.00	10	7.00	5	8.00

Instructions: 1. Use a form similar to the one below. Figure the inventory values using the fifo, lifo, and weighted-average inventory costing methods.

Stock No.	Dec. 31 Inventory	Inventory Costing Method					
		Fifo		Lifo		Weighted-Average	
		Unit Cost	Value	Unit Cost	Value	Unit Cost	Value
Total Values							

2. Total the three Value columns.

3. Assume that the weighted-average unit cost figured in Instruction 1 is the cost price and use the market price given in the form at the beginning of the problem. Use a form similar to the one below to figure the inventory values for each item using the lower of cost or market method. Also, total the Total Value column.

Stock No.	Inventory	Price to Use		Total Value
		Cost	Market	
Total				

4. Figure the corporation's estimated ending inventory using the gross profit method. The following information is obtained from the corporation's records on December 31 of the current year.

Item	Cost	Retail
Beginning merchandise inventory	$19,400.00	$ 48,740.00
Net purchases to date	68,000.00	142,800.00
Net sales to date....................	97,200.00	129,300.00
Gross profit percentage	40%	

5. Figure the corporation's estimated ending inventory using the retail method.

6. Use the information and the estimated inventory figured in Instruction 4. Figure the corporation's merchandise inventory turnover ratio.

7. Use the merchandise inventory turnover ratio figured in Instruction 6. Figure the corporation's average number of days' sales in merchandise inventory.

CHALLENGE PROBLEM 16-C **Valuing merchandise inventory; figuring merchandise inventory turnover ratio and average number of days' sales in merchandise inventory**

On January 31 of the current year, Minder, Inc., takes a periodic inventory. The following selected information was obtained from Minder's records.

Stock No.	January 1 Inventory		During January				January 31 Inventory
			First Purchase		Second Purchase		
	No.	Cost	No.	Cost	No.	Cost	
H15	2,400	$ 7.00	1,500	$ 8.00	1,500	$ 9.00	2,500
J35	1,600	5.00	1,000	5.00	1,000	8.00	2,500
M40	800	12.00	150	11.00	150	11.00	250
Q75	700	8.00	300	8.00	300	8.00	650
V22	500	4.00	100	6.00	100	7.00	400

Instructions: 1. Use a form similar to the one below. Figure the inventory values using the fifo, lifo, and weighted-average inventory costing methods.

Stock No.	Jan. 31 Inventory	Inventory Costing Method					
		Fifo		Lifo		Weighted-Average	
		Unit Cost	Value	Unit Cost	Value	Unit Cost	Value
Total Values							

2. Total the three Value columns.

3. On December 31 of the current year, Minder takes another periodic inventory. The following information was obtained.

Stock No.	Dec. 31 Inventory	Cost Price	Market Price
H15	2,000	$ 9.00	$10.00
J35	1,500	5.00	7.00
M40	200	10.00	9.00
Q75.	300	8.00	8.00
V22	300	4.00	8.00

Use a form similar to the one below to figure the inventory values for each item using the lower of cost or market method. Also, total the Total Value column.

Stock No.	Inventory	Price to Use		Total Value
		Cost	Market	
Total				

4. Figure the corporation's estimated ending inventory using the gross profit method. The following information is obtained from the corporation's records on December 31 of the current year.

Item	Cost	Retail
Beginning merchandise inventory.............	$ 42,000.00	$135,420.00
Net purchases to date	150,320.00	377,300.00
Net sales to date	213,900.00	319,200.00
Gross profit percentage	45%	

5. Figure the corporation's estimated ending inventory using the retail method.

6. Use the information and the estimated inventory figured in Instruction 4. Figure the corporation's merchandise inventory turnover ratio.

7. Use the merchandise inventory turnover ratio figured in Instruction 6. Figure the corporation's average number of days' sales in merchandise inventory.

17 Budgetary Planning and Control

ENABLING PERFORMANCE TASKS

After studying Chapter 17, you will be able to:
a. Define accounting terms related to budgetary planning and control.
b. Identify accounting concepts and practices related to preparing and analyzing budgeted income statements and cash budgets.
c. Prepare a budgeted income statement.
d. Prepare a cash budget.

An important goal of a successful business is to improve profitability. *(CONCEPT: Going Concern)* Effective planning is important to profitability improvement. Financial planning is a part of a business' overall planning process. Planning the financial operations of a business is called budgeting. A written financial plan of a business for a specific period of time, expressed in dollars, is called a budget. *(CONCEPT: Unit of Measurement)*

BUDGET FUNCTIONS

Budgets are estimates of what will happen in the future expressed in financial terms. A carefully prepared budget reflects the best predictions possible by those persons who prepare the plan. A completed budget shows the expected course of action for a business.

A budget serves three important business functions. (1) Planning. (2) Operational control. (3) Departmental coordination.

Planning

In preparing a budget, managers must anticipate what probably will happen in the future. This view of the future helps a manager plan actions that will meet desired goals. The budgeting process forces a manager to decide which actions should be emphasized to achieve the desired goals.

Operational control

A budget includes a business' expected accomplishments — the kind as well as amount of expected activities. By comparing actual production with expected budgeted production, a manager can judge how well a business is achieving its planned performance.

By comparing actual expenses with expected or budgeted expenses, a business also can identify where action is needed to control expenses. Comparison of actual amounts with budgeted amounts identifies items for which costs are higher than expected. After high cost items are identified, a business can concentrate on actions to reduce the unexpected high costs.

Departmental coordination

Profitable business growth requires that all managers be aware of the company's future plans. A budget reflects these plans. Each phase of a business operation must be coordinated with all other related phases. For example, if estimated sales are to be achieved, the purchasing department must know when and how much merchandise to purchase. Therefore, all management personnel must help plan and use a budget as a guide to control and to coordinate revenue and expenses.

BUDGET DESIGN PROCEDURES

A budget is a view into the future, a plan of expected financial activities. Therefore, budget preparation begins with company goals. Company goals might be to increase sales, to reduce cost of merchandise sold, or to increase net income. All of these goals affect budget preparation because the budget is a business' financial plan.

Budget period

The length of time covered by a budget is called the budget period. Usually this period is one year. Some companies also prepare a long-range budget of five years or more for special projects and plant and equipment purchases. However, the annual budget is the one used to compare current financial performance with budget plans.

An annual budget normally is prepared for a company's fiscal year. The annual budget commonly is divided into quarterly and monthly budgets. Such budget subdivisions provide frequent opportunities to evaluate how actual operations compare with budgeted operations.

A budget must be prepared in sufficient time to be communicated to the appropriate managers prior to the beginning of a budget period. If a company is large and complex, gathering budget information will start long before the beginning of a new budget year. Gathering information, making analyses, making decisions, preparing the budget, and approving and communicating the budget take considerable time.

Budget type

Businesses frequently prepare two types of annual budgets. (1) Budgeted income statement. (2) Cash budget.

Budgeted income statement. A budgeted income statement is an estimate of a business' expected revenue, expenses, and net income for a fiscal period. The budgeted income statement is similar to a regular income statement and is sometimes known as an operating budget or a revenue and expenses budget.

Cash budget. A cash budget is an estimate of a business' expected cash receipts and payments for a fiscal period. For example, if a cash budget shows an expected cash shortage as of May 31, the company can arrange prior to May 31 to borrow cash. If a cash budget shows an expected surplus of cash on June 30, the company can plan how to invest the extra cash.

Information sources

Budgets should be based on information from company records of past operations, current general economic information, consultation with company personnel, and good judgment. Budgets cannot be exact since only expected revenue and expenses are shown. However, a company's best estimate of what will occur in future operations should be made.

Company records. A company's accounting and sales records contain much of the information needed to prepare budgets. Accounting information about previous years' operations is used to determine trends in sales, purchases, and operating expenses. Expected price changes, sales promotion plans, and market research studies also are important in predicting activity for a budget period.

General economic information. A general slowdown or speedup in the national economy may affect budget decisions. Unusually high inflation rates will affect amounts budgeted. A labor strike may affect some related industry and thus affect company operations. New product development, changes in consumer buying habits, availability of merchandise, international trade, and general business conditions all must be considered when preparing budgets.

Company staff and managers. Sales personnel estimate the amount of expected sales. Considering estimated sales for the new budget period, other departmental managers estimate anticipated essential budget items for each of their areas of the business.

Good judgment. Good judgment by the individuals preparing the budgets is essential to realistic budgets. Even after evaluating all available information, there is seldom an obvious answer to many budget questions. Since some information will be in conflict with other information, budget decisions are based finally on good judgment.

Preparation for budget planning

All available financial information should be analyzed as a basis for preparing new budgets. An analysis of previous years' revenue and expense amounts is an important part of budget preparation. A variety of other sources of information may also be used.

Suntrol, Inc., is a corporation that sells, assembles, and installs custom-made louvered blinds. Suntrol makes the following decisions and analyses as a basis for preparing its annual budget.

1. Previous years' revenue and expenses are analyzed.
2. General and industry economic conditions are analyzed to determine probable changes in costs and sales volume for the coming year.
3. Company goals are set for sales and net income as a percent of sales.

An income statement containing revenue, cost, and expense information for two or more years is called a comparative income statement. A comparative income statement provides the information for Suntrol's analysis of previous years' revenue, costs, and expenses. This statement shows trends that may be taking place in certain revenue, cost, or expense items. The statement also highlights revenue, cost, or expense items that may be increasing or decreasing at a higher rate than other items on the statement. Suntrol's comparative income statement is shown in Illustration 17-1.

The first column of Suntrol's comparative income statement shows actual revenue, costs, and expenses for 1987. The second column shows actual amounts for 1988, the current year. The third column shows the amount of increase or decrease from the previous year, 1987, to the current year, 1988. (For example, 1988 sales, $1,425,000.00 *less* 1987 sales, $1,290,750.00, *equals* the increase, $134,250.00.) The fourth column shows the percentage the current year amount, 1988, increased or decreased from the previous year amount, 1987. (For example, sales increase, $134,250.00 *divided by* previous year amount, $1,290,750.00 *equals* percent of increase, 10.4%.) Suntrol rounds percentages to the nearest 0.1%.

Each increase or decrease amount on the comparative income statement is carefully reviewed. The percent of increase or decrease provides an indication of whether the change is favorable, unfavorable, or normal compared with revenue. Net income is the difference between total revenue and combined costs and expenses when total revenue is greater. If a cost or expense item increase is a higher percentage than the revenue increase, net income is unfavorably affected by this change. However, if the revenue increase is a higher percentage than cost and expense items, net income is

Suntrol, Inc.
Comparative Income Statement
For Years Ended December 31, 1987 and 1988

	1987 Actual	1988 Actual	Increase/ Decrease From 1987	*% of Increase/ Decrease From 1987
Operating Revenue:				
Sales	$1,290,750	$1,425,000	+ $134,250	+ 10.4%
Cost of Merchandise Sold	558,500	641,250	+ 82,750	+ 14.8%
Gross Profit on Operations	$ 732,250	$ 783,750	+ $ 51,500	+ 7.0%
Operating Expenses:				
Selling Expenses:				
Advertising Expense	$ 9,465	$ 11,360	+ $ 1,895	+ 20.0%
Delivery Expense	18,650	21,450	+ 2,800	+ 15.0%
Depr. Expense — Delivery Equipment	14,250	17,000	+ 2,750	+ 19.3%
Depr. Expense — Warehouse Equipment	11,000	11,300	+ 300	+ 2.7%
Miscellaneous Expense — Sales	7,770	8,600	+ 830	+ 10.7%
Salary Expense — Commissions	103,260	114,000	+ 10,740	+ 10.4%
Salary Expense — Regular	226,100	263,630	+ 37,530	+ 16.6%
Supplies Expense — Sales	17,640	18,520	+ 880	+ 5.0%
Total Selling Expenses	$ 408,135	$ 465,860	+ $ 57,725	+ 14.1%
Administrative Expenses:				
Bad Debts Expense	$ 4,130	$ 5,700	+ $ 1,570	+ 38.0%
Depr. Expense — Office Equipment	5,200	5,660	+ 460	+ 8.8%
Insurance Expense	1,200	1,500	+ 300	+ 25.0%
Miscellaneous Expense — Administrative	3,140	3,420	+ 280	+ 8.9%
Payroll Taxes Expense	37,130	42,320	+ 5,190	+ 14.0%
Rent Expense	20,000	24,000	+ 4,000	+ 20.0%
Salary Expense — Administrative	83,220	92,620	+ 9,400	+ 11.3%
Supplies Expense — Office	2,720	2,850	+ 130	+ 4.8%
Utilities Expense	5,110	6,130	+ 1,020	+ 20.0%
Total Administrative Expenses	$ 161,850	$ 184,200	+ $ 22,350	+ 13.8%
Total Operating Expenses	$ 569,985	$ 650,060	+ $ 80,075	+ 14.0%
Income from Operations	$ 162,265	$ 133,690	− $ 28,575	− 17.6%
Other Expenses:				
Interest Expense	$ (1,860)	$ (2,440)	+ $ 580	+ 31.2%
Net Income before Federal Income Tax	$ 160,405	$ 131,250	− $ 29,155	− 18.2%
Federal Income Tax	53,535	40,125	− 13,410	− 25.0%
Net Income after Federal Income Tax	$ 106,870	$ 91,125	− $ 15,745	− 14.7%
Net Income % of Sales	8.3%	6.4%	− 1.9%	− 22.9%
Units (sq. ft.) of Blinds Sold	172,100	190,000	17,900	+ 10.4%

*Percentages rounded to nearest 0.1%.

Illustration 17-1
Comparative income statement

favorably affected. Decreases have the opposite effect. If a cost or expense item decrease is a higher percentage than the revenue decrease, net income is favorably affected. If the revenue decrease is a higher percentage than cost and expense items, net income is unfavorably affected.

Suntrol analyzes each item on its comparative income statement. If an item's trend is unfavorable, further inquiry is made to determine why the trend is unfavorable.

Suntrol made the following analysis of the 1987-1988 comparative income statement. First, a review of the 1988 financial goals showed that the goals were a sales increase of 10% and a net income of 9% of sales. Previous years had annual sales increases of 2% to 3%. Net income as a percent of sales had been increasing about 0.1% annually when it reached the highest percentage, 8.3% in 1987. Suntrol had decided to make a major effort in 1988 to increase the company's market share. Thus, the goal was to increase sales 10%. A review of the 1988 financial goals may help identify reasons for some increases and decreases on the comparative income statement.

The first items reviewed on the comparative income statement were major category totals—sales, cost of merchandise sold, selling expenses, administrative expenses, and net income. All three cost and expense categories had a higher percentage increase than sales, 10.4% (cost of merchandise sold, 14.8%; selling expenses, 14.1%; administrative expenses, 13.8%). Thus, net income was significantly reduced in 1988 even though sales increased.

Suntrol analyzed sales and each cost and expense item on its 1987-88 comparative income statement that exceeded the percent of increase in sales by more than 0.5%. Therefore, each cost and expense item with a 10.9% (10.4% + 0.5%) increase or greater was analyzed in more detail. Further inquiries to departmental managers revealed the following reasons for some of the significant changes.

a. Sales: The 10.4% increase in sales resulted from an increase in units sold (172,100 in 1987 to 190,000 in 1988) with no increase in unit sales price of $7.50.

b. Cost of merchandise sold: The 14.8% increase in cost of merchandise sold resulted from a 10.4% increase in units purchased and an increase in purchase price per unit ($3.245 in 1987 to $3.375 in 1988).

c. Advertising expense: The 20.0% increase in advertising expense resulted from expanded efforts to increase sales.

d. Delivery expense: The 15.0% increase in delivery expense resulted from increased volume of sales. Also, before Suntrol added another delivery truck to handle the increased sales, the company used a commercial carrier to deliver some units.

e. Depreciation expense—delivery equipment: The 19.3% increase in depreciation expense—delivery equipment resulted from depreciation on an additional delivery truck bought in 1988.

f. Salary expense—regular: The 16.6% increase in regular sales salary expense resulted from a 6% rate increase plus 10% more hours worked to install the increased number of blinds sold.

g. Bad debts expense: The 38.0% increase in bad debts expense resulted primarily from taking some higher credit risks in an effort to increase sales. Bad debt loss increased from 0.8% to 1.0% of sales on account.

h. Insurance expense: The 25.0% increase in insurance expense resulted from an increase in fire and casualty coverage for additional warehouse facilities and merchandise inventory.

i. Payroll taxes expense: The 14.0% increase resulted from the increases in all salaries paid. Payroll tax rates remained the same.

j. Rent expense: The 20.0% increase in rent expense resulted from renting additional warehouse space to store and assemble blinds for the increased units sold.

k. Salary expense—administrative: The 11.3% increase in administrative salary expense resulted from a 6% rate increase plus an additional part-time employee to help with additional customer billings for the increased sales.

l. Utilities expense: The 20.0% increase in utilities expense resulted from an 8% increase in utility rates plus utilities for the additional warehouse space and to operate machinery for the additional blinds assembled.

m. Interest expense: The 31.2% increase in interest expense resulted from additional amounts borrowed to buy increased merchandise inventory for the second and third high sales quarters and to buy a new delivery truck.

Summary of analyses: The significant reduction in 1988 net income, 14.7% decrease, appears to be caused by two major factors. (1) The cost of merchandise purchased increased in unit cost, yet Suntrol did not increase the unit sales price. (2) Eleven expense categories increased at a rate higher than sales primarily because of special efforts to increase sales.

BUDGETED INCOME STATEMENT PLANNING

After previous years' records have been analyzed, a business may set goals, develop operational plans, and prepare estimates of revenue, costs, and expenses for the coming year.

A business' executive officers and planners generally determine the goals and operational plan. The operational plan is converted to a more precise plan expressed in dollars by preparing a budgeted income statement. Suntrol prepares separate schedules for the major parts of the budgeted income statement. Separate schedules are prepared for sales, purchases, selling expenses, administrative expenses, and other revenue and expenses. To permit more frequent comparisons with budgeted amounts, schedules for the budget are separated into quarterly estimates.

At Suntrol, the accounting department is responsible for coordinating budget preparation. The sales manager is responsible for preparing the sales, purchases, and selling expenses budget schedules. The administrative manager is responsible for preparing the administrative expenses budget and the other expenses budget schedules. The accounting department then prepares the budgeted income statement from the budget schedules. The completed budget with attached schedules is submitted to the budget committee for approval. The budget committee consists of the president and two members of Suntrol's board of directors.

Annual operational plans and goals

Annual company goals establish targets the company will work toward in the coming year. Goals help a company coordinate the efforts of all areas toward a common direction. An operational plan provides general guidelines for achieving the company's goals. Operational plans and goals generally are determined by a planning group consisting of the company's executive officers and departmental managers.

At Suntrol, the company planning group includes the president and all departmental managers. The company planning group reviews the analysis of the previous years' comparative income statement and considers possible changes in economic conditions that may affect the company. From these discussions, the company's operational plan and goals are determined for the coming year.

Planning analysis. After reviewing company records and considering general economic conditions, Suntrol's planning group made the following observations.

a. The 1988 goal of increasing sales 10% was exceeded by 0.4%. However, the goal of a 9% net income as a percent of sales was not achieved. In fact, the percent decreased significantly from 8.3% in 1987 to 6.4% in 1988.

b. Cost of merchandise sold increased at a much higher rate than sales. Unit costs of blinds increased from $3.245 per square foot to $3.375, a 4% increase. However, Suntrol continued selling its blinds at the same unit price in 1988, $7.50 per square foot.

c. A major sales effort and the resulting increase in sales units in 1988 caused several expense items to increase at a higher percentage than sales.

d. Salary expenses and payroll taxes were about 36% of sales in 1988 — by far the largest expense item and exceeded only by cost of merchandise sold.

e. Area economic projections indicate new construction of homes and office buildings will increase 6% to 8% in 1989.

Budget guidelines. After the planning group's analyses, Suntrol issues the following budget planning guidelines.

a. Sales goal is to increase units sold to 200,000 units, about a 5.25% increase. Increase selling price per unit 4%, to $7.80 per unit, to recover merchandise cost increases of 1988 and expected increases in 1989.

b. A profitability goal is set to increase net income to 7.5% of net sales.

c. Sales distribution by quarters is expected to be: 1st quarter — 20%; 2d quarter — 30%; 3d quarter — 30%; and 4th quarter — 20%.

d. Cost of merchandise is expected to increase about 2.2% to $3.45 per unit.

e. An automated assembler machine has been ordered. The machine will cost $25,000.00 and is expected to save approximately $25,000.00 per year in salary expense.

f. All employees on salary will receive a 5% increase in wage rate.

g. Rigid controls on all expenditures will be exercised.

Sales budget schedule

A sales budget schedule shows the estimated sales for a budget period. The sales budget schedule is usually the first one prepared because the other schedules are affected by the expected sales revenue. Before a business can estimate the merchandise to purchase, an accurate estimate is needed for expected sales. Expected sales revenue also determines the amount that may be spent for salaries, advertising, and other selling and administrative expenses.

Suntrol's sales manager, with knowledge of the budget guidelines and with the assistance of sales representatives, prepares a sales budget schedule. In preparing a sales budget schedule, sales and the trend in sales for a period of several years are considered. Also considered are general economic conditions, consumer buying trends, competition, new products on the market, and such activities as planned special sales.

Previous years' income statement trends, the current economic conditions, and the competitive situation support Suntrol's planning group goal of a 5.25% increase in unit sales. Sales personnel also estimate a 5.25% increase in units sold during 1989. Based on a projected 5.25% increase, the 1989 sales estimate is set at 200,000 units.

After considering the budget guidelines, reviewing competitors' selling prices, and analyzing expected costs of merchandise, the sales manager sets the 1989 unit sales price at $7.80. Total revenue from sales is estimated as $1,560,000.00. When all factors that may affect sales have been considered, the sales budget schedule is prepared. Accurate estimates are important for effective budgeting. However, since budgets are based on estimates, most businesses round the estimated amounts to simplify the budgeting process. Suntrol rounds unit estimates to the nearest hundred and dollar estimates to the nearest $10.00.

Suntrol prepares its annual budget in quarterly segments to provide more frequent opportunities to compare actual with budgeted operations.

Quarterly amounts are based on an estimated percentage of the annual budget similar to previous years' quarterly percentages and on projected activities for specific quarters. The 1989 sales budget schedule for Suntrol is shown in Illustration 17-2.

	1988 Actual		1989 Budget	
	Units (sq. ft.)*	Actual Amount @ 7.50/unit	Units (sq. ft.)*	Estimated Amount @ 7.80/unit
1st Quarter........	37,240	$ 279,300	40,000	$ 312,000
2d Quarter	55,480	416,100	60,000	468,000
3d Quarter	58,520	438,900	60,000	468,000
4th Quarter........	38,760	290,700	40,000	312,000
Year.............	190,000	$1,425,000	200,000	$1,560,000

Suntrol, Inc.
Sales Budget Schedule
For Year Ended December 31, 1989   Schedule 1

*Louvered blinds are measured in square feet.

Illustration 17-2
Sales budget schedule

Once the sales budget is approved, the sales manager knows the company's 1989 goal is to sell 200,000 units. The annual budget is subdivided into estimates for each quarter of the budget year. Thus, of the estimated annual sale of 200,000 units, 20% are estimated to be sold during the first and fourth quarters. During the second and third quarters, 30% of annual sales are estimated to be sold. For example, 40,000 units of blinds must be sold at $7.80 per unit during the first quarter to achieve budget. Sales activities will be planned to achieve the quarterly goals.

Purchases budget schedule

A purchases budget schedule is prepared to show the anticipated amount of purchases that will be required during a budget period. Since the amount of purchases depends on estimated sales, the purchases budget schedule is prepared after the sales budget schedule.

In planning a purchases budget schedule, the following factors are considered.

1. The estimate of unit sales as shown in the sales budget schedule.
2. The quantity of merchandise on hand at the beginning of the budget period.
3. The quantity of merchandise needed to fill expected sales without having too much inventory on hand at any one time.
4. The price trends of merchandise to be purchased.

The sales manager prepares the 1989 purchases budget schedule shown in Illustration 17-3.

	Ending Inventory +	Sales	= Total Needed −	Beginning Inventory	= Purchases	Unit × Cost	= Cost of Purchases
			Suntrol, Inc.				
			Purchases Budget Schedule				
			For Year Ended December 31, 1989				Schedule 2
1st Quarter	24,000	+ 40,000 =	64,000 −	16,000	= 48,000	× $3.45 =	$165,600
2d Quarter	24,000	+ 60,000 =	84,000 −	24,000	= 60,000	× 3.45 =	207,000
3d Quarter	16,000	+ 60,000 =	76,000 −	24,000	= 52,000	× 3.45 =	179,400
4th Quarter	16,800*	+ 40,000 =	56,800 −	16,000	= 40,800	× 3.45 =	140,760
Year	16,800	+ 200,000 =	216,800 −	16,000	= 200,800	× 3.45 =	692,760

*First quarter, 1990: estimated sales of 42,000 units.

Preparation of a purchases budget schedule is much the same as the preparation of a sales budget schedule. However, purchases are made in advance of sales to allow for delivery of the merchandise. For example, merchandise that is to be sold in April must be ordered in an earlier month. The exact date depends on the time required for delivery.

Illustration 17-3
Purchases budget schedule

Beginning and ending inventories used in figuring the estimated cost of purchases must be the appropriate inventories for the accounting period figured. The beginning inventory used to figure a year's estimated purchases is the same as the first quarter's beginning inventory. The ending inventory used to figure a year's estimated purchases is the same as the last quarter's ending inventory.

Enough total units are needed to meet sales demand while new units are being purchased. Estimated unit sales are shown in the sales budget schedule. Beginning inventory is the same amount as the ending inventory for the previous period. Sales estimates are needed also for first quarter, 1990, to figure estimated ending inventory for fourth quarter, 1989. Suntrol's sales manager estimates 1990 first quarter sales as 42,000 units. Estimated units of purchases are multiplied by the estimated cost per unit to figure the estimated cost of purchases.

Suntrol's sales manager estimates that 1989 materials costs will be $3.45 per unit. The sales manager also estimates that the desired number of units for ending inventory should be about 40% of the number of units estimated to be sold in the next quarter.

Selling expenses budget schedule

A selling expenses budget schedule is prepared to show expected expenditures related directly to the selling operations. The sales manager estimates the information for the selling expenses budget schedule. However, other sales personnel may provide specific information. For example, the advertising manager supplies much of the advertising expense information. After selling expenses information has been estimated, a selling expenses budget schedule is prepared.

Some selling expense items are relatively stable and require little budget planning. For example, warehouse and delivery equipment depreciation expenses are reasonably stable from year to year unless new equipment is bought. On the other hand, several selling expenses increase and decrease in relation to sales increases and decreases. Suntrol has a seasonal business with higher sales during the second and third quarters. The company hires more personnel and spends more for advertising and sales supplies during the heavy sales season. All of these factors are considered in making a selling expenses budget schedule. Suntrol's 1989 selling expenses budget schedule is shown in Illustration 17-4.

Suntrol, Inc.
Selling Expenses Budget Schedule
For Year Ended December 31, 1989   Schedule 3

| | 1989 Budget | 1989 — By Quarters | | | |
		1st	2d	3d	4th
Advertising Expense	$ 12,480	$ 2,500	$ 3,740	$ 3,740	$ 2,500
Delivery Expense	21,600	4,320	6,480	6,480	4,320
Depr. Expense — Delivery Equipment	17,000	4,250	4,250	4,250	4,250
Depr. Expense — Warehouse Equipment	13,800	3,450	3,450	3,450	3,450
Miscellaneous Expense — Sales	7,800	1,560	2,340	2,340	1,560
Salary Expense — Commissions	124,800	24,960	37,440	37,440	24,960
Salary Expense — Regular	250,560	50,110	75,170	75,170	50,110
Supplies Expense — Sales	20,280	4,060	6,080	6,080	4,060
Total Selling Expenses	$468,320	$95,210	$138,950	$138,950	$95,210

Illustration 17-4
Selling expenses budget schedule

Suntrol's sales manager uses a number of approaches to estimate the various 1989 selling expenses. For example, advertising expense is closely related to sales and sales promotions for the year. Sales promotion emphasis will be maintained at about the same level as 1988. Regular salary expense is determined by salary increases and changes in the amount of activity which affects the number of people employed. The new automated assembler will reduce regular salary expense in 1989. Delivery expenses are related closely to the number of units sold and delivered. The 1988 delivery expenses increased significantly because an external freight company was used for increased deliveries until Suntrol could acquire an additional truck. Rigid cost control measures will be applied to bring the unit delivery expense cost down in 1989. Other selling expenses are linked closely to the amount of sales. Some, such as depreciation expenses, remain the same unless equipment is added or deleted. No new delivery equipment will be added. Thus Depreciation Expense—Delivery Equipment will remain the same as 1988. However, acquisition of the automated assembler will increase Depreciation Expense—Warehouse Equipment by $2,500.00 in 1989.

Suntrol uses the following estimation guides to prepare its selling expenses budget schedule.

Advertising expense: 0.8% of sales.

Delivery expense: 10.8 cents per unit (sq. ft.) sold.

Depreciation expense—delivery equipment and depreciation expense—warehouse equipment: Straight-line depreciation. Annual depreciation divided equally among four quarters.

Miscellaneous expense—sales: 0.5% of sales.

Salary expense—commissions: 8.0% of sales.

Salary expense—regular: Reduced salaries $25,000.00 at 1988 rates, then provided 5% rate increase. Budgeted amount is figured as follows.

1988 salary expense	$263,630
Less reduction	25,000
Total	$238,630
Plus 5% rate increase	11,930
1989 budgeted amount	$250,560

Budgeted amount is allocated among the four quarters in relation to amount of budgeted sales.

Supplies expense—sales: 1.3% of sales; about the same percentage as 1988.

Administrative expenses budget schedule

An administrative expenses budget schedule shows the expected expenses for all operating expenses not directly related to selling operations. The administrative manager is responsible for estimating most of the information in this budget. Information for this budget schedule comes from a study of past records, an evaluation of company plans, the sales budget schedule, and discussions with other managers. After the administrative expenses have been estimated, the administrative expenses budget schedule is prepared. Suntrol's 1989 administrative expenses budget schedule is shown in Illustration 17-5.

Several administrative expenses are fixed so that the amounts are known and remain the same each period. For example, Suntrol leases the building in which it is located. The company pays annual rent of $24,000.00. This includes the additional warehouse space rented in 1988, which will again be needed in 1989. Since the amount is known and is used equally each time period, rent expense can be budgeted accurately at $6,000.00 each quarter and $24,000.00 each year. A few administrative expenses need to be budgeted as a percent of another amount. For example, the amount of bad

	1989 Budget	1989 — By Quarters			
		1st	2d	3d	4th
Bad Debts Expense	$ 6,240	$ 1,250	$ 1,870	$ 1,870	$ 1,250
Depr. Expense — Office Equipment	5,800	1,450	1,450	1,450	1,450
Insurance Expense	1,800	450	450	450	450
Miscellaneous Expense — Administrative. . . .	3,600	860	1,010	1,010	720
Payroll Taxes Expense.	42,530	8,860	12,580	12,590	8,500
Rent Expense	24,000	6,000	6,000	6,000	6,000
Salary Expense — Administrative.	97,250	23,370	27,220	27,240	19,420
Supplies Expense — Office	3,120	620	940	940	620
Utilities Expense	6,820	1,500	1,840	1,910	1,570
Total Administrative Expenses	$191,160	$44,360	$53,360	$53,460	$39,980

Suntrol, Inc.
Administrative Expenses Budget Schedule
For Year Ended December 31, 1989   Schedule 4

Illustration 17-5
Administrative expenses
budget schedule

debts expense probably will be related to the amount of sales. Payroll taxes will be related to salary expenses. Utilities will be determined by the rate and amount of power, heat, and other utilities used.

Suntrol's administrative manager uses a number of approaches to estimate expenses. The 1989 administrative expenses at Suntrol are estimated in the following manner.

Bad debts expense: 1.0% of credit sales. Credit sales are estimated as 40% of total sales.

Depreciation expense — office equipment: Straight-line depreciation. New office equipment bought at the end of 1988 increases annual depreciation by $140.00. Annual depreciation divided equally over the four quarters.

Insurance expense: Amount to increase $300.00 from 1988 primarily because of added coverage for the new automated assembler. An equal amount is paid in each quarter.

Miscellaneous expense — administrative: 3.7% of administrative salaries; same percentage as 1988.

Payroll taxes expense: 9.0% of all salaries.

Rent expense: Known rental, $24,000.00, divided equally over the four quarters.

Salary expense — administrative: 5.0% increase over last year, a result of a salary rate increase. Administrative salary expenses for 1988 were:

1st Quarter	$22,260.00
2d Quarter	25,925.00
3d Quarter	25,940.00
4th Quarter.	18,495.00
Total for 1988	$92,620.00

Supplies expense — office: 0.2% of sales; same percentage as 1988.
Utilities expense: 11.3% increase over last year, a result of 5.0%
projected increase in activity and a 6.0% increase in rates.
Utilities expenses for 1988 were:

1st Quarter...................................	$1,347.00
2d Quarter	1,653.00
3d Quarter	1,720.00
4th Quarter..................................	1,410.00
Total for 1988	$6,130.00

After Suntrol's administrative manager has completed the expense estimates, the administrative expenses budget schedule is prepared.

Other revenue and expenses budget schedule

Budgeted revenue and expenses from activities other than normal operations are shown in an other revenue and expenses budget schedule. Typical
items in this budget are interest income, interest expense, and gains or
losses on the sale of plant assets. Suntrol's 1989 other revenue and expenses
budget schedule is shown in Illustration 17-6. Suntrol has only one expense
item and no other revenue items.

<table>
<tr><td colspan="6">Suntrol, Inc.
Other Revenue and Expenses Budget Schedule
For Year Ended December 31, 1989   Schedule 5</td></tr>
<tr><td rowspan="2"></td><td rowspan="2">1989
Budget</td><td colspan="4">1989 — By Quarters</td></tr>
<tr><td>1st</td><td>2d</td><td>3d</td><td>4th</td></tr>
<tr><td>Other Expenses:
  Interest Expense ....</td><td>$2,250</td><td>$750</td><td>$750</td><td>$750</td><td></td></tr>
</table>

Suntrol's administrative manager is responsible for estimating the information in the other revenue and expenses budget schedule. Estimated
interest expense, the only item in the 1989 budget, is based on a $25,000.00
loan that was used to acquire the automated assembler machine. Suntrol
plans to repay the loan at the beginning of the fourth quarter.

Illustration 17-6
Other revenue and
expenses budget schedule

Budgeted income statement

A budgeted income statement shows estimated sales, costs, expenses,
and net income of a company. Suntrol prepares the budgeted income statement from information in the sales, purchases, selling expenses, administrative expenses, and other revenue and expenses budget schedules. Since
the budget schedules contain detailed items, Suntrol prepares a shortened
budgeted income statement and then attaches the budget schedules.

Suntrol's 1989 budgeted income statement is shown in Illustration 17-7.

Suntrol, Inc.
Budgeted Income Statement
For Year Ended December 31, 1989

	Total for Year****	1989 — By Quarters***			
		1st	2d	3d	4th
Operating Revenue:					
Sales (Schedule 1)	$1,560,000	$312,000	$468,000	$468,000	$312,000
Cost of Merchandise Sold:					
Beginning Inventory (Schedule 2)	$ *54,000	$ *54,000	$ *82,800	$ *82,800	$ *55,200
Purchases (Schedule 2)	692,760	165,600	207,000	179,400	140,760
Total Merchandise Available	$ 746,760	$219,600	$289,800	$262,200	$195,960
Less Ending Inventory (Schedule 2) . .	57,960	82,800	82,800	55,200	57,960
Cost of Merchandise Sold	$ 688,800	$136,800	$207,000	$207,000	$138,000
Gross Profit on Operations	$ 871,200	$175,200	$261,000	$261,000	$174,000
Operating Expenses:					
Selling Expenses (Schedule 3)	$ 468,320	$ 95,210	$138,950	$138,950	$ 95,210
Administrative Expenses (Schedule 4)	191,160	44,360	53,360	53,460	39,980
Total Operating Expenses	$ 659,480	$139,570	$192,310	$192,410	$135,190
Income from Operations	$ 211,720	$ 35,630	$ 68,690	$ 68,590	$ 38,810
Other Expense Deduction (Schedule 5)	$ (2,250)	$ (750)	$ (750)	$ (750)	
Net Income before Federal Income Tax	$ 209,470	$ 34,880	$ 67,940	$ 67,840	$ 38,810
Federal Income Tax	76,110	**12,670	**24,690	**24,650	**14,100
Net Income after Federal Income Tax	$ 133,360	$ 22,210	$ 43,250	$ 43,190	$ 24,710

*Inventory January 1 cost $3.375 per unit. All other inventories cost $3.45 per unit.
**Quarterly estimate of federal income tax is same percentage of quarterly Net Income before Federal Income Tax as annual tax is of Annual Net Income before Federal Income Tax, 36.335%.
***Sum of quarterly amounts may not equal annual budget because of rounding.
****Budgeted amounts rounded to nearest $10.00.

Illustration 17-7
Budgeted income
statement

CASH BUDGET PLANNING

Good management requires the planning and controlling of cash so that cash will be available to meet obligations when due. Reliable cash management requires a knowledge of beginning cash balances, expected cash receipts, and expected cash payments during a budget period.

Suntrol's cash budget is prepared by the treasurer in consultation with the budget committee. A corporation treasurer is an officer of the corporation who is usually responsible for planning the corporation's requirement for and use of cash. A detailed analysis is made of expected receipts from cash sales, from customers on account, and from other sources. Also, an analysis is made of the expected cash payments for ordinary expenses such as rent, payroll, and payments to vendors on account. In addition, consideration is given to other cash payments, such as buying plant assets or supplies. Since a cash budget reports estimated cash receipts and payments, Suntrol prepares two budget schedules, one for cash receipts and one for cash payments. Total amounts are then entered in the cash budget.

Cash receipts budget schedule

Expected cash receipts for a budget period are reported on a cash receipts budget schedule. The following estimates are made in preparing a cash receipts budget schedule.

1. An estimate of quarterly cash sales.
2. An estimate of quarterly collections on account from customers. The amounts received from customers will not be the same as the amount of sales on account. Normally, cash is received for sales on account made during the previous one or two months. Also, some sales returns and allowances and uncollectible accounts are likely.
3. An estimate of cash to be received quarterly from other sources.

Suntrol's 1989 cash receipts budget schedule is shown in Illustration 17-8.

<table>
<tr><td colspan="5" align="center">Suntrol, Inc.
Cash Receipts Budget Schedule
For Year Ended December 31, 1989</td><td align="right">Schedule A</td></tr>
<tr><td></td><td colspan="4" align="center">Quarters</td></tr>
<tr><td></td><td align="center">1st</td><td align="center">2d</td><td align="center">3d</td><td align="center">4th</td></tr>
<tr><td>From Sales:</td><td></td><td></td><td></td><td></td></tr>
<tr><td>Cash Sales.............................</td><td>$187,200</td><td>$280,800</td><td>$280,800</td><td>$187,200</td></tr>
<tr><td>Accts. Rec. Collections—This Quarter Sales....</td><td>62,400</td><td>93,600</td><td>93,600</td><td>62,400</td></tr>
<tr><td>Accts. Rec. Collections—Last Quarter Sales....</td><td>55,860</td><td>61,150</td><td>91,730</td><td>91,730</td></tr>
<tr><td>Total Receipts from Sales....................</td><td>$305,460</td><td>$435,550</td><td>$466,130</td><td>$341,330</td></tr>
<tr><td>From Other Sources:</td><td></td><td></td><td></td><td></td></tr>
<tr><td>Note Payable to Bank ....</td><td>25,000</td><td></td><td></td><td></td></tr>
<tr><td>Total Cash Receipts..........................</td><td>$330,460</td><td>$435,550</td><td>$466,130</td><td>$341,330</td></tr>
</table>

An analysis of Suntrol's sales for previous years shows the following pattern of total sales. In a quarter, about 60% of all sales are cash sales. About 20% are sales on account collected in the quarter. About 19.6% are collected in the following quarter. About 0.4% are sales on account that prove to be uncollectible. For example, an analysis of cash receipts from sales for the first quarter, 1989, shows expected cash receipts of $330,460.00. This amount is figured as follows.

Illustration 17-8
Cash receipts budget schedule

Cash sales (60% × $312,000.00, first quarter sales from 1989 budgeted income statement, Illustration 17-7)	$187,200.00
Plus cash collected on account, this quarter's sales (20% × $312,000.00 first quarter sales from 1989 budgeted income statement, Illustration 17-7).	62,400.00
Plus cash collected on account, previous quarter's sales (19.6% × $285,000.00 fourth quarter's sales from previous quarter's 1988 income statement)	55,860.00
Equals estimated cash received from sales in first quarter, 1989	$305,460.00
Plus cash from a note payable, first quarter, 1989	25,000.00
Equals estimated total cash received in first quarter, 1989	$330,460.00

Cash sales and collections on account generally provide most of the cash receipts. However, if additional cash is needed, other sources of cash should be planned. After preliminary planning of estimated cash receipts and cash payments, the treasurer determines that cash on hand will be reduced in the first quarter to an unusually low level. This condition could prevent the company from making timely payments for its expenditures. Therefore, the treasurer makes arrangements to borrow $25,000.00 during the first quarter.

Cash payments budget schedule

Expected cash payments for a budget period are reported on a cash payments budget schedule. To prepare a cash payments budget schedule, the accountant and treasurer estimate quarterly cash payments. The following estimates are made in preparing a cash payments budget schedule.

1. An estimate of quarterly cash payments for accounts payable or notes payable to vendors.
2. An estimate of quarterly cash payments for each expense item. This estimate requires an analysis of the selling expenses, administrative expenses, and other revenue and expenses budgets.
3. An estimate of quarterly cash payments for buying equipment and other assets.
4. An estimate of quarterly cash payments for dividends.
5. An estimate of quarterly cash payments for investments.

Suntrol's 1989 cash payments schedule is shown in Illustration 17-9.

An analysis of past records for payments to vendors on account shows the following cash payment pattern. About 10% of all purchases are cash purchases. About 60% are purchases on account paid for in the quarter. About 30% are purchases on account paid for in the following quarter. An analysis of cash payments for purchases for the first quarter, 1989, shows expected cash payments of $154,880.00. This amount is figured as follows. Suntrol rounds dollar amounts to the nearest $10.00.

Suntrol, Inc.
Cash Payments Budget Schedule
For Year Ended December 31, 1989   Schedule B

	Quarter			
	1st	2d	3d	4th
For Merchandise:				
Cash Purchases	$ 16,560	$ 20,700	$ 17,940	$ 14,080
Payment on Accts. Pay.—This Quarter Purch.	99,360	124,200	107,640	84,460
Payment on Accts. Pay.—Last Quarter Purch.	38,960	49,680	62,100	53,820
Total Cash Payments for Purchases.	$154,880	$194,580	$187,680	$152,360
For Operating Expenses:				
Cash Selling Expenses:				
Advertising Expense.	$ 2,500	$ 3,740	$ 3,740	$ 2,500
Delivery Expense	4,320	6,480	6,480	4,320
Miscellaneous Expense—Sales	1,560	2,340	2,340	1,560
Salary Expense—Commissions	24,960	37,440	37,440	24,960
Salary Expense—Regular	50,110	75,170	75,170	50,110
Supplies Expense—Sales	4,060	6,080	6,080	4,060
Total Cash Selling Expenses	$ 87,510	$131,250	$131,250	$ 87,510
Cash Administrative Expenses:				
Insurance Expense.	$ 450	$ 450	$ 450	$ 450
Miscellaneous Expense—Administrative.	860	1,010	1,010	720
Payroll Taxes Expense	8,860	12,580	12,590	8,500
Rent Expense	6,000	6,000	6,000	6,000
Salary Expense—Administrative.	23,370	27,220	27,240	19,420
Supplies Expense—Office	620	940	940	620
Utilities Expense	1,500	1,840	1,910	1,570
Total Cash Administrative Expenses.	$ 41,660	$ 50,040	$ 50,140	$ 37,280
For Other Cash Payments:				
Federal Income Tax	$ 12,670	$ 24,690	$ 24,650	$ 14,100
Assembler Equipment	25,000			
Cash Dividend.		50,000	50,000	
Investment				35,000
Note Payable and Interest.				27,250
Total Other Cash Payments	$ 37,670	$ 74,690	$ 74,650	$ 76,350
Total Cash Payments.	$321,720	$450,560	$443,720	$353,500

Cash purchases (10% × $165,600.00, first quarter purchases from 1989 budgeted income statement, Illustration 17-7) . .	$ 16,560.00
Plus cash payments on account, this quarter's purchases (60% × $165,600.00, first quarter purchases from 1989 budgeted income statement, Illustration 17-7)	99,360.00
Plus cash payments on account, previous quarter's purchases (30% × $129,860.00, fourth quarter purchases from 1988 income statement)	38,960.00
Equals estimated total cash payments for purchases in first quarter, 1989.	$154,880.00

Illustration 17-9
Cash payments budget
schedule

The selling expenses budget schedule, Illustration 17-4, and the administrative expenses budget schedule, Illustration 17-5, include estimated items for which cash will not be paid. For example, cash will not be paid for depreciation or for bad debts expense. Therefore, these items do not appear in the cash payments budget schedule.

Suntrol also plans for cash payments other than for merchandise, selling expenses, and administrative expenses. An estimate is made of the 1989 income tax payments to be made throughout the year. The company also plans in the first quarter to buy new automated assembler equipment for $25,000.00. The company expects to pay a $50,000.00 cash dividend to stockholders in each of the second and third quarters. Plans call for repaying at the beginning of the fourth quarter the promissory note and interest, $27,250.00. Also, since a large cash balance is projected for the fourth quarter, Suntrol plans a $35,000.00 interest-earning investment.

The last line of the cash payments schedule shows the total cash payments expected each quarter. This total indicates the minimum amount of cash that must be available each quarter.

Cash budget

A cash budget shows for each month or quarter an estimate of a company's beginning cash balance, cash receipts, cash payments, and ending cash balance. Suntrol's cash budget is prepared from the information in the cash receipts schedule and cash payments schedule. Suntrol's 1989 cash budget is shown in Illustration 17-10.

Suntrol, Inc.
Cash Budget
For Year Ended December 31, 1989

	Quarter			
	1st	2d	3d	4th
Cash Balance — Beginning...............	$ 41,420	$ 50,160	$ 35,150	$ 57,560
Cash Receipts (Schedule A).............	330,460	435,550	466,130	341,330
Cash Available........................	$371,880	$485,710	$501,280	$398,890
Less Cash Payments (Schedule B)......	321,720	450,560	443,720	353,500
Cash Balance — Ending................	$ 50,160	$ 35,150	$ 57,560	$ 45,390

Illustration 17-10
Cash budget

At the end of each quarter of a budget period, Suntrol compares the actual cash balance with the estimated cash balance as shown in the cash budget. If the actual cash balance is less than the estimated balance, the reasons for the decrease are determined and action is taken to correct the problem. One reason may be that some customers are not paying their accounts when they should. Another may be that expenses are exceeding budget estimates. If the decrease continues, the company could have a quarter in which there is not enough cash to make all the required cash payments. If this shortage does occur, the business will have to borrow money until receipts and payments are brought into balance.

PERFORMANCE REPORT PREPARATION AND ANALYSIS

At the end of each quarter, a business prepares an income statement that compares actual amounts with the budgeted income statement for that period. This comparison shows variations between actual and budgeted items. A report showing a comparison of budgeted and actual amounts for a specific period of time is called a performance report

Suntrol prepares a quarterly performance report. This report is sent to the sales manager and the administrative manager. Knowing about significant differences between budgeted and actual amounts helps the managers identify areas that need to be reviewed. By identifying large cost variations early, managers may be able to make changes that will correct negative effects on net income for the year. If conditions change significantly, the budget for the remainder of the year can be revised. For the first quarter, 1989, Suntrol prepares the performance report shown in Illustration 17-11.

Preparation of a performance report is similar to preparation of a comparative income statement. However, a performance report compares actual amounts with budgeted amounts for the same fiscal period. A comparative income statement compares actual amounts of one fiscal period with actual amounts of a previous fiscal period.

The first amount column of the performance report shows the amounts budgeted for the first quarter of 1989. The second amount column shows the actual revenue, costs, and expenses for the first quarter of 1989. The third amount column shows how much the actual amount varies from the budgeted amount. (For example, actual sales, $313,560.00 *less* budgeted sales, $312,000.00 *equals* increase, $1,560.00.) The fourth column shows the percent the actual amount increased or decreased from the budgeted amount. (For example, sales increase, $1,560.00 *divided by* budgeted sales, $312,000.00 *equals* percent of increase, 0.5%.) Percentages are rounded to the nearest 0.1%.

Suntrol made the following analysis of the 1989 first quarter performance report. First, major category totals are reviewed—sales, cost of merchandise sold, selling expenses, administrative expenses, and net income. Suntrol considers 2% or more as a significant difference between budgeted and actual amounts. An analysis is made of all significant differences to determine why they occurred.

Differences between budgeted and actual amounts appear to be insignificant except for two items, utilities expense and income from operations. This report alerts the managers to changes in revenues and costs as well as how those changes affect net income. Gross profit is 1.2% over budget, a favorable variance. Normally, Suntrol considers significant only changes of

Suntrol, Inc.
Performance Report
For Quarter Ended March 31, 1989

	Budget 1989 1st Qtr.	Actual 1989 1st Qtr.	Increase/ Decrease From Budget	**% of Increase/ Decrease From Budget
Sales (sq. ft.)	40,000	40,200	+ 200	+0.5%
Operating Revenue:				
Sales	$312,000	$313,560	+$1,560	+0.5%
Cost of Merchandise Sold....................	136,800	136,270	− 530	−0.4%
Gross Profit on Operations	$175,200	$177,290	+$2,090	+1.2%
Operating Expense:				
Selling Expenses:				
Advertising Expense........................	$ 2,500	$ 2,530	+$ 30	+1.2%
Delivery Expense	4,320	4,337	+ 17	+0.4%
Depr. Expense—Delivery Equipment........	4,250	4,250		
Depr. Expense—Warehouse Equipment.....	3,450	3,450		
Miscellaneous Expense—Sales	1,560	1,548	− 12	−0.8%
Salary Expense—Commissions	24,960	25,085	+ 125	+0.5%
Salary Expense—Regular	50,110	50,110		
Supplies Expense—Sales	4,060	3,986	− 74	−1.8%
Total Selling Expenses....................	$ 95,210	$ 95,296	+$ 86	+0.1%
Administrative Expenses:				
Bad Debts Expense	$ 1,250	$ 1,240	−$ 10	−0.8%
Depr. Expense—Office Equipment..........	1,450	1,450		
Insurance Expense........................	450	450		
Miscellaneous Expense—Administrative.....	860	858	− 2	−0.2%
Payroll Taxes Expense	8,860	8,869	+ 9	+0.1%
Rent Expense	6,000	6,000		
Salary Expense—Administrative............	23,370	23,370		
Supplies Expense—Office	620	617	− 3	−0.5%
Utilities Expense	1,500	1,598	+ 98	+6.5%
Total Administrative Expenses	$ 44,360	$ 44,452	+$ 92	+0.2%
Total Operating Expenses......................	$139,570	$139,748	+$ 178	+0.1%
Income from Operations	$ 35,630	$ 37,542	+$1,912	+5.4%
Other Expenses:				
Interest Expense...........................	$ (750)	$ (750)		
Net Income before Federal Income Tax..........	$ 34,880	$ 36,792	+$1,912	+5.5%
Federal Income Tax	12,670	*13,368	+ 698	+5.5%
Net Income after Federal Income Tax	$ 22,210	$ 23,424	+$1,214	+5.5%
Net Income % of Sales	7.1%	7.5%		

*Amount of federal income tax paid is same percentage of net income as budgeted tax is of budgeted net income.
**Percentages rounded to the nearest 0.1%.

Illustration 17-11
Performance report

2.0% or more. However, because the items influencing gross profit are large dollar amounts, small percentage changes affect net income significantly. Therefore, Suntrol's sales manager reviews carefully gross profit results regardless of the amount of change. The 1.2% increase over budget in gross profit is the result of two factors. These factors are a small increase in sales, 0.5% over budget, and a small decrease in cost of merchandise sold, 0.4% under budget. However, these small percentage changes resulted in a gross profit increase of $2,090.00 over budget, the primary contribution to the significant 5.5% increase in net income. The sales manager should determine what actions caused the favorable results in sales and cost of merchandise, then encourage a continuation of those favorable actions.

The administrative manager needs to review the reason for the rapid rise in utility costs. If the utility service cost has increased, the manager cannot change that. However, if power is being wasted, procedures may need to be changed to avoid the waste.

The 5.5% increase in net income enabled Suntrol to meet its profitability goal for the first quarter of 1989 by achieving 7.5% net income as a percent of sales. All managers will be encouraged to continue these positive results.

ACCOUNTING TERMS

What is the meaning of each of the following?

1. budgeting
2. budget
3. budget period
4. comparative income statement
5. performance report

QUESTIONS FOR INDIVIDUAL STUDY

1. What is an important goal for a successful business?
2. Expressing financial information in dollars on a budget is an application of which accounting concept?
3. What three important functions does a budget serve for management?
4. How does preparing a budget require a manager to plan?
5. How does the budgeting process help control expenses?
6. What is the length of time generally covered by a company's budget?
7. Why are annual budgets commonly divided into quarterly and monthly budgets?
8. What is a budgeted income statement?
9. What is a cash budget?
10. What are the four main sources of information for budgeting?

11. Why are general and economic conditions analyzed when preparing a budget?
12. What kind of information does a comparative income statement show?
13. What kind of information about revenue, cost, and expense items is highlighted on a comparative income statement?
14. What action does Suntrol take when analysis of a comparative income statement shows that an item's trend is unfavorable?
15. How do annual goals help a company?
16. Why is the sales budget schedule prepared first?
17. What factors are considered in preparing a sales budget?
18. What factors are considered in preparing a purchases budget?
19. Why do some items in a selling expenses budget stay about the same from period

to period, while other items vary a great deal?

20. What factors are considered in preparing an administrative expenses budget schedule?

21. What are three typical items in an other revenue and expenses budget schedule?

22. Why is a cash budget important?

23. What estimates are made in preparing a cash receipts budget schedule?

24. What estimates are made in preparing a cash payments budget schedule?

25. Why do many companies prepare a performance report at the end of each quarter?

CASES FOR MANAGEMENT DECISION

CASE 1 Jane Rost, president of Soar Corporation, says she has observed that an increase in sales almost always results in an increase in net income. Therefore, she is considering recommending the company set a sales goal increase of 15% for next year and "spare no expense" to achieve this goal. Ms. Rost asks for your opinion regarding her recommendation. How would you respond?

CASE 2 Olivia Moyer, new sales manager for Condor Corporation, recommends to you a new procedure for preparing the company's budgeted income statement. Miss Moyer's suggested procedure is to determine the percent change in actual cost of merchandise for last year compared with the projected cost of merchandise for the budget year. Then adjust each item on the budgeted income statement by the same percentage change. Miss Moyer says her recommended procedure will be "more accurate and simpler to prepare."

Do you agree? Explain the reason for your response.

CASE 3 Ted Grable owns and manages an appliance store. He states that because the business is small, he does not prepare a budgeted income statement. He does not think the time spent in the extra activity is justified since he has not needed a budget in the past. What is Mr. Grable overlooking in his consideration of a budgeted income statement?

CASE 4 Joyce Kingston is general manager of Barre Corporation. She suggests that the budgeted income statement and the cash budget seem to show the same information. Therefore, she recommends that one of the statements be eliminated to reduce accounting costs. What response would you make to Mrs. Kingston?

APPLICATION PROBLEMS

PROBLEM 17-1   Preparing a sales budget schedule and a purchases budget schedule

At the end of 1988, Harrison Corporation plans to prepare a sales budget schedule and a purchases budget schedule for 1989. The accounting records show that sales units have increased about 5% each year over the past four years. This increase is expected to continue in 1989. After reviewing price trends the sales manager estimates that Harrison Corporation will need to increase its sales price per unit of merchandise from $5.70 to $6.00 in 1989.

The sales manager, after checking with the company's merchandise suppliers, estimates that the cost of merchandise will increase from the 1988 cost of $3.45 per unit to $3.60 per unit in 1989.

The accounting records show the following quarterly unit sales in 1988. Ending inventory for 1988 is 52,700 units.

1st quarter	92,900 units	3d quarter	90,600 units
2d quarter	95,200 units	4th quarter	99,500 units

After considering the time required to reorder merchandise, the sales manager established the following desired levels of quarterly ending inventories for 1989.

1st quarter	62,600 units	3d quarter	65,400 units
2d quarter.	60,000 units	4th quarter.	65,400 units

Instructions: 1. Prepare a sales budget schedule for the year ended December 31, 1989, similar to the one illustrated in this chapter. Round all estimates to the nearest 100 units and to the nearest $10.00.
  2. Prepare a purchases budget schedule for the year ended December 31, 1989, similar to the one illustrated in this chapter. Round all estimates to the nearest $10.00.

PROBLEM 17-2 Preparing a budgeted income statement

The sales manager and administrative manager of Samson Company have made the following estimates to be used in preparing a budgeted income statement for 1989.

a. Total net sales for 1989 are estimated to be $1,200,000.00. In each quarter the following percentages of total sales were made.

1st quarter	20%	3d quarter	30%
2d quarter.	25%	4th quarter.	25%

b. Purchases and merchandise ending inventories for 1989 are estimated to be as shown below. Ending inventory for 1988 is $88,250.00.

	Purchases	Ending Inventory
1989	$749,750.00	$ 99,250.00
1st quarter	162,000.00	111,500.00
2d quarter.	208,500.00	132,500.00
3d quarter.	203,000.00	110,500.00
4th quarter	176,250.00	99,250.00

c. Expenses for the year are estimated as shown below. (Percentages are based on quarterly net sales estimated for 1989. Dollar amounts are divided equally among the four quarters.)

Selling Expenses		Administrative Expenses	
Advertising Expense	1.6%	Bad Debts Expense	0.5%
Delivery Expense	0.6%	Depreciation Expense—	
Depreciation Expense—		Office Equipment	$3,280.00
Delivery Equipment	$2,880.00	Insurance Expense	$7,280.00
Depreciation Expense—		Miscellaneous Expense—	
Store Equipment.	$4,560.00	Administrative.	$5,520.00
Miscellaneous Expense—		Payroll Taxes Expense . . .	9% of total
Sales.	$4,320.00		salaries
Salary Expense—Sales . . .	5.0%	Rent Expense.	$15,840.00
Supplies Expense—Sales .	1.0%	Salary Expense—	
		Administrative.	$45,000.00
		Supplies Expense—	
		Office	$6,640.00
		Utilities Expense	$19,680.00

Federal income tax is 25% of each quarter's estimated net income before income tax.

Instructions: 1. Prepare a selling expenses budget schedule and an administrative expenses budget schedule for the year ended December 31, 1989, similar to those illustrated in this chapter. Round amounts to the nearest $10.00.

2. Prepare a budgeted income statement for the year ended December 31, 1989, similar to the one illustrated in this chapter. There are no other revenue and expenses. Round amounts to the nearest $10.00.

PROBLEM 17-3   Preparing a cash budget with supporting schedules

The following table shows Giant Mart's estimated sales, purchases, and cash payments for expenses for 1989.

Quarter	Estimated Sales	Estimated Purchases	Estimated Cash Payments for Expenses
1st	$557,600.00	$469,100.00	$64,100.00
2d	574,900.00	471,600.00	70,200.00
3d	561,800.00	461,200.00	82,400.00
4th	581,600.00	482,300.00	76,800.00

Additional information is listed below.

a. Actual amounts for the 4th quarter of 1988 are: sales, $529,800.00; purchases, $438,240.00.
b. The balance of cash on hand on January 1, 1989, is $45,720.00.
c. In each quarter, cash sales are 10% and collections of accounts receivable are 50% of the total estimated sales for the current quarter. Collections from the preceding quarter's total sales are 39.5% of that quarter. Bad debt losses are 0.5% of total sales.
d. In each quarter, cash payments for cash purchases are 10% and for accounts payable 40% of the purchases for the current quarter. Cash payments for purchases of the preceding quarter are 50% of that quarter.
e. Estimated cash payments for expenses are listed in the table above. Record only total cash payments for expenses.
f. In the second quarter, $24,000.00 will be borrowed on a promissory note, and equipment costing $21,600.00 will be purchased for cash. In the third quarter dividends of $28,800.00 will be paid in cash. In the fourth quarter, the promissory note plus interest will be paid in cash, $26,880.00.
g. Cash payments for estimated income tax are: first quarter, $4,800.00; second quarter, $6,720.00; third quarter, $3,600.00; fourth quarter, $4,560.00.

Instructions: Prepare the following schedules and budget for the four quarters ending December 31, 1989. Round all amounts to the nearest $10.00.
1. Prepare a cash receipts budget schedule (A) similar to the one illustrated in this chapter.
2. Prepare a cash payments budget schedule (B) similar to the one illustrated in this chapter.
3. Prepare a cash budget similar to the one illustrated in this chapter.

ENRICHMENT PROBLEMS

MASTERY PROBLEM 17-M   Preparing a budgeted income statement and a cash budget with supporting schedules

On December 31, 1988, the accounting records of Zack's Sporting Goods show the following unit sales for 1988.

1st quarter	22,000 units	3d quarter	28,000 units
2d quarter	26,600 units	4th quarter	30,500 units
1988 ending inventory			12,500 units

The following are additional actual amounts for the 4th quarter of 1988.

Sales (30,500 units @ $5.60)	$170,800.00
Purchases (26,400 units @ $4.00)	105,600.00

The records also show that sales units have increased about 2% each year over the past five years. This increase is expected to continue in 1989.

The sales manager, after reviewing price trends and checking with the company's merchandise suppliers, estimates the cost of merchandise will increase from the 1988 cost of $4.00 per unit to $4.50 per unit in 1989. Because of the increase in costs, the company will need to increase its sales price per unit of merchandise from $5.60 to $6.30 in 1989.

After considering the time required to reorder merchandise, the sales manager established the following desired levels of quarterly ending inventories for 1989.

1st quarter	13,700 units	3d quarter	15,600 units
2d quarter..............	14,000 units	4th quarter.............	13,300 units

Expenses for 1989 are estimated as shown below. (Percentages are based on quarterly net sales estimated for 1989 unless otherwise noted. Dollar amounts are divided equally among the four quarters.)

Selling Expenses		Administrative Expenses	
Advertising Expense	1.0%	Bad Debts Expense	0.6%
Delivery Expense	0.6%	Depreciation Expense—	
Depreciation Expense—		Office Equipment......	$1,800.00
Delivery Equipment	$1,760.00	Insurance Expense	$2,680.00
Depreciation Expense—		Miscellaneous Expense—	
Store Equipment........	$5,360.00	Administrative.........	$3,000.00
Miscellaneous Expense—		Payroll Taxes Expense...	9% of total
Sales..................	0.4%		salaries
Salary Expense—Sales ...	5.0%	Rent Expense...........	$9,600.00
Supplies Expense—Sales .	0.8%	Salary Expense—	
		Administrative.........	$25,200.00
		Supplies Expense—	
		Office	$2,800.00
		Utilities Expense	1.8%

Interest expense for the year ended December 31, 1989 is $750.00 each quarter.
Federal income tax is 25% of each quarter's estimated net income before income tax.

Additional information is listed below.
a. The balance of cash on hand on January 1, 1989, is $32,300.00.
b. In each quarter, cash sales are 10% and collections of accounts receivable are 40% of the total estimated sales for the current quarter. Collections from the preceding quarter's total sales are 49.4% of that quarter. Bad debt losses are 0.6% of total sales.
c. In each quarter, cash payments for cash purchases are 10% and for accounts payable 55% of the purchases for the current quarter. Cash payments for purchases of the preceding quarter are 35% of that quarter.
d. Selling and administrative expenses are paid in the quarter incurred. Cash is not paid for depreciation and bad debt expenses.
e. In the first quarter, $20,000.00 will be borrowed on a promissory note, and equipment costing $30,000.00 will be purchased for cash. In each quarter, dividends of $10,000.00 will be paid in cash. In the fourth quarter, the promissory note plus interest will be paid in cash, $23,000.00.

Instructions: Prepare the following schedules and budgets for the year ended December 31, 1989. Round all estimates to the nearest 100 units and to the nearest $10.00.

1. Prepare a sales budget schedule (1). Figure total budgeted sales units for the year based on a 2% estimated increase. This estimate may not equal the sum of the four quarterly estimates due to rounding differences.

2. Prepare a purchases budget schedule (2).

3. Prepare a selling expenses budget schedule (3).

4. Prepare an administrative expenses budget schedule (4).

5. Prepare an other revenue and expenses budget schedule (5).

6. Prepare a budgeted income statement.

7. Prepare a cash receipts schedule (A).

8. Prepare a cash payments schedule (B).

9. Prepare a cash budget.

CHALLENGE PROBLEM 17-C Preparing a budgeted income statement and a cash budget with supporting schedules

On December 31, 1988, the accounting records of Brownwood Industries show the following unit sales for 1988. Ending inventory for 1988 is 63,400 units.

1st quarter	112,200 units	3d quarter	110,200 units
2d quarter	115,300 units	4th quarter	120,400 units

Because of increased competition, sales units are projected to decrease about 2% in 1989 from 1988.

The sales manager, after reviewing price trends and checking with the company's merchandise suppliers, estimates the cost of merchandise will increase from the 1988 cost of $2.60 per unit to $2.80 per unit in 1989. Because of the increased competition, Brownwood plans to hold the sales price per unit of merchandise in 1989 to the 1988 price, $4.50 per unit.

After considering the time required to reorder merchandise, the sales manager established the following desired levels of quarterly ending inventories for 1989.

1st quarter	71,600 units	3d quarter	74,800 units
2d quarter	68,400 units	4th quarter	71,200 units

Expenses for 1989 are estimated as shown below. (Percentages are based on quarterly net sales estimated for 1989 unless otherwise noted. Dollar amounts are divided equally among the four quarters.)

Selling Expenses		Administrative Expenses	
Advertising Expense	1.8%	Bad Debts Expense	0.6%
Delivery Expense	1.4%	Depreciation Expense —	
Depreciation Expense —		Office Equipment	$4,680.00
Delivery Equipment	$4,320.00	Insurance Expense	$13,800.00
Depreciation Expense —		Miscellaneous Expense —	
Store Equipment	$5,560.00	Administrative	$16,100.00
Miscellaneous		Payroll Taxes Expense . .	9% of total
Expense — Sales	1.0%		salaries
Salary Expense — Sales . . .	8.0%	Rent Expense	$27,600.00
Supplies Expense — Sales .	1.4%	Salary Expense —	
		Administrative	$132,400.00
		Supplies Expense —	
		Office	$11,280.00
		Utilities Expense	$44,300.00

The following is the interest expense for the year ended December 31, 1989.

1st quarter	None	3d quarter	$1,500.00
2d quarter.	$1,500.00	4th quarter.	$1,500.00

The following are the annual federal income tax rates.

15% of first $25,000.00 net income before taxes
18% of net income over $25,000.00 to $50,000.00
30% of net income over $50,000.00 to $75,000.00
40% of net income over $75,000.00 to $100,000.00
46% of net income over $100,000.00

Allocate the quarterly tax estimate in relation to the quarter's net income before taxes as a percent of the year's net income. Round the percent to the nearest 0.1%.

Additional information needed to prepare the cash budget is listed below.

a. Actual amounts for the 4th quarter of 1988 are: sales, $541,800.00; purchases, $314,200.00.
b. The balance of cash on hand on January 1, 1989, is $49,820.00.
c. In each quarter, cash sales are 10% and collections of accounts receivable are 50% of the total estimated sales for the current quarter. Collections from the preceding quarter's total sales are 39.4% of that quarter. Bad debt losses are 0.6% of total sales.
d. In each quarter, cash payments for cash purchases are 10% and for accounts payable 40% of the purchases for the current quarter. Cash payments for purchases of the preceding quarter are 50% of that quarter.
e. Selling and administrative expenses are paid in the quarter incurred.
f. In the first and third quarters, dividends of $35,000.00 will be paid in cash. In the second quarter, equipment costing $40,000.00 will be purchased for cash and $40,000.00 will be borrowed on a promissory note. In the fourth quarter, the promissory note plus interest will be paid in cash, $44,500.00.

Instructions: Prepare the following schedules and budget for the year ended December 31, 1989. Round all estimates to the nearest 100 units and to the nearest $10.00.

1. Prepare a sales budget schedule (1).
2. Prepare a purchases budget schedule (2).
3. Prepare a selling expenses budget schedule (3).
4. Prepare an administrative expenses budget schedule (4).
5. Prepare an other revenue and expenses budget schedule (5).
6. Prepare a budgeted income statement.
7. Prepare a cash receipts schedule (A).
8. Prepare a cash payments schedule (B).
9. Prepare a cash budget.

18 Accounting Information for Management Decisions

ENABLING PERFORMANCE TASKS

After studying Chapter 18, you will be able to:
a. Define accounting terms related to accounting information for management decisions.
b. Identify accounting concepts and practices related to preparing accounting information for management decisions.
c. Prepare an income statement reporting contribution margin.
d. Figure the breakeven point in sales volume and sales units.
e. Determine the effect of changes in volume, cost, unit price, and sales mix on net income.

Sound management decisions frequently determine whether a business earns a favorable net income. Earning a favorable net income is necessary for a business to continue to grow and prosper. Thus, earning a favorable net income is a major business objective. Previous performance as well as comparisons to industry standards usually determine what is considered to be a favorable net income for a given business. Many management decisions therefore are dependent upon complete and accurate information about revenues and costs. (CONCEPT: Adequate Disclosure)

COST CHARACTERISTICS THAT INFLUENCE DECISIONS

A manager increases company net income by making decisions that (a) increase revenues, and/or (b) decrease costs. Managers, with the advice and assistance of accountants, identify a company's strengths and weaknesses by analyzing sales and cost information. An income statement is one source of information on which a manager can base decisions. An income statement includes information about sales, cost of merchandise sold, gross profit, selling and administrative expenses, and net income. All of these items are important indicators that a company is earning a favorable net income. However, if net income is going down, an income statement may not help a manager identify causes for the decline. A manager may need greater detail about costs than typical financial reports contain. *(CONCEPT: Adequate Disclosure)*

Total costs versus unit cost

All costs for a specific period of time are called total costs. The abbreviated income statement in Illustration 18-1 shows the cost of merchandise sold, $54,000.00, one part of total costs for the period October 1 through October 31. The $38,800.00 selling expenses for October are another part of total costs. Total costs show how many total dollars were spent for all activities during a specific period of time. *(CONCEPT: Accounting Period Cycle)*

Suntrol, Inc.		
Income Statement		
For Month Ended October 31, 1988		
Operating Revenue:		
Sales		$120,000.00
Cost of Merchandise Sold		54,000.00
Gross Profit on Operations		$ 66,000.00
Operating Expenses:		
Selling Expenses	$38,800.00	
Administrative Expenses	16,200.00	
Total Operating Expenses		55,000.00
Income from Operations		$ 11,000.00
Other Expenses		200.00
Net Income		$ 10,800.00

Illustration 18-1
Abbreviated income
statement

An amount spent for one of a specific product or service is called a unit cost. Suntrol sold 16,000 square feet of blinds in October at a $54,000.00 total cost. The unit cost of each square foot of blinds is $3.375 ($54,000.00 total costs ÷ 16,000 square feet).

Suntrol's sales personnel made 500 sales contacts during October to sell blinds. The selling expense unit cost per sales contact for blinds is $77.60 ($38,800.00 total selling expenses ÷ 500 contacts).

Units may be expressed in many different terms. However, units should be expressed in terms that are meaningful to the people who are responsible for the costs. Some examples of other unit terms are gallons, liters, pounds, kilograms, inches, yards, meters, and hours. Knowing unit costs can be helpful to a manager in setting unit selling prices and in planning cost control.

Variable costs

Costs may be separated into two parts: variable and fixed. Costs which change in direct proportion to the change in number of units are called variable costs.

For example, a business buys one microcomputer diskette at a cost of $4.00. Later the business buys ten more diskettes at a cost of $40.00 (10 × $4.00). The cost of the diskettes is a variable cost. The change in cost is the same percentage of increase as the percentage of increase in the number of units. The second purchase is ten times the first in both units and total cost.

Suntrol's louvered blind purchases for the months January through June, 1988, are shown in Illustration 18-2.

Suntrol, Inc. Louvered Blind Purchases For Period January 1-June 30, 1988			
Month	Units Purchased	Unit Cost per sq. ft.	Total Cost
January	12,000	$3.375	$40,500.00
February	13,400	3.375	45,225.00
March	16,400	3.375	55,350.00
April	17,400	3.375	58,725.00
May	20,200	3.375	68,175.00
June	22,800	3.375	76,950.00

Illustration 18-2
Louvered blind purchases

The volume of blinds purchased ranges from a low of 12,000 square feet in January to a high of 22,800 square feet in June. However, the price paid per square foot (unit cost) remained at $3.375 throughout the six month period. A comparison of the relationship of *total cost* per month to *units purchased* per month shows that both change in the same proportion. For example, the 22,800 units purchased in June is 1.9 times greater than the 12,000 units purchased in January (22,800 ÷ 12,000 = 1.9). The $76,950.00 paid for the June purchases is also 1.9 times greater than the $40,500.00 paid for the January purchases ($76,950.00 ÷ $40,500.00 = 1.9). The unit cost is $3.375 per square foot in each instance. Therefore, these costs have the characteristics of variable costs.

Suntrol's monthly costs for purchases of blinds are plotted on a graph as shown in Illustration 18-3. The line drawn between the plotted points is a straight, sloped line.

The line is straight because Suntrol's unit cost per square foot remained the same even though the number of units purchased per month varied. The change is in *direct proportion* to the quantities purchased. This situation results in a straight line on a graph that rises as quantities increase from month to month.

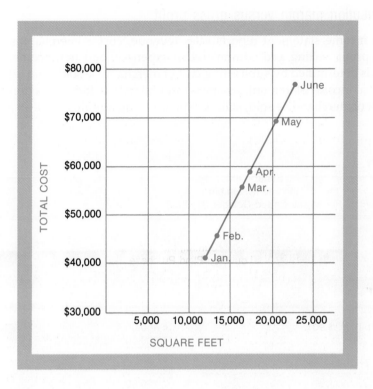

Illustration 18-3
Variable costs
characteristics

Fixed costs

Costs that remain constant regardless of change in business activity are called fixed costs. For example, if Suntrol's rent is $2,000.00 per month, the rent is a fixed cost. Rent is *fixed* because the amount has been set at $2,000.00 per month regardless of how many square feet of blinds are sold. If each monthly rental cost is plotted on a graph and connected, the chart will appear as shown in Illustration 18-4. The fixed cost line is a straight line parallel to the base of the graph.

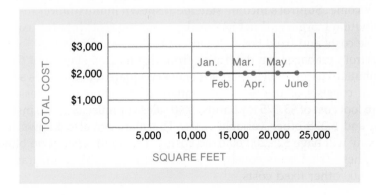

Illustration 18-4
Fixed costs characteristics

Contribution margin versus gross profit

An income statement reports sales revenue, cost of merchandise sold, gross profit, selling and administrative expenses, and net income. Gross profit is determined by subtracting cost of merchandise sold from sales. On a typical income statement, as shown in Illustration 18-5, costs are shown as cost of merchandise sold, selling expenses, and administrative expenses.

Suntrol, Inc.
Income Statement
For Month Ended October 31, 1988

Operating Revenue:			
Sales (16,000 sq. ft. @ $7.50)			$120,000.00
Cost of Merchandise Sold (16,000 sq. ft. @ $3.375)............			54,000.00
Gross Profit on Operations			$ 66,000.00
Operating Expenses:			
Selling Expenses:			
Sales Commission (16,000 sq. ft. @ $.60)	$ 9,600.00		
Installation Costs (16,000 sq. ft. @ $.90)....................	14,400.00		
Other Selling Expenses.......................................	14,800.00	$38,800.00	
Administrative Expenses:			
Rent...	$2,000.00		
Insurance	125.00		
Other Administrative Expenses	14,075.00	16,200.00	
Total Operating Expenses.....................................			55,000.00
Income from Operations			$ 11,000.00
Other Expenses..			200.00
Net Income...			$ 10,800.00

Illustration 18-5
Abbreviated income
statement with gross
profit

Income determined by subtracting all variable costs from sales revenue is called contribution margin. Contribution margin is also known as marginal income. Suntrol's income statement shown in Illustration 18-6 reports contribution margin and net income by grouping costs into two categories: variable costs and fixed costs. *(CONCEPT: Adequate Disclosure)*

Suntrol's manager can determine from this income statement that $2.25 contribution margin will be earned for every square foot of blinds sold. This amount consists of the $7.50 per square foot selling price, less the per square foot cost of $3.375 for blinds, $.60 sales commission, $.90 installation costs, and $.375 other variable costs. The manager also knows that the company will have $25,200.00 fixed costs each month even if no blinds are sold. These fixed costs consist of $2,000.00 rent, $125.00 insurance, and $23,075.00 other fixed costs.

Suntrol, Inc.
Income Statement
For Month Ended October 31, 1988

Operating Revenue:		
Sales (16,000 sq. ft. @ $7.50)		$120,000.00
Less Variable Costs:		
Cost of Blinds (16,000 sq. ft. @ $3.375)	$54,000.00	
Sales Commission (16,000 sq. ft. @ $.60)	9,600.00	
Installation Costs (16,000 sq. ft. @ $.90).	14,400.00	
Other Variable Costs (16,000 sq. ft. @ $.375)	6,000.00	
Total Variable Costs		84,000.00
Contribution Margin.		$ 36,000.00
Less Fixed Costs:		
Rent.	$ 2,000.00	
Insurance	125.00	
Other Fixed Costs.	23,075.00	
Total Fixed Costs		25,200.00
Net Income.		$ 10,800.00

Illustration 18-6
Abbreviated income
statement with
contribution margin

DECISIONS THAT AFFECT INCOME

If a manager is to make decisions that yield a favorable net income for a company, two important kinds of information are needed. (1) The amount of merchandise or services the company must sell to make a favorable net income. (2) The factors that contribute most to net income.

Figuring the breakeven point

The amount of sales at which sales revenue is exactly the same as total costs is called the breakeven point. At the breakeven point, neither a net income nor a net loss will occur. Suntrol figures the breakeven point to determine how many dollars worth of merchandise must be sold before the company begins to earn a net income.

Three amounts are required to figure a breakeven point.

1. Total revenue.
2. Total variable costs.
3. Total fixed costs.

A breakeven point is figured in three steps.

1 *Figure the contribution margin.* Suntrol's contribution margin for October, $36,000.00, is shown on the income statement, Illustration 18-6. Contribution margin is figured as follows.

Total Revenue	−	**Total Variable Costs**	=	**Contribution Margin**
$120,000.00	−	$84,000.00	=	$36,000.00

2 *Figure the contribution margin rate.* Contribution margin rate is figured as follows.

Contribution Margin	÷	Total Revenue	=	Contribution Margin Rate
$36,000.00	÷	$120,000.00	=	.30 or 30%

Variable costs change in direct proportion to changes in sales activity. Therefore, the contribution margin rate means that for every $1.00 of revenue, $0.70 is required for variable costs. Also for every $1.00 of revenue, $0.30 is contribution margin. The contribution margin is available to pay for fixed costs and provide net income.

3 *Figure the breakeven point.* The breakeven point is the amount of sales at which the entire contribution margin is used to pay for fixed costs. The contribution margin rate for Suntrol is 30%. The breakeven point is figured as follows.

Total Fixed Costs	÷	Contribution Margin Rate	=	Breakeven Point
$25,200.00	÷	.30 or 30%	=	$84,000.00

Suntrol must have total sales revenue of $84,000.00 just to recover the costs of doing business. Suntrol's manager knows that more than $84,000.00 in sales must be made if the company is to earn a net income.

Sales dollar breakeven point versus product unit breakeven point. A manager also is interested in how many units of merchandise must be sold to break even. Four steps are used to figure a product unit breakeven point.

1 *Determine sales price per unit.* Suntrol's sales price per unit, $7.50, is shown on the income statement, Illustration 18-6.

2 *Determine the variable costs per unit.* Unit costs are added for all items with variable costs.

Item	Variable Costs per Unit
Blinds..	$3.375
Sales commission...................................	.60
Installation costs	.90
Other variable costs	.375
Total variable costs per square foot.................	$5.25

3 *Figure the contribution margin per unit.* Contribution margin per unit is figured as follows.

Sales Price per Square Foot	−	Variable Costs per Unit	=	Contribution Margin per Unit
$7.50	−	$5.25	=	$2.25

4 *Figure the breakeven point in units.* The breakeven point is figured as follows.

Total Fixed Costs	÷	Contribution Margin per Unit	=	Breakeven Point in Units
$25,200.00	÷	$2.25	=	11,200 units

Suntrol must sell more than 11,200 square feet of blinds per month before the company begins to make a net income.

Breakeven point computation verification. The simplest way to verify the breakeven figure's accuracy is to prepare an income statement using the breakeven point numbers. If the breakeven point is accurate, net income will be zero. The breakeven income statement in Illustration 18-7 shows the proof for Suntrol's breakeven point figures.

Suntrol, Inc.
Breakeven Income Statement
For a Projected Month

Operating Revenue:		
Sales (11,200 sq. ft. @ $7.50)		$84,000.00
Less Variable Costs:		
Cost of Blinds (11,200 sq. ft. @ $3.375)	$37,800.00	
Sales Commission (11,200 sq. ft. @ $.60)	6,720.00	
Installation Costs (11,200 sq. ft. @ $.90)	10,080.00	
Other Variable Costs (11,200 sq. ft. @ $.375)	4,200.00	
Total Variable Costs		58,800.00
Contribution Margin...............................		$25,200.00
Less Fixed Costs:		
Rent...	$ 2,000.00	
Insurance	125.00	
Other Fixed Costs................................	23,075.00	
Total Fixed Costs		25,200.00
Net Income..		-0-

Illustration 18-7
Breakeven income statement

The breakeven point in units (11,200 square feet) times the normal sales price per unit ($7.50 per square foot) equals the breakeven point in sales dollars ($84,000.00). Also, the contribution margin of $25,200.00 is 30% of sales ($84,000.00). This verifies Suntrol's contribution margin rate of 30%.

Determining the effect of changes on net income

Knowing the breakeven point for October will not help a manager plan business activities for October. However, the October information may have implications for November activity. Managers making decisions about future activities need information that helps predict future events. Since actual information is not available for the future, the next best thing, information from the past, is used.

To more accurately plan, Suntrol needs estimated answers to questions such as the following. What will be the net income if 14,400 square feet of blinds are sold rather than 16,000 square feet? If 17,600 square feet of blinds are sold? What will happen to net income if the sales price per square foot is increased from $7.50 to $8.25? Decreased from $7.50 to $6.75? How will net income be affected if the cost of merchandise increases from $3.375 to $3.75 per square foot? Decreases from $3.375 to $3.00 per square foot?

Volume changes. The relationship of sales to costs and net income is shown below.

$$\text{Sales} = \text{Variable Costs} + \text{Fixed Costs} + \text{Net Income}$$

Also, variable costs are always a percentage of each sales dollar regardless of the sales amount. The remainder, contribution margin, is available to pay fixed costs and contribute to net income. Fixed costs must be paid first and any amount remaining is net income. *(CONCEPT: Matching Expenses with Revenue)*

Illustration 18-8 shows how net income changes as units sold change.

1	2	3	4	5
	Per Unit	Number of Units		
		10,100 sq. ft.	11,200 sq. ft.	12,300 sq. ft.
Sales	$7.50	$75,750.00	$84,000.00	$92,250.00
Variable Costs	5.25	53,025.00	58,800.00	64,575.00
Contribution Margin. .	$2.25	$22,725.00	$25,200.00	$27,675.00
Fixed Costs		25,200.00	25,200.00	25,200.00
Net Income (Loss). . .		($ 2,475.00)	-0-	$ 2,475.00

Illustration 18-8
Effect of volume changes
on net income

From every square foot of blinds Suntrol sells, $2.25 contribution margin is available for fixed costs and net income. The manager knows that there are $25,200.00 fixed costs each month. Therefore, the entire $2.25 per square foot contribution margin will be applied to fixed costs until the $25,200.00 has been paid. For every square foot of blinds sold above 11,200 (the breakeven point), the $2.25 per square foot contribution margin will be net income. Therefore, when 12,300 square feet of blinds are sold, as shown in column 5, contribution margin from the first 11,200 units will pay the fixed costs. Contribution margin from the remaining 1,100 square feet of blinds will result in a net income of $2,475.00 (1,100 square feet × $2.25). *(CONCEPT: Matching Expenses with Revenue)*

If only 10,100 square feet of blinds are sold during the month, the contribution margin of $22,725.00 will not cover the fixed costs of $25,200.00. At this sales volume, a net loss of $2,475.00 will result, as shown in column 3.

The graph, Illustration 18-9, shows the relationship of sales, costs, and net income as the volume of units changes.

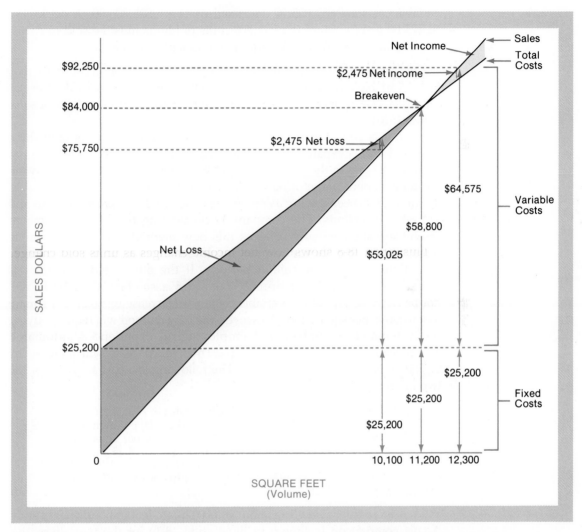

The sales line, beginning at zero, represents unit sales price times number of units sold. The total costs line starting at $25,200.00 (total fixed costs) represents the total amount of costs for the number of units sold. The variable cost area represents 70% of sales regardless of volume. The fixed costs are $25,200.00. No matter what the sales volume is, the fixed costs remain constant, as shown by the horizontal line at the bottom of the graph.

If 11,200 square feet of blinds are sold for $84,000.00, the variable costs are $58,800.00 and fixed costs are $25,200.00. No net income is earned. If 12,300 square feet of blinds are sold, the sales revenue, $92,250.00, is composed of variable costs, $64,575.00, fixed costs, $25,200.00, and net income, $2,475.00. If only 10,100 square feet of blinds are sold for $75,750.00, the

Illustration 18-9
Effect of sales volume on net income

variable costs are $53,025.00 and fixed costs are $25,200.00. A net loss of $2,475.00 results. More than 11,200 units of blinds must be sold to earn a net income. *(CONCEPT: Matching Expenses with Revenue)*

Cost changes. Two types of costs influence the decisions a company may make: variable costs and fixed costs. Variable costs increase or decrease as sales increase or decrease. Fixed costs remain constant regardless of sales amount. *(CONCEPT: Consistent Reporting)*

Suntrol is considering a sales alternative. The company is only three years old and is expanding sales each year. However, the net income has been decreasing in the current year, 1988. Suntrol is searching for ways to improve its percentage of net income per sales dollar.

Suntrol has been paying a crew $.30 per square foot to manually cut and assemble the blinds. The company is considering buying an automated assembler. The company believes this new method will make assembly more efficient and permit regular employees to assist with the assembly operation during slow selling periods. If the automated assembler is bought, the crew that manually cuts and assembles the blinds will not be needed. Therefore, variable costs will decrease by $0.30 per square foot to $4.95 per square foot. However, the new method will require buying the automated assembler and employing an experienced automated assembler operator at a fixed salary. Thus, fixed costs will increase by $4,800.00 per month to $30,000.00. The following is a cost analysis for the two alternatives.

Alternative 1: *Manual assembly.* Variable costs per square foot of blinds are $5.25. Fixed costs are $25,200.00 per month.

Alternative 2: *Automated assembly.* Variable costs per square foot of blinds are estimated to be $4.95 ($5.25 minus $0.30 savings). Fixed costs are estimated to be $30,000.00 per month. ($25,200.00 plus $4,800.00 additional fixed costs).

Sales have been averaging about 16,000 square feet of blinds per month. A cost comparison is shown in Illustration 18-10 for the two alternative plans assuming sales volume continues at 16,000 square feet per month.

	Alternative 1 Manual Assembly			Alternative 2 Automated Assembly		
	Per Unit	Units Sold	Total	Per Unit	Units Sold	Total
Sales	$7.50	16,000	$120,000.00	$7.50	16,000	$120,000.00
Variable Costs	5.25	16,000	84,000.00	4.95	16,000	79,200.00
Contribution Margin	$2.25	16,000	$ 36,000.00	$2.55	16,000	$ 40,800.00
Fixed Costs			25,200.00			30,000.00
Net Income (Loss) . .			$ 10,800.00			$ 10,800.00

Illustration 18-10
Effect of variable and
fixed costs — average
volume

At a 16,000 unit sales level, net income is the same for both alternatives. With Alternative 2, the contribution margin is higher, but fixed costs also are higher. Thus, the higher fixed costs cancel out the higher contribution margin.

If Suntrol expects increased sales, a cost comparison may be made for a higher sales rate. Cost comparisons with a 20% sales increase to 19,200 units are shown in Illustration 18-11.

	Alternative 1 Manual Assembly			Alternative 2 Automated Assembly		
	Per Unit	Units Sold	Total	Per Unit	Units Sold	Total
Sales	$7.50	19,200	$144,000.00	$7.50	19,200	$144,000.00
Variable Costs	5.25	19,200	100,800.00	4.95	19,200	95,040.00
Contribution Margin	$2.25	19,200	$ 43,200.00	$2.55	19,200	$ 48,960.00
Fixed Costs			25,200.00			30,000.00
Net Income (Loss). .			$ 18,000.00			$ 18,960.00

Illustration 18-11
Effect of variable and fixed costs — above average volume

With the increased sales volume, Alternative 2 earns a higher net income. If Suntrol expects a sales increase, Alternative 2 would be more profitable than Alternative 1.

However, if there is doubt whether sales will increase, the results could be much different. From the previous cost comparison, one may conclude that Alternative 2 will earn about 5% more than Alternative 1. However, if the number of units actually sold is 20% less (12,800 units) than previous average sales, the results will favor Alternative 1. At the lower volume, shown in Illustration 18-12, Alternative 1 will earn $3,600.00 net income while Alternative 2 will earn only $2,640.00 net income.

	Alternative 1 Manual Assembly			Alternative 2 Automated Assembly		
	Per Unit	Units Sold	Total	Per Unit	Units Sold	Total
Sales	$7.50	12,800	$96,000.00	$7.50	12,800	$96,000.00
Variable Costs	5.25	12,800	67,200.00	4.95	12,800	63,360.00
Contribution Margin	$2.25	12,800	$28,800.00	$2.55	12,800	$32,640.00
Fixed Costs			25,200.00			30,000.00
Net Income (Loss). .			$ 3,600.00			$ 2,640.00

Illustration 18-12
Effect of variable and fixed costs — below average volume

What is the reason for the change in favorable alternatives? The contribution margin rate favors Alternative 2.

Illustration 18-13 shows that the contribution margin rate for Alternative 1 is 30% ($36,000.00 ÷ $120,000.00) versus 34% ($40,800.00 ÷ $120,000.00) for Alternative 2. This means that for every $1.00 of sales from Alternative 1, $0.30 is available for fixed costs and net income. But for every $1.00 of sales from Alternative 2, $0.34 is available for fixed costs and net income. *(CONCEPT: Matching Expenses with Revenue)*

Illustration 18-13
Effects of different
variable costs on
contribution margin rate

	Alternative 1 Manual Assembly		Alternative 2 Automated Assembly	
	Dollars	Percent	Dollars	Percent
Sales	$120,000.00	100%	$120,000.00	100%
Variable Costs	84,000.00	70%	79,200.00	66%
Contribution Margin ..	$ 36,000.00	30%	$ 40,800.00	34%

A high contribution margin rate is desirable. However, fixed costs must also be reasonable since the contribution margin must cover the fixed costs before any net income is earned. The contribution margin rate for the automated assembly method is more favorable (34%). But, as shown in the cost comparison charts, fixed costs are $30,000.00, $4,800.00 more than fixed costs for the manual assembly method. Thus, if sales volume is reduced as shown in Illustration 18-12, the increased contribution margin is not enough to recover the increased fixed costs and a reduction in net income occurs. By comparison, the manual assembly method with a lower fixed cost is a more profitable operation when sales volume declines 20%.

A logical conclusion is that: "Everything else being equal, the activity with the higher contribution margin rate is more profitable." If "everything else" is equal, selecting the more profitable choice is very simple. However, alternatives normally are not that simple because fixed costs probably will differ for each alternative. Therefore, an effective business looks for the best combination of fixed and variable costs.

Unit price changes. Setting the selling price of products is extremely important for a business that expects to make a reasonable net income. If the price is set too high, potential customers will buy from another business. If the price is set too low, the company may lose money. The objective then is to set selling prices which provide a reasonable amount of net income while keeping prices competitive.

Illustration 18-14 shows Suntrol's October net income based on 16,000 units at the current price.

Suntrol decides that although a monthly net income of $10,800.00 is acceptable, an increase in net income is more desirable. Company prices are compared with those of competitors. Suntrol then predicts that a 10% reduction in selling price will result in a 20% increase in the number of units

	Per Unit			No. Units Sold	Total		
	Sales Price	Variable Costs	Contr. Margin		Sales	Variable Costs	Contr. Margin
Blinds, sq. ft.	$7.50	$5.25	$2.25	16,000	$120,000.00	$84,000.00	$36,000.00
Less Fixed Costs. . . .							25,200.00
Net Income (Loss). . .							$10,800.00

sold. Before making these changes, the schedule shown in Illustration 18-15 is prepared to estimate the effect of this price change on sales volume and net income. As the schedule shows, a 10% reduction in unit price and a 20% increase in volume results in a significant reduction in net income.

Illustration 18-14
Net income at current price

	Per Unit			No. Units Sold	Total		
	Sales Price	Variable Costs	Contr. Margin		Sales	Variable Costs	Contr. Margin
Blinds, sq. ft.	$6.75	$5.25	$1.50	19,200	$129,600.00	$100,800.00	$28,800.00
Less Fixed Costs. . . .							25,200.00
Net Income (Loss). . .							$ 3,600.00

Price cutting can be dangerous. In October, Suntrol had a $2.25 contribution margin per square foot of blinds sold. Sales of 16,000 units resulted in $36,000.00 total contribution margin. A price reduction of 10% ($0.75 per unit) reduces the contribution margin to $1.50. The contribution margin would be reduced 33⅓% (from $2.25 to $1.50) even though the total selling price would be reduced only 10%.

Illustration 18-15
Effect of 10% reduction in sales price and 20% increase in units sold

The potential results of a price cut can be figured as follows. Divide total contribution margin (or desired contribution margin) by new contribution margin per unit to determine number of units to be sold.

October Contribution Margin		New Contribution Margin Per Unit		Unit Sales Required to Maintain Net Income
$36,000.00	÷	$1.50	=	24,000 units

A decrease in price from $7.50 to $6.75 is estimated to increase sales from 16,000 to 19,200 units. However, at $6.75, a total of 24,000 units would have to be sold to maintain the same net income as current sales at the $7.50 price. Reducing the selling price by $0.75 would not be a profitable decision if only 19,200 units can be sold.

Sales mix changes. If price increases could be freely made, each product could be priced to yield a desired amount of net income. However, competition frequently prevents a desired price increase. For example, a sports equipment store prices an exercise bicycle at $175.00. A bicycle of similar quality is priced at $140.00 by competitors. The first store probably will not sell many bicycles at $175.00.

Relative distribution of sales among various products is called sales mix A company's sales mix is determined by figuring the relationship of each product's sales dollars to total sales dollars. Sales mix is important in maintaining net income. If products with the highest contribution margin can be identified and sales increased for those products, overall net income should increase.

Suntrol has been selling only aluminum blinds during the first four years of the company's life. Sales revenue is always low during the winter months. In an effort to increase sales, the company tested the market in December, a slow sales month, by selling vinyl blinds. The effect of the sales mix for December when both aluminum and vinyl blinds were sold is shown in Illustration 18-16.

	Per Unit			No. Units Sold	Total		
	Sales Price	Variable Costs	Contr. Margin		Sales	Variable Costs	Contr. Margin
Aluminum Blinds	$7.50	$5.25	$2.25	9,000	$67,500.00	$47,250.00	$20,250.00
Vinyl Blinds.	5.00	2.75	2.25	1,000	5,000.00	2,750.00	2,250.00
Totals.					$72,500.00	$50,000.00	$22,500.00
Less Fixed Costs. . . .							25,200.00
Net Income (Loss). . .							($ 2,700.00)

Illustration 18-16
Effect of sales mix on net income

Suntrol lost $2,700.00 during December operations. After reviewing the December contribution margin and net loss, Suntrol made the following observations.

1. An increase in the price of blinds is probably unacceptable because competitors would then be selling similar blinds at a lower price.
2. Variable costs are as low as possible.
3. Fixed costs cannot be reduced.

Can Suntrol operate profitably during the winter months? Suntrol's manager noticed that each unit of aluminum blinds sold for $7.50 and earned $2.25 contribution margin—a contribution margin of 30%. However, each unit of vinyl blind sold for only $5.00 and also earned $2.25 contribution margin—a contribution margin of 45%. Why not, during the slow, winter months, change the sales emphasis to sell more vinyl blinds? What changes would be necessary if Suntrol decided to change the sales mix? What would be the impact if they were successful in making the change? A larger variety of vinyl blinds would need to be stocked in inventory. Advertising emphasis would need to be changed from aluminum to vinyl blinds. Sales personnel would need to call on more potential vinyl blind customers.

Illustration 18-17 shows what the December results would have been with the same amount of sales if the sales mix had been changed.

	Per Unit			No. Units Sold	Total		
	Sales Price	Variable Costs	Contr. Margin		Sales	Variable Costs	Contr. Margin
Aluminum Blinds	$7.50	$5.25	$2.25	5,800	$43,500.00	$30,450.00	$13,050.00
Vinyl Blinds.	5.00	2.75	2.25	5,800	29,000.00	15,950.00	13,050.00
Totals.					$72,500.00	$46,400.00	$26,100.00
Less Fixed Costs. . . .							25,200.00
Net Income (Loss). . .							$ 900.00

In evaluating the effect of a sales mix change, the amount of sales is assumed to be the same as October sales, $72,500.00. The unit sales prices, unit variable costs, and fixed costs remain the same. The only change is the sales mix. Fewer units of aluminum blinds would be sold but more units of vinyl blinds, with a higher contribution margin rate, would be sold. The change in sales mix would change operating results from a $2,700.00 net loss to a $900.00 net income.

Illustration 18-17
Effect of change in sales mix

ACCOUNTING TERMS

What is the meaning of each of the following?

1. total costs
2. unit cost
3. variable costs
4. fixed costs
5. contribution margin
6. breakeven point
7. sales mix

QUESTIONS FOR INDIVIDUAL STUDY

1. What is a major objective for most businesses?
2. Providing complete and accurate information about revenues and costs for managers' decisions is an application of which accounting concept?
3. How can a manager identify a company's strengths and weaknesses?
4. What additional information not provided on an income statement may a manager need to identify a declining net income problem?
5. Reporting dollars spent for all activities during a specific period of time is an application of which accounting concept?
6. What are the differences between variable and fixed costs?
7. If total monthly variable costs for a company were plotted on a graph for six months, what kind of line would connect the plotted points? Would the line be parallel to the base or sloped? Explain why.

8. If total monthly fixed costs for a company were plotted on a graph for six months, what kind of line would connect the plotted points? Would the line be parallel to the base or sloped? Explain why.

9. How does contribution margin differ from gross profit?

10. What financial information is required to figure a company's breakeven point?

11. How is contribution margin figured?

12. How is the contribution margin rate figured?

13. What does the contribution margin rate represent?

14. How is the breakeven point figured?

15. How is the breakeven point in product units figured?

16. What is the simplest way to verify a breakeven figure's accuracy?

17. Why is knowledge of the contribution margin rate helpful to a business?

18. Which of the following changes will have the most significant effect on net income?
    a. 20% reduction in sales price.
    b. 20% increase in variable costs.
    c. 20% increase in fixed costs.

19. How can a company with no change in sales amount increase its net income by changing its sales mix?

CASES FOR MANAGEMENT DECISION

CASE 1 Sally Akins, the new accountant for Americo Company, has recommended that income statements reporting contribution margin be prepared rather than statements reporting gross profit. She states that the income statement with contribution margin is better information. Jeff Bauman, the manager, disagrees that one statement is better than the other. He says gross profit is the same as contribution margin so it does not make any difference which statement is prepared. Which person is correct? Explain.

CASE 2 Concrete Supreme has been earning approximately $75,000.00 per month. The following information is from a typical abbreviated monthly income statement.

Sales.................	$600,000.00
Variable Costs..........	450,000.00
Contribution Margin	$150,000.00
Fixed Costs............	75,000.00
Net Income	$ 75,000.00

A new concrete mixing process has been introduced. Concrete Supreme is considering changing to the new process. You are asked to evaluate the financial effects. At the same level of sales, variable costs will be reduced to $360,000.00 but fixed costs will increase to $180,000.00. What is your recommendation? Explain your reasons. Under what conditions would you recommend the change?

CASE 3 Gus MacRae manages a paint store. He has been selling about 3,000 gallons of paint each month at $10.00 per gallon. His variable costs are $8.40 per gallon and fixed costs are $2,500.00 per month. Mr. MacRae is searching for a way to improve sales volume and net income. He estimates that cutting the unit price of paint about 10% ($10.00 to $9.00), will increase sales 20% (3,000 to 3,600 gallons). Is this a wise decision? Explain.

APPLICATION PROBLEMS

PROBLEM 18-1   Preparing an income statement reporting contribution margin

Pebble Creek Glass Company's income statement has been prepared for November of the current year.

Pebble Creek Glass Company
Income Statement
For Month Ended November 30, 19--

Operating Revenue:
Sales (14,400 units @ $16.20) $233,280.00
Cost of Merchandise Sold
(14,400 units @ $7.20) 103,680.00
Gross Profit. $129,600.00
Operating Expenses:
Selling Expenses:
Sales Commission
(14,400 @ $1.30). $18,720.00
Installation Costs (14,400 @ $1.80).   25,920.00
Other Variable Costs
(14,400 @ $0.62). 8,928.00
Fixed Costs. 11,970.00 $65,538.00
Administrative Expenses:
Variable Costs (14,400 @ $0.42) . . . . . $ 6,048.00
Rent 2,700.00
Insurance. 180.00
Other Fixed Costs 17,955.00   26,883.00
Total Operating Expenses 92,421.00
Net Income . . . . $ 37,179.00

Instructions: Prepare Pebble Creek Glass Company's November income statement reporting contribution margin. Use Illustration 18-6 as a guide.

PROBLEM 18-2   Figuring contribution margin and breakeven point

Seagrove Landscape Company sells and plants landscape trees. The company recorded the following sales and costs from last year's records.

Sales, 900 units @ $1,500.00
Variable costs, 900 units @ $1,200.00
Fixed costs, $190,200.00

Instructions: 1. Figure the contribution margin.
2. Figure the contribution margin rate.
3. Figure the breakeven point (a) in sales dollars and (b) in units.

PROBLEM 18-3   Figuring plans for net income

Mrs. Debra Johnson, manager of Parker Paint Supply, is planning her net income potential for the coming year. Sales prices and expenses for last year are as follows.

Variable Data	Per Gallon of Paint	Annual Fixed Costs	
Selling price.	$12.00	Rent	$16,000.00
Cost of paint	$ 8.40	Salaries	67,000.00
Sales commission.	.60	Miscellaneous.	16,000.00
Total variable costs	$ 9.00	Total fixed costs	$99,000.00

2. Figure the planned net income for each of the following changes. Consider each case independently.

a. Unit selling price increases 10%.

b. Unit selling price decreases 10%.

c. Unit variable costs increase 10%.

d. Unit variable costs decrease 10%.

e. Total fixed costs increase 10%.

f. Total fixed costs decrease 10%.

g. Unit selling price decreases 10% and units sold increase 20%.

h. Unit selling price increases 10%; unit variable costs increase 10%; and total fixed costs increase 10%.

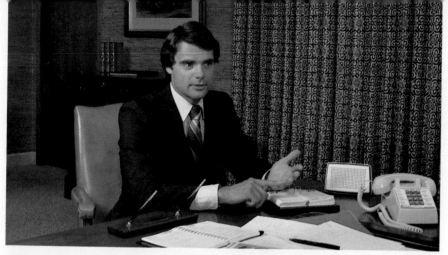

19 Financial Statement Analysis

ENABLING PERFORMANCE TASKS

After studying Chapter 19, you will be able to:
a. Define accounting terms related to financial statement analysis.
b. Identify accounting concepts and practices related to financial statement analysis.
c. Analyze financial statements.
d. Figure earnings performance analysis.
e. Figure efficiency analysis.
f. Figure financial strength analysis.

Financial information is needed by managers to make better decisions about operating a business. Owners and potential owners use the information to decide whether to buy, sell, or keep their investment. Banks and lending agencies use the information to decide whether to loan money to a business. Each group of people may need different financial information about a business. *(CONCEPT: Adequate Disclosure)* Therefore, each group may analyze the financial information in a different way to provide the best help in making decisions.

FINANCIAL ANALYSIS

Before financial information can be analyzed effectively, several questions must be answered. (a) What are the objectives for making the analysis? (b) What sources of information are needed to make the analysis? (c) What kind of analysis is to be made? (d) What level of performance is acceptable?

Financial analysis objectives

Financial analysis objectives are determined by a business' characteristics and achievements that are important to the person making the analysis. Information is analyzed to obtain more knowledge about the business'

413

strengths and weaknesses. Common objectives for analyzing financial information are to determine (a) profitability, (b) efficiency, (c) short-term financial strength, and (d) long-term financial strength.

Financial information sources

Financial statements, with supporting schedules, are the primary information sources to be analyzed. A statement showing two or more years' information permits a reader to compare year to year differences. Financial statements providing information for each of two or more years are called comparative financial statements. Thus, consistent preparation and reporting of financial information are essential. *(CONCEPT: Consistent Reporting)*

Financial analysis procedures

Comparative financial statements report a business' current and past activity. However, most financial statement readers are also interested in how well a business will do in the future. Therefore, financial statements are analyzed to help predict how well a business will perform in the future. *(CONCEPT: Adequate Disclosure)*

Several different comparisons may be made to analyze financial statements. Three common comparisons are (1) ratio analysis, (2) trend analysis, and (3) component percentage analysis.

Ratio analysis. A comparison between two numbers showing how many times one number exceeds the other is known as a ratio. A ratio may be expressed as a stated ratio, a percentage, or a fraction. For a business with net sales of $1,000,000.00 and net income of $100,000.00, the relationship may be stated as any of the following ratios.

a.	**Net Sales**	÷	**Net Income**	=	**Stated Ratio**
	$1,000,000.00	÷	$100,000.00	=	10 times (often stated as 10 to 1 or 10:1)

The stated ratio of sales to net income is 10 times; that is, sales is 10 times net income. Another way of stating this ratio is 10:1, or for each $10.00 of sales, the business earns $1.00 of net income.

b.	**Net Income**	÷	**Net Sales**	=	**Percentage Ratio**
	$100,000.00	÷	$1,000,000.00	=	.10 or 10%

Net income is 10% of sales.

c.	**Net Income**	÷	**Net Sales**	=	**Fractional Ratio**
	$100,000.00	÷	$1,000,000.00	=	1/10

Net income is one tenth of sales.

All three methods of figuring and expressing ratios are correct and essentially the same. The method selected is usually determined by the statement user's preference.

Trend analysis. Trends in a business' financial condition and operating results may not be apparent from a single year's financial information. Comparison of information for two or more fiscal periods may be needed to determine whether a business is making satisfactory progress. A comparison of the relationship between one item on a financial statement and the same item on a previous year's financial statement is called trend analysis. Trend analysis is sometimes known as horizontal analysis. A trend analysis can be figured for any financial statement item. A trend analysis for Maverick Corporation's net sales is figured as follows.

Current Year's Net Sales	−	Previous Year's Net Sales	=	Increase or Decrease in Net Sales	÷	Previous Year's Net Sales	=	% Increase or Decrease in Net Sales
$3,178,100.00	−	$2,422,000.00	=	$756,100.00	÷	$2,422,000.00	=	31.2% Increase

Maverick's net sales increased 31.2% from last year's net sales, a favorable trend. The trend for each item on Maverick's income statement is shown in Illustration 19-1, page 416. Some items are reported in condensed form. For example, a number of selling expenses are combined under the income statement heading Other Selling Expenses. Also, a number of administrative expenses are combined under the heading Other Administrative Expenses.

The trend in stockholders' equity can be determined from information on Maverick's comparative statement of stockholders' equity, Illustration 19-2. Total stockholders' equity increased 27.1% from December 31, 1988, to December 31, 1989. Further review shows the increase in stockholders' equity was caused by an increase in both capital stock and net income. Maverick's 1988 stockholders' equity was unsatisfactorily low; thus, the trend is favorable.

Illustration 19-2
Comparative statement of stockholders' equity with trend analysis

Maverick Corporation
Comparative Statement of Stockholders' Equity
For Years Ended December 31, 1989 and 1988

	1989	1988	Increase/Decrease Amount	Increase/Decrease Percentage*
Capital Stock, January 1	$320,000	$320,000	-0-	0.0
Additional Capital Stock Issued	80,000	-0-	$ 80,000	—
Capital Stock, December 31	$400,000	$320,000	$ 80,000	25.0
Retained Earnings, January 1	$272,500	$213,900	$ 58,600	27.4
Net Income after Federal Income Tax	168,300	106,600	61,700	57.9
Total	$440,800	$320,500	$120,300	37.5
Less Dividends Declared	88,000	48,000	40,000	83.3
Retained Earnings, December 31	$352,800	$272,500	$ 80,300	29.5
Total Stockholders' Equity, December 31	$752,800	$592,500	$160,300	27.1

*Rounded to nearest 0.1%.

Maverick Corporation
Comparative Income Statement
For Years Ended December 31, 1989 and 1988

	1989	1988	Increase/Decrease Amount	Increase/Decrease Percentage*
Operating Revenue:				
Net Sales	$3,178,100	$2,422,000	$756,100	31.2
Cost of Merchandise Sold:				
Merchandise Inventory, Jan. 1	$ 282,500	$ 88,200	$194,300	220.3
Net Purchases	1,684,600	1,504,600	180,000	12.0
Cost of Merchandise Available	$1,967,100	$1,592,800	$374,300	23.5
Less Merchandise Inventory, Dec. 31 . . .	298,600	282,500	16,100	5.7
Cost of Merchandise Sold	$1,668,500	$1,310,300	$358,200	27.3
Gross Profit on Operations	$1,509,600	$1,111,700	$397,900	35.8
Operating Expenses:				
Selling Expenses:				
Advertising Expense	$ 29,800	$ 20,500	$ 9,300	45.4
Delivery Expense	47,700	36,600	11,100	30.3
Salary Expense — Sales	610,900	465,200	145,700	31.3
Supplies Expenses	53,700	41,200	12,500	30.3
Other Selling Expenses	74,600	57,100	17,500	30.6
Total Selling Expenses	$ 816,700	$ 620,600	$196,100	31.6
Administrative Expenses:				
Bad Debts Expense	$ 17,800	$ 11,400	$ 6,400	56.1
Salary Expense — Administrative	200,100	155,700	44,400	28.5
Other Administrative Expenses	158,300	128,100	30,200	23.6
Total Administrative Expenses	$ 376,200	$ 295,200	$ 81,000	27.4
Total Operating Expenses	$1,192,900	$ 915,800	$277,100	30.3
Income from Operations	$ 316,700	$ 195,900	$120,800	61.7
Other Expenses:				
Interest Expense	$ 42,600	$ 36,000	$ 6,600	18.3
Net Income before Federal Income Tax	$ 274,100	$ 159,900	$114,200	71.4
Federal Income Tax	105,800	53,300	52,500	98.5
Net Income after Federal Income Tax	$ 168,300	$ 106,600	$ 61,700	57.9

*Rounded to nearest 0.1%.

Illustration 19-1
Comparative income
statement with trend
analysis

Changes in Maverick's balance sheet accounts are shown in Illustration 19-3. Accounts Receivable and Plant Assets are reported at book value. Information on this statement shows that total assets increased 17.6% during 1989. This increase was caused by an 8.4% increase in total liabilities and a 27.1% increase in stockholders' equity. This trend is considered favorable because assets are increasing and the increase came principally from the significant increase in stockholders' equity.

Maverick Corporation
Comparative Balance Sheet
December 31, 1989 and 1988

	1989	1988	Increase/Decrease Amount	Increase/Decrease Percentage*
ASSETS				
Current Assets:				
Cash	$ 144,800	$ 75,800	$ 69,000	91.0
Accounts Receivable (book value)	329,300	386,100	−56,800	−14.7
Merchandise Inventory.................	298,600	282,500	16,100	5.7
Other Current Assets	17,400	14,200	3,200	22.5
Total Current Assets..................	$ 790,100	$ 758,600	$ 31,500	4.2
Plant Assets (book value)	620,000	440,000	180,000	40.9
Total Assets	$1,410,100	$1,198,600	$ 211,500	17.6
LIABILITIES				
Current Liabilities:				
Notes Payable......................	$ 108,100	$ 160,300	$−52,200	−32.6
Interest Payable.....................	8,600	13,800	− 5,200	−37.7
Accounts Payable	229,500	275,500	−46,000	−16.7
Income Tax Payable—Federal	7,500	2,200	5,300	240.9
Other Current Liabilities...............	3,600	4,300	− 700	−16.3
Total Current Liabilities...............	$ 357,300	$ 456,100	$−98,800	−21.7
Long-Term Liability:				
Mortgage Payable...................	300,000	150,000	150,000	100.0
Total Liabilities.......................	$ 657,300	$ 606,100	$ 51,200	8.4
STOCKHOLDERS' EQUITY				
Capital Stock	$ 400,000	$ 320,000	$ 80,000	25.0
Retained Earnings.....................	352,800	272,500	80,300	29.5
Total Stockholders' Equity	$ 752,800	$ 592,500	$ 160,300	27.1
Total Liabilities and Stockholders' Equity ...	$1,410,100	$1,198,600	$ 211,500	17.6
Capital Stock Shares Outstanding.........	4,000	3,200	800	25.0

*Rounded to nearest 0.1%.

Component percentage analysis. The percentage relationship between one financial statement item and the total that includes that item is known as component percentage. Component percentage analysis is also known as vertical analysis.

Component percentages for items on an income statement normally are figured as a percentage of net sales. Maverick figures component percentages as described for Supergolf in Chapter 5 and Computex in Chapter 8. The component percentage is shown in a separate percentage column. For example, Maverick's 1989 income statement component percentage column, Illustration 19-4, shows that cost of merchandise sold was 52.5% of net sales.

Illustration 19-3
Comparative balance
sheet with trend analysis

Maverick Corporation
Comparative Income Statement
For Years Ended December 31, 1989 and 1988

	1989		1988	
	Amount	Percentage of Sales*	Amount	Percentage of Sales*
Operating Revenue:				
Net Sales	$3,178,100	100.0	$2,422,000	100.00
Cost of Merchandise Sold:				
Merchandise Inventory, Jan. 1	$ 282,500	8.9	$ 88,200	3.6
Net Purchases......................	1,684,600	53.0	1,504,600	62.1
Cost of Merchandise Available.........	$1,967,100	61.9	$1,592,800	65.8
Less Merchandise Inventory, Dec. 31...	298,600	9.4	282,500	11.7
Cost of Merchandise Sold.............	$1,668,500	52.5	$1,310,300	54.1
Gross Profit on Operations	$1,509,600	47.5	$1,111,700	45.9
Operating Expenses:				
Selling Expenses:				
Advertising Expense...................	$ 29,800	0.9	$ 20,500	0.8
Delivery Expense	47,700	1.5	36,600	1.5
Salary Expense—Sales	610,900	19.2	465,200	19.2
Supplies Expense....................	53,700	1.7	41,200	1.7
Other Selling Expenses...............	74,600	2.3	57,100	2.4
Total Selling Expenses................	$ 816,700	25.7	$ 620,600	25.6
Administrative Expenses:				
Bad Debts Expense	$ 17,800	0.6	$ 11,400	0.5
Salary Expense—Administrative.......	200,100	6.3	155,700	6.4
Other Administrative Expenses	158,300	5.0	128,100	5.3
Total Administrative Expenses	$ 376,200	11.8	$ 295,200	12.2
Total Operating Expenses.................	$1,192,900	37.5	$ 915,800	37.8
Income from Operations	$ 316,700	10.0	$ 195,900	8.1
Other Expenses:				
Interest Expense	$ 42,600	1.3	$ 36,000	1.5
Net Income before Federal Income Tax.....	$ 274,100	8.6	$ 159,900	6.6
Federal Income Tax	105,800	3.3	53,300	2.2
Net Income after Federal Income Tax	$ 168,300	5.3	$ 106,600	4.4

*Rounded to nearest 0.1%.
Percentage totals may not equal sum of parts because of rounding.

Illustration 19-4
Comparative income
statement with
component percentage
analysis

In addition, component percentages on comparative statements show changes in a specific item from year to year. For example, Maverick's cost of merchandise sold was 54.1% and 52.5% of net sales for the years 1988 and 1989 respectively as shown in Illustration 19-4. These percentages show a favorable trend. The 1989 percentage, 52.5%, is lower than the 1988 percentage, 54.1%. This change indicates that the cost of merchandise sold took a smaller part of each sales dollar in 1989 than in 1988. Similar comparisons can be made for each item on the comparative income statement. Significant unfavorable changes should be investigated further to determine the cause so that corrective action can be taken.

Component percentages for items on a comparative statement of stockholders' equity normally are figured as a percentage of total stockholders' equity. As shown in Illustration 19-5, 53.1% of Maverick's 1989 stockholders' equity consists of capital stock and 46.9% consists of retained earnings. Respective percentages for 1988 are 54.0% and 46.0%. Thus, little change has occurred in the component makeup of total equity from 1988 to 1989. However, the percentage of dividends declared increased significantly from 8.1% in 1988 to 11.7% in 1989, a favorable trend for stockholders.

Maverick Corporation
Comparative Statement of Stockholders' Equity
For Years Ended December 31, 1989 and 1988

	1989		1988	
	Amount	Percentage*	Amount	Percentage*
Capital Stock, January 1	$320,000	42.5	$320,000	54.0
Additional Capital Stock Issued	80,000	10.6	-0-	-0-
Capital Stock, December 31	$400,000	53.1	$320,000	54.0
Retained Earnings, January 1	$272,500	36.2	$213,900	36.1
Net Income after Federal Income Tax	168,300	22.4	106,600	18.0
Total.....................................	$440,800	58.6	$320,500	54.1
Less Dividends Declared..................	88,000	11.7	48,000	8.1
Retained Earnings, December 31	$352,800	46.9	$272,500	46.0
Total Stockholders' Equity, December 31....	$752,800	100.0	$592,500	100.0

*Rounded to nearest 0.1%.

Component percentages for asset amounts on a comparative balance sheet normally are figured as a percentage of total assets. Liabilities and stockholders' equity amounts are figured as a percentage of total liabilities and stockholders' equity. Information on Maverick's comparative balance sheet, Illustration 19-6, page 420, shows current liabilities in 1989 were 25.3% of total liabilities and stockholders' equity, down from 38.1% in 1988.

Since current liabilities were at a high percentage in 1988, Maverick considers the reduction from 38.1% to 25.3% as a very favorable change. Similar comparisons can be made for each item on the comparative balance sheet.

Illustration 19-5
Comparative statement of stockholders' equity with component percentage analysis

Acceptable levels of financial performance

Analyzing financial information shows relationships among parts of the information analyzed. However, for an analysis to be useful, a company

Maverick Corporation
Comparative Balance Sheet
December 31, 1989 and 1988

	1989		1988	
	Amount	Percentage*	Amount	Percentage*
ASSETS				
Current Assets:				
Cash	$ 144,800	10.3	$ 75,800	6.3
Accounts Receivable (book value)	329,300	23.4	386,100	32.2
Merchandise Inventory.................	298,600	21.2	282,500	23.6
Other Current Assets	17,400	1.2	14,200	1.2
Total Current Assets..................	$ 790,100	56.0	$ 758,600	63.3
Plant Assets (book value)	620,000	44.0	440,000	36.7
Total Assets	$1,410,100	100.0	$1,198,600	100.0
LIABILITIES				
Current Liabilities:				
Notes Payable........................	$ 108,100	7.7	$ 160,300	13.4
Interest Payable......................	8,600	0.6	13,800	1.2
Accounts Payable.....................	229,500	16.3	275,500	23.0
Income Tax Payable—Federal	7,500	0.5	2,200	0.2
Other Current Liabilities...............	3,600	0.3	4,300	0.4
Total Current Liabilities	$ 357,300	25.3	$ 456,100	38.1
Long-Term Liability:				
Mortgage Payable....................	300,000	21.3	150,000	12.5
Total Liabilities........................	$ 657,300	46.6	$ 606,100	50.6
STOCKHOLDERS' EQUITY				
Capital Stock	$ 400,000	28.4	$ 320,000	26.7
Retained Earnings......................	352,800	25.0	272,500	22.7
Total Stockholders' Equity................	$ 752,800	53.4	$ 592,500	49.4
Total Liabilities and Stockholders' Equity ...	$1,410,100	100.0	$1,198,600	100.0
Capital Stock Shares Outstanding.........	4,000		3,200	

*Rounded to nearest 0.1%.
Percentage totals may not equal sum of parts because of rounding.

Illustration 19-6
Comparative balance
sheet with component
percentage analysis

needs to know what level of performance is acceptable for each analysis made. For example, Norris Grocery considers a 3% rate earned on net sales to be very good. The rate earned on net sales is found by dividing net income after federal income tax by net sales. The rate earned on net sales is also referred to as the ratio of net income to net sales as described in Chapter 5. Fieldwood Manufacturing Company considers a 3% rate earned on net sales to be very poor. A 9% rate earned for Fieldwood would be more desirable because the two companies have different financial characteristics. The grocery company has low investment in plant assets and sells its inventory quickly. The manufacturing company has high investment in plant assets and holds its inventory much longer because of the time required to manufacture a finished product. Because of the manufacturing company's larger investment per sales dollar, the company must earn a higher rate on sales. Each company's management must determine the acceptable levels of performance for each financial analysis made.

Many businesses use two major guides to determine acceptable levels of performance. (a) Trends are compared with previous company performances. (b) Company results are compared with industry performance standards that are published by industry organizations.

Other frequently used sources of performance guides are as follows. (a) Financial and credit reporting companies such as Dun and Bradstreet. (b) The company's planned objectives. (c) Current interest rates that could be earned by investing capital elsewhere.

Each company's management should determine the acceptable performance level for each financial analysis made by the company.

EARNINGS PERFORMANCE ANALYSIS

Amount and consistency of earnings are important measures of a business' success. A business' earnings must be satisfactory to continue operations. *(CONCEPT: Going Concern)* Consequently, managers, owners, and creditors are interested in an analysis of earnings performance. Maverick figures five earnings performance ratios for the two most recent years. (1) Rate earned on average total assets. (2) Rate earned on average stockholders' equity. (3) Rate earned on net sales. (4) Earnings per share. (5) Price-earnings ratio.

Rate earned on average total assets

A business uses its assets to earn net income. If all assets are used as efficiently as possible, a business should earn the best possible net income. The rate found by dividing net income after federal income tax by average total assets is known as the rate earned on average total assets. The rate earned on average total assets shows how well a business is using its assets to earn net income. Average total assets is the average amount of assets held during a year.

From income statement and balance sheet information, Illustrations 19-4 and 19-6, Maverick figures its 1989 rate of return on average total assets.

Step 1:	$\begin{pmatrix} \textbf{January 1} \\ \textbf{Total Assets} \end{pmatrix}$	$+$	$\begin{pmatrix} \textbf{December 31} \\ \textbf{Total Assets} \end{pmatrix}$	$\div$	2	$=$	$\begin{matrix} \textbf{Average} \\ \textbf{Total Assets} \end{matrix}$
	($1,198,600.00	+	$1,410,100.00)	÷	2	=	$1,304,350.00

Step 2:	$\begin{matrix} \textbf{Net Income} \\ \textbf{after Federal} \\ \textbf{Income Tax} \end{matrix}$	$\div$	$\begin{matrix} \textbf{Average} \\ \textbf{Total Assets} \end{matrix}$	$=$	$\begin{matrix} \textbf{Rate Earned} \\ \textbf{on Average} \\ \textbf{Total Assets} \end{matrix}$
	$168,300.00	÷	$1,304,350.00	=	12.9%

January 1 total assets are the same as the total assets on the previous year's December 31 balance sheet.

A 12.9% rate earned on average total assets means that for each $1.00 of assets the business earned 12.9 cents. The following rates earned on average total assets are figured from Maverick's financial statement information, Illustrations 19-4 and 19-6. (Some information for 1988 is taken from 1987 financial statements that are not illustrated.)

	1989	1988
Net Income after Federal Income Tax	$ 168,300.00	$ 106,600.00
January 1 Total Assets.	1,198,600.00	958,400.00
December 31 Total Assets	1,410,100.00	1,198,600.00
Average Total Assets.	1,304,350.00	1,078,500.00
Rate Earned on Average Total Assets	12.9%	9.9%

Maverick determines an acceptable rate of return on total assets by reviewing the company's previous results and comparing rates of return on alternative investments. Maverick's goal is to earn a rate of return on average total assets at least as high as investments available elsewhere. For example, if Maverick can earn more by placing extra cash in savings deposits or government bonds, the company is not meeting its earnings goal.

Investment sources available to Maverick are earning 12%. Also, the trend in rate earned is up significantly from 9.9% to 12.9%. Therefore, Maverick believes a rate earned on total assets of 12.9% is satisfactory.

Rate earned on average stockholders' equity

Stockholders are particularly interested in knowing how much net income their investment is earning. Also, potential investors may compare the rate earned on stockholders' equity for several businesses to determine which business to invest in. The rate found by dividing net income after federal income tax by average stockholders' equity is known as the rate earned on average stockholders' equity.

The following analysis is made from Maverick's 1989 income statement and stockholders equity statement, Illustrations 19-4 and 19-5.

Step 1:	January 1 Stockholders' Equity	+	December 31 Stockholders' Equity	÷	2	=	Average Stockholders' Equity
	($592,500.00	+	$752,800.00)	÷	2	=	$672,650.00

Step 2:	Net Income after Federal Income Tax	÷	Average Stockholders' Equity	=	Rate Earned on Average Stockholders' Equity
	$168,300.00	÷	$672,650.00	=	25.0%

January 1 stockholders' equity is the same as the stockholders' equity on the previous year's December 31 statement of stockholders' equity.

From information on Maverick's financial statements, rates earned on average stockholders' equity are figured for 1989 and 1988. (Some information for 1988 is taken from 1987 financial statements that are not illustrated.)

	1989	1988
Net Income after Federal Income Tax.........	$168,300.00	$106,600.00
January 1 Stockholders' Equity..............	592,500.00	503,600.00
December 31 Stockholders' Equity...........	752,800.00	592,500.00
Average Stockholders' Equity...............	672,650.00	548,050.00
Rate Earned on Average Stockholders' Equity .	25.0%	19.5%

Maverick determines an acceptable rate earned on stockholders' equity by reviewing the company's previous results. The company also compares its rate earned on stockholders' equity with rates earned by other companies in the same industry. Minimum industry standards for the last two years have been 20%.

A review of the analysis shows 1988 did not meet the minimum acceptable rate of earnings on stockholders' equity. However, the rate of earnings increased significantly from 19.5% in 1988 to 25.0% in 1989. Based upon the trend and comparison with industry standards, Maverick achieved a satisfactory rate earned on stockholders' equity in 1989.

Rate earned on net sales

A business that carefully controls costs should earn about the same or higher percentage of net income compared to sales dollar from year to year. However, if costs suddenly change, the rate earned on net sales will change also.

The 1989 rate earned on net sales is figured as follows.

Net Income after Federal Income Tax	÷	Net Sales	=	Rate Earned on Net Sales
$168,300.00	÷	$3,178,100.00	=	5.3%

The following rates earned on Maverick's net sales are figured from information on the comparative income statement, Illustration 19-4.

	1989	1988
Net Income after Federal Income Tax......	$ 168,300.00	$ 106,600.00
Net Sales	3,178,100.00	2,422,000.00
Rate Earned on Net Sales................	5.3%	4.4%

The component percentage for net income after federal income tax, Illustration 19-4, is the same percentage as the rate earned on net sales figured above. In both computations, net income is figured as a percentage of net sales.

When evaluating an acceptable rate earned on sales, Maverick considers what is normal for other similar businesses and the company's own past experience. Businesses similar to Maverick have been earning about a 5.0%

rate on sales for the last two or three years. Based on a comparison of similar businesses, Maverick's 1988 rate earned on net sales of 4.4% was unsatisfactory. The trend in rate earned increased to 5.3% in 1989, a satisfactory rate. This trend should be watched closely for any future declines. When a rate earned on net sales declines, the company must increase sales or reduce costs to overcome the lower rate.

Earnings per share

The amount of net income earned on one common stock share during a fiscal period is known as earnings per share. Stockholders and management frequently use earnings per share as a measure of success. As earnings per share increase, more people become interested in buying stock. This demand for stock causes stock prices to go up. The company then finds it easier to issue stock or borrow money.

Maverick's 1989 earnings per share are figured as follows.

Net Income after Federal Income Tax	÷	Shares of Stock Outstanding	=	Earnings Per Share
$168,300.00	÷	4,000	=	$42.08

From financial statement information, Illustrations 19-4 and 19-6, the earnings per share are figured.

	1989	1988
Net Income after Federal Income Tax	$168,300.00	$106,600.00
Shares of Stock Outstanding.................	4,000	3,200
Earnings Per Share	$42.08	$33.31

A trend of increasing earnings per share is important to stockholders. This trend is one signal to stockholders that the company is continuing to increase the net income earned for each share. Therefore, Maverick considers a trend of increasing earnings per share important to the company. Earnings per share increased significantly from $33.31 in 1988 to $42.08 in 1989, a very favorable trend.

Price-earnings ratio

Investors want to buy stock in companies that will earn a reasonable return on their investment. The relationship between the earnings per share and the market value per share of stock is known as the price-earnings ratio. As described in Chapter 15, the price-earnings ratio of a company's stock relates profitability to the amount the investors currently pay for the stock. The price-earnings ratio is usually expressed as a stated ratio.

Maverick's capital stock sold for $442.00 per share on December 31, 1989. Maverick's December 31, 1989, stated price-earnings ratio is figured as follows.

Market Price Per Share	÷	Earnings Per Share	=	Price-Earnings Ratio
$442.00	÷	$42.08	=	10.5 times

Earnings per share is figured on page 424.

Price-earnings ratios on December 31, 1989 and 1988, are as follows.

	1989	1988
Market Price Per Share........................	$442.00	$313.50
Earnings Per Share	42.08	33.31
Price-Earnings Ratio	10.5 times	9.4 times

The market price of a share of stock is determined by the amount investors are willing to pay for the stock. If investors think a company's profitability is increasing, they will pay more for the stock. Thus, the market price of a company's stock is influenced strongly by what potential investors think the company's earnings will be in the future. Maverick's price-earnings ratio increased from 9.4 in 1988 to 10.5 in 1989. This change indicates investors considered the stock more valuable and were willing to pay more for the stock per dollar earned by the corporation in 1989 than in 1988. This increased demand is a favorable trend for Maverick.

EFFICIENCY ANALYSIS

The profitability and continued growth of a business are influenced by how efficiently the business utilizes its assets. A business' operating cycle consists of three phases. (1) Purchase merchandise. (2) Sell merchandise, frequently on account. (3) Collect the accounts receivable. Much of a business' assets are in accounts receivable and merchandise inventory. The quicker a business can convert these assets to cash and begin another operating cycle, the more efficient and profitable the business is.

Maverick uses two ratios to measure its efficiency. (1) Accounts receivable turnover ratio. (2) Merchandise inventory turnover ratio.

Accounts receivable turnover ratio

Accounts receivable normally do not contribute to a business' earnings. A business accepts accounts receivable to encourage sales. However, once the sale has been made, earnings are not increased by holding accounts receivable. Thus, an efficient company will monitor closely the length of time required to collect its receivables. The number of times the average amount of accounts receivable is collected annually is known as the accounts receivable turnover ratio. The accounts receivable turnover ratio can be used to monitor a business' accounts receivable collection efficiency.

Accounts receivable turnover is described in Chapter 9. Maverick uses information from Illustrations 19-4 and 19-6 to figure its 1989 stated accounts receivable turnover ratio.

Step 1:	Beginning Book Value of Accounts Receivable		Ending Book Value of Accounts Receivable				Average Book Value of Accounts Receivable
	($386,100.00	+	$329,300.00)	÷	2	=	$357,700.00

Step 2:	Net Sales on Account	÷	Average Book Value of Accounts Receivable	=	Accounts Receivable Turnover Ratio
	$3,178,100.00	÷	$357,700.00	=	8.9 times

The beginning book value of accounts receivable is the same as the ending book value of accounts receivable for the previous year. All of Maverick's sales are on account.

Maverick's 1989 turnover ratio of 8.9 indicates accounts are being collected 8.9 times a year. The average number of days for customers to pay their accounts based on an 8.9 turnover ratio is figured as follows.

Days in Year	÷	Accounts Receivable Turnover Ratio	=	Average Number of Days for Payment
365	÷	8.9	=	41 days

During 1989, Maverick had an average of 41 days from date of sale to date of collection for the average account receivable. Accounts receivable turnover ratio and average number of days for payment are figured for 1989 and 1988 from information in Illustrations 19-4 and 19-6. (Some information for 1988 is taken from 1987 financial statements that are not illustrated.)

	1989	1988
Beginning Book Value of Accounts Receivable.................	$ 386,100.00	$ 308,900.00
Ending Book Value of Accounts Receivable.	329,300.00	386,100.00
Average Book Value of Accounts Receivable.................	357,700.00	347,500.00
Net Sales on Account.....................	3,178,100.00	2,422,000.00
Accounts Receivable Turnover Ratio.......	8.9 times	7.0 times
Average Number of Days for Payment.....	41 days	52 days

The larger the accounts receivable turnover ratio, the more favorable the results. That is, accounts have been collected more times in a year. The fewer the average number of days for payment, the more favorable the results. The accounts are being collected quicker.

Maverick's credit terms are n/30. Thus, the company's goal is to collect accounts receivable in 30 days or less. Neither 1988 nor 1989 have met that goal, an unfavorable result. However, Maverick increased its accounts receivable turnover ratio from 7.0 to 8.9. This favorable trend means the company is improving its collection efficiency by reducing collection of its accounts receivable from 52 to 41 days.

Merchandise inventory turnover ratio

A company earns income when merchandise is sold. Therefore, the quicker a business can sell its merchandise inventory, the more efficient and generally more profitable is the business. The number of times the average amount of merchandise inventory is sold annually is known as the merchandise inventory turnover ratio. The merchandise inventory turnover ratio can be used to monitor a business' merchandise inventory efficiency.

The merchandise inventory turnover ratio is described in Chapter 16. Maverick uses information from the financial statements, Illustrations 19-4 and 19-6, to figure its 1989 merchandise inventory turnover ratio.

Step 1:	January 1 Merchandise Inventory	+	December 31 Merchandise Inventory	÷ 2 =	Average Merchandise Inventory
	($282,500.00	+	$298,600.00)	÷ 2 =	$290,550.00

Step 2:	Cost of Merchandise Sold	÷	Average Merchandise Inventory	=	Merchandise Inventory Turnover Ratio
	$1,668,500.00	÷	$290,550.00	=	5.7 times

January 1 merchandise inventory is the same as the merchandise inventory on the previous year's December 31 balance sheet.

Maverick's 1989 merchandise inventory turnover ratio of 5.7 indicates that the average amount of inventory is being sold 5.7 times in a year. The average number of days' sales in merchandise inventory based on a 5.7 turnover ratio is figured as follows.

Days in Year	÷	Merchandise Inventory Turnover Ratio	=	Average Number of Days' Sales in Merchandise Inventory
365	÷	5.7	=	64 days

During 1989 Maverick had an average of 64 days' sales in merchandise inventory. Merchandise inventory ratios and average number of days' sales in merchandise inventory are figured for 1989 and 1988 from information in Illustrations 19-4 and 19-6.

	1989	1988
January 1 Merchandise Inventory	$ 282,500.00	$ 88,200.00
December 31 Merchandise Inventory	298,600.00	282,500.00
Average Merchandise Inventory	290,550.00	185,350.00
Cost of Merchandise Sold	1,668,500.00	1,310,300.00
Merchandise Inventory Turnover Ratio	5.7 times	7.1 times
Average Number of Days' Sales in Merchandise Inventory.................	64 days	51 days

An optimum merchandise inventory turnover ratio is determined by two factors: (1) amount of sales, and (2) number of days needed to replenish inventory. A business needs as a minimum enough merchandise on hand to fill all sales orders during the time required to order and receive new merchandise. If the inventory level gets too low, a business risks running out of merchandise to sell before new merchandise is received. If the inventory level is much higher than needed, a business has more money invested in inventory than is necessary which adds additional costs. An efficient business tries to maintain an optimum level of merchandise inventory — enough to meet sales demand but no more than is needed.

Previous experience has shown that Maverick needs to maintain an inventory turnover ratio of about 6.0. This 6.0 ratio equates to an average number of days' sales in merchandise inventory of 61 days. Maverick's 1988 days' sales in inventory was 51 days. This lower than desired level of inventory resulted in lost sales because some items were out of stock before new inventory arrived. However, the 1989 inventory level is back to a satisfactory amount.

SHORT-TERM FINANCIAL STRENGTH ANALYSIS

A successful business needs adequate capital. A business gets capital from two sources. (1) Owners' investments and retained earnings. (2) Loans. Some capital, either owned or borrowed, is to be used for long periods of time. Also, some capital is borrowed for short periods of time. A business can invest long-term capital in some assets (such as equipment and buildings) for long periods of time. A business also invests in assets (such as merchandise) that will be converted back to cash in a short period of time. Short-term assets are known as current assets because they are consumed in a business' daily activities or exchanged for cash. Long-term assets are known as plant assets and are used over a long period of time.

Maverick uses two common ratios to analyze short-term financial strength: (1) current ratio and (2) acid-test ratio.

Current ratio

A ratio that shows the numeric relationship of current assets to current liabilities is called the current ratio. Normally, current liabilities are expected to be paid from cash on hand plus cash soon to be received from other current assets.

The current ratio is figured by dividing total current assets by total current liabilities. Based on the balance sheet information, Illustration 19-6, Maverick's 1989 stated current ratio is figured as follows.

Total Current Assets	÷	Total Current Liabilities	=	Current Ratio
$790,100.00	÷	$357,300.00	=	2.2 times

The current ratio of 2.2 means that Maverick owns $2.20 in current assets for each $1.00 needed to pay current liabilities.

Businesses similar to Maverick try to maintain a current ratio of 2.0 times. Industry experience has shown that a business with a current ratio less than 2.0 times will have difficulty raising ready cash to pay current liabilities on time. At the same time, industry experience shows that a current ratio can be too high. If the current ratio is 3.0 times, the business has more capital invested in current assets than is needed to run the business.

A current ratio becomes more meaningful when compared to current ratios for other years. From Maverick's balance sheet information, Illustration 19-6, the following current ratios are figured for 1989 and 1988.

	1989	1988
Total Current Assets	$790,100.00	$758,600.00
Total Current Liabilities	$357,300.00	$456,100.00
Current Ratio	2.2 times	1.7 times

In 1988, Maverick's current ratio, 1.7, was significantly below the desired ratio. However, the 1989 ratio, 2.2, is back to a satisfactory level. A review of other financial information suggests that part of the reason for 1988's lower current ratio was the company's fast expansion. Frequently, when a business expands too rapidly, money is borrowed to buy more inventory and to pay more employees. The rate of increased costs for merchandise and payroll may be greater initially than the rate of increase in sales and net income. Maverick took action in 1989 to lower its current liabilities by issuing more capital stock and long-term liabilities.

Acid-test ratio

Those current assets that are cash or that can be quickly turned into cash are called quick assets. Quick assets include cash, receivables, and marketable securities, but not merchandise or prepaid expenses. Merchandise inventory is a current asset that is expected to be turned into cash. The merchandise first has to be sold and then receivables have to be collected before cash is available. Therefore, merchandise inventory is not considered to be a quick asset. Also prepaid expenses will seldom be converted to cash.

A ratio that shows the numeric relationship of quick assets to current liabilities is called the acid-test ratio. This ratio shows the ability of a business to pay all current liabilities almost immediately if necessary.

Based on the balance sheet information, Illustration 19-6, Maverick figures the 1989 stated acid-test ratio as follows.

Total Quick Assets (Cash + Accounts Receivable)	÷	Total Current Liabilities	=	Acid-Test Ratio
($144,800.00 + $329,300.00)	÷	$357,300.00	=	1.3 times

The ratio indicates that for each $1.00 needed to pay current liabilities, Maverick has available $1.30 in quick assets. For companies similar to Maverick, the desired industry standard for an acid-test ratio is between 1.2 and 1.4.

Based on the balance sheet information, Illustration 19-6, the acid-test ratios for 1989 and 1988 are as follows.

	1989	1988
Total Quick Assets............................	$474,100.00	$461,900.00
Total Current Liabilities	$357,300.00	$456,100.00
Acid-Test Ratio.............................	1.3 times	1.0 times

Maverick's acid-test ratios show considerable change from 1988 to 1989. In 1988, the ratio was at an unacceptable level. However, the ratio for 1989 is at a satisfactory level. A review of financial statements shows that Maverick issued additional capital stock and long-term liabilities in 1989. Part of the cash received from these stock and long-term liabilities issues was used to reduce the level of current liabilities and improve the acid-test ratio.

LONG-TERM FINANCIAL STRENGTH ANALYSIS

Businesses that are successful and are able to continue in business through both strong and weak economic periods usually have long-term financial strength. Long-term financial strength requires a balance between stockholders' capital and borrowed capital. A profitable business can be even more profitable by using borrowed capital wisely. However, borrowed capital must be repaid with interest. Continuing operation of a business with a large percentage of borrowed capital may be jeopardized if net income declines and loan payments cannot be made. Also, creditors are reluctant to loan additional money to companies with a high level of liabilities. A well-managed company monitors its long-term financial strength to insure that a reasonable balance between stockholders' capital and borrowed capital is maintained.

Maverick uses three measures to analyze long-term financial strength. (1) Debt ratio. (2) Equity ratio. (3) Equity per share.

Debt ratio

The ratio found by dividing total liabilities by total assets is called the debt ratio. This ratio shows the percentage of assets that are financed with borrowed capital (liabilities).

Maverick's 1989 percentage debt ratio is figured from information on the comparative balance sheet, Illustration 19-6.

Total Liabilities	÷	Total Assets	=	Debt Ratio
$657,300.00	÷	$1,410,100.00	=	46.6%

This ratio, 46.6%, indicates that for each $1.00 of assets owned by Maverick, the company has borrowed 46.6 cents.

Based on the balance sheet information, Illustration 19-6, debt ratios for 1989 and 1988 are as follows.

	1989	1988
Total Liabilities	$ 657,300.00	$ 606,100.00
Total Assets	1,410,100.00	1,198,600.00
Debt Ratio	46.6%	50.6%

The debt ratio for companies similar to Maverick is 43%. Maverick's 1989 and 1988 ratios are both above the industry average, an unfavorable condition. Rapid growth over the past two or three years, financed primarily through borrowed capital, has caused the unfavorable liabilities level. However, Maverick issued additional capital stock in 1989 which helped lower the debt ratio by 4%. The company plans to issue more capital stock in 1990 to reduce the total liabilities to an industry average of 43%.

Equity ratio

The ratio found by dividing stockholders' equity by total assets is called the equity ratio. This ratio shows the percentage of assets that are provided by stockholders' equity.

Maverick's 1989 percentage equity ratio is figured from information on the comparative balance sheet, Illustration 19-6.

Total Stockholders' Equity	÷	Total Assets	=	Equity Ratio
$752,800.00	÷	$1,410,100.00	=	53.4%

Maverick's ratio, 53.4%, indicates that for each $1.00 of assets owned by the company, 53.4 cents worth was acquired with stockholders' capital.

Based on the balance sheet information, Illustration 19-6, equity ratios for 1989 and 1988 are figured as follows.

	1989	1988
Total Stockholders' Equity	$ 752,800.00	$ 592,500.00
Total Assets	1,410,100.00	1,198,600.00
Equity Ratio.	53.4%	49.4%

The average equity ratio for companies similar to Maverick is 57%. Maverick's 1989 and 1988 ratios are below the industry average, an unfavorable condition. A review of two ratios, debt ratio and equity ratio, shows the mix of capital provided by borrowing and capital provided by stockholders. These 1989 and 1988 ratios for Maverick are as follows.

	1989	1988
Debt Ratio	46.6%	50.6%
Equity Ratio...................................	53.4%	49.4%
Totals...	100.0%	100.0%

The sum of the two ratios equals 100%. This fact is always true because the total liabilities and stockholders' equity represent the source of all asset ownership. However, the relationship between the two ratios at Maverick is changing. In 1989, a higher percentage of ownership comes from stockholders' equity. Maverick's 1988 stockholders' equity had declined to a level the company considered unfavorable. The company took action to increase the percentage of ownership provided by stockholders' equity by issuing more capital stock. Maverick could also increase the equity ratio by paying some of its liabilities. However, Maverick is expanding and needs the additional capital. Additional capital stock has been issued to regain a favorable balance of stockholders' equity and liabilities.

Equity per share

The amount of total stockholders' equity belonging to a single share of stock is known as equity per share. Equity per share is also known as book value per share.

Maverick's 1989 equity per share is figured from information on the comparative balance sheet, Illustration 19-6.

Total Stockholders' Equity	÷	Shares of Capital Stock Outstanding	=	Equity Per Share
$752,800.00	÷	4,000	=	$188.20

Maverick's equity per share, $188.20, indicates that on December 31, 1989, each share of capital stock represents ownership in $188.20 of the assets.

Based on balance sheet information, Illustration 19-6, equity per share for 1989 and 1988 is figured as follows.

	1989	1988
Total Stockholders' Equity	$752,800.00	$592,500.00
Shares of Capital Stock Outstanding..........	4,000	3,200
Equity Per Share............................	$188.20	$185.16

Equity per share provides more meaningful information for individual stockholders. With this additional information, a stockholder knows how much ownership of a company each share represents. For example, a stockholder of Maverick knows that each share of stock in 1989 represents $188.20 ownership of the total company assets. Also, this ownership has increased from $185.16 per share in 1988, a favorable trend.

ACCOUNTING TERMS

What is the meaning of each of the following?

1. comparative financial statements   **4.** quick assets   **6.** debt ratio
2. trend analysis   **5.** acid-test ratio **7.** equity ratio
3. current ratio

QUESTIONS FOR INDIVIDUAL STUDY

1. Why do managers, owners, and lending agencies need a business' financial information?

2. Providing each group of financial statement users with the financial information the group needs is an application of which accounting concept?

3. What questions should be answered to effectively analyze financial information?

4. What are four common objectives for analyzing a business' financial information?

5. Which accounting concept must be followed if comparative financial statements are to provide useful information for statement users?

6. What three types of comparisons are commonly used to analyze financial statements?

7. How may ratios be expressed?

8. Which method of expressing ratios is best?

9. How can trends in financial condition and operating results of a business be determined?

10. How is the percentage increase or decrease in net sales figured?

11. Which comparative analysis should be used to determine whether cost of merchandise sold is too high a percentage of net sales compared with other years?

12. What two major guides are used to determine acceptable levels of performance?

13. What are five ratios that can be used to analyze earnings performance of a business?

14. What does a rate earned on average total assets show?

15. How should a company determine an acceptable rate earned on total assets?

16. What does a rate earned on average stockholders' equity show?

17. How should a company determine an acceptable rate of earnings on stockholders' equity?

18. What determines the market price of a share of stock?

19. How does efficient management of accounts receivable and merchandise inventory contribute to a business' profitability?

20. What are two ratios that can be used to analyze the efficiency of a business?

21. What factors determine the optimum merchandise inventory turnover ratio for a business?

22. What two ratios can be used to analyze short-term financial strength?

23. Would the trend in the following current ratios be considered favorable or unfavorable? Why?

1988	2.0 times
1987	1.5 times
1986	1.1 times

24. What is the major difference between current assets and quick assets?

25. What is the characteristic of most successful businesses that are able to continue in business through strong and weak economic periods?

26. What three ratios can be used to analyze long-term financial strength?

27. What is the relationship between the two ratios, debt ratio and equity ratio?

CASES FOR MANAGEMENT DECISION

CASE 1 Pappago Corporation has had declining net income the past four years. The company president employs you as a consultant to review the company's operations in an effort to identify the reason for the decline. As part of your analysis, you make a component percentage analysis of the company's four most recent income statements. A part of that analysis is shown below. What are the implications from the information? What are the problems or potential problems evident from this analysis? What are your suggestions to the company?

CASE 2 Ben Monet has received year-end information from his accountant, including financial statements. Among the information is a report that the accounts receivable turnover ratio in the previous year was 8.9 and for the current year is 6.5. Mr. Monet is overjoyed at the favorable trend of the accounts receivable turnover ratio. Do you agree with Monet's interpretation? Explain your answer.

	1989	1988	1987	1986
Cost of Merchandise Sold..........	65.1%	61.4%	58.2%	55.5%
Total Selling Expenses.............	10.3%	12.2%	13.9%	15.6%

APPLICATION PROBLEMS

PROBLEM 19-1   Preparing comparative financial statements with trend analysis

The following information is taken from the financial records of Metrocom on December 31, 1989 and 1988.

	1989	1988
Cash..	$149,740.00	$153,030.00
Accounts Receivable (book value)....................	82,760.00	81,220.00
Merchandise Inventory	309,820.00	203,840.00
Other Current Assets...............................	10,800.00	10,570.00
Plant Assets (book value)...........................	211,980.00	216,940.00
Notes Payable.....................................	86,250.00	57,530.00
Interest Payable	5,460.00	4,720.00
Accounts Payable..................................	164,660.00	161,080.00
Income Tax Payable—Federal	5,220.00	2,130.00
Other Current Liabilities............................	21,080.00	16,270.00
Mortgage Payable (long-term liability)	95,830.00	101,670.00
Capital Stock.....................................	250,000.00	200,000.00
Retained Earnings (after net income and dividend entries are made)....................	136,600.00	122,200.00
Net Sales..	919,980.00	828,800.00
Net Purchases....................................	777,560.00	747,890.00
Advertising Expense	7,360.00	5,800.00
Delivery Expense	13,800.00	12,430.00
Salary Expense—Sales	59,800.00	49,730.00
Supplies Expense.................................	2,760.00	2,490.00
Other Selling Expenses............................	3,680.00	3,310.00
Bad Debts Expense	9,200.00	4,140.00
Salary Expense—Administrative	22,080.00	20,720.00
Other Administrative Expenses	11,040.00	9,950.00
Interest Expense..................................	18,400.00	15,750.00
Federal Income Tax...............................	25,880.00	10,660.00

	1989	1988
Dividends declared and paid	$ 60,000.00	$ 40,000.00
Shares of capital stock outstanding	5,000	4,000

Additional information:

Accounts receivable (book value), January 1.........	$ 81,220.00	$ 77,160.00
Merchandise inventory, January 1...................	203,840.00	102,410.00
Total assets, January 1...........................	665,600.00	544,200.00
Capital stock, January 1..........................	200,000.00	200,000.00
Retained earnings, January 1	122,200.00	114,840.00
Market price per share of stock Dec. 31	220.00	150.00

Instructions: 1. Prepare a comparative income statement with trend analysis, similar to the one in this chapter, for the years 1989 and 1988. Round percentage computations to the nearest 0.1%.

2. Prepare a comparative stockholders' equity statement with trend analysis, similar to the one in this chapter, for the years 1989 and 1988. Round percentage computations to the nearest 0.1%.

3. Prepare a comparative balance sheet with trend analysis, similar to the one in this chapter, for the years 1989 and 1988. Round percentage computations to the nearest 0.1%.

4. Use the financial statements' trend analyses to determine if the trend from 1988 to 1989 for each of the following items appears to be favorable or unfavorable. Give reasons for these trends.

a. Net sales
b. Net income
c. Total stockholders' equity
d. Total assets

The comparative financial statements prepared in Problem 19-1 are needed to complete Problems 19-3, 19-4, 19-5, and 19-6.

PROBLEM 19-2 Preparing comparative financial statements with component percentage analysis

Use the information for Metrocom given in Problem 19-1 to complete the following instructions.

Instructions: 1. Prepare a comparative income statement with component percentage analysis, similar to the one in this chapter, for the years 1989 and 1988. Round percentage computations to the nearest 0.1%.

2. Prepare a comparative stockholders' equity statement with component percentage analysis, similar to the one in this chapter, for the years 1989 and 1988. Round percentage computations to the nearest 0.1%.

3. Prepare a comparative balance sheet with component percentage analysis, similar to the one in this chapter, for the years 1989 and 1988. Round percentage computations to the nearest 0.1%.

4. Use the financial statements' component percentage analyses to determine if 1989 results for the following items appear to be favorable or unfavorable compared with 1988. Give reasons for your responses.

a. As a percentage of net sales:
(1) Cost of merchandise sold
(2) Gross profit on operations
(3) Total operating expenses
(4) Net income after federal income tax

b. As a percentage of total stockholders' equity:
(1) Retained earnings
(2) Capital stock

c. As a percentage of total assets:
   (1) Current assets
   (2) Current liabilities

PROBLEM 19-3   Analyzing earnings performance from comparative financial statements

The comparative statements prepared in Problem 19-1 are needed to complete this problem.

Instructions: 1. Based on Metrocom's comparative financial statements prepared in Problem 19-1, and the additional information given in Problem 19-1, figure the following for each year.

a. Rate earned on average total assets
b. Rate earned on average stockholders' equity
c. Rate earned on net sales
d. Earnings per share
e. Price-earnings ratio

   2. For each of the analyses, indicate if there appears to be a favorable or an unfavorable trend from 1988 to 1989. Give reasons for these trends.

PROBLEM 19-4   Analyzing efficiency from comparative financial statements

The comparative statements prepared in Problem 19-1 are needed to complete this problem.

Instructions: 1. Based on Metrocom's comparative financial statements prepared in Problem 19-1, and the additional information given in Problem 19-1, figure the following for each year. All of Metrocom's sales are on account.

a. Accounts receivable turnover ratio
b. Average number of days for payment
c. Merchandise inventory turnover ratio
d. Average number of days' sales in merchandise inventory

   2. For each of the analyses, indicate if there appears to be a favorable or an unfavorable trend from 1988 to 1989. Give reasons for these trends.

PROBLEM 19-5   Analyzing short-term financial strength from a comparative balance sheet

The comparative balance sheet prepared in Problem 19-1 is needed to complete this problem.

Instructions: 1. Based on Metrocom's comparative balance sheet prepared in Problem 19-1, figure the following for each year.

a. Current ratio
b. Acid-test ratio

   2. For each of the analyses, indicate if there appears to be a favorable or an unfavorable trend from 1988 to 1989. Give reasons for these trends.

PROBLEM 19-6   Analyzing long-term financial strength from a comparative balance sheet

The comparative balance sheet prepared in Problem 19-1 is needed to complete this problem.

Instructions: 1. Based on Metrocom's comparative balance sheet prepared in Problem 19-1, figure the following for each year.

a. Debt ratio
b. Equity ratio
c. Equity per share

2. For each of the analyses, indicate if there appears to be a favorable or an unfavorable trend from 1988 to 1989. Give reasons for these trends.

ENRICHMENT PROBLEMS

MASTERY PROBLEM 19-M   Preparing and analyzing comparative financial statements

The following information is taken from the financial records of Customaire on December 31, 1989 and 1988.

	1989	1988
Cash	$ 86,880.00	$ 45,480.00
Accounts Receivable (book value)	198,300.00	231,660.00
Merchandise Inventory	179,200.00	169,500.00
Other Current Assets	10,920.00	8,520.00
Plant Assets (book value)	372,000.00	264,000.00
Notes Payable	64,860.00	93,370.00
Interest Payable	5,160.00	8,040.00
Accounts Payable	136,700.00	160,470.00
Income Tax Payable—Federal	5,500.00	1,280.00
Other Current Liabilities	2,160.00	2,500.00
Mortgage Payable (long-term liability)	180,000.00	90,000.00
Capital Stock	240,000.00	200,000.00
Retained Earnings (after net income and dividend entries are made)	212,920.00	163,500.00
Net Sales	1,907,000.00	1,453,000.00
Net Purchases	1,201,600.00	1,047,110.00
Advertising Expense	15,260.00	10,170.00
Delivery Expense	22,880.00	17,440.00
Salary Expense—Sales	286,050.00	216,500.00
Supplies Expense	13,350.00	10,170.00
Other Selling Expenses	38,140.00	30,510.00
Bad Debts Expense	11,440.00	7,270.00
Salary Expense—Administrative	80,090.00	63,930.00
Other Administrative Expenses	57,210.00	47,950.00
Interest Expense	25,560.00	22,500.00
Federal Income Tax	55,700.00	23,540.00
Dividends declared and paid	60,000.00	40,000.00
Shares of capital stock outstanding	4,800	4,000

Additional information:		
Accounts receivable (book value), January 1	$231,660.00	$222,400.00
Merchandise inventory, January 1	169,500.00	53,760.00
Total assets, January 1	719,160.00	693,200.00
Capital stock, January 1	200,000.00	200,000.00
Retained earnings, January 1	163,500.00	131,850.00
Market price per share of stock Dec. 31	367.00	300.00

Instructions: 1. Prepare a comparative income statement with trend analysis, similar to the one in this chapter, for the years 1989 and 1988. Round percentage computations to the nearest 0.1%.

2. Prepare a comparative stockholders' equity statement with trend analysis, similar to the one in this chapter, for the years 1989 and 1988. Round percentage computations to the nearest 0.1%.

3. Prepare a comparative balance sheet with trend analysis, similar to the one in this chapter, for the years 1989 and 1988. Round percentage computations to the nearest 0.1%.

4. Use the financial statements' trend analyses to determine if the trend from 1988 to 1989 for each of the following items appears to be favorable or unfavorable. Give reasons for these trends.

a. Net sales
b. Net income
c. Total stockholders' equity
d. Total assets

5. Prepare a comparative income statement with component percentage analysis, similar to the one in this chapter, for the years 1989 and 1988. Round percentage computations to the nearest 0.1%.

6. Record from the statement prepared in Instruction 5 or figure the component percentages for 1989 and 1988 for each of the following.

a. As a percentage of net sales:
    (1) Cost of merchandise sold
    (2) Gross profit on operations
    (3) Total operating expenses
    (4) Net income after federal income tax

b. As a percentage of total stockholders' equity:
    (1) Retained earnings
    (2) Capital stock

c. As a percentage of total assets:
    (1) Current assets
    (2) Current liabilities

7. State whether the 1989 results for each of the items figured in Instruction 6 appear to be favorable or unfavorable compared with 1988. Give reasons for your responses.

8. Based on Customaire's comparative financial statements for the years ended December 31, 1989 and 1988, figure the following earnings performance ratios for each year.

a. Rate earned on average total assets
b. Rate earned on average stockholders' equity
c. Rate earned on net sales
d. Earnings per share
e. Price-earnings ratio

9. For each of the items in Instruction 8, indicate if there appears to be a favorable or an unfavorable trend from 1988 to 1989. Give reasons for these trends.

10. Based on Customaire's comparative financial statements for the years ended December 31, 1989 and 1988, figure the following efficiency ratios for each year. All of Customaire's sales are on account.

a. Accounts receivable turnover ratio
b. Merchandise inventory turnover ratio

11. For each of the items in Instruction 10, indicate if there appears to be a favorable or an unfavorable trend from 1988 to 1989. Give reasons for these trends.

12. Based on Customaire's comparative balance sheet as of December 31, 1989 and 1988, figure the following short-term financial strength ratios for each year.

a. Current ratio
b. Acid-test ratio

13. For each of the items in Instruction 12, indicate if there appears to be a favorable or an unfavorable trend from 1988 to 1989. Give reasons for these trends.

14. Based on Customaire's comparative balance sheet as of December 31, 1989 and 1988, figure the following long-term financial strength ratios for each year.

a. Debt ratio
b. Equity ratio
c. Equity per share

15. For each of the items in Instruction 14, indicate if there appears to be a favorable or an unfavorable trend from 1988 to 1989. Give reasons for these trends.

CHALLENGE PROBLEM 19-C   Preparing and analyzing comparative financial statements

The following information is taken from the financial records of ExCell on December 31, 1989 and 1988.

	1989	1988
Cash	$ 157,760.00	$ 173,850.00
Accounts Receivable (book value)	77,200.00	118,800.00
Merchandise Inventory	361,580.00	352,420.00
Other Current Assets	145,830.00	125,130.00
Plant Assets (book value)	270,930.00	278,600.00
Notes Payable	142,000.00	112,200.00
Interest Payable	3,100.00	2,600.00
Accounts Payable	130,400.00	198,220.00
Income Tax Payable — Federal	500.00	3,000.00
Other Current Liabilities	34,330.00	24,880.00
Mortgage Payable (long-term liability)	120,000.00	132,000.00
Capital Stock	500,000.00	500,000.00
Retained Earnings (after net income and dividend entries are made)	82,970.00	75,900.00
Net Sales	1,070,000.00	1,320,000.00
Net Purchases	705,730.00	918,640.00
Advertising Expense	20,330.00	26,400.00
Delivery Expense	33,170.00	40,920.00
Salary Expense — Sales	86,670.00	116,160.00
Supplies Expense	8,560.00	10,560.00
Other Selling Expenses	37,450.00	46,200.00
Bad Debts Expenses	4,280.00	9,240.00
Salary Expense — Administrative	64,200.00	77,880.00
Other Administrative Expenses	55,640.00	66,000.00
Interest Expense	31,030.00	26,400.00
Federal Income Tax	5,030.00	17,960.00
Dividends declared and paid	20,000.00	40,000.00
Shares of capital stock outstanding	20,000	20,000

Additional information:		
Accounts receivable (book value), January 1	$ 118,800.00	$ 126,400.00
Merchandise inventory, January 1	352,420.00	253,500.00
Total assets, January 1	1,048,800.00	1,052,400.00
Capital stock, January 1	500,000.00	500,000.00
Retained earnings, January 1	75,900.00	53,340.00
Market price per share of stock Dec. 31	6.50	32.00

Instructions: 1. Prepare a comparative income statement with trend analysis, similar to the one in this chapter, for the years 1989 and 1988. Round percentage computations to the nearest 0.1%.

2. Prepare a comparative stockholders' equity statement with trend analysis, similar to the one in this chapter, for the years 1989 and 1988. Round percentage computations to the nearest 0.1%.

3. Prepare a comparative balance sheet with trend analysis, similar to the one in this chapter, for the years 1989 and 1988. Round percentage computations to the nearest 0.1%.

4. Use the financial statements' trend analyses to determine if the trend from 1988 to 1989 for each of the following items appears to be favorable or unfavorable. Give reasons for these trends.

a. Net sales
b. Net income

c. Total stockholders' equity
d. Total assets

5. Prepare a comparative income statement with component percentage analysis, similar to the one in this chapter for the years 1989 and 1988. Round percentage computations to the nearest 0.1%.

6. Record from the statement prepared in Instruction 5 or figure the component percentages for 1989 and 1988 for each of the following:

a. As a percentage of net sales:
  (1) Cost of merchandise sold
  (2) Gross profit on operations

  (3) Total operating expenses
  (4) Net income after federal income tax

b. As a percentage of total stockholders' equity:
  (1) Retained earnings

  (2) Capital stock

c. As a percentage of total assets:
  (1) Current assets

  (2) Current liabilities

7. State whether the 1989 results for each of the items figured in Instruction 6 appear to be favorable or unfavorable compared with 1988. Give reasons for your responses.

8. Based on ExCell's comparative financial statements for the years ended December 31, 1989 and 1988, figure the following earnings performance ratios for each year.

a. Rate earned on average total assets
b. Rate earned on average stockholders' equity
c. Rate earned on net sales

d. Earnings per share
e. Price-earnings ratio

9. For each of the items in Instruction 8, indicate if there appears to be a favorable or an unfavorable trend from 1988 to 1989. Give reasons for these trends.

10. Based on ExCell's comparative financial statements for the years ended December 31, 1989 and 1988, figure the following efficiency ratios for each year. All of ExCell's sales are on account.

a. Accounts receivable turnover ratio

b. Merchandise inventory turnover ratio

11. For each of the items in Instruction 10, indicate if there appears to be a favorable or an unfavorable trend from 1988 to 1989. Give reasons for these trends.

12. Based on ExCell's comparative balance sheet as of December 31, 1989 and 1988, figure the following short-term financial strength ratios for each year.

a. Current ratio

b. Acid-test ratio

13. For each of the items in Instruction 12, indicate if there appears to be a favorable or an unfavorable trend from 1988 to 1989. Give reasons for these trends.

14. Based on ExCell's comparative balance sheet as of December 31, 1989 and 1988, figure the following long-term financial strength ratios for each year.

a. Debt ratio
b. Equity ratio

c. Equity per share

15. For each of the items in Instruction 14, indicate if there appears to be a favorable or an unfavorable trend from 1988 to 1989. Give reasons for these trends.

Computer Application 6
Automated Accounting Cycle for a
Corporation: Financial Statement Analysis

Manual accounting procedures for analyzing financial statements are described in Chapter 19. Four financial statements are prepared to determine profitability, efficiency, short-term financial strength, and long-term financial strength. (1) Comparative income statement with trend analysis. (2) Comparative income statement with component percentage analysis. (3) Comparative balance sheet with trend analysis. (4) Comparative balance sheet with component percentage analysis. Ratios are also figured to compare selected items for determining how many times one number exceeds another number.

Computer Application 6 provides for the use of a microcomputer to complete financial statement analysis. Computer Application 6 contains instructions for using a microcomputer to solve Mastery Problem 19-M, Chapter 19.

COMPUTER APPLICATION PROBLEM

COMPUTER APPLICATION PROBLEM 6   Financial statement analysis

Instructions. 1. Load the Systems Selection Menu from the *Advanced Automated Accounting* diskette according to the instructions for the computer being used. Select Problem CA-6. The general ledger chart of accounts and account balances have been entered and stored on the template diskette.

  2. Display/Print the comparative income statement with trend analysis.

  3. Display/Print the comparative income statement with component percentage analysis.

  4. Display/Print the comparative balance sheet with trend analysis.

  5. Display/Print the comparative balance sheet with component percentage analysis.

  6. Key-enter ratio data given in Mastery Problem 19-M.

  7. Display/Print the ratio analysis.

7
Cost Accounting

GENERAL BEHAVIORAL GOALS

1. Know accounting terminology related to cost accounting.
2. Understand accounting concepts and practices related to cost accounting.
3. Demonstrate cost accounting procedures.

WATERCRAFT, INC.
Chart of Accounts

Balance Sheet Accounts

(1000) ASSETS

1100	Current Assets
1105	Cash
1110	Accounts Receivable
1115	Allowance for Uncollectible Accounts
1120	Merchandise Inventory — Accessories
1125	Merchandise Inventory — Boats
1130	Supplies
1135	Prepaid Insurance
1200	Plant Assets
1205	Delivery Equipment — Boats
1210	Accumulated Depreciation — Delivery Equipment, Boats
1215	Office Equipment
1220	Accumulated Depreciation — Office Equipment
1225	Store Equipment — Accessories
1230	Accumulated Depreciation — Store Equipment, Accessories
1235	Store Equipment — Boats
1240	Accumulated Depreciation — Store Equipment, Boats

(2000) LIABILITIES

2100	Current Liabilities
2105	Accounts Payable
2110	Employees Income Tax Payable
2115	Federal Income Tax Payable
2120	FICA Tax Payable
2125	Salaries Payable
2130	Sales Tax Payable
2135	Unemployment Tax Payable — Federal
2140	Unemployment Tax Payable — State
2145	Dividends Payable

(3000) CAPITAL

3105	Capital Stock
3110	Retained Earnings
3115	Dividends
3120	Income Summary — Accessories
3125	Income Summary — Boats
3130	Income Summary — General

Income Statement Accounts

(4000) OPERATING REVENUE

4105	Sales — Accessories
4110	Sales Returns and Allowances — Accessories
4115	Sales Discount — Accessories
4120	Sales — Boats
4125	Sales Returns and Allowances — Boats
4130	Sales Discount — Boats

(5000) COST OF MERCHANDISE

5105	Purchases — Accessories
5110	Purchases Returns and Allowances — Accessories
5115	Purchases Discount — Accessories
5120	Purchases — Boats
5125	Purchases Returns and Allowances — Boats
5130	Purchases Discount — Boats

(6000) DIRECT EXPENSES

6100	Direct Expenses — Accessories
6105	Advertising Expense — Accessories
6110	Depreciation Expense — Store Equipment, Accessories
6115	Insurance Expense — Accessories
6120	Payroll Taxes Expense — Accessories
6125	Salary Expense — Accessories
6130	Supplies Expense — Accessories
6200	Direct Expenses — Boats
6205	Advertising Expense — Boats
6210	Bad Debts Expense — Boats
6215	Delivery Expense — Boats
6220	Depreciation Expense — Delivery Equipment, Boats
6225	Depreciation Expense — Store Equipment, Boats
6230	Insurance Expense — Boats
6235	Payroll Taxes Expense — Boats
6240	Salary Expense — Boats
6245	Supplies Expense — Boats

(7000) INDIRECT EXPENSES

7105	Credit Card Fee Expense
7110	Depreciation Expense — Office Equipment
7115	Insurance Expense — Administrative
7120	Miscellaneous Expense
7125	Payroll Taxes Expense — Administrative
7130	Rent Expense
7135	Salary Expense — Administrative
7140	Supplies Expense — Administrative
7145	Utilities Expense

(8000) INCOME TAX

8105	Federal Income Tax

The chart of accounts for Watercraft, Inc., is illustrated above for ready reference as you study Chapter 20 of this textbook.

20 Cost Accounting for a Merchandising Business

ENABLING PERFORMANCE TASKS

After studying Chapter 20, you will be able to:
a. Define accounting terms related to cost accounting for a departmentalized merchandising business.
b. Identify accounting concepts and practices related to cost accounting for a departmentalized merchandising business.
c. Record cost transactions.
d. Complete selected end-of-fiscal-period work for a departmentalized merchandising business using departmental margins.

Providing consumers with a variety and a choice of products requires a number of businesses. Manufacturing businesses make the products which are needed by consumers. Merchandising businesses purchase and display products from many different manufacturers to provide consumers a selection of products in one location. Regardless of the type of business, a company needs accurate, timely statements of revenue, costs, and expenses to operate a profitable business. *(CONCEPT: Adequate Disclosure)*

RESPONSIBILITY ACCOUNTING FOR A MERCHANDISING BUSINESS

Controlling costs is essential to a business' success. The question is, who should control a business' costs? Good management practices prescribe that each manager is responsible for controlling all costs incurred by the manager's business unit. Assigning control of business revenues, costs, and expenses as a responsibility of a specific manager is called responsibility accounting.

Merchandising businesses with effective cost controls generally use some kind of responsibility accounting. A successful responsibility accounting system has two important features.

1. Each manager is assigned responsibility for only those revenues, costs, and expenses for which the manager can make decisions and affect the outcome.
2. The revenues, costs, and expenses for which a manager is responsible must be readily identifiable with the manager's unit. For example, if a manager is responsible for supplies expense, that manager should make decisions about the use of supplies. Also, a separate record should be kept for the manager's supplies expense. Thus, responsibility accounting traces revenues, costs, and expenses to the individual managers who are responsible for making decisions about those revenues, costs, and expenses. (CONCEPT: Adequate Disclosure)

A typical merchandising business income statement reports net income earned during a fiscal period. (CONCEPT: Accounting Period Cycle) However, an income statement usually does not report specific information which a departmental manager can use to control departmental costs. Therefore, merchandising businesses often prepare departmental statements to show each department's contribution to the net income earned by the business.

In responsibility accounting, operating expenses are classified as either direct or indirect expenses. An operating expense identifiable with and chargeable to the operation of a specific department is called a direct expense. An operating expense chargeable to overall business operations and not identifiable with a specific department is called an indirect expense. The cost of supplies used by a specific department is an example of a direct expense. The cost of electricity used by a business' overall operation is an example of an indirect expense.

The revenue earned by a department less its cost of merchandise sold and less its direct expenses is called departmental margin. A statement that reports departmental margin for a specific department is called a departmental margin statement.

Watercraft, Inc., uses responsibility accounting to help control costs and expenses. Watercraft has two merchandising departments: accessories and boats. Each department's revenue, cost of merchandise sold, and direct expenses are recorded in separate departmental general ledger accounts as shown in Watercraft's chart of accounts.

Each business develops a chart of accounts that best accommodates its accounting transactions and financial statements. Supergolf, in Part 2, and Watercraft, in this chapter, are both departmentalized businesses. Supergolf adds a −1 and −2 to the separate departmental accounts to permit sorting by departments. Watercraft prefers to group accounts by types of accounts, such as revenue, cost of merchandise, direct expenses, and indirect expenses. For example, Direct Expenses — Accessories are 6100 numbers. Direct Expenses — Boats are 6200 numbers. Each business develops a chart of accounts that best meets its needs.

REVENUE, COST, AND EXPENSE TRANSACTIONS FOR A DEPARTMENTALIZED MERCHANDISING BUSINESS

Procedures for recording revenue, cost, and expense transactions are similar for most merchandising businesses. Journalizing procedures used by Supergolf in Chapters 2 and 3 are similar to procedures used by Watercraft. Watercraft has separate accounts as does Supergolf for each department's merchandise inventory, sales, and purchases. Supergolf uses these departmentalized accounts to figure and report gross profit for each department. In addition to these accounts, Watercraft has separate accounts in the general ledger for each department's direct expenses, such as advertising, salaries, and supplies. Separate departmental accounts for sales, merchandise inventory, purchases, and direct expenses provide information needed to prepare departmental margin statements.

A journal entry prepared by Watercraft to record a direct expense is shown in Illustration 20-1.

	DATE	ACCOUNT TITLE	CK. NO.	POST. REF.	GENERAL DEBIT	GENERAL CREDIT	ACCOUNTS PAYABLE DEBIT	PURCH. DISCOUNT CR. ACCESS.	PURCH. DISCOUNT CR. BOATS	CASH CREDIT	
1	1989 Apr. 6	Advertising Exp. — Access.	820		35000					35000	1
2											2

CASH PAYMENTS JOURNAL — PAGE 30

Watercraft's accessories department manager decided to buy the advertising services recorded in Illustration 20-1. The advertising promotes the department's sale of boat accessories. Since the departmental manager controls the advertising expense and the department receives the benefits, the expense is classified as a direct expense. So that such expenses can be recorded as direct expenses, the account title also includes the department's name, Advertising Expense — Accessories.

A journal entry prepared by Watercraft to record rent expense for April is shown in Illustration 20-2.

Illustration 20-1
Entry to record a direct expense

Illustration 20-2
Entry to record an indirect expense

	DATE	ACCOUNT TITLE	CK. NO.	POST. REF.	GENERAL DEBIT	GENERAL CREDIT	ACCOUNTS PAYABLE DEBIT	PURCH. DISCOUNT CR. ACCESS.	PURCH. DISCOUNT CR. BOATS	CASH CREDIT	
1	1989 Apr. 1	Rent Expense	796		59000					59000	1
2											2

CASH PAYMENTS JOURNAL — PAGE 29

The accessories department uses a portion of the space rented by Watercraft. However, the decision to rent the specific facility was made by the company president, not the accessories department manager. Also, the rent expense is not separated by departments but is one payment for the entire facility used by all departments. Since this expense is not separated by departments, the expense is recorded as an indirect expense. Indirect expenses are reported in the company's income statement but not in departmental margin statements. Direct and indirect expenses are reported in the same way each fiscal period. *(CONCEPT: Consistent Reporting)*

END-OF-FISCAL-PERIOD WORK FOR A MERCHANDISING BUSINESS USING RESPONSIBILITY ACCOUNTING

Watercraft uses an expanded work sheet to help sort information needed for departmental margin statements. The twelve-column work sheet prepared by Watercraft on April 30, 1989, is shown in Illustration 20-3, pages 450 and 451.

Eight amount columns on the work sheet are the same as described previously. Four additional columns are used by Watercraft: Departmental Margin Statement—Accessories Debit and Credit and Departmental Margin Statement—Boats Debit and Credit. Information in these four additional columns is used to prepare departmental margin statements.

Trial balance on a work sheet

A trial balance is prepared by Watercraft in the same way as previously described for other kinds of businesses. The trial balance prepared by Watercraft on April 30, 1989, is on the work sheet, Illustration 20-3. All general ledger accounts are listed whether they have balances or not. Three income summary accounts are used. Two are used for adjusting inventory accounts related to separate departments, Income Summary— Accessories and Income Summary—Boats. They are also used to close revenue, cost, and direct expense accounts of both departments. Income Summary— General is used for other closing entries.

Watercraft writes the account Federal Income Tax on the work sheet two lines below Departmental Margin—Boats. This location simplifies subtotaling the income statement columns and figuring additional income tax expense. Procedures for figuring corporate income tax are described in Chapter 15.

Adjustments on a work sheet with departmental margins

The following information is needed for adjusting Watercraft's general ledger accounts for the month ended April 30, 1989.

Bad debts expense—boats	$ 714.40
Merchandise inventory—accessories	160,291.20
Merchandise inventory—boats	209,175.00
Supplies used—accessories	1,219.50
Supplies used—boats	1,067.90
Supplies used—administrative	877.00
Insurance expired—accessories	108.40
Insurance expired—boats	144.50
Insurance expired—administrative	27.10
Depreciation expense—delivery equipment, boats	540.00
Depreciation expense—office equipment	190.00
Depreciation expense—store equipment, accessories	481.60
Depreciation expense—store equipment, boats	120.00
Federal income tax for April	12,898.90

Watercraft's adjustments are in the work sheet's Adjustments columns, Illustration 20-3. The departmental merchandise inventory adjustments are recorded in each department's appropriate income summary account.

Adjustments are made for bad debts expense, changes in departmental merchandise inventory, supplies used, insurance used, depreciation, and estimated federal income tax.

Watercraft keeps a record of supplies used by each department so supplies expense can be charged to the appropriate department. The effect of the supplies adjusting entry for April is shown in the T accounts.

Supplies Expense—Accessories		Supplies Expense—Administrative	
Adj. 1,219.50		Adj. 877.00	

Supplies Expense—Boats		Supplies	
Adj. 1,067.90		Apr. 1 Bal. 5,977.40	Adj. 3,164.40

Watercraft also analyzes insurance records each month to determine how much insurance expense each department has incurred. The effect of the adjusting entry to record insurance expired by each department is shown in the T accounts.

Insurance Expense—Accessories		Insurance Expense—Administrative	
Adj. 108.40		Adj. 27.10	

Insurance Expense—Boats		Prepaid Insurance	
Adj. 144.50		Apr. 1 Bal. 2,240.00	Adj. 280.00

These adjustments record expenses associated with producing revenue for a fiscal period. (CONCEPT: *Matching Expenses with Revenue*)

Bad Debts Expense is included in the direct expenses section of Watercraft's departmental margin statement—boats because only boats are sold on credit. Therefore, bad debts expense is charged only to this department. In some companies bad debts expense is divided among various departments. In other companies bad debts expense is considered an administrative expense and is listed in the indirect expenses section of the income statement.

Watercraft, Inc.
Work Sheet
For Month Ended April 30, 1989

| | Trial Balance | | Adjustments | | Departmental Margin Statements — Accessories | | Departmental Margin Statements — Boats | | Income Statement | | Balance Sheet | |
Account Title	Debit	Credit	Debit	Credit	Debit	Credit	Debit	Credit	Debit	Credit	Debit	Credit
1 Cash	9934850										9934850	
2 Accounts Receivable	6495600										6495600	
3 Allow. for Uncoll. Accts.		12840		(a)71440								84280
4 Mdse. Invr.-Accessories	14841720		(b)1187400								16029120	
5 Mdse. Invr.-Boats	19368000		(c)1549500								20917500	
6 Supplies	597740			(d)316440							281300	
7 Prepaid Insurance	224000			(e)28000							196000	
8 Delivery Equip.-Boats	3234000										3234000	
9 Accum. Depr.-Del. Equip.-Boats		970000		(f)54000								1024000
10 Office Equipment	1141680										1141680	
11 Accum. Depr.-Office Equip.		171100		(g)19000								190100
12 Store Equipment-Accessories	2882850										2882850	
13 Accum. Depr.-Store Equip., Access.		864840		(h)48160								913000
14 Store Equipment-Boats	723360										723360	
15 Accum. Depr.-Store Equip.-Boats		217000		(i)12000								229000
16 Accounts Payable		9382070										9382070
17 Employees Income Tax Payable		513690										513690
18 Federal Income Tax Payable				(j)1289890								1289890
19 FICA Tax Payable		345160										345160
20 Salaries Payable												
21 Sales Tax Payable		1607320										1607320
22 Unemploy. Tax Payable-Fed.		34190										34190
23 Unemploy. Tax Payable-State		230290										230290
24 Dividends Payable												
25 Capital Stock		30000000										30000000
26 Retained Earnings		16612210										16612210
27 Dividends	2500000										2500000	
28 Income Summary-Access.			(b)1187400			1187400						
29 Income Summary-Boats			(c)1549500					1549500				
30 Income Summary-General												
31 Sales-Accessories		12553560				12553560						
32 Sales Ret.& Allow.-Access.	10590				10590							
33 Sales Discount-Accessories	42350				42350							
34 Sales-Boats		44029380						44029380				

Line	Account Title	Amount
35	Sales Ret. & Allow. – Boats	69160
36	Sales Discount – Boats	72150
37	Purchases – Accessories	8410780
38	Purch. Ret. & Allow. – Accessories	37240
39	Purch. Discount – Accessories	42050
40	Purchases – Boats	8549100
41	Purch. Ret. & Allow. – Boats	34580
42	Purch. Discount – Boats	51300
43	Advertising Exp. – Accessories	157220
44	Depr. Exp. – Store Equip., Access.	(a) 48160
45	Insurance Exp. – Accessories	(a) 10840
46	Payroll Taxes Exp. – Access.	178330
47	Salary Exp. – Accessories	1927880
48	Supplies Exp. – Accessories	(a) 121950
49	Advertising Exp. – Boats	222350
50	Bad Debts Exp. – Boats	(c) 71440
51	Delivery Exp. – Boats	452440
52	Depr. Exp. – Del. Equip., Boats	(b) 54000
53	Depr. Exp. – Store Equip., Boats	(c) 12000
54	Insurance Exp. – Boats	(a) 14450
55	Payroll Taxes Exp. – Boats	164460
56	Salary Expense – Boats	1783520
57	Supplies Expense – Boats	(d) 106790
58	Credit Card Fee Expense	351070
59	Depr. Exp. – Office Equip.	(g) 19000
60	Insurance Exp. – Admin.	(a) 2710
61	Miscellaneous Expense	480760
62	Payroll Taxes Exp. – Admin.	201940
63	Rent Expense	590000
64	Salary Expense – Admin.	2219370
65	Supplies Expense – Admin.	(d) 87700
66	Utilities Expense	281550
67		88108820 88108820 10908100 15711860 6064760
68	Dept. Margin – Accessories	2912150
69	Dept. Margin – Boats	4492900
70		13820250 13820250 13820250 13820250 6064760 6064760
71	Federal Income Tax	1289890
72		5523990 7405050 6436260 8455200
73		7405050 7405050 6436260 6436260
74	Net Inc. after Fed. Inc. Tax	1881060 1881060

Illustration 20-3   Work sheet with departmental margin statement columns

Completing a work sheet with departmental margin columns

Seven basic steps are followed in completing a work sheet with departmental margin columns. Watercraft's work sheet is shown in Illustration 20-3.

1 Extend balance sheet items to the Balance Sheet Debit and Credit columns. (Lines 1-27.)

- The procedure for extending the balance sheet amounts is the same as described previously in this textbook. When an account is not affected by an adjustment, the amount in the Trial Balance Debit or Credit column is extended to either the Balance Sheet Debit or Credit column. When an account is affected by an adjustment, the new balance is figured and extended to either the Balance Sheet Debit or Credit column.

2 Extend revenue, cost, and direct expense items for the accessories department to the Departmental Margin — Accessories Debit and Credit columns. (Lines 28, 31–33, 37–39, and 43–48.)

- The procedure for extending these income statement amounts is the same as described previously. The difference is that the amounts are extended to the Departmental Margin Statements — Accessories Debit and Credit columns.

3 Extend the revenue, cost, and direct expense items for the boats department to the Departmental Margin Statements — Boats Debit and Credit columns. (Lines 29, 34–36, 40–42, and 49–57.)

- The procedure for extending these income statement amounts is the same as that for the accessories department amounts described in Step 2.

4 Extend the indirect expense items to the Income Statement Debit columns. (Lines 58–66.)

5 Figure the departmental margin for each department. (Lines 68 and 69.)

- Rule a single line across the Departmental Margin Statements — Accessories Debit and Credit columns on the line with the last expense account, line 66. Add each column and write the totals under the ruled line. Subtract the smaller total from the larger total ($138,202.50 − $109,081.00 = $29,121.50). Write the difference, *$29,121.50*, in the Departmental Margin Statements — Accessories Debit column on the next line, line 68. Also, write the same amount in the Income Statement Credit column on the same line. Write the words *Dept. Margin — Accessories* on the same line in the Account Title column. The amount written on this line, $29,121.50, is the departmental margin for the accessories department for the month ended April 30, 1989.

- The same procedure is followed to figure departmental margin for the boats department. The totals for the Boats Debit and Credit columns are written on the same line as the totals of the Accessories columns. This departmental margin is recorded in the work sheet's Departmental Margin Statements—Boats Debit column and in the Income Statement Credit column. The amounts are written on the line below the departmental margin for the accessories department, line 69.
- The Departmental Margin Statements columns for the two departments are totaled and ruled as shown on line 70.

6 Figure the federal income tax and record it on the work sheet. The procedure is the same as described in Chapter 15.

7 Total the Adjustments, Income Statement, and Balance Sheet columns. Figure and record net income after federal income tax. Rule the work sheet as shown on lines 72–74.

Generally, procedures for completing a twelve-column work sheet are the same as for work sheets previously described. The differences are (a) extending amounts to Departmental Margin Statements columns, (b) figuring departmental margin, and (c) extending departmental margins to Income Statement columns.

RESPONSIBILITY STATEMENTS FOR A MERCHANDISING BUSINESS

Financial statements reporting revenue, costs, and direct expenses under a specific department's control are called responsibility statements. Watercraft prepares the usual end-of-fiscal-period financial statements: income statement, stockholders' equity statement, and balance sheet. In addition, Watercraft prepares two responsibility statements: (1) departmental margin statement—accessories, and (2) departmental margin statement—boats. *(CONCEPT: Adequate Disclosure)*

Departmental margin statements

Major responsibility for improving Watercraft's financial condition rests with the management, including the departmental managers. To help these managers make management decisions, two responsibility statements are prepared to provide information about the two departments' progress.

Watercraft's departmental margin statement—accessories for the month ended April 30, 1989, is shown in Illustration 20-4. Information for this statement is obtained from the Departmental Margin Statements—Accessories columns of the work sheet, Illustration 20-3.

The departmental margin statement, Illustration 20-4, includes information about operating revenue, cost of merchandise sold, and the

Watercraft, Inc.
Departmental Margin Statement—Accessories
For Month Ended April 30, 1989

			*% of Net Sales
Operating Revenue:			
Sales......................................		$125,535.60	100.4
Less: Sales Returns & Allowances...........	$ 105.90		0.1
Sales Discount.......................	423.50	529.40	0.3
Net Sales..................................		$125,006.20	100.0
Cost of Merchandise Sold:			
Merchandise Inventory, April 1, 1989..........		$148,417.20	118.7
Purchases..............................	$84,107.80		67.3
Less: Purchases Returns & Allowances	$372.40		0.3
Purchases Discount	420.50	792.90	0.3
Net Purchases		83,314.90	66.6
Total Cost of Mdse. Avail. for Sale............		$231,732.10	185.4
Less Mdse. Inventory, April 30, 1989..........		160,291.20	128.2
Cost of Merchandise Sold		71,440.90	57.1
Gross Profit on Operations		$ 53,565.30	42.9
Direct Expenses:			
Advertising Expense		$ 1,572.20	1.3
Depreciation Expense—Store Equip.		481.60	0.4
Insurance Expense		108.40	0.1
Payroll Taxes Expense......................		1,783.30	1.4
Salary Expense............................		19,278.80	15.4
Supplies Expense..........................		1,219.50	1.0
Total Direct Expenses......................		24,443.80	19.6
Departmental Margin		$ 29,121.50	23.3

*Rounded to nearest 0.1%

Illustration 20-4
Departmental margin
statement for a
merchandising business

direct expenses which can be identified with Watercraft's accessories department. The departmental margin statement is similar to an income statement for the accessories department. The statement is prepared in much the same format as an income statement. However, only direct expenses for the accessories department are included on the departmental margin statement.

Watercraft includes a Percentage of Net Sales column on departmental margin statements to help interpret the information. The percentages are figured by dividing the amount on each line by the amount of departmental net sales. For the departmental margin statement—accessories, the departmental margin percentage is figured as below.

Departmental Margin	÷	Net Sales	=	Percentage of Net Sales
$29,121.50	÷	$125,006.20	=	23.3%

A company may set departmental margin goals for each of its departments to encourage and determine acceptable performance by each department. Watercraft has set a minimum departmental margin goal of 22.0% for the accessories department. Departmental goals are determined by reviewing the department's previous achievements and evaluating changes in selling prices and department costs.

Percentages for the current fiscal period also are compared to similar percentages for previous fiscal periods. The accessories department's departmental margin percentages for the current and two preceding months are shown below.

	Percentages for		
	April	**March**	**February**
Departmental Margin	23.3%	22.7%	22.5%

Since a department has control of and can affect its departmental margin by specific departmental action, this percentage is an excellent measure of a department's performance. Watercraft's accessories department manager can determine if the department is performing satisfactorily by making two comparisons. (1) Current period's departmental margin percentage compared with the company assigned goal of at least 22.0% departmental margin. The department exceeded the company assigned goal February through April, a desirable result. (2) Current period's departmental margin percentage compared with previous periods' departmental margin percentages. The supplies department increased its departmental margin percentage from 22.5% to 23.3% in two months, a favorable trend.

When changes in percentages occur for an item on the departmental margin statement, the departmental manager seeks the reasons for the changes. If changes are good, the policies resulting in favorable changes are continued. If changes are not good, the manager seeks to change policies to prevent unfavorable changes.

Sometimes departmental revenue increases because of special sales and advertising programs. Sometimes the cost of merchandise changes because lower prices are obtained when merchandise is purchased. At other times the percentages change because of an increase or decrease in direct expenses. Without the information on the departmental margin statement, a departmental manager will not know which policies to continue and which to change. (CONCEPT: Adequate Disclosure)

Thus, departmental margin statements provide information to help managers identify unusual changes in revenue and cost amounts. The statements also provide information to assist company officers as well as departmental managers in evaluating departmental performance.

Watercraft prepares a departmental margin statement for the boats department as well as for the accessories department. The departmental margin statement — boats for the month ended April 30, 1989, is shown in Illustration 20-5.

Watercraft, Inc.
Departmental Margin Statement — Boats
For Month Ended April 30, 1989

				*% of Net Sales
Operating Revenue:				
Sales....................................			$144,293.80	101.0
Less: Sales Returns & Allowances...........		$ 691.60		0.5
Sales Discount........................		721.50	1,413.10	0.5
Net Sales.................................			$142,880.70	100.0
Cost of Merchandise Sold:				
Merchandise Inventory, April 1, 1989..........			$193,680.00	135.6
Purchases................................		$85,491.00		59.8
Less: Purchases Returns & Allowances	$345.80			0.2
Purchases Discount	513.00	858.80		0.4
Net Purchases			84,632.20	59.2
Total Cost of Mdse. Avail. for Sale............			$278,312.20	194.8
Less Mdse. Inventory, April 30, 1989..........			209,175.00	146.4
Cost of Merchandise Sold			69,137.20	48.4
Gross Profit on Operations			$ 73,743.50	51.6
Direct Expenses:				
Advertising Expense		$ 2,223.50		1.6
Bad Debts Expense.........................		714.40		0.5
Delivery Expense...........................		4,524.40		3.2
Depreciation Expense — Delivery Equip........		540.00		0.4
Depreciation Expense — Store Equip.		120.00		0.1
Insurance Expense		144.50		0.1
Payroll Taxes Expense		1,644.60		1.2
Salary Expense.............................		17,835.20		12.5
Supplies Expense...........................		1,067.90		0.7
Total Direct Expenses			28,814.50	20.2
Departmental Margin			$ 44,929.00	31.4

*Rounded to nearest 0.1%

Illustration 20-5
Departmental margin
statement for a
merchandising business

Income statement

Watercraft's income statement reports operating revenue, cost of merchandise sold, gross profit, direct expenses, departmental margin, indirect expenses, federal income tax, and net income. Watercraft's income statement for the month ended April 30, 1989, is shown in Illustration 20-6.

The information for Watercraft's income statement is obtained from the two departmental margin statements, Illustration 20-4 and 20-5, and from the Income Statement columns of the work sheet, Illustration 20-3.

The income statement is prepared with five columns: two for departmental amounts and three for company amounts and percentages. The income statement is prepared as follows.

Watercraft, Inc.
Income Statement
For Month Ended April 30, 1989

| | Departmental | | | Company | |
	Accessories	Boats		Amounts	*% of Net Sales
Net Sales	$125,006.20	$142,880.70		$267,886.90	100.0
Cost of Merchandise Sold..................	71,440.90	69,137.20		140,578.10	52.5
Gross Profit on Operations	$ 53,565.30	$ 73,743.50		$127,308.80	47.5
Direct Expenses	24,443.80	28,814.50		53,258.30	19.9
Departmental Margin	$ 29,121.50	$ 44,929.00		$ 74,050.50	27.6
Indirect Expenses:					
Credit Card Fee Expense.......................				$ 3,510.70	1.3
Depreciation Expense—Office Equipment........................				190.00	0.1
Insurance Expense—Administrative				27.10	0.0
Miscellaneous Expense........................				4,807.60	1.8
Payroll Taxes Expense—Administrative..........................				2,019.40	0.8
Rent Expense...............................				5,900.00	2.2
Salary Expense—Administrative				22,193.70	8.3
Supplies Expense—Administrative				877.00	0.3
Utilities Expense............................				2,815.50	1.1
Total Indirect Expenses........................				42,341.00	15.8
Net Income before Federal Income Tax.............................				$ 31,709.50	11.8
Less Federal Income Tax				12,898.90	4.8
Net Income after Federal Income Tax				$ 18,810.60	7.0

*Rounded to nearest 0.1%
Percentage totals may not equal sum of parts due to rounding.

Illustration 20-6
Income statement with departmental margin

1 Write the heading. Use the same format as for income statements previously described.

2 Prepare the net sales section. Information is obtained from the departmental margin statements.

3 Prepare the cost of merchandise sold section. Information is obtained from the departmental margin statements.

4 Prepare the gross profit section. Information is obtained from the departmental margin statements.

5 Prepare the direct expenses section. Information is obtained from the departmental margin statements.

   Details about direct expenses are not listed. If managers need these figures, they refer to departmental margin statements.

6 Prepare the departmental margin section. Information is obtained from the departmental margin statements.

Company amounts in steps 2 through 6 are totals of departmental amounts.

7 Prepare the indirect expenses section. Account titles and balances are obtained from the Income Statement columns of the work sheet, Illustration 20-3.

8 Complete the income statement. The procedure is the same as for income statements previously described. Watercraft has no *Other Revenue* or *Other Expenses*. However, if these items are included, the same procedure as previously described is followed.

9 Prepare the Percentage of Net Sales column. The procedure is the same as figuring the percentage of net sales on departmental margin statements. However, the percentages are based on company net sales.

ACCOUNTING TERMS

What is the meaning of each of the following?

1. responsibility accounting
2. direct expense
3. indirect expense
4. departmental margin
5. departmental margin statement
6. responsibility statements

QUESTIONS FOR INDIVIDUAL STUDY

1. What part do merchandising businesses play in providing consumers with a choice of products?

2. Why does a company need financial statements?

3. According to good management practices, who should control a business' costs?

4. What two important features does a successful responsibility accounting system have?

5. Reporting a business' net income earned for each fiscal period is an application of which accounting concept?

6. What is the major difference between a direct expense and an indirect expense?

7. How are supplies that are a specific department's direct expenses accounted for differently from supplies for the entire business?

8. To prepare departmental margin statements, what separate departmental accounts are needed?

9. What two factors should exist for an expense to be classified as a direct expense of a department?

10. How should an expense that is not separated by departments be reported on a company's income statement?

11. A business that reports direct and indirect expenses in the same way each fiscal period is applying which accounting concept?

12. Why does Watercraft use an expanded work sheet?

13. Why does Watercraft have three income summary accounts?

14. To which column on a work sheet is the balance of Insurance Expense— Accessories extended?

15. How do the procedures for completing the twelve-column work sheet described in this chapter differ from completing work sheets previously described?
16. What is the difference between a departmental margin statement and a company income statement?
17. Why should a company set departmental margin goals for each of its departments?
18. What two comparisons can be made to determine if a department is performing satisfactorily?
19. Departmental margin statements provide information to help managers in what two ways?

CASES FOR MANAGEMENT DECISION

CASE 1 Redding Corporation prepares departmental margin statements for each of its four departments. A new company accountant listed the sum of the departmental margins as the company's net income on the tax return. Is the accountant's procedure correct? Explain.

CASE 2 ClearVu Corporation, a retail paint and glass business, recently decided to prepare departmental margin statements in addition to an income statement. At the end of the first fiscal period, expenses for the company totaled $29,800.00. The abbreviated departmental margin statements below were prepared. The company president criticized Liz Phillips, paint department manager, for poor financial performance. Miss Phillips responded that since her department had fewer employees, less store equipment, and used fewer supplies, she did not think her department used $14,900.00 of expenses. Had she been charged only with expenses actually incurred by her department, the departmental margin would have been as high as the glass department. Further review showed that half of total company expenses had been allocated to each department. Does Miss Phillips have a valid argument? Explain.

CASE 3 Benson's Hardware has three departments: plumbing, electrical, and household. The departmental margins reported for the three departments for the year ended December 31 are: plumbing, $46,740.00; electrical, $49,420.00; household, $1,620.00. These amounts are similar to the departmental margins reported for the past four years. The owner is considering closing the household department because of the consistently low departmental margin. Before taking action, he asks for your recommendation. What is your reply? What factors should be considered before a decision is made to close the department?

	Paint Department	Glass Department	ClearVu Corporation
Revenue	$34,200.00	$39,500.00	$73,700.00
Cost of Merchandise Sold	18,480.00	20,100.00	38,580.00
Gross Profit	$15,720.00	$19,400.00	$35,120.00
Expenses	14,900.00	14,900.00	29,800.00
Departmental Margin	$ 820.00	$ 4,500.00	$ 5,320.00

APPLICATION PROBLEMS

PROBLEM 20-1   Recording direct and indirect expenses

Type-right, an office machinery and supplies merchandising business, uses an accounting system that provides information needed to prepare departmental margin statements as well as an income statement. The company has two departments: machinery and supplies.

Instructions: Record the following selected transactions on page 16 of a cash payments journal. Expenses not identified with a specific department are recorded as indirect expenses.

Mar. 1. Paid March rent, $6,145.00. C334. (Used by all departments.)
      5. Paid advertising for supplies department, $54.00. C362.
     12. Paid delivery expense for machinery department, $93.20. C416.
     15. Paid telephone bill, $132.10. C431. (A miscellaneous expense used by all departments.)
     23. Paid advertising for machinery department, $82.90. C494.
     30. Paid utility bill, $3,011.60. C537. (Amount used cannot be identified with each department.)
     31. Paid payroll for machinery department, $3,916.77. C586. (Gross salaries, $4,776.53; federal income tax withheld, $525.40; FICA tax withheld, $334.36.)

PROBLEM 20-2   Preparing a work sheet with departmental margins

Lone Oak Lumber is a merchandising business selling hardware and lumber. The company uses a monthly fiscal period. Lone Oak Lumber's June 30 trial balance is recorded on a twelve-column work sheet in the working papers accompanying this textbook.

Instructions: 1. Use the following information to plan adjustments on the work sheet for the month ended June 30 of the current year.

Bad debts expense — lumber	$ 185.20
Merchandise inventory — hardware	37,821.30
Merchandise inventory — lumber	55,978.80
Supplies used — hardware	288.40
Supplies used — lumber	370.80
Supplies used — administrative	164.80
Insurance expired — hardware	60.30
Insurance expired — lumber	120.60
Insurance expired — administrative	20.10
Depreciation expense — delivery equipment, lumber	198.00
Depreciation expense — office equipment	23.00
Depreciation expense — store equipment, hardware	185.50
Depreciation expense — store equipment, lumber	32.00
Federal income tax for the month	2,592.52

2. Complete the work sheet. Extend proper amounts to debit and credit columns for Departmental Margin Statement — Hardware, Departmental Margin Statement — Lumber, Income Statement, and Balance Sheet. Accounts on trial balance lines 58–66 are classified as indirect expenses.

The work sheet prepared in this problem is needed to complete Problems 20-3 and 20-4.

PROBLEM 20-3   Preparing departmental margin statements

The work sheet prepared in Problem 20-2 is needed to complete this problem.

Instructions: Prepare departmental margin statements for Lone Oak Lumber's hardware department and lumber department. Prepare statements similar to the ones described in this chapter. Figure the percentage of net sales, rounding to the nearest 0.1%.

The statements prepared in this problem are needed to complete Problem 20-4.

PROBLEM 20-4   Preparing an income statement with departmental margins

The work sheet prepared in Problem 20-2 and statements prepared in Problem 20-3 are needed to complete this problem.

Instructions: Prepare an income statement for Lone Oak Lumber. Prepare a statement similar to the one described in this chapter. Figure the percentage of net sales, rounding to the nearest 0.1%.

ENRICHMENT PROBLEMS

MASTERY PROBLEM 20-M   Completing end-of-fiscal-period work for a merchandising business using departmental margins

Playtime, Inc., is a merchandising business specializing in children's clothing and toys. The company uses a yearly fiscal period. Playtime's December 31 trial balance is recorded on a twelve-column work sheet in the working papers accompanying this textbook.

Instructions: 1. Use the following information to plan adjustments on the work sheet for the year ended December 31 of the current year.

Bad debts expense—clothing	$ 81.60
Merchandise inventory—clothing	112,350.90
Merchandise inventory—toys	46,543.80
Supplies used—clothing	1,409.00
Supplies used—toys	986.30
Supplies used—administrative	422.70
Insurance expired—clothing	1,395.00
Insurance expired—toys	1,395.00
Insurance expired—administrative	310.00
Depreciation expense—office equipment	529.50
Depreciation expense—store equipment, clothing	2,131.30
Depreciation expense—store equipment, toys	981.70
Federal income tax for the year	2,888.49

2. Complete the work sheet. Extend proper amounts to debit and credit columns for Departmental Margin Statement—Clothing, Departmental Margin Statement—Toys, Income Statement, and Balance Sheet. Accounts on trial balance lines 54–62 are classified as indirect expenses.

3. Prepare departmental margin statements for each department. Figure the percentage of net sales, rounding to the nearest 0.1%.

4. Prepare an income statement similar to the one described in this chapter. Figure the percentage of net sales, rounding to the nearest 0.1%.

CHALLENGE PROBLEM 20-C   Analyzing a departmental margin statement

The following departmental margin statement is for the luggage department of Leathercraft, Inc., for the years 1988 and 1989. The company has set a goal for the luggage department to contribute a minimum of 25.0% departmental margin. For the years 1983 through 1988, the departmental margin for the luggage department has varied from 25.0% to 28.8% of net sales.

Leathercraft, Inc.
Departmental Margin Statement—Luggage
For Years Ended December 31, 1989 and 1988

	1989 Amounts	*% of Net Sales	1988 Amounts	*% of Net Sales
Operating Revenue:				
Sales..............................	$431,411.90		$384,805.90	100.4
Less Sales Returns & Allowances	1,718.80		1,533.10	0.4
Net Sales..........................		$429,693.10	$383,272.80	100.0
Cost of Merchandise Sold:				
Merchandise Inventory, Jan. 1.........	$ 45,566.80		$ 41,010.20	10.7
Purchases	237,204.90		203,901.10	53.2
Total Cost of Mdse. Avail. for Sale.....	$282,771.70		$244,911.30	63.9
Less Mdse. Inventory, Dec. 31	42,048.50		45,609.50	11.9
Cost of Merchandise Sold		240,723.20	199,301.80	52.0
Gross Profit on Operations		$188,969.90	$183,971.00	48.0
Direct Expenses:				
Advertising Expense	$ 4,325.90		$ 3,449.50	0.9
Bad Debts Expense..................	4,899.60		3,827.90	1.0
Delivery Expense	10,237.20		8,432.00	2.2
Depreciation Exp.—Delivery Equip.....	5,960.10		4,599.30	1.2
Depreciation Exp.—Store Equip.......	3,901.60		3,432.60	0.9
Insurance Expense	3,398.20		3,023.70	0.8
Payroll Taxes Expense	2,864.30		2,579.40	0.7
Salary Expense.....................	50,243.70		42,960.00	11.2
Supplies Expense...................	3,922.80		2,981.90	0.8
Total Direct Expenses		89,753.40	75,286.30	19.6
Departmental Margin		$ 99,216.50	$108,684.70	28.4

*Rounded to nearest to 0.1%

Instructions: 1. Figure the percentage of net sales for each item on the 1989 departmental margin statement. Round to the nearest 0.1%.

2. Figure the changes in "% of Net Sales" from 1988 to 1989 for the following items: (a) cost of merchandise sold, (b) gross profit, (c) total direct departmental expenses, and (d) departmental margin.

3. From an analysis of the departmental margin statement and the amounts obtained from Instructions 1 and 2, answer the following questions.

a. Is the departmental margin for the luggage department at a satisfactory percentage of sales? Explain why it is or is not satisfactory.
b. Is the trend of the cost of merchandise sold percentage favorable or unfavorable? Explain why it is or is not favorable. Can you suggest some possible reasons for the change in cost of merchandise sold from 1988 to 1989?
c. Is the trend of the total direct departmental expenses percentage favorable or unfavorable? Explain why the trend is or is not favorable.

COMVU, INC.
Chart of Accounts

Balance Sheet Accounts	Income Statement Accounts

Balance Sheet Accounts

(1000) ASSETS

1100	Current Assets
1105	Cash
1110	Petty Cash
1115	Accounts Receivable
1120	Allowance for Uncollectible Accounts
1125	Materials
1130	Work in Process
1135	Finished Goods
1140	Supplies—Factory
1145	Supplies—Sales
1150	Supplies—Administrative
1155	Prepaid Insurance

1200	Plant Assets
1205	Factory Equipment
1210	Accumulated Depreciation—Factory Equipment
1215	Office Equipment
1220	Accumulated Depreciation—Office Equipment
1225	Store Equipment
1230	Accumulated Depreciation—Store Equipment
1235	Building
1240	Accumulated Depreciation—Building
1245	Land

(2000) LIABILITIES

2100	Current Liabilities
2105	Accounts Payable
2110	Employees Income Tax Payable
2115	Federal Income Tax Payable
2120	FICA Tax Payable
2125	Salaries Payable
2130	Unemployment Tax Payable—Federal
2135	Unemployment Tax Payable—State
2140	Dividends Payable

2200	Long-Term Liability
2205	Mortgage Payable

(3000) CAPITAL

3105	Capital Stock
3110	Retained Earnings
3115	Dividends
3120	Income Summary

Income Statement Accounts

(4000) OPERATING REVENUE

4105	Sales

(5000) COST OF SALES

5105	Cost of Goods Sold

(5500) MANUFACTURING COSTS

5505	Factory Overhead
5510	Depreciation Expense—Factory Equipment
5515	Depreciation Expense—Building
5520	Heat, Light, and Power Expense
5525	Insurance Expense—Factory
5530	Miscellaneous Expense—Factory
5535	Payroll Taxes Expense—Factory
5540	Property Tax Expense—Factory
5545	Supplies Expense—Factory

(6000) OPERATING EXPENSES

6100	Selling Expenses
6105	Advertising Expense
6110	Delivery Expense
6115	Depreciation Expense—Store Equipment
6120	Miscellaneous Expense—Sales
6125	Salary Expense—Sales
6130	Supplies Expense—Sales

6200	Administrative Expenses
6205	Bad Debts Expense
6210	Depreciation Expense—Office Equipment
6215	Insurance Expense—Administrative
6220	Miscellaneous Expense—Administrative
6225	Payroll Taxes Expense—Administrative
6230	Property Tax Expense—Administrative
6235	Salary Expense—Administrative
6240	Supplies Expense—Administrative
6245	Utilities Expense—Administrative

(7000) OTHER REVENUE

7105	Gain on Plant Assets
7110	Miscellaneous Revenue

(8000) OTHER EXPENSES

8105	Interest Expense
8110	Loss on Plant Assets

(9000) INCOME TAX

9105	Federal Income Tax

The chart of accounts for ComVu, Inc., is illustrated above for ready
reference as you study Chapters 21 and 22 of this textbook.

21 Cost Accounting for a Manufacturing Business

ENABLING PERFORMANCE TASKS

After studying Chapter 21, you will be able to:
a. Define accounting terms related to cost accounting for a manufacturing business.
b. Identify accounting concepts and practices related to cost accounting for a manufacturing business.
c. Identify the elements of manufacturing costs: (a) direct materials, (b) direct labor, and (c) factory overhead.
d. Identify the flow of costs through the manufacturing process.
e. Record entries related to cost records for a manufacturing business.
f. Prepare selected ledger and cost sheets for a manufacturing business.

Merchandising and manufacturing businesses are similar in several ways. Both types of businesses sell products. Both types earn revenue and incur expenses. Both types intend to earn a net income. (CONCEPT: Going Concern)

These businesses differ however in one significant way. A merchandising business purchases products and, without changing the products' form, sells those products to customers. Department stores and grocery stores are examples of merchandising businesses.

A manufacturing business buys materials and, by using labor and machines, changes the form of the materials into a finished product. After changing the form of materials into a finished product, a manufacturing business sells the product. A manufacturing business generally sells the finished product to a merchandising business which then sells the product to consumers. ComVu, Inc., a satellite antenna manufacturing business, buys antenna dishes, polarizers, control consoles, receivers, and other materials. By using labor and machines, ComVu combines the materials to make satellite antenna systems. The form of the antenna dishes, polarizers, control consoles, receivers, and other materials is changed into a single

product—a satellite antenna system. Merchandising businesses buy the satellite antenna systems from ComVu for resale to consumers.

A merchandising business needs to know the cost of merchandise sold in order to figure net income. For the same reason, a manufacturing company needs to know the cost of finished products sold. To know how much finished products cost, ComVu keeps records of all costs involved in making the products.

Selling and administrative activities of a manufacturing business normally are similar to those of a merchandising business. Procedures for recording the selling and administrative expenses are also similar in both types of businesses.

ELEMENTS OF MANUFACTURING COST

The manufacturing cost of any finished product includes three cost elements. These cost elements are (1) direct materials, (2) direct labor, and (3) factory overhead.

Direct materials

Materials that are of significant value in the cost of and that become an identifiable part of a finished product are called direct materials. Direct materials include all items used in the manufacturing process that have sufficient value to justify charging the cost directly to the product. *(CONCEPT: Materiality)* Examples of direct materials are the antenna dishes and receivers used in the manufacture of satellite antenna systems.

Direct labor

Salaries of factory workers who make a product are called direct labor. Direct labor includes only salaries of persons working directly on a product. Salaries of supervisors, maintenance workers, and others whose efforts do not apply directly to the manufacture of a product are not direct labor.

Factory overhead

All expenses other than direct materials and direct labor that apply to the making of products are called factory overhead.

Some materials used in manufacturing a product cost a very small amount for each unit produced. Materials used in the completion of a product but that are of insignificant value to justify accounting for separately are called indirect materials. Indirect materials may include items such as glue, nails, thread, and rivets.

Some factory workers devote their time to supervisory, clerical, and maintenance tasks necessary to operate the factory. Such workers include time clerks, supervisors, maintenance people, receiving clerks, and inspectors. Salaries paid to factory workers who are not actually making products are called indirect labor.

Other costs also are incurred in the manufacturing process. (a) Supplies used in the factory. (b) Depreciation of factory buildings and equipment. (c) Repairs to factory buildings and equipment. (d) Insurance on building, equipment, and stock. (e) Taxes on property owned. (f) Heat, light, and power. All of these expenses, including indirect materials and indirect labor, make up factory overhead.

INVENTORIES FOR A MANUFACTURING BUSINESS

A merchandising business normally has one general ledger account for merchandise inventory. However, a manufacturing business has three inventory accounts related to the products manufactured. (1) Materials. (2) Work in Process. (3) Finished Goods.

A materials inventory account shows the costs of materials on hand that have not yet been used in making a product. Products that are being manufactured but are not yet complete are called work in process. A work in process inventory account therefore shows all costs that have been spent on products that are not yet complete. Manufactured products that are fully completed are called finished goods. A finished goods inventory account therefore shows the cost of completed products still on hand and unsold.

COST RECORDS

Manufacturing businesses keep detailed cost records for three purposes. (1) To determine accurate costs for each product made. (2) To provide specific cost information to managers who must identify high cost areas so that corrective action can be taken. (3) To provide cost summary information for journal entries.

Subsidiary cost ledgers

Three subsidiary ledgers are kept to provide detailed cost information for the three manufacturing inventory accounts.

Materials ledger. Merchandise inventory determined by keeping a continuous record of increases, decreases, and balance on hand is known as perpetual inventory. ComVu uses a perpetual inventory system for materials. A perpetual inventory record is kept to provide detailed cost information about each kind of material. A ledger containing all records of materials is called a materials ledger.

Cost ledger. A record is kept of all charges for direct materials, direct labor, and factory overhead for each specific job. The record is known as a cost sheet. A cost sheet is maintained for each manufacturing job. A ledger containing all cost sheets for products in the process of being manufactured is called a cost ledger.

Finished goods ledger. A record is kept of each kind of finished good to provide a perpetual inventory of each product produced and its cost. A ledger containing records of all finished goods on hand is called a finished goods ledger. This ledger is similar to a materials ledger.

Manufacturing cost flows

Illustration 21-1
Cost flow and forms used
to record manufacturing
costs

Manufacturing costs are recorded on cost forms as costs occur. The forms used and sequence of steps followed for recording ComVu's manufacturing costs are shown in Illustration 21-1.

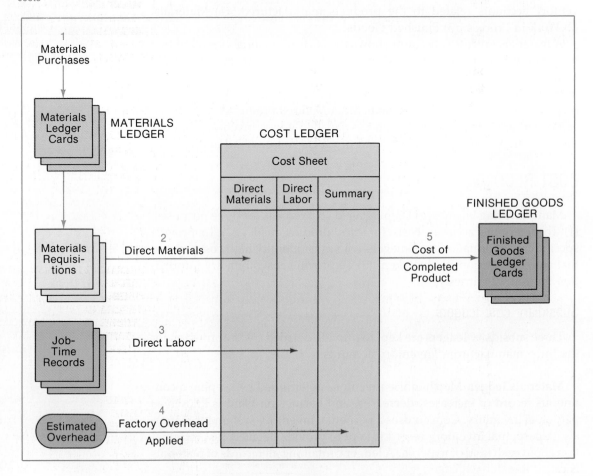

1 When materials are purchased, the number and cost of each kind of material are recorded on materials ledger cards.

2 When direct materials are issued for use in the factory, a materials requisition is prepared. The amount of direct materials issued is recorded as a reduction on the materials ledger card and an increase in the Direct Materials column of the cost sheet.

3 When direct labor is used, job-time records are prepared. Time record amounts are recorded in the Direct Labor column of the cost sheet.

4 When a product is completed, the amount of factory overhead is estimated and recorded in the Summary column of the cost sheet. Estimating factory overhead is described later in this chapter.

5 When a product is completed, amounts on the cost sheet are totaled and recorded on a finished goods ledger card.

Journal entries for job costs are described in Chapter 22.

RECORDS FOR MATERIALS

A manufacturing business keeps a record of materials used in the manufacturing process. In addition, sufficient materials should be on hand so that the manufacturing process will not be interrupted. However, too great a stock of materials requires needless investment in inventory. To provide a perpetual inventory and detailed cost information about materials, ComVu keeps a materials ledger card for each kind of material.

Preparing a materials ledger

A materials ledger contains a materials ledger card for each kind of material kept in the storeroom. ComVu's materials ledger card is shown in Illustration 21-2.

Illustration 21-2
Materials ledger card

MATERIALS LEDGER CARD

Article _96A Satellite Dish_   Acct. No. _115_
Reorder _140_   Minimum _110_   Location _A-12_

ORDERED			RECEIVED					ISSUED					BALANCE			
Date	Purchase Order No.	Quantity	Date	Purchase Order No.	Quantity	Unit Price	Value	Date	Requisition No.	Quantity	Unit Price	Value	Date	Quantity	Unit Price	Value
													1989 Jan.3	110	201.00	22,110.00
1989 Jan.3	572	140						1989 Jan.4	841	50	201.00	10,050.00	4	60	201.00	12,060.00
								11	863	50	201.00	10,050.00	11	10	201.00	2,010.00
			1989 Jan.14	572	140	201.00	28,140.00						14	150	201.00	30,150.00

The name and account number of the item are entered at the top of each materials ledger card. The reorder quantity and minimum quantities to be kept in stock are shown on the second line. When the number on hand equals the minimum, the materials clerk notifies the purchasing agent and a new order is placed.

Recording purchases of materials

On January 3, 1989, ComVu orders 140 satellite dishes from Cosmos Company on Purchase Order No. 572. A completed form authorizing a seller to deliver goods with payment to be made later is called a purchase order. The date of the order, the purchase order number, and the quantity ordered are recorded on the materials ledger card in the Ordered columns, as shown in Illustration 21-2. Information about quantities ordered is recorded on the card to avoid placing duplicate orders.

When the items ordered are received, an entry is made in the Received columns on the card as shown in Illustration 21-2. The quantity and value are added to the previous balance and extended into the Balance columns. The total value for all the materials ledger cards equals the balance of the materials general ledger account.

The relationship of the general ledger accounts to the forms and ledgers described in this chapter is explained in Chapter 22.

RECORDS FOR WORK IN PROCESS

During the manufacturing process, all costs of making a product must be recorded. All charges for direct materials, direct labor, and factory overhead for a particular job are recorded on a cost sheet. A job number is recorded on each cost sheet to identify the specific job.

Preparing cost sheets

When a factory department is ready to start a new job, the factory department supervisor requests a job number from the cost accounting department. The cost accounting department assigns a job number and prepares a cost sheet for the job. All costs then can be charged to a specific job number.

On January 18, ComVu starts Job No. 902 for 10 AG96 Satellite Antennas. The heading of the cost sheet for Job No. 902 is shown in Illustration 21-3.

Recording direct materials requisitions

Direct materials, when needed, are requested from the storeroom. A materials requisition form is used to authorize transfer of items from the storeroom to the factory. The materials requisition is prepared in triplicate

COST SHEET

Job No. _902_   Date _January 18, 1989_
Item _AG 96 Satellite Antenna_   Date wanted _January 25, 1989_
No. of items _10_   Date completed _____
Ordered for _Stock_

DIRECT MATERIALS		DIRECT LABOR				SUMMARY	
Req. No.	Amount	Date	Amount	Date	Amount	Item	Amount

and signed by a person in authority, usually the factory superintendent or factory department supervisor.

Illustration 21-3
Cost sheet

A materials requisition prepared by a factory department supervisor is shown in Illustration 21-4.

MATERIALS REQUISITION

Requisition No. **885**   Date _January 18_   19_89_
Requisitioned By _Phillip Hall_   Position _Supervisor_

JOB NO.	QUANTITY	DESCRIPTION	UNIT PRICE	TOTAL COST
902	10	96A Satellite Dish		

Materials Issued _____ 19____   Recorded:
By _____
            Materials Clerk

Illustration 21-4
Materials requisition submitted by factory department supervisor

One copy of a materials requisition is kept in the factory. Two copies are sent to the materials storeroom. The materials issued date, unit price, and total cost are recorded on both storeroom requisition copies. The materials clerk initials the requisition to show that the materials have been issued. One copy of the completed materials requisition is kept in the storeroom. The original requisition is sent to the cost accounting department. The completed Materials Requisition No. 885 is shown in Illustration 21-5.

MATERIALS REQUISITION

Requisition No. **885**   Date _January 18_   19 _89_

Requisitioned By _Phillip Hall_   Position _Supervisor_

JOB NO.	QUANTITY	DESCRIPTION	UNIT PRICE	TOTAL COST
902	10	96A Satellite Dish	201.00	2,010 00

Materials Issued _January 18_ 19 _89_   Recorded:
By _SLA_

Materials Clerk

Illustration 21-5
Completed materials
requisition

From the materials requisition copy, an entry is made in the materials ledger. The entry for Materials Requisition No. 885 on the materials ledger card is shown in Illustration 21-6. The requisition is first summarized in the Issued columns. Then the quantity and value entered in the Issued columns are subtracted from the amounts in the Balance columns to show the new balance.

MATERIALS LEDGER CARD

Article _96A Satellite Dish_   Acct. No. _115_

Reorder _140_   Minimum _110_   Location _A-12_

ORDERED			RECEIVED					ISSUED					BALANCE			
Date	Purchase Order No.	Quantity	Date	Purchase Order No.	Quantity	Unit Price	Value	Date	Requisition No.	Quantity	Unit Price	Value	Date	Quantity	Unit Price	Value
			1989 Jan. 14	572	140	201.00	28,140.00						14	150	201.00	30,150.00
								18	885	10	201.00	2,010.00	18	140	201.00	28,140.00

Illustration 21-6
Materials ledger card after
entering a materials
requisition

Recording direct materials on a cost sheet

The original copy of each materials requisition is sent to the cost accounting department. As requisitions are received, they are recorded on the cost sheets for the jobs to be charged. For example, Materials Requisition No. 885 is for direct materials, $2,010.00, Job No. 902. The entries for direct materials are in the Direct Materials columns of the cost sheet shown in Illustration 21-7.

COST SHEET

Job No. *902* Date *January 18, 1989*
Item *AG 96 Satellite Antenna* Date wanted *January 25, 1989*
No. of items *10* Date completed _____
Ordered for *Stock*

DIRECT MATERIALS		DIRECT LABOR				SUMMARY	
Req. No.	Amount	Date	Amount	Date	Amount	Item	Amount
884	$ 98.50	Jan. 18	$ 278.00				
885	2,010.00	19	483.00				
889	310.30	20	474.50				
890	319.90	21	496.00				
894	405.50	24	505.00				
897	178.40	25	275.50				
898	622.20		$ 2,512.00				
	$ 3,944.80						

Illustration 21-7
Cost sheet with direct materials and direct labor entries

Recording direct labor on a cost sheet

Factory employees may work on a number of different jobs each day. Therefore, a job-time record is kept showing the amount of time spent on each job. At the end of each day, all job-time records are summarized. The total direct labor cost for each job is recorded on each job's cost sheet. A job-time record for one ComVu employee working 4 hours on Job No. 902 is shown in Illustration 21-8.

JOB – TIME RECORD

Employee Number *21* Job Number *902*
Date *1-18-89*
Time started *8 a.m.*
Time finished *12 noon*
Total time spent on job .... *4.0 hrs.*

Illustration 21-8
Job-time record

All the direct labor costs for Job No. 902 are in the Direct Labor columns of the cost sheet shown in Illustration 21-7.

Figuring and recording factory overhead on a cost sheet

Some factory overhead expenses occur regularly throughout a fiscal period while others occur irregularly. Also, many factory overhead expenses are not known until the end of a fiscal period. Therefore, factory overhead expenses normally are charged to jobs by using an application rate based on a known cost such as direct labor. This method applies factory overhead expenses to all jobs and permits a company to record overhead on a cost sheet when a job is completed. The estimated amount of factory overhead recorded on cost sheets is called applied overhead.

Applied overhead is recorded on cost sheets during the fiscal period and before all factory overhead for the current period is known. (CONCEPT: Matching Expenses with Revenue) Therefore, the factory overhead applied rate used to determine applied overhead is figured before the fiscal period begins.

Three steps are followed to determine a factory overhead applied rate.

1 Estimate amount of factory overhead costs for the next fiscal period. Generally three factors are considered in estimating factory overhead. (a) Amount of factory overhead for the past several fiscal periods. (b) Number of products the factory expects to produce in the next fiscal period. (c) Expected increase in unit costs of factory overhead items. ComVu expects to produce 2,500 satellite antennas in 1989. Considering this volume, previous years' overhead, and anticipated cost increases, ComVu estimates 1989 factory overhead as $375,000.00.

2 Estimate number of base units that will be used in the next fiscal period. Base units are usually cost items that can be identified easily. Direct labor cost, direct labor hours, and direct material cost are common bases. A base unit should be selected that most closely relates to actual overhead costs. ComVu uses direct labor cost as a base unit because there is a close relationship between the amount of direct labor cost and factory overhead costs. ComVu estimates 1989 direct labor cost as $625,000.00. This amount is determined as follows.

Estimated No. of Units (Antennas) Produced		Estimated Direct Labor Hours Per Unit		Estimated Salary Rate Per Hour		Estimated Total Direct Labor Cost
2,500	×	25	×	$10.00	=	$625,000.00

3 Figure factory overhead applied rate. Divide estimated factory overhead costs by estimated base units. ComVu's factory overhead applied rate is 60% of direct labor cost. The rate is figured as follows.

Estimated Factory Overhead		Estimated Direct Labor Cost		Factory Overhead Applied Rate
$375,000.00	÷	$625,000.00	=	.60 or 60%

During 1989, ComVu will record factory overhead costs of 60% of direct labor costs on each cost sheet. This overhead amount is the applied overhead. The total direct labor for Job No. 902 is $2,512.00 as shown in Illustration 21-7. The amount of applied overhead, $1,507.20, recorded on the cost sheet for Job No. 902 is figured as follows.

Total Direct Labor Costs (Job No. 902)	×	Factory Overhead Applied Rate	=	Applied Overhead (Job No. 902)
$2,512.00	×	60%	=	$1,507.20

Completing a cost sheet

The completed cost sheet for Job No. 902 is shown in Illustration 21-9.

COST SHEET

Job No. *902*

Item *AG 96 Satellite Antenna*

No. of items *10*

Ordered for *Stock*

Date *January 18, 1989*

Date wanted *January 25, 1989*

Date completed *January 25, 1989*

DIRECT MATERIALS		DIRECT LABOR				SUMMARY	
Req. No.	Amount	Date	Amount	Date	Amount	Item	Amount
884	$ 98.50	Jan. 18	$ 278.00			Direct Materials	$ 3,944.80
885	2,010.00	19	483.00			Direct Labor	2,512.00
889	310.30	20	474.50			Factory Overhead	
890	319.90	21	496.00			(60% of direct	
894	405.50	24	505.00			labor costs)	1,507.20
897	178.40	25	275.50			Total Cost	$ 7,964.00
898	622.20		$ 2,512.00				
	$ 3,944.80					No. units finished	10
						Cost per unit	$ 796.40

When a job is completed, total costs are figured and recorded in the Summary columns of the cost sheet. Direct Materials and Direct Labor columns on the cost sheet are totaled and the totals are recorded in the Summary columns. For Job No. 902, ComVu recorded Direct Materials, $3,944.80, and Direct Labor, $2,512.00, in the Summary columns. Applied overhead is figured and recorded in the cost sheet's Summary columns. ComVu records factory overhead for Job No. 902, $1,507.20, which is 60% of direct labor cost ($2,512.00 × 60% = $1,507.20).

Illustration 21-9
Completed cost sheet

Next, the three cost element amounts recorded in the cost sheet's Summary columns, direct materials, direct labor, and factory overhead, are totaled. This total amount is the total cost of the job. Total cost for ComVu's Job No. 902 is $7,964.00 as shown in Illustration 21-9.

The cost of each satellite antenna manufactured in Job No. 902, $796.40, is figured as follows.

Total Costs (Job No. 902)	÷	No. of Units	=	Cost Per Unit
$7,964.00	÷	10	=	$796.40

This information is recorded on Job No. 902's cost sheet so that the cost per unit is available when needed.

The total value for all cost sheets for work still in process equals the balance of the work in process account in the general ledger. Thus, at the end of a fiscal period, cost sheets for work in process are totaled to determine ending inventory for the general ledger account Work in Process.

RECORDS FOR FINISHED GOODS

When a job is completed, the finished goods are placed in the finished goods stock area until shipped to customers. When finished goods are moved to the stock area, summary information from the cost sheet is recorded on the completed product's finished goods ledger card.

The entry for the completed Job No. 902 is recorded on the finished goods ledger card shown in Illustration 21-10.

Illustration 21-10
Finished goods ledger
card

FINISHED GOODS LEDGER CARD

Description _Satellite Antenna_   Stock No. _AG 96_
Minimum _15_   Location _T-4_

MANUFACTURED/RECEIVED					SHIPPED/ISSUED					BALANCE			
Date	Job No.	Quantity	Unit Cost	Total Cost	Date	Sales Invoice No.	Quantity	Unit Cost	Total Cost	Date	Quantity	Unit Cost	Total Cost
										1989 Jan. 1	24	795.50	19,092.00
					1989 Jan. 7	626	8	795.50	6,364.00	7	16	795.50	12,728.00
1989 Jan. 11	877	28	801.60	22,444.80						11	16	795.50	
											28	801.60	35,172.80
					12	632	12	795.50	9,546.00	12	4	795.50	
											28	801.60	25,626.80
					18	639	4	795.50					
							6	801.60	7,991.60	18	22	801.60	17,635.20
25	902	10	796.40	7,964.00						25	22	801.60	
											10	796.40	25,599.20

When ComVu's Job No. 902 is complete, five cost sheet items are recorded in the Manufactured/Received columns of the AG96 Satellite Antenna finished goods ledger card. (1) Date job is completed, 25. (2) Job number, 902. (3) Quantity of products, 10. (4) Unit cost of product, $796.40. (5) Total cost of the job, $7,964.00.

The Balance columns are figured by adding costs of Job No. 902 to the previous balance. Since unit costs for each job frequently are different amounts, unit costs are kept separate. However, the total cost balance is combined for all units in the finished goods inventory. ComVu uses the first-in, first-out inventory method. Thus, the cost recorded first is the cost removed from inventory first when units are sold.

The total value for all finished goods ledger cards equals the finished goods inventory account balance in the general ledger. After ComVu's Job No. 902 is completed and recorded, the company has 32 AG96 Satellite Antennas on hand at a total cost of $25,599.20 (22 units @ $801.60 plus 10 units @ $796.40).

> Different amounts of direct materials and direct labor cause the difference in unit costs of different jobs.

ACCOUNTING TERMS

What is the meaning of each of the following?

1. direct materials
2. direct labor
3. factory overhead
4. indirect materials

5. indirect labor
6. work in process
7. finished goods
8. materials ledger

9. cost ledger
10. finished goods ledger
11. purchase order
12. applied overhead

QUESTIONS FOR INDIVIDUAL STUDY

1. How is a merchandising business similar to a manufacturing business?
2. How does a merchandising business differ from a manufacturing business?
3. What are the three cost elements of manufacturing any finished product?
4. Recording only the identifiable part of a finished product as direct materials that have sufficient value to justify charging directly to the product is an application of which accounting concept?
5. Why are the salaries of a manufacturing plant's maintenance workers not recorded as direct labor?
6. What are some of the overhead expenses incurred in manufacturing?
7. What three inventory accounts does a

manufacturing company generally keep?
8. Why do manufacturing businesses keep detailed cost records?
9. What are the three subsidiary cost ledgers that are kept to provide detailed cost information of the manufacturing inventory accounts?
10. Why do manufacturers usually maintain records that show the quantity and value of materials on hand?
11. What information is recorded on each card in a materials ledger?
12. What is the relationship between the total value balances for all the materials ledger cards and the general ledger?
13. What is the process generally used to authorize transfer of direct materials from

the storeroom to the factory?
14. Where is the information obtained for the Direct Materials section of each cost sheet?
15. What information is recorded daily on each cost sheet?
16. Where is the information obtained for the Direct Labor section of each cost sheet?
17. How are factory overhead expenses normally distributed to a specific job?
18. Recording applied overhead on cost sheets during a fiscal period is an application of which accounting concept?
19. What three factors generally are considered in estimating factory overhead?
20. What are some common base units used in figuring the applied overhead?
21. How is a factory overhead applied rate figured?
22. How is ComVu's applied overhead figured?
23. What is the total amount recorded in a cost sheet's Summary column?
24. What is the source of information for making entries in the finished goods ledger for newly completed products?

CASES FOR MANAGEMENT DECISION

CASE 1 DeLan Cabinet Company manufactures kitchen cabinets. During the current year, payments were made for the following items. A new clerk classified the cost items. Are the cost items classified correctly? If not, give the correct classification and explain the reason for your corrected classification. 1. Wood to be used in the cabinets. (Factory Overhead) 2. Insurance premium on the factory building. (Direct Materials) 3. Salary of cabinet maker. (Factory Overhead) 4. Nails used in assembling the cabinets. (Direct Materials) 5. Salary of factory supervisor. (Direct Labor) 6. Brooms used to sweep the factory floors. (Direct Materials) 7. Salary of packer who packs cabinets in crates for shipping. (Direct Labor) 8. Paint and stain to be used on the cabinets. (Direct Materials)

CASE 2 Evergreen Implement Company manufactures garden tools and implements. The company maintains one inventory account titled Merchandise. All costs of manufac-

turing are charged to this inventory account. Comment on this accounting procedure used by Evergreen. What procedure do you recommend for recording inventory? Give the reasons for your recommendation.

CASE 3 All Star Company has found that total factory overhead is usually about 60% of direct labor cost. The business manufactures one product that is processed in three different manufacturing departments: A, B, and C. In Department A, much expensive machinery is used. In Department B, some machinery is used. In Department C, virtually no machinery is used, all the work being manual work. There is a great difference in the amount of time required to process various jobs in the different departments. Under these circumstances do you believe that the company should charge factory overhead to each job at the rate of 60% of direct labor? If not, what would you recommend?

APPLICATION PROBLEMS

PROBLEM 21-1   Recording entries in a materials ledger

Telec, Inc., manufactures business telephone and communication systems. The company maintains a materials ledger for all direct materials.

Instructions: 1. Prepare a materials ledger card similar to the one described in this chapter for D-14 coiled cords. The cord is Account No. 91. Reorder quantity is set at 2,500 cords; minimum at 200 cords. Inventory location is Area B-42.

2. Record the beginning balance on August 1 of the current year of 340 D-14 cords at a unit price of $3.70. Telec uses the first-in, first-out inventory method.

3. Record the following transactions.

Aug. 1. Ordered 2,500 D-14 cords; unit cost, $3.75. Purchase Order No. 174.
     2. Issued 50 D-14 cords. Materials Requisition No. 149.
     4. Received 2,500 D-14 cords; unit cost, $3.75. Purchase Order No. 174.
     8. Issued 314 D-14 cords. Materials Requisition No. 157.
    16. Issued 250 D-14 cords. Materials Requisition No. 163.
    22. Issued 70 D-14 cords. Materials Requisition No. 178.
    30. Issued 320 D-14 cords. Materials Requisition No. 192.

PROBLEM 21-2   Figuring factory overhead applied rate

CalFast, Inc., a manufacturer of small electronic calculators, uses a factory overhead applied rate to charge overhead costs to its manufactured products.

The company manager estimates CalFast will manufacture 30,000 units next year. For this amount of production, the cost accountant estimates total factory overhead costs to be $283,500.00. Estimated direct labor cost for next year is $405,000.00.

Instructions: Figure CalFast's factory overhead applied rate for next year as a percentage of direct labor cost.

PROBLEM 21-3   Preparing a cost sheet

On August 1, Security, Inc., began work on Job No. 298. The order is for 90 No. SF52 smoke detectors for stock, to be completed by August 10.

Instructions: 1. Open a cost sheet similar to the one described in this chapter and record the following items.

Aug. 1. Direct materials, $427.50. Materials Requisition No. 321.
     1. Direct labor, $310.00. Daily summary of job-time records.
     2. Direct materials, $230.00. Materials Requisition No. 327.
     2. Direct labor, $243.00. Daily summary of job-time records.
     3. Direct labor, $201.00. Daily summary of job-time records.
     4. Direct materials, $174.00. Materials Requisition No. 336.
     4. Direct labor, $190.00. Daily summary of job-time records.
     5. Direct labor, $134.00. Daily summary of job-time records.

2. Complete the cost sheet, recording factory overhead at the applied rate of 75% of direct labor costs.

PROBLEM 21-4   Recording entries in a finished goods ledger

TDX, Inc., maintains a finished goods ledger for all of its manufactured products.

Instructions: 1. Prepare a finished goods ledger card similar to the one described in this chapter for Stock No. JK10 telescopes. Minimum quantity is set at 80. Inventory location is Area C-23.

2. Record the beginning balance on August 1 of the current year for 170 JK10 telescopes at a unit cost of $30.20. TDX uses the first-in, first-out method to record inventory costs.

3. Record the following transactions.

Aug. 1. Sold 60 JK10 telescopes. Sales Invoice No. 423.
       4. Sold 30 JK10 telescopes. Sales Invoice No. 436.
       5. Received 90 JK10 telescopes; unit cost, $30.20. Job No. 298.
       9. Sold 40 JK10 telescopes. Sales Invoice No. 451.
   12. Received 100 JK10 telescopes, unit cost, $31.50. Job No. 307.
   19. Sold 52 JK10 telescopes. Sales Invoice No. 479.
   23. Received 90 JK10 telescopes; unit cost, $31.50. Job No. 321.
   26. Sold 136 JK10 telescopes. Sales Invoice No. 482.
   30. Received 50 JK10 telescopes; unit cost, $32.00. Job No. 335.

ENRICHMENT PROBLEMS

MASTERY PROBLEM 21-M   Preparing cost records

Bright Lights manufactures lighting fixtures and lamps. The company records manufacturing costs by job number and uses a factory overhead applied rate to charge overhead costs to its products.

The company estimates Bright Lights will manufacture 25,000 light fixtures and lamps next year. For this amount of production, total factory overhead is estimated to be $423,725.00. Estimated direct labor costs for next year are $498,500.00.

Instructions: 1. Figure Bright Lights' factory overhead applied rate for next year as a percentage of direct labor cost.

On June 4, Bright Lights began work on Job No. 172. The order is for 72 No. 48Z floor lamps for stock, to be completed by June 14.

2. Open a cost sheet for Job No. 172 similar to the one described in this chapter and record the following items.

June 4. Direct materials, $860.00. Materials Requisition No. 281.
      4. Direct labor, $129.00. Daily summary of job-time records.
      5. Direct labor, $248.00. Daily summary of job-time records.
      6. Direct materials, $471.00. Materials Requisition No. 288.
      6. Direct labor, $175.00. Daily summary of job-time records.
      7. Direct labor, $192.00. Daily summary of job-time records.
      8. Direct labor, $295.00. Daily summary of job-time records.
   11. Direct materials, $359.00. Materials Requisition No. 317.
   11. Direct labor, $165.00. Daily summary of job-time records.
   12. Direct labor, $152.00. Daily summary of job-time records.
   13. Direct labor, $124.00. Daily summary of job-time records.

3. Complete the cost sheet, recording factory overhead at the rate figured in Instruction 1.

4. Prepare a finished goods ledger card similar to the one described in this chapter for Stock No. 48Z floor lamp. Minimum quantity is set at 50. Inventory location is Area E-40.

5. Record on the finished goods ledger card the beginning balance on June 1. The June 1 balance of 48Z floor lamps is 70 units at a unit cost of $60.90. Bright Lights uses the first-in, first-out method to record inventory costs.

6. Record the following transactions on the finished goods ledger card for 48Z floor lamps.

June 6. Sold 30 48Z floor lamps. Sales Invoice No. 522.
   13. Received 72 48Z floor lamps. Record cost from cost sheet for Job No. 172.
   18. Sold 15 48Z floor lamps. Sales Invoice No. 541.

CHALLENGE PROBLEM 21-C Preparing cost records

SiteNSound manufactures video cassette recorders. The company records manufacturing costs by job number and uses a factory overhead applied rate to charge overhead costs to its products.

The company estimates SiteNSound will manufacture 12,500 items of recording equipment next year. For this amount of production, total factory overhead is estimated to be $750,000.00. Estimated direct materials costs for next year are $75.00 for each item manufactured. Estimated direct labor for next year is 4.8 labor hours for each recording equipment item at $10.00 per hour.

Instructions: 1. Figure SiteNSound's factory overhead applied rate for next year for each of the following three bases. (a) Direct materials cost. (b) Direct labor cost. (c) Direct labor hours.

On April 8, SiteNSound began work on Job No. 254. The order is for 60 No. VC32 recorders for stock, to be completed by April 18.

2. Open a cost sheet for Job No. 254 similar to the one described in this chapter and record the following items.

Apr. 8. Direct materials, $1,160.00. Materials Requisition No. 310.
     8. Direct labor, $275.00. Daily summary of job-time records.
     9. Direct labor, $441.00. Daily summary of job-time records.
    10. Direct materials, $2,320.00. Materials Requisition No. 319.
    10. Direct labor, $392.00. Daily summary of job-time records.
    11. Direct labor, $423.00. Daily summary of job-time records.
    12. Direct labor, $440.00. Daily summary of job-time records.
    15. Direct materials, $1,020.00. Materials Requisition No. 327.
    15. Direct labor, $370.00. Daily summary of job-time records.
    16. Direct labor, $352.00. Daily summary of job-time records.
    17. Direct labor, $181.00. Daily summary of job-time records.

3. Complete the cost sheet, recording factory overhead at the direct materials cost rate figured in Instruction 1.

4. Prepare a finished goods ledger card similar to the one described in this chapter for Stock No. VC32 recorder. Minimum quantity is set at 30. Inventory location is Area B-28.

5. Record on the finished goods ledger card the beginning balance on April 1. The April 1 balance of VC32 recorders is 50 units at a unit cost of $181.50. SiteNSound uses the last-in, first-out method to record inventory costs.

6. Record the following transactions on the finished goods ledger card for VC32 recorders.

Apr. 10. Sold 10 VC32 recorders. Sales Invoice No. 339.
    17. Received 60 VC32 recorders. Record cost from cost sheet for Job No. 254.
    22. Sold 30 VC32 recorders. Sales Invoice No. 383.
    24. Sold 25 VC32 recorders. Sales Invoice No. 412.

22 Accounting Transactions and Financial Reporting for a Manufacturing Business

ENABLING PERFORMANCE TASKS

After studying Chapter 22, you will be able to:

a. Define accounting terms related to accounting transactions and financial reporting for a manufacturing business.

b. Identify accounting concepts and practices related to accounting transactions and financial reporting for a manufacturing business.

c. Record accounting transactions for a manufacturing business.

d. Prepare selected financial statements for a manufacturing business.

Accounting for a manufacturing business is more complex than accounting for a merchandising business. To provide usable financial information for a manufacturing business, detailed cost records must be maintained throughout the manufacturing process from direct materials to the finished product. These detailed manufacturing cost records provide a business with information needed to price its product, analyze manufacturing costs, and make other important management decisions. Procedures for maintaining detailed factory cost records are described in Chapter 21.

In addition to detailed cost records, a manufacturing business also needs accurate financial statements. To provide financial statements, journal entries must be made to reflect cost transactions in general ledger accounts.

Factory cost records generally are recorded daily to provide up-to-date cost information. However, most general ledger entries for manufacturing costs are made only when up-to-date account balances are needed to prepare financial statements. These end-of-fiscal-period journal entries update the general ledger manufacturing accounts before financial statements are prepared.

RECORDING MANUFACTURING ACCOUNTING TRANSACTIONS

All manufacturing costs flow through the manufacturing accounts. Therefore, journal entries are made to record these costs through each phase of the manufacturing process. The flow of manufacturing costs through the general ledger accounts is shown in Illustration 22-1. Seven journal entries involving manufacturing accounts normally are recorded.

Illustration 22-1
Flow of manufacturing costs through general ledger accounts

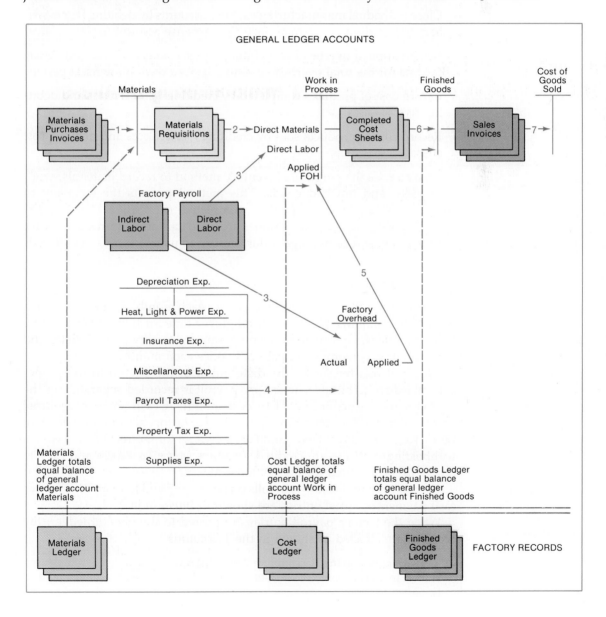

1 Record materials purchases by debiting Materials and crediting Accounts Payable.

2 Record direct materials transferred to the factory by crediting Materials and debiting Work in Process.

3 Record factory payroll by debiting direct labor to Work in Process, debiting indirect labor to Factory Overhead, crediting payroll liability accounts, and crediting Cash.

4 Close individual manufacturing expense accounts by debiting Factory Overhead and crediting each manufacturing expense account for its balance.

5 Record applied overhead by debiting Work in Process and crediting Factory Overhead for the total overhead amount applied during the fiscal period.

6 Record cost of products completed by crediting Work in Process and debiting Finished Goods.

7 Record cost of products sold by crediting Finished Goods and debiting Cost of Goods Sold.

ComVu uses the perpetual inventory method to record materials, work in process, and finished goods. This method permits the company to charge costs to jobs when jobs are completed. *(CONCEPT: Matching Expenses with Revenue)* Also, inventories are up to date after journal entries are posted. Thus, end-of-fiscal-period inventory adjustments are not required.

Payroll transactions

ComVu pays all factory employees twice each month. At the end of each pay period, amounts on all factory employee time cards are totaled. These totals provide the information for preparing the factory payroll. Sales and administrative personnel are paid only once each month.

A payroll register shows the distribution of the payroll to the proper general ledger accounts. The factory payroll is recorded separately in the payroll register since it is paid twice a month. A cash payments journal entry is prepared for each factory payroll. Two factory accounts are debited: Work in Process for direct labor, and Factory Overhead for indirect labor. Two tax withholding accounts are credited: Employees Income Tax Payable and FICA Tax Payable. Cash is credited for the net amount.

ComVu prepared factory payrolls on January 15 and January 31. The two cash payments journal entries are shown in Illustration 22-2.

When the factory payroll entries are posted to the general ledger, the accounts are affected as shown in the T accounts.

Two amounts in the T account for Cash are shown to illustrate the complete entries. In practice, only the total of the journal's Cash Credit column would be posted to Cash.

CASH PAYMENTS JOURNAL   PAGE 26

	DATE	ACCOUNT TITLE	CHECK NO.	POST. REF.	GENERAL DEBIT	GENERAL CREDIT	ACCOUNTS PAYABLE DEBIT	PURCHASES DISCOUNT CREDIT	CASH CREDIT	
1	1989 Jan. 15	Work in Process	1083		3922840				4103930	1
2		Factory Overhead			1081960					2
3		Employees Income Tax Payable				550530				3
4		FICA Tax Payable				350340				4
19	31	Work in Process	1133		4314760				4514100	19
20		Factory Overhead			1190240					20
21		Employees Income Tax Payable				605550				21
22		FICA Tax Payable				385350				22
23										23

Work in Process			FICA Tax Payable		
Bal.	75,072.20		Jan. 15	3,503.40	
Jan. 15	39,228.40		Jan. 31	3,853.50	
Jan. 31	43,147.60				

Factory Overhead			Cash		
Jan. 15	10,819.60		Jan. 15	41,039.30	
Jan. 31	11,902.40		Jan. 31	45,141.00	

Employees Income Tax Payable		
	Jan. 15	5,505.30
	Jan. 31	6,055.50

Illustration 22-2
Entries to record factory payrolls for a month

Materials transactions

ComVu records the amount of materials purchased and used in the general ledger account Materials. ComVu uses a perpetual inventory in the factory which permits the company to charge cost of materials to a job as materials are used. *(CONCEPT: Matching Expenses with Revenue)*

Materials purchases. Purchases of materials are frequent. Thus, ComVu uses a special materials purchases journal to record materials purchases. The journal has a single amount column headed Materials Dr./Accts. Pay. Cr. All purchases on account of direct materials are debited to Materials and credited to Accounts Payable in the general ledger. An entry for materials is on line 1 of the materials purchases journal shown in Illustration 22-3.

MATERIALS PURCHASES JOURNAL   PAGE 24

	DATE	ACCOUNT CREDITED	PURCH. NO.	POST. REF.	MATERIALS DR. ACCTS. PAY. CR.	
1	1989 Jan. 3	Galaxy Parts and Supplies	510		645250	1
24	31	Total			14967510	24

Illustration 22-3
Entry to record purchase of materials

At the end of a month, the total of the materials purchases journal is posted to the two general ledger accounts, Materials and Accounts Payable. The effect of posting the January total of the materials purchases journal is shown in the T accounts.

In the materials account, the January 1 debit balance, $110,210.20, is the materials inventory at the beginning of the month. The January 31 debit, $149,675.10, is the total posted from the materials purchases journal. This last entry is the total cost of materials purchased during the month.

Materials	
Bal. 110,210.20	
Jan. 31 149,675.10	

Accounts Payable	
	Jan. 31 149,675.10

Materials requisitions. A materials requisition is prepared for direct materials used on a specific job. After materials are issued, the requisition amount is recorded on a cost sheet and the requisition placed in a materials requisitions file. At the end of a month, the total value of all direct materials transferred to specific jobs must be transferred from Materials to Work in Process. ComVu prepares a memorandum with monthly summary information of the materials requisitions total, $142,251.90. The general journal entry to transfer this amount is shown in Illustration 22-4.

	GENERAL JOURNAL			PAGE 20	
DATE	ACCOUNT TITLE	POST. REF.	DEBIT	CREDIT	
1989 Jan. 31	Work in Process		142251 90		1
	Materials			142251 90	2
	M129				3
					4

Illustration 22-4
Entry to record materials requisition for a month

The effect of posting this journal entry is shown in the T accounts. The first debit amount in the work in process account, $75,072.20, is the beginning inventory of work in process. The second and third debit amounts, $39,228.40 and $43,147.60, are the total amounts of direct labor used for all jobs during the month. The last debit amount, $142,251.90, is the total amount of direct materials placed in process on all jobs during the month.

Work in Process	
Bal. 75,072.20	
Jan. 15	
Dir. Lab. 39,228.40	
Jan. 31	
Dir. Lab. 43,147.60	
Jan. 31	
Dir. Mat. 142,251.90	

Materials	
Bal. 110,210.20	Jan. 31
Jan. 31	Used 142,251.90
Purch. 149,675.10	

The first debit amount in the materials account, $110,210.20, is the materials inventory at the beginning of the month. The second debit amount, $149,675.10, is the total amount of materials purchased during the month. The credit amount, $142,251.90, is the total amount of all direct materials placed in process on all jobs during the month.

Materials account. The materials account is a controlling account for the materials ledger described in Chapter 21. The materials purchases total as shown in the materials purchases journal is debited to the general ledger account Materials. Each materials purchase is also recorded in the Received columns of a materials ledger account after the invoice has been received.

The total of all materials requisitions is recorded in the general journal as a credit to the general ledger account Materials. Each materials requisition is recorded in the Issued columns of a materials ledger account. Therefore, the balance of the general ledger account Materials should equal the sum of the balances of all accounts in the materials ledger.

Factory overhead transactions

Factory overhead includes various indirect factory expenses such as indirect labor, taxes, depreciation, and insurance. Actual factory overhead expenses are summarized in an account titled Factory Overhead.

Recording actual factory overhead. Indirect labor is posted directly to the factory overhead account from the factory payroll entry shown in Illustration 22-2. Other indirect expenses are recorded throughout the month in other manufacturing expense accounts. At the end of each month, these indirect expense account balances are all transferred to the factory overhead account. The actual overhead can then be compared with the estimated amount of overhead recorded on the job cost sheets. The general journal entry to transfer actual overhead expenses to the factory overhead account is shown in Illustration 22-5.

	DATE	ACCOUNT TITLE	POST. REF.	DEBIT	CREDIT	
		GENERAL JOURNAL			PAGE 20	
4	31	Factory Overhead		2682840		4
5		Depr. Exp. – Factory Equip.			250000	5
6		Depr. Exp. – Building			130000	6
7		Heat, Light, and Power Exp.			568780	7
8		Insurance Exp. – Factory			51770	8
9		Miscellaneous Exp. – Factory			48230	9
10		Payroll Taxes Exp. – Factory			1387290	10
11		Property Tax Exp. – Factory			75450	11
12		Supplies Expense – Factory			171320	12
13		M130				13

Illustration 22-5
Entry to close actual monthly factory overhead expenses to the factory overhead account

Adjusting entries are made at the end of a fiscal period prior to the entry to transfer actual factory overhead expenses to the factory overhead account. These adjusting entries resulted in amounts being debited to the depreciation expense, insurance expense, and supplies expense accounts.

After posting the cash payments journal shown in Illustration 22-2 and the general journal shown in Illustration 22-5, all factory overhead expense

Factory Overhead

Jan. 15	
Ind. Lab. 10,819.60	
Jan. 31	
Ind. Lab. 11,902.40	
Jan. 31	
Act. OH 26,828.40	

accounts are summarized in the factory overhead account. The factory overhead account is debited for the actual overhead expenses for the month. These expenses are indirect labor, $10,819.60 and $11,902.40, plus the other actual factory overhead expenses, $26,828.40. The effect of these entries on the factory overhead account is shown in the T account.

Recording applied overhead to work in process. ComVu distributes estimated factory overhead as described in Chapter 21. Factory overhead is applied to each job at the rate of 60% of direct labor charges on each cost sheet.

At the end of each month, the factory overhead recorded on all job cost sheets during the month is totaled. ComVu's applied overhead cost for January is $49,425.60. The general journal entry to record this applied overhead is shown in Illustration 22-6.

GENERAL JOURNAL				PAGE 20	
DATE	ACCOUNT TITLE	POST. REF.	DEBIT	CREDIT	
31	Work in Process		4942560		14
	Factory Overhead			4942560	15
	M131				16
					17

Illustration 22-6
Entry to record applied overhead

The effect of this entry is shown in the T accounts.

Work in Process

Bal. 75,072.20	
Jan. 15	
Dir. Lab. 39,228.40	
Jan. 31	
Dir. Lab. 43,147.60	
Jan. 31	
Dir. Mat. 142,251.90	
Jan. 31	
Applied OH 49,425.60	

Factory Overhead

Jan. 31	Jan. 31
Act. OH 49,550.40	Applied OH 49,425.60

The work in process account now shows beginning inventory, direct labor cost, direct materials cost, and applied overhead.

The factory overhead account debit, $49,550.40, is the actual factory overhead expense for the month. The credit, $49,425.60, is the applied overhead recorded on cost sheets during the month. The factory overhead account ending balance is a $124.80 debit. This debit balance results from recording less applied overhead than the amount of actual overhead expenses.

Disposing of overapplied and underapplied factory overhead balances. In theory, applied overhead should be equal to the actual overhead expenses. However, the rate used to figure applied overhead is estimated and may not be absolutely accurate. Therefore, the factory overhead account may have an ending balance. The amount by which applied overhead is less than actual overhead is called underapplied overhead. The debit balance, $124.80, in ComVu's account indicates underapplied overhead for January. This balance is closed to the income summary account. The general journal entry to close the factory overhead account at the end of January is shown in Illustration 22-7.

	GENERAL JOURNAL		PAGE 20	
DATE	ACCOUNT TITLE	POST. REF.	DEBIT	CREDIT
31	Income Summary		12480	
	Factory Overhead			12480
	M132			

Illustration 22-7
Entry to close the factory overhead account with underapplied overhead

A credit balance in the factory overhead account indicates that applied overhead is more than actual overhead. The amount by which applied overhead is more than actual overhead is called overapplied overhead. A credit ending balance in the factory overhead account indicates overapplied overhead. If the factory overhead account has a credit balance, Factory Overhead is debited and Income Summary is credited for the overapplied overhead amount.

If an overapplied or underapplied overhead amount is large, factory expense accounts should be reviewed to determine the reason for the significant difference. ComVu considers the amount to be significant if overapplied or underapplied overhead is 3% or more of actual factory overhead. Two situations may cause overapplied or underapplied overhead. (1) Actual expenses may be higher or lower than normal. This event requires closer control of expenditures. (2) The overhead applied rate may be inaccurate. This event requires more accurate estimating and figuring of the applied rate.

Finished goods transactions

After a cost sheet is completed, the sheet is filed. At the end of the month, total amounts on all cost sheets completed during the current month are totaled. The total of ComVu's completed cost sheets for January, $254,865.90, is the cost of work finished during the month. This total amount is transferred from Work in Process to Finished Goods to update these two inventory accounts. This entry is recorded in the general journal as shown in Illustration 22-8.

		GENERAL JOURNAL			PAGE 20	
DATE		ACCOUNT TITLE	POST. REF.	DEBIT	CREDIT	
20	31	*Finished Goods*		2548 65 90		20
21		*Work in Process*			2548 65 90	21
22		*M133*				22
23						23
24						24

Illustration 22-8
Entry to record finished goods completed during a month

The effect of this entry is shown in the T accounts.

Finished Goods		Work in Process	
Bal. 104,643.00		Bal. 75,072.20	Jan. 31
Jan. 31		Jan. 15	Finished
Completed Cost		Dir. Lab. 39,228.40	Goods 254,865.90
Sheets 254,865.90		Jan. 31	
		Dir. Lab. 43,147.60	
		Jan. 31	
		Dir. Mat. 142,251.90	
		Jan. 31	
		Applied	
		OH 49,425.60	
		Bal. Jan. 31 94,259.80	

The first debit in the finished goods account, $104,643.00, is the beginning inventory of finished goods. The second debit, $254,865.90, is the cost of goods finished during the month. The credit to Work in Process, $254,865.90, is the cost of finished goods transferred from the factory to the stockroom. The work in process account balance, $94,259.80, is the value of the ending inventory of work in process.

Sales and cost of goods sold transactions

ComVu's procedures for recording sales are similar to those described in Chapter 3. However, since ComVu uses a perpetual inventory, a different procedure is used to determine and record cost of goods sold.

For each sale, a sales invoice is sent to the finished goods stockroom. A sales invoice provides authorization and information for shipping products. The number of products shipped is posted to the finished goods ledger from the sales invoice. The unit cost and total amount of products sold is recorded on the sales invoice. The sales invoice is then filed until the end of the month.

At the end of the month, cost information on all sales invoices is totaled. The total costs recorded on all of ComVu's sales for January, $176,381.40, is the cost of goods sold during the month. This total cost is transferred from the inventory account Finished Goods to the cost account Cost of Goods Sold. This general journal entry is shown in Illustration 22-9.

		GENERAL JOURNAL			PAGE 20	
	DATE	ACCOUNT TITLE	POST. REF.	DEBIT	CREDIT	
23	31	*Cost of Goods Sold*		176 381 40		23
24		*Finished Goods*			176 381 40	24
25		*M134*				25
26						26

Illustration 22-9
Entry to record cost of goods sold for month

The effect of this entry is shown in the T accounts.

Cost of Goods Sold	
Jan. 31 from Finished Goods 176,381.40	

Finished Goods	
Bal. 104,643.00 Jan. 31 Completed Cost Sheets 254,865.90 *Bal. Jan. 31 183,127.50*	Jan. 31 Cost of Goods Sold 176,381.40

The debit to Cost of Goods Sold, $176,381.40, is the cost of goods sold during the month. The credit to Finished Goods, $176,381.40, is the cost of finished goods sold during the month and removed from inventory. The finished goods account balance, $183,127.50, is the ending inventory of finished goods.

Manufacturing accounts in the general ledger

After the entries described in this chapter are posted, ComVu's manufacturing accounts in the general ledger appear as shown in Illustration 22-10.

Illustration 22-10
Manufacturing accounts

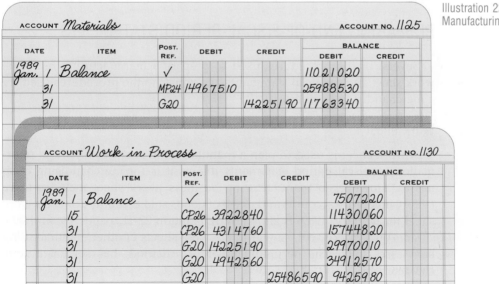

ACCOUNT *Materials*   ACCOUNT NO. 1125

DATE	ITEM	POST. REF.	DEBIT	CREDIT	BALANCE DEBIT	BALANCE CREDIT
1989 Jan. 1	Balance	✓			110 210 20	
31		MP24	149 675 10		259 885 30	
31		G20		142 251 90	117 633 40	

ACCOUNT *Work in Process*   ACCOUNT NO. 1130

DATE	ITEM	POST. REF.	DEBIT	CREDIT	BALANCE DEBIT	BALANCE CREDIT
1989 Jan. 1	Balance	✓			75 072 20	
15		CP26	39 228 40		114 300 60	
31		CP26	43 147 60		157 448 20	
31		G20	142 251 90		299 700 10	
31		G20	49 425 60		349 125 70	
31		G20		254 865 90	94 259 80	

Illustration 22-10
Manufacturing accounts
(concluded)

PREPARING END-OF-FISCAL-PERIOD STATEMENTS

Several of the procedures used to prepare a manufacturing business' work sheet and financial statements are similar to the procedures used for a merchandising business.

Work sheet

A work sheet is used to plan a manufacturing business' financial information for fiscal period statements just as it is for merchandising businesses. However, a manufacturing business' work sheet includes three factory inventory accounts and a cost of goods sold account. ComVu's work sheet for January, 1989, is shown in Illustration 22-11, pages 494 and 495.

ComVu's work sheet, similar to the work sheets of other manufacturing businesses using the perpetual inventory method, has several unique characteristics.

1. The entries to record direct materials, work in process, and finished goods bring manufacturing inventory accounts up to date on January 31. Thus, the balances of Materials, Work in Process, and Finished Goods are brought up to date before a work sheet is prepared. Adjustments for these inventory accounts do not need to be planned on a work sheet.
2. Perpetual inventory subsidiary ledgers and detailed cost records are kept in the factory. Based on these subsidiary records, summary journal entries are made that record the flow of costs through the manufacturing process to the cost of goods sold account.
3. Since all manufacturing costs flow toward the account Cost of Goods Sold, no manufacturing cost accounts on the work sheet have balances. Amounts in these accounts have been transferred to either one of the inventory accounts or the cost of goods sold account. The cost of goods sold amount, $176,381.40, is extended to the Income Statement Debit column.
4. Income Summary has a debit balance of $124.80. This balance resulted from closing the underapplied overhead to Income Summary. The amount represents additional manufacturing costs that are not already in the inventory or cost of goods sold account. The amount is extended to the Income Statement Debit column.
5. Extending other accounts to the Income Statement and Balance Sheet columns and figuring net income are similar to the procedures described for corporations in Chapter 15.

Financial statements

A manufacturing business prepares an income statement, a statement of stockholders' equity, and a balance sheet. These statements are similar to those described previously for other kinds of businesses. Many manufacturing businesses also prepare a statement of cost of goods manufactured.

> A statement of stockholder's equity for a manufacturing business is similar to that of a merchandising business described in Chapter 15. This statement is not illustrated in Chapter 22.

Statement of cost of goods manufactured. An additional statement is prepared by many manufacturing businesses to report greater detail about costs of finished goods. A statement showing details about the cost of finished goods is called a statement of cost of goods manufactured. This statement shows the details of the cost elements—materials, direct labor, and factory overhead—spent on the goods completed in a fiscal period. A statement of cost of goods manufactured supplements the income statement. ComVu's statement of cost of goods manufactured is shown in Illustration 22-12, page 496.

ComVu, Inc.
Work Sheet
For Month Ended January 31, 1989

ACCOUNT TITLE	TRIAL BALANCE DEBIT	TRIAL BALANCE CREDIT	ADJUSTMENTS DEBIT	ADJUSTMENTS CREDIT	INCOME STATEMENT DEBIT	INCOME STATEMENT CREDIT	BALANCE SHEET DEBIT	BALANCE SHEET CREDIT
1 Cash	15219470						15219470	
2 Petty Cash	30000						30000	
3 Accounts Receivable	18683960						18683960	
4 Allow. for Uncoll. Accts.		4136350		(a) 1362200				5498650
5 Materials	11763340						11763340	
6 Work in Process	9425980						9425980	
7 Finished Goods	18312750						18312750	
8 Supplies - Factory	604890						604890	
9 Supplies - Sales	759500			(b) 119420			640080	
10 Supplies - Administrative	194140			(c) 31020			163120	
11 Prepaid Insurance	347660			(d) 8650			339010	
12 Factory Equipment	15170000						15170000	
13 Accum. Depr. - Fact. Equip.		4551000						4551000
14 Office Equipment	2105000						2105000	
15 Accum. Depr. - Office Equip.		526000		(e) 35000				561000
16 Store Equipment	1910000						1910000	
17 Accum. Depr. - Store Equip.		573000		(f) 32000				605000
18 Building	33080000						33080000	
19 Accum. Depr. - Building		4962000						4962000
20 Land	14750000						14750000	
21 Accounts Payable		15808220						15808220
22 Employees Income Tax Pay.		969550						969550
23 Federal Income Tax Pay.		1654580		(g) 1654580				1654580
24 FICA Tax Payable		1233820						1233820
25 Salaries Payable								
26 Unemploy. Tax Pay. - Fed.		84080						84080
27 Unemploy. Tax Pay. - State		567530						567530
28 Dividends Payable								
29 Mortgage Payable		10000000						10000000
30 Capital Stock		60000000						60000000
31 Retained Earnings		38341780						38341780

No.	Account	Trial Balance Dr.	Trial Balance Cr.	Adjustments Dr.	Adjustments Cr.	Income Statement Dr.	Income Statement Cr.	Balance Sheet Dr.	Balance Sheet Cr.
32	Dividends	12480						12480	
33	Income Summary								
34	Sales		27246000				27246000		
35	Cost of Goods Sold	17638140				17638140			
36	Factory Overhead								
37	Depr. Exp. – Factory Equip.								
38	Depr. Exp. – Building								
39	Heat, Lights & Power Expense								
40	Insurance Exp. – Factory								
41	Miscellaneous Exp. – Factory								
42	Payroll Taxes Exp. – Factory								
43	Property Tax Exp. – Factory								
44	Supplies Exp. – Factory								
45	Advertising Expense	314760				314760			
46	Delivery Expense	727540				727540			
47	Depr. Exp. – Store Equip.			(b) 32000		32000			
48	Miscellaneous Exp. – Sales	102270				102270			
49	Salary Expense – Sales	1847250				1847250			
50	Supplies Expense – Sales			(a) 119420		119420			
51	Bad Debts Expense			(a) 136200		136200			
52	Depr. Exp. – Office Equip.			(a) 35000		35000			
53	Insurance Exp. – Admin.			(a) 8650		8650			
54	Miscellaneous Exp. – Admin.	144650				144650			
55	Payroll Taxes Exp. – Admin.	436650				436650			
56	Property Tax Exp. – Admin.	10580				10580			
57	Salary Expense – Admin.	1460750				1460750			
58	Supplies Expense – Admin.			(c) 31020		31020			
59	Utilities Expense – Admin.	102240				102240			
60	Gain on Plant Assets								
61	Miscellaneous Revenue								
62	Interest Expense	100000				100000			
63	Loss on Plant Assets	22630				22630			
64	Federal Income Tax			(d) 1654580		1654580			
65		1652766630	1652766630	2016870	2016870	24936810			39888410
66	Net Inc. after Fed. Inc. Tax					2309190			2309190
67						27246000	27246000	42197600	42197600
68									

Illustration 22-11   Work sheet for a manufacturing business

ComVu, Inc.
Statement of Cost of Goods Manufactured
For Month Ended January 31, 1989

Direct Materials:		
Materials Inventory, Jan. 1, 1989................	$110,210.20	
Materials Purchased...........................	149,675.10	
Total Materials Available During January..........	$259,885.30	
Less Materials Inventory, Jan. 31, 1989.........	117,633.40	
Cost of Direct Materials Placed in Process........		$142,251.90
Direct Labor......................................		82,376.00
Factory Overhead Applied.........................		49,425.60
Total Cost of Work Placed in Process		$274,053.50
Work in Process Inventory Jan. 1, 1989............		75,072.20
Total Cost of Work in Process During January.......		$349,125.70
Less Work in Process Inventory, Jan. 31, 1989		94,259.80
Cost of Goods Manufactured		$254,865.90

Illustration 22-12
Statement of cost of
goods manufactured

Information for the statement of cost of goods manufactured comes from four sources. Materials inventory and work in process inventory come from the general ledger accounts, Illustration 22-10. Materials purchased comes from the materials purchases journal, Illustration 22-3. Direct labor comes from the cash payments journal, Illustration 22-2. Factory overhead applied comes from the general journal entry applying factory overhead to the work in process account, Illustration 22-6. The amount of factory overhead, $49,425.60, is the total estimate recorded on cost sheets and not the actual overhead debited to Factory Overhead. The total amount to be included in cost of goods manufactured is therefore the total applied overhead and not the actual overhead.

Income statement. ComVu's income statement for the month of January, 1989, is shown in Illustration 22-13.

Information for ComVu's income statement comes from three sources. Finished goods inventory comes from the general ledger account, Illustration 22-10. Cost of goods manufactured comes from the statement of cost of goods manufactured, Illustration 22-12. All other amounts come from the Income Statement columns of the work sheet, Illustration 22-11.

This income statement differs in two ways from the income statements of merchandising businesses shown in previous chapters.

1. Cost of goods manufactured is used instead of purchases. Details of the cost of goods manufactured are given on the statement of cost of goods manufactured.
2. The amount of underapplied overhead, $124.80, is added to the cost of goods sold. The amount is added because applied overhead, $49,425.60, is less than the actual overhead, $49,550.40.

ComVu, Inc.
Income Statement
For Month Ended January 31, 1989

			*% of Net Sales
Operating Revenue:			
Sales		$272,460.00	100.00
Cost of Goods Sold:			
Finished Goods Inventory, Jan. 1, 1989	$104,643.00		
Cost of Goods Manufactured	254,865.90		
Total Cost of Finished Goods Available for Sale	$359,508.90		
Less Finished Goods Inventory, Jan. 31, 1989	183,127.50		
Cost of Goods Sold	$176,381.40		
Underapplied Overhead	124.80		
Net Cost of Goods Sold		176,506.20	64.8
Gross Profit on Operations		$ 95,953.80	35.2
Operating Expenses:			
Selling Expenses:			
Advertising Expense	$ 3,147.60		
Delivery Expense	7,275.40		
Depreciation Expense—Store Equipment	320.00		
Miscellaneous Expense—Sales	1,022.70		
Salary Expense—Sales	18,472.50		
Supplies Expense—Sales	1,194.20		
Total Selling Expenses		$ 31,432.40	
Administrative Expenses:			
Bad Debts Expense	$ 1,362.00		
Depreciation Expense—Office Equipment	350.00		
Insurance Expense—Administrative	86.50		
Miscellaneous Expense—Administrative	1,446.50		
Payroll Taxes Expense—Administrative	4,366.50		
Property Tax Expense—Administrative	105.80		
Salary Expense—Administrative	14,607.50		
Supplies Expense—Administrative	310.20		
Utilities Expense—Administrative	1,022.40		
Total Administrative Expenses		23,657.40	
Total Operating Expenses		55,089.80	20.2
Net Income from Operations		$ 40,864.00	
Other Expenses:			
Interest Expense	$ 1,000.00		
Loss on Plant Assets	226.30		
Net Deduction		1,226.30	
Net Income before Federal Income Tax		$ 39,637.70	14.5
Less Federal Income Tax		16,545.80	6.1
Net Income after Federal Income Tax		$ 23,091.90	8.5

*Rounded to nearest 0.1%

Illustration 22-13
Income statement of a manufacturing business

If there had been overapplied overhead, the overhead included in the cost of goods manufactured would have been more than the actual overhead expenses. In that case, the amount of the overapplied overhead would have been subtracted from the cost of goods sold on the income statement.

Balance sheet. The balance sheet prepared by ComVu on January 31, 1989, is shown in Illustration 22-14.

Except for the listing of inventories, the balance sheet of a manufacturing business is similar to the balance sheet of a merchandising business. In a manufacturing business, the current assets section of the balance sheet lists three types of inventories. (1) Materials. (2) Work in Process. (3) Finished Goods.

ACCOUNTING TERMS

What is the meaning of each of the following?

1. underapplied overhead
2. overapplied overhead

3. statement of cost of goods manufactured

QUESTIONS FOR INDIVIDUAL STUDY

1. What is needed to provide usable financial information for a manufacturing business?
2. When are most general ledger entries made for manufacturing costs?
3. What seven journal entries involving manufacturing accounts normally are made to record manufacturing costs through each phase of the manufacturing process?
4. What are two reasons for a manufacturing company to use the perpetual inventory method to record materials, work in process, and finished goods?
5. What two accounts are debited when a factory payroll is recorded in a cash payments journal?
6. Charging cost of materials to a job as materials are used is an application of

which accounting concept?
7. What accounts are affected, and how, in an entry for the purchase of materials?
8. What accounts are affected, and how, when the total value of all materials requisitions is recorded in the general journal at the end of a month?
9. What amount does the balance of the general ledger account Materials equal?
10. What are some examples of factory overhead expenses?
11. What accounts are affected, and how, when overhead is applied for the month?
12. After the journal entry for applied overhead has been posted, what do the debit and credit amounts in the factory overhead account represent?
13. When there is underapplied overhead at the end of a month, does the factory

ComVu, Inc.
Balance Sheet
January 31, 1989

ASSETS

Current Assets:

Cash		$152,194.70
Petty Cash		300.00
Accounts Receivable	$186,839.60	
Less Allowance for Uncollectible Accounts	5,498.50	181,341.10
Materials		117,633.40
Work in Process		94,259.80
Finished Goods		183,127.50
Supplies — Factory		6,048.90
Supplies — Sales		6,400.80
Supplies — Administrative		1,631.20
Prepaid Insurance		3,390.10
Total Current Assets		$ 746,327.50

Plant Assets:

Factory Equipment	$151,700.00		
Less Accumulated Depreciation — Factory Equipment	45,510.00	$106,190.00	
Office Equipment	$ 21,050.00		
Less Accumulated Depreciation — Office Equipment	5,610.00	15,440.00	
Store Equipment	$ 19,100.00		
Less Accumulated Depreciation — Store Equipment	6,050.00	13,050.00	
Building	$330,800.00		
Less Accumulated Depreciation — Building	49,620.00	281,180.00	
Land		147,500.00	
Total Plant Assets			563,360.00
Total Assets			$1,309,687.50

LIABILITIES

Current Liabilities:

Accounts Payable	$158,082.20	
Employees Income Tax Payable	9,695.50	
Federal Income Tax Payable	16,545.80	
FICA Tax Payable	12,338.20	
Unemployment Tax Payable — Federal	840.80	
Unemployment Tax Payable — State	5,675.30	
Total Current Liabilities		$ 203,177.80

Long-Term Liability:

Mortgage Payable		100,000.00
Total Liabilities		$ 303,177.80

STOCKHOLDERS' EQUITY

Capital Stock	$600,000.00	
Retained Earnings	406,509.70	
Total Stockholders' Equity		1,006,509.70
Total Liabilities and Stockholders' Equity		$1,309,687.50

Illustration 22-14   Balance sheet of a manufacturing business

overhead account have a debit balance or a credit balance?

14. What accounts are affected, and how, in an entry to close the factory overhead account when there is overapplied overhead?

15. What two reasons may cause a difference between actual and applied overhead? What should be done to correct the difference?

16. How does ComVu determine the amount of work finished during a month?

17. What accounts are affected, and how, in an entry to record the finished goods manufactured during the month?

18. What accounts are affected, and how, in an entry to record costs of sales for a business using a perpetual inventory?

19. What is reported on a statement of cost of goods manufactured?

20. What four sources of information are used to prepare a statement of cost of goods manufactured?

21. What three sources of information are used to prepare ComVu's income statement?

22. ComVu's income statement differs in what two ways from income statements of merchandising businesses shown in previous chapters?

23. How does ComVu's balance sheet differ from a merchandising business' balance sheet?

CASES FOR MANAGEMENT DECISION

CASE 1 Fairmont Corporation, a manufacturing company, uses the perpetual inventory method for all inventory accounts. Direct materials, direct labor, and applied overhead are recorded on cost sheets similar to ComVu's. At the end of each month, general journal entries are made to update the general ledger manufacturing accounts. Overapplied or Underapplied Overhead is closed to Income Summary and reported separately on the income statement as an adjustment to the cost of goods sold.

A new accountant suggests that the company could save considerable time if a number of accounting changes are made: (a) Use the periodic inventory method, (b) drop the use of applied overhead, and (c) close all manufacturing accounts into Income Summary similar to the procedure used by merchandising businesses. The accountant indicates that these new procedures would provide adequate information to prepare the income statement with a substantial time and cost saving.

Should the changes in accounting procedures be made? Will the changes provide adequate information? How will the changes affect the information now provided?

CASE 2 Jupiter Corporation is a small manufacturing company. During 1989 the company had underapplied and overapplied overhead as listed below.

Underapplied

January	$ 288.00
February	184.50
March	18.00
November	207.00
December	360.00
	$1,057.50

Overapplied

April	$ 141.00
May	204.00
June	432.00
July	99.00
August	324.00
September	186.00
October	30.00
	$1,416.00

Jupiter Corporation closes the books and prepares financial statements at the end of each calendar year. (a) On December 31 is the factory overhead for 1989 underapplied or overapplied? (b) How will the balance of the factory overhead account be listed on the income statement for 1989?

In 1987 and 1988, the company had under-applied and overapplied overhead amounts as listed below.

	Underapplied	Overapplied
1987........	$ 923.50	$1,230.00
1988........	1,042.00	1,374.50

(c) Considering the relationship between underapplied and overapplied overhead for the three years, would you make any recommendations to the factory manager? Explain.

CASE 3 Northwest Corporation is a small manufacturing company. At the end of each fiscal period, the company prepares an income statement and a balance sheet. However, the company does not prepare a statement of cost of goods manufactured. A consultant told the company president that a statement of cost of goods manufactured is absolutely essential. Do you agree with the consultant or not? Explain.

APPLICATION PROBLEMS

PROBLEM 22-1   Journalizing cost accounting transactions for a manufacturing company

Stewart, Inc., manufacturing business, completed the following selected factory cost transactions during February of the current year.

Instructions: 1. Record the following selected transactions completed during February of the current year. Use page 15 of a materials purchases journal and page 15 of a cash payments journal. Source documents are abbreviated as follows: check, C; purchase invoice, P.

Feb. 6. Purchased materials on account from Cheetah Company, $3,694.00. P171.
  10. Paid cash for machinery repairs, $186.90. C333. (Miscellaneous Expense — Factory)
  15. Paid cash for factory supplies, $412.90. C341.
  22. Purchased materials on account from Norte Company, $1,394.70. P172.
  23. Paid cash for a new stitching machine, $1,265.30. C352. (Factory Equipment)
  25. Paid factory payroll: direct labor, $5,100.00; indirect labor, $1,956.00; employees income tax, $776.20; FICA tax, $493.90. C367.

2. Total and rule the materials purchases journal.
3. Prove and rule the cash payments journal.

PROBLEM 22-2   Journalizing entries that summarize cost records at the end of a fiscal period

On April 30 of the current year, Macomber Corporation has the following information. The accounts and balances needed to complete this problem are given in the working papers accompanying this textbook.

(a) The total of the materials purchases journal for April is $46,519.00.
(b) The total factory payroll for the month according to the payroll register is $122,531.50, distributed as follows.

Work in Process	$102,570.00
Factory Overhead...	19,961.50
Cash	100,475.80
Employees Income Tax Payable	13,478.50
FICA Tax Payable	8,577.20

(c) The total of all requisitions of direct materials issued during the month is $139,419.80.
(d) The factory overhead to be charged to Work in Process is 63% of the direct labor cost.
(e) The total of all cost sheets completed during the month is $289,185.00.
(f) The total of costs recorded on all sales invoices for April is $388,050.00.

Instructions: 1. Record the factory payroll entry on page 11 of a cash payments journal. C371. Post the general debit and general credit amounts.
2. Record the following entries on page 9 of a general journal. Post the entries.

a. An entry to transfer the total of all materials requisitions from Materials to Work in Process. M34.
b. An entry to close all individual manufacturing expense accounts to Factory Overhead. M35.
c. An entry to record applied overhead to Work in Process. M36.

3. Record and post the entry to close the balance of the factory overhead account to Income Summary. M37.
4. Record and post the entry to transfer the total of all cost sheets completed from Work in Process to Finished Goods. M38.
5. Record and post the entry to transfer the cost of products sold from Finished Goods to Cost of Goods Sold. M39.

The ledger and journals prepared in this problem are needed to complete Problem 22-3.

PROBLEM 22-3   Preparing a statement of cost of goods manufactured

The ledger and journals prepared in Problem 22-2 are needed to complete this problem.

Instructions: Prepare for Macomber Corporation a statement of cost of goods manufactured similar to the one illustrated in this chapter. The statement is for the month ended April 30 of the current year. Use the information from Problem 22-2.

ENRICHMENT PROBLEMS

MASTERY PROBLEM 22-M   Journalizing entries that summarize cost records at the end of a fiscal period

On March 31 of the current year, Tanner Corporation has the following information. The accounts and balances needed to complete this problem are given in the working papers accompanying this textbook.

(a) The total of the materials purchases journal for March is $61,584.00.
(b) The total factory payroll for the month according to the payroll register is $78,432.00, distributed as follows.

Work in Process	$58,272.00
Factory Overhead	20,160.00
Cash	64,314.30
Employees Income Tax Payable	8,627.50
FICA Tax Payable	5,490.20

(c) The total of all requisitions of direct materials issued during the month is $64,344.00.

(d) The factory overhead to be charged to Work in Process is 70% of the direct labor cost.

(e) The total of all cost sheets completed during the month is $159,000.00.

(f) The total of costs recorded on all sales invoices for March is $251,280.00.

Instructions: 1. Record the entry for the factory payroll on page 14 of a cash payments journal. C711. Post the general debit and general credit amounts.

2. Record the following entries on page 8 of a general journal. Post the debit and credit amounts.

a. An entry to transfer the total of all materials requisitions from Materials to Work in Process. M211.

b. An entry to close all individual manufacturing expense accounts to Factory Overhead. M212.

c. An entry to record applied overhead to Work in Process. M213.

3. Record and post the entry to close the balance of the factory overhead account to Income Summary. M214.

4. Record and post the entry to transfer the total of all cost sheets completed from Work in Process to Finished Goods. M215.

5. Record and post the entry to transfer the cost of products sold from Finished Goods to Cost of Goods Sold. M216.

6. Prepare for Tanner Corporation a statement of cost of goods manufactured for the month ended March 31 of the current year.

CHALLENGE PROBLEM 22-C   Journalizing entries that summarize cost records at the end of a fiscal period; preparing financial statements

On May 31 of the current year, Advant Company has the following information. The accounts and balances needed to complete this problem are given in the working papers accompanying this textbook.

(a) The total of the materials purchases journal for May is $77,534.38.

(b) The total factory payroll for the month according to the payroll register is $63,121.21, distributed as follows.

Work in Process	$46,604.25
Factory Overhead	16,516.96
Cash	51,759.40
Employees Income Tax Payable	6,943.33
FICA Tax Payable	4,418.48

(c) The total of all requisitions of direct materials issued during the month is $74,750.94.

(d) The factory overhead to be charged to Work in Process is 67% of the direct labor cost.

(e) The total of all cost sheets completed during the month is $134,934.05.

(f) The total of costs recorded on all sales invoices for May is $106,126.54.

Instructions: 1. Record the factory payroll entry on page 22 of a cash payments journal. C341. Post the general debit and general credit amounts.

2. Record the following entries on page 19 of a general journal. Post the entries.

a. An entry to transfer the total of all materials requisitions from Materials to Work in Process. M698.

b. An entry to close all individual manufacturing expense accounts to Factory Overhead. M699.

c. An entry to record applied overhead to Work in Process. M700.

3. Record and post the entry to close the balance of the factory overhead account to Income Summary. M701.

4. Record and post the entry to transfer the total of all cost sheets completed from Work in Process to Finished Goods. M702.

5. Record and post the entry to transfer the cost of products sold from Finished Goods to Cost of Goods Sold. M703.

6. Prepare for Advant Company a statement of cost of goods manufactured for the month ended May 31 of the current year.

After the transactions in Instructions 2 through 6 are posted, the accounts and their balances in Advant's general ledger appear as below on May 31 of the current year. (The Employees Income Tax Payable and FICA Tax Payable balances differ from your ledger account balances due to additional postings completed for payroll taxes and sales and administrative salaries.)

Account Title	Balance	Account Title	Balance
Cash	$ 62,261.46	Sales	$159,822.56
Petty Cash	375.00	Cost of Goods Sold	106,126.54
Accounts Receivable	115,300.30	Factory Overhead	—
Allow. for Uncoll. Accts.	2,819.65	Depr. Exp. — Factory Equip.	—
Materials	44,112.28	Depr. Exp. — Building	—
Work in Process	37,860.10	Heat, Light, and Power Exp.	—
Finished Goods	67,216.45	Insurance Exp. — Factory	—
Supplies — Factory	2,474.55	Misc. Exp. — Factory	—
Supplies — Sales	3,107.03	Payroll Taxes Exp. — Factory	—
Supplies — Admin.	794.20	Property Tax Exp. — Factory	—
Prepaid Insurance	1,422.23	Supplies Exp. — Factory	—
Factory Equipment	103,005.00	Advertising Expense	2,416.05
Accum. Depr. — Factory Equip.	28,116.00	Delivery Expense	5,842.24
Office Equipment	8,613.00	Depr. Exp. — Store Equip.	—
Accum. Depr. — Office Equip.	2,769.30	Misc. Exp. — Sales	1,500.33
Store Equipment	7,771.50	Salary Expense — Sales	11,604.38
Accum. Depr. — Store Equip.	2,884.56	Supplies Expense — Sales	—
Building	237,600.00	Bad Debts Expense	—
Accum. Depr. — Building	23,760.00	Depr. Exp. — Office Equip.	—
Land	99,445.89	Insurance Exp. — Admin.	—
Accounts Payable	16,535.86	Misc. Exp. — Admin.	1,561.41
Employees Income Tax Pay.	9,903.90	Payroll Taxes Exp. — Admin.	2,529.95
Federal Income Tax Pay.	—	Property Tax Exp. — Admin.	92.59
FICA Tax Payable	12,604.97	Salary Expense — Admin.	15,309.90
Unemploy. Tax Pay. — Fed.	588.32	Supplies Expense — Admin.	—
Unemploy. Tax Pay. — State	3,971.14	Gain on Plant Assets	155.93
Mortgage Payable	56,250.00	Miscellaneous Revenue	—
Capital Stock	450,000.00	Interest Expense	468.74
Retained Earnings	168,359.21	Loss on Plant Assets	—
Income Summary	269.72	Federal Income Tax	—

7. Prepare an eight-column work sheet for the month ended May 31 of the current year. Use as a guide the work sheet illustrated in this chapter. The following information is needed for adjustments.

Bad debts expense (estimated)	$ 762.75
Sales supplies inventory, May 31	1,762.50
Administrative supplies inventory, May 31	520.74
Value of insurance policies, May 31	1,383.30
Monthly depreciation expense on office equipment	68.51
Monthly depreciation expense on store equipment	61.88
Federal income tax estimated for the month	3,025.67

8. From the work sheet, prepare an income statement for the month ended May 31 of the current year. As part of the income statement figure the following items. (a) Ratio of net cost of merchandise sold to net sales. (b) Ratio of gross profit to net sales. (c) Ratio of total operating expenses to net sales. (d) Ratio of net income before federal income tax to net sales. (e) Ratio of federal income tax to net sales. (f) Ratio of net income after federal income tax to net sales.

9. Prepare a balance sheet for May 31 of the current year.

Reinforcement Activity 3
Processing and Reporting Cost Accounting Data for a Manufacturing Business

This activity reinforces selected learnings from Chapters 21 and 22. Job cost accounting processing and reporting is emphasized for a manufacturing company organized as a corporation.

LEISURETIME, INC.

Leisuretime, Inc., is a corporation that manufactures patio furniture. Leisuretime uses a job cost accounting system to record manufacturing costs. The fiscal year is from January 1 through December 31. Monthly financial statements are prepared.

PART A: RECORDING COST ACCOUNTING ACTIVITIES

In Part A of this reinforcement activity, Leisuretime's daily cost accounting activities for one month will be recorded.

Leisuretime uses the chart of accounts shown on the following page. The journals and ledgers used by Leisuretime are similar to those illustrated in Chapters 21 and 22. The job cost sheets, selected general ledger accounts, and other accounting records or forms needed to do the cost accounting activities are provided in the working papers accompanying this textbook. Beginning balances have been recorded.

The January 31 balances are the result of posting completed during the month of January. Note that Accounts Payable has a debit balance for this reason. Also, the balances of the payroll liability accounts are the amounts posted for sales and administrative salaries for January.

Figuring factory overhead applied rate

Instructions: 1. Figure the factory overhead applied rate based on direct labor costs. Estimated annual factory overhead costs for the current year are $100,500.00. Estimated direct labor hours to be used during the current year are 13,400 hours at an estimated rate of $10.00 per hour. Retain the calculations for use later in this reinforcement activity.

Recording transactions

Instructions: 2. Record and post the following selected transactions for January of the current year. Posting instructions are provided only for the first occurrence of each kind of transaction. Source documents are abbreviated as follows: check, C; memorandum, M; materials requisition, MR; purchase order, PO; sales invoice, S.

LEISURETIME, INC.
Chart of Accounts

Balance Sheet Accounts	Income Statement Accounts

(1000) ASSETS

1100	Current Assets
1105	Cash
1110	Petty Cash
1115	Accounts Receivable
1120	Allowance for Uncollectible Accounts
1125	Materials
1130	Work in Process
1135	Finished Goods
1140	Supplies — Factory
1145	Supplies — Sales
1150	Supplies — Administrative
1155	Prepaid Insurance
1200	Plant Assets
1205	Factory Equipment
1210	Accumulated Depreciation — Factory Equipment
1215	Office Equipment
1220	Accumulated Depreciation — Office Equipment
1225	Store Equipment
1230	Accumulated Depreciation — Store Equipment
1235	Building
1240	Accumulated Depreciation — Building
1245	Land

(2000) LIABILITIES

2100	Current Liabilities
2105	Accounts Payable
2110	Employees Income Tax Payable
2115	Federal Income Tax Payable
2120	FICA Tax Payable
2125	Salaries Payable
2130	Unemployment Tax Payable — Federal
2135	Unemployment Tax Payable — State
2140	Dividends Payable
2200	Long-Term Liability
2205	Mortgage Payable

(3000) CAPITAL

3105	Capital Stock
3110	Retained Earnings
3115	Dividends
3120	Income Summary

(4000) OPERATING REVENUE

4105	Sales

(5000) COST OF SALES

5105	Cost of Goods Sold

(5500) MANUFACTURING COSTS

5505	Factory Overhead
5510	Depreciation Expense — Factory Equipment
5515	Depreciation Expense — Building
5520	Heat, Light, and Power Expense
5525	Insurance Expense — Factory
5530	Miscellaneous Expense — Factory
5535	Payroll Taxes Expense — Factory
5540	Property Tax Expense — Factory
5545	Supplies Expense — Factory

(6000) OPERATING EXPENSES

6100	Selling Expenses
6105	Advertising Expense
6110	Delivery Expense
6115	Depreciation Expense — Store Equipment
6120	Miscellaneous Expense — Sales
6125	Salary Expense — Sales
6130	Supplies Expense — Sales
6200	Administrative Expenses
6205	Bad Debts Expense
6210	Depreciation Expense — Office Equipment
6215	Insurance Expense — Administrative
6220	Miscellaneous Expense — Administrative
6225	Payroll Taxes Expense — Administrative
6230	Property Tax Expense — Administrative
6235	Salary Expense — Administrative
6240	Supplies Expense — Administrative
6245	Utilities Expense — Administrative

(7000) OTHER REVENUE

7105	Gain on Plant Assets
7110	Miscellaneous Revenue

(8000) OTHER EXPENSES

8105	Interest Expense
8110	Loss on Plant Assets

(9000) INCOME TAX

9105	Federal Income Tax

Jan. 2. Opened a cost sheet for Job No. 321, 250 G110 chairs, ordered for stock; date wanted, January 10.
    2. Issued direct materials to factory for Job No. 321, $937.50. MR862.
        Materials list: 6,250 feet tubular aluminum @ $0.15 per foot
        Posting. Post to materials ledger and cost ledger.
    3. Opened a cost sheet for Job No. 322, 175 E610 chaise lounges; ordered for stock; date wanted, January 13.
    3. Issued direct materials to factory for Job No. 322, $3,456.25. MR863.
        Materials list: 6,125 feet tubular aluminum @ $0.15 per foot
                      1,050 square yards polyester fabric @ 1.00 per square yard
                      175 18 × 18 inch cushions @ $2.50 each
                      175 18 × 42 inch cushions @ $5.00 each
                      350 spools thread @ $0.50 each
    3. Ordered materials (35,000 feet tubular aluminum). P0630.
        Posting. Post to materials ledger.
    3. Ordered materials (600 spools thread). P0631.
    3. Ordered materials (1,500 square yards polyester fabric). P0632.
    3. Ordered materials (650 18 × 18 inch cushions). P0633.
    5. Issued direct materials to factory for Job No. 321, $900.00. MR864.
        Materials list: 15,000 feet vinyl straps @ $0.05 per foot
                      1,000 glides @ $0.15 each
    5. Ordered materials (175 18 × 42 inch cushions). P0634.
    6. Issued direct materials to factory for Job No. 322, $507.50. MR865.
        Materials list: 7,000 feet vinyl straps @ $0.05 per foot
                      1,050 glides @ $0.15 each
    6. Ordered materials (50,000 feet vinyl straps). P0635.
    6. Posted weekly summary of job-time records to cost ledger.
            Job No. 321 $1,250.00
            Job No. 322   1,710.00
    9. Sold 100 G110 chairs to Patio Shop. S433.
        Record only the cost in the finished goods ledger. Sales on account have been recorded in the sales journal. Leisuretime uses the first-in, first-out inventory method. Thus, the cost recorded first is the cost removed from inventory first when units are sold.
        Posting. Post to finished goods ledger.
    9. Ordered materials (5,000 glides). P0636.
    9. Received at materials stockroom 600 spools of thread @ $0.50 per spool; purchased on account from Thread Unlimited, $300.00. P0631. (Record all receipts of materials ordered in the materials purchases journal.)
        Posting. Post to materials ledger. Posting to accounts payable ledger is completed. You will post to the general ledger when you post the column total of the materials purchases journal at the end of the month.
    10. Opened a cost sheet for Job No. 323, 85 E710 tables; ordered for stock; date wanted, January 17.
    10. Issued direct materials to factory for Job No. 323, $272.00. MR866.
        Materials list: 1,530 feet tubular aluminum @ $0.15 per foot
                      170 square feet sheet aluminum @ $0.25 per square foot
    10. Received at materials stockroom 35,000 feet of tubular aluminum @ $0.15 per foot; purchased on account from Metals, Inc., $5,250.00. P0630.
    10. Received at materials stockroom 1,500 square yards of polyester fabric @ $1.00 per

square yard; purchased on account from Cloth World, $1,500.00. P0632.

10. Received at materials stockroom 650 18 × 18 inch cushions @ $2.50 each; purchased on account from A. J. Moore Company, $1,625.00. P0633.

10. Completed Job No. 321. Apply factory overhead to job. Use the rate figured in Instruction 1. Complete the cost sheet. Interim summary of job-time records for Job No. 321, $500.00.

      When jobs are completed in the middle of a week, Leisuretime makes a special interim summary of job-time records for these jobs. Therefore, direct labor costs will be complete.

      Posting. Post to finished goods ledger.

11. Opened a cost sheet for Job No. 324, 340 E510 chairs; ordered for stock; date wanted, January 26.

11. Issued direct materials to factory for Job No. 324, $4,505.00. MR867.

      Materials list: 8,500 feet tubular aluminum @ $0.15 per foot

               1,360 square yards polyester fabric @ $1.00 per square yard

               680 18 × 18 inch cushions @ $2.50 each

               340 spools thread @ $0.50 per spool

13. Issued direct materials to factory for Job No. 323, $1,326.00. MR868.

      Materials list: 85 tempered glass table tops @ $15.00 each

               340 glides @ $0.15 each

13. Posted weekly summary of job-time records to cost ledger.

      Job No. 322 $2,140.00

      Job No. 323   1,020.00

      Job No. 324   1,270.00

13. Completed Job No. 322.

15. Recorded total factory payroll for January 1–15 according to the payroll register, $9,784.00. C891. Payroll distribution is below.

Work in Process................................	$7,890.00
Factory Overhead	1,894.00
Cash..	8,022.90
Employees Income Tax Payable...................	1,076.22
FICA Tax Payable	684.88

      Posting. Post the general debit and general credit entries from the cash payments journal to the general ledger.

15. Recorded factory payroll tax expenses for January 1–15, $1,291.49. M417.

FICA Tax Payable	$684.88
Unemployment Tax Payable — Federal................	78.27
Unemployment Tax Payable — State	528.34

      Posting. Post the general journal entry.

16. Ordered materials (650 18 × 18 inch cushions). P0637.

16. Ordered materials (125 tempered glass table tops). P0638.

17. Sold 125 E610 chaise lounges to Discount Mart. S434.

17. Completed Job No. 323. Interim summary of job-time record for Job No. 323, $510.00.

18. Opened a cost sheet for Job No. 325, 200 G210 chaise lounges; ordered for stock; date wanted, January 28.

18. Issued direct materials to factory for Job No. 325, $1,050.00. MR869.

      Materials list: 7,000 feet tubular aluminum @ $0.15 per foot

19. Issued direct materials to factory for Job No. 324, $629.00. MR870.

      Materials list: 8,500 feet vinyl straps @ $0.05 per foot

              1,360 glides @ $0.15 each

19. Sold 25 G310 tables to Patio Shop. S435.
20. Received at materials stockroom 50,000 feet vinyl straps @ $0.05 per foot; purchased on account from Plastics, Etc., $2,500.00. P0635.
20. Received at materials stockroom 5,000 glides @ $0.15 each; purchased on account from Plastics, Etc., $750.00. P0636.
20. Posted weekly summary of job-time records to cost ledger.
    Job No. 324 $2,165.00
    Job No. 325   750.00
23. Ordered materials (1,500 square yards polyester fabric). P0639.
23. Ordered materials (600 spools thread). P0640.
24. Issued direct materials to factory for Job No. 325, $1,080.00. MR871.
    Materials list: 18,000 feet vinyl straps @ $0.05 per foot
                    1,200 glides @ $0.15 each
24. Opened a cost sheet for Job No. 326, 100 G310 tables; ordered for stock; date wanted, January 31.
24. Issued direct materials to factory for Job No. 326, $270.00. MR872.
    Materials list: 1,800 feet tubular aluminum @ $0.15 per foot
24. Received at materials stockroom 175 18 × 42 inch cushions @ $5.00 each; purchased on account from A. J. Moore Company, $875.00. P0634.
25. Sold 50 E710 tables to Wings Department Store. S436.
25. Completed Job No. 324. Interim summary of job-time records for Job No. 324, $1,325.00.
26. Sold 400 E510 chairs to Discount Mart. S437.
27. Issued direct materials to factory for Job No. 326, $510.00. MR873.
    Materials list: 1,800 square feet sheet aluminum @ $0.25 per square foot
                    400 glides @ $0.15 each
27. Opened a cost sheet for Job No. 327, 250 G110 chairs; ordered for stock; date wanted, February 7.
27. Issued direct materials to factory for Job No. 327, $937.50. MR874.
    Materials list: 6,250 feet tubular aluminum @ $0.15 per foot
27. Posted weekly summary of job-time records to cost ledger.
    Job No. 325 $1,250.00
    Job No. 326   665.00
    Job No. 327   290.00
27. Completed Job No. 325.
30. Sold 100 G210 chaise lounges to Patio Shop. S438.
30. Received at materials stockroom 650 18 × 18 inch cushions @ $2.50 each; purchased on account from A. J. Moore Company, $1,625.00. P0637.
30. Received at materials stockroom 125 tempered glass table tops @ $15.00 each; purchased on account from Sparkle Glass Company, $1,875.00. P0638.
31. Issued direct materials to factory for Job No. 327, $900.00. MR875.
    Materials list: 15,000 feet vinyl straps @ $0.05 per foot
                    1,000 glides @ $0.15 each
31. Posted summary of job-time records for January 30–31 to cost ledger.
    Job No. 326 $335.00
    Job No. 327   585.00
31. Sold 200 G110 chairs to Outdoors, Inc. S439.
31. Completed Job No. 326.
31. Recorded total factory payroll for January 16–31 according to the payroll register, $9,765.00. C965. Payroll distribution is as follows.

Work in Process...................................	$7,875.00
Factory Overhead	1,890.00
Cash..	8,007.30
Employees Income Tax Payable...................	1,074.15
FICA Tax Payable	683.55

31. Recorded factory payroll tax expenses for January 16–31, $1,288.98. M432.

FICA Tax Payable	$683.55
Unemployment Tax Payable—Federal................	78.12
Unemployment Tax Payable—State	527.31

Completing cost records

Instructions: 3. Jobs not completed on January 31 are work in process. The factory overhead for the month of January on work in process must be recorded. Apply the factory overhead rate to the direct labor costs recorded on the cost sheet for work in process. Record this amount in the Summary column with the item description Factory Overhead for January and the explanation of how this was figured.

4. Total and rule the materials purchases journal. Post the total. Use MP as the abbreviation for this journal.

5. Prove the cash payments journal. The individual amounts from this journal and the column totals from the complete journal have been posted. Therefore, no additional posting from this journal is needed.

6. Record the following general journal entries. Use January 31 as the date. Post after recording each entry.
a. An entry to transfer the total of all materials requisitions from Materials to Work in Process. The total of all materials requisitions for January is $17,280.75. M435.
b. An entry to close all individual manufacturing expense accounts to Factory Overhead. M436.
c. An entry to record applied overhead to Work in Process. (Sum of factory overhead applied to cost sheets for the month.) M437.
d. An entry to close the balance of the factory overhead account to Income Summary. M438.
e. An entry to transfer the total of all cost sheets completed from Work in Process to Finished Goods. M439.
f. An entry to transfer the cost of products sold from Finished Goods to Cost of Goods Sold. The total of all cost amounts recorded on the sales invoices for January is $34,839.25. M440.

7. Prove the subsidiary ledgers as follows.
a. Add the ending balances in the materials ledger. This total should equal the ending balance of Materials in the general ledger.
b. Add the costs recorded on all cost sheets in the cost ledger that have not been completed. This total should equal the ending balance of Work in Process in the general ledger.
c. Add the ending balances in the finished goods ledger. This total should equal the ending balance of Finished Goods in the general ledger.

8. Prepare a statement of cost of goods manufactured for the month ended January 31 of the current year.

PART B: COMPLETING END-OF-FISCAL-PERIOD ACTIVITIES

In Part B of this reinforcement activity, all accounting activities have been completed up to but not including a trial balance for the month of January.

The January 31 balances of the general ledger accounts not provided in Part A are recorded on an eight-column work sheet in the working papers accompanying this textbook.

Instructions: 9. Record the January 31 balances from the general ledger accounts used in Part A on the work sheet. Complete the Trial Balance columns of the work sheet.

10. Complete the work sheet for the month ended January 31 of the current year. The following information is needed for adjustments.

Bad debts expense	$ 270.00
Sales supplies inventory, January 31	1,111.35
Administrative supplies inventory, January 31	302.47
Value of office insurance policies, January 31	257.40
Monthly depreciation expense on office equipment	34.25
Monthly depreciation expense on store equipment	31.00
Federal income tax	2,092.76

11. Prepare an income statement for the month ended January 31 of the current year. As part of the income statement figure the following items. (a) Ratio of net cost of merchandise sold to net sales. (b) Ratio of gross profit to net sales. (c) Ratio of total operating expenses to net sales. (d) Ratio of net income before federal income tax to net sales. (e) Ratio of federal income tax to net sales. (f) Ratio of net income after federal income tax to net sales.

12. Prepare a balance sheet for January 31 of the current year. A statement of stockholders' equity is not prepared. Therefore, add the amount of net income after taxes to the beginning balance of Retained Earnings to obtain the ending balance.

TEMPO LUGGAGE INC

A BUSINESS SIMULATION

Tempo Luggage, Inc., is a manufacturing business organized as a corporation. This business simulation covers the realistic transactions completed by Tempo Luggage, Inc., which manufactures suitcases, garment bags, and briefcases. The activities included in the accounting cycle for Tempo Luggage, Inc., are listed below. This simulation is available from the publisher.

Activities in Tempo Luggage, Inc.

1. Recording selected transactions in special journals and a general journal.
2. Posting items to be posted individually to a general ledger and subsidiary ledgers (accounts receivable, accounts payable, materials, cost, and finished goods).
3. Proving and ruling the journals.
4. Recording and posting general journal entries that summarize cost records.
5. Proving the subsidiary ledgers.
6. Preparing a trial balance on a work sheet.
7. Planning adjustments and completing a work sheet.
8. Preparing financial statements.
9. Recording and posting adjusting entries.
10. Recording and posting closing entries.
11. Preparing a post-closing trial balance.

513

8
Other Accounting Systems

GENERAL BEHAVIORAL GOALS

1. Know accounting terminology related to partnership accounting and accounting for not-for-profit organizations.
2. Understand accounting concepts and practices related to partnership accounting and accounting for not-for-profit organizations.
3. Demonstrate accounting procedures unique to partnerships and not-for-profit organizations.

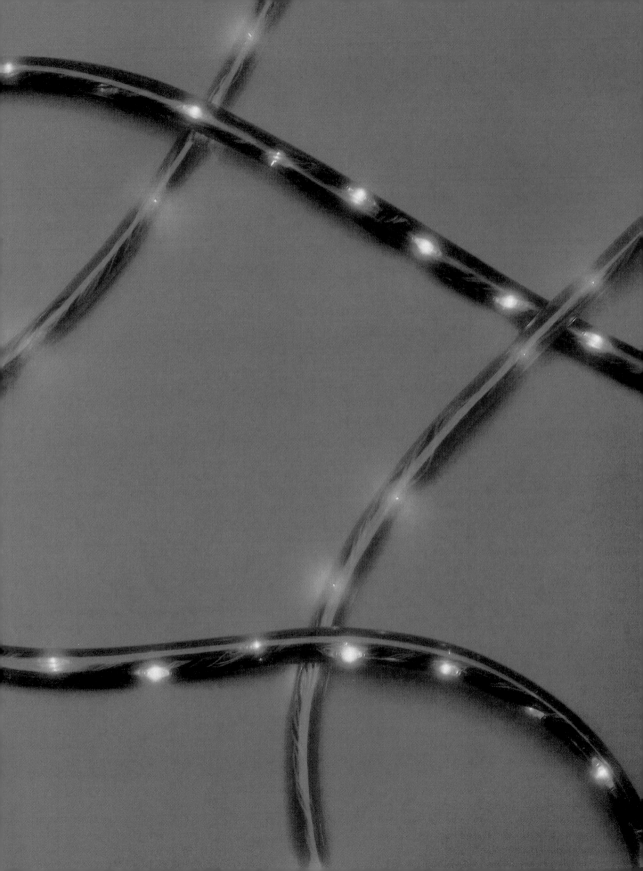

S & W ELECTRIC
Chart of Accounts

Balance Sheet Accounts	Income Statement Accounts

(1000) ASSETS

1100	Current Assets		
1105	Cash		
1110	Petty Cash		
1115	Accounts Receivable		
1120	Allowance for Uncollectible Accounts		
1125	Supplies — Electrical		
1130	Supplies — Office		
1135	Prepaid Insurance		
1200	Plant Assets		
1205	Equipment		
1210	Accumulated Depreciation — Equipment		
1215	Truck		
1220	Accumulated Depreciation — Truck		

(2000) LIABILITIES

2100	Current Liabilities
2105	Accounts Payable
2110	Sales Tax Payable

(3000) CAPITAL

3105	James Sutter, Capital
3110	James Sutter, Drawing
3115	Jane Woodrow, Capital
3120	Jane Woodrow, Drawing
3125	Income Summary

(4000) OPERATING REVENUE

4105	Sales

(5000) OPERATING EXPENSES

5105	Advertising Expense
5110	Bad Debts Expense
5115	Depreciation Expense — Equipment
5120	Depreciation Expense — Truck
5125	Insurance Expense
5130	Miscellaneous Expense
5135	Rent Expense
5140	Supplies Expense — Electrical
5145	Supplies Expense — Office
5150	Truck Expense
5155	Utilities Expense

The chart of accounts for S & W Electric is illustrated above for ready reference as you study Chapters 23 and 24 of this textbook.

23 Organizational Structure of a Partnership

ENABLING PERFORMANCE TASKS

After studying Chapter 23, you will be able to:
a. Define accounting terms related to forming and expanding a partnership.
b. Identify accounting concepts and practices related to forming and expanding a partnership.
c. Record selected transactions related to forming and expanding a partnership.

An organization with the legal rights of a person and which may be owned by many persons is known as a corporation. Another form of business may also have more than one owner. A business in which two or more persons combine their assets and skills is known as a partnership. Each member of a partnership is known as a partner. Except for recording owners' equity and income taxes, accounting procedures for a partnership are similar to those for a corporation.

FORMING A PARTNERSHIP

A partnership is created when two or more persons agree orally or in writing to form a business using the partnership form of organization. A partnership's financial records are kept separate from those of the partners. *(CONCEPT: Business Entity)*

James Sutter and Jane Woodrow agree to form a partnership called S & W Electric. Prior to forming the partnership, Mr. Sutter owned a similar business and Miss Woodrow was employed as an electrician.

S & W Electric provides electricians' services to homeowners, housing developers, and businesses. The business does not sell merchandise. For this reason, the business does not need general ledger accounts for merchandise inventory, purchases, purchases returns and allowances, and purchases discount. The partners, who provide all the service to customers, are not considered employees of the partnership. The Internal Revenue Service does not consider the money partners receive from a partnership to be salaries. Therefore, the business does not need accounts for recording salaries and payroll taxes.

Partnership agreement

A written agreement setting forth the conditions under which a partnership is to operate is known as a partnership agreement. A partnership's life is limited to the length of time agreed on by the partners. A partnership is terminated by the partners' mutual agreement, by death of a partner, by withdrawal of one partner, or by admission of a new partner. In comparison, a corporation has unlimited life.

Each partner can bind a partnership to any contract. The right of all partners to contract for a partnership is called mutual agency. Each partner is an agent of the partnership unless restricted by agreement.

Legally, a partnership agreement may be either written or oral. Some but not all states require that a partnership agreement be in writing. However, to avoid misunderstandings, a partnership agreement should be in writing.

With an attorney's assistance, Mr. Sutter and Miss Woodrow prepare the partnership agreement shown in Illustration 23-1.

Both partners sign three copies of the partnership agreement. Each partner receives a copy for personal records and the third copy becomes part of the partnership's records.

Partnership capital accounts

The capital division of a partnership's general ledger has two accounts for each partner.

1. An account in which to record a partner's equity includes the word *capital* in the title. The two accounts in S & W's general ledger are titled James Sutter, Capital and Jane Woodrow, Capital.
2. An account in which the earnings taken out of the partnership during the fiscal period are recorded includes the word *drawing* in the title. Assets taken out of a business for the owner's personal use are called withdrawals. The two accounts in S & W's general ledger used to record withdrawals are titled James Sutter, Drawing and Jane Woodrow, Drawing.

Partners' withdrawals can be a cause of misunderstandings. For this reason, most partnership agreements include a statement controlling withdrawals. S & W's partnership agreement has a controlling statement in item six as shown in Illustration 23-1.

Partners' initial investments

Mr. Sutter invests the assets of his existing business in the new partnership. According to item two of the partnership agreement, Mr. Sutter

PARTNERSHIP AGREEMENT

THIS CONTRACT is made and entered into this thirty-first day of December, 1988, by and between James T. Sutter and Jane C. Woodrow, of Charleston, South Carolina.

WITNESSETH: That the said parties have this date formed a partnership to engage in and conduct a business under the following stipulations which are a part of this contract. The partnership will begin operation January 1, 1989.

FIRST: The business shall be conducted under the name of S & W Electric, located initially at 1927 Ashley Avenue, Charleston, South Carolina, 29407-3737.

SECOND: The investment of each partner is: James T. Sutter: Equity in a business located at 1927 Ashley Avenue, Charleston, South Carolina, 29407-3737, and as shown in a balance sheet to be provided by Mr. Sutter on December 31, 1988. Total investment, $22,885.50. Jane C. Woodrow: Cash equal to one-half of the initial investment of Mr. Sutter. Total investment, $11,442.75.

THIRD: Both partners are to (a) participate in all general policy-making decisions, (b) devote full time and attention to the partnership business, and (c) engage in no other business enterprise without the written consent of the other partner. Mr. Sutter is to be general manager of the business' operations.

FOURTH: Neither partner is to become a surety or bonding agent for anyone without the written consent of the other partner.

FIFTH: The partners' shares in earnings and losses of the partnership are: Mr. Sutter: 5% interest on equity as of January 1 of each year; salary, $5,000.00 per year; remaining income or loss, 50%. Miss Woodrow: 5% interest on equity as of January 1 of each year; salary, $3,000.00 per year; remaining income or loss, 50%.

SIXTH: No partner is to withdraw assets in excess of the agreed upon interest and salary without the other partner's written consent.

SEVENTH: All partnership transactions are to be recorded in accordance with standard and generally accepted accounting procedures and concepts. The partnership records are to be open at all times for inspection by either partner.

EIGHTH: In case of either partner's death or legal disability, the equity of the partners is to be determined as of the time of the death or disability of the one partner. The continuing partner is to have first option to buy the deceased/disabled partner's equity at recorded book value.

NINTH: This partnership agreement is to continue indefinitely unless (a) terminated by death of one partner, (b) terminated by either partner by giving the other partner written notice at least ninety (90) days prior to the termination date, or (c) terminated by written mutual agreement signed by both partners.

TENTH: At the termination of this partnership agreement, the partnership's assets, after all liabilities are paid, will be distributed according to the balance in partners' capital accounts.

IN WITNESS WHEREOF, the parties to this contract have set their hands and seals on the date and year written.

Signed _James T. Sutter_ (Seal) Date _December 31, 1988_

Signed _Jane C. Woodrow_ (Seal) Date _December 31, 1988_

will provide a December 31, 1988, balance sheet for his existing business. Mr. Sutter's balance sheet is shown in Illustration 23-2.

Illustration 23-1
Partnership agreement

A value for all invested assets is agreed on by the two partners on the date the partnership begins, January 1, 1989. Mr. Sutter's initial investment is $22,885.50, the agreed upon value of his equity in his previous business. Miss Woodrow's initial cash investment, $11,442.75, is equal to one-half of Mr. Sutter's initial investment.

Sutter's Electric		
Balance Sheet		
December 31, 1988		

ASSETS

Current Assets:			
Cash		$ 9,097.48	
Accounts Receivable	$1,953.44		
Less Allowance for Uncollectible Accounts	58.76	1,894.68	
Supplies — Electrical.		2,194.39	
Supplies — Office.		900.00	
Prepaid Insurance.		116.86	
Total Current Assets.			$14,203.41
Plant Assets:			
Equipment.		$10,881.73	
Truck		4,900.00	
Total Plant Assets.			15,781.73
Total Assets			$29,985.14

LIABILITIES

Current Liabilities:		
Accounts Payable.		$ 7,099.64

CAPITAL

James Sutter, Capital.		22,885.50
Total Liabilities and Capital		$29,985.14

Illustration 23-2
Balance sheet of an
existing business invested
in a partnership

Entries to record partners' initial investments

A separate journal entry is made for each partner's initial investment.

Recording initial investment of cash only. A journal entry is made for Miss Woodrow's initial cash investment.

January 1, 1989.
Received from Jane Woodrow as an initial investment,
$11,442.75. Receipt No. 1.

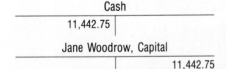

The analysis of this transaction is shown in the T accounts. Miss Woodrow's initial investment involves only cash and is recorded on line 1 of a cash receipts journal as shown in Illustration 23-3.

Recording initial investment of cash, other assets, and liabilities. Mr. Sutter's investment includes cash, other assets, and liabilities from his prior existing business. A copy of the balance sheet from Mr. Sutter's previous business, Illustration 23-2, is attached to a receipt to provide needed details. *(CONCEPT: Objective Evidence)*

			CASH RECEIPTS JOURNAL						PAGE /		
					1	2	3	4	5	6	
	DATE	ACCOUNT TITLE	DOC. NO.	POST. REF.	GENERAL		ACCOUNTS RECEIVABLE CREDIT	SALES CREDIT	SALES TAX PAYABLE CREDIT	CASH DEBIT	
					DEBIT	CREDIT					
1	1989 Jan. 1	Jane Woodrow, Capital	R1			1144275				1144275	1
2	1	Accounts Receivable	R2		195344					909748	2
3		Supplies—Electrical			219439						3
4		Supplies—Office			90000						4
5		Prepaid Insurance			11686						5
6		Equipment			1088173						6
7		Truck			490000						7
8		Allow. for Uncoll. Accts.				5876					8
9		Accounts Payable				709964					9
10		James Sutter, Capital				2288550					10
11											11
12											12
13											13
14											14
15											15

January 1, 1989.
Accepted assets and liabilities of James Sutter's existing business as an initial investment, $22,885.50. Receipt No. 2.

Illustration 23-3
Entries for partners' initial investments

The analysis of this transaction is shown in the T accounts.

Cash	
9,097.48	

Equipment	
10,881.73	

Accounts Receivable	
1,953.44	

Truck	
4,900.00	

Supplies — Electrical	
2,194.39	

Allowance for Uncollectible Accounts	
	58.76

Supplies — Office	
900.00	

Accounts Payable	
	7,099.64

Prepaid Insurance	
116.86	

James Sutter, Capital	
	22,885.50

The entry to record Mr. Sutter's initial investment is shown on lines 2 through 10 of the cash receipts journal shown in Illustration 23-3.

ADMITTING PARTNERS TO EXISTING PARTNERSHIPS

Any change in the number of partners terminates an existing partnership agreement. When a new partner is admitted, a new partnership agreement is signed by the new partners.

When a new partner is admitted, the old partnership's accounting records are often continued for the new partnership. As a result, initial investment entries for all partners are not always needed. Entries are needed however to show clearly how the partners' equity has changed. One or both of the following entries may be needed.

1. An entry to show how much the new partner invests.
2. An entry to show how the new partner's admission affects existing partners' capital accounts.

Admitting a partner with no change in total equity

Pauline Lowe and Josephine Svendater are partners in an existing business. John Karlsen has considerable experience in the same kind of business and desires to join the partnership. The two existing partners agree that Mr. Karlsen's skills are needed by the partnership. However, the business does not need additional capital at the present time. Therefore, Ms. Lowe and Mrs. Svendater agree to sell part of their existing equity to Mr. Karlsen.

The existing partners each have $30,000.00 equity in the existing partnership. The three partners of the new partnership agree that Mr. Karlsen is to pay $20,000.00 for a one-third equity in the new partnership. The two partners personally receive cash from Mr. Karlsen for equity in the partnership. The partnership does not receive the cash from the sale of equity. The equity for Mr. Karlsen is figured as follows.

$$\left(\begin{array}{c}\text{Lowe's}\\\text{Existing}\\\text{Equity}\\(\$30,000.00\end{array} + \begin{array}{c}\text{Svendater's}\\\text{Existing}\\\text{Equity}\\\$30,000.00\ )\end{array}\right) \div 3 = \begin{array}{c}\text{Karlsen's}\\\text{Equity}\\\$20,000.00\end{array}$$

The two existing partners are each entitled to one-half of the price Mr. Karlsen pays to buy a one-third share of the partnership. Therefore, Mr. Karlsen pays $10,000.00 to each of the existing partners. Also, $20,000.00 of the existing equity is transferred to Mr. Karlsen on the partnership's records.

June 1, 1989.
Recorded personal sale of equity to new partner, John Karlsen, $20,000.00, distributed as follows: from Pauline Lowe, $10,000.00; from Josephine Svendater, $10,000.00. Memorandum No. 23.

Pauline Lowe, Capital	
10,000.00	Bal. 30,000.00

Josephine Svendater, Capital	
10,000.00	Bal. 30,000.00

John Karlsen, Capital	
	20,000.00

The analysis of this transaction is shown in the T accounts. The receipt of cash, a personal transaction between Ms. Lowe, Mrs. Svendater, and Mr. Karlsen, is not recorded on the partnership's records. However, the redistribution of capital is a partnership entry and is recorded as shown in Illustration 23-4.

	GENERAL JOURNAL			PAGE 6	
DATE	ACCOUNT TITLE	POST. REF.	DEBIT	CREDIT	
1989 June 1	Pauline Lowe, Capital		10 000 00		1
	Josephine Svendater, Capital		10 000 00		2
	John Karlsen, Capital			20 000 00	3
	M23				4
					5
					6

Illustration 23-4
Entry to admit new partner with no change in total equity

Admitting a partner with equity equal to new partner's investment

Art Downs and Muriel Ortiz are partners in an existing partnership. Each partner's equity is $15,000.00 for a total equity of $30,000.00. The existing partners agree to admit Jeri Moore as a partner with a one-fourth interest for a $10,000.00 cash investment.

Jeri Moore's equity is figured as follows.

$$\left(\begin{matrix} \textbf{Downs'} \\ \textbf{Equity} \\ (\$15,000.00 \end{matrix} + \begin{matrix} \textbf{Ortiz's} \\ \textbf{Equity} \\ \$15,000.00 \end{matrix} + \begin{matrix} \textbf{Moore's} \\ \textbf{Investment} \\ \$10,000.00 \end{matrix} \right) \div 4 = \begin{matrix} \textbf{Moore's} \\ \textbf{Equity} \\ \$10,000.00 \end{matrix}$$

August 1, 1989.
Received from new partner, Jeri Moore, for a one-fourth equity in the business, $10,000.00. Receipt No. 150.

The analysis of this entry is shown in the T accounts.

Cash		Muriel Ortiz, Capital	
10,000.00			Bal. 15,000.00

Art Downs, Capital		Jeri Moore, Capital	
	Bal. 15,000.00		10,000.00

The transaction does not change the equity of Mr. Downs or Ms. Ortiz. The entry to record receipt of cash from Mrs. Moore is shown in Illustration 23-5.

Illustration 23-5
Entry to record cash investment of a new partner

		CASH RECEIPTS JOURNAL				1	2	3	4	PAGE 8 5	6	
	DATE	ACCOUNT TITLE	DOC. NO.	POST. REF.		GENERAL DEBIT	GENERAL CREDIT	ACCOUNTS RECEIVABLE CREDIT	SALES CREDIT	SALES TAX PAYABLE CREDIT	CASH DEBIT	
1	1989 Aug. 1	Jeri Moore, Capital	R150				10 000 00				10 000 00	1
2												2
3												3
4												4

Admitting a partner with equity greater than new partner's investment

David Waters and Jane Reidy have equity of $22,000.00 each in an existing partnership. The existing partners agree to admit Teri Wise as a partner with a one-third interest for a $16,000.00 cash investment. Miss Wise's equity is figured as follows.

$$\left(\begin{array}{c}\text{Waters'} \\ \text{Equity} \\ (\$22,000.00\end{array} + \begin{array}{c}\text{Reidy's} \\ \text{Equity} \\ \$22,000.00\end{array} + \begin{array}{c}\text{Wise's} \\ \text{Investment} \\ \$16,000.00 \end{array}\right) \div \begin{array}{c} \\ 3 \\ \div \ 3\end{array} = \begin{array}{c} \\ = \\ =\end{array} \begin{array}{c}\text{Wise's} \\ \text{Equity} \\ \$20,000.00\end{array}$$

Cash

| 16,000.00 | |

Teri Wise, Capital

| | 16,000.00 |

September 1, 1989.
Received from new partner, Teri Wise, for a one-third equity in the business, $16,000.00; existing equity redistributed as follows: from David Waters, $2,000.00; from Jane Reidy, $2,000.00. Receipt No. 125 and Memorandum No. 40.

The analysis of the receipt of cash is shown in the T accounts. The entry to record the receipt of cash is shown in Illustration 23-6.

	DATE	ACCOUNT TITLE	DOC. NO.	POST. REF.	GENERAL DEBIT	GENERAL CREDIT	ACCOUNTS RECEIVABLE CREDIT	SALES CREDIT	SALES TAX PAYABLE CREDIT	CASH DEBIT	
1	1989 Sept. 1	Teri Wise, Capital	R125			1600000				1600000	1
2											2
3											3
4											4
5											5
6											6
7											7
8											8
9											9
10											10

CASH RECEIPTS JOURNAL   PAGE 9

Illustration 23-6
Entry to record a cash investment by a new partner

David Waters, Capital

| 2,000.00 | Bal. | 22,000.00 |

Jane Reidy, Capital

| 2,000.00 | Bal. | 22,000.00 |

Teri Wise, Capital

| | Bal. | 16,000.00 |
| | | 4,000.00 |

The analysis of the redistribution of equity as a result of admitting Miss Wise as a partner is shown in the T accounts.

Miss Wise paid $16,000.00 for a one-third equity share which is worth $20,000.00. The additional $4,000.00 above Miss Wise's cash investment comes from the equity of the two existing partners. The existing partnership agreement between Mr. Waters and Mrs. Reidy provides that they share equally in equity increases and decreases. Therefore, half of the $4,000.00, or $2,000.00, is transferred from the capital account of each partner to Miss Wise's capital account.

The entry to record the redistribution of equity is shown in Illustration 23-7.

GENERAL JOURNAL				PAGE 8	
DATE	ACCOUNT TITLE	POST. REF.	DEBIT	CREDIT	
1989 Sept. 1	David Waters, Capital		2000 00		1
	Jane Reidy, Capital		2000 00		2
	Teri Wise, Capital			4000 00	3
	M40				4
					5

Illustration 23-7
Entry to record transfer of equity to a new partner admitted with equity greater than investment

Admitting a partner when goodwill is recognized

Jake Hugo and Albert Goode are partners in an existing business. Each partner's equity is $40,000.00, for a total equity of $80,000.00. The existing partners agree to admit Ruby Stone as a partner with a one-third interest for a $50,000.00 cash investment. Ms. Stone is willing to pay $50,000.00 for a one-third equity. She believes the total equity value is worth $150,000.00 after her investment. This value is figured as follows.

				Total Agreed Value of
Stone's Total Equity	×	**3**	=	**Equity of Partnership**
$50,000.00	×	3	=	$150,000.00

The value of a business in excess of the total investment of owners is called goodwill. The partners agree that Ms. Stone's willingness to pay $50,000.00 for a one-third interest is evidence that goodwill exists. After Ms. Stone invests her $50,000.00, the total capital on record is $130,000.00 ($40,000.00 + $40,000.00 + $50,000.00). The value of goodwill is figured as follows.

Total Agreed Value of Equity	−	**Total Recorded Equity**	=	**Increase in Equity from Goodwill**
$150,000.00	−	$130,000.00	=	$20,000.00

The $20,000.00 amount of equity in excess of the total recorded investment of the three partners is the value of goodwill.

September 1, 1989.
Received from new partner, Ruby Stone, for a one-third equity in the business, $50,000.00. Goodwill, $20,000.00, is distributed as follows: Jake Hugo, $10,000.00; Albert Goode, $10,000.00. Receipt No. 110 and Memorandum No. 50.

Cash	
50,000.00	

Ruby Stone, Capital	
	50,000.00

The analysis of the entry to record the cash investment is shown in the T accounts. The entry to record this cash investment is similar to the one shown in Illustration 23-6.

Based on prior partnership agreement, the goodwill is divided equally between Mr. Hugo and Mr. Goode with each partner receiving $10,000.00. The total equity after admission of Ms. Stone as a partner is distributed as follows.

	Previous Equity	+	Share of Goodwill	=	New Equity
Hugo	$ 40,000.00	+	$10,000.00	=	$ 50,000.00
Goode	40,000.00	+	10,000.00	=	50,000.00
Stone	50,000.00	+	—	=	50,000.00
Total	$130,000.00	+	$20,000.00	=	$150,000.00

Goodwill

20,000.00	

Jake Hugo, Capital

	Bal.	40,000.00
		10,000.00

Albert Goode, Capital

	Bal.	40,000.00
		10,000.00

The analysis of the entry to distribute goodwill is shown in the T accounts. None of the goodwill is recorded in Ruby Stone's capital account. She invests $50,000.00 for a one-third share of the business. One-third of the total equity, $150,000.00, equals the current balance of Ms. Stone's capital account, $50,000.00.

When used, the account Goodwill is located in a general ledger's *Intangible Assets* section. If S & W Electric has goodwill to record, this account will be added to its general ledger.

The entry to record the goodwill is shown in Illustration 23-8.

	DATE	ACCOUNT TITLE	POST. REF.	DEBIT	CREDIT	
		GENERAL JOURNAL			PAGE 8	
1	1989 Sept. 1	Goodwill		2000000		1
2		Jake Hugo, Capital			1000000	2
3		Albert Goode, Capital			1000000	3
4		M50				4
5						5
6						6
7						7

Illustration 23-8
Entry to record goodwill

ACCOUNTING TERMS

What is the meaning of each of the following?

1. mutual agency   **2.** withdrawals   **3.** goodwill

QUESTIONS FOR INDIVIDUAL STUDY

1. In what way do accounting procedures for a partnership differ from accounting procedures for a corporation?

2. When does a partnership come into existence?

3. Keeping partnership records separate from those of the partners is an application of which accounting concept?

4. What happens to an existing partnership if a partner dies?

5. Why should a partnership agreement be in writing?

6. Which two capital accounts for each partner are kept in a partnership's general ledger?

7. What accounts are affected, and how, when Partner A invests only cash to form a partnership?

8. What accounts are affected, and how, when Partner B invests cash, equipment, and accounts payable to form a partnership?

9. What happens to the existence of a partnership when a new partner is admitted?

10. When a new partnership is created and the records of a previous partnership are continued, what two kinds of entries may be needed?

11. What accounts are affected, and how, when cash is paid to Partners A and B for admission of Partner C with no change in total equity?

12. What accounts are affected, and how, when Partners A and B admit Partner C with an equity equal to Partner C's cash investment?

13. What accounts are affected, and how, when Partners A and B admit Partner C for an equity share greater than Partner C's cash investment?

14. What accounts are affected, and how, to record goodwill when Partner C's investment creates goodwill?

15. What is the general ledger classification of the goodwill account?

CASES FOR MANAGEMENT DECISION

CASE 1 Partner A contracts with a vendor to buy a delivery truck for the partnership. Partner A did not discuss the transaction with Partner B nor get Partner B's approval. Partner B refuses to approve payment for the truck when it is delivered claiming the vendor cannot force payment because all partners did not agree to buy the truck. The vendor claims that the transaction is valid and the partnership must pay for the truck. Is Partner B or the vendor correct? Explain.

CASE 2 Betty Cowan, her husband, and her son were partners in a business. Mrs. Cowan's husband died leaving his equity in the partnership to Mrs. Cowan. Mrs. Cowan and her son plan to form a new partnership and continue the business. Mrs. Cowan's brother owns a similar business. The brother suggests that they combine the two businesses into a corporation. What questions do you suggest Mrs. Cowan answer before she decides whether to form a partnership with her son or a corporation with her son and brother?

APPLICATION PROBLEMS

PROBLEM 23-1   Forming a partnership

Ruth Wilson and Mary Chang agree to form a partnership on July 1 of the current year. The partnership assumes the assets and liabilities of Ms. Wilson's existing business. Miss Chang invests cash equal to the investment of Ms. Wilson. Partners share equally in all changes in equity. The June 30 balance sheet for Ms. Wilson's existing business is on page 528.

Instructions: Record the following entries. Use page 1 of a cash receipts journal. Use July 1 of the current year as the date. The abbreviation for receipt is R.

July 1. Received from Mary Chang as an initial investment, $31,875.00. R1.
    1. Accepted assets and liabilities of Ruth Wilson's existing business as an initial investment, $31,875.00. R2.

Wilson's Boutique
Balance Sheet
June 30, 19--

ASSETS

Current Assets:
Cash		$11,639.44
Accounts Receivable	$2,775.16	
Less Allowance for Uncollectible Accounts	55.49	2,719.67
Merchandise Inventory		19,480.25
Supplies		496.73
Total Current Assets		$34,336.09

Plant Assets:
Equipment		7,023.04
Total Assets		$41,359.13

LIABILITIES

Accounts Payable	$ 9,484.13

CAPITAL

Ruth Wilson, Capital	31,875.00
Total Liabilities and Capital	$41,359.13

PROBLEM 23-2   Admitting a partner with no change in total equity

Harold Miller and Thad Roman are partners in an existing business. Each partner has capital of $45,000.00. On October 1 of the current year, the two partners agree to admit Jean Dawson as a third partner. The partners agree to personally sell Mrs. Dawson $15,000.00 each of their equity and to give her a one-third share of ownership. Mrs. Dawson is to pay the money directly to the two original partners.

Instructions: Record the following transaction. Use page 2 of a general journal. The abbreviation for memorandum is M.

Oct. 1. Recorded personal sale of equity to new partner, Jean Dawson, $30,000.00, distributed as follows: from Harold Miller, $15,000.00; from Thad Roman, $15,000.00. M14.

PROBLEM 23-3   Admitting a partner with equity equal to investment

Alice Wickersham and Candice Beech are partners in an existing business. Each partner has $50,000.00 equity in the partnership. Partners share equally in all changes in equity. On March 1 of the current year, the two partners agree to admit Jon Wall as a partner with a one-third share of the total equity.

Instructions: Record the following transaction. Use page 3 of a cash receipts journal. The abbreviation for receipt is R.

Mar. 1. Received from new partner, Jon Wall, for a one-third equity in the business, $50,000.00. R100.

PROBLEM 23-4   Admitting a partner with equity greater than investment

Donald Newsome and Teresa Jones each have $35,000.00 investment in a partnership. Partners share equally in all changes in equity. On September 1 of the current year, the existing partners agree to admit Quint Taylor with a one-third share of the total equity.

Instructions: Record the following transaction. Use page 5 of a cash receipts journal and page 2 of a general journal. Source documents are abbreviated as follows: memorandum, M; receipt, R.

Sept. 1. Received from new partner, Quint Taylor, for a one-third equity in the business, $20,000.00. R127 and M30.

Problem 23-5   Admitting a partner when goodwill is recognized

Ken Jamison and Bond Treacher are partners, with $21,000.00 equity each in an existing business. Partners share equally in all changes in equity. On February 1 of the current year, Sean McDowell is admitted as a new partner with a one-third share of the total equity.

Instructions: Record the following transaction. Use page 9 of a cash receipts journal and page 2 of a general journal. Source documents are abbreviated as follows: memorandum, M; receipt, R.

Feb. 1. Received from new partner, Sean McDowell, for a one-third equity in the business, $25,000.00. Partners agree that the investment results in goodwill. R56 and M9.

ENRICHMENT PROBLEMS

MASTERY PROBLEM 23-M   Forming and expanding a partnership

On June 1 of the current year, George Heatherton and Carol Anderson form a partnership. Partners share equally in all changes in equity. The partnership assumes the assets and liabilities of Mr. Heatherton's existing business. Ms. Anderson invests cash equal to Mr. Heatherton's investment. The May 31 balance sheet for Mr. Heatherton's existing business is on page 530.

Instructions: Record the following transactions. Use page 4 of a cash receipts journal and page 2 of a general journal. Source documents are abbreviated as follows: memorandum, M; receipt, R.

June   1. Received from Carol Anderson as an initial investment, $9,000.00. R1.
       1. Accepted assets and liabilities of George Heatherton's existing business as an initial investment, $9,000.00. R2.
July   1. Recorded personal sale of equity to new partner, Allan Bortz, $6,000.00, distributed as follows: from Carol Anderson, $3,000.00; from George Heatherton, $3,000.00. M8.
Sept. 1. Received from new partner, Jose Morales, for a one-fourth equity in the business, $6,000.00. R80.
Sept. 20. Received from new partner, Susan Wires, for a one-fifth equity in the business, $5,000.00. R92 and M18.
Nov.   5. Received from new partner, Wilma Mason, for a one-sixth equity in the business, $6,000.00. Partners agree that investment results in goodwill. R118 and M24.

George Heatherton
Balance Sheet
May 31, 19--

ASSETS

Current Assets:			
Cash		$3,291.23	
Accounts Receivable	$2,303.60		
Less Allowance for Uncollectible Accounts	35.79	2,267.81	
Supplies		290.19	
Total Current Assets			$5,849.23
Plant Assets:			
Equipment			3,367.14
Total Assets			$9,216.37

LIABILITIES

Accounts Payable			$ 216.37

CAPITAL

George Heatherton, Capital			9,000.00
Total Liabilities and Capital			$9,216.37

CHALLENGE PROBLEM 23-C   Forming and expanding a partnership

On July 1 of the current year, Martha Heath and James Wood form a partnership. The partnership assumes the assets and liabilities of the two partners' existing businesses. Partners share equally in all changes in equity. The July 1 balance sheets for the existing businesses are as follows.

Martha Heath
Balance Sheet
July 1, 19--

ASSETS

Current Assets:			
Cash		$3,258.32	
Accounts Receivable	$2,280.56		
Less Allowance for Uncollectible Accounts	35.43	2,245.13	
Merchandise Inventory		5,237.29	
Total Current Assets			$10,740.74
Plant Assets:			
Office Equipment			1,943.49
Total Assets			$12,684.23

LIABILITIES

Accounts Payable			$ 3,684.23

CAPITAL

Martha Heath, Capital			9,000.00
Total Liabilities and Capital			$12,684.23

James Wood
Balance Sheet
July 1, 19--

ASSETS

Current Assets:

Cash	$3,323.49	
Supplies	2,075.21	
Merchandise Inventory...........................	5,342.04	
Total Current Assets.............................		$10,740.74
Plant Assets:		
Office Equipment................................		1,959.88
Total Assets		$12,700.62

LIABILITIES

Accounts Payable....................................	$3,700.62

CAPITAL

James Wood, Capital................................	9,000.00
Total Liabilities and Capital.........................	$12,700.62

Instructions: Record the following transactions. Use page 4 of a cash receipts journal and page 2 of a general journal. Source documents are abbreviated as follows: memorandum, M; receipt, R.

July 1. Accepted assets and liabilities of Martha Heath's existing business as an initial investment. R1.

July 1. Accepted assets and liabilities of James Wood's existing business as an initial investment. R2.

Sept. 1. Accepted assets of Richard Oliver's existing business as an investment of new partner for a one-third equity in the business. M80. Mr. Oliver's September 1 balance sheet is as follows.

Richard Oliver
Balance Sheet
September 1, 19--

ASSETS

Merchandise Inventory	$9,000.00

CAPITAL

Richard Oliver, Capital................................	$9,000.00

Sept. 20. Received from new partner, Mindy Woke, for a one-fourth equity in the business, $12,000.00. R24 and M85.

Oct. 5. Accepted assets of Tom Shirer's existing business as an investment of new partner for a one-fifth equity in the business. Partners agree that the investment results in goodwill. R92 and M90. Mr. Shirer's October 5 balance sheet is as follows.

Tom Shirer
Balance Sheet
October 5, 19--

ASSETS

Cash . . . . $ 3,000.00
Merchandise Inventory 7,000.00
Total Assets $10,000.00

CAPITAL

Tom Shirer, Capital $10,000.00

24 Financial Reporting for a Partnership

ENABLING PERFORMANCE TASKS

After studying Chapter 24, you will be able to:
a. Define accounting terms related to distributing earnings and completing end-of-fiscal-period work for a partnership.
b. Identify accounting concepts and practices related to distributing earnings and completing end-of-fiscal-period work for a partnership.
c. Prepare a distribution of net income statement for a partnership.
d. Complete selected end-of-fiscal-period work for a partnership.
e. Record entries for liquidating a partnership.

Some, but usually not all, of a corporation's earnings are distributed to stockholders as dividends. All of a partnership's earnings are distributed to partners. To avoid possible misunderstandings, most partnership agreements state how partnership earnings are to be distributed.

DISTRIBUTION OF PARTNERSHIP EARNINGS

All earnings of a partnership are distributed to the partners. Five methods are commonly used for figuring how partnership earnings are distributed.

1. Fixed percentage.
2. Each partner's percentage of total equity.
3. Interest on each partner's equity.
4. Salaries for partners.
5. A combination of methods.

Distribution of partnership earnings—fixed percentage

The basis on which a partnership's earnings are distributed is usually stated in the partnership agreement. If a partnership agreement does not indicate how to divide the earnings, most state laws stipulate that partners share the earnings equally. For example, if there are two partners, earnings are shared on a fixed percentage of 50% and 50%. The law applies regardless of the differences in partners' investments, abilities, or time devoted to partnership business.

John Carlson and Saul Mentuso are partners. On January 1, 1989, the partners' equities are: Mr. Carlson, $50,000.00; Mr. Mentuso, $30,000.00. The net income for the year ended December 31, 1989, is $16,000.00. The partnership agreement states that Mr. Carlson is to receive 60% and Mr. Mentuso is to receive 40% of the net income or net loss. The distribution of net income is figured as follows.

	Total Net Income	×	Fixed Percentage	=	Share of Net Income
Carlson	$16,000.00	×	60%	=	$ 9,600.00
Mentuso	$16,000.00	×	40%	=	6,400.00
Total...........					$16,000.00

Distribution of partnership earnings— each partner's percentage of total equity

Partners often agree to use capital account balances on the first day of a fiscal year as the basis for this method. If Mr. Carlson and Mr. Mentuso had agreed to use the percentage of total equity method, the amounts would be figured as follows.

	Partner's Equity	÷	Total Equity	=	Percentage of Total Equity
Carlson	$50,000.00	÷	$80,000.00	=	62.5%
Mentuso	30,000.00	÷	$80,000.00	=	37.5%
Total...........	$80,000.00				

	Total Net Income	×	Percentage of Total Equity	=	Share of Net Income
Carlson	$16,000.00	×	62.5%	=	$10,000.00
Mentuso	$16,000.00	×	37.5%	=	6,000.00
Total...........					$16,000.00

Distribution of partnership earnings—interest on each partner's equity

Interest on equity is often used when partners invest different amounts in a partnership. Partners often agree to use capital account balances on the first day of a fiscal year as the basis for this method. The partnership agreement states the interest rate.

S & W Electric's partnership agreement, item five, Illustration 23-1, Chapter 23, stipulates that each partner is to receive 5% interest on equity. On January 1, 1989, Mr. Sutter's equity is $22,885.50 and Miss Woodrow's equity is $11,442.75. The interest on equity is figured as follows.

	Partner's Equity	×	5%	=	Interest on Equity
Sutter.............	$22,885.50	×	5%	=	$1,144.28
Woodrow	$11,442.75	×	5%	=	$ 572.14

When interest on equity is used, the remaining net income or net loss is distributed using some other method as described later in this chapter.

Distribution of partnership earnings—salaries for partners

Salaries are often used when partners contribute different amounts of personal service or bring different prior experience to a partnership. The amount of salary for each partner is stated in the partnership agreement.

S & W's partnership agreement states that salaries are to be paid as follows: Mr. Sutter, $5,000.00; Miss Woodrow, $3,000.00.

When salaries are used, the remaining net income or net loss is distributed using some other method as described later in this chapter.

Distribution of partnership earnings—combination of methods

A combination of methods may be used for distributing partnership earnings. S & W's partnership agreement states the earnings distribution as follows.

	Interest on Equity	Salary	Distribution of Remaining Net Income or Net Loss
Sutter........	5%	$5,000.00	50%
Woodrow	5%	$3,000.00	50%

The distribution of S & W's 1989 net income, $37,194.82, is figured as follows.

	Sutter	Woodrow	Distribution
Total Net Income........................			$37,194.82
Interest on Equity	$ 1,144.28	$ 572.14	
Salary.................................	5,000.00	3,000.00	
Total	$ 6,144.28	$ 3,572.14	9,716.42
Remaining Net Income			$27,478.40
Distribution of Remaining Net Income	13,739.20	13,739.20	
Total Distribution	$19,883.48	$17,311.34	$37,194.82

DISTRIBUTION OF NET INCOME STATEMENT FOR A PARTNERSHIP

A partnership financial statement showing distribution of net income or net loss to partners is called a distribution of net income statement.

Distribution of net income statement showing net income

S & W's distribution of net income statement is shown in Illustration 24-1.

S & W Electric
Distribution of Net Income Statement
For Year Ended December 31, 1989

James Sutter:		
5% Interest on Equity	$ 1,144.28	
Salary	5,000.00	
Share of Remaining Net Income.................	13,739.20	
Total Share of Net Income		$19,883.48
Jane Woodrow:		
5% Interest on Equity	$ 572.14	
Salary	3,000.00	
Share of Remaining Net Income.................	13,739.20	
Total Share of Net Income		17,311.34
Total Net Income.................................		$37,194.82

Illustration 24-1
Distribution of net income
statement showing net
income

Distribution of net income statement showing a deficit

When salaries or interest on equity are stipulated, the amounts are allowed whether or not there is sufficient net income available. The amount by which allowances to partners exceed net income is called a deficit. If the net income is less than the total allowed, partners share in the resulting deficit according to the partnership agreement.

On January 1, 1989, the equity of two partners is as follows: Eli Freund, $60,000; Alice Patzol, $48,000.00. The partners each receive a 10% annual interest on equity and share any remaining income or deficit on a fixed percentage of 60% and 40%, respectively. For the month of January, the partnership earns a net income of $800.00. The monthly amounts due each partner are figured as follows.

	⎛ Partner's Equity	×	Interest ⎞ Rate	×	Time	=	Monthly Interest
Freund....	($60,000.00	×	10%)	×	$1/12$	=	$500.00
Patzol.....	($48,000.00	×	10%)	×	$1/12$	=	400.00
Total...							$900.00

The 10% interest rate on equity is for a year. To find the monthly interest, the annual amount is multiplied by the time expressed as a fraction of a year. One month is one-twelfth of a year.

Total Net Income	−	Total Allowance	=	Deficit
$800.00	−	$900.00	=	$100.00

The total interest is more than the net income available. The difference between the net income available and the allowances is a deficit.

	Deficit	×	Fixed Percentage	=	Partner's Share of Deficit
Freund..........	$100.00	×	60%	=	$60.00
Patzol..........	$100.00	×	40%	=	$40.00

The partnership's distribution of net income statement is shown in Illustration 24-2.

Freund and Patzol		
Distribution of Net Income Statement		
For Month Ended January 31, 1989		
Eli Freund:		
10% Interest on Equity	$500.00	
Less Share of Deficit	60.00	
Total Share of Net Income		$440.00
Alice Patzol:		
10% Interest on Equity	$400.00	
Less Share of Deficit	40.00	
Total Share of Net Income		360.00
Total Net Income		$800.00

Illustration 24-2
Distribution of net income statement showing a deficit

WITHDRAWAL OF PARTNERSHIP EARNINGS

A partner often needs a portion of the annual net income before the end of a fiscal year when the actual net income is known. Thus, during a fiscal year, partners take assets out of the partnership in anticipation of the net income for the year. Assets taken out of a business for the owner's personal use are known as withdrawals. Usually the partnership agreement indicates the limits on how much may be withdrawn.

Withdrawal of cash

May 20, 1989.
Paid to James Sutter, partner, for personal use, $500.00. Check No. 56.

The analysis of this transaction is shown in the T accounts. James Sutter, Drawing is debited for $500.00. Cash is credited for $500.00. The account balance of James Sutter, Drawing, a contra capital account, is a deduction from the account balance of James Sutter, Capital.

The entry to record this transaction is shown in Illustration 24-3.

James Sutter, Drawing	
500.00	

Cash	
	500.00

		CASH PAYMENTS JOURNAL					PAGE 5	
					1 GENERAL	2	3 ACCOUNTS PAYABLE	4
	DATE	ACCOUNT TITLE	CK. NO.	POST. REF.	DEBIT	CREDIT	DEBIT	CASH CREDIT
21	20	James Sutter, Drawing	56		500.00			500.00

Illustration 24-3   Entry to record withdrawal of cash by a partner

Withdrawal of assets other than cash

November 2, 1989.
Jane Woodrow, partner, withdrew office supplies for personal use, $100.00.
Memorandum No. 29.

Because office supplies withdrawn from a partnership are not a business expense, the amount cannot be debited to the office supplies expense account. This transaction reduces the partnership's office supplies inventory and therefore Supplies — Office is credited.

Jane Woodrow, Drawing	
100.00	

Supplies — Office	
	100.00

The analysis of this transaction is shown in the T accounts. Jane Woodrow, Drawing is debited for $100.00. Supplies — Office is credited for $100.00.

The entry to record this transaction is shown in Illustration 24-4.

Illustration 24-4
Entry to record
withdrawal of assets other
than cash by a partner

	DATE	ACCOUNT TITLE	POST. REF.	DEBIT	CREDIT	
1	*1989* *Nov.* 2	*Jane Woodrow, Drawing*		1 00 00		1
2		*Supplies — Office*			1 00 00	2
3		*M29*				3
4						4

GENERAL JOURNAL   PAGE 7

END-OF-FISCAL-PERIOD WORK FOR A PARTNERSHIP

End-of-fiscal-period work for a partnership is similar to that for a corporation. In preparing partnership financial statements, accounting principles are applied in the same way during each fiscal period. *(CONCEPT: Consistent Reporting)*

Partnership work sheet

S & W's work sheet is shown in Illustration 24-5. All accounts in S & W's general ledger are listed in the Account Title column. This procedure is the same as used by corporations.

Needed adjustments are planned on a partnership work sheet in the same manner as on a corporate work sheet with one exception. No adjustment for accrued federal income tax is *ever* planned on a partnership work sheet because partnerships do not pay federal income tax.

As described later in this chapter, partnership net income is reported to the Internal Revenue Service on the partners' personal tax returns.

Because S & W Electric does not sell merchandise, an adjustment for merchandise inventory is not needed.

B & W Electric
Work Sheet
For Year Ended December 31, 1989

	ACCOUNT TITLE	TRIAL BALANCE DEBIT	TRIAL BALANCE CREDIT	ADJUSTMENTS DEBIT	ADJUSTMENTS CREDIT	INCOME STATEMENT DEBIT	INCOME STATEMENT CREDIT	BALANCE SHEET DEBIT	BALANCE SHEET CREDIT	
1	Cash	4177747						4177747		1
2	Petty Cash	20000						20000		2
3	Accounts Receivable	1199251						1199251		3
4	Allow. for Uncoll. Accts.		1992		(a) 11955				13947	4
5	Supplies - Electrical	930500			(b) 767650			162850		5
6	Supplies - Office	184500			(c) 142000			42500		6
7	Prepaid Insurance	134970			(d) 50320			84650		7
8	Equipment	1250497						1250497		8
9	Accum. Depr. - Equipment				(e) 125050				125050	9
10	Truck	612500						612500		10
11	Accum. Depr. - Truck				(f) 91875				91875	11
12	Accounts Payable		884139						884139	12
13	Sales Tax Payable		7677						7677	13
14	James Sutter, Capital		2288550						2288550	14
15	James Sutter, Drawing	450000						450000		15
16	Jane Woodrow, Capital		1144275						1144275	16
17	Jane Woodrow, Drawing	275000						275000		17
18	Income Summary									18
19	Sales		7181509				7181509			19
20	Advertising Expense	98500				98500				20
21	Bad Debts Expense			(a) 11955		11955				21
22	Depr. Exp. - Equipment			(e) 125050		125050				22
23	Depr. Exp. - Truck			(f) 91875		91875				23
24	Insurance Expense			(d) 50320		50320				24
25	Miscellaneous Expense	286921				286921				25
26	Rent Expense	840000				840000				26
27	Supplies Exp. - Electrical			(b) 767650		767650				27
28	Supplies Exp. - Office			(c) 142000		142000				28
29	Truck Expense	847756				847756				29
30	Utilities Expense	200000				200000				30
31		11508142	11508142	1188850	1188850	3462027	7181509	8274995	4555513	31
32	Net Income					3719482			3719482	32
33						7181509	7181509	8274995	8274995	33

Illustration 24-5
Partnership work sheet

Partnership income statement

S & W's income statement is shown in Illustration 24-6.

S & W Electric Income Statement For Year Ended December 31, 1989		*% of Net Sales
Operating Revenue:		
Net Sales...	$71,815.09	100.0
Operating Expenses:		
Advertising Expense	$ 985.00	
Bad Debts Expense...	119.55	
Depreciation Expense—Equipment.............................	1,250.50	
Depreciation Expense—Truck	918.75	
Insurance Expense	503.20	
Miscellaneous Expense...	2,869.21	
Rent Expense...	8,400.00	
Supplies Expense—Electrical...................................	7,676.50	
Supplies Expense—Office.......................................	1,420.00	
Truck Expense	8,477.56	
Utilities Expense..	2,000.00	
Total Operating Expenses	34,620.27	48.2
Net Income..	$37,194.82	51.8

*Rounded to the nearest 0.1%.

Illustration 24-6
Partnership income
statement

Because S & W does not sell merchandise, the income statement does not include a cost of merchandise sold section. S & W needs relatively few expense accounts. Therefore, the partnership does not subdivide the operating expenses.

S & W figures two ratios based on its income statement.

1. The ratio of total operating expenses to net sales. S & W expects an average of between 45.0% and 50.0% for this ratio. Therefore, S & W's ratio of 48.2% is acceptable.
2. The ratio of net income to net sales. S & W expects an average of between 50.0% and 55.0% for this ratio. Therefore, S & W's ratio of 51.8% is acceptable.

The ratio of net income to net sales is often high for partnerships that sell only services of the partners. The partners' salaries are not included as part of the partnership expenses, and there is no cost of merchandise sold.

Partnership distribution of net income statement

S & W's distribution of net income statement is shown in Illustration 24-1.

Partnership capital statement

A corporation's equity is reported on a statement of stockholders' equity. The statement summarizes changes in equity during a fiscal year. A similar statement is prepared for a partnership. A financial statement that summarizes the changes in capital during a fiscal period is called a capital statement. The partners review the capital statement to determine the changes occurring in equity.

S & W's capital statement is shown in Illustration 24-7.

S & W Electric Capital Statement For Year Ended December 31, 1989			
James Sutter:			
Capital, January 1, 1989		$22,885.50	
Share of Net Income	$19,883.48		
Less Withdrawals	4,500.00		
Net Increase in Capital		15,383.48	
Capital, December 31, 1989			$38,268.98
Jane Woodrow:			
Capital, January 1, 1989		$11,442.75	
Share of Net Income	$17,311.34		
Less Withdrawals	2,750.00		
Net Increase in Capital		14,561.34	
Capital, December 31, 1989			26,004.09
Total Capital, December 31, 1989			$64,273.07

The following information is reported on a partnership's capital statement.

Illustration 24-7
Partnership capital statement

1. Each partner's capital at the beginning of the fiscal period. This balance is found by referring to each partner's capital account in the general ledger.
2. Each partner's total share of net income. These amounts are obtained from the distribution of net income statement.
3. Each partner's withdrawals during the fiscal period. This amount is found by referring to the work sheet.
4. Each partner's net increase in equity during the fiscal period.
5. Each partner's capital on the last day of the fiscal period.
6. The partnership's total capital on the last day of the fiscal period.

Partnership balance sheet

A partnership balance sheet is similar to a balance sheet for a corporation. The major difference is how the owners' equity is reported. On a corporate balance sheet, summarized information about capital stock is reported under the heading Stockholders' Equity. No information is reported about the equity of individual stockholders. On a partnership balance sheet, each partner's ending capital is reported under the heading Capital. The amount of ending capital is obtained from the capital statement.

S & W's balance sheet is shown in Illustration 24-8.

S & W Electric Balance Sheet December 31, 1989			
ASSETS			
Current Assets:			
Cash...		$41,777.47	
Petty Cash..		200.00	
Accounts Receivable...............................	$11,992.51		
Less Allowance for Uncollectible Accounts...................	139.47	11,853.04	
Supplies—Electrical.................................		1,628.50	
Supplies—Office....................................		425.00	
Prepaid Insurance..................................		846.50	
Total Current Assets...............................			$56,730.51
Plant Assets:			
Equipment..	$12,504.97		
Less Accumulated Depreciation—Equipment.................	1,250.50	$11,254.47	
Truck...	$ 6,125.00		
Less Accumulated Depreciation—Truck.....................	918.75	5,206.25	
Total Plant Assets..................................			16,460.72
Total Assets..			$73,191.23
LIABILITIES			
Current Liabilities:			
Accounts Payable...................................		$ 8,841.39	
Sales Tax Payable..................................		76.77	
Total Current Liabilities.............................			$ 8,918.16
CAPITAL			
James Sutter, Capital...............................		$38,268.98	
Jane Woodrow, Capital..............................		26,004.09	
Total Capital.......................................			64,273.07
Total Liabilities and Capital........................			$73,191.23

Illustration 24-8
Partnership balance sheet

Partnership adjusting entries

S & W's adjusting entries are made to record expenses in the fiscal period to which they apply. (CONCEPT: Matching Expenses with Revenue)

Partnerships often need to make the same adjusting entries made by corporations. However, S & W does not sell merchandise, does not accept notes receivable, has not issued any notes payable, and does not pay federal income tax. Also, because the business has no employees, no accrued salaries need to be recorded. Therefore, S & W does not need adjusting entries for merchandise inventory, prepaid interest expense, accrued interest expense, interest income, accrued federal income tax, or accrued payroll.

S & W's adjusting entries are shown in Illustration 24-9.

	DATE		ACCOUNT TITLE	POST. REF.	DEBIT	CREDIT	
1			Adjusting Entries				1
2	1989 Dec.	31	Bad Debts Expense		11955		2
3			Allow. for Uncoll. Accts.			11955	3
4		31	Supplies Expense – Electrical		767650		4
5			Supplies – Electrical			767650	5
6		31	Supplies Expense – Office		142000		6
7			Supplies – Office			142000	7
8		31	Insurance Expense		50320		8
9			Prepaid Insurance			50320	9
10		31	Depreciation Expense – Equipment		125050		10
11			Accum. Depr. – Equipment			125050	11
12		31	Depreciation Expense – Truck		91875		12
13			Accum. Depr. – Truck			91875	13
14							14

GENERAL JOURNAL   PAGE *13*

Illustration 24-9
Partnership adjusting entries

Partnership closing entries

A partnership's closing entries are similar to those of a corporation. The major difference is in recording distribution of earnings to the partners.

S & W's closing entries recorded on December 31, 1989, are shown in Illustration 24-10.

S & W records five closing entries.

1. The first entry closes income statement accounts with credit balances as shown on lines 15-16.
2. The second entry closes income statement accounts with debit balances as shown on lines 17-28.
3. The third entry closes the income summary account and distributes earnings to the partners' capital accounts as shown on lines 29-31. The amount credited to each partner's capital account is obtained from the distribution of net income statement, Illustration 24-1. When this closing entry is posted, the income summary account is closed. Each partner's capital account is increased by the partner's share of the net income for 1989.

\multicolumn{2}{c}{GENERAL JOURNAL}				PAGE *13*
DATE	ACCOUNT TITLE	POST. REF.	DEBIT	CREDIT	

14		*Closing Entries*			14
15	31	*Sales*		7 1 8 1 5 0 9	15
16		*Income Summary*			7 1 8 1 5 0 9	16
17	31	*Income Summary*		3 4 6 2 0 2 7		17
18		*Advertising Expense*			9 8 5 0 0	18
19		*Bad Debts Expense*			1 1 9 5 5	19
20		*Depr. Exp.—Equipment*			1 2 5 0 5 0	20
21		*Depr. Exp.—Truck*			9 1 8 7 5	21
22		*Insurance Expense*			5 0 3 2 0	22
23		*Miscellaneous Expense*			2 8 6 9 2 1	23
24		*Rent Expense*			8 4 0 0 0 0	24
25		*Supplies Exp.—Electrical*			7 6 7 6 5 0	25
26		*Supplies Exp.—Office*			1 4 2 0 0 0	26
27		*Truck Expense*			8 4 7 7 5 6	27
28		*Utilities Expense*			2 0 0 0 0 0	28
29	31	*Income Summary*		3 7 1 9 4 8 2		29
30		*James Sutter, Capital*			1 9 8 8 3 4 8	30
31		*Jane Woodrow, Capital*			1 7 3 1 1 3 4	31
32	31	*James Sutter, Capital*		4 5 0 0 0 0		32
33		*James Sutter, Drawing*			4 5 0 0 0 0	33
34	31	*Jane Woodrow, Capital*		2 7 5 0 0 0		34
35		*Jane Woodrow, Drawing*			2 7 5 0 0 0	35
36						36
37						37

Illustration 24-10
Partnership closing
entries

4. The fourth and fifth entries close each partner's drawing account
   and transfer the balances to each partner's capital account as shown on
   lines 32-35.

Partnership post-closing trial balance

After adjusting and closing entries have been posted, S & W prepares a
post-closing trial balance listing all general ledger accounts with balances.
S & W's post-closing trial balance is similar to that of a corporation.

FEDERAL INCOME TAXES OF A PARTNERSHIP

S & W's distribution of net income statement, Illustration 24-1, shows
salaries for each of the partners. However, the Internal Revenue Service
does not consider partners to be employees of the partnership they own.
The IRS classifies the partners as self-employed persons whose salaries are

not an expense of the partnership. Therefore, partners' salaries are considered to be withdrawals of partnership earnings and not expenses.

A partnership does not pay income tax on its earnings. However, a partnership does submit to the IRS a partnership tax return which reports earnings distributed to each partner. Partners include their share of the partnership net income or net loss on their personal income tax returns.

As self-employed persons, partners are entitled to old-age, survivors, disability, and hospitalization insurance benefits known as social security. Each partner personally pays a self-employment tax in order to qualify for social security coverage. The self-employment tax rate is higher than an individual's FICA tax rate. Part of an individual's FICA tax rate is paid by the employer. The self-employment taxes are personal expenses of the partners and not of the partnership. Therefore, partners' self-employment FICA taxes are not recorded on partnership records. *(CONCEPT: Business Entity)*

LIQUIDATION OF A PARTNERSHIP

If a partnership goes out of business, the assets are distributed to the creditors and partners. The process of paying a partnership's liabilities and distributing remaining assets to the partners is called liquidation of a partnership.

Recording realization

Cash received from the sale of assets during liquidation of a partnership is called realization. Typically, when a partnership is liquidated, the non-cash assets are sold and the available cash is used to pay the creditors. Any remaining cash is distributed to the partners according to each partner's total equity.

On July 31, 1989, James Walden and Betsy Joiner decide to liquidate their partnership. At that time, financial statements are prepared and adjusting and closing entries are recorded and posted. After the end-of-fiscal-period work is completed, the partnership has account balances as shown in the T accounts.

Cash		Accounts Payable	
11,000.00			2,500.00

Supplies		James Walden, Capital	
900.00			10,000.00

Truck		Betsy Joiner, Capital	
15,000.00			9,500.00

Accumulated Depreciation — Truck	
	4,900.00

Gain on Realization. Noncash assets might be sold for more than the recorded book value. When this happens, the value received in excess of the book value is recorded as a gain on realization. The gain is recorded in an account titled Loss and Gain on Realization.

August 1, 1989.
Received from sale of truck, $12,000.00. Cost, $15,000.00; accumulated depreciation recorded to date, $4,900.00. Receipt No. 204.

The partnership's gain on the sale of the truck is figured as follows.

Cash Received for Truck		Cost of Truck		Accumulated Depreciation		Gain on Realization
$12,000.00	−	($15,000.00	−	$4,900.00)	=	$1,900.00

Cash

Bal. 11,000.00	
12,000.00	

Accumulated Depreciation — Truck

4,900.00	Bal. 4,900.00

Truck

Bal. 15,000.00	15,000.00

Loss and Gain on Realization

	1,900.00

The analysis of this transaction is shown in the T accounts. Cash is debited for the total amount received, $12,000.00. Accumulated Depreciation — Truck, is debited for the total depreciation recorded to date, $4,900.00. Truck is credited for the cost of the truck, $15,000.00. Loss and Gain on Realization is credited for the amount received in excess of the truck's book value, $1,900.00.

The entry to record this transaction is shown in Illustration 24-11, lines 1-3.

CASH RECEIPTS JOURNAL   PAGE 1

	DATE	ACCOUNT TITLE	DOC. NO.	POST. REF.	GENERAL DEBIT	GENERAL CREDIT	ACCOUNTS RECEIVABLE CREDIT	SALES CREDIT	SALES TAX PAYABLE CREDIT	CASH DEBIT	
1	1989 Aug. 1	Accum. Depr. — Truck	R204		490000					1200000	1
2		Truck				1500000					2
3		Loss & Gain on Realization				190000					3
4	1	Loss & Gain on Realization	R205		10000					80000	4
5		Supplies				90000					5
6											6

Illustration 24-11
Entries to record loss and gain on realization

Loss on Realization. Sometimes, during liquidation, the sale of an asset brings in less cash than the recorded book value.

Cash

Bal. 23,000.00	
800.00	

Loss and Gain on Realization

100.00	Bal. 1,900.00

Supplies

Bal. 900.00	900.00

August 1, 1989.
Received from sale of supplies, $800.00; balance of supplies account, $900.00. Receipt No. 205.

The analysis of this transaction is shown in the T accounts. Cash is debited for the amount received, $800.00. Loss and Gain on Realization is debited for the amount received that is less than the recorded value of the supplies, $100.00. Supplies is credited for the recorded value of the supplies sold, $900.00.

The entry to record this transaction is shown on lines 4 and 5, Illustration 24-11. After these entries are recorded, the balance of Loss and Gain on Realization, $1,800.00, is the amount received in excess of the value of the truck and supplies combined.

Liquidating liabilities

After all noncash assets are sold, the available cash is used to pay creditors.

August 4, 1989.
Paid all creditors the amounts owed, $2,500.00. Check No. 357.

The analysis of this transaction is shown in the T accounts. Accounts Payable is debited for $2,500.00. Cash is credited for the same amount.

The entry to record this transaction is shown in Illustration 24-12.

Accounts Payable		
2,500.00	Bal.	2,500.00

Cash		
Bal.	23,800.00	2,500.00

CASH PAYMENTS JOURNAL							PAGE 8	
					1	2	3	4
DATE	ACCOUNT TITLE	CK. NO.	POST. REF.	GENERAL		ACCOUNTS PAYABLE DEBIT	CASH CREDIT	
				DEBIT	CREDIT			
1989 Aug. 4	Accounts Payable	357		250000			250000	1
								2
								3
								4
								5
								6
								7
								8

When this transaction has been recorded and posted, the partnership has only four general ledger accounts with balances as shown in the T accounts.

Illustration 24-12
Entry to record liquidation of liabilities

Cash			Betsy Joiner, Capital		
Bal.	21,300.00			Bal.	9,500.00

James Walden, Capital			Loss and Gain on Realization		
	Bal.	10,000.00		Bal.	1,800.00

Distributing loss or gain on realization to partners

When all creditors have been paid, the balance of Loss and Gain on Realization is distributed to the partners. A credit balance indicates a gain on realization. A debit balance indicates a loss. The distribution is based on the method of distributing net income or net loss as stated in the partnership agreement. The percentages for the Walden and Joiner partnership are: Mr. Walden, 55%; Ms. Joiner, 45%. The distribution of the balance of Loss and Gain on Realization is figured as follows.

	Balance of Loss and Gain on Realization	×	Fixed Percentage	=	Share of the Balance of Loss and Gain on Realization
Walden ...	$1,800.00	×	55%	=	$ 990.00
Joiner.....	$1,800.00	×	45%	=	810.00
Total...					$1,800.00

Loss and Gain on Realization

1,800.00	Bal.	1,800.00

James Walden, Capital

	Bal.	10,000.00
		990.00

Betsy Joiner, Capital

	Bal.	9,500.00
		810.00

August 6, 1989.
Recorded distribution of gain on realization: to James Walden, $990.00; to Betsy Joiner, $810.00. Memorandum No. 351.

The analysis of this transaction is shown in the T accounts. Loss and Gain on Realization is debited for $1,800.00 to close this account. James Walden, Capital is credited for $990.00, his share of the gain on realization. Betsy Joiner, Capital is credited for $810.00, her share of the gain on realization.

The entry to record this transaction is shown in Illustration 24-13.

	GENERAL JOURNAL				PAGE 7	
DATE	ACCOUNT TITLE	POST. REF.	DEBIT		CREDIT	
1989 Aug. 6	Loss & Gain on Realization		1800 00			1
	James Walden, Capital				990 00	2
	Betsy Joiner, Capital				810 00	3
	M351					4

Illustration 24-13
Entry to record distribution of gain on realization

If a loss on realization is distributed to the partners, Loss and Gain on Realization is credited to close the account. Each partner's capital account is debited for the partner's share of the loss on realization.

Distributing remaining cash to partners

The final step in liquidating a partnership is to distribute any remaining cash to the partners. The cash is distributed according to each partner's capital account balance regardless of the method used to distribute net income or net loss.

August 6, 1989.
Recorded final distribution of remaining cash to partners: to James Walden, $10,990.00; to Betsy Joiner, $10,310.00. Check Nos. 358 and 359.

James Walden, Capital		
10,990.00	Bal.	10,990.00

Betsy Joiner, Capital		
10,310.00	Bal.	10,310.00

Cash		
Bal. 21,300.00		21,300.00

The analysis of this transaction is shown in the T accounts. James Walden, Capital is debited for $10,990.00. Betsy Joiner, Capital is debited for $10,310.00. Cash is credited for $21,300.00.

The entry to record this transaction is shown in Illustration 24-14.

					CASH PAYMENTS JOURNAL				PAGE 8		
						1	2	3	4		
	DATE	ACCOUNT TITLE	CK. NO.	POST. REF.	GENERAL DEBIT	GENERAL CREDIT	ACCOUNTS PAYABLE DEBIT	CASH CREDIT			
2	6	James Walden, Capital	358		1099000			2130000			2
3		Betsy Joiner, Capital	359		1031000						3
4											4
5											5
6											6
7											7
8											8
9											9
10											10
11											11
12											12

After this entry is recorded and posted, all of the partnership's general ledger accounts will have zero balances. The partnership is liquidated.

Illustration 24-14
Entry to record distribution of remaining cash to partners

ACCOUNTING TERMS

What is the meaning of each of the following?

1. distribution of net income statement
2. deficit
3. capital statement
4. liquidation of a partnership
5. realization

QUESTIONS FOR INDIVIDUAL STUDY

1. What are five common methods of dividing partnership earnings?
2. If a partnership agreement does not state how earnings are distributed, how are the earnings distributed?
3. What is the formula for figuring each partner's percentage of total equity?
4. Why might each partner receive a different salary?
5. What is done when there are insufficient earnings to cover the salaries or interest allowed to partners?
6. What accounts are affected, and how, when Partner A withdraws office supplies for personal use?
7. When partnership financial statements are prepared using the same procedures in each fiscal period, which accounting concept is being applied?
8. What adjustment planned on a corporate work sheet is never found on a partnership work sheet? Why not?
9. Recording adjusting entries is an application of which accounting concept?
10. What are the five closing entries recorded by S & W Electric?
11. What accounts are affected, and how, by S & W's closing entry to record distribution of the partnership's net income?
12. Why are partners' salaries not recorded as a partnership expense?
13. What information does a partnership report to the IRS?
14. How do partners obtain social security coverage?
15. What accounts are affected, and how, when a truck is sold for more than its book value during liquidation?
16. What accounts are affected, and how, when supplies are sold for less than their book value during liquidation?
17. What accounts are affected, and how, when distributing a gain on realization to partners?
18. What accounts are affected, and how, when distributing remaining cash to partners during liquidation?

CASES FOR MANAGEMENT DECISION

CASE 1 Carlos Suarez invests $20,000.00 in a partnership. His partner, Daniel Sampson, invests $30,000.00. Mr. Suarez has 20 years experience in a similar business and Mr. Sampson has no experience. Mr. Suarez is to spend about 20 hours a week working for the partnership. Mr. Sampson is to spend full time. Which method of distributing partnership earnings would you suggest for this partnership? Explain your answer.

CASE 2 The R & W partnership does not prepare a distribution of net income statement or a capital statement at the end of a fiscal period. Instead, the information is all reported in detail on the partnership's balance sheet. Is this an acceptable practice? Explain your answer.

APPLICATION PROBLEMS

PROBLEM 24-1   Distributing partnership earnings

Olive Smith and George King are partners in a business called Smith and King. On December 31 of the current year, the partners' equities are: Miss Smith, $40,000.00; Mr. King, $60,000.00. The net income for the year is $35,000.00.

Instructions: 1. For each of the following cases, figure how the $35,000.00 net income will be distributed to the two partners.

a. Each partner receives a fixed percentage of 50% of net income.
b. Each partner receives a percentage of net income based on the percentage of the partner's equity to total equity.
c. Each partner receives 10% interest on equity. The partners share remaining net income, net loss, or deficit equally.
d. Miss Smith receives a salary of $10,000.00; Mr. King receives a salary of $15,000.00. The partners share remaining net income, net loss, or deficit on a fixed percentage of Miss Smith, 40%, and Mr. King, 60%.
e. Miss Smith is to receive 5% interest on equity and a salary of $10,000.00. Mr. King is to receive 5% interest on equity and a salary of $15,000.00. The partners share remaining net income, net loss, or deficit equally.
f. Miss Smith is to receive 10% interest on equity and a salary of $12,000.00. Mr. King is to receive 10% interest on equity and a salary of $17,000.00. The partners share remaining net income, net loss, or deficit equally.

2. From the information figured in case e in Instruction 1, prepare a distribution of net income statement.

3. From the information figured in case f in Instruction 1, prepare a distribution of net income statement.

PROBLEM 24-2   Recording partners' withdrawals

Milisa Matthews and Bruce Gibson are partners in a business. Each partner withdraws assets during May of the current year.

Instructions: Record the following selected transactions. Use page 6 of a cash payments journal and page 5 of a general journal. Source documents are abbreviated as follows: check, C; memorandum, M.

May   5. Milisa Matthews, partner, withdrew office supplies for personal use, $200.00. M25.
        26. Paid to Bruce Gibson, partner, for personal use, $400.00. C205.

PROBLEM 24-3   Completing financial statements for a partnership

Linda Placer and Tina Dettermeyer are partners in a business called Green Grass Care. The partnership's work sheet for the year ended December 31 of the current year is given in the working papers accompanying this textbook.

Instructions: 1. Prepare an income statement. As part of the income statement, report the ratios of total operating expenses to net sales and net income to net sales. Round percentage computations to the nearest 0.1%.

2. Prepare a distribution of net income statement. The partners share in net income, net loss, or deficit according to each partner's percentage of total equity. The January 1 equity is: Ms. Placer, $23,125.00; Mrs. Dettermeyer, $12,500.00. Round percentage computations to the nearest 0.1%.

3. Prepare a capital statement.

4. Prepare a balance sheet.

5. Record the adjusting entries. Use page 12 of a general journal.

6. Continue using page 12 of the general journal. Record the closing entries.

PROBLEM 24-4   Liquidating a partnership

Richard Wilson and Michelle Ring agree to liquidate their partnership on June 30 of the current year. On that date, after financial statements are prepared and closing entries are posted, general ledger accounts have the following balances.

Cash	$ 5,000.00
Supplies	500.00
Office Equipment	8,000.00
Accum. Depreciation—Office Equip.	5,500.00
Truck	15,000.00
Accum. Depreciation—Truck	12,200.00
Accounts Payable	500.00
Richard Wilson, Capital	5,300.00
Michelle Ring, Capital	5,000.00

Instructions: Record the following transactions. Use page 7 of a cash receipts journal, page 6 of a cash payments journal, and page 4 of a general journal. Source documents are abbreviated as follows: check, C; memorandum, M; receipt, R.

July 1. Received from sale of office equipment, $2,000.00. R102.
  1. Received from sale of supplies, $400.00. R103.
  3. Received from sale of truck, $3,000.00. R104.
  5. Paid all creditors the amounts owed. C123.
  6. Recorded distribution of balance of Loss and Gain on Realization: to Richard Wilson, 60%; to Michelle Ring, 40%. M34.
  6. Recorded final distribution of remaining cash to partners. C124 and C125.

ENRICHMENT PROBLEMS

MASTERY PROBLEM 24-M   Completing end-of-fiscal-period work for a partnership

Alicia Ross and Don Sands are partners in a business called A & D Service. The partnership's work sheet for the year ended December 31 of the current year is given in the working papers accompanying this textbook.

Instructions: 1. Prepare an income statement. As part of the income statement report the ratios of total operating expenses to net sales and net income to net sales. Round percentage computations to the nearest 0.1%.

2. Prepare a distribution of net income statement. Each partner is to receive 5% interest on January 1 equity. The January 1 equity is: Miss Ross, $12,000.00; Mr. Sands, $12,000.00. Also, partners' salaries are: Miss Ross, $6,000.00; Mr. Sands, $8,000.00. The partners share remaining net income, net loss, or deficit equally.

3. Prepare a capital statement.

4. Prepare a balance sheet.

5. Record the adjusting entries. Use page 12 of a general journal.

6. Continue using page 12 of the general journal. Record the closing entries.

CHALLENGE PROBLEM 24-C   Completing end-of-fiscal-period work for a partnership

Doris Waiser and Rolf Schermer are partners in a business called W & S Sales. The partnership's work sheet for the year ended December 31 of the current year is given in the working papers accompanying this textbook.

Instructions: 1. Prepare an income statement. As part of the income statement, report the ratios of cost of merchandise sold to net sales, gross profit on operations to net sales, total operating expenses to net sales, and net income or net loss to net sales. Round percentage computations to the nearest 0.1%. If there is a net loss, use a minus sign with the ratio of net loss to net sales.

2. Prepare a distribution of net income statement. Each partner is to receive 5% interest on January 1 equity. The January 1 equity is: Mrs. Waiser, $24,250.00; Mr. Schermer, $21,500.00. Also, partners' salaries are: Mrs. Waiser, $5,000.00; Mr. Schermer, $4,000.00. The partners share remaining net income, net loss, or deficit equally.

3. Prepare a capital statement.

4. Prepare a balance sheet.

TOWN OF OAKWOOD GENERAL FUND
Chart of Accounts

Balance Sheet Accounts

(1000) ASSETS

1010	Cash
1020	Taxes Receivable — Current
1030	Allowance for Uncollectible Taxes — Current
1040	Taxes Receivable — Delinquent
1050	Allowance for Uncollectible Taxes — Delinquent
1060	Interest Receivable
1070	Allowance for Uncollectible Interest
1080	Inventory of Supplies
1090	Investments — Short Term

(2000) LIABILITIES

2010	Accounts Payable
2020	Notes Payable

(3000) FUND EQUITY

3010	Unreserved Fund Balance
3020	Reserve for Encumbrances — Current Year
3030	Reserve for Encumbrances — Prior Year
3040	Reserve for Inventory of Supplies

Revenue and Expenditure Accounts

(4000) REVENUES

4010	Property Tax Revenue
4020	Interest Revenue
4030	Other Revenue

(5000) EXPENDITURES

5100	General Government
5110	Expenditure — Personnel, General Government
5120	Expenditure — Supplies, General Government
5130	Expenditure — Other Charges, General Government
5140	Expenditure — Capital Outlays, General Government
5200	Public Safety
5210	Expenditure — Personnel, Public Safety
5220	Expenditure — Supplies, Public Safety
5230	Expenditure — Other Charges, Public Safety
5240	Expenditure — Capital Outlays, Public Safety
5300	Public Works
5310	Expenditure — Personnel, Public Works
5320	Expenditure — Supplies, Public Works
5330	Expenditure — Other Charges, Public Works
5340	Expenditure — Capital Outlays, Public Works

Revenue and Expenditure Accounts (cont.)

(5000) EXPENDITURES (cont.)

5400	Recreation
5410	Expenditure — Personnel, Recreation
5420	Expenditure — Supplies, Recreation
5430	Expenditure — Other Charges, Recreation
5440	Expenditure — Capital Outlays, Recreation

Budgetary Accounts

(6000) BUDGETARY

6010	Estimated Revenues
6020	Appropriations
6030	Budgetary Fund Balance
6100	General Government
6110	Encumbrance — Personnel, General Government
6120	Encumbrance — Supplies, General Government
6130	Encumbrance — Other Charges, General Government
6140	Encumbrance — Capital Outlays, General Government
6200	Public Safety
6210	Encumbrance — Personnel, Public Safety
6220	Encumbrance — Supplies, Public Safety
6230	Encumbrance — Other Charges, Public Safety
6240	Encumbrance — Capital Outlays, Public Safety
6300	Public Works
6310	Encumbrance — Personnel, Public Works
6320	Encumbrance — Supplies, Public Works
6330	Encumbrance — Other Charges, Public Works
6340	Encumbrance — Capital Outlays, Public Works
6400	Recreation
6410	Encumbrance — Personnel, Recreation
6420	Encumbrance — Supplies, Recreation
6430	Encumbrance — Other Charges, Recreation
6440	Encumbrance — Capital Outlays, Recreation

The chart of accounts for Oakwood is illustrated above for ready reference as you study Chapters 25 and 26 of this textbook.

25 Budgeting and Accounting for a Not-for-Profit Organization

ENABLING PERFORMANCE TASKS

After studying Chapter 25, you will be able to:
a. Define accounting terms related to budgeting and accounting for a not-for-profit governmental organization.
b. Identify accounting concepts and practices related to budgeting and accounting for a not-for-profit governmental organization.
c. Record budget, revenues, expenditures, encumbrances, and other transactions for a not-for-profit governmental organization.

Businesses are organized as proprietorships, partnerships, or corporations. These business organizations differ in their kinds of ownership but they have a common objective — to earn a profit. Other kinds of organizations are formed for purposes other than earning a profit. An organization providing goods or services with neither a conscious motive nor expectation of earning a profit is called a not-for-profit organization. Not-for-profit organizations are also known as nonprofit organizations.

Both businesses and not-for-profit organizations provide goods or services. Business owners generally invest in a business for the purpose of earning a profit. Not-for-profit organizations however are formed to provide needed goods or services to a group of individuals without regard to earning a profit. The primary purpose of the organization is to make available the needed goods or services that may not be available otherwise.

THE NATURE OF NOT-FOR-PROFIT ORGANIZATIONS

Not-for-profit organizations may differ in types of goods or services provided, sources of revenues, or procedures for selecting their leaders or managers. Major types of not-for-profit organizations are as follows.

1. Government, such as federal, state, county, city, town, and village.
2. Education, such as elementary, secondary, and post-secondary schools.
3. Health, such as hospitals and nursing homes.
4. Charitable, such as United Way, United Fund, and American Red Cross.
5. Foundations, including trusts and corporations organized for charitable and educational purposes such as the Carnegie Foundation and Ford Foundation.
6. Religious, such as churches and other religious organizations.

Since not-for-profit organizations have a common objective, they all have many of the same needs for financial information. Thus, the accounting system and many of the financial reports are similar for all not-for-profit organizations. However, because of differences in goods or services provided, sources of revenues, or leadership selection, accounting procedures and reports are modified for the specific type of organization.

All individuals are affected by and are members of one or more governmental organizations. Also, more individuals are employed by governmental organizations than any other type of not-for-profit organization. Therefore, Chapters 25 and 26 emphasize accounting for local governmental organizations.

Characteristics of governmental organizations that affect the accounting system

A governmental organization's purpose normally is to provide needed goods or services that would be impossible for individuals to provide for themselves. For example, the federal government provides national defense for all citizens of the nation. Individual states and cities would find it difficult and very inefficient to provide for their own defense from foreign pressures. Cities provide police and fire protection that would be very expensive and inefficient for individuals to provide for themselves.

There are four major characteristics of a governmental organization that affect the accounting system.

1. No profit motive exists. A business' success can be measured by whether or not a profit is earned. If a business is inefficient and not competitive, a profit will not be earned. Without profits, a business will soon be unable to continue operations. However, since a governmental organization does not intend to earn a profit, success is much more difficult to measure. As long as money is available, a governmental organization can continue to operate regardless of its efficiency or inefficiency.
2. Leadership is subject to frequent change. Policy-making bodies of governmental organizations generally are elected by popular vote of the group's members. Thus, the leadership is dependent upon the political process and may change frequently. Therefore, policies and long-range

goals may change when the leadership changes. These frequent changes make effective long-range planning difficult.

3. Users of services do not necessarily pay for the services. Revenues for governmental organizations are provided primarily by taxation on property, retail sales, or income. Organization members who have the greatest amount of property or income provide the greatest amount of revenues. However, the goods or services normally are provided to all members of the organization based on need. The amount individuals pay is not directly related to the benefits they receive. Therefore, individuals have decreased incentive for insuring that services are administered efficiently.

4. Conflicting pressures for differing objectives. No direct relationship exists between who pays for and who receives the services provided by a governmental organization. Therefore, individuals generally support the organizational objective most advantageous to themselves. For example, some citizens of a city may place the construction of a city library high on their list of priorities. Others who seldom use a library may place this project low on their list of priorities. Consequently, services provided by a governmental organization are usually determined through negotiation and compromise among the different interest groups. This procedure does not necessarily provide for the best services or the most efficiency.

The characteristics of governmental organizations have affected the development of governmental accounting systems. As a result, numerous financial and legal regulations for determining the source and amount of revenues and for planning and executing expenditures of funds are required.

Characteristics of governmental accounting systems

Several accounting practices are similar for business and governmental organizations. The following practices are applied by both kinds of organizations.

1. Apply the accounting equation, assets equal equities.
2. Analyze transactions into debit and credit parts.
3. Use similar procedures to journalize transactions from source documents, post to ledgers, and prepare a trial balance to assure equality of debits and credits.
4. Prepare an appropriate chart of accounts.
5. Apply most of the same accounting concepts.
6. Prepare financial statements for each fiscal period.

The characteristics of governmental organizations and the conditions in which they operate create information and control requirements different from those of businesses. Because of these differences, governmental accounting and financial reporting differ in several ways from business accounting and financial reporting.

Fund accounting. The accounting system for a business includes a single accounting entity. That is, all accounts used to record accounting transactions for the entire business are part of a single set of accounts. Within this set of accounts, assets must equal equities. Governmental accounting systems are organized and operated on a fund basis. A governmental accounting entity with a set of accounts in which assets always equal equities is called a fund. A governmental unit, such as a city, may have several different funds.

A fund accounting system emphasizes strong controls on the use of funds. The amount in a fund can be spent only for the specified purpose of the fund. Different funds may be created for different purposes. For example, the town of Westview has two funds: (1) a general fund, and (2) a library fund. Balance sheets for the two funds are shown in Illustration 25-1.

Westview General Fund	
ASSETS	
Cash	$300,000.00
Taxes Receivable	50,000.00
Total Assets	$350,000.00
LIABILITIES AND FUND EQUITY	
Liabilities:	
Accounts Payable	$ 60,000.00
Fund Equity:	
Fund Balance..............	290,000.00
Total Liabilities and Fund Equity	$350,000.00

Westview Library Fund	
ASSETS	
Cash	$60,000.00
LIABILITIES AND FUND EQUITY	
Liabilities:	
Accounts Payable	$ 5,000.00
Fund Equity:	
Fund Balance................	55,000.00
Total Liabilities and Fund Equity .	$60,000.00

Illustration 25-1
Balance sheets for two funds

The town of Westview has total assets of $410,000.00 (general fund, $350,000.00, *plus* library fund, $60,000.00). However, the assets are accounted for separately. Assets in the library fund may be used for library purposes only. General fund assets may be used for other authorized town expenditures. Each fund is kept as a separate entity with a separate set of accounts.

The fund equity, similar to owner's equity for a business, is the net amount of assets available for use. For example, Westview's library fund equity is $55,000.00 (assets, $60,000.00, *less* liabilities, $5,000.00). If $6,000.00 cash is spent for library salaries, assets available for spending would be reduced to $54,000.00 ($60,000.00 *less* $6,000.00) and the fund equity account, Fund Balance, would be reduced to $49,000.00 (assets, $54,000.00, *less* liabilities, $5,000.00). After this transaction, the fund remains in balance. Assets equal liabilities plus fund equity as shown on the balance sheet in Illustration 25-2.

Westview Library Fund	
ASSETS	
Cash	$54,000.00
LIABILITIES AND FUND EQUITY	
Liabilities:	
Accounts Payable	$ 5,000.00
Fund Equity:	
Fund Balance	49,000.00
Total Liabilities and Fund Equity	$54,000.00

Illustration 25-2
Balance sheet for a fund

Types of funds vary with the type of not-for-profit organization and the types of goods or services provided. A unique set of funds normally is used for each type of organization — federal government, state and local governments, hospitals, schools, etc.

Modified accrual accounting. Most businesses use accrual accounting so that revenue and expenses incurred during a fiscal period determine the resulting net income for the period. *(CONCEPT: Matching Expenses with Revenue)* In governmental accounting revenues are recorded in the accounting period in which they become measurable and available. For example, property taxes become measurable and available as soon as the amount is determined and tax statements are sent to property owners. However, sales taxes cannot be determined until sales are made. Thus, sales tax revenue is recognized when the taxes are received from merchants.

Governmental organizations record expenditures rather than expenses. Cash disbursements and liabilities incurred for the cost of goods delivered or services rendered are called expenditures. An important distinction is made between expenditures and expenses. Businesses emphasize matching expenses with revenue in each fiscal period. However, governmental accounting emphasizes determining and controlling revenues and expenditures during a fiscal period. For example, if a business buys a truck, Plant Asset or Truck is debited and Cash or Notes Payable is credited. No expense is incurred until the truck is used. If a governmental organization buys a truck, Expenditure is debited and Cash or Notes Payable is credited. The amount of money spent or liability incurred is recorded, not the expense. Thus, expenditures are decreases in net financial resources. Emphasis is placed on control of the net financial resources, not on matching expenses with revenue. Thus, modified accrual accounting is used for measuring financial position and operating results of governmental organizations.

Financial reporting emphasis. Business and governmental organizations both prepare financial statements at the end of a fiscal period. *(CONCEPT: Accounting Period Cycle)* However, because the organizations have different objectives, the statements also differ. The two most common financial statements prepared by businesses are an income statement and a balance sheet. The two most common financial statements prepared by governmental organizations are a statement of revenues, expenditures, and changes in fund balance and a balance sheet.

Businesses prepare income statements to report the amount of net income earned during a fiscal period. Earning a net income is not an objective of governmental organizations. However, identifying and controlling the sources of revenues and the expenditure of funds is emphasized as part of the control process. Therefore, a statement of revenues, expenditures, and changes in fund balance is prepared.

A business' balance sheet reports the assets, liabilities, and owners' equity of the business at the end of a fiscal period. A governmental organization's balance sheet also reports the current assets and liabilities of the organization at the end of a fiscal period. However, no specific ownership of a governmental organization exists. Therefore, assets less liabilities is reported as fund equity.

Budgeting. Budgets are prepared by both businesses and governmental organizations. The primary purpose of all budgets is planning and control. For businesses, planning is required to prepare the budget. During the fiscal period, budgeted amounts are compared with actual amounts to provide information to management about the effectiveness of cost control. Planning also is required to prepare a budget for a governmental organization. However, an approved governmental budget becomes (a) a legal authorization to spend, and (b) a legal limit on the amount that can be spent.

DEVELOPING AN ANNUAL GOVERNMENTAL OPERATING BUDGET

A plan of current expenditures and the proposed means of financing those expenditures is called an operating budget. A governmental fund's annual operating budget authorizes and provides the basis for control of financial operations during a fiscal year. Since each governmental fund is a separate accounting entity, an operating budget is normally prepared for each fund. The general procedures for preparing an annual governmental operating budget are as follows.

1   Departments of the governmental organization submit budget requests to the chief executive of the organization. Requests are based on an analysis of expenditures for the previous year and expected changes in expenditures for the coming year.

2 The chief executive reviews budget requests with department heads. When budget requests are acceptable to the chief executive, departmental requests are consolidated into a single budget request for the organization. The chief executive then submits the operating budget to the legislative body. The legislative body is a group of persons normally elected by the citizens of the organization and granted authority to make laws for the organization.

3 The legislative body approves the operating budget. The approved operating budget becomes an authorization to spend the amounts listed in the budget. Before the operating budget can be approved, revenues plus the available amount of fund equity must be at least as great as the expenditures. If the expenditures are more than the total of expected revenues and available fund equity, the expected sources of revenue must be increased or expenditures decreased.

In some states, the operating budget is not officially approved until reviewed by tax committees at the county and state level.

Oakwood is a small town with a town manager and five town council members. The council members are elected to their positions. One member of the council serves as mayor. The council serves as the legislative body for Oakwood. The council appoints the town manager who works full time as chief executive of the town. Oakwood has three department heads: public safety director, public works director, and recreation director. Because Oakwood is small and most of its revenues come from property taxes, the accounting system contains only one fund—a general fund.

At the request of the town manager, Oakwood's three department heads prepare budget requests for 1989 after analyzing the current year's expenditures and expected changes for 1989. The town manager reviews the budget requests with each department head. The requests are then combined into a single operating budget for Oakwood's 1989 general fund and submitted to the town council. The town council represents the interests of all the town's citizens. Thus, the council should evaluate the operating budget from at least four viewpoints. (1) Are adequate services being provided? (2) Are the services desired by a majority of citizens? (3) Are the amounts requested essential to provide the desired level of services? (4) Does the city have the financial capacity to support the budget?

The approved operating budget determines the amount of revenues needed for the year. The town tax rate needed to provide the necessary funds for the approved operating budget is then determined.

After completing their review, the Oakwood council formally approves the 1989 governmental operating budget. The approved governmental operating budget becomes authorization for the town manager and department heads to make expenditures as specified in the budget. The approved annual governmental operating budget for Oakwood's general fund is shown in Illustration 25-3.

Town of Oakwood
Annual Operating Budget—General Fund
For Year Ended December 31, 1989

ESTIMATED REVENUES

Property Tax	$1,494,000.00	
Interest	6,000.00	
Other	2,500.00	
Total Estimated Revenues		$1,502,500.00

ESTIMATED EXPENDITURES AND BUDGETARY FUND BALANCE

General Government:		
Personnel	$ 263,280.00	
Supplies	12,150.00	
Other Charges	113,400.00	
Capital Outlays	16,220.00	
Total General Government		$ 405,050.00
Public Safety:		
Personnel	$ 489,200.00	
Supplies	20,000.00	
Other Charges	153,150.00	
Capital Outlays	90,300.00	
Total Public Safety		752,650.00
Public Works:		
Personnel	$ 113,400.00	
Supplies	5,600.00	
Other Charges	47,500.00	
Capital Outlays	51,500.00	
Total Public Works		218,000.00
Recreation:		
Personnel	$ 58,260.00	
Supplies	1,970.00	
Other Charges	25,250.00	
Capital Outlays	11,620.00	
Total Recreation		97,100.00
Total Estimated Expenditures		$1,472,800.00
Budgetary Fund Balance		29,700.00
Total Estimated Expenditures and Budgetary Fund Balance		$1,502,500.00

Illustration 25-3
Annual governmental
operating budget for
general fund

Oakwood organizes revenue accounts by source of revenue. Expenditure accounts are organized by department and type of expenditure. Some organizations maintain subsidiary accounts for each of the general ledger accounts to provide greater detail about the sources of revenues and types of expenditures. Because of its small size, Oakwood maintains only the general ledger accounts listed in its chart of accounts.

RECORDING ACCOUNTING TRANSACTIONS

Governmental organizations, just as businesses, record accounting transactions initially in a journal. Also, source documents are the basis for recording the journal entries. Governmental organizations may use a multi-column journal, a general journal, or special journals adapted to the organization's needs. Oakwood uses a multi-column journal to record all its journal entries.

Recording an approved annual governmental operating budget

Approval of an annual governmental operating budget by the proper authorities provides legal authorization for expenditures to be made in accordance with the approved budget. Authorizations to make expenditures for specified purposes are called appropriations. Oakwood's approved 1989 operating budget has appropriations that authorize expenditures up to the amounts stated in the budget. The tax rate is then set at a rate that will raise at least enough revenue to cover the appropriations.

Many governmental organizations have restrictions on the amount of tax increase permitted. Public hearings may be required to increase taxes. A formal vote in an election may also be required. If a proposed operating budget exceeds the amount of taxes and other estimated revenue, the budget may need to be reduced to the level of available revenues.

As an additional control measure, Oakwood records its approved operating budget in the budgetary accounts, Estimated Revenues and Appropriations. Budgetary accounts are for control purposes and are closed at the end of a fiscal period.

Total estimated revenues, as shown on Oakwood's 1989 operating budget, Illustration 25-3, are $1,502,500.00. Oakwood's appropriations (total estimated expenditures) are $1,472,800.00.

January 2, 1989.
Recorded Oakwood's approved 1989 operating budget: estimated revenues, $1,502,500.00; appropriations, $1,472,800.00; budgetary fund balance, $29,700.00. Memorandum No. 25.

The analysis of this transaction is shown in the T accounts. Estimated Revenues is increased by a debit for the amount of budgeted revenues, $1,502,500.00. Estimated Revenues has a normal debit balance. This debit balance is opposite the normal credit balance of an actual revenue account. Appropriations is increased by a credit for the amount of Oakwood's budgeted expenditures, $1,472,800.00. Appropriations has a normal credit balance. This credit balance is opposite the normal debit balance of the actual expenditure accounts. Budgetary Fund Balance is increased by a credit, $29,700.00 (estimated revenues, $1,502,500.00, *less* appropriations, $1,472,800.00).

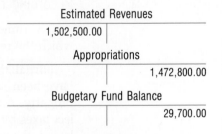

Estimated Revenues	
1,502,500.00	

Appropriations	
	1,472,800.00

Budgetary Fund Balance	
	29,700.00

The journal entry to record Oakwood's approved operating budget is shown in Illustration 25-4.

					1 GENERAL 2		3 CASH 4	
								PAGE 12
DATE	ACCOUNT TITLE	DOC. NO.	POST. REF.	DEBIT	CREDIT	DEBIT	CREDIT	
1989 Jan. 2	Estimated Revenues	M25		15025000				1
	Appropriations				14728000			2
	Budgetary Fund Balance				297000			3
								4
								5
								6

Illustration 25-4
Entry to record an
approved annual
governmental operating
budget

A separate revenue account will be credited as revenues are earned. Balances of the two accounts, Estimated Revenues and Revenues, can be reviewed to determine the amount of actual revenues earned compared with the amount of revenues estimated to be earned. If actual revenues are not as great as expected, expenditures may need to be reduced to avoid exceeding available funds. Recording the estimated revenues in the budgetary account Estimated Revenues provides this additional planning and control information.

Separate expenditure accounts will be debited as actual expenditures are made. Insuring that expenditures do not exceed the appropriations (budgeted expenditures) is essential for governmental organizations. Periodically, the appropriations account balance can be compared with the total of expenditure account balances to avoid overspending appropriations. Appropriations less total expenditures is the amount still available for spending. Recording appropriations in the budgetary account Appropriations provides this additional control information. Each department also keeps records of its appropriated and expended amounts to insure each department's appropriation amounts are not exceeded.

If appropriations exceed estimated revenues, Budgetary Fund Balance is debited to make the total debits equal the total credits. However, most governmental organizations normally set their revenue sources slightly above appropriations to avoid exceeding appropriations.

Recording revenues

Governmental fund revenues are recorded in the accounting period in which the revenues become measurable and available.

Journalizing current property tax revenue. When property tax rates have been set and tax amounts figured, taxes are levied on all taxable property. Authorized action taken by a governmental organization to collect taxes by legal authority is called a tax levy. When property taxes are levied, the taxes are considered measurable and available because they are now a legal obligation of property owners. When the levy is made, property tax revenue is recorded. On January 2, 1989, Oakwood authorizes its tax levy and sends out property tax statements to property owners. Although tax levies are legal obligations of property owners, some property owners do not pay their taxes. Legal action may eventually be taken against these property owners in an effort to collect the taxes. Even with these actions, a government generally does not collect all the taxes levied. Oakwood estimates that $15,000.00 of property taxes will not be collected.

January 2, 1989.
Recorded 1989 property tax levy: taxes receivable—current, $1,509,000.00; allowance for uncollectible taxes—current, $15,000.00; property tax revenue, $1,494,000.00. Memorandum No. 26.

The analysis of this transaction is shown in the T accounts. Taxes Receivable—Current is increased by a debit for the total amount of tax levied, $1,509,000.00. This amount is the total of the tax statements sent to taxpayers. The contra asset account Allowance for Uncollectible Taxes—Current is increased by a credit for the amount of estimated loss, $15,000.00. The revenue account Property Tax Revenue is increased by a credit for the amount of revenue recognized, $1,494,000.00. This amount is the difference between the total tax levy, $1,509,000.00, and the allowance for current uncollectible taxes, $15,000.00.

Taxes Receivable—Current	
1,509,000.00	

Allowance for Uncollectible Taxes—Current	
	15,000.00

Property Tax Revenue	
	1,494,000.00

The journal entry to record this transaction is shown in Illustration 25-5.

	DATE	ACCOUNT TITLE	DOC. NO.	POST. REF.	GENERAL DEBIT	GENERAL CREDIT	CASH DEBIT	CASH CREDIT	
4	2	Taxes Receivable – Current	M26		1509000 00				4
5		Allow. for Uncoll. Taxes – Current				15000 00			5
6		Property Tax Revenue				1494000 00			6

Journalizing collection of current property taxes. Cash received for property taxes reduces the taxes receivable account. Revenue was recorded when property taxes were levied.

Illustration 25-5
Entry to record current property tax revenue

January 10, 1989.
Received for current taxes receivable, $182,000.00. Receipt No. 356.

The analysis of this transaction is shown in the T accounts. Cash is increased by a debit for the amount of cash received, $182,000.00. Taxes Receivable—Current is decreased by a credit for the same amount, $182,000.00.

The journal entry to record this transaction is shown in Illustration 25-6.

Cash	
182,000.00	

Taxes Receivable—Current	
Bal. 1,509,000.00	182,000.00

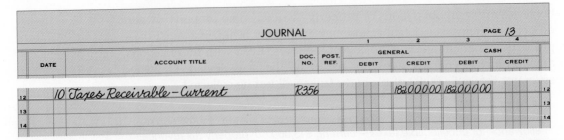

Journalizing other revenue. Some revenues, such as fines, inspection charges, parking meter receipts, and penalties, are normally not known, and thus not measurable, until cash is received. Such revenues therefore are generally recorded only when cash is received.

January 15, 1989.
Received from traffic fines, $75.00. Receipt No. 361.

Cash

| 75.00 | |

Other Revenue

| | 75.00 |

The analysis of this transaction is shown in the T accounts. Cash is increased by a debit for the amount of cash received, $75.00. Other Revenue is increased by a credit for the same amount, $75.00.

The journal entry to record this transaction is shown in Illustration 25-7.

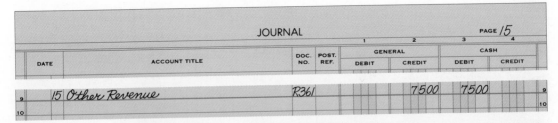

Journalizing delinquent property taxes. Property taxes normally are due and payable by a date specified on the tax statements. Taxes not paid by the specified date are reclassified as delinquent to distinguish them from current taxes. Oakwood's property taxes are due on February 28. On March 1, taxes not paid are considered delinquent. On that date, a journal entry is made to transfer uncollected taxes from current to delinquent status.

Taxes that Oakwood expects to collect are accounted for by using two accounts, Taxes Receivable—Current and Allowance for Uncollectible Taxes—Current. On March 1 of each year, the remaining balance of Taxes Receivable—Current is considered to be a delinquent amount. Delinquent taxes are accounted for by using two accounts, Taxes Receivable—Delinquent and Allowance for Uncollectible Taxes—Delinquent. Thus, on March 1 of each year, the balances of the two current accounts are transferred to the two delinquent accounts.

March 1, 1989.
Recorded reclassification of current taxes receivable to delinquent status,
$74,200.00, and the accompanying allowance for uncollectible accounts,
$15,000.00. Memorandum No. 55.

The analysis of this transaction is shown in the T accounts.
Taxes Receivable—Delinquent is increased by a debit for the
amount of current taxes becoming delinquent, $74,200.00.
The contra asset account Allowance for Uncollectible Taxes—
Current is decreased by a debit for the balance in that
account, $15,000.00. Taxes Receivable—Current is decreased by a
credit for the amount of current taxes becoming delinquent,
$74,200.00. Allowance for Uncollectible Taxes—Delinquent is in-
creased by a credit for the amount of allowance on the
delinquent taxes, $15,000.00. When this entry is posted,
the delinquent taxes and the accompanying uncollectible
allowance amount will be transferred from current to delinquent status.

Taxes Receivable — Delinquent	
74,200.00	

Allowance for Uncollectible Taxes — Current	
15,000.00	Bal. 15,000.00

Taxes Receivable — Current	
Bal. 74,200.00	74,200.00

Allowance for Uncollectible Taxes — Delinquent	
	15,000.00

The journal entry to record this transaction is shown in Illustration 25-8.

	DATE	ACCOUNT TITLE	DOC. NO.	POST. REF.	GENERAL DEBIT	GENERAL CREDIT	CASH DEBIT	CASH CREDIT	
15	Mar. 1	Taxes Receivable—Delinquent	M55		7420000				15
16		Allow. for Uncoll. Taxes—Current			1500000				16
17		Taxes Receivable—Current				7420000			17
18		Allow. for Uncoll. Taxes—Delinquent				1500000			18
19									19
20									20
21									21

Journalizing collection of delinquent property taxes. Even though
some taxes become delinquent, Oakwood continues efforts to collect these
taxes. Cash received for delinquent taxes reduces the taxes receivable—
delinquent account.

Illustration 25-8
Entry to record delinquent
property taxes

March 20, 1989.
Received for delinquent taxes receivable, $12,000.00. Receipt No. 410.

The analysis of this transaction is shown in the T accounts.
Cash is increased by a debit for the amount of cash received,
$12,000.00. Taxes Receivable—Delinquent is decreased by a credit
for the same amount, $12,000.00.

The journal entry to record this transaction is shown in
Illustration 25-9.

Cash	
12,000.00	

Taxes Receivable — Delinquent	
Bal. 74,200.00	12,000.00

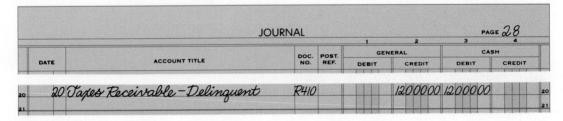

			JOURNAL				PAGE 28
				1	2	3	4
		DOC.	POST.	GENERAL		CASH	
DATE	ACCOUNT TITLE	NO.	REF.	DEBIT	CREDIT	DEBIT	CREDIT
20	20 *Taxes Receivable—Delinquent*	R410				1200000	1200000	20
21								21

Illustration 25-9
Entry to record collection
of delinquent property
taxes

Recording expenditures and encumbrances

A primary objective of governmental accounting is to control the financial resources. Governmental accounting focuses on measuring changes in financial resources rather than determining net income. Therefore, in governmental accounting, expenditures rather than expenses are recorded.

Control of expenditures is enhanced by the use of two special accounting procedures.

1. Expenditures are classified into several categories to assign specific responsibility for the expenditure and to analyze the purpose of the expenditure. For example, Expenditure—Personnel, Public Safety is one of Oakwood's expenditure accounts. Personnel indicates the type of expenditure (salaries for personnel). Public Safety indicates the department for which the personnel expenditures were made.

2. Budgetary accounts are used to record estimated amounts of expenditures to protect against overspending the budgeted amounts. To accomplish this control procedure, encumbrance accounts are used. A commitment to pay for goods or services which have been ordered but not yet provided is called an encumbrance. When an order is placed that will require a future expenditure, a budgetary encumbrance account is debited for the estimated amount. This entry reduces the fund balance and insures that commitments and expenditures will not be greater than funds available.

Journalizing expenditures. Exact amounts of some expenditures are known as soon as the obligation is determined. For example, the amount and due date of payment for utility costs is known when the utility statement is received.

January 10, 1989.
Paid for electrical service in public safety department, $270.00. Check No. 345.

Expenditure—Other Charges,
Public Safety

| 270.00 | |

Cash

| | 270.00 |

The analysis of this transaction is shown in the T accounts. Expenditure—Other Charges, Public Safety is increased by a debit for the cost of the electrical service, $270.00. Cash is decreased by a credit for the same amount, $270.00.

The journal entry to record this transaction is shown in Illustration 25-10.

						GENERAL		CASH	
DATE	**ACCOUNT TITLE**		**DOC. NO.**	**POST. REF.**	**DEBIT**	**CREDIT**	**DEBIT**	**CREDIT**	
1989 *Jan.* 10	*Expenditure—Other Charges, Public Safety*		C345		270 00			270 00	1
									2
									3

JOURNAL PAGE *13*

Illustration 25-10
Entry to record an
expenditure for electrical
service

The major control of expenditures is achieved by holding department heads accountable for expenditures in their unit. Classification of expenditures is used to analyze major types of expenditures within each department. For Oakwood, each department's expenditures are recorded in one of four classifications: personnel, supplies, other charges, or capital outlays. Other charges is used for all expenditures, except salaries and related personnel expenditures, supplies, and capital outlays. Capital outlays is used for expenditures that will benefit future years.

Journalizing encumbrances. To avoid spending more resources than are available, encumbrance accounts are used. When goods or services are ordered that will be provided at a later date, an obligation for a future expenditure is made. Resources have not yet been used but there is a promise to give up those resources when ordered goods or services are delivered. Encumbering resources is a way of setting aside the amount estimated to be needed to pay for the ordered goods or services. When the goods or services are delivered, the estimated amount is removed from the encumbrance account and the exact amount of the expenditure is recorded in an expenditure account.

January 12, 1989.
Encumbered estimated amount for supplies in public works department,
$360.00. Memorandum No. 30.

The analysis of this transaction is shown in the T accounts. The budgetary account Encumbrance—Supplies, Public Works is increased by a debit for the amount of the order, $360.00. The fund equity account Reserve for Encumbrances—Current Year is increased by a credit for the amount of the supplies order, $360.00. This account serves as an offsetting account for the encumbrance account and shows that this amount of the fund equity is reserved for an encumbrance.

Encumbrance—Supplies, Public Works	
360.00	

Reserve for Encumbrances—Current Year	
	360.00

The journal entry to record this transaction is shown in Illustration 25-11.

Expenditures plus encumbrances for a specific account equal the total commitments that have been made against the appropriated amount for that account. The appropriated amount less the encumbrances and expenditures equals the amount that can still be spent. For example, Oakwood appropriated $5,600.00 for supplies for the public works department. If expenditures are $800.00, and encumbrances are $360.00, then $4,440.00

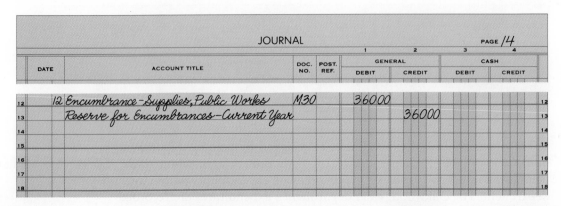

DATE	ACCOUNT TITLE	DOC. NO.	POST. REF.	GENERAL DEBIT	GENERAL CREDIT	CASH DEBIT	CASH CREDIT	
12	12	Encumbrance—Supplies, Public Works	M30		360.00				12
13		Reserve for Encumbrances—Current Year				360.00			13

Illustration 25-11
Entry to record an
encumbrance for supplies
ordered

is still available for public works supplies expenditures ($5,600.00 *less* $800.00 *less* $360.00).

Journalizing expenditures for amounts encumbered. When goods or services that have been encumbered are received, two entries must be made. First, the encumbrance entry is reversed to remove the estimated amount from the encumbrance and reserve for encumbrance accounts. Second, the expenditure is recorded.

January 25, 1989.
Paid for public works department supplies, $356.00, encumbered January 12 per Memorandum No. 30. Memorandum No. 36 and Check No. 352.

Reserve for Encumbrances — Current Year

360.00	Bal. 360.00

Encumbrance — Supplies, Public Works

Bal. 360.00	360.00

The analysis of the first entry to reverse the encumbrance entry for the supplies ordered is shown in the T accounts. The encumbrance was for an estimated amount, $360.00. When the supplies were delivered, the actual cost was $356.00. The actual amount of an expenditure sometimes differs from the amount estimated when an order is placed. Reserve for Encumbrances — Current Year is decreased by a debit for the amount of the entry made to this fund equity account when the encumbrance was initially recorded, $360.00. Encumbrance — Supplies, Public Works is credited for the amount of the encumbrance in this budgetary account, $360.00. This entry cancels the encumbrance which is no longer needed. The order has been received and the expenditure will be recorded. Thus, an encumbrance is no longer outstanding.

Expenditure — Supplies, Public Works

356.00	

Cash

	356.00

The analysis of the entry to record the supplies expenditure is shown in the T accounts. Expenditure — Supplies, Public Works is increased by a debit for the actual cost of supplies, $356.00. Cash is decreased by a credit for the same amount, $356.00.

The journal entries to record reversing the encumbrance and to record the actual expenditure for supplies are shown in Illustration 25-12.

		JOURNAL						PAGE 17
					1	2	3	4
					GENERAL		CASH	
DATE	ACCOUNT TITLE		DOC. NO.	POST. REF.	DEBIT	CREDIT	DEBIT	CREDIT
10	25 Reserve for Encumbrances–Current Year		M36		36000				10
11	Encumbrance–Supplies, Public Works					36000			11
12	25 Expenditure– Supplies, Public Works		C352		35600			35600	12
13									13

Journalizing expenditures benefiting future periods. Governmental organizations are formed to provide needed services for their members, not to earn a profit. A business records the cost of property, such as a typewriter, as an asset. The business then depreciates the asset over its useful life. Recording depreciation spreads the cost of the asset over the asset's life. The depreciation expense is matched with revenue earned in each fiscal period. Since governmental organizations do not earn net income, they have no need for expense information. However, controlling the expenditure of funds is important. When money is spent for capital outlays, the amount is recorded as an expenditure in the period spent, even though the item may benefit several accounting periods.

On March 10, Oakwood's general government department bought a new typewriter.

March 10, 1989.
Paid for typewriter for general government department, $700.00. Check No. 390.

The analysis of this transaction is shown in the T accounts. Expenditure—Capital Outlays, General Government is increased by a debit for the cost of the typewriter, $700.00. Cash is decreased by a credit for the same amount, $700.00.

The journal entry to record the expenditure for property that will benefit future periods is shown in Illustration 25-13.

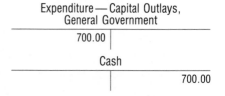

Illustration 25-12
Entries to record reversing an encumbrance and to record an actual expenditure

Expenditure — Capital Outlays, General Government

700.00	

Cash

	700.00

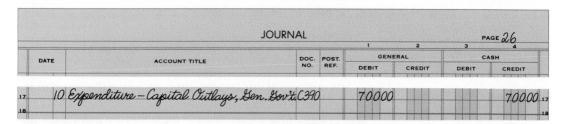

		JOURNAL						PAGE 26
					1	2	3	4
					GENERAL		CASH	
DATE	ACCOUNT TITLE		DOC. NO.	POST. REF.	DEBIT	CREDIT	DEBIT	CREDIT
17	10 Expenditure—Capital Outlays, Gen. Gov't.		C390		70000			70000	17
18									18

Governmental properties that benefit future periods are called general fixed assets. Most governmental organizations keep some kind of record of general fixed assets. The purpose of the record is to help safeguard the

Illustration 25-13
Entry to record an expenditure benefiting future periods

government's ownership of the property. Oakwood keeps a card file with needed information about each general fixed asset.

Recording other transactions

Sometimes governmental organizations need to borrow cash for short periods until tax money is received. At other times, these organizations have cash to invest for short periods until the cash is needed to pay expenditures.

Journalizing issuance and payment of liabilities. Oakwood sends tax statements to property owners on January 1 each year. Taxes can be paid anytime from January 1 through February 28. Consequently, the town may need to borrow cash until taxes are received.

January 4, 1989.
Issued a one-month, 12% note payable to Second National Bank, $100,000.00. Note Payable No. 16.

Cash	
100,000.00	

Notes Payable	
	100,000.00

The analysis of this transaction is shown in the T accounts. Cash is increased by a debit for the amount of cash received, $100,000.00. Notes Payable is increased by a credit for the same amount, $100,000.00.

The journal entry to record this transaction is shown in Illustration 25-14.

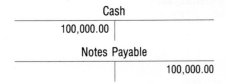

					GENERAL		CASH		
DATE	ACCOUNT TITLE	DOC. NO.	POST. REF.	DEBIT	CREDIT	DEBIT	CREDIT	
4 Notes Payable		NP16				10000000	10000000	

JOURNAL PAGE 12

Illustration 25-14
Entry to record issuance
of a note payable

When Oakwood's note payable is due on February 4, the amount of the note plus interest is paid to the bank.

February 4, 1989.
Paid Note Payable No. 16, $100,000.00, plus interest, $1,000.00; total, $101,000.00. Check No. 360.

Notes Payable	
100,000.00	

Expenditure — Other Charges, General Government	
1,000.00	

Cash	
	101,000.00

The analysis of this transaction is shown in the T accounts. Notes Payable is decreased by a debit, $100,000.00. Expenditure — Other Charges, General Government is increased by a debit for the amount of interest, $1,000.00. Cash is decreased by a credit for the total amount paid, $101,000.00.

The journal entry to record payment of the note payable is shown in Illustration 25-15.

		JOURNAL							PAGE 20	
							1	2	3	4
DATE	ACCOUNT TITLE		DOC. NO.	POST. REF.	GENERAL		CASH			
					DEBIT	CREDIT	DEBIT	CREDIT		
22	4 Notes Payable		C360		10000000			10100000		22
23	Expenditure—Other Charges, Gen. Gov't.				100000					23
24										24

Journalizing short-term investments. Most of Oakwood's property taxes, the major portion of the town's revenue, are collected by March 1 each year. Cash that will not be needed for several months is placed in short-term investments. Interest on these investments provides additional revenue.

March 1, 1989.
Paid for a 4-month, 8% certificate of deposit, $240,000.00. Check No. 375.

A document issued by a bank as evidence of money invested with the bank is called a certificate of deposit. The time and interest rate to be paid are included on the certificate.

The analysis of this transaction is shown in the T accounts. Investments—Short Term is increased by a debit for the amount of the certificate, $240,000.00. Cash is decreased by a credit for the same amount, $240,000.00.

The journal entry to record this transaction is shown in Illustration 25-16.

Illustration 25-15
Entry to record payment of a note payable with interest

Investments — Short Term	
240,000.00	

Cash	
	240,000.00

		JOURNAL							PAGE 24	
							1	2	3	4
DATE	ACCOUNT TITLE		DOC. NO.	POST. REF.	GENERAL		CASH			
					DEBIT	CREDIT	DEBIT	CREDIT		
19	Mar. 1 Investments — Short Term		C375		24000000			24000000		19
20										20

When the certificate of deposit is due on July 1, cash is received for the original cost of the investment plus interest revenue earned.

July 1, 1989.
Received for certificate of deposit due today, $240,000.00, plus interest, $6,400.00; total, $246,400.00. Receipt No. 562.

The analysis of this transaction is shown in the T accounts. Cash is increased by a debit for the amount of cash received, $246,400.00. Investments—Short Term is decreased by a credit for the certificate of deposit's original cost, $240,000.00. Interest Revenue is increased by a credit for the amount of interest earned, $6,400.00.

Illustration 25-16
Entry to record a short-term investment

Cash	
246,400.00	

Investments — Short Term	
	240,000.00

Interest Revenue	
	6,400.00

The journal entry to record this transaction is shown in Illustration 25-17.

DATE	ACCOUNT TITLE	DOC. NO.	POST. REF.	GENERAL DEBIT	GENERAL CREDIT	CASH DEBIT	CASH CREDIT	
22 July 1	Investments – Short Term	R562			2400000	2464000		22
23	Interest Revenue				64000			23
24								24
25								25

JOURNAL   PAGE 51

Illustration 25-17
Entry to record cash
received for a short-term
investment plus interest

ACCOUNTING TERMS

What is the meaning of each of the following?

1. not-for-profit organization
2. fund
3. expenditures
4. operating budget
5. appropriations
6. tax levy
7. encumbrance
8. general fixed assets
9. certificate of deposit

QUESTIONS FOR INDIVIDUAL STUDY

1. What is the major objective of a not-for-profit organization?
2. What are six types of not-for-profit organizations?
3. What are the four characteristics of a governmental organization that affect the accounting system?
4. How have the characteristics of governmental organizations affected the development of governmental accounting systems?
5. Which accounting practices are applied by both businesses and governmental organizations?
6. What restriction does a fund accounting system emphasize?
7. What is the accounting equation for governmental organizations?
8. When are governmental fund revenues recorded?
9. Preparing financial statements at the end of a fiscal period is an application of which accounting concept?
10. What are the two most common financial statements prepared by governmental organizations?
11. What is the primary purpose of budgets for all organizations?
12. What two control functions does an approved governmental budget serve?
13. What are the general procedures followed to prepare a governmental operating budget?
14. What accounts are affected, and how, by an entry to record the operating budget in a governmental organization?
15. When is property tax revenue recorded?
16. What accounts are affected, and how, when a governmental organization levies property taxes?

17. When are traffic fines recorded as revenue?
18. What accounts are affected, and how, when Oakwood collects traffic fines?
19. What do governmental organizations do with the current taxes that are not collected by the due date?
20. What is the purpose of using encumbrance accounts?
21. What two entries must be made when goods or services are received that have been encumbered?
22. Why may the amounts for an encumbrance entry and the related expenditure entry not always be the same amount?
23. What accounts are affected, and how, when a governmental organization buys a typewriter?
24. What accounts are affected, and how, when a governmental organization issues a note payable?
25. What accounts are affected, and how, when a governmental organization pays a note payable plus interest?
26. What accounts are affected, and how, when a governmental organization receives cash for its short-term investment plus interest?

CASES FOR MANAGEMENT DECISION

CASE 1 The town of Clifton has three funds in its accounting system—general, library, and roads. Clifton's new town manager, Jane Wilson, has questioned the necessity of having three separate governmental funds. Mrs. Wilson suggests combining all the funds into a single general fund. What do you recommend? Explain your answer.

CASE 2 Stephen Rehl, a new accounting clerk with the town of Bayside, has been struggling with accounting entries involving encumbrances. He suggests that no entries be made until goods or services are received. When goods are received then an expenditure would be recorded. Encumbrances would not be necessary and the final results would be the same. What is your response to Mr. Rehl's suggestion? Explain your answer.

APPLICATION PROBLEMS

PROBLEM 25-1   Recording governmental operating budgets

Three towns, Center, Tower, and Parker, approved their annual general fund operating budgets effective January 1 of the current year.

Instructions: Record the following operating budgets for each of the three towns on page 5 of a journal.

	Estimated Revenues	Appropriations	Budgetary Fund Balance
Center.........................	$1,056,000.00	$ 989,000.00	$67,000.00
Tower	793,500.00	789,200.00	4,300.00
Parker........................	1,764,000.00	1,722,500.00	41,500.00

PROBLEM 25-2   Recording governmental revenue

Lakeview's town council recently approved the town's general fund operating budget for the current year.

Instructions: Record the following selected transactions on page 15 of a journal. Source documents are abbreviated as follows: memorandum, M; receipt, R.

Jan. 1. Recorded current year's property tax levy: taxes receivable — current, $1,250,000.00; allowance for uncollectible taxes — current, $9,400.00; property tax revenue, $1,240,600.00. M78.
    8. Received for current taxes receivable, $97,600.00. R124.
  14. Received from traffic fines, $46.00. R137. (Other Revenue)
Feb. 11. Received for current taxes receivable, $72,350.00. R184.
  16. Received from parking meter receipts, $174.50. R202. (Other Revenue)
Mar. 1. Recorded reclassification of current taxes receivable to delinquent status, $46,800.00, and the accompanying allowance for uncollectible accounts, $9,400.00. M97.
  12. Received for delinquent taxes receivable, $9,700.00. R249.

PROBLEM 25-3   Recording governmental encumbrances, expenditures, and other transactions

The town of Plainville uses a general fund for all financial transactions. Expenditures are recorded by type of expenditure and by department. The four categories of expenditures are: personnel, supplies, other charges, and capital outlays. Departments are: General Government, Public Safety, Public Works, and Recreation.

Instructions: Record the following selected transactions completed during the current year. Use page 21 of a journal. Source documents are abbreviated as follows: check, C; memorandum, M; note payable, NP; receipt, R.

Jan. 11. Paid for electrical service in public works department, $185.00. C234.
  14. Encumbered estimated amount for supplies in public safety department, $125.00. M23.
  15. Issued a one-month, 10% note payable to First State Bank, $150,000.00. NP5.
  28. Paid for public safety department supplies, $128.00, encumbered January 14 per M23. M30 and C248.
Feb. 5. Paid for calculator for general government department, $255.00. C257. (Capital Outlays)
  15. Paid NP5, $150,000.00, plus interest, $1,250.00; total, $151,250.00. C269.
  28. Encumbered estimated amount for supplies in public works department, $176.00. M39.
Mar. 15. Paid for a 3-month, 6% certificate of deposit, $200,000.00. C286.
  18. Paid for public works department supplies, $169.50, encumbered February 28 per M39. M48 and C305.
  21. Paid for consultant's services in recreation department, $350.00. C312. (Personnel)
June 15. Received for certificate of deposit due today, $200,000.00, plus interest, $3,000.00; total, $203,000.00. R174.

ENRICHMENT PROBLEMS

MASTERY PROBLEM 25-M   Recording governmental transactions

The town of Elkton uses a general fund for all financial transactions. Expenditures are recorded by type of expenditure and by department. The four categories of expenditures are: personnel, supplies, other charges, and capital outlays. Departments are: General Government, Public Safety, Public Works, and Recreation.

Instructions: Record the following selected transactions completed during the current year. Use page 21 of a journal. Source documents are abbreviated as follows: check, C; memorandum, M; note payable, NP; receipt, R.

Jan. 2. Recorded current year's approved operating budget: estimated revenues, $1,265,000.00; appropriations, $1,214,000.00; budgetary fund balance, $51,000.00. M32.

2. Recorded current year's property tax levy: taxes receivable—current, $1,215,000.00; allowance for uncollectible taxes—current, $12,200.00; property tax revenue, $1,202,800.00. M33.

6. Received for current taxes receivable, $47,300.00. R95.

10. Paid for gas utility service in general government department, $224.00. C158.

12. Issued a 2-month, 9% note payable to First National Bank, $200,000.00. NP7.

16. Encumbered estimated amount for supplies in public works department, $155.00. M44.

20. Received from traffic fines, $125.00. R101. (Other Revenue)

30. Paid for lawn mower for public works department, $350.00. C172.

Feb. 6. Paid for public works department supplies, $160.00, encumbered January 16 per M44. M48 and C180.

24. Encumbered estimated amount for supplies in recreation department, $123.00. M59.

Mar. 1. Recorded reclassification of current taxes receivable to delinquent status, $61,400.00, and the accompanying allowance for uncollectible accounts, $12,200.00. M66.

12. Paid NP7, $200,000.00, plus interest, $3,000.00; total, $203,000.00. C212.

20. Paid for a 4-month, 6% certificate of deposit, $400,000.00. C224.

22. Paid for recreation department supplies, $121.00, encumbered February 24 per M59. M78 and C231.

Apr. 10. Received for delinquent taxes receivable, $11,000.00. R345.

25. Paid for consultant's services in recreation department, $400.00. C256. (Personnel)

July 20. Received for certificate of deposit due today, $400,000.00, plus interest, $8,000.00; total, $408,000.00. R487.

CHALLENGE PROBLEM 25-C   Recording governmental transactions

The town of Middleton uses a general fund for all financial transactions. Expenditures are recorded by type of expenditure and by department. The four categories of expenditures are: personnel, supplies, other charges, and capital outlays. Departments are: General Government, Public Safety, Public Works, and Recreation.

Instructions: Record the following selected transactions completed during the current year. Use page 32 of a journal. Source documents are abbreviated as follows: check, C; memorandum, M; note payable, NP; receipt, R.

Jan. 2. Recorded current year's approved operating budget: estimated revenues, $1,518,000.00; appropriations, $1,542,100.00; budgetary fund balance, $24,100.00. M78.

> (Note: Most towns prohibit deficit spending. In this case, a town would be prohibited from having a debit balance in the budgetary fund balance account. However, if sufficient fund equity is available at the beginning of a year, a town council may choose to appropriate more than the estimated revenues. The available fund equity would then be used for the amount that expenditures exceed revenues for the current period.)

2. Recorded current year's property tax levy: total amount of tax statements sent, $1,442,000.00; uncollectible taxes estimated at 2% of total tax levy. M79.

9. Received for current taxes receivable, $54,700.00. R101.

17. Paid for electric utility service in public works department, $276.00. C121.

20. Issued a 2-month, 10% note payable to Merchants National Bank, $150,000.00. NP12.

25. Encumbered estimated amount for supplies in public safety department, $160.00. M92.

Feb. 3. Received from parking meter receipts, $1,058.00. R142.

10. Paid for public safety department supplies, $152.00, encumbered January 25 per M92. M120 and C178.

21. Paid for swing set for recreation department, $475.00. C189. (Capital Outlays)

Mar. 1. Recorded reclassification of current taxes receivable to delinquent status, $173,100.00, and the accompanying allowance for uncollectible accounts, $28,840.00. M144.

15. Paid for a 4-month, 6% certificate of deposit, $500,000.00. C210.

20. Paid NP12, $150,000.00, plus interest. C220.

20. Received for delinquent taxes receivable, $12,500.00. R196.

Apr. 4. Encumbered estimated amount for printer in general government department, $580.00. M168. (Capital Outlays)

16. Paid for general government department printer, $598.00, encumbered April 4 per M168. M180 and C257.

July 15. Received for certificate of deposit due today, $500,000.00, plus interest. R279.

26 Financial Reporting for a Not-for-Profit Organization

ENABLING PERFORMANCE TASKS

After studying Chapter 26, you will be able to:
a. Identify accounting concepts and practices related to financial reporting for a not-for-profit governmental organization.
b. Complete selected end-of-fiscal-period work for a not-for-profit governmental organization.

Not-for-profit organizations report financial information, as do business organizations, by preparing financial statements periodically. *(CONCEPT: Accounting Period Cycle)* However, financial information needed for not-for-profit organizations differs from that needed for businesses. A business' performance is measured primarily through determining the amount of net income. Thus, the accounting records are designed to emphasize the measurement of net income. However, a not-for-profit organization's performance is measured primarily by the services provided and the efficiency with which resources are used. Therefore, a not-for-profit organization's financial statements are designed to provide information for the following purposes.

1. To make decisions about the use of resources.
2. To assess services provided and the ability to provide those services.
3. To assess management's financial accountability and performance.
4. To determine the assets, liabilities, and fund equity of the organization.

PREPARING A WORK SHEET FOR A GOVERNMENTAL ORGANIZATION

The town of Oakwood uses an eight-column work sheet similar to the one used by AquaPro, Inc., in Part 5. The work sheets differ in one set of columns. Oakwood's work sheet has Revenues/Expenditures Debit and Credit columns. AquaPro's work sheet has Income Statement Debit and Credit columns.

Recording a trial balance on a work sheet

A trial balance is entered in the Trial Balance columns as the first step in preparing a work sheet. All general ledger accounts except encumbrances are listed in the Account Title column in the same order as they appear in the general ledger. Only encumbrance accounts with balances are listed. The Trial Balance columns are totaled to prove the equality of debits and credits.

Oakwood's trial balance on December 31, 1989, is shown on the work sheet, Illustration 26-1.

Preparing adjustments on a work sheet

Some general ledger accounts for governmental funds need to be brought up to date before financial statements are prepared. Since governmental funds report expenditures and not expenses, no adjustments are needed for expense accounts. The actual amounts that have been spent and recorded as expenditures are the amounts reported.

Since governmental funds recognize revenues when the revenues become measurable and available, an adjusting entry may be needed to record some revenues.

Adjusting entries are planned on a work sheet. Oakwood makes adjustments to three accounts. (1) Inventory of Supplies. (2) Interest Revenue. (3) Reserve for Encumbrances—Current Year.

Inventory of supplies adjustment. When supplies are bought, an expenditure account is debited. Some supplies may be unused at the end of a fiscal period. These unused supplies should be reported as an asset. (CONCEPT: *Adequate Disclosure*) Thus, an adjustment is made at the end of a fiscal period to record the amount of supplies on hand as an asset. Expenditure accounts debited when supplies were bought are not adjusted. When an expenditure is made during a fiscal period, the expenditure is reported regardless of the purpose.

The total account balances of a governmental fund represent the equity of that fund. Thus, assets less liabilities equal total fund equity. However, unless reserved for a specified purpose, fund equity should represent resources that are available for appropriations and spending. The inventory of supplies will be used by the organization. Therefore, this asset is not available for spending. To show that this asset, Inventory of Supplies, is not available for other uses, an equal amount of fund equity is reserved. Thus, the amount is credited to a restricted fund equity account titled Reserve for Inventory of Supplies.

The analysis of the adjustment for supplies on hand is shown in the T accounts. Inventory of Supplies, an asset account, is increased by a debit for the amount of supplies on hand, $3,120.00. Reserve for Inventory of Supplies is increased by a credit for the same amount, $3,120.00.

Inventory of Supplies	
Adj. 3,120.00	

Reserve for Inventory of Supplies	
	Adj. 3,120.00

The adjustment for inventory of supplies is shown as adjustment (a) on the work sheet, lines 8 and 15, Illustration 26-1.

Illustration 26-1
Work sheet for a governmental organization

Town of Oakwood General Fund
Work Sheet
For Year Ended December 31, 1989

#	Account Title	Trial Balance Debit	Trial Balance Credit	Adjustments Debit	Adjustments Credit	Revenues/Expenditures Debit	Revenues/Expenditures Credit	Balance Sheet Debit	Balance Sheet Credit
1	Cash	74360.00						74360.00	
2	Taxes Receivable – Current								
3	Allow. for Uncoll. Taxes – Cur.								
4	Taxes Receivable – Delinquent	18640.00						18640.00	
5	Allow. for Uncoll. Taxes – Delin.		8750.00						8750.00
6	Interest Receivable			(b) 2940.00				2940.00	
7	Allow. for Uncoll. Interest				(b) 588.00				588.00
8	Inventory of Supplies			(a) 3120.00				3120.00	
9	Investments – Short Term								
10	Accounts Payable		36125.00						36125.00
11	Notes Payable								
12	Unreserved Fund Balance		157050.0						157050.0
13	Res. for Encum. – Current Year		2640.00	(c) 2640.00					
14	Res. for Encum. – Prior Year				(c) 2640.00		2640.00		
15	Reserve for Inv. of Supplies				(a) 3120.00				3120.00
16	Property Tax Revenue		1494000.00				1494000.00		
17	Interest Revenue		3785.00		(b) 2352.00		6137.00		
18	Other Revenue		2625.00				2625.00		
19	Expend.-Personnel, Gen. Govt.	263175.00				263175.00			
20	Expend.-Supplies, Gen. Govt.	11940.00				11940.00			
21	Expend.-Other Chgs. Gen. Govt.	112380.00				112380.00			
22	Expend.- Cap. Outlays, Gen. Gov't	16000.00				16000.00			
23	Expend.-Personnel, Public Safety	488650.00				488650.00			
24	Expend.-Supplies, Public Safety	19790.00				19790.00			
25	Expend.- Other Chgs. Public Safety	152635.00				152635.00			
26	Expend.- Cap. Outlays, Public Safety	89350.00				89350.00			
27	Expend.-Personnel, Public Works	113300.00				113300.00			
28	Expend.- Supplies, Public Works	5540.00				5540.00			
29	Expend.-Other Chgs. Public Works	47340.00				47340.00			
30	Expend.- Cap. Outlays, Public Works	51175.00				51175.00			
31	Expend.-Personnel, Recreation	58110.00				58110.00			
32	Expend.-Supplies, Recreation	1960.00				1960.00			
33	Expend.- Other Chgs. Recreation	25105.00				25105.00			
34	Expend.- Cap. Outlays, Recreation	11540.00				11540.00			
35	Estimated Revenues	1502500.00				1502500.00			
36	Appropriations		1472800.00				1472800.00		
37	Budgetary Fund Balance		29700.00				29700.00		
38	Encum.-Supplies, Public Safety	2640.00				2640.00			
39		3066130.00	3066130.00	8700.00	8700.00	2973130.00	3007902.00	99060.00	64288.00
40	Excess of Revenues Over Expend.					34772.00			34772.00
41						3007902.00	3007902.00	99060.00	99060.00

Interest revenue adjustment. Interest is assessed on all delinquent taxes. Interest becomes measurable and available when it occurs. Thus, to bring the accounts up to date and record revenue earned but not collected at the end of the year, an adjustment is made.

Oakwood's interest due but not yet collected on December 31, 1989, is $2,940.00. Past experience has shown that approximately 20% of this amount, $588.00 ($2,940.00 × 20%), will not be collected. Thus, the amount expected to be collected, $2,352.00 ($2,940.00 − $588.00), is recorded as revenue.

Interest Receivable	
Adj. 2,940.00	

Allowance for Uncollectible Interest	
	Adj. 588.00

Interest Revenue	
	Adj. 2,352.00

The analysis of the adjustment for interest revenue and allowance for uncollectible interest is shown in the T accounts. Interest Receivable, an asset account, is increased by a debit for the amount earned but not collected, $2,940.00. Allowance for Uncollectible Interest, a contra asset account, is increased by a credit for the amount of interest that is not expected to be collected, $588.00. Interest Revenue is increased by a credit for the amount of interest that is expected to be collected, $2,352.00.

The adjustment for interest revenue is shown as adjustment (b) on the work sheet, lines 6, 7, and 17, Illustration 26-1.

Reserve for encumbrances — current year adjustment. At the end of a fiscal year, a governmental organization may have outstanding encumbrances — orders that have not yet been delivered. When goods are delivered that were encumbered against the preceding year's appropriations, the amount should not be recorded as an expenditure of the current period. Therefore, at the end of a fiscal period, the balance of Reserve for Encumbrances — Current Year, the amount of encumbrances outstanding, should be reclassified to prior year status. When prior year's orders arrive, they can be debited to Reserve for Encumbrances — Prior Year, rather than current year's expenditures. This procedure prevents charging expenditures of one year to another year's appropriations.

On December 31, 1989, the balance of Oakwood's Reserve for Encumbrances — Current Year is $2,640.00. The analysis of the adjustment to reclassify this fund equity account is shown in the T accounts.

Reserve for Encumbrances — Current Year	
Adj. 2,640.00	Bal. 2,640.00

Reserve for Encumbrances — Prior Year	
	Adj. 2,640.00

Reserve for Encumbrances — Current Year is decreased by a debit, $2,640.00. Reserve for Encumbrances — Prior Year is increased by a credit, $2,640.00. Reserve for Encumbrances — Current Year has a zero balance after this adjustment. Reserve for Encumbrances — Prior Year has a $2,640.00 balance after this adjustment.

The adjustment for reserve for encumbrances — current year is shown as adjustment (c) on the work sheet, lines 13 and 14, Illustration 26-1.

Extending amounts to Revenues/ Expenditures and Balance Sheet columns

All asset, liability, and fund equity account balances except Reserve for Encumbrances — Prior Year are extended to the Balance Sheet columns as shown on the work sheet, lines 1 through 12 and line 15, Illustration 26-1.

The reserve for encumbrances accounts are listed as balance sheet accounts in the chart of accounts. During a fiscal period, the current year reserve for encumbrances account is used as a balancing account for the encumbrance accounts. Fund equity is not actually reduced when encumbrances are recorded. Therefore, the current year reserve for encumbrances account is considered to be a budgetary account until accounts are closed at the end of a fiscal period. Therefore, the balance of Reserve for Encumbrances — Prior Year is extended to the Revenues/Expenditures columns as shown on the work sheet, line 14.

The balances of all temporary accounts are also extended to a work sheet's Revenues/Expenditures columns. Temporary accounts are those accounts that are closed at the end of each fiscal period. Temporary accounts include all revenue, expenditure, and budgetary accounts. Revenue accounts are extended to the Revenues/Expenditures columns as shown on the work sheet, lines 16 through 18. Expenditure accounts are shown on lines 19 through 34. Budgetary accounts are shown on line 14 and lines 35 through 38.

Completing a governmental organization's work sheet

The Revenues/Expenditures and Balance Sheet columns are totaled. Totals are written as shown on the work sheet, line 39, Illustration 26-1. The difference between the Revenues/Expenditures Credit column total and the Debit column total is the excess of revenues over expenditures. If the Debit column total is larger, the difference is the excess of expenditures over revenues.

Oakwood has an excess of revenues over expenditures figured as follows.

Revenues/Expenditures Credit column total (line 39)............	$3,007,902.00
Less Revenues/Expenditures Debit column total (line 39)	2,973,130.00
Equals excess of revenues over expenditures	$ 34,772.00

The excess of revenues over expenditures, *$34,772.00*, is written under the work sheet's Revenues/Expenditures Debit column total on line 40 to make the two Revenues/Expenditures columns balance. The words *Excess of Revenues Over Expend.* are written in the Account Title column on the same line.

Oakwood's excess of revenues over expenditures, $34,772.00, is also written under the Balance Sheet Credit column total on line 40 to make the two Balance Sheet columns balance.

> When there is an excess of expenditures over revenues, the excess amount is written on a work sheet in the Revenues/Expenditures Credit and Balance Sheet Debit columns.

After the excess of revenues over expenditures is recorded on the work sheet, the last four columns are totaled again. Each pair of these new totals, as shown on line 41, must be the same. Oakwood's Revenues/Expenditures column totals are the same, $3,007,902.00. The Balance Sheet column totals are the same, $99,060.00. When the totals of each pair of columns are the same, the work sheet is assumed to be correct. The work sheet is then ruled as shown on line 41.

After the work sheet is completed, expenditures in the Revenues/Expenditures Debit column are totaled for each department. These totals are used in the preparation of financial statements. Departmental totals are written in small numbers below the amount of the last listed expenditure for the department. For General Government, lines 19 through 22, the total, $403,495.00, is written below line 22. For Public Safety, lines 23 through 26, the total, $750,425.00, is written below line 26. For Public Works, lines 27 through 30, the total, $217,355.00, is written below line 30. For Recreation, lines 31 through 34, the total, $96,715.00, is written below line 34.

PREPARING FINANCIAL STATEMENTS FOR A GOVERNMENTAL ORGANIZATION

Financial statements are prepared to report a governmental organization's financial activity for a fiscal period and financial condition on a specific date. Financial statements are prepared for each governmental fund. (CONCEPT: Adequate Disclosure) Oakwood prepares two financial statements for its general fund. (1) Statement of revenues, expenditures, and changes in fund balance—budget and actual. (2) Balance sheet. In the preparation of financial statements, accounting concepts are applied the same way from one fiscal period to the next. (CONCEPT: Consistent Reporting)

Statement of revenues, expenditures, and changes in fund balance—budget and actual

A statement of revenues, expenditures, and changes in fund balance— budget and actual reports the amount of revenues earned and expenditures made for a fiscal period. The changes in the unreserved fund balance from the beginning to the end of the fiscal period are also reported. (CONCEPT:

Accounting Period Cycle) In addition, actual revenues, expenditures, and unreserved fund balance are compared with budgeted amounts for a fiscal period. *(CONCEPT: Accounting Period Cycle)*

Oakwood's general fund statement of revenues, expenditures, and changes in fund balance—budget and actual for the fiscal year ended December 31, 1989, is shown in Illustration 26-2.

	Budget	Actual	Variance—Favorable (Unfavorable)
Town of Oakwood General Fund Statement of Revenues, Expenditures, and Changes in Fund Balance—Budget and Actual For Year Ended December 31, 1989			
Revenues:			
Property Tax Revenue.................................	$1,494,000.00	$1,494,000.00	—
Interest Revenue	6,000.00	6,137.00	$ 137.00
Other Revenue	2,500.00	2,625.00	125.00
Total Revenues..	$1,502,500.00	$1,502,762.00	$ 262.00
Expenditures:			
General Government..................................	$ 405,050.00	$ 403,495.00	$1,555.00
Public Safety...	752,650.00	750,425.00	2,225.00
Public Works...	218,000.00	217,355.00	645.00
Recreation	97,100.00	96,715.00	385.00
Total Expenditures....................................	$1,472,800.00	$1,467,990.00	$4,810.00
Excess of Revenues Over Expenditures	$ 29,700.00	$ 34,772.00	$5,072.00
Less Outstanding Encumbrances, Dec. 31, 1989...........	—	2,640.00	(2,640.00)
Increase in Unreserved Fund Balance for Year	$ 29,700.00	$ 32,132.00	$2,432.00
Unreserved Fund Balance, Jan. 1, 1989	15,705.00	15,705.00	—
Unreserved Fund Balance, Dec. 31, 1989................	$ 45,405.00	$ 47,837.00	$2,432.00

This statement has three sections: (1) revenues, (2) expenditures, and (3) changes in unreserved fund balance. This statement has three amount columns: (1) Budget, (2) Actual, and (3) Variance—Favorable (Unfavorable).

Information used to prepare the Budget column is obtained from the annual operating budget. Information needed to prepare the Actual column is obtained from the work sheet's Revenues/Expenditures columns. The beginning fund balance that is used in both the Budget and Actual columns is obtained from the previous year's balance sheet.

The following steps are used to prepare a statement of revenues, expenditures, and changes in fund balance—budget and actual.

Illustration 26-2
Statement of revenues, expenditures, and changes in fund balance—budget and actual

1 List revenues by source. Oakwood has three sources of revenues: property taxes, interest, and other. The total of all three sources of revenues is also shown.

2 List expenditures as totals for each department. Departments are responsible for controlling expenditures through budgeting and appropriations of specific amounts for each department. Thus, to aid the control process, amounts actually spent are reported for each responsible department. The total expenditures for the whole fund are also shown on the statement.

3 Figure the excess of revenues over expenditures.

If expenditures exceed revenues, the difference is labeled "excess of expenditures over revenues."

4 Figure the changes in the unreserved fund balance.
- Record any outstanding encumbrances for the current year. Outstanding encumbrances are not deducted in figuring excess of revenues over expenditures. However, funds will be required in the future when the goods for which the encumbrances were made are delivered. Therefore, current year's encumbrances should be reported as a reduction in the current year's excess of revenues rather than in the next year when goods are paid for. Because no amount is budgeted for the encumbrances, the amount shown in the budget column is zero.
- Deduct outstanding encumbrances from excess of revenues over expenditures to determine the change in the unreserved fund balance for the year. The remaining excess of revenues over expenditures is an increase in the unreserved fund balance for the current year.
- Record the beginning unreserved fund balance. This January 1 balance is obtained from the previous year's balance sheet.
- Figure the ending unreserved fund balance. The increase in the unreserved fund balance for the year plus the beginning unreserved fund balance equals the ending unreserved fund balance.

Each amount recorded in the Variance column is the difference between the budget and actual amounts for the item. For example, the variance for other revenue is $125.00 (actual, $2,625.00, *less* budget, $2,500.00). Variances are considered favorable if actual results are better than the amount budgeted for that item. When actual revenues are *more than* budgeted revenues, variances are favorable. When actual revenues are *less* than budgeted revenues, variances are unfavorable. When actual expenditures are *less than* budgeted expenditures, variances are favorable. When actual expenditures are *more* than budgeted expenditures, variances are unfavorable. A reserve for encumbrances variance has the same effect as an expenditure variance. Because encumbrances are not budgeted, any variance will be unfavorable since an actual encumbrance will cause an increase. Unfavorable variances are indicated by placing the amounts in parentheses.

Balance sheet for a governmental organization

A governmental fund balance sheet reports information about assets, liabilities, and fund equity for a specific date, usually the last day of a fiscal period. *(CONCEPT: Adequate Disclosure)*

Assets and liabilities reported on a governmental fund balance sheet have similar characteristics to those reported on a corporation's balance sheet. However, a governmental fund does not have specific owners. Therefore, a governmental fund has no owner's equity section. Instead, the difference between assets and liabilities is reported as fund equity. Thus, unless restricted, fund equity represents the amount that is available for expenditures or encumbrances.

Oakwood's general fund balance sheet for December 31, 1989, is shown in Illustration 26-3.

Town of Oakwood General Fund Balance Sheet December 31, 1989		
ASSETS		
Cash		$74,360.00
Taxes Receivable—Delinquent	$18,640.00	
Less Allowance for Uncollectible Taxes—Delinquent	8,750.00	9,890.00
Interest Receivable	$ 2,940.00	
Less Allowance for Uncollectible Interest	588.00	2,352.00
Inventory of Supplies		3,120.00
Total Assets		$89,722.00
LIABILITIES AND FUND EQUITY		
Liabilities:		
Accounts Payable		$36,125.00
Fund Equity:		
Unreserved Fund Balance	$47,837.00	
Reserve for Encumbrances—Prior Year	2,640.00	
Reserve for Inventory of Supplies	3,120.00	
Total Fund Equity		53,597.00
Total Liabilities and Fund Equity		$89,722.00

Illustration 26-3
Balance sheet for a
governmental organization

On December 31, 1989, Oakwood's fund equity, consisting of three fund equity account balances, is $53,597.00. The unreserved fund balance, $47,837.00, represents equity in the fund that has no restrictions. With proper authorization, Oakwood may appropriate this amount for expenditures.

Two of the fund equity account balances are reserved for specific purposes. The reserve for encumbrances—prior year, $2,640.00, is an amount

Reserve for Encumbrances — Prior Year

Jan. 1990	2,640.00	Bal.	2,640.00

Cash

	Jan. 1990	2,640.00

of equity set aside for an encumbrance outstanding on December 31, 1989. This encumbrance will be paid for when the order arrives in 1990. When goods arrive and are paid for in 1990 for an order that was encumbered in 1989, Reserve for Encumbrances — Prior Year is debited rather than Expenditures. This transaction is analyzed in the T accounts.

Payment of the prior year's order closes the reserve for encumbrances account. The entry also avoids recording an expenditure in 1990 for goods ordered in 1989.

The reserve for inventory of supplies, $3,120.00, represents the equity in inventory of supplies. Although supplies are assets, they are available for use, not spending. Therefore, part of the fund equity is reserved for the amount of supplies on hand. This reserve avoids appropriating the amount of equity that is represented by the asset supplies.

On a governmental fund balance sheet, total assets must equal total liabilities and fund equity. Oakwood's balance sheet has total assets of $89,722.00. The total liabilities and fund equity is the same amount. The balance sheet is in balance and assumed to be correct.

RECORDING ADJUSTING AND CLOSING ENTRIES FOR A GOVERNMENTAL ORGANIZATION

Adjusting and closing entries are journalized and posted to the general ledger accounts for governmental funds as they are for businesses.

Adjusting entries for a governmental organization

Illustration 26-4
Adjusting entries for a
governmental organization

Oakwood's adjusting entries recorded on December 31, 1989, are shown in Illustration 26-4.

	DATE	ACCOUNT TITLE	DOC. NO.	POST. REF.	GENERAL DEBIT	GENERAL CREDIT	CASH DEBIT	CASH CREDIT	
1	1989	*Adjusting Entries*							1
2	Dec. 31	Inventory of Supplies			3 1 2 0 00				2
3		Reserve for Inventory of Supplies				3 1 2 0 00			3
4	31	Interest Receivable			2 9 4 0 00				4
5		Allowance for Uncollectible Interest				5 8 8 00			5
6		Interest Revenue				2 3 5 2 00			6
7	31	Reserve for Encumbrances—Current Year			2 6 4 0 00				7
8		Reserve for Encumbrances—Prior Year				2 6 4 0 00			8
9									9
10									10
11									11

JOURNAL — PAGE 102

Information needed for Oakwood's adjusting entries is obtained from the work sheet's Adjustments columns, Illustration 26-1.

Closing entries for a governmental organization

Oakwood's closing entries recorded on December 31, 1989, are shown in Illustration 26-5.

							GENERAL		CASH	
	DATE	ACCOUNT TITLE	DOC. NO.	POST. REF.			DEBIT	CREDIT	DEBIT	CREDIT
9		*Closing Entries*								
10	31	Property Tax Revenue					1494000000			
11		Interest Revenue					613700			
12		Other Revenue					262500			
13		Unreserved Fund Balance						150276200		
14	31	Unreserved Fund Balance					146799000			
15		Expenditure—Personnel, Gen. Gov't.						2631 7500		
16		Expenditure—Supplies, Gen. Gov't.						1194000		
17		Expenditure—Other Charges, Gen. Gov't.						1123 8000		
18		Expenditure—Capital Outlays, Gen. Gov't.						1600000		
19		Expenditure—Personnel, Public Safety						4886500		
20		Expenditure—Supplies, Public Safety						1979000		
21		Expenditure—Other Charges, Public Safety						1526 3500		
22		Expenditure—Capital Outlays, Public Safety						8935000		
23		Expenditure—Personnel, Public Works						1133 0000		
24		Expenditure—Supplies, Public Works						554000		
25		Expenditure—Other Charges, Public Works						4734000		
26		Expenditure—Capital Outlays, Public Works						5117500		
27		Expenditure—Personnel, Recreation						5811000		
28		Expenditure—Supplies, Recreation						196000		
29		Expenditure—Other Charges, Recreation						251 0500		
30		Expenditure—Capital Outlays, Recreation						1154000		
31	31	Appropriations					1472 80000			
32		Budgetary Fund Balance					2970000			
33		Estimated Revenues						150250000		
34	31	Unreserved Fund Balance					264000			
35		Encumbrance—Supplies, Public Safety						264000		

JOURNAL — PAGE 102 — 1 2 3 4

Information needed for Oakwood's closing entries is obtained from the work sheet's Revenues/Expenditures columns. Oakwood records four entries to close the temporary and budgetary accounts.

Illustration 26-5
Closing entries for a governmental organization

1. Close all revenue accounts to the unreserved fund balance account as shown on lines 10 through 13 of the journal, Illustration 26-5.
2. Close all expenditure accounts to the unreserved fund balance account as shown on lines 14 through 30 of the journal.
3. Close the budgetary accounts. At the beginning of the fiscal year, estimated revenues and appropriations were recorded based on the approved operating budget. This entry provides control by permitting comparisons of estimated versus actual revenue and appropriations versus expenditures. At the end of the fiscal year, these budgetary accounts are no longer needed. Thus they are closed as shown on lines 31 through 33 of the journal. This entry is the opposite of the original entry to record the operating budget.
4. Close the outstanding encumbrance accounts to the unreserved fund balance account as shown on lines 34 and 35 of the journal. This entry reduces the unreserved fund balance account by the amount of the outstanding encumbrance for supplies, public safety, $2,640.00.

The balance of Reserve for Encumbrances — Prior Year, $2,640.00, shown in the Revenues/Expenditures Credit column of Oakwood's work sheet, Illustration 26-1, has been a budgetary account balance. Thus the account balance is listed in the work sheet's Revenue column. However, after the outstanding encumbrance account is closed to Unreserved Fund Balance, Reserve for Encumbrances — Prior Year is considered a fund equity account. The account therefore is not closed even though it has an amount in the work sheet's Revenues/Expenditures Credit column. This account balance now is the amount of total fund equity that is reserved for outstanding encumbrances.

After closing entries are posted, all temporary accounts have zero balances and are prepared for a new fiscal period. The difference between revenues and expenditures has been transferred to the unreserved fund balance account. Fund equity amounts that are not available for appropriations are recorded in reserve accounts.

PREPARING A POST-CLOSING TRIAL BALANCE FOR A GOVERNMENTAL ORGANIZATION

After all end-of-fiscal-period activities are complete, a post-closing trial balance is prepared to prove the equality of debits and credits in the account balances. Oakwood's post-closing trial balance is shown in Illustration 26-6.

Debits and credits on Oakwood's post-closing trial balance both equal $99,060.00. Debit and credit accounts are in balance. The general ledger accounts are ready for the new fiscal period. (CONCEPT: Accounting Period Cycle)

Town of Oakwood General Fund
Post-Closing Trial Balance
December 31, 1989

Cash	$74,360.00	
Taxes Receivable — Delinquent	18,640.00	
Allowance for Uncollectible Taxes — Delinquent		$ 8,750.00
Interest Receivable	2,940.00	
Allowance for Uncollectible Interest		588.00
Inventory of Supplies	3,120.00	
Accounts Payable		36,125.00
Reserve for Encumbrances — Prior Year		2,640.00
Reserve for Inventory of Supplies		3,120.00
Unreserved Fund Balance		47,837.00
	$99,060.00	$99,060.00

Illustration 26-6
Post-closing trial balance
for a governmental
organization

QUESTIONS FOR INDIVIDUAL STUDY

1. How is a not-for-profit organization's performance measured?
2. For what purposes are financial statements prepared for a not-for-profit organization?
3. What is the first step in preparing a work sheet for a governmental organization?
4. For what three accounts does Oakwood make adjustments on its work sheet before financial statements are prepared?
5. What is the purpose of an adjustment for Inventory of Supplies?
6. What two accounts are affected, and how, when an inventory of supplies adjustment is recorded for a governmental organization?
7. What is the purpose of an adjustment for Interest Revenue?
8. What accounts are affected, and how, when an interest revenue adjustment is recorded?
9. What is the purpose of an adjustment for Reserve for Encumbrances — Current Year?

10. What accounts are affected, and how, when an adjustment for Reserve for Encumbrances — Current Year is recorded?
11. What are the temporary accounts of a governmental organization?
12. How is the excess of revenue over expenditures figured on a work sheet of a governmental organization?
13. Preparing financial statements for each governmental fund is an application of which accounting concept?
14. What two financial statements does Oakwood prepare for its general fund?
15. Preparing financial statements the same way from one fiscal period to the next is an application of which accounting concept?
16. What does a statement of revenues, expenditures, and changes in fund balance — budget and actual report?
17. What are the three sections of a statement of revenues, expenditures, and changes in fund balance — budget and actual?

18. What are the three amount columns on a statement of revenues, expenditures, and changes in fund balance — budget and actual?

19. From where is the information obtained to prepare a statement of revenues, expenditures, and changes in fund balance — budget and actual?

20. What steps are followed in preparing a statement of revenues, expenditures, and changes in fund balance — budget and actual?

21. What does the amount in the Variance column of the statement of revenues,

expenditures, and changes in fund balance — budget and actual represent?

22. What are favorable variances on a statement of revenues, expenditures and changes in fund balance — budget and actual?

23. What does a governmental fund balance sheet report?

24. How is the difference between assets and liabilities reported on a governmental fund balance sheet?

25. What does fund equity on a governmental fund balance sheet represent?

CASES FOR MANAGEMENT DECISION

CASE 1 The town of Piketown's statement of revenue, expenditures, and changes in fund balance — budget and actual lists expenditures by type of expenditure. Expenditures listed are personnel, supplies, other charges, and capital outlays. Ben Zelhart, a new accountant, suggested that expenditures be reported on this statement by departmental organization. Do you agree with Mr. Zelhart? Explain your response.

CASE 2 Jill Embry, a new accounting clerk for the town of Plainville, recorded the closing

entries for the current year. Miss Embry questions the necessity of making a closing entry for encumbrance accounts with balances. She suggests not closing the encumbrances. Then when items are received for which the encumbrances were recorded, make the regular journal entries. That is, (1) reverse the encumbrance entry and (2) debit Expenditures and credit Cash. Do you agree with Miss Embry? Explain your response.

APPLICATION PROBLEMS

PROBLEM 26-1   Preparing a work sheet for a governmental organization

The town of Fairview uses a general fund. The trial balance for December 31 of the current year is recorded on a work sheet in the working papers accompanying this textbook.

Instructions: Complete the work sheet. The following information is needed for the adjustments.

Unused supplies on hand $3,430.00
Interest revenue due but not collected 2,780.00
An estimated 20% of interest revenue due will not be collected.
Reserve for encumbrances for current year is reclassified to prior-year status.

The work sheet prepared in this problem is needed to complete Problems 26-2, 26-3, and 26-4.

PROBLEM 26-2   Preparing a statement of revenues, expenditures, and changes in fund balance — budget and actual for a governmental organization

The work sheet prepared in Problem 26-1 is needed to complete this problem.

The town of Fairview's general fund operating budget for the current fiscal year is as follows.

Town of Fairview
Annual Operating Budget — General Fund
For Year Ended December 31, 19--

ESTIMATED REVENUES

Property Taxes...	$1,459,000.00	
Interest	7,200.00	
Other	8,750.00	
Total Estimated Revenues................................		$1,474,950.00

ESTIMATED EXPENDITURES AND BUDGETARY FUND BALANCE

General Government:		
Personnel..	$ 250,120.00	
Supplies	13,360.00	
Other Charges	124,740.00	
Capital Outlays	14,600.00	
Total General Government		$ 402,820.00
Public Safety:		
Personnel..	$ 464,740.00	
Supplies	22,000.00	
Other Charges	168,460.00	
Capital Outlays	81,270.00	
Total Public Safety		736,470.00
Public Works:		
Personnel..	$ 107,730.00	
Supplies	6,160.00	
Other Charges	52,250.00	
Capital Outlays	46,350.00	
Total Public Works		212,490.00
Recreation:		
Personnel..	$ 55,350.00	
Supplies	2,170.00	
Other Charges	27,780.00	
Capital Outlays	10,460.00	
Total Recreation		95,760.00
Total Estimated Expenditures		$1,447,540.00
Budgetary Fund Balance................................		27,410.00
Total Estimated Expenditures and Budgetary Fund Balance ...		$1,474,950.00

Instructions: Prepare a statement of revenues, expenditures, and changes in fund balance— budget and actual for the year ended December 31 of the current year. The unreserved fund balance on January 1 was $39,244.00.

The statement of revenues, expenditures, and changes in fund balance—budget and actual prepared in this problem is needed to complete Problem 26-3.

PROBLEM 26-3   Preparing a balance sheet for a governmental organization

The work sheet and statement of revenues, expenditures, and changes in fund balance—budget and actual prepared in Problems 26-1 and 26-2 are needed to complete this problem.

Instructions: Prepare a balance sheet for December 31 of the current year.

PROBLEM 26-4   Recording adjusting and closing entries for a governmental organization

The work sheet prepared in Problem 26-1 is needed to complete this problem.

Instructions: 1. Record the adjusting entries on page 10 of a journal.
2. Record the closing entries. Continue using page 10 of the journal.

ENRICHMENT PROBLEMS

MASTERY PROBLEM 26-M   Completing end-of-fiscal-period work for a governmental organization

The town of Belton uses a general fund. The trial balance for December 31 of the current year is recorded on a work sheet in the working papers accompanying this textbook.

Instructions: 1. Complete the work sheet. The following information is needed for the adjustments.

Unused supplies on hand $2,900.00
Interest revenue due but not collected 2,350.00
An estimated 20% of interest revenue due will not be collected.
Reserve for encumbrances for current year is reclassified to prior-year status.

Belton's general fund operating budget for the current fiscal year is as follows.

Town of Belton
Annual Operating Budget—General Fund
For Year Ended December 31, 19--

ESTIMATED REVENUES

Property Taxes	$1,275,000.00	
Interest	7,250.00	
Other	7,750.00	
Total Estimated Revenues		$1,290,000.00

ESTIMATED EXPENDITURES AND BUDGETARY FUND BALANCE

General Government:		
Personnel..	$ 213,750.00	
Supplies...	11,360.00	
Other Charges	106,700.00	
Capital Outlays....................................	12,390.00	
Total General Government...........................		$ 344,200.00
Public Safety:		
Personnel..	$ 397,590.00	
Supplies...	18,900.00	
Other Charges	144,290.00	
Capital Outlays....................................	69,320.00	
Total Public Safety................................		630,100.00
Public Works:		
Personnel..	$ 92,270.00	
Supplies...	5,280.00	
Other Charges	44,770.00	
Capital Outlays....................................	39,680.00	
Total Public Works.................................		182,000.00
Recreation:		
Personnel..	$ 47,220.00	
Supplies...	1,880.00	
Other Charges	23,690.00	
Capital Outlays....................................	8,910.00	
Total Recreation		81,700.00
Total Estimated Expenditures.......................		$1,238,000.00
Budgetary Fund Balance.............................		52,000.00
Total Estimated Expenditures and Budgetary Fund Balance...		$1,290,000.00

2. Prepare a statement of revenues, expenditures, and changes in fund balance—budget and actual for the year ended December 31 of the current year. The unreserved fund balance on January 1 was $33,550.00.

3. Prepare a balance sheet for December 31 of the current year.

4. Record the adjusting and closing entries on page 12 of a journal.

CHALLENGE PROBLEM 26-C   Completing end-of-fiscal-period work for a governmental organization

The town of Copperhill uses a general fund. The trial balance for December 31 of the current year is recorded on a work sheet in the working papers accompanying this textbook.

Instructions: 1. Complete the work sheet. The following information is needed for adjustments.

Unused supplies on hand...	$3,582.00
Interest revenue due but not collected................................	5,080.00

An estimated 20% of interest revenue due will not be collected.
Reserve for encumbrances for current year is reclassified to prior-year status.

Copperhill's general fund operating budget for the current fiscal year follows. Copperhill's town council permits departmental managers to exceed budgeted amounts for supplies, other charges, and capital outlays. However, total amounts expended for these three types of expenditure must be within the total budget amounts for these three items within each department.

Copperhill is prohibited from deficit spending. However, if sufficient funds are on hand at the beginning of a year, the town council may choose to appropriate more than the estimated revenues. Sufficient funds are on hand when the beginning fund balance plus estimated revenues equals or exceeds appropriations.

Town of Copperhill
Annual Operating Budget—General Fund
For Year Ended December 31, 19--

ESTIMATED REVENUES AND BUDGETARY FUND BALANCE

Property Taxes	$1,457,900.00	
Interest	13,160.00	
Other	16,580.00	
Total Estimated Revenues		$1,487,640.00
Budgetary Fund Balance		23,620.00
Estimated Revenues and Budgetary Fund Balance		$1,511,260.00

ESTIMATED EXPENDITURES

General Government:		
Personnel	$ 260,480.00	
Supplies	14,280.00	
Other Charges	130,240.00	
Capital Outlays	15,130.00	
Total General Government		$ 420,130.00
Public Safety:		
Personnel	$ 484,610.00	
Supplies	23,080.00	
Other Charges	176,920.00	
Capital Outlays	84,620.00	
Total Public Safety		769,230.00
Public Works:		
Personnel	$ 113,300.00	
Supplies	6,660.00	
Other Charges	53,320.00	
Capital Outlays	48,875.00	
Total Public Works		222,155.00
Recreation:		
Personnel	$ 56,855.00	
Supplies	2,990.00	
Other Charges	28,925.00	
Capital Outlays	10,975.00	
Total Recreation		99,745.00
Total Estimated Expenditures		$1,511,260.00

2. Prepare a statement of revenues, expenditures, and changes in fund balance—budget and actual for the year ended December 31 of the current year. The unreserved fund balance on January 1 was $60,450.00.

3. Prepare a balance sheet for December 31 of the current year.

4. Record the adjusting and closing entries on page 18 of a journal.

Appendix
Electronic Spreadsheet Accounting

Accountants regularly use paper with lines, columns, and rows to organize, record, and analyze financial data. This paper is frequently referred to as work sheet paper, columnar paper, or analysis paper. Computer software is available that provides a form on the computer monitor similar to the accountant's analysis paper. A form generated by computer software and consisting of multiple rows and columns in which data can be entered and analyzed is called an electronic spreadsheet. An electronic spreadsheet can be used the same way analysis paper is used for preparing financial statements, work sheets, and budgets, as well as comparing alternatives and measuring results. However, an electronic spreadsheet is faster, more efficient, and more versatile than analysis paper.

ELECTRONIC SPREADSHEETS

Analysis paper has been used for years to answer "what if" kinds of business questions. Answering these "what if" questions requires a number of changes in numeric data. When changes are made manually, amounts must be erased and new amounts must be entered. Also, totals must be recalculated, which increases the possibility of errors. A new version must also be manually prepared for each different change of data if several different "what if" questions are being compared. Therefore, many hours may be spent in preparing a number of versions manually.

Using an electronic spreadsheet eliminates the need to manually erase data and recalculate totals when a change is made. New data are entered into the computer to replace existing data. Formulas are entered into the spreadsheet to tell the computer to recalculate totals in a matter of seconds each time a change is made. Therefore, several versions of the spreadsheet can be prepared in minutes. In addition, most spreadsheet software has the ability to print the results appearing on the computer monitor.

Parts of an electronic spreadsheet

The arrangement of an electronic spreadsheet is similar to analysis paper except a spreadsheet may have more columns and rows available for recording data. The basic parts of a typical electronic spreadsheet are shown in Illustration A-1.

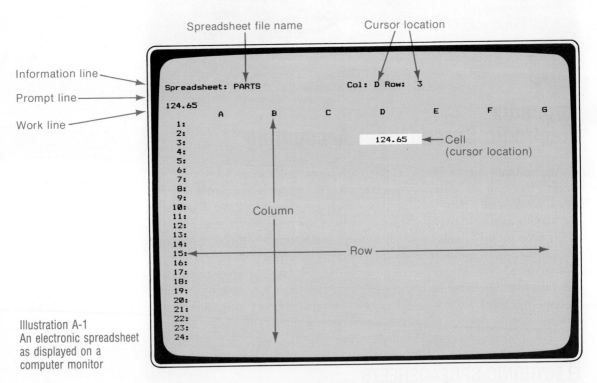

Illustration A-1
An electronic spreadsheet as displayed on a computer monitor

Columns and rows. Columns are vertical spaces on an electronic spreadsheet. Each column is identified by a letter. Rows are horizontal spaces on an electronic spreadsheet. Each row is identified by a number. The space where a column intersects with a row is called a cell. Data may be entered in any one of the cells just as data may be entered on a line under a specified column of analysis paper.

Cells are identified by referring to the cell's column and row. For example, in Illustration A-1, the highlighted space under column D in row 3 is referred to as cell *D3*. Words, formulas, or amounts may be entered in any cell. Entries on an electronic spreadsheet that begin with a letter are called labels. Entries on an electronic spreadsheet that begin with a number or arithmetic symbol are called values.

Information line. The information line of a spreadsheet shows information about the spreadsheet. The first item in the information line is the name of the spreadsheet. The name of the spreadsheet in Illustration A-1 is *Parts*, since this spreadsheet was created to illustrate the parts of a spreadsheet. The name should give a good description of the spreadsheet so that different spreadsheets may be distinguished easily from each other.

The second item in the information line shows the location of the cursor. The cursor is indicated on the spreadsheet as a highlighted area. In Illustration A-1, the information line shows that the cursor is located in column D in row 3.

Prompt line. The prompt line is used to give operating commands for the spreadsheet. This line is used for functions such as saving the spreadsheet to disk, copying or moving one part of the spreadsheet to another, or starting a new spreadsheet. In Illustration A-1, the prompt line is blank.

Work line. The work line of a spreadsheet shows the contents of the cell at the cursor location. If there is nothing already entered in the cell, words, formulas, or amounts can be entered from the work line. In Illustration A-1, the work line shows the contents of cell D3, $124.65.

Calculating amounts on an electronic spreadsheet

Illustration A-2 shows an electronic spreadsheet with a list of amounts and the total of the amounts.

```
Spreadsheet: ADDING              Col: B Row:  5

+B1+B2+B3
            A       B       C       D       E       F       G
     1:            145
     2:            233
     3:            357
     4:            ---
     5: Total      735
     6:
     7:
     8:
     9:
    10:
    11:
    12:
    13:
    14:
    15:
    16:
    17:
    18:
    19:
    20:
    21:
    22:
    23:
    24:
```

Illustration A-2
Calculating the total of amounts on an electronic spreadsheet

The amounts 145, 233, and 357 are entered in cells B1, B2, and B3. A calculator could be used to determine the total of the three amounts, 735. This total could then be entered directly in cell B5.

However, an electronic spreadsheet can use a formula to total the amounts. In Illustration A-2, the total is the sum of the amounts in cells B1,

B2, and B3. A formula can be entered in cell B5. The formula tells the computer to add the amounts that are in cells B1, B2, and B3, and record that total in cell B5. The formula for adding the amounts in cells B1, B2, and B3 is +B1+B2+B3.

If the first character of a formula is a letter, the software reads the entry as a label rather than a value and will not calculate the formula. Therefore, a plus symbol is entered first before the letter to identify the formula as a value.

Once the formula has been entered in cell B5, the total of cells B1, B2, and B3 will always appear in cell B5 of the spreadsheet. If the amount in cell B1 is changed to 164, the total that appears in cell B5 will automatically change to the new total, 754, as shown in Illustration A-3.

```
Spreadsheet: ADDING                    Col: B Row:  5

+B1+B2+B3
                A        B        C        D        E        F        G
   1:                   164
   2:                   233
   3:                   357
   4:                   ---
   5:  Total            754
   6:
   7:
   8:
   9:
  10:
  11:
  12:
  13:
  14:
  15:
  16:
  17:
  18:
  19:
  20:
  21:
  22:
  23:
  24:
```

Illustration A-3
Changing an amount and
recalculating the total on
an electronic spreadsheet

If a long list of amounts is to be added, the formula may also be written as @SUM(B1 . . B8). This formula will add the amounts in cells B1, B2, B3, B4, B5, B6, B7, and B8. The total of these eight amounts will appear in the cell in which the formula was entered.

Differences between electronic spreadsheets

Many different electronic spreadsheets are available from software publishers. One particular spreadsheet software package was used to create the spreadsheets illustrated in this appendix. However, other spreadsheets may have a different appearance on the computer monitor. In addition, other spreadsheets may use different commands or symbols and may even identify the columns and rows differently. Regardless of the spreadsheet software used, the basic spreadsheet concepts in this appendix still apply.

PREPARING A SALES BUDGET SCHEDULE USING AN ELECTRONIC SPREADSHEET

In Chapter 17, Suntrol, Inc., prepared a sales budget schedule for 1989 as shown in Illustration A-4.

	1988 Actual		1989 Budget	
	Units (sq. ft.)*	Actual Amount @ 7.50/unit	Units (sq. ft.)*	Estimated Amount @ 7.80/unit
1st Quarter........	37,240	$ 279,300	40,000	$ 312,000
2d Quarter	55,480	416,100	60,000	468,000
3d Quarter	58,520	438,900	60,000	468,000
4th Quarter........	38,760	290,700	40,000	312,000
Year..............	190,000	$1,425,000	200,000	$1,560,000

Suntrol, Inc.
Sales Budget Schedule
For Year Ended December 31, 1989   Schedule 1

*Louvered blinds are measured in square feet.

Illustration A-4
Sales budget schedule

The 1989 budget is based on Suntrol's 1988 actual results plus some estimates as to the changes that will occur in 1989. Suntrol made the following estimates.

1. Total units sold will increase from 190,000 in 1988 to 200,000 in 1989.
2. The selling price per unit will increase from $7.50 in 1988 to $7.80 in 1989.
3. The distribution of unit sales will be 20% in the first quarter, 30% in the second and third quarters, and 20% in the fourth quarter.

Suntrol prepared its budget manually by figuring the amounts with a calculator and recording with pencil and paper. Then after checking the accuracy, the budget was typed and proofread carefully. A microcomputer with spreadsheet software can improve the efficiency and accuracy of preparing Suntrol's budget. In addition, estimates can be changed and the entire budget recalculated with little additional work. Also, the same model can be saved and used every year.

Preparing a sales budget schedule on an electronic spreadsheet

When Suntrol's sales budget schedule is entered on an electronic spreadsheet, the schedule will appear as shown on the computer monitor in Illustration A-5.

```
Spreadsheet: SALESBUD                    Col: A Row:  2

Units sold, budget year
          A            B            C            D            E            F            G
 1: Data section:
 2: Units sold, budget year                         200000
 3:      1st quarter                                 40000
 4:      2d quarter                                  60000
 5:      3d quarter                                  60000
 6:      4th quarter                                 40000
 7: Price, actual year                                7.50
 8: Price, budget year                                7.80
 9:
10:                          Suntrol, Inc.
11:                       Sales Budget Schedule
12:              For Year Ended December 31, 1989      Schedule 1
13:
14:                         1988 Actual              1989 Budget
15:
16:                        Units    Actual         Units    Estimated
17:                       (sq. ft.)  Amount       (sq. ft.)   Amount
18:                                 (dollars)                (dollars)
19: 1st Quarter           37240     279300        40000      312000
20: 2d Quarter            55480     416100        60000      468000
21: 3d Quarter            58520     438900        60000      468000
22: 4th Quarter           38760     290700        40000      312000
23:                       ---------------------------------------------
24: Year                 190000    1425000       200000     1560000
```

Illustration A-5
Electronic spreadsheet for
a sales budget schedule

Estimates and other data used to calculate the budgeted amounts are entered as shown in rows 2 through 8 of the spreadsheet. Additional information for the sales budget schedule is entered as shown in rows 10 through 24 of the spreadsheet. The following procedures are used to enter the data to prepare Suntrol's sales budget schedule.

1 All labels are entered as words at the desired location. For example, with the cursor at cell A2, the label *Units sold, budget year* is entered. A label may overlap another cell if the other cell does not contain data. The label entered in cell A2 overlaps cell B2.

2 All values that are not the result of a calculation from a formula are entered as numbers at the desired location. For example, with the cursor located at cell D2, the number of units sold in the budget year, 200,000, is entered. In Illustration A-5, the amounts in cells D2, D7, D8, C19, C20, C21, and C22 are values that do not require the calculation of a formula.

3 All values requiring calculations to determine the amount are entered as formulas. The following formulas and their cell locations are entered in Suntrol's sales budget schedule.

- Quarterly unit sales are calculated as a percentage of annual unit sales. The estimates for the four quarters are 20%, 30%, 30%, and 20% respectively. The formula for the first quarter's unit sales is entered in cell D3 as .2*D2. The percentage is entered as a decimal, .2. The asterisk is the symbol for multiplication. Therefore, .2 (20%) *times* the contents of cell D2, 200,000, *equals* the budgeted first quarter unit sales, 40,000. This amount is displayed in cell D3 on the computer monitor. Similar formulas are entered in cells D4, D5, and D6 to calculate the budgeted quarterly unit sales for the second, third, and fourth quarters respectively.

- Actual dollar sales amounts are calculated by multiplying the actual units sold times the actual unit price. The formula for the first quarter's actual dollar amount of sales is entered in cell D19 as +C19*D7. The contents of cell C19, 37,240, *times* the contents of cell D7, $7.50, *equals* the first quarter's actual sales, $279,300. This amount is displayed in cell D19 on the computer monitor. Similar formulas are entered in cells D20, D21, and D22 to calculate the actual dollar sales amounts for the second, third, and fourth quarters respectively.

- Budgeted unit sales amounts by quarters are displayed in cells E19, E20, E21, and E22. These same amounts were calculated in cells D3 through D6. An entry can be made that will obtain the amount from cell D3 and display the amount in cell E19. When +D3 is entered in cell E19, the amount in cell D3, 40,000, is displayed in cell E19. Similar entries are made in cells E20, E21, and E22 to obtain the amounts from cells D4, D5, and D6 respectively.

- Budgeted dollar sales amounts are calculated by multiplying the budgeted units times the budgeted unit price. The formula for the first quarter's budgeted dollar amount of sales is entered in cell F19 as +E19*D8. The contents of cell E19, 40,000, *times* the amount in cell D8, $7.80, *equals* the first quarter's budgeted sales amount, $312,000. This amount is displayed in cell F19. Similar formulas are entered in cells F20, F21, and F22 to calculate the budgeted dollar sales amounts for the second, third, and fourth quarters respectively.

- Yearly totals of unit and dollar amounts for 1988 actual and 1989 budget are calculated by adding the quarterly totals for each column. The formula for the 1988 actual sales in units is entered in cell C24 as @SUM(C19..C22). Similar formulas are entered in cells D24, E24, and F24 to calculate the other yearly totals.

Changing estimates on an electronic spreadsheet

With the power of an electronic spreadsheet, estimates can be changed and the results recalculated quickly on the computer. This capability permits budget preparers to see the results of many different estimates without the time-consuming efforts of manually recalculating all the amounts.

Suntrol estimated that unit sales would be 200,000 in 1989 when the budget was prepared. If Suntrol wants to see the effect on the budget if 205,000 unit sales are estimated rather than 200,000, only one change needs to be made. When the amount in cell D2 is changed to the new estimate, 205,000, all amounts in the budget are quickly recalculated and displayed as shown in Illustration A-6.

```
Spreadsheet: SALESBUD                Col: D Row:  2

205000
              A           B           C           D           E           F           G
  1: Data section:
  2: Units sold, budget year                205000
  3:    1st quarter                          41000
  4:    2d quarter                           61500
  5:    3d quarter                           61500
  6:    4th quarter                          41000
  7: Price, actual year                       7.50
  8: Price, budget year                       7.80
  9:
 10:                         Suntrol, Inc.
 11:                      Sales Budget Schedule
 12:           For Year Ended December 31, 1989       Schedule 1
 13:
 14:                       1988 Actual           1989 Budget
 15:
 16:                     Units    Actual      Units    Estimated
 17:                    (sq. ft.) Amount     (sq. ft.)  Amount
 18:                              (dollars)            (dollars)
 19: 1st Quarter         37240    279300      41000     319800
 20: 2d Quarter          55480    416100      61500     479700
 21: 3d Quarter          58520    438900      61500     479700
 22: 4th Quarter         38760    290700      41000     319800
 23:                    --------------------------------------
 24: Year               190000   1425000     205000    1599000
```

Illustration A-6
Electronic spreadsheet for a sales budget recalculated with a change in estimated unit sales

If Suntrol wants to see the effect on the budget of a change in the estimated unit selling price from $7.80 to $7.95, only one change needs to be made. When the amount in cell D8 is changed to the new estimate, $7.95, all amounts in the budget are recalculated and displayed as shown in Illustration A-7.

```
Spreadsheet: SALESBUD                Col: D Row:  8

7.95
              A           B           C           D           E           F           G
  1: Data section:
  2: Units sold, budget year                200000
  3:    1st quarter                          40000
  4:    2d quarter                           60000
  5:    3d quarter                           60000
  6:    4th quarter                          40000
  7: Price, actual year                       7.50
  8: Price, budget year                       7.95
  9:
 10:                         Suntrol, Inc.
 11:                      Sales Budget Schedule
 12:           For Year Ended December 31, 1989       Schedule 1
 13:
 14:                       1988 Actual           1989 Budget
 15:
 16:                     Units    Actual      Units    Estimated
 17:                    (sq. ft.) Amount     (sq. ft.)  Amount
 18:                              (dollars)            (dollars)
 19: 1st Quarter         37240    279300      40000     318000
 20: 2d Quarter          55480    416100      60000     477000
 21: 3d Quarter          58520    438900      60000     477000
 22: 4th Quarter         38760    290700      40000     318000
 23:                    --------------------------------------
 24: Year               190000   1425000     200000    1590000
```

Illustration A-7
Electronic spreadsheet for a sales budget recalculated with a change in estimated unit selling price

ACCOUNTING TERMS

What is the meaning of each of the following?

1. electronic spreadsheet

2. cell

3. labels

4. values

Recycling Problems

NOTE: No recycling problems are provided for Chapter 1.

RECYCLING PROBLEM 2-R 1   **Journalizing departmental purchases and cash payments**

Household, Inc., has two departments: Appliances and Furniture. All purchases on account are subject to a 2% discount if payment is made within the discount period.

Instructions: 1. Record the following selected transactions for November of the current year. Use page 17 of a purchases journal, page 5 of a purchases returns and allowances journal, and page 18 of a cash payments journal. Source documents are abbreviated as follows: check, C; debit memorandum, DM; purchase invoice, P.

Nov. 1. Paid November rent, $1,200.00. C301.
   2. Bought supplies for cash, $52.50. C302.
   2. Purchased appliances on account from Queen Appliances, $3,740.00. P178.
   4. Paid on account to Len-Mar Furniture, covering P176 for furniture, $1,820.00, less 2% discount. C303.
   7. Purchased furniture on account from Minx Furniture, $2,180.00. P179.
   7. Paid on account to Comfort Craft, Inc., covering P177 for furniture, $1,685.00, less 2% discount. C304.
   8. Returned defective appliance to Queen Appliances, $186.00, from P178. DM19.
  11. Purchased appliances on account from Trimline Appliances, $2,670.00. P180.
  12. Paid on account to Queen Appliances, covering P178 for appliances, less DM19 for $186.00 and less 2% discount. C305.
  14. Paid for advertising, $92.50. C306.
  15. Purchased furniture on account from Minx Furniture, $1,360.00. P181.
  15. Returned defective furniture to Comfort Craft, Inc., $212.40, from P177. DM20.
  15. Returned defective appliance to Trimline Appliances, $450.00, from P180. DM21.
  17. Paid on account to Minx Furniture, covering P179 for furniture, $2,180.00, less 2% discount. C307.
  19. Bought supplies for cash, $62.75. C308.
  21. Paid on account to Trimline Appliances, covering P180 for appliances, $2,670.00, less DM21 for $450.00 and less 2% discount. C309.
  23. Purchased appliances on account from Queen Appliances, $925.00. P182.
  25. Paid on account to Minx Furniture, covering P181 for furniture, $1,360.00, less 2% discount. C310.

28. Replenished petty cash. Charge the following accounts: Supplies, $55.50; Advertising Expense, $87.30; Miscellaneous Expense, $61.20. C311.
28. Recorded bank service charge, $11.20. M22.
28. Recorded bank credit card charge, $467.50. M23.
30. Purchased furniture on account from Len-Mar Furniture, $3,340.00. P183.

2. Prove and rule the journals.

RECYCLING PROBLEM 2-R 2   Reconciling a bank statement

On September 30 of the current year, Trudeau, Inc., received its bank statement from Century State Bank.

Instructions: Prepare a bank statement reconciliation using the following information. The bank statement is dated September 29.

Bank statement balance, September 29	$28,160.00
Bank service charge for September	9.40
Bank credit card charge for September	393.80
Balance on Check Stub No. 233	29,640.00
Outstanding deposit, September 29	3,157.20
Outstanding checks:	
No. 231	1,220.00
No. 232	860.40

RECYCLING PROBLEM 3-R 1   Journalizing departmental sales, sales returns and allowances, and cash receipts

Crown Office Products has two departments: Furniture and Supplies. A 5% sales tax is charged on all sales. A 2% sales discount is granted to customers for early payment of their accounts.

Instructions: 1. Record the following selected transactions for April of the current year. Use page 11 of a sales journal, page 6 of a sales returns and allowances journal, and page 13 of a cash receipts journal. Source documents are abbreviated as follows: credit memorandum, CM; receipt, R; sales invoice, S; cash register tape, T.

Apr. 1. Sold furniture on account to Ricardo Diaz, $1,140.00, plus sales tax. S119.
2. Recorded cash and credit card sales for April 1–2: furniture, $2,170.00; supplies, $1,690.00; plus sales tax. T2.
5. Received on account from Westen Co., covering S116 for supplies ($168.00 plus sales tax) less discount and less sales tax. R72.
5. Granted credit to Carol Keto for defective supplies returned, $28.00, plus sales tax, from S118. CM21.
8. Sold supplies on account to Geig Enterprises, $580.00, plus sales tax. S120.
8. Received on account from Dominick Lanz, covering S117 for furniture ($870.00 plus sales tax) less discount and less sales tax. R73.
9. Received on account from Carol Keto, covering S118 for supplies ($168.00 plus sales tax) less CM21 ($28.00 plus sales tax) less discount and less sales tax. R74.
9. Recorded cash and credit card sales for April 4–9: furniture, $5,780.00; supplies, $4,620.00; plus sales tax. T9.
11. Received on account from Ricardo Diaz, covering S119 for furniture ($1,140.00 plus sales tax) less discount and less sales tax. R75.
13. Sold supplies on account to Doris Ashton, $75.00, plus sales tax. S121.
15. Sold furniture on account to Dominick Lanz, $480.00, plus sales tax. S122.

16. Recorded cash and credit card sales for April 11–16: furniture, $6,210.00; supplies, $5,030.00; plus sales tax. T16.

18. Received on account from Geig Enterprises, covering S120 for supplies ($580.00 plus sales tax) less discount and less sales tax. R76.

19. Granted credit to Doris Ashton for defective supplies returned, $18.00, plus sales tax, from S121. CM22.

22. Sold furniture on account to Mason Schools, $1,640.00; no sales tax. S123.

23. Received on account from Doris Ashton, covering S121 for supplies ($75.00 plus sales tax) less CM22 ($18.00 plus sales tax) less discount and less sales tax. R77.

23. Recorded cash and credit card sales for April 18–23: furniture, $6,630.00; supplies, $4,720.00; plus sales tax. T23.

25. Received on account from Dominick Lanz, covering S122 for furniture ($480.00 plus sales tax) less discount and less sales tax. R78.

27. Sold supplies on account to Carol Keto, $50.00, plus sales tax. S124.

30. Recorded cash and credit card sales for April 25–30: furniture, $5,890.00; supplies, $4,930.00; plus sales tax. T30.

2. Prove and rule the sales journal and the sales returns and allowances journal.

3. Prove the cash receipts journal.

4. Prove cash. The balance on the last check stub is $57,647.16. Additional information is given below.

Cash on hand at the beginning of the month $46,930.00
Cash paid during the month 42,870.95

5. Rule the cash receipts journal.

RECYCLING PROBLEM 4-R 1 **Completing payroll records; paying payroll; and recording taxes**

Sound Center has two departments: Stereo and Television. A biweekly payroll system of 26 pay periods per year is used. Salesclerks and employees in the accounting department are paid on an hourly basis and receive 1.5 times the regular hourly rate for all hours worked over 80 each pay period. A time card is used for hourly employees to record hours worked. Departmental supervisors are paid a biweekly salary and receive monthly commissions of 1% of net sales. Commissions are paid in the first pay period of the following month.

Sound Center provides the same employee benefits as Supergolf in Chapter 4. The employee benefits provided are in the employee benefits schedule shown in Illustration 4-1.

Instructions: 1. Prepare Mayna Able's benefits record for the first four biweekly pay periods of the current year. Information needed to complete the record is as follows.

Employee Name: Mayna C. Able Date of Initial Employment: November 1, 1985				Department: Television Employee No.: 1		
Pay Period	Regular Hours	Employee Benefits Available			Employee Benefits Used		
1/2	80	V63	S38	P16	V8	S0	P2
1/16	80	———	———	———	V0	S3	P4
1/30	80	———	———	———	V24	S4	P0
2/13	80	———	———	———	V4	S0	P3
V = Vacation time; S = Sick leave time; P = Personal leave time						

2. Prepare the commissions record for each departmental supervisor for the month ended January 31 of the current year. Use the basic payroll information given in the table below. The following additional information is needed to complete the commissions records.

    a. Stereo department: sales on account, $6,440.30; cash and credit card sales, $8,320.70; sales discounts, $104.20; sales returns and allowances, $362.10.

    b. Television department: sales on account, $7,212.50; cash and credit card sales, $8,920.40; sales discounts, $116.30; sales returns and allowances, $625.60.

Employee No.	Employee Name	Position	Dept.	Marital Status	Allow.	Total Hours	Regular Pay	Overtime Pay
1	Able, Mayna C.	Salesclerk	T	M	2	83	$480.00	$27.00
2	Betts, Alan F.	Supervisor	S	S	1	—	525.00	—
3	Cheng, Yu-lan	Clerk	A	S	2	82	520.00	19.50
4	Ebner, Leo T.	Salesclerk	S	M	3	80	464.00	—
5	Janson, Cora L.	Salesclerk	T	M	2	84	432.00	32.40
6	Neal, Debra S.	Supervisor	T	M	4	—	550.00	—
7	Petrosky, Karl E.	Salesclerk	S	S	1	84	440.00	33.00
8	Redmond, Joseph P.	Clerk	A	M	3	82	448.00	16.80
9	Tifft, John B.	Salesclerk	S	S	1	83	456.00	25.65
10	Wolf, Cindy A.	Salesclerk	T	M	2	83	448.00	25.20

Departments: Stereo, S; Television, T; Accounting, A

3. Prepare Sound Center's payroll register for the biweekly pay period ended February 13 and paid February 20 of the current year. The following additional data is needed to complete the payroll register.

    a. A deduction is to be made from each employee's pay for federal income tax. Use the appropriate income tax withholding tables shown in Chapter 4, Illustration 4-7.

    b. A deduction of 4.5% is to be made from each employee's pay for state income tax.

    c. A deduction of 7% is to be made from each employee's pay for FICA tax.

    d. All employees have dental insurance, $9.10, and hospital insurance, $13.40, deducted from their pay each biweekly pay period. The letter D is to be written in front of the dental insurance deduction. The letter H is to be written in front of the hospital insurance deduction.

4. Complete Mayna Able's employee's earnings record for the fourth pay period ended February 13 of the current year. The following data about Mayna Able is needed to complete the record.

    a. Hourly rate, $6.00.

    b. Social Security number, 514-30-2258.

    c. Accumulated earnings for the first three payroll periods, $1,503.00.

5. Record the February 20 payroll payment on page 7 of a cash payments journal. The source document is Check No. 125.

6. Record the employer's payroll taxes on page 4 of a general journal. Use February 20 of the current year as the date. The source document is Memorandum No. 10. Employer tax rates are: FICA, 7%; federal unemployment, 0.8%; state unemployment, 5.4%. The employee's FICA tax withheld and the employer's share of FICA tax will not be equal due to rounding differences.

RECYCLING PROBLEM 5-R 1   Estimating ending merchandise inventory; preparing an interim departmental statement of gross profit; figuring and recording percentage ratios

Reela Photo Center has two departments: Cameras and Photo Supplies. The following data was obtained from the accounting records on March 31 of the current year.

	Cameras	Photo Supplies
Beginning inventory, January 1	$64,340.30	$57,120.50
Estimated beginning inventory, March 1	62,200.83	61,474.92
Net purchases to date	22,178.40	25,420.60
Net sales to date	39,680.20	41,520.70
Net purchases for March	9,746.00	6,270.60
Net sales for March	13,480.00	15,200.00
Gross profit on operations (percentage based on records of previous years' operations)		45% of sales

Instructions: 1. Prepare an estimated merchandise inventory sheet for each department similar to the one in Chapter 5. Use March 31 of the current year as the date.

2. Prepare an interim departmental statement of gross profit for the month ended March 31 of the current year. Figure and enter departmental and total percentage ratios of cost of merchandise sold and gross profit on operations to net sales. Round percentage computations to the nearest 0.1%.

RECYCLING PROBLEM 5-R 2   Completing end-of-fiscal-period work for a departmentalized business

Antone Decorating, Inc., has two departments: Paint and Wallpaper. The general ledger accounts and their balances on December 31 of the current year are as follows.

Account Title	Account Balance
Cash	$ 46,320.68
Petty Cash	500.00
Accounts Receivable	23,470.20
Allowance for Uncollectible Accounts	296.60
Merchandise Inventory—Paint	190,382.60
Merchandise Inventory—Wallpaper	163,740.30
Supplies—Office	12,930.00
Supplies—Store	10,640.30
Prepaid Insurance	7,560.00
Office Equipment	16,820.00
Accumulated Depreciation—Office Equipment	8,760.00
Store Equipment	19,380.00
Accumulated Depreciation—Store Equipment	11,270.00
Accounts Payable	26,438.00
Employees Income Tax Payable—Federal	1,630.60
Employees Income Tax Payable—State	960.50
Federal Income Tax Payable	—
FICA Tax Payable	1,102.00
Sales Tax Payable	7,108.10
Unemployment Tax Payable—Federal	21.30
Unemployment Tax Payable—State	143.78

Account Title	Account Balance
Hospital Insurance Premiums Payable.............................	$ 1,630.00
Life Insurance Premiums Payable..................................	1,180.60
Capital Stock...	200,000.00
Retained Earnings	142,181.92
Income Summary—Paint....................................	—
Income Summary—Wallpaper	—
Income Summary—General	—
Sales—Paint...	369,891.10
Sales—Wallpaper	352,840.30
Sales Returns and Allowances—Paint	2,830.60
Sales Returns and Allowances—Wallpaper..................	3,060.00
Sales Discount—Paint....................................	3,120.50
Sales Discount—Wallpaper................................	2,910.30
Purchases—Paint	194,938.72
Purchases—Wallpaper....................................	193,696.10
Purchases Returns and Allowances—Paint..................	3,480.60
Purchases Returns and Allowances—Wallpaper	4,260.00
Purchases Discount—Paint................................	2,940.20
Purchases Discount—Wallpaper	3,180.90
Advertising Expense	6,340.00
Credit Card Fee Expense	5,210.30
Depreciation Expense—Store Equipment	—
Salary Expense—Paint	76,920.00
Salary Expense—Wallpaper	73,680.00
Supplies Expense—Store	—
Bad Debts Expense	—
Depreciation Expense—Office Equipment	—
Insurance Expense.......................................	—
Miscellaneous Expense...................................	3,960.40
Payroll Taxes Expense	17,420.00
Rent Expense	15,600.00
Salary Expense—Administrative	38,320.00
Supplies Expense—Office.................................	—
Federal Income Tax......................................	9,565.50

Instructions: 1. Complete Antone's departmental work sheet for the year ended December 31 of the current year. The adjustment information for December 31 is as follows.

Bad debts expense	$ 2,140.60
Merchandise inventory—paint.............................	186,740.20
Merchandise inventory—wallpaper	165,460.70
Office supplies inventory.................................	2,610.30
Store supplies inventory	3,260.20
Value of prepaid insurance...............................	2,520.00
Depreciation expense—office equipment...................	1,320.00
Depreciation expense—store equipment	1,480.00
Federal income tax for the year...........................	13,945.13

2. Prepare a departmental statement of gross profit for the year ended December 31 of the current year. Figure and record the percentage ratios of cost of merchandise sold and gross profit on operations to net sales. Round percentage computations to the nearest 0.1%.

3. Prepare an income statement for the year ended December 31 of the current year. Record the percentage ratios of total cost of merchandise sold and total gross profit on operations to net sales from the departmental statement of gross profit. Figure and record the percentage ratio of total operating expenses to net sales. Figure and record the percentage ratio of net income to net sales. Round percentage computations to the nearest 0.1%.

4. Prepare a statement of stockholders' equity for the year ended December 31 of the current year. The following additional information is needed.

> January 1 balance of capital stock account $200,000.00
>   (2,000 shares at $100.00 per share)
> No additional stock issued.

5. Prepare a balance sheet.

6. Record adjusting and closing entries on pages 14 and 15 of a general journal.

RECYCLING PROBLEM 6-R 1   Performing file maintenance activities

The following is a partial general ledger chart of accounts for Midstate Sports Center.

1120 Merchandise Inventory	5105 Purchases
2145 Unemployment Tax	5110 Purchases Returns and
Payable — State	Allowances
2150 Savings Bonds Payable	5115 Purchases Discount
3120 Income Summary	6115 Salary Expense
4105 Sales	6245 Utilities Expense
4110 Sales Returns and Allowances	
4115 Sales Discount	

<table>
<tr><th>Accounts Added</th><th>Accounts Deleted</th></tr>
<tr><td>Hospital Insurance Premiums Payable</td><td>Savings Bonds Payable</td></tr>
<tr><td>Life Insurance Premiums Payable</td><td>Utilities Expense</td></tr>
</table>

Accounts Departmentalized

Merchandise Inventory	Purchases
Income Summary	Purchases Returns and Allowances
Sales	Purchases Discount
Sales Returns and Allowances	Salary Expense
Sales Discount	

Instructions: 1. Prepare a general ledger file maintenance input form to add, delete, and departmentalize the appropriate accounts. Midstate Sports Center will have two departments: Camping Gear and Hunting Gear. Use October 1 of the current year as the run date. Use Computex's chart of accounts at the beginning of Part 3 as a guide for adding and departmentalizing general ledger accounts.

2. Prepare a journal entries input form to divide the merchandise inventory account balance, $386,420.60, between the two departmental merchandise inventory accounts. The division of the account balance is as follows: Camping Gear, $186,310.20; Hunting Gear, $200,110.40. The remaining departmental accounts have zero balances because October 1 is the start of a new monthly fiscal period. Use October 1 of the current year as the run date. Batch No. 1. Memorandum No. 47.

3. Prepare a general ledger file maintenance input form to delete the related nondepartmental accounts. Use October 1 of the current year as the run date.

4. Prepare a vendor file maintenance input form to add and delete the appropriate accounts from the following vendor list. Use October 1 of the current year as the run date.

Partial Vendor List

210 Ampco Tents, Inc.   240 National Sporting Goods
220 Concord Hunting Products   245 Sandar Office Products
230 Gino's Camping Gear   250 Taylor Hunting Equipment

Accounts Added	Accounts Deleted
Lewis Store Supplies	Concord Hunting Products
Wyco Hunting Equipment	Sandar Office Products

RECYCLING PROBLEM 7-R 1   Recording departmental business transactions

Photocenter, Inc., has two departments: Accessories and Cameras. A 2% purchases discount is allowed for prompt payment. A 5% sales tax is charged on all sales. A 2% sales discount is granted to customers for early payment of their accounts. A partial general ledger chart of accounts and partial vendor and customer lists are given below.

General Ledger Chart of Accounts

1105	Cash	4115-1	Sales Discount—Accessories
1115	Accounts Receivable	4115-2	Sales Discount—Cameras
1140	Supplies—Office	5105-1	Purchases—Accessories
2105	Accounts Payable	5105-2	Purchases—Cameras
2110	Employees Income Tax Payable—Federal	5110-1	Purchases Returns and Allowances—Accessories
2115	Employees Income Tax Payable—State	5110-2	Purchases Returns and Allowances—Cameras
2125	FICA Tax Payable	5115-1	Purchases Discount—Accessories
2130	Sales Tax Payable		
2145	Dental Insurance Premiums Payable	5115-2	Purchases Discount—Cameras
		6105	Advertising Expense
2150	Hospital Insurance Premiums Payable	6115-1	Salary Expense—Accessories
		6115-2	Salary Expense—Cameras
4105-1	Sales—Accessories	6225	Miscellaneous Expense
4105-2	Sales—Cameras	6235	Rent Expense
4110-1	Sales Returns and Allowances—Accessories	6240	Salary Expense—Administrative
4110-2	Sales Returns and Allowances—Cameras		

Customer List		Vendor List	
110	Hamad Abry	210	Cross Photo, Inc.
120	Lisa Devoe	220	Di-Fo Photo Products
130	Betty Latoski	230	Kufner Cameras
140	John Teyner	240	Ultra Photo Supplies
150	Teresa Yurik	250	Yeager Camera House

Instructions: 1. Record the following selected transactions on journal entries input forms. Use October 15 of the current year as the run date. Batch No. 3. Source documents are abbreviated as follows: check, C; credit memorandum, CM; debit memorandum, DM; purchase invoice, P; receipt, R; sales invoice, S; and cash register tape, T.

Oct. 10. Paid October rent, $1,400.00. C259.
     10. Purchased cameras on account from Kufner Cameras, $1,940.00. P151.
     11. Purchased accessories on account from Cross Photo, Inc., $930.00. P152.
     11. Sold cameras on account to John Teyner, $925.00, plus sales tax, $46.25. S220.

12. Returned defective camera to Yeager Camera House, $260.00, from P145. DM35.

12. Paid on account to Ultra Photo Supplies, $1,313.20, covering P148 for accessories, $1,340.00, less 2% discount, $26.80. C260.

13. Received on account from Hamad Abry, $329.28, covering S217 for a camera ($320.00 plus sales tax, $16.00) less 2% discount, $6.40, and less sales tax, $0.32. R192.

14. Sold accessories on account to Lisa Devoe, $125.00, plus sales tax, $6.25. S221.

15. Paid semimonthly payroll: accessories, $3,640.00; cameras, $3,920.00; administrative, $2,730.00 (less deductions: employees' income tax—federal, $1,110.60; employees' income tax—state, $514.20; FICA tax, $720.30; dental insurance, $96.00; hospital insurance, $136.00); total, $7,712.90. C261.

15. Granted credit to John Teyner for damaged camera, $155.00, plus sales tax, $7.75, from S220. CM15.

15. Bought office supplies for cash, $83.00. C262.

15. Recorded cash and credit card sales for October 10–15: accessories, $4,860.00; cameras, $5,430.00, plus sales tax, $514.50. T15.

2. Total the Debit and Credit columns. Prove the equality of debits and credits.

3. Record the following selected transactions on a journal entries input form. Use October 22 of the current year as the run date. Batch No. 4.

Oct. 17. Purchased cameras on account from Di-Fo Photo Products, $1,780.00. P153.

18. Replenished petty cash. Charge the following accounts: Supplies—Office, $112.50; Advertising Expense, $78.50; Miscellaneous Expense, $110.25; total, $301.25. C263.

20. Returned defective accessories to Cross Photo, Inc., $140.00, from P152. DM36.

20. Paid on account to Kufner Cameras, $1,901.20, covering P151 for cameras, $1,940.00, less 2% discount, $38.80. C264.

21. Paid on account to Cross Photo, Inc., $774.20, covering P152 for accessories, $930.00, less DM36, $140.00, and less 2% discount, $15.80. C265.

22. Received on account from John Teyner, $792.33, covering S220 for cameras ($925.00 plus sales tax, $46.25) less CM15 ($155.00 plus sales tax, $7.75), less 2% discount, $15.40, and less sales tax, $0.77. R193.

22. Recorded cash and credit card sales for October 17–22: accessories, $5,230.00; cameras, $6,180.00; plus sales tax, $570.50. T22.

4. Total the Debit and Credit columns. Prove the equality of debits and credits.

RECYCLING PROBLEM 8-R 1   Recording adjusting entries on a journal entries input form

Safama Art Gallery has two departments: Frames and Prints. The following general ledger accounts need adjustment at the end of the fiscal period.

Account Number	Account Title	Account Balance
1120	Allowance for Uncollectible Accounts	$ 212.40
1125-1	Merchandise Inventory—Frames	132,520.40
1125-2	Merchandise Inventory—Prints	187,210.60
1130	Supplies—Office	7,940.80
1135	Supplies—Store	10,560.20
1140	Prepaid Insurance	4,200.00
1210	Accumulated Depreciation—Computer Equipment	3,400.00
1220	Accumulated Depreciation—Office Equipment	9,320.00
1230	Accumulated Depreciation—Store Equipment	11,840.00
2120	Federal Income Tax Payable	—

Account Number	Account Title	Account Balance
3120-1	Income Summary — Frames	—
3120-2	Income Summary — Prints	—
6110	Depreciation Expense — Store Equipment	—
6120	Supplies Expense — Store	—
6205	Bad Debts Expense	—
6210	Depreciation Expense — Computer Equipment	—
6215	Depreciation Expense — Office Equipment	—
6220	Insurance Expense	—
6245	Supplies Expense — Office	—
9105	Federal Income Tax	—

Adjustment information, July 31

Bad debts expense	$ 325.40
Merchandise inventory — frames	130,820.60
Merchandise inventory — prints	183,940.60
Office supplies inventory	7,360.20
Store supplies inventory	9,740.80
Value of prepaid insurance	3,780.00
Depreciation expense — computer equipment	390.00
Depreciation expense — office equipment	350.00
Depreciation expense — store equipment	430.00
Federal income tax	1,480.00

Instructions: 1. Record the adjusting entries on a journal entries input form. Use July 31 of the current year as the run date. Batch No. 5.

2. Total and prove the Debit and Credit columns.

RECYCLING PROBLEM 9-R 1   Estimating and recording uncollectible accounts using a percentage of net sales — allowance method

Selected transactions for Masters, Inc., for the current year are given below.

Instructions: 1. Record the following transactions. Use page 12 of a general journal and page 24 of a cash receipts journal. Source documents are abbreviated as follows: memorandum, M; receipt, R.

Jan. 18. Wrote off past due account of Jane Tressler as uncollectible, $33.96. M25.

Mar. 4. Wrote off past due account of John Young as uncollectible, $80.85. M34.

Mar. 28. Received full payment for Jane Tressler's account, previously written off as uncollectible, $33.96. M45 and R83.

June 20. Wrote off past due account of Betty Armstrong as uncollectible, $17.16. M63.

Oct. 7. Wrote off past due account of Tina Worth as uncollectible, $108.15. M79.

Dec. 11. Received full payment for John Young's account, previously written off as uncollectible, $80.85. M87 and R97.

2. Continue using page 12 of the general journal. Record the adjusting entry needed for bad debts expense. Use December 31 of the current year as the date. Selected account balances for Masters before adjustments are recorded on December 31 of the current year are as follows.

Accounts Receivable	$19,768.25
Sales	94,463.79
Sales Returns and Allowances	901.42
Sales Discount	1,573.58

Masters uses the percentage of net sales method. The percentage is 0.5%.

3. If all the entries recorded in the general journal and cash receipts journal were posted, including the adjusting entry, what would be the new balance of Allowance for Uncollectible Accounts? The January 1 balance of Uncollectible Accounts, before the transactions for the year were recorded, was $1,434.61.

RECYCLING PROBLEM 10-R 1   Recording transactions for plant assets

Phillips, Inc., completed the selected transactions given below.

Instructions: Record the following transactions. Record an entry for additional depreciation if needed. Phillips uses the straight-line method of figuring depreciation. Use page 3 of a general journal, page 4 of a cash receipts journal, and page 2 of a cash payments journal. Source documents are abbreviated as follows: check, C; memorandum, M; receipt, R.

Jan.   5, 1986.   Paid cash for office chair: cost, $150.00; estimated salvage value, none; estimated useful life, 2 years; Serial No., none. C30.

Mar.   3, 1986.   Paid cash for new office desk: cost, $600.00; estimated salvage value, 150.00; estimated useful life, 4 years; Serial No., D125. C45.

Jan.   5, 1987.   Paid cash for office file cabinet: cost, $300.00; estimated salvage value, $75.00; estimated useful life, 5 years; Serial No., F325. C115.

July   3, 1987.   Paid cash for office table: cost, $270.00; estimated salvage value, $20.00; estimated useful life, 10 years; Serial No., none. C170.

Jan.   3, 1988.   Discarded chair bought on January 5, 1986. M50.

Mar.   5, 1988.   Received $300.00 for office desk, Serial No., D125. M55 and R50.

June 29, 1988.   Paid cash, $180.00, plus old file cabinet, Serial No. F325, for new office file cabinet: estimated salvage value of new cabinet, $80.00; estimated useful life of new cabinet, 5 years; Serial No. of new cabinet, F915. M70 and C200.

July   1, 1988.   Paid cash for typewriter: cost, $1,000.00; estimated salvage value, $200.00; estimated useful life, 5 years; Serial No., A6501M341. C230.

RECYCLING PROBLEM 10-R 2   Figuring depreciation expense

On January 5 of the current year, Boulder, Inc., bought a new company car. Cost, $9,500.00; estimated salvage value, $800.00; estimated useful life, 5 years.

Instructions: 1. Prepare a depreciation table similar to Illustration 10-16, showing the straight-line, declining-balance, and sum-of-the-years-digits methods of figuring depreciation.

2. Assume that Boulder's car has an estimated useful life of 100,000 miles. Also assume that the car is driven the following number of miles: 1st year, 27,000; 2nd year, 23,000; 3rd year, 15,000; 4th year, 20,000; 5th year, 15,000. Prepare a table similar to Illustration 10-17, using the production-unit method of figuring depreciation.

RECYCLING PROBLEM 10-R 3   Figuring property tax

Anderson, Inc., has real property assessed at $300,000.00. The business is located in a city with a tax rate of 5% of assessed value.

Instructions: 1. Figure the total annual property tax on Anderson's property.

2. Record the entry for the payment of the first half of Anderson's annual property tax. Use page 5 of a cash payments journal. Use May 1 of the current year as the date. Check No. 142.

RECYCLING PROBLEM 11-R 1   Recording adjusting and reversing entries for prepaid expenses recorded initially as expenses and for accrued expenses

Mandol, Inc., completed the following selected transactions during the current year. Mandol records prepaid expenses initially as expenses. Source documents are abbreviated as follows: check, C; note payable, NP.

Aug. 1. Issued a 1-month, 10% note to Clymer Trust Bank, $600.00. NP1.
Sept. 1. Paid Clymer Trust Bank $605.00 for NP1, $600.00, plus interest, $5.00. C95.
Sept. 1. Issued a 150-day, 10% note to Clymer State Bank, $1,000.00. NP2.
Oct. 1. Issued a 120-day, 12% note to Clymer Bank and Trust Company, $1,500.00. NP3.
Dec. 1. Discounted at 12% at Clymer State Bank a 60-day note, $600.00; discount, $11.84; proceeds, $588.16. NP4.

Instructions: 1. Figure the maturity dates for Notes Payable Nos. 2, 3, and 4.

2. Record the transactions on page 12 of a cash receipts journal and page 10 of a cash payments journal.

3. Record the adjusting entries for prepaid and accrued expenses on page 12 of a general journal. Use December 31 of the current year as the date. The following information is from the business' records on December 31 of the current year before adjusting entries are recorded.

General ledger account balances:	
Supplies Expense—Sales	$ 800.00
Supplies Expense—Administrative	500.00
Insurance Expense	700.00
Notes Payable	3,800.00
Inventories, December 31:	
Sales supplies	250.00
Administrative supplies	200.00
Unused insurance premiums	300.00
Remaining prepaid interest	5.92
Accrued interest on notes payable	78.03
Accrued payroll:	
Sales salaries	115.00
Administrative salaries	150.00
Accrued employer's payroll taxes:	
FICA tax	18.55
Federal unemployment tax	1.33
State unemployment tax	14.84
Accrued federal income tax	300.00

4. Record the needed reversing entries on page 1 of a general journal. Use January 1 of the next year as the date.

RECYCLING PROBLEM 12-R 1   Recording entries for notes receivable, unearned revenue, and accrued revenue

Munster, Inc., completed the transactions given below during the current year. Munster records prepaid and unearned items initially as expenses and revenue.

Instructions: 1. Record the following transactions. Use page 3 of a general journal and page 4 of a cash receipts journal. Source documents are abbreviated as follows: memorandum, M; note receivable, NR; receipt, R.

July   1. Received a 60-day, 10% note receivable from Jon Benson for an extension of time on his account, $100.00. NR20.
July   5. Received a 2-month, 12% note receivable from Don Schenck for an extension of time on his account, $300.00. NR21.
Aug. 30. Jon Benson dishonored NR20 due today: principal, $100.00; interest, $1.64. M39.
Sept. 5. Received from Don Schenck in settlement of NR21: $300.00, plus interest, $6.00. R70.
Nov.   1. Received three months' rent in advance from Chang, Inc., $1,500.00. R75.
Nov. 29. Received from Jon Benson for dishonored NR20: principal, $101.64, plus additional interest, $2.53. R90.

2. Continue using page 3 of the general journal. Record the needed adjusting entries using the following information. Use December 31 of the current year as the date.

Accrued interest on notes receivable, December 31 . . . . $ 16.43
Rent received in advance and still unearned 500.00

3. Record the needed reversing entries. Use page 4 of a general journal. Use January 1 of the next year as the date.

RECYCLING PROBLEM 13-R 1   Recording transactions for starting a corporation

Nelson, Inc., received its charter on June 1 of the current year. The corporation is authorized to issue 80,000 shares of $10.00 stated-value common stock and 30,000 shares of 10%, $100.00 par-value, noncumulative, participating preferred stock.

Instructions: 1. Record the following selected transactions on page 1 of a cash receipts journal, page 1 of a cash payments journal, and page 1 of a general journal. Source documents are abbreviated as follows: check, C; memorandum, M; receipt, R.

June   2. Received from two incorporators for 60,000 shares of $10.00 stated-value common stock, $600,000.00. R1-2.
June   2. Paid to Mildred Shear as reimbursement for organization costs, $1,200.00. C1.
June   7. Received a subscription from Edith Earl for 10,000 shares of $10.00 stated-value common stock, $100,000.00. M1.
June 25. Received a subscription from Ron Bestor for 500 shares of $10.00 stated-value common stock, $5,000.00. M2.
Aug. 10. Received from Ron Bestor in payment of stock subscription, $5,000.00. R3.
Aug. 10. Issued Stock Certificate No. 3 to Ron Bestor for 500 shares of $10.00 stated-value common stock, $5,000.00. M3.
Sept. 1. Received from Edith Earl in partial payment of stock subscription, $50,000.00. R4.
Sept. 15. Received a subscription from Tony Robinson for 3,000 shares of $10.00 stated-value common stock, $30,000.00. M4.
Oct.   1. Received from Edith Earl in final payment of stock subscription, $50,000.00. R5.
Oct.   1. Issued Stock Certificate No. 4 to Edith Earl for 10,000 shares of $10.00 stated-value common stock, $100,000.00. M5.

2. Prepare a balance sheet for Nelson, Inc., as of October 2 of the current year.

3. At the end of the following year, Nelson has outstanding 73,500 shares of $10.00 stated-value common stock and 1,000 shares of $100.00 par-value preferred stock. At the end of the fiscal year, the corporation's board of directors votes $25,000.00 to be used as dividends. No additional stock has been sold. Figure the total amount of dividends for preferred stock and for common stock.

RECYCLING PROBLEM 14-R 1 **Recording transactions for stocks and bonds**

Gormatt, Inc., is authorized to issue 60,000 shares of $20.00 stated-value common stock and 30,000 shares of 10%, $200.00 par-value preferred stock.

Instructions: Record the following selected transactions using page 3 of a cash receipts journal, page 2 of a cash payments journal, and page 1 of a general journal. Source documents are abbreviated as follows: check, C; memorandum, M; receipt, R.

Jan.   2, 1989.   Received for the face value of a 10-year, 10%, $1,000.00 par-value bond issue, $200,000.00. R104.

Jan.   6, 1989.   Received from Bill Wilcox for 600 shares of $20.00 stated-value common stock, $12,000.00. R110.

Jan. 21, 1989.   Paid to Frank Ketter for 700 shares of $20.00 stated-value common stock at $21.00 per share, $14,700.00. C141.

Mar. 13, 1989.   Received from Andrew Twomey for 100 shares of $20.00 stated-value common stock at $21.00 per share, $2,100.00. R143.

Mar. 22, 1989.   Received from Ethel Holston for 200 shares of treasury stock at $21.00 per share, $4,200.00. Treasury stock was bought on January 21 at $21.00 per share. R149.

Apr. 15, 1989.   Received from Connie Dwyer for 100 shares of treasury stock at $22.00 per share, $2,200.00. Treasury stock was bought on January 21 at $21.00 per share. R155.

Apr. 15, 1989.   Received from Doris Rossi for 300 shares of $200.00 par-value preferred stock at $202.00 per share, $60,600.00. R156.

June   5, 1989.   Received from Samuel Waite for 400 shares of $200.00 par-value preferred stock at $200.00 per share, $80,000.00. R173.

June 30, 1989.   Paid to bond trustee for semiannual interest on bond issue, $10,000.00. C308.

June 30, 1989.   Paid to bond trustee for semiannual deposit to bond sinking fund, $10,000.00. C309.

July   1, 1989.   Received store equipment from Kevin Tate at an agreed value of $40,000.00 for 200 shares of $200.00 par-value preferred stock. M107.

July 30, 1989.   Received from Larry Ross for 100 shares of treasury stock at $20.50 per share, $2,050.00. Treasury stock was bought on January 21 at $21.00 per share. R215.

Dec. 31, 1989.   Paid to bond trustee for semiannual interest on bond issue, $10,000.00. C519.

Dec. 31, 1989.   Paid to bond trustee for semiannual deposit to bond sinking fund, $10,000.00, less interest earned on bond sinking fund, $1,100.00. C520.

Jan.   2, 1999.   Received notice from bond trustee that bond issue was retired using bond sinking fund, $200,000.00. M492.

RECYCLING PROBLEM 15-R 1 **End-of-fiscal-period work for a corporation**

Fine, Inc., has the following general ledger account balances on December 31, 1989.

Cash	$ 96,923.38	Supplies—Administrative	$ 11,031.27
Petty Cash	600.00	Prepaid Insurance	8,933.30
Notes Receivable	2,030.37	Prepaid Interest	—
Interest Receivable	—	Bond Sinking Fund	9,000.00
Accounts Receivable	67,676.52	Store Equipment	66,932.08
Allow. for Uncoll. Accounts	203.03	Accum. Depr.—Store Equip	6,760.14
Subscriptions Receivable	—	Delivery Equipment	60,435.13
Merchandise Inventory	113,290.49	Accum. Depr.—Delivery	
Supplies—Sales	6,361.59	Equip.	3,686.54
Supplies—Delivery	8,053.51	Office Equipment	29,913.02

Accum. Depr.—Office Equip. .	$ 2,871.65	Sales	$439,897.38
Building	63,000.00	Sales Returns and	
Accum. Depr.—Building......	6,993.00	Allowances	1,319.69
Land......................	47,170.53	Sales Discount	879.79
Organization Costs	400.00	Purchases	202,352.79
Notes Payable	676.77	Purch. Returns and	
Interest Payable............	—	Allowances	1,214.12
Accounts Payable	609.09	Purchases Discount.........	3,440.00
Employees Income		Advertising Expense	5,143.42
Tax Payable	541.41	Credit Card Fee Expense.....	5,820.18
Federal Income Tax Payable..	—	Depr. Expense—Store Equip.	—
FICA Tax Payable	326.64	Misc. Expense—Sales.......	2,504.03
Salaries Payable	—	Salary Expense—Sales......	30,725.14
Sales Tax Payable..........	947.47	Supplies Expense—Sales....	—
Unemploy. Tax		Depr. Expense—Delivery	
Pay.—Federal	108.01	Equip.....................	—
Unemploy. Tax Pay.—State ..	730.50	Misc. Expense—Delivery	6,564.62
Hosp. Insurance Premiums		Salary Expense—Delivery ...	13,670.66
Pay.......................	203.03	Supplies Expense—Delivery .	—
Dividends Payable...........	19,419.64	Bad Debts Expense..........	—
Bonds Payable..............	90,000.00	Depr. Expense—Office	
Capital Stock—Common.....	240,000.00	Equip.....................	—
Stock Subscribed—Common .	—	Depr. Expense—Building	—
Capital Stock—Preferred.....	94,000.00	Insurance Expense	—
Stock Subscribed—Preferred.	—	Misc. Expense—	
Paid-in Capital in Excess of		Administrative	7,173.71
Par/Stated Value	2,400.00	Payroll Taxes Expense.......	7,423.57
Discount on Sale of Capital		Property Tax Expense........	3,000.00
Stock	4,000.00	Salary Expense—Admin.	11,843.39
Treasury Stock..............	1,600.00	Supplies Expense—Admin. ..	—
Paid-in Capital from Sale of		Utilities Expense............	12,114.10
Treasury Stock		Gain on Plant Assets	—
(credit balance)............	320.00	Interest Income..............	270.71
Retained Earnings...........	29,439.29	Interest Expense	5,752.50
Dividends—Common Stock ..	10,019.64	Loss on Plant Assets	—
Dividends—Preferred Stock ..	9,400.00	Organization Expense........	—
Income Summary............	—	Federal Income Tax..........	12,000.00

Instructions: 1. Complete the work sheet. The following additional information is needed.

Accrued interest income	$ 22.33
Bad debts expense	2,774.74
Inventories, December 31:	
Merchandise inventory.......................................	112,939.29
Sales supplies...	2,640.06
Delivery supplies...	2,311.36
Administrative supplies	2,106.97
Value of prepaid insurance....................................	3,153.46
Prepaid interest expense	4.06
Depreciation expense:	
Store equipment	6,626.28
Delivery equipment..	6,043.51
Office equipment..	2,841.74
Building...	3,150.00
Organization expense	100.00

Accrued interest expense...	$ 9,005.64
Accrued salaries:	
Sales	337.98
Delivery	150.38
Administrative..	1,302.77
Accrued payroll taxes:	
FICA tax payable..	125.38
Unemployment tax payable — federal	14.33
Unemployment tax payable — state................................	96.72
Accrued federal income tax.......................................	2,691.75

2. Prepare an income statement for the year ended December 31, 1989. As part of the income statement figure the following items. (a) Ratio of cost of merchandise sold to net sales. (b) Ratio of gross profit to net sales. (c) Ratio of total operating expenses to net sales. (d) Ratio of net income before federal income tax to net sales. (e) Ratio of federal income tax to net sales. (f) Ratio of net income after federal income tax to net sales. (g) Earnings per share. Fine has 24,000 shares of $10.00 stated-value common stock issued and 940 shares of $100.00 par-value preferred stock issued. Treasury stock consists of 160 shares of common stock. The dividend rate on preferred stock is 10%.

3. Prepare a statement of stockholders' equity for the year ended December 31, 1989. Use the following additional information.

	January 1 Balance	Issued During the Year	December 31 Balance
Common stock:			
No. of shares...................	20,000	4,000	24,000
Amount.......................	$200,000.00	$40,000.00	$240,000.00
Preferred stock:			
No. of shares...................	900	40	940
Amount.......................	$ 90,000.00	$ 4,000.00	$ 94,000.00

The January 1 balance of Retained Earnings was $29,439.29

4. Figure the following items based on information from the statement of stockholders' equity. (a) Equity per share of stock. (b) Price-earnings ratio. The market price of common stock on December 31 is $10.00.

5. Prepare a balance sheet for December 31, 1989.

6. Figure the following items based on information from the balance sheet. (a) Rate earned on average stockholders' equity. Total stockholders' equity on January 1 was $316,559.29. (b) Rate earned on average total assets. Total assets on January 1 were $493,695.43.

7. Record the adjusting entries on pages 12 and 13 of a general journal.

8. Record the closing entries on pages 13 and 14 of a general journal.

9. Record the reversing entries. Continue to use page 14 of the general journal. Use January 1, 1990, as the date.

10. Record the following selected transactions on page 17 of a general journal and page 21 of a cash payments journal. Source documents are abbreviated as follows: check, C; memorandum, M.

Dec. 1, 1990. Fine's board of directors voted to declare dividends on preferred stock, $9,400.00, and common stock, $10,012.80; date of record, December 31, 1990; date of payment, February 1, 1991. M81.

Feb. 1, 1991. Paid the dividends declared December 1, 1990, $19,412.80. C179.

RECYCLING PROBLEM 16-R 1   **Valuing merchandise inventory; figuring merchandise inventory turnover ratio and average number of days' sales in merchandise inventory**

On December 31 of the current year, Endal, Inc., takes a periodic inventory. The following selected information is obtained from Endal's records.

Stock No.	January 1 Inventory		First Purchase		Second Purchase		December 31 Inventory	Market Price
	No.	Cost	No.	Cost	No.	Cost		
A50	24	$ 5.00	10	$ 5.00	10	$ 6.00	20	$ 6.00
C25	20	10.00	10	9.00	10	8.00	15	8.00
F21	12	15.00	15	14.00	15	13.00	20	12.00
K55	10	10.00	10	8.00	10	10.00	5	10.00
P12	25	4.00	10	5.00	10	6.00	15	6.00

Instructions: 1. Use a form similar to the one below. Figure the inventory values using the fifo, lifo, and weighted-average inventory costing methods.

Stock No.	Dec. 31 Inventory	Inventory Costing Method					
		Fifo		Lifo		Weighted-Average	
		Unit Cost	Value	Unit Cost	Value	Unit Cost	Value
Total Values							

2. Total the three Value columns.

3. Assume that the weighted-average unit cost figured in Instruction 1 is the cost price and use the market price given in the form at the beginning of the problem. Use a form similar to the one below to figure the inventory values for each item using the lower of cost or market method. Also, total the Total Value column.

Stock No.	Inventory	Price to Use		Total Value
		Cost	Market	
Total				

4. Figure the corporation's estimated ending inventory using the gross profit method. The following information is obtained from the corporation's records on December 31 of the current year.

Item	Cost	Retail
Total beginning merchandise inventory.............	$ 400.00	$1,004.00
Net purchases to date	1,400.00	3,514.00
Net sales to date.................................	2,000.00	2,980.00
Gross profit percentage	40%	

5. Figure the corporation's estimated ending inventory using the retail method.

6. Use the information and the estimated inventory figured from Instruction 4. Figure the corporation's merchandise inventory turnover ratio.

7. Use the merchandise inventory turnover ratio figured in Instruction 6. Figure the corporation's average number of days' sales in merchandise inventory.

RECYCLING PROBLEM 17-R 1   **Preparing a budgeted income statement and a cash budget with supporting schedules**

On December 31, 1988, the accounting records of Dee's Drapery show the following unit sales for 1988.

1st quarter	22,100 units	3d quarter	25,000 units
2d quarter.	24,000 units	4th quarter.	27,900 units
1988 ending inventory			11,500 units

The following are additional actual amounts for the 4th quarter of 1988.

Sales (27,900 units @ $5.50)	$153,450.00
Purchases (22,600 units @ $3.75)	84,750.00

The records also show that sales units have increased about 4% each year over the past five years. This increase is expected to continue in 1989.

The sales manager, after reviewing price trends and checking with the company's merchandise suppliers, estimates the cost of merchandise will increase from the 1988 cost of $3.75 per unit to $4.20 per unit in 1989. Because of the increase in costs, the company will need to increase its sales price per unit of merchandise from $5.50 to $6.20 in 1989.

After considering the time required to reorder merchandise, the sales manager established the following desired levels of quarterly ending inventories for 1989.

1st quarter	12,600 units	3d quarter	14,400 units
2d quarter.	13,000 units	4th quarter.	12,200 units

Expenses for 1989 are estimated as shown below. (Percentages are based on quarterly net sales estimated for 1989 unless otherwise noted. Dollar amounts are divided equally among the four quarters.)

Selling Expenses		Administrative Expenses	
Advertising Expense	1.4%	Bad Debts Expense	0.5%
Delivery Expense	0.6%	Depreciation Expense—	
Depreciation Expense—		Office Equipment	$1,680.00
Delivery Equipment	$4,040.00	Insurance Expense	$4,320.00
Depreciation Expense—		Miscellaneous Expense—	
Store Equipment.	$2,200.00	Administrative.	$2,800.00
Miscellaneous Expense—		Payroll Taxes Expense . . .	9% of total
Sales.	0.3%		salaries
Salary Expense—Sales . . .	5.6%	Rent Expense.	$8,640.00
Supplies Expense—Sales .	0.8%	Salary Expense—	
		Administrative.	$24,000.00
		Supplies Expense—	
		Office	$1,320.00
		Utilities Expense	1.8%

Interest expense for the year ended December 31, 1989, is $450.00 each quarter. Federal income tax is 25% of each quarter's estimated net income before income tax.

Additional information is listed below.

a. The balance of cash on hand on January 1, 1989, is $18,540.00.
b. In each quarter, cash sales are 10% and collections of accounts receivable are 35% of the total estimated sales for the current quarter. Collections from the preceding quarter's total sales are 54.5% of that quarter. Bad debt losses are 0.5% of total sales.
c. In each quarter, cash payments for cash purchases are 10% and for accounts payable 50% of the purchases for the current quarter. Cash payments for purchases of the preceding quarter are 40% of that quarter.
d. Selling and administrative expenses are paid in the quarter incurred. Cash is not paid for depreciation and bad debt expenses.
e. In the first quarter, $12,000.00 will be borrowed on a promissory note, and equipment costing $15,000.00 will be purchased for cash. In each quarter, dividends of $12,500.00 will be paid in cash. In the fourth quarter, the promissory note plus interest will be paid in cash, $16,800.00.

Instructions: Prepare the following schedules and budgets for the year ended December 31, 1989. Round all estimates to the nearest 100 units and to the nearest $10.00.

1. Prepare a sales budget schedule (1). Figure total budgeted sales units for the year based on a 4% estimated increase. This estimate may not equal the sum of the four quarterly estimates due to rounding differences.

2. Prepare a purchases budget schedule (2).

3. Prepare a selling expenses budget schedule (3).

4. Prepare an administrative expenses budget schedule (4).

5. Prepare an other revenue and expenses budget schedule (5).

6. Prepare a budgeted income statement.

7. Prepare a cash receipts schedule (A).

8. Prepare a cash payments schedule (B).

9. Prepare a cash budget.

RECYCLING PROBLEM 18-R 1   Figuring the effects on net income of changes in selling price, variable costs, fixed costs and volume

Cherokee Aluminum sold 180,000 square meters (m²) of siding last year with the results shown in the following income statement. Jim Thompson, manager of Cherokee Aluminum, is anticipating changing prices next year. Thus, he is doing some advance planning.

Cherokee Aluminum Income Statement For Year Ended December 31, 19--	
Sales (180,000 m² siding @ $25.00)	$4,500,000.00
Less Variable Costs (180,000 m² siding @ $15.00)	2,700,000.00
Contribution Margin	$1,800,000.00
Less Fixed Costs	840,000.00
Net Income	$ 960,000.00

Instructions: 1. Figure the required (a) sales dollars and (b) number of square meters of siding to increase net income by $160,000.00.

2. Figure the net income for each of the following changes. Consider each case independently.
a. Unit selling price increases 20%.
b. Unit variable costs increase 20%.
c. Total fixed costs increase 20%.
d. Unit selling price decreases 10% and units sold increase 20%.

RECYCLING PROBLEM 18-R 2   Figuring effects of sales mix changes

Wilderness Camping sells tents and camp stoves. The following information is from the January income statement. Wilderness Camping is considering changing its sales mix to increase its net income.

Sales:		
Stoves (5,000 @ $20.00)	$100,000.00	
Tents (500 @ $50.00)	25,000.00	
Total Sales		$125,000.00
Variable Costs:		
Stoves (5,000 @ $14.00)	$ 70,000.00	
Tents (500 @ $25.00)	12,500.00	
Total Variable Costs		82,500.00
Contribution Margin		$ 42,500.00
Less Fixed Costs		20,000.00
Net Income		$ 22,500.00

Instructions: Figure the net income for Wilderness Camping using the following assumptions.
a. Total sales remain $125,000.00.
b. Sales mix to be equal: stoves, $62,500.00; tents, $62,500.00.
c. All unit prices, unit costs, and fixed costs remain the same.

RECYCLING PROBLEM 19-R 1   Preparing and analyzing comparative financial statements

The following information is taken from the financial records of Genco on December 31, 1989 and 1988.

	1989	1988
Cash	$ 76,340.00	$ 55,760.00
Accounts Receivable (book value)	63,840.00	41,530.00
Merchandise Inventory	297,960.00	179,690.00
Other Current Assets	8,320.00	8,470.00
Plant Assets (book value)	136,800.00	147,360.00
Notes Payable	66,530.00	10,830.00
Interest Payable	2,500.00	1,800.00
Accounts Payable	125,100.00	45,020.00
Income Tax Payable — Federal	600.00	600.00

	1989	**1988**
Other Current Liabilities.	$ 19,110.00	$ 1,940.00
Mortgage Payable (long-term liability)	73,920.00	83,130.00
Capital Stock	240,000.00	240,000.00
Retained Earnings (after net income and dividend		
entries are made)	55,500.00	49,490.00
Net Sales	709,600.00	630,800.00
Net Purchases.	633,440.00	554,840.00
Advertising Expense	14,190.00	13,880.00
Delivery Expense	15,610.00	14,500.00
Salary Expense — Sales	50,380.00	47,310.00
Supplies Expense.	2,130.00	2,520.00
Other Selling Expenses.	4,260.00	4,420.00
Bad Debts Expense	8,520.00	3,780.00
Salary Expense — Administrative	29,090.00	32,170.00
Other Administrative Expenses	16,320.00	17,030.00
Interest Expense.	17,030.00	11,990.00
Federal Income Tax	5,890.00	5,950.00
Dividends declared and paid	25,000.00	25,000.00
Shares of capital stock outstanding	2,400	2,400
Additional information:		
Accounts receivable (book value) January 1	$ 41,530.00	$ 38,480.00
Merchandise inventory, January 1.	179,690.00	70,830.00
Total assets, January 1	432,810.00	421,200.00
Capital stock, January 1	240,000.00	240,000.00
Retained earnings, January 1	49,490.00	43,220.00
Market price per share of stock Dec. 31	125.00	130.00

Instructions: 1. Prepare a comparative income statement with trend analysis, similar to the one in Chapter 19, for the years 1989 and 1988. Round percentage computations to the nearest 0.1%.

2. Prepare a comparative stockholders' equity statement with trend analysis, similar to the one in Chapter 19, for the years 1989 and 1988. Round percentage computations to the nearest 0.1%.

3. Prepare a comparative balance sheet with trend analysis, similar to the one in Chapter 19, for the years 1989 and 1988. Round percentage computations to the nearest 0.1%.

4. Use the financial statements' trend analyses to determine if the trend from 1988 to 1989 for each of the following items appears to be favorable or unfavorable. Give reasons for these trends.

a. Net sales
b. Net income
c. Total stockholders' equity
d. Total assets

5. Prepare a comparative income statement with component percentage analysis, similar to the one in Chapter 19, for the years 1989 and 1988. Round percentage computations to the nearest 0.1%.

6. Record from the statement prepared in Instruction 5 or figure the component percentages for 1989 and 1988 for each of the following:

a. As a percentage of net sales:
  (1) Cost of merchandise sold
  (2) Gross profit on operations
  (3) Total operating expenses
  (4) Net income after federal income tax

b. As a percentage of total stockholders' equity:
   (1) Retained earnings
   (2) Capital stock

c. As a percentage of total assets:
   (1) Current assets
   (2) Current liabilities

   7. State whether the 1989 results for each of the items figured in Instruction 6 appear to be favorable or unfavorable compared with 1988. Give reasons for your responses.
   8. Based on Genco's comparative financial statements for the years ended December 31, 1989 and 1988, figure the following earnings performance ratios for each year.

a. Rate earned on average total assets
b. Rate earned on average stockholders' equity
c. Rate earned on net sales
d. Earnings per share
e. Price-earnings ratio

   9. For each of the items in Instruction 8, indicate if there appears to be a favorable or an unfavorable trend from 1988 to 1989. Give reasons for these trends.
   10. Based on Genco's comparative financial statements for the years ended December 31, 1989 and 1988, figure the following efficiency ratios for each year. All of Genco's sales are on account.

a. Accounts receivable turnover ratio
b. Merchandise inventory turnover ratio

   11. For each of the items in Instruction 10, indicate if there appears to be a favorable or an unfavorable trend from 1988 to 1989. Give reasons for these trends.
   12. Based on Genco's comparative balance sheet as of December 31, 1989 and 1988, figure the following short-term financial strength ratios for each year.

a. Current ratio
b. Acid-test ratio

   13. For each of the items in Instruction 12, indicate if there appears to be a favorable or an unfavorable trend from 1988 to 1989. Give reasons for these trends.
   14. Based on Genco's comparative balance sheet as of December 31, 1989 and 1988, figure the following long-term financial strength ratios for each year.

a. Debt ratio
b. Equity ratio
c. Equity per share

   15. For each of the items in Instruction 14, indicate if there appears to be a favorable or an unfavorable trend from 1988 and 1989. Give reasons for these trends.

RECYCLING PROBLEM 20-R 1   Completing end-of-fiscal-period work for a merchandising business using departmental margins

Ski Chalet is a merchandising business specializing in snow skis and ski wear. Ski Chalet's account balances for the current year ended December 31 are as follows.

Account Title	Balance
Cash	$ 66,976.80
Accounts Receivable	53,312.60
Allowance for Uncollectible Accounts	71.30
Merchandise Inventory — Skis	65,251.50
Merchandise Inventory — Ski Wear	51,732.70
Supplies	9,776.00
Prepaid Insurance	9,300.00
Office Equipment	3,694.20
Accumulated Depreciation — Office Equipment	396.30
Store Equipment — Skis	10,584.60
Accumulated Depreciation — Store Equipment, Skis	2,449.40
Store Equipment — Ski Wear	7,595.90
Accumulated Depreciation — Store Equipment, Ski Wear	1,542.00
Accounts Payable	16,287.40
Employees Income Tax Payable	1,064.30
Federal Income Tax Payable	—
FICA Tax Payable	1,105.80
Salaries Payable	—
Sales Tax Payable	1,728.90
Unemployment Tax Payable — Federal	55.30
Unemployment Tax Payable — State	221.10
Dividends Payable	—
Capital Stock	150,000.00
Retained Earnings	68,779.10
Dividends	10,000.00
Income Summary — Skis	—
Income Summary — Ski Wear	—
Income Summary — General	—
Sales — Skis	242,546.90
Sales Returns and Allowances — Skis	400.90
Sales Discount — Skis	601.20
Sales — Ski Wear	281,081.30
Sales Returns and Allowances — Ski Wear	631.70
Sales Discount — Ski Wear	772.00
Purchases — Skis	138,980.60
Purchases Returns and Allowances — Skis	401.70
Purchases Discount — Skis	267.80
Purchases — Ski Wear	144,213.20
Purchases Returns and Allowances — Ski Wear	271.10
Purchases Discount — Ski Wear	331.20
Advertising Expense — Skis	2,957.60
Delivery Expense — Skis	6,114.40
Depreciation Expense — Store Equipment, Skis	—
Insurance Expense — Skis	—
Payroll Taxes Expense — Skis	3,007.10
Salary Expense — Skis	34,219.00
Supplies Expense — Skis	—
Advertising Expense — Ski Wear	4,239.60
Depreciation Expense — Store Equipment, Ski Wear	—
Insurance Expense — Ski Wear	—
Payroll Taxes Expense — Ski Wear	2,878.60
Salary Expense — Ski Wear	31,628.00

Account Title	Balance
Supplies Expense—Ski Wear	—
Bad Debts Expense	—
Credit Card Fee Expense	$ 5,263.70
Depreciation Expense—Office Equipment	—
Insurance Expense—Administrative	—
Miscellaneous Expense	18,318.20
Payroll Taxes Expense—Administrative	3,809.30
Rent Expense	23,440.00
Salary Expense—Administrative	44,733.00
Supplies Expense—Administrative	—
Utilities Expense	8,621.50
Federal Income Tax	5,547.00

Instructions: 1. Prepare a trial balance on a twelve-column work sheet. List all accounts with or without a balance. Skip four lines after Utilities Expense before entering Federal Income Tax.

2. Use the following information to plan adjustments on the work sheet for the year ended December 31 of the current year.

Bad debts expense	$ 757.20
Merchandise inventory—skis	68,123.30
Merchandise inventory—ski wear	52,211.10
Supplies used—skis	2,413.80
Supplies used—ski wear	4,023.00
Supplies used—administrative	1,609.20
Insurance expired—skis	2,220.00
Insurance expired—ski wear	2,775.00
Insurance expired—administrative	555.00
Depreciation expense—office equipment	123.90
Depreciation expense—store equipment, skis	896.10
Depreciation expense—store equipment, ski wear	232.30
Federal income tax for the year	6,057.00

3. Complete the work sheet. Extend proper amounts to debit and credit columns for Departmental Margin Statement—Skis, Departmental Margin Statement—Ski Wear, Income Statement, and Balance Sheet. Accounts on trial balance lines 54–63 are classified as indirect expenses.

4. Prepare a departmental margin statement for each department for the year ended December 31. Figure the percentage of net sales, rounding to the nearest 0.1%.

5. Prepare an income statement for the year ended December 31. Figure the percentage of net sales, rounding to the nearest 0.1%.

RECYCLING PROBLEM 21-R 1   Preparing cost records

Windows, Etc., manufactures thermal storm window units. The company records manufacturing costs by job number and uses a factory overhead applied rate to charge overhead costs to its products.

The company estimates it will manufacture 10,000 units of windows next year. For this amount of production, total factory overhead is estimated to be $164,500.00. Estimated direct labor costs for next year are $235,000.00.

Instructions: 1. Figure Windows' factory overhead applied rate for next year as a percentage of direct labor cost.

On October 5, Windows began work on Job No. 642. The order is for 60 No. MP-64 window units for stock, to be completed by October 20.

2. Open a cost sheet for Job No. 642 similar to the one described in Chapter 21 and record the following items.

Oct. 5. Direct materials, $760.00. Materials Requisition No. 413.
      5. Direct labor, $120.00. Daily summary of job-time records.
      6. Direct labor, $190.00. Daily summary of job-time records.
      7. Direct materials, $230.00. Materials Requisition No. 424.
      7. Direct labor, $136.00. Daily summary of job-time records.
      8. Direct labor, $126.00. Daily summary of job-time records.
      9. Direct materials, $185.00. Materials Requisition No. 431.
      9. Direct labor, $210.00. Daily summary of job-time records.
    12. Direct materials, $156.00. Materials Requisition No. 437.
    12. Direct labor, $198.00. Daily summary of job-time records.
    13. Direct materials, $112.00. Materials Requisition No. 445.
    13. Direct labor, $186.00. Daily summary of job-time records.
    14. Direct materials, $145.00. Materials Requisition No. 452.
    14. Direct labor, $112.00. Daily summary of job-time records.
    15. Direct labor, $52.00. Daily summary of job-time records.

3. Complete the cost sheet, recording factory overhead at the rate figured in Instruction 1.

4. Prepare a finished goods ledger card similar to the one described in Chapter 21 for Stock No. MP-64 window unit. Minimum quantity is set at 20. Inventory location is Area G-9.

5. Record on the finished goods ledger card the beginning balance on October 1. The October 1 balance of MP-64 window units is 40 units at a unit cost of $63.50. Windows uses the first-in, first-out method to record inventory costs.

6. Record the following transactions on the finished goods ledger card for MP-64 window units.

Oct. 9. Sold 16 MP-64 window units. Sales Invoice No. 632.
    15. Received 60 MP-64 window units. Record cost from cost sheet for Job No. 642.
    20. Sold 38 MP-64 window units. Sales Invoice No. 646.

RECYCLING PROBLEM 22-R 1   **Journalizing entries that summarize cost records at the end of a fiscal period**

On March 31 of the current year, Soloman Company has the following information.

(a) The various general ledger accounts used in recording actual factory overhead expenses during the month have the following balances.

5510	Depreciation Expense—Factory Equipment	$ 2,885.12
5515	Depreciation Expense—Building	1,411.20
5520	Heat, Light, and Power Expense	4,527.60
5525	Insurance Expense—Factory	752.64
5530	Miscellaneous Expense—Factory	8,467.20
5535	Payroll Taxes Expense—Factory	20,291.04
5540	Property Tax Expense—Factory	3,044.16
5545	Supplies Expense—Factory	9,031.68

(b) Inventory accounts have the following balances.

Materials, $272,244.00. (March 1 balance, $151,539.36, plus March purchases, $120,704.64.) Account No. 1125.
Work in Process, March 1 balance, $95,961.60. Account No. 1130.
Finished Goods, March 1 balance, $71,442.00. Account No. 1135.

(c) The following accounts are needed for completing the posting (no beginning balances are needed).

2110	Employees Income Tax Payable	5105	Cost of Goods Sold
2120	FICA Tax Payable	5505	Factory Overhead
3120	Income Summary		

(d) The total factory payroll for the month according to the payroll register is $153,720.00, distributed as follows.

Work in Process	$114,240.00
Factory Overhead.	39,480.00
Cash	126,050.40
Employees Income Tax Payable	16,909.20
FICA Tax Payable	10,760.40

(e) The total of all requisitions of direct materials issued during the month is $126,114.80.
(f) The factory overhead to be charged to Work in Process is 78% of the direct labor cost.
(g) The total of all cost sheets completed during the month is $311,640.00.
(h) The total of costs recorded on all sales invoices for March is $327,026.00.

Instructions: 1. Open ledger accounts and record balances for information items in (a), (b), and (c).

2. Record the factory payroll entry on page 29 of a cash payments journal. C901. Post the general debit and general credit amounts.

3. Record the following entries on page 13 of a general journal. Post the entries.

a. An entry to transfer the total of all materials requisitions from Materials to Work in Process. M733.

b. An entry to close all individual manufacturing expense accounts to Factory Overhead. M734.

c. An entry to record applied overhead to Work in Process. M735.

4. Record and post the entry to close the balance of the factory overhead account to Income Summary. M736.

5. Record and post the entry to transfer the total of all cost sheets completed from Work in Process to Finished Goods. M737.

6. Record and post the entry to transfer the cost of products sold from Finished Goods to Cost of Goods Sold. M738.

7. Prepare for Soloman Company a statement of cost of goods manufactured for the month ended March 31 of the current year.

RECYCLING PROBLEM 23-R 1 Forming and expanding a partnership

On January 1 of the current year, Gene Mint and Alice Rutgers form a partnership. The partnership accepts the assets and liabilities of Mr. Mint's existing business. Miss Rutgers invests cash equal to Mr. Mint's investment. Partners share equally in all changes in equity. The January 1 balance sheet for Mr. Mint's existing business is as follows.

Gene Mint
Balance Sheet
January 1, 19--

ASSETS

Current Assets:		
Cash		$2,791.23
Accounts Receivable	$1,800.00	
Less Allowance for Uncollectible Accounts	15.39	1,784.61
Supplies		300.00
Total Current Assets...............................		$4,875.84
Plant Assets:		
Equipment		1,200.00
Total Assets		$6,075.84

LIABILITIES

Accounts Payable....................................	$1,575.84

CAPITAL

Gene Mint, Capital	4,500.00
Total Liabilities and Capital.........................	$6,075.84

Instructions: Record the following transactions. Use page 4 of a cash receipts journal and page 2 of a general journal. Source documents are abbreviated as follows: memorandum, M; receipt, R.

Jan. 1. Received from Alice Rutgers as an initial investment, $4,500.00. R1.
    1. Accepted assets and liabilities of Gene Mint's existing business as an initial investment, $4,500.00. R2.
Mar. 1. Recorded personal sale of equity to new partner, Albert Cruz, $3,000.00, distributed as follows: from Gene Mint, $1,500.00; from Alice Rutgers, $1,500.00. M18.
Aug. 1. Received from new partner, Edna Capio, for a one-fourth equity in the business, $3,000.00. R92.
Sept. 2. Received from new partner, Charles Black, for a one-fifth equity in the business, $2,500.00. R121 and M32.
Nov. 1. Received from new partner, Jane Lewis, for a one-sixth equity in the business, $3,000.00. Partners agree that the investment results in goodwill. R181 and M42.

RECYCLING PROBLEM 24-R 1   Completing end-of-fiscal-period work for a partnership

Kimberly Day and Susan Ness are partners in a partnership called First Call Plumbing. The partnership's work sheet for the year ended December 31 of the current year is shown on the following page.

Instructions: 1. Prepare an income statement. As part of the income statement, report the ratios of total operating expenses to net sales and net income to net sales. Round percentage computations to the nearest 0.1%.

2. Prepare a distribution of net income statement. Each partner is to receive 5% interest on January 1 equity. The January 1 equity is: Ms. Day, $22,000.00; Ms. Ness, $20,000.00. Also, the partners' salaries are: Ms. Day, $5,000.00; Ms. Ness, $4,000.00. The partners share remaining net income, net loss, or deficit equally.

First Call Plumbing
Work Sheet
For Year Ended December 31, 19--

		1	2	3	4	5	6	7	8
	Account Title	Trial Balance		Adjustments		Income Statement		Balance Sheet	
		Debit	Credit	Debit	Credit	Debit	Credit	Debit	Credit
1	Cash.........................	23 762 02						23 762 02	
2	Petty Cash...................	300 00						300 00	
3	Accounts Receivable..........	1 529 47						1 529 47	
4	Allow. for Uncoll. Accts........		32 15		(a) 90 00				122 15
5	Supplies—Plumbing...........	7 142 61			(b) 5 892 56			1 250 05	
6	Supplies—Office..............	1 360 00			(c) 1 088 76			271 24	
7	Prepaid Insurance.............	1 236 00			(d) 383 82			852 18	
8	Equipment....................	21 527 00						21 527 00	
9	Accum. Depr.—Equip..........		4 305 00		(e) 2 152 70				6 457 70
10	Truck........................	17 000 00						17 000 00	
11	Accum. Depr.—Truck..........		3 400 00		(f) 1 700 00				5 100 00
12	Accounts Payable..............		4 616 25						4 616 25
13	Sales Tax Payable.............		61 40						61 40
14	Kimberly Day, Capital..........		22 000 00						22 000 00
15	Kimberly Day, Drawing.........	7 000 00						7 000 00	
16	Susan Ness, Capital...........		20 000 00						20 000 00
17	Susan Ness, Drawing..........	7 000 00						7 000 00	
18	Income Summary..............								
19	Sales........................		49 793 30				49 793 30		
20	Advertising Expense...........	600 00				600 00			
21	Bad Debts Expense...........			(a) 90 00		90 00			
22	Depr. Exp.—Equipment.......			(e) 2 152 70		2 152 70			
23	Depr. Exp.—Truck............			(f) 1 700 00		1 700 00			
24	Insurance Expense............			(d) 383 82		383 82			
25	Miscellaneous Expense........	900 00				900 00			
26	Rent Expense.................	8 400 00				8 400 00			
27	Supplies Exp.—Plumbing......			(b) 5 892 56		5 892 56			
28	Supplies Exp.—Office.........			(c) 1 088 76		1 088 76			
29	Truck Expense................	5 126 00				5 126 00			
30	Utilities Expense..............	1 325 00				1 325 00			
31		104 208 10	104 208 10	11 307 84	11 307 84	27 658 84	49 793 30	80 491 96	58 357 50
32	Net Income					22 134 46			22 134 46
33						49 793 30	49 793 30	80 491 96	80 491 96

3. Prepare a capital statement.
4. Prepare a balance sheet.
5. Record the adjusting entries. Use page 6 of a general journal.
6. Record the closing entries. Use page 7 of a general journal.

RECYCLING PROBLEM 25-R 1   Recording governmental transactions

The town of Summit uses a general fund for all financial transactions. Expenditures are recorded by type of expenditure and by department. The four categories of expenditures are: personnel, supplies, other charges, and capital outlays. Departments are: General Government, Public Safety, Public Works, and Recreation.

Instructions: Record the following selected transactions completed during the current year. Use page 24 of a journal. Source documents are abbreviated as follows: check, C; memorandum, M; note payable, NP; receipt, R.

Jan. 2. Recorded current year's approved operating budget: estimated revenues, $1,138,500.00; appropriations, $1,093,000.00; budgetary fund balance, $45,500.00. M25.

2. Recorded current year's property tax levy: taxes receivable—current, $1,093,000.00; allowance for uncollectible taxes—current, $16,400.00; property tax revenue, $1,076,600.00. M26.

9. Paid for gas utility service in recreation department, $172.00. C124.

16. Received for current taxes receivable, $51,200.00. R75.

19. Encumbered estimated amount for supplies in general government department, $120.00. M42.

20. Issued a 45-day, 9% note payable to Farmers State Bank, $100,000.00. NP6.

31. Received from traffic fines, $590.00. R90. (Other Revenue)

Feb. 3. Paid for general government department supplies, $118.00, encumbered January 19 per M42. M51 and C145.

22. Paid for library books for recreation department, $425.00. C162. (Capital Outlays)

Mar. 1. Recorded reclassification of current taxes receivable to delinquent status, $82,000.00, and the accompanying allowance for uncollectible accounts, $16,400.00. M63.

6. Paid NP6, $100,000.00, plus interest, $1,109.59; total, $101,109.59. C179.

15. Paid for a 4-month, 6% certificate of deposit, $300,000.00. C199.

Apr. 5. Encumbered estimated amount for supplies in public safety department, $240.00. M84.

18. Received for delinquent taxes receivable, $14,500.00. R245.

26. Paid for public safety department supplies, $244.00, encumbered April 5 per M84. M92 and C234.

May 8. Paid for consultant's services in general government department, $600.00. C255. (Personnel)

July 15. Received for certificate of deposit due today, $300,000.00, plus interest, $6,000.00; total $306,000.00. R304.

RECYCLING PROBLEM 26-R 1   Completing end-of-fiscal-period work for a governmental organization

The town of Cascade uses a general fund. The general ledger trial balance for December 31 of the current year is as follows.

Account Title	Trial Balance Debit	Credit
Cash	$ 89,390.00	
Taxes Receivable—Current	—	—
Allow. for Uncoll. Taxes—Current	—	—
Taxes Receivable—Delinquent	22,760.00	
Allow. for Uncoll. Taxes—Delinquent		$ 7,950.00
Interest Receivable	—	—
Allow. for Uncoll. Interest	—	—
Inventory of Supplies	—	—
Investments—Short Term	—	—
Accounts Payable		25,640.00
Notes Payable	—	—
Unreserved Fund Balance		33,450.00
Reserve for Encumbrances—Current Year		780.00
Reserve for Encumbrances—Prior Year	—	—

| | Trial Balance | |
Account Title	Debit	Credit
Reserve for Inventory of Supplies	—	—
Property Tax Revenue		$1,138,200.00
Interest Revenue		6,610.00
Other Revenue...		13,840.00
Expenditure—Personnel, Gen. Gov't........................	$ 193,560.00	
Expenditure—Supplies, Gen. Gov't.........................	10,580.00	
Expenditure—Other Charges, Gen. Gov't.	96,700.00	
Expenditure—Capital Outlays, Gen. Gov't...................	11,240.00	
Expenditure—Personnel, Public Safety	351,150.00	
Expenditure—Supplies, Public Safety	16,690.00	
Expenditure—Other Charges, Public Safety..................	128,170.00	
Expenditure—Capital Outlays, Public Safety	61,300.00	
Expenditure—Personnel, Public Works	85,120.00	
Expenditure—Supplies, Public Works.......................	4,190.00	
Expenditure—Other Charges, Public Works	40,120.00	
Expenditure—Capital Outlays, Public Works.................	36,750.00	
Expenditure—Personnel, Recreation	44,490.00	
Expenditure—Supplies, Recreation........................	2,290.00	
Expenditure—Other Charges, Recreation	22,610.00	
Expenditure—Capital Outlays, Recreation...................	8,580.00	
Estimated Revenues......................................	1,161,300.00	
Appropriations...		1,115,000.00
Budgetary Fund Balance		46,300.00
Encumbrance—Supplies, Public Works.....................	780.00	

Instructions: 1. Complete the work sheet. The following information is needed for adjustments.

Unused supplies on hand..	$2,380.00
Interest revenue due but not collected...............................	3,650.00

An estimated 20% of interest revenue due will not be collected.
Reserve for encumbrances for current year is reclassified to prior-year status.

Cascade's general fund operating budget for the current fiscal year is shown below and on the following page.

2. Prepare a statement of revenues, expenditures, and changes in fund balance—budget and actual for the year ended December 31 of the current year. The unreserved fund balance on January 1 was $33,450.00.

3. Prepare a balance sheet for December 31 of the current year.

4. Record the adjusting and closing entries on page 22 of a journal.

Town of Cascade
Annual Operating Budget—General Fund
For Year Ended December 31, 19--

ESTIMATED REVENUES

Property Taxes...	$1,138,200.00	
Interest	9,500.00	
Other	13,600.00	
Total Estimated Revenues		$1,161,300.00

ESTIMATED EXPENDITURES AND BUDGETARY FUND BALANCE

General Government:

Personnel...	$ 193,560.00	
Supplies..	10,610.00	
Other Charges	96,780.00	
Capital Outlays.....................................	11,250.00	
Total General Government.............................		$ 312,200.00
Public Safety:		
Personnel...	$ 351,220.00	
Supplies..	16,730.00	
Other Charges	128,220.00	
Capital Outlays.....................................	61,330.00	
Total Public Safety..................................		557,500.00
Public Works:		
Personnel...	$ 85,300.00	
Supplies..	5,020.00	
Other Charges	40,140.00	
Capital Outlays.....................................	36,790.00	
Total Public Works		167,250.00
Recreation:		
Personnel...	$ 44,490.00	
Supplies..	2,340.00	
Other Charges	22,630.00	
Capital Outlays.....................................	8,590.00	
Total Recreation		78,050.00
Total Estimated Expenditures.............................		$1,115,000.00
Budgetary Fund Balance................................		46,300.00
Total Estimated Expenditures and Budgetary Fund Balance...		$1,161,300.00

Index

Acknowledgments

For permission to reproduce the photographs on the pages indicated, acknowledgment is made to the following:

© Peter Garfield/THE STOCK MARKET 3
Rhoda Sidney/Monkmeyer Press Photo Service 4
Marc St. Gil/West Stock... 7
Photri 13
Matt Brown/West Stock 23
Richard Wood/THE PICTURE CUBE 39
Bill Gallery/Stock Boston 122
© Joel Gordon 1986 159
James F. Housel/West Stock 160
© Peter Garfield/THE STOCK MARKET 178
Marc St. Gil/West Stock... 183
© 1986 Joel Baldwin/THE STOCK MARKET 226
Matt Brown/West Stock 302
Blumebild/H. Armstrong Roberts 363
CRADOC BAGSHAW 368
Compliments of ROBERT F. UHRIG COMPANY, Certified Public Accountants 441
Florida Department of Commerce/Division of Tourism 446
M. Uselmann/H. Armstrong Roberts 465
Photo Courtesy of TRW, Inc.. 466
Thanks to the College of Business Administration, Xavier University,
    Cincinnati, Ohio.. 517
CRADOC BAGSHAW 533
© Joel Gordon 1985 603